FROMMER'S

COMPREHENSIVE TRAVEL GUIDE

THAILAND

2ND Edition

by John Levy
and Kyle McCarthy

MACMILLAN • USA

About the Authors   **Kyle McCarthy** has been a travel writer since 1979. When she isn't on the go in Asia, she's on the road in the U.S. as an assistant director for film and television. **John Levy** has traveled extensively throughout Europe and Asia and has produced a feature film shot in Sri Lanka. They are also the authors of *Frommer's Greece on $45 a Day* and *Frommer's Bangkok*.

Macmillan Travel
A Prentice Hall Macmillan Company
15 Columbus Circle
New York, NY 10023

Copyright © 1992, 1994 by Simon & Schuster Inc.

All rights reserved. No part of this book may be reproduced or transmitted in any form or by any means, electronic or mechanical, including photocopying, recording, or by any information storage and retrieval system, without permission in writing from the Publisher.

Macmillan is a registered trademark of Macmillan, Inc.

ISBN 0-671-84913-1
ISSN 1055-5412

Design by Robert Bull Design
Maps by Geografix, Inc.

SPECIAL SALES

Bulk purchases (10+ copies) of Frommer's Travel Guides are available to corporations at special discounts. The Special Sales Department can produce custom editions to be used as premiums and/or for sales promotion to suit individual needs. Existing editions can be produced with custom cover imprints such as corporate logos. For more information write to: Special Sales, Prentice Hall, 15 Columbus Circle, New York, NY 10023.

Manufactured in the United States of America

CONTENTS

LIST OF MAPS

ACKNOWLEDGEMENTS

This first update of the Thailand Guide owes its spirit and enthusiasm to our co-writers, John Bozman and Ariel Zeitlin, as well as Kyle and Ron's 20-month old son, Regan, who delighted in the many "Buddha houses" and "tuk-tuks" he saw throughout our research. Their fresh outlook, combined with the Thais' boundless affection, renewed our love for this rapidly-changing country and its gracious people.

In addition, we owe tremendous gratitude to Khun Sumontha Nakornthab and her excellent staff at the TAT: our old friend Peck Chalermlap, Chattan Kunjara, and Suraphon Svetasreni and Mr. Nat in the TAT New York office.

We'd also like to thank some of our many friends throughout Thailand for revealing their favorite haunts and sharing their hard-won insights into a sometimes frustrating and mysterious place. Kanchari Buranasomphob, Frederic Lucron, Jonathan Hayssen, and Jane Puranananda came up with the hot and new; Imtiaz Muqbil and Israporn Posayanond provided an overview on Bangkok's socio-political scene; Lem Morgan passed on his travel tips.

KHOP KHUN KRAP—for the many kindnesses extended by Michael Bamberg, Alan Guignon, Marion Darby, Sakchai Srongprapa, Kathy Barbour, Marion Harris, Caroline Ward, Matthias Wiesmann, and Supachawee Bunyaketu—for their diligence, Junpen Tangjitvisuth and Chalida Thana-kitcharoensuk—and for their continuous support, everyone at Prentice Hall.

WHAT THE SYMBOLS MEAN

What is a Frommer Guide? It's a comprehensive, easy-to-use guide to the best travel values in all price ranges—from very expensive to budget. The one guidebook to take along on any trip.

 FROMMER'S FAVORITES—hotels, restaurants, attractions, and entertainment you should not miss

 SUPER-SPECIAL VALUES—really exceptional values

 FROMMER'S SMART TRAVELER TIPS—hints on how to secure the best value for your money

IN HOTEL AND OTHER LISTINGS

The following symbols refer to the standard amenities available in all rooms:

A/C air conditioning   TEL telephone   TV television
MINIBAR refrigerator stocked with beverages and snacks

The following abbreviations are used for credit cards:

AE American Express   DISC Discover   EU Eurocard
CB Carte Blanche   ER enRoute   MC MasterCard
DC Diners Club   V VISA

TRIP PLANNING WITH THIS GUIDE

Use the following features:

What Things Cost In . . . to help you plan your daily budget
Calendar of Events . . . to plan for or avoid
Suggested Itineraries . . . for seeing the country
What's Special About Checklist . . . a summary of a city's or region's highlights—which lets you check off those that appeal most to you
Easy-to-Read Maps . . . regional attractions, walking tours, city sights, hotel and restaurant locations—all referring to or keyed to the text
Distances and Transportation . . . at the beginning of each town section
Fast Facts . . . all the essentials at a glance: currency, embassies, emergencies, and more

OTHER SPECIAL FROMMER FEATURES

Did You Know . . . ?—offbeat, fun facts
Impressions—what others have said

INVITATION TO THE READERS

In researching this book, we have come across many wonderful establishments, the best of which we have included here. We are sure that many of you will also come across appealing hotels, inns, restaurants, guest houses, shops, and attractions. Please don't keep them to yourself. Share your experiences, especially if you want to comment on places included in this edition that have changed for the worse. You can address your letters to:

John Levy and Kyle McCarthy
Frommer's Thailand, 2nd Edition
Macmillan Travel
15 Columbus Circle
New York, NY 10023

A DISCLAIMER

Readers are advised that prices fluctuate in the course of time, and travel information changes under the impact of the varied and volatile factors that affect the travel industry. Neither the author nor the publisher can be held responsible for the experiences of readers while traveling. Readers are invited to write to the Publisher with ideas, comments, and suggestions for future editions.

SAFETY ADVISORY

Whenever you're traveling in an unfamiliar city or country, stay alert. Be aware of your immediate surroundings. Wear a money belt and keep a close eye on your possessions. Be particularly careful with cameras, purses, and wallets, all favorite targets of thieves and pickpockets.

CHAPTER 1

GETTING TO KNOW THAILAND

When Thailand was still called Siam, it figured in the imagination of adventurers and poets as a land of golden temples, royal white elephants, bejeweled palaces, and dense teak forests. The country maintained a cautious relation with the outside world. In particular, the West, and few visitors actually explored the territory. Even during the 19th-century, travel to the distant kingdom was arduous and forbidding.

Those who managed the journey returned home painting different images of the Land of Smiles, marveling as much at the physical riches of the country as by the serenity and inner security of its people. Travelers would remark on the Thais' fiercely enduring independence ("Thailand" means "Land of the Free") and ancient Buddhist culture, a mix that resulted in deeply gracious hospitality that's seemed neither subservient or obsequious. Travelers today are still impressed. Old Siam is certainly gone, but its natural and cultural wonders survive alongside the warmth of the Thai people. It's little wonder that many a modern traveler falls in love with both the country and its cordial hosts.

1. GEOGRAPHY, HISTORY & PEOPLE

GEOGRAPHY

Thailand is located roughly equidistant from China and India, in the center of Southeast Asia. It borders Myanmar (Burma) to the north and west, Laos to the northeast, Cambodia to the east, and Malaysia to the south. Thailand's southwestern coast stretches along the Andaman Sea, and its southern and southeastern coastlines border the Gulf of Thailand.

Thailand covers approximately 180,000 square miles—about the size of France. The country is divided into six major geographic zones. The north (really the foothills of the Himalayas) is a mountainous belt where elephants have traditionally provided the heavy labor needed to harvest teak and other hardwoods. Fluorite, wolfram, and tungsten are mined in this region. And, as with much of Thailand, the cool hills in the north are well suited for farming, particularly for strawberries, asparagus, peaches, litchis, and other fruits. At higher elevations, many hill-tribe farmers cultivate opium poppies. The major cities in the north are Chiang Rai, Chiang Mai, Lamphun, Lampang, and Mae Hong Son.

? DID YOU KNOW . . . ?

- Chang and Eng, joined at birth (1811) by cartilage linking their chests, were made famous by the Barnum & Bailey Circus as the "Siamese Twins."
- Ancestors of the Siamese cat came from China but their earliest mention is at the royal court at Ayutthaya in 1350.
- All statues of the Buddha are leased from their makers because the image, considered too sacred to have material value, can never be "bought' or "sold."
- White elephants (called Chang Puak or strange colored) are traditionally the very auspicious and revered property of royalty. They can have any of seven skin colors but must have white eyes, palate, testicles, and toenails.
- Bird's-nest specialties served in Chinese restaurants throughout the world are make from swallow spittle harvested in caves off Ko Pi Pi, and islands off of Chumphon.
- In Phitsanulok's Night Market, morning glory greens are sautéed in a wok, tossed 65 feet into the air, then caught on a serving dish by a waiter poised on a nearby rooftop.
- Thailand is the world's largest tuna fish processor and Bumble Bee tuna, one of the largest retail brands in the world, is Thai owned.

The broad and relatively infertile northeast plateau, perhaps the least developed of any region in Thailand, is bordered by the Mae Khlong (Khlong River)—one of the country's four great rivers—on the north and northeast boundaries, separating the country from neighboring Laos. This brittle plain, called Isan by villagers, is home to the most ancient Bronze Age village in the country (if not the world), at Ban Chiang, dating back more than 5,600 years. The area's major Khmer ruins are at Phimai and outside Surin and Buriram. Other than potash mining and subsistence farming the region has little economic development, although industrial inroads are being made in and around Khorat and Khon Kaen.

In contrast to the poor soil of Isan, Thailand's central plain is a fantastically fertile region, providing the country with its massive rice crop. The main city in the central plain is Phitsanulok; nearby is the ancient city of Si Satchanalai and Thailand's first capital, Sukhothai; to the south is Lopburi, an ancient Mon/Khmer settlement.

The southeastern coast is lined with seaside resorts, such as Pattaya and the islands Ko Samet and Ko Chang. Farther east, in the mountains, is the greatest concentration of Thailand's sapphire-and-ruby mines. And recently natural gas deposits were discovered off the southeastern coast.

On the opposite side of the country, west of Bangkok, are mountains and valleys carved by the Kwai River, made infamous during World War II by the "Death Railway" and a bridge over the river near Kanchanaburi (made famous by the film *Bridge on the River Kwai*). Just to the north of Bangkok (which is in the center of the country, along the Chao Phraya River banks) is Ayutthaya, Thailand's capital after Sukhothai.

A long, skinny, southern peninsula extends to the Malaysian border, bisecting the Andaman Sea and the Gulf of Thailand. The eastern coastline along the gulf extends more than 1,125 miles; while the western shoreline runs 445 miles along the Andaman Sea. This region is the most tropical in the country and experiences heavy rainfall during the monsoon season. There are glamorous beach resorts here (glamorous during the dry seasons, that is), such as the western islands of Phuket and nearby Ko Pi Pi, Krabi, and Ko Tarutao as well as Ko Samui on the eastern shore. The primary industries in this region are tin mining, rubber production, fishing, and of course, tourism.

HISTORY

While the origin of the Thai people is debated, the history of the country is very much a source of national pride. Thailand is the only Asian country never to have been occupied by a Western power. In fact, the country has never been completely overrun by any foreign power since national unification during the Sukhothai period in the 13th century—the Japanese exercised control during World War II but never

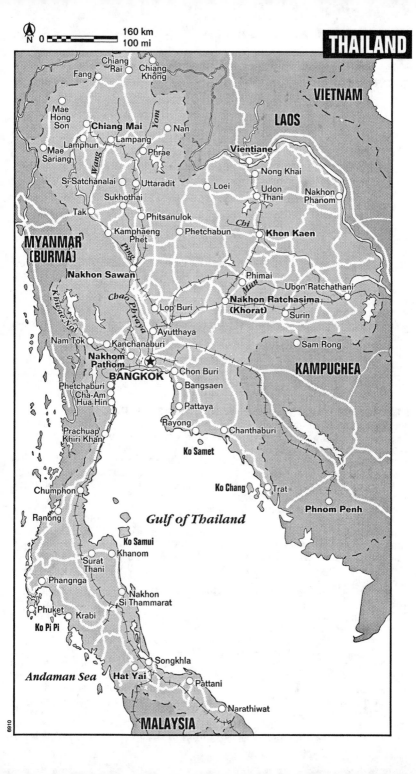

fully occupied the territory. Independence, and the determination to maintain it, explains much about the development of the Thai nation.

EARLY HISTORY Remains of neolithic villages scatter the country, and those at Ban Chiang in the northeast have attracted particular attention, providing evidence of a highly evolved civilization that dates back to 4,000 B.C. The agrarian villagers' sophisticated metallurgy predates by hundreds of years similar examples from China. The Ban Chiang people are thought to have migrated to this fertile region from Vietnam. Their enigmatic disappearance is linked possibly to an ecological disaster and may have been related to their slash-and-burn agriculture.

Other tribes coexisted with the Ban Chiang people, though none left such a lasting legacy. Among them were various tribes that migrated south from China and the predecessors of the ethnic Malays, who may have lived in the verdant Chao Phraya River basin.

Important to the spiritual development of Thailand was the spreading of Buddhism by missionaries sent by the Indian emperor Aśoka, who reigned during the 3rd century B.C. These Buddhist leaders formed small, politically independent states, though none had any degree of permanency.

Among those tribes that directly affected Thailand's early development, the most significant were the Khmer and the Mon. Both originally lived in southern China and migrated further south during the 1st century B.C. The Khmer ultimately settled in Thailand's northeastern section and mostly built villages in what is now Cambodia, where they also built their magnificent capital at Angkor. The Mon concentrated along the Chao Phraya River valley and built their capital near Nakhon Pathom, which was already a major Buddhist center. Both the Khmer and the Mon, through their art, language, religion, and architecture, influenced later Thai culture.

During the height of the Mon Empire in the so-called Dvaravati period (6th to 11th centuries), the first Tibeto-Burman people settled in the northern hills. These people were the original hill-tribe dwellers and roamed throughout the northern part of Indochina for centuries.

THE SVARATI PERIOD TO THE SUKHOTHAI PERIOD It was also during the Dvaravati period, in the 7th century, that inhabitants of the Nanchao Kingdom in southern China banded together to live as a common Thai people. But because of economically oppressive Chinese policies, it wasn't long before Thais began migrating south to the Indochinese peninsula. Over 200 years (beginning in the 11th century) these pioneers established small, independent states in the north. The settlers had a ready trade network with Chinese merchants from Yunnan Province, and brought with them improved methods of irrigation and rice cultivation. It wasn't long before these northern dominions grew affluent and influential.

By the 13th century the final wave of immigrants moved south. The Mon Empire was already in decline, but it was the imminent assault by Kublai Khan, in nearby Burma, that finally moved the Thai states together to form three great 13th-century kingdoms: Lanna Thai (based in Chiang Mai), Phayao, and Sukhothai. Of these, Sukhothai was the most powerful military state and was expected to protect the other kingdoms from attack.

At the outset of the Sukhothai period (13th to 14th centuries), the Khmer kings, based in Angkor, controlled much of Thailand. No single Thai state could defeat the Khmer armies, but in 1238 two local headmen combined forces to expel a Khmer division—a victory that led to the founding of the Kingdom of Sukhothai, "Dawn of Happiness" as it is known in Pali. Khun Bang Klang became the first king of Sukhothai and was called by the title "Sri Inthrathit."

The apex of the Sukhothai period was reached during the reign of the third ruler, King Ramkamhaeng (1275–1317). After expelling the Khmer forces, the remaining independent Thai kingdoms made alliances with Sukhothai, which led a unified Thai state. Ramkamhaeng—in addition to his military conquests during 42 years as King—was responsible for creating the Thai alphabet, establishing Theravacla Buddhism as the dominant religion (and at the same time, creating a religious connection with Sri Lanka), promoting the growth of the Sangkalok ceramics industry, expanding trade throughout all of Asia (especially with Burma and India, with whom he made separate treaties), as well as sending ambassadors to the Chinese court.

THE 14TH CENTURY TO THE 17TH CENTURY After Ramkamhaeng followed a series of kings with diminishing influence, leading Sukhothai into vassalage under the rising power of 14th-century Ayutthaya. The last Sukhothai king, Phra Ramesun, was an Ayutthaya prince.

Ayutthaya, 400km (240 miles) south of Sukhothai in the Chao Phraya valley, was the capital of Thailand from 1350 until 1767. At its height in the 17th century, the city's population was greater than that of contemporary London. Not only was Ayutthaya populous, it was cosmopolitan, attracting citizens from as far away as England, Holland, France, Spain, Portugal, Japan, China, and Persia. So entrenched were these outsiders that a Japanese merchant was promoted commander of the King's Cavalry.

It was during this period that Thailand enacted its first civil laws and greatly expanded its boundaries to Angkor, Cambodia. King Naresuan also neutralized the Burmese, considered Thailand's greatest remaining military threat. (The Burmese had ruled Thailand from 1569 to 1584.)

King Ekatosarot (Naresuan's successor) and King Narai opened Thailand politically to the West in the 17th century, receiving Dutch, French, and Portuguese ambassadors. Still, the Ayutthaya government was wary of Western colonists and kept a check on their influence. After King Narai's suspicious death, most Europeans were expelled and trade with the West all but ceased for 100 years.

One important legacy of the Ayutthaya period was the changing attitude toward the king. During the Sukhothai period, the king lived by the principles of Buddhism as the "King of Righteousness," and was expected to embody the basic tenets of Buddhism. During the Ayutthaya period, the king was thought to have been divinely appointed, and followed Brahman or Hinduism. Being close to gods, kings lived in corresponding opulence. They awarded themselves names such as "King Ramathipodi I," derived from the Hindu epic, *Ramayana*.

This change in attitude concentrated power on the throne and led to a series of corrupt, and dictatorial rulers. Such irresponsibility ultimately contributed to Ayutthaya's final destruction by the Burmese in the 18th century.

Before Burma destroyed Ayutthaya, the city had more than a million inhabitants; after the invasion only a few thousand were left and the social order was thrown into chaos. Nearly every institution, including royalty, was in shambles.

King Taksin, last of the great Ayutthaya rulers, moved the capital south to safer ground, at Thonburi. For the next 15 years he fought the Burmese and reformed the country's political and social system. As a final blow to the Ayutthaya period, Taksin proclaimed a new royal line. Taksin's most powerful general, Chao Phrya Chakri, was crowned Rama I in 1782.

During that year, Rama I relocated the capital across the Chao Phraya River to the merchant village Bangkok (Village of the Wild Plums). For the next 27 years, Rama I laid the groundwork for a city that was to surpass the grandeur of Ayutthaya. At the same time, he enacted laws designed to correct the underlying weaknesses of the previous empire, thus beginning a new administrative and economic order.

THE 18TH CENTURY TO THE PRESENT By the 18th century, Thailand felt secure enough to ever so slightly reopen its doors to the outside world. Christian missionaries from England and America brought Thailand modern Western medicine, education, and agriculture.

IMPRESSIONS

It is a country of perpetual symbol. Mermaids and sirens in the waters, ogres and giants on the land, nymphs in the forests, ghosts and spirits everywhere, dragons and fire-spitting serpents. . . . A country of unceasing pageantry.
—BISHOP PALLEGOIX, *DESCRIPTION DU ROYAUME THAI*, 1854

King Mongkut (Rama IV) and his son, King Chulalongkorn (Rama V), were the architects of Thailand's emergence, during the 19th century, into the modern world as a completely independent nation. Slavery was abolished and a technologically modern infrastructure established; civil laws were reformed and trade treaties signed with most global powers of the time; and a strong army guaranteed national security.

The following two reigns brought declining royal power, which coincided with rising expectations among the military, government officials, and growing merchant class. These three factions banded together to topple the king in 1932, creating a democratic, parliamentary form of government with the king as the nominal head of state.

The country's attempts to establish a firm political base were set back by Japanese occupation during World War II, which began in the Pacific on December 8, 1941. Against Japan's overwhelming power, Thailand gave up quickly, entering into an alliance with them on December 21. After British and American planes bombed Bangkok, Thailand declared war against the Allies on January 25, 1942. But at war's end, no punitive treaties were imposed on Thailand, thanks to the Free Thai Movement that had been organized abroad by M. R. Seni Pramoj, then Thai consul in Washington, and the underground resistance led by Dr. Pridi Panomyong. Parliamentary democracy reasserted itself and was accepted, with changes brought about by socially active students.

Since the late 1940s, the government has been led by a series of military field marshals and generals (brought to power through coups), with short intervening periods of civilian control. Thailand managed to stay out of the Vietnam War (though it continues to feel repercussions from it) and because of this was largely responsible for forming the Association of Southeast Asian Nations (ASEAN).

During the mid-1970s, as a result of more student uprisings, the country was led by academic and political figures unassociated with the military. But the country has been ruled by the military since 1977, following the coup by Gen. Kriengsak Chammanand and subsequent administration by General Premadasa. The most recent government was toppled in a coup during 1991.

In May of 1992, after mounting protest and calls for democratic reforms, the military cracked down on public demonstrations and several students were killed. The king managed to quell the ensuing violence by publicly scolding both the prime minister, as head of the military, and opposition leaders. A compromise was reached; General Suchinda stepped down and businessman Anand Panyarachun, who had run the interim government after the coup, resumed the post of prime minister.

General elections were held in September 1992 and Chuan Leekpai was elected the new prime minister, heading a very fragile five-party coalition. At our recent visit, the most pressing issues on his agenda were decentralization of the economy (currently strong with a GDP of 7.5% and inflation at 3.6%), equalizing the wealth in the rural areas, solving Bangkok's traffic and environment problems, and ridding the government of corruption.

It is a tribute to the Thai people that the nation has never been ruled by a foreign power. Thais protect their political structure and freedom under the central triad of nation, king, and religion. The political system is relatively fluid, responding to the changing needs of the times. Even during periods of open government, the military has played an influential role, as has the royal family (often steering in different directions from each other), in the maintenance of a semblance of stability.

The government is now a constitutional monarchy, with King Bhumibol Adulyadej the head of state and chief of staff of the armed forces. The administrative, judicial, and ministerial bodies all operate semiautonomously, under the king's nominal supervision. Bangkok is the capital city; the rest of the country is organized into 73 provinces (*changwat*). These geographic regions are further organized into districts (*amphoe*) and villages (*muban*).

PEOPLE

Thailand's population was estimated at 60 million in 1990. The lineage of the Thai people is still a matter of dispute. (Approximately 90% of the population are ethnically Thai, 9% Chinese or Indian, and 1% come from the various hill tribes.) The prevailing theory is that the Thais, who had a unified culture by the 7th century, migrated south from the Nanchao Kingdom in the Yunnan Province of China. They settled in independent states throughout the north during the 11th and 12th centuries, and were united during the Sukhothai period, beginning in the 13th century. Thai culture was influenced primarily by settlers from the great Mon and Khmer civilizations, but individual Tibeto-Burman tribes also played a role in shaping Thai culture.

Others believe the Thai people were Thailand's indigenous inhabitants, forced out of the country by more powerful Mon and Khmer invaders. They fled north to Yunnan Province and returned to their homeland, under pressure from the Mongolians during the 11th and 12th centuries.

Although they number a relatively small 575,000 households (according to the Tribal Research Institute's 1993 study), the six main hill tribes of the north contribute a great deal to Thailand's ethnic diversity. The principal groups are the Karen, Hmong, Lahu, Mien, Akha, and Lisu, and all of them live in the hills around Chiang Mai.

In the past 15 years Thailand has accepted over a million refugees from surrounding Indo-Chinese countries. Since the Vietnam War, Laotians, Vietnamese, and Cambodians flocked to Thailand, where many of these displaced persons were housed in camps along the eastern border. The Thai government and various international aid organizations are attempting to repatriate them in the wake of the Cambodian Peace Accord.

2. ART, ARCHITECTURE & LITERATURE

ART & ARCHITECTURE

Most accounts of Thai art history begin with the so-called Nanchao period. (A.D. 650–1250) during which Chinese and associated ethnic minorities migrated south into the land that would become a unified country during the early years of the 13th century. Yet the real story begins during the neolithic era in which such places as the Spirit Cave in Mae Hong Son and the settlements in and around Ban Chiang in the Northeast which developed into sophisticated agrarian cultures. Their religion was animistic and its art is exceedingly similar to the geometric period in early Greek art; large primitively fired ceramic red vessels are painted with bold, black spirals and other abstract designs. Opened graves indicate some aesthetically crude but sophisticated metal sculpture, mostly of animals, as well as finely crafted jewelry.

A gulf of over 2,000 years separates the neolithic period with the Nanchao era; there are few extant art forms from this early time though it's thought that Buddhist missionaries from India and Sri Lanka imported aesthetic ideas from the subcontinent. Only with the direct connection between Thailand and China, Burma, Indonesia, Cambodia, and most importantly, Sri Lanka and India, is there solid evidence of a true Thai art in the making. Indian art spawned locally assimilated styles in the Southeast Asian territory: Dvaravati (Mon), Khmer (Cambodia), Burmese, and

IMPRESSIONS

The lowest peasant considers himself superior to the proudest and most elevated subject of any other country.
—JOHN CRAWFURD, 1830

Srivijaya (Javanese), all of whom either settled in or traded with the Thai people. Of these, the Dvaravati were initially the most influential. This style, from the 6th–10th century, is most similar to the so-called Gupta style of traditional Indian art and architecture and is most evident in the central and northeast section of the country. Unfortunately, the vast majority of sculpture and painting was destroyed when most Dvaravati influenced buildings were either left to ruin or converted to Mahayana Buddhist structures, but what survives are the precursors to the Khmer *prang* or cactus-shaped towers with carved images of Hindu and Sri Lankan forms, with most buildings made from carved sandstone.

The Khmer (Cambodian/Hindu) Empire was well established within Thailand from the 11th to the 13th century and with it came the country's second significant influence. The two most important aspects of Khmer art and architecture (as they relate to later Thai styles) are the fluid, sinewy shapes evident in Khmer stone religious sculpture and the layout of both civil and religious buildings. Khmer stone carvers incorporated the elaborate ornamentation of Indian art with the abstract style of Chinese sculpture; friezes above lintels in such temples as Phimai are examples of the former, while the serene Khmer figural representation on display in Jim Thompson's House are excellent examples of the latter. Khmer architects (both in Cambodia at Angkor, the capital, and in the satellite towns in Thailand, such as Prasat Hin Phanom Rung) built travel halts and religious complexes that would later serve as models for the Thai "wat" (a cluster of religious buildings surrounded by a wall and gateways) and its individual buildings. Both Phanom Rung and Phimai are excellent examples of the stone vaulted Khmer "stone castles," some of which were later incorporated into the much larger Thai wat.

The kingdoms in Chiang Mai and Sukhothai swept away Hindu cultural hegemony and brought forward the next major advances in Thai art and architecture. One of the lasting legacies of the Sukhothai period is its sculpture, characterized by the parrot-nose Buddha, either sitting or, more typically, walking. These Buddhas are considered the best ever produced, and the period is regarded as the zenith of Thai culture. Both cities expanded and furthered the layout and decorative style of the Khmer capitals. With the inclusion of Chinese wooden building techniques and polychromatic schemes and Japanese influenced carved flowing lines, the wat, with its murals, Buddhist sculpture, and spacious religious and administrative buildings, defined the first "pure" Thai Buddhist style. During this period came the mainstays of Thai wat architecture (in order of artistic importance): the *phra chedi* (*stupa*), *bot*, *vihara*, *phra prang*, *mondop*, and *prasat*.

The *phra chedi* or stupa is the most venerated structure. Originally it enshrined relics of the Buddha, later of holy men and kings, and is the equivalent symbolically of the Christian cross. The structure consists of a drum (basement) and dome (tumulus) surmounted by a cubical chair representative of the seated Buddha and over it the *chatra* or umbrella in one or many tiers. There are many different forms extant in Thailand.

The *bot* is where the *bhikku* (monks) meditate and all ceremonies are performed. It consists of either one large nave or one nave with lateral aisles. The Buddha image is enshrined here. It is built on a rectangular plan. At the end of each ridge of the roof are graceful finials, called *chofa*, "sky tassle" which are reminiscent of animal horns but are thought to represent celestial geese or the Garmda. The triangular gables are enriched with gilded wooden ornamentation and glass mosaic.

The *vihara* or *viharm* is a replica of the bot that is used to keep Buddha images.

The *Phra Prang* which originated with the corner tower of the Khmer temple is a new form of Thai stupa elliptical in shape. The interior contains images of the Buddha.

The *mondop* may be of wood or brick. On a square pillared base the pyramidal roof is formed by a series of receding stories, enriched with the same decoration tapering off in a pinnacle. It may serve to enshrine some holy object as at Saraburi where it enshrines the footprint of the Lord Buddha or it may serve as a kind of library and storeroom for religious ceremonial objects as it does at Wat Phra Kaeo in Bangkok.

The *prasat* is a direct descendant of the Greek-cross shaped Khmer temple. At the center is a square sanctuary with a domed sikhara and four porchlike antechambers which project from the main building giving the whole a steplike contour. The *prasat* serves either as the royal throne hall or as a shrine for some venerated objects such as the *prasat* of Wat Phra Kaeo in Bangkok which enshrines the statues of the kings of the present dynasty.

Less important architectural structures include the *ho trai* or library housing palm-leave books; the sala an open pavilion used for resting; and the *ho rakhang* the Thai belfry.

The Ayutthaya and Bangkok periods furthered the Sukhothai style, bringing refinements in materials and design. During the Ayutthaya period there was a Khmer revival; the Ayutthaya kings briefly flirted with Hinduism with the result that they built a number of Neo-Khmer style temples and edifices. The art and architecture evident in early Bangkok was directly inspired by the dominant styles in Ayutthaya, the country's earlier capital. After the destruction of Ayutthaya in the 18th century, the new leaders, having established their foothold in Thonburi (and soon to move across the Chao Praya to Bangkok), tried to rebuild many of the most distinctive buildings in the so-called Ayutthaya mold. This meant incorporating older Khmer (such as Wat Arun), Chinese, northern Thai, and (to a lesser degree), Western modes into contemporary wats, palaces, sculpture, and murals.

The last major influence in Thailand's architectural and artistic development was of Western origin—many would say that it is the single most important style today. Beginning with the opening up to Europe during the latter days of the Ayutthaya period, Jesuit missionaries and French merchants brought with them decidedly baroque fashions. Although the country was circumspect about its continuing relations with the West, it did follow and incorporate many of the prevailing styles of the day. The Marble Wat in Bangkok is an obvious example of this melding of Thai/European style.

The modern modes are almost indistinguishable from other fast growing Asian capitals, particularly Hong Kong and Singapore. Typical Thai wooden house blocks are cleared, klongs are filled in, and wide boulevards are created. In place of traditional Thai architecture are highrise office and apartment complexes that bear little connection to past traditions.

PAINTING Murals, paintings on cloth, and manuscripts are the largest and most important examples of Thai painting along with the designs in gold leaf and black lacquer found on doors, bookcases, chests, and screens.

The subjects of traditional Thai painting are mainly religious scenes depicting the life of the Buddha, the Jataka scenes narrating the many lives of the Buddha prior to his Enlightenment, or scenes from the Ramakien already discussed.

Usually, though not always, the murals are placed as follows. On the top part of the wall facing the main image of the Buddha there is a scene representing the unsuccessful temptation of the Buddha by Mara. Behind the Buddha image will probably be scenes of the Buddhist cosmos or of Hell. Scenes from the life of the Buddha or from the Jataka stories—the most famous being the Mahachat (the final life of the Buddha before his Enlightenment) or the Thotsachat (the last 10 lives of the Buddha)—are usually pictured on the other two walls. These murals are often surmounted by rows of seated Buddhas.

IMPRESSIONS

Publicly the Thai remain more Victorian than the Victorians. . . . it is viewed as improper and inappropriate to even hold hands in public.
One of the most pervasive of Thai cultural imperatives is the avoidance of social confrontation. One is expected to mask one's emotions especially socially destructive ones like anger, hatred, annoyance.
—WILLIAM J. KLAUSNER, *REFLECTIONS ON THAI CULTURE*, 1976

In Thai painting there is no Western perspective or shadow. Landscape in itself is not considered important, being only the background setting for the action of the story. In mural painting the paint (traditionally made of mineral and earth pigments) is applied to dry plaster. The brushes which are made of tree roots, are what give Thai painting its distinctive solid wirelike line compared to Chinese and other Oriental brush painting. The wooden brushes are used for broad lines and stippling; cow's hair brushes are used for detail and finer work.

Only a few examples of pre-17th century work have survived the humid climate. The first fairly well-preserved painting was found at Ayutthaya at Wat Ratachaburana and in a chedi at Wat Mahathat. From the fall of Ayutthaya to the mid-19th century murals grew in their complexity and richness of color, which was heightened by lavish use of gold leaf. Good examples can be seen in Thonburi at Wat Suwannaram and in Bangkok at Wat Suthat and in the Buddhaisawan chapel in the National Museum.

In Northern Thailand painting is more Burmese in style, less luxurious and cooler in tone than the Bangkok school. In Wat Pra Sing in Chiang Mai, one of the walls narrates the story of Sang Thong about a prince born in a golden conch shell. Look at them closely and you will find humorous touches even in the most reverent scenes, like the man flirting with a group of girls while a cat stalks a female on the roof above his head.

Traditional Thai painting began to die in the mid-19th century when Western oil paints and techniques were introduced. An interesting early example of this development incorporating some elements of shading and perspective can be seen on the upper portion of walls at Wat Bovornivet, where King Mongkut ordered the painting of Western scenes including a windmill, Mount Vernon, and Versailles as an educational mural.

LITERATURE

Although there are several great works of literature that are representative of the Thai cultural tradition, there are two that are best known in the West and that visitors will most likely come across either portrayed artistically in murals or dramatically in the khon and in shadow plays. The first is the *Ramakien* which is based on the Hindu epic, the *Ramayana*, and tells the story of the triumph of Rama, rightful king of Ayutthays, over Tosakanth, the evil king of the island of Longka—the triumph of good over evil. Derived from the sacred book of the Hindus, the *Ramakien* as such has no sanctity to a Thai; rather it's profane entertainment. The second is the *Mahachat*, a story beloved of the Thai people. It is the story of the Lord Buddha in his last-incarnation-but-one-on-earth as Prince Wetsandon before he attained his Buddhahood. This selfless life which prepared him for his final enlightenment represents to the Thais an ideal for faith and it is recited at the midyear Autumnal Festival by specially trained monks. Originally composed in Pali, it has been a source of great inspiration for Thai art and poetry and exists in many versions. Prior to 1828 when the Thai language was first set in print, works of literature were written on folded scrolls, which are both difficult and expensive to produce.

Among the current generation of Thai writers, none is better known to both readers in Thai and English than Pira Sudham, whose most recent work, *Monsoon Country* (Bangkok: Shire Books), has been translated into French and Thai (it was written in English). Mr. Pira hails from Isan and his books reflect the struggles of living between the Western and Thai worlds. In 1990, Mr. Pira was nominated for the Nobel Prize in literature; his other titles are *People of Esarn* and *Siamese Drama*. Among the better books by other well regarded contemporary writers available in translation are *Four Reigns and Red Bamboo*, by Kukrit Pramoj (Bangkok: D.K. Books), and *A Man Called Karn*, by Suwanee Sukonta (Bangkok: Bannakarn).

3. RELIGION, MYTH & FOLKLORE

RELIGION

Anyone visiting Thailand cannot fully appreciate the culture without some under-standing of Buddhism, which is followed by 90% of the population. Buddha was a great Indian sage born in the 6th century B.C. Born Siddhartha Gautama, a noble prince sheltered from the outside world, he left the palace and outside its walls he encountered first an old man, then a sick man, and then a corpse. He concluded that all is suffering and resolved to search for relief from that suffering. He went into the forest and lived there for many years as a solitary ascetic and ultimately achieved enlightenment while sitting under a sacred fig tree. The highlights of his life were his temptation by Mara (evil), who sent his daughters to seduce him; his pro-tection by serpent king Mucalinda from raging floods that followed a seven-day storm; the first sermon on the Wheel of Law given in the Deer Park at Sarnath, In-dia; and his death and cremation. After his death two schools arose. The oldest and probably closest to the original is Theravada (Doctrine of the Elders), sometimes re-ferred to less correctly as Hinayana (the Small Vehicle), which prevails in Sri Lanka, Burma, Thailand, and Cambodia, and Mahayana (the Large Vehicle), which is prac-ticed in China, Korea, and Japan. In addition, Tibetan Buddhism and Zen Buddhism could be considered schools of their own.

The basic document is the Pali canon, which was recorded in writing in the 1st century A.D. The doctrine is essentially an ethical and psychological system in which no deity plays a role. It is a religion without a God; mystical in the sense that it strives for the intuitive realization of the oneness of the universe. It has no pope, no earthly authority, and no priests. It requires that individuals work out their own sal-vation as commanded by the Buddha himself, to "look within, thou art the Bud-dha," and in his final works, to "work out your own salvation with diligence." The open pagoda design of the temples reflects the openness and accessibility to all of the teaching which admits to no caste, no sex, no race superiority, and has no priest guarding the entrance to its portals. It is tolerant and seeks no converts.

So you may ask what are the people doing who enter the temple and prostrate themselves before the Buddha, place their hands together in a gesture of worship, light incense, and make offerings of fruit and flowers? What role exactly does the Buddha image play and how did the image become so prevalent? Here's how it hap-pened. At his death his disciples were distraught at the prospect of losing their great and beloved teacher and they asked how they might remember him. Buddha granted them permission to make pilgrimages to the Great Events of his career and to gather his bodily relics and place them in stupas or mounds to remind them of his life and his teachings and to make their hearts glad and happy. And so stupas were built and the events of his life remembered by making symbolic representations of the ele-ments of those events, and it was a short step from there to making representations of the Buddha himself. Buddha images were first invented about the beginning of the Christian era and have been created by artists ever since. The images are honored in the same way that any great teacher is honored and revered in the Eastern tradition; they are not idols of worship but images that in their physical form radiate spiritual-ity and convey the essence of Buddhist teachings—serenity, enlightenment, purity of mind, purity of tongue, and purity of action. They are therefore often presented with robes. For example, the Emerald Buddha has three changes of costume: a princely attire for the hot season, monastic robe for the rainy season, and a mantle of gold mesh for the cool season. Similar energy is felt to inhere in the miniature Buddhas which are worn as talismans to protect against evil spirits.

Buddhism has one aim and one aim only: to abolish suffering. It proposes to do so by the purely human means of ridding oneself of the causes of suffering which are craving, malice, and delusion. All Buddhist individuals are expected to eliminate craving and malice by exercising self-restraint and showing kindness to all creatures or "sentient beings." Only the monks though, are able to participate directly in the struggle against delusion.

Other aspects of the philosophy include the law of karma whereby every action has effects and the energy of past action, good or evil, continues forever and is 'reborn." (Some argue though that the Buddha took transmigration quite literally.) As a consequence "tam bun" or making merit is taken very seriously. This can be done by entering the monkhood for a few days or months, helping in the construction of a monastery or a stupa, contributing to education, giving alms, or performing any act of kindness no matter how small. When the monks go daily with their begging bowls from house to house they are giving the people an opportunity to make merit; similarly the boys who you will see carrying caged birds which people then free for a fee are allowing people to merit by freeing the bird from the cage. When making merit it is the motive that is all important—the intention of the mind at the time of the action determines the karmic outcome, not the action itself. Buddhism calls for self reliance; the individual embarks alone on the Noble Eightfold Path to Nirvana following the teachings that include the exhortations "to cease to do evil, learn to do good, cleanse your own heart."

Much of the ritual that you will observe in Thailand is also derived from Chinese and Indian traditions (including Confucianism and Brahmanism). For a living example of the Brahminical tradition stop by the Erawan shrine in Bangkok and watch the supplicants lighting joss sticks and asking for the god's help. (One of the reasons why the crowds are so thick here is that one man won the lottery after worshiping at the shrine.)

Although Buddhism first came to Thailand in the 3rd century B.C., when missionaries sent by King Asoka of India arrived at Suvannabhumi, near present-day Nakhon Pathom, not until the 14th century when the then king sent to Ceylon for a Theravadan Bhikku was the sangha (monastic order) established. The king entered the order, thus beginning the close connection between the royal house and the sangha which continues to this day.

Most Chinese and Vietnamese living in Thailand follow Mahayana Buddhism (there are 34 such monasteries in the country.)

Other religions and philosophies are also followed in Thailand including Islam, Christianity, Hinduism, and Sikhism. Sunni Islam is followed by more than two million Thais, mostly in the south. Most are of Malay origin and are descendants of the Muslim traders and missionaries who spread their teachings in the southern peninsula in the early 13th century. There are approximately 2,000 mosques in Thailand.

Christianity has been spread throughout Thailand since the 16th century by generations of Jesuit, Dominican, and Franciscan missionaries from Europe and America. Even with centuries of evangelism, there are only a quarter of a million Christians living in the country. Yet Thais have accepted much that has come from the Christian missionaries, particularly ideas on education, health, and science. Part of the reason that Christianity has failed to establish itself in the country is that the Thai inner spirit is unwilling to accept a limited or exclusive faith. One of our favorite stories is about a remark by King Mongkut (the king in *Anna and the King of Siam*) to a group of visiting missionaries: "What you teach us to do is admirable, but what you teach us to believe is foolish."

The king is dubbed "Upholder of All Religions" and, though a Buddhist, he is a testament to the Thai sense of tolerance and diversity that charges him to protect all beliefs. Still, it is the network of more than 27,000 Buddhist monasteries that most occupies that attention of the king and government.

IMPRESSIONS

Fundamentally the culture of Thailand may be summed up in one word, religion. For everything, arts and literature, social system, habits and customs is developed around her religion . . . to the people as a whole religious culture is still a living force.
—Phya Anuman Rajadhon, *Essay on Thai Folklore*, 1968

MYTH & FOLKLORE

Thai myth is principally derived from the Indian epic, the *Ramayana*. The Thai version, called the *Ramakien*, is a restatement of the epic text that is best known in Indonesian culture, especially as it is dramatized in the wayang kulit or shadow puppet plays. These stories involve brave kings and queens, heroic deeds, historical battles, animals that are transformed into people (and vice versa), clowns, and touching love stories. Many of the country's writers have taken classic stories from the *Ramakien* and updated them.

There is so much that could be classified as folklore or superstition in Thai village life, particularly in rural areas. It's too vast a topic to go into here, but there are some elements that you will certainly notice on your travels. For example, ancestor and spirit worship exists everywhere even in Bangkok where you will see "spirit houses," small replicas of houses standing on a pedestal that are filled with flowers, fruit, ribbons, and burning incense. There are shelters for gods who watch over the household; if a householder adds to his house then he will also expand the spirit house too so as not to alienate them. There are family spirits, rice spirits, tree spirits, village spirits—all kinds of spirits which inform many village customs. They are vestiges of the animism which was practiced before the advent of Buddhism. In some ways these spirits help to encourage social harmony and the resolution of village conflicts insofar as an individual who alienates the local spirits is a threat to the safety and well-being of the community.

Many of the festivals that are celebrated in Thailand derive from the same animistic roots, like the rain-generating Skyrocket festival *bun bang fai* in Northeast Thailand or Loy Krathong when offerings are made to the water goddess. For further discussion of this fascinating topic, see "Recommended Books & Films" below.

A rich folklore tradition also exists among the ethnic hill tribes in the north of Thailand. Each culture has its own story about the creation of the world and that people's place in the universe. The characters, rituals, and traditions within this much studied segment are well described in Paul and Elaine Lewis's *Peoples of the Golden Triangle*.

4. PERFORMING ARTS & EVENING ENTERTAINMENT

PERFORMING ARTS

There is much to see throughout the country in performing arts, particularly during the many festivals and holidays. Thai dance, which incorporates the subtlety of south Indian Kathakali gestures and elegant costumes dating from over 300 years, is most well known and is often performed. In the north, there are dances performed by members of the hill tribes; these are more closely related to traditional folk dance than to the so-called Thai classical style.

The *khon*, the dramatic masked performance of the *Ramakien*, is what most visitors will encounter. The performance dramatizes incidents from the story that tells of the war between Rama, rightful king of Ayutthaya, and Tosakanth, evil king of the island of Lonka, who abducts Rama's wife Sita. Rama is aided by his brother Lakshman and several monkey chieftains, including Hanuman with troops of monkeys. Tosakanth's allies are various demons (*Asuras, Rakshas,* and *Yakshas*). At one time all the performers wore masks, but generally speaking today the players of divine and human roles no longer wear masks; only the simians and demons do. The masks are magnificent. There are 100 masks for the demons alone and each mask is distinguished by its shape, color, and facial characteristics. The *Ramakien* stories are also told in shadow plays.

Thai musical composition uses the diatonic scale of seven full tones (no semitones) within an octave and uses simple duple time not compound time.

It is performed by a piphat band consisting of woodwind and percussion. The first is represented solely by the *pi-nai*, a cylindrical rosewood instrument with a reed that produces a piercing tone similar to a bagpipe. The percussion is divided into gongs, drums, and other metal percussive instruments. The *ranad ek*, is shaped like a wooden boat on a stand. Across it are hung 21 graduated resonance bars (like a xylophone). Its cousin is the *ranad thong* which is shaped like a tapered box. There are also deep-toned versions of both of these. The *gong wong yai*, which plays the principal melody, consists of a large oval frame of rattan or cane about two feet high and five feet from front to back which is strung with 16 metal discs of different pitches. The player sits in the circle beating them with hard and soft sticks. The *gong wong lek* is similar but smaller, while the *gong hoi* is a set of three very sonorous gongs, often beautifully decorated, which are suspended from a strand and played with padded sticks. The drums are represented by the *tapone*, a bulging drum on a stand that has different-size ends, one covered with ox or wild goat, the other with calf skin. Its sound effects are regulated by the application of a thick rice and ash paste. The *song na* is a thinner version of the tapone that is played on the lap. The *klong thad* is a very large drum that stands up on end. Both ends are the same size and only one size is beaten with thick bamboo sticks. *Charb lek* and *charb yai* are small and large cymbals, respectively. The *ching* are small heavy cup-shaped cymbals that are much more resonant than the triangle. These play the role of the conductor by setting the rhythm and the pace of the orchestra.

EVENING ENTERTAINMENT

Other than the performing arts, sports, and movies, many travelers to Thailand expect to visit the bawdy districts of such places as Patpong or Soi Cowboy in Bangkok, the bars in Pattaya, or the night market in Patong Beach on Phuket for sexually explicit entertainment. Most of this is discussed in other sections of this guide, but suffice to say, Thailand has a huge and growing problem with AIDS and those who engage in sexual activity are strongly encouraged to make use of condoms.

5. SPORTS & RECREATION

SPORTS

When most Thais get together to participate or watch a sporting event, there is often as much activity on the sidelines as on the field. This commotion relates to one of the country's grand passions: gambling. Thais love to wager, so that nearly any activity can be organized into a bet. Among the favorites are Thai boxing, fish-and-kite fighting, and net takraw, a Southeast Asian game that involves kicking a loosely woven rattan ball over a net à la volleyball or badminton (truly fantastic to watch and impossible, for us, to play).

Thai boxing is one of the great pastimes and is now included in many international competitions. The main difference between Western and Thai boxing is that the fighters are allowed to use their feet, requiring an entirely different set of rules, strategies, skill, and physique. Thai boxing reputedly began during the reign of King Naresuan, who in 1560 won his freedom in a hand-to-hand fight with the best of Burma. Since then, Thai boxing has been included in military training and has become the national sport.

Kite fighting is a seasonal sport that takes place in the spring. Teams are divided between Chula or male and Pakpao or female kites. The former is a pentagular kite fitted with sharp bamboo hooks, while the latter is half the size but drags a long, starched cotton tail with a string loop designed to snare its opponent. There are elaborate rules for Chula and Pakpao teams, and each kite has its own handling and flying crews.

Fish (as well as cock-and-cricket) fighting is another of the gambling sports. You'll likely have to travel outside of Bangkok to witness a bout, as such contests are illegal in the city. Most fish fights are conducted within a tall glass bowl and are fought to the death, with both sides chewing off fins, tails, and scales; obviously this is not for the faint of heart. Cock fighting is equally gruesome, although there are at least a few fights in which the loser merely loses. Not so with crickets. When one side wins the other is often devoured.

RECREATION

Thai recreational activities are numerous and similar to those available in most countries. Swimming, windsurfing, snorkeling and scuba diving, golfing, bicycling, jogging (although we wouldn't recommend this in Bangkok), tennis, squash, and racquetball are all available in most tourist destinations. For distinctly Asian activities we would recommend trying a game of takraw (if you're more physically adept than John) or an early morning t'ai chi session, a Chinese style of exercise and stretching. If you fashion yourself a good Ping-Pong player, watch out for the 10- to 15-year-old hustlers; they're much better than you!

6. FOOD & DRINK

FOOD

Food is one of the true joys of traveling in Thailand. If you aren't familiar with Thai cooking, imagine the best of Chinese food ingredients and preparation combined with the sophistication of Indian spicing and topped off with red and green chili. The styles of cooking available in Thailand run the gamut from northern khan toke to southern tiger prawns; in other words, you can find nearly any style of Thai (and Western) cooking in the capital. Basic ingredients include a cornucopia of shellfish, fresh fruits, and vegetables—lime, asparagus, tamarind, bean sprouts, carrots, mushrooms (many different kinds), morning glory, spinach, and bamboo shoots—and spices, including basil, lemongrass, mint, chili, garlic, and coriander. Thai cooking also uses coconut milk, curry paste, peanuts, and a large variety of noodles and rice.

Among the dishes you'll find throughout the country are: *tom yum goong*, a Thai hot-and-sour shrimp soup; *satay*, charcoal-broiled chicken, beef, or pork strips skewered on a bamboo stick and dipped in a peanut-coconut curry sauce; spring rolls, similar to egg rolls but thinner and usually containing only vegetables; *larb*, a spicy chicken or ground-beef concoction with mint-and-lime flavoring; salads, made with nearly any ingredient as the prime flavor, but most have a dressing made with onion, chili pepper, lime juice, and fish sauce; *pad thai*, literally "Thai noodles" (this is one of our favorites and you can find it everywhere), with rice noodles, large shrimp, eggs, peanuts, fresh bean sprouts, lime, and a delicious sauce; *khao soi*, a northern curried soup served at small food stalls; a wide range of curries, flavored with coriander, chili, garlic, and fish sauce or coconut milk; *tod man pla*, one of many preparations of fish, this one is spicy; sticky rice, served in the north and made from glutinous rice, prepared with vegetables and wrapped in a banana leaf; and Thai fried rice, a simple rice dish made with whatever the kitchen has on hand.

As a word of caution, the Thai palate relishes incredibly spicy food, normally much hotter than is tolerated in even the most piquant Western cuisine. Protect your palate with "mai phet, farang" meaning "not spicy, foreigner." If you begin to suffer from Thai-food burnout, visit a Chinese restaurant. Most of the Chinese cuisine in

Thailand is from Yunnan Province or Canton, meaning delicious food with restrained spices. However, most Thai and Chinese food, particularly in the cheaper restaurants and food stalls, is cooked with lots of MSG (known locally as "Ajinomoto" because of the popular Japanese brand widely used), and it's almost impossible to avoid.

Traditionally, Thai menus don't offer fancy desserts. The most you'll find are coconut milk–based sweets or a variety of fruit-flavored custards, but the local fruit is luscious enough for a perfect dessert. Familiar fruits are pineapple (eaten with salt to heighten the flavor), mangoes, bananas, guava, papaya, coconut, and watermelon, as well as the latest rage, apples grown in the royal orchards. Less familiar is durian, in season during June and July, which tastes wonderful but smells odious; mangosteen, a purplish, hard-skinned fruit with delicate, whitish-pink segments that melt in the mouth, available April to September; jackfruit, which is large, yellow-brown with a thick, thorned skin that envelops tangy-flavored flesh, available year-round; litchie; longan, a small, brown-skinned fruit with very sweet white flesh available July to October; tamarind, a spicy little fruit in a pod that you can eat fresh; rambutan, which is small, red, and hairy, with transparent sweet flesh clustered round a woody seed, available May to July; and pomelo, similar to a grapefruit, but less juicy, available October to December. By the way, some of these fruits are served as salads— the raw green papaya, for example, is particularly delicious.

With a strong resident international community, Thailand has a large assortment of European-style restaurants. Don't be surprised if your Thai host suggests visiting a French or Italian restaurant (the latter has become the dining fad of the mid-1990s in Thailand's major cities and resorts). They are extremely popular and often quite good. If you do visit a Western-style restaurant, try those unique dishes that combine traditional European recipes with native Thai ingredients.

Thailand also has many Indian restaurants, with a wide variety of vegetarian dishes. We've found that most of the Indian restaurants serve less spicy, northern cuisine, not the fiery dishes from the south.

DINING CUSTOMS The Thai family usually has an early breakfast of *khao tom*, a rice soup (made from leftovers) to which chicken, seafood, or meat may be added. Typically, it's served with a barely cooked egg floating on top and a variety of pickled vegetables, relishes, and spicy condiments to add flavor. It's our favorite breakfast, and widely available at even the poshest hotels.

The Thais take eating very seriously, so business people allow two to three hours for lunch. A formal business luncheon consists of several dishes, but most casual diners have a one-course rice, noodle, or curry dish. For two tourists, two hot dishes and perhaps a cold salad (mostly of the "not spicy" variety) are a satisfying way to sample new foods. Most restaurants offer lunch from noon to 2pm; in fact, many close until 6 or 7pm before reopening for dinner.

Thais usually stop at one of the ubiquitous food stalls for a large bowl of noodle soup (served with meat, fish, or poultry), or dine at a department store food hall or market where they can buy snacks from many different vendors and have a seat. Snacking from streetside food stalls—some would claim the source of the best Thai food—is popular throughout the day.

Dinner is the main meal, and consists of a soup (*gaeng jued*); curried dish (*gaeng ped*); steamed, fried, stir-fried, or grilled dish (*nueng, thod, paad,* or *yaang*); a side dish of salad or condiments (*krueang kiang*), steamed rice (*khao*), and some fruit (*polamai*). Two Thais dining out may share four of five dishes (typically balanced as sweet, salty, sour, bitter, and piquant), always helping themselves to a little portion at a time (so as not to appear gluttonous). Dishes are brought to the table as they're cooked and eaten in any order.

Bangkok's elite often follow the lead of their Singapore and Hong Kong neighbors by entertaining guests at Chinese, French, or continental restaurants, often located in the city's best hotels. For those at the other end of the economic spectrum, American-style fast-food restaurants have become popular dating venues. Many travelers use their evening meals to sample Thai buffets or banquet menus, prepared in conjunction with classical music and dance performances.

**FROMMER'S SMART TRAVELER:
RESTAURANTS**

1. If you can't eat Thai food at the extremely hot (spicy) level that is served in most restaurants outside the major tourist centers, inform the waiter that you want it "MAI PHET, FARANG." (Not spicy, foreigner.) If you forget to add the "farang," the chef may assume you're a Thai diner with a subtler palate, rather than a foreigner who's serious about the request.

2. Splurge on a Thai or Chinese feast rather than gourmet continental fare, as these are the least-expensive (and usually better-prepared) cuisines throughout the country.

3. There's no need to save those fresh fish and lobster specials for the beach resorts, because most seafood is shipped to Bangkok where competition keeps seafood prices lower.

4. Thai food is served family style, so the greater the number of diners, the cheaper the meal and the greater the variety. Dishes are often priced according to size: small (two person), medium (four to six portions), or large (six or more) orders.

5. Single travelers will find rice dishes (such as *khao pad kai*, chicken fried rice) or noodle dishes (such as *goon kuai tiao*, prawns with rice noodles) the cheapest, most satisfying, one-plate dinners. A soup (such as *tom yom pla*, spicy fish soup, or *khao soi*, spicy Northern curried soup) or salad (such as *yam nua*, beef salad) can be a filling one-plate lunch served with rice.

6. The traditional Thai breakfast of *khao tom* (a bland rice soup served with either pork, chicken, crab, or fish, vegetables, an egg, and several condiments for flavor) is cheaper at most hotels than a skimpy continental or mediocre American breakfast and provides more sustenance for a morning of sightseeing.

7. In the cities, the food courts in the major department stores are the cheapest places to eat. In smaller towns, you can dine for next to nothing at the Night Markets, though hygiene is sometimes questionable.

8. "MAI SAI PHONG CHU ROD" means "Please don't add MSG." If you get that fuzzy-brained, dull headache from a monosodium glutamate rush after eating most Asian foods, be warned—the Thais use a lot of it. Most chefs know it as "Ajinomoto," the Japanese brand which has become a generic name for this flavor enhancer. At all but the finest restaurants, it's usually premixed with seasonings and sauces, but it never hurts to ask. Drinking water seems to dispel the MSG haze more quickly.

9. If you want an alcoholic beverage with your meal, you'll find Thai beer (usually the price of an average main dish) is the best value, because imported beer, liquor, and wine are extremely expensive.

DRINK

You won't have a problem finding alcohol, as nearly every town in Thailand has an ample supply of bars, and liquor and beer are widely available in stores, restaurants, and hotels. Several fine varieties of beer are brewed in the country; the best known are Sigha and a locally brewed German beer, Kloste (our favorite). There isn't much in the way of Thai wine. Most wine is imported and incredibly expensive; it's readily available in Bangkok, Chiang Mai, and at the beach resorts but not in the countryside, except in Western restaurants. Be warned that the storage of fine wines is rarely up to snuff and the result is that your favorite red may be undrinkable. Local whisky, such as Mekong, is very popular. Johnnie Walker Black is still one of the most highly prized gifts you can give.

7. RECOMMENDED BOOKS & FILMS

BOOKS

If you're planning an extensive tour of the country, we recommend the *APA Insight Guide on Thailand* (published in the United States and Canada by Random House) for in-depth historical and cultural background. The low-budget tourist on an extended tour of off-the-beaten-track destinations would do well to purchase Lonely Planet's *Thailand: A Travel Survival Kit*, by Joe Cummings. If you plan to travel to out-of-the-way upcountry villages, try John Hoskin's *Guide to Chiang Mai & Northern Thailand* (Hong Kong: Hong Kong Publishing Co., 1986).

For an entertaining and well-written history of Bangkok, read Alec Waugh's *Bangkok, Story of a City* (Boston: Little Brown, 1971). William Warren's *Bangkok's Waterways* (Bangkok: Asian Books) provides an entertaining tour of the river and klongs of contemporary Bangkok. For a more in-depth travel guide to the capital, read *Frommer's Bangkok* (New York: Macmillan Travel). We also suggest Collin Piprell's *Bangkok Knights* (Editions Duang Kamol, D. K. Books, 1991), a collection of short stories by a Canadian resident, set in contemporary Bangkok.

For a historical overview of the region, try D. G. E. Hall's *A History of Southeast Asia* (London: Macmillan, 1977); or for more specifics, M. L. Jumsai's *Popular History of Thailand* (Bangkok: Chalermnit, 1970), or W. A. R. Wood's *A History of Siam* (London: Unwin, 1979).

For 19th-century descriptions of travel in Thailand, we recommend *Temples and Elephants* (Oxford: Oxford University Press), a delightful account written during King Chulalongkorn's reign by Carl Bock.

Among the best works on art and sculpture are Piriya Krairiksh's *The Sacred Image and Art in Thailand Since 1932* (Bangkok: White Lotus, 1980), as well as Reginald LeMay's *The Culture of Southeast Asia* (London: Unwin, 1954).

Literary works in English include *Anna and the King of Siam*, by Margaret Landon, and the related and recently reprinted *The English Governess at the Siamese Court*, by Anna Leonowens (London: Oxford University Press); William Warren's *Jim Thompson: The Legendary American* (Boston: Houghton Mifflin; now out-of-print but available in libraries); Reginald Campbell's *Teak-Wallah* (Oxford: Oxford University Press, 1985); and Ernest Young's *The Kingdom of the Yellow Robe* (Oxford: Oxford University Press). Many of these books can be ordered from Paragon Book Gallery Ltd., 2130 Broadway, Mezzanine, New York, NY 10023 (tel. 212/496-2378), or Traveller's Bookstore, 22 West 52nd St., New York, NY 10019 (tel. 212/664-0995).

Thai literary suggestions include translations of the epic Sanskrit work, *Ramakien*, based on the Ramayana; *Four Reigns* and *Red Bamboo*, by Kukrit Pramoj (Bangkok: D. K. Books), a contemporary novelist; and *A Man Called Karn*, by Suwanee Sukonta (Bangkok: Bannakarn). Pira Sudham's *Monsoon Country* (Bangkok: Shire Books) is written in English and is a good literary companion for those traveling through the Northeast.

For a better understanding of Buddhism and the customs and culture of the country the following titles are all filled with fascinating material. The first two are easily available; the rest can be found in English bookstores in Thailand. *Buddhism* by Christmas Humphreys (Penguin, 1987) gives a good, clear explanation of Buddhism, including an extensive discussion of Theravada. *Three Ways of Asian Wisdom* by

Nancy Wilson Ross (Simon & Schuster, 1966) is a classic, providing brilliant explication of the complex intuitions at the heart of Hinduism, Buddhism, and Zen. *Essays on Thai Folklore* (Bangkok: Editions Duang Kamol) by Phya Anuman Rajadhon, who was president of the Siam Society, is filled with descriptions and explanations of rites, rituals, ceremonies, superstitions, and traditional folktales. His *Some Traditions of the Thai* concentrates on birth customs. *Reflections on Thai Culture* by William J. Klausner (Siam Society, 1987) is a collection of essays about traditional village life, popular Buddhism, the law, and customs covering everything from *krengjai* (deference and consideration), gift-giving, and the meaning of *sanuk* (fun), to bargaining, body language, taboos, and eating habits. *More Thai Ways* (Allied Newspapers, 1982) by Denis Segaller, an Englishman now living in Thailand, takes a living look at Thai people and customs touching on all kinds of things: the royal barge procession, the relationship of the people to the monarchy, language, fruits, flowers, ceremonies, and much more.

A good introduction for businesspeople who intend to work in the country is *Conflict or Communication*, reprinted from Business in Thailand (Business Information and Research Co., Phetchaburi Road, Bangkok), or the newly revised edition of *Culture Shock: Thailand* (Singapore: Times Books). If you plan to live in Thailand—particularly in Bangkok—for an extended amount of time, the *Bangkok Guide* (compiled by the Australian–New Zealand Women's Group, Bangkok, 1990) is an excellent reference handbook that will ease your move.

For an overview of the hill tribes in Thailand, we recommend Paul and Elaine Lewis's excellent *Peoples of the Golden Triangle* (London and New York: Thames and Hudson, 1984), with detailed descriptions and color photographs of the main tribes in and around the north; George Young's *The Hill Tribes of Northern Thailand* (Bangkok: Siam Society, 1966); and the Technical Service Club's *The Hill Tribes of Thailand* (Thailand, 1986).

Samitsuda Ekachai's collection of interviews with residents of Isan in *Behind the Smile* (Development Support Committee, 1990) is a fascinating look at life in the Northeast.

FILMS

Few films have been made about Thailand, but recently a spate of Vietnam War pictures have been shot in the country to replicate other Southeast Asian areas. *The Killing Fields* deals with the mass murder of Cambodians during the Pol Pot regime and takes place along the Thai-Cambodian border. Monologist Spalding Gray describes his experiences in Thailand on the production of the same film in *Swimming to Cambodia*. *Casualties of War* was shot on the island of Phuket and *Air America* was filmed in Mae Hong Son and Chiang Mai.

Robert De Niro starred in the Academy Award–winning *The Deer Hunter*, which was partially filmed in Thailand. Robin Williams played a disc jockey during the war in *Good Morning Vietnam*, another feature shot in Thailand. *Rambo III* was shot in Bangkok and Chiang Mai. Oliver Stone shot *Heaven and Earth* in Thailand during 1993. *Pirates* was partially filmed in Phuket. The James Bond thriller *The Man with the Golden Gun*, used Phangnga Bay as a backdrop for an exciting chase sequence.

Going further back, *The Ugly American* was shot in Bangkok in 1963. On a more lurid note, you might look for *Emmanuelle in Bangkok* in the adult section of your video store.

On a more classical note, the Rex Harrison and Linda Darnell version of *Anna and the King of Siam*, followed by the musical version with Yul Brynner and Deborah Kerr, *The King and I*, were both shot in Hollywood on a soundstage; both are banned in Thailand as they are considered disrespectful to the monarchy.

CHAPTER 2

PLANNING A TRIP TO THAILAND

This chapter is devoted to the where, when, and how of your trip—the advance planning issues required to get it together and take it on the road. It should help you budget your trip and resolve other important questions: when to go; whether or not to take a tour; what other alternative travel vacations are available; what pretrip health precautions to take; what insurance coverage is needed; where to obtain more information about the destination; and so on.

1. INFORMATION, ENTRY REQUIREMENTS & MONEY

SOURCES OF INFORMATION

A major source of free and excellent information is the **Tourist Authority of Thailand** (TAT), with offices throughout the country and abroad. Consult the TAT on travel plans, hotels, transportation options, and current schedules for festivals and holidays. A multilingual Tourist Police force is part of the TAT in all major tourist areas within Thailand. They are helpful in emergencies (such as filing police reports for theft) and can provide local information.

You'll find TAT offices at 3440 Wilshire Blvd., Suite 1100, Los Angeles, CA 90010 (tel. 213/382-2353); 303 Wacker Dr., Suite 400, Chicago, IL 60601 (tel. 312/819-3990); 5 World Trade Center, Suite 3443, New York, NY 10048 (tel. 212/432-0433); 49 Albemarle St., London WIX 3FE, England, United Kingdom (tel. 071/499-7679); and Royal Exchange Building, 12th floor, 56 Pitt St., Sydney 2000, Australia (tel. 02/247-7549).

You can also contact the **Royal Thai Consulate General** at 351 E. 52nd St., New York, NY 10022 (tel. 212/754-1770); 35 E. Wacker Dr., Suite 1834, Chicago, IL 60601 (tel. 312/236-2447); 801 N. La Brea Ave., Los Angeles, CA 90038 (tel. 213/937-1894); and the Royal Thai Embassy at 2300 Kalorama Rd. NW, Washington, DC 20008 (tel. 202/483-7200), or the **Royal Thai Embassy** in your home country. For additional information in other Asian cities, contact the local **Thai Airways International** office.

Follow your local newspapers for current information about the state of affairs in Thailand and Southeast Asia. Travelers should contact the **Travel Advisory**

Service of the U.S. Department of State (tel. 202/647-5225) to see if any recent travel advisories have been issued about the area.

ENTRY REQUIREMENTS

All visitors to Thailand must carry a valid passport with proof of onward passage (either a return or through ticket). Visas are not required if you are staying up to 15 days and are a national of 41 designated countries. Fifteen-day visas can be issued at Don Muang airport to nationals of 80 other countries with proof of return passage.

Visa-free entry cannot be extended. Entry and departure must be through the airport or one of the major ports of entry; check with the Thai consulate or embassy in your country if you plan to enter Thailand via an exotic port. To stay longer than 15 days, you need to apply for a 60-day tourist visa or 30-day transit visa at any Thai embassy or consulate. A valid passport, two photographs, and $10 are required for a transit visa, $15 for a tourist visa, and $20 for a nonimmigrant (business) visa. Business people need a visa for making business contacts, calls, or meetings, as well as employment. A nonimmigrant visa for up to 90 days can be obtained with a letter from your employer, stating the purpose and length of stay. If you have a question as to which type is required (if any), call or write to the nearest Thai embassy or consulate. The entire process takes one business day when you apply in person, and all visas must be used within 90 days of issuance.

Check at the consulate or embassy for up-to-date information about health certificates that may be required for entry.

There are no restrictions on the import of foreign currencies or traveler's checks; but, you cannot export foreign currency in excess of $10,000 unless declared to Customs upon arrival. Individuals may bring a maximum of 2,000B (4,000B per family) into the country and may take out a maximum of 500B (1,000B per family) upon exit.

MONEY

CASH & CURRENCY

The Thai unit of currency is the **baht** (written B) divided into 100 **satang** (though you'll rarely see a satang coin). Copper-colored coins represent 25 and 50 satang; silver-colored coins are 1B, 2B, and 5B (note: the 1B and old 5B coins are the same size). Baht notes come in denominations of 10B (brown), 20B (green), 100B (red), and 500B (purple). The exchange rate at the time of publication was 25B = $1 U.S., making 1B equal to 4 cents.

WHAT THINGS COST IN BANGKOK	U.S. $
Taxi from the airport to the city center	12.00
Local Telephone Call (private pay phone)	.20
Double at The Oriental (deluxe)	300.00
Double at Wall Street Inn (moderate)	86.00
Double at Peachy Guesthouse (budget)	6.20
Lunch for one at Ban Chiang (inexpensive)	9.00
Lunch for one at Suda (budget)	5.00
Dinner for one, without wine, at Sala Thip (moderate)	20.00
Dinner for one, without wine, at Lemongrass (inexpensive)	17.00
Dinner for one, without wine, at M. K. Restaurant (budget)	6.50
Pint of beer	3.20
Coca-Cola	.95
Cup of coffee	.60

Roll of ASA 100 Kodacolor film, 36 exposures	4.80
Admission to the National Museum	1.00
Movie ticket	2.00

WHAT THINGS COST IN MAE HONG SON — U.S. $

Taxi from the airport to the city center	5.00
Local Telephone Call (pay phone)	.04
Double at Mae Hong Son Resort (deluxe)	104.00
Double at Maehongson Resort (moderate)	64.00
Double at Piya Complex (budget)	10.00
Lunch for one at Kai-mook (moderate)	5.00
Dinner for one, without beer, Night Market (budget)	2.00
Pint of beer	2.00
Coca-Cola	.60
Cup of coffee	.50
Roll of ASA 100 Kodacolor film, 36 exposures	7.00
Fee for a day trek to tribal villages	27.00

TRAVELER'S CHECKS & CREDIT CARDS

Traveler's checks are negotiable in most banks, hotels, restaurants, and tourist-oriented shops, but you'll receive a better rate cashing them at commercial banks.

Nearly all international hotels and larger businesses accept major credit cards, but few accept personal checks. Despite protest from credit-card companies, most establishments add a 3% to 5% surcharge for payment by credit card. In smaller towns and remote provinces, baht will be the only acceptable currency.

CURRENCY EXCHANGE RATES

At this writing $1 equals approximately 25B (or 1B = 4 cents), and this was the rate of exchange used to calculate the dollar values given in this book. The rate fluctuates from time to time and may not be the same when you travel to Thailand. Therefore, the following table should be used only as a guide:

THE BAHT & THE DOLLAR

Baht	U.S.$	Baht	U.S.$
1	0.04	500	20.00
4	0.20	750	30.00
10	0.40	1,000	40.00
15	0.60	1,250	50.00
20	0.80	1,500	60.00
25	1.00	1,750	70.00
50	2.00	2,000	80.00
75	3.00	2,250	90.00
100	4.00	2,500	100.00

Baht	U.S.$	Baht	U.S.$
125	5.00	2,750	110.00
150	6.00	3,000	120.00
175	7.00	3,250	130.00
200	8.00	3,500	140.00
225	9.00	3,750	140.00
250	10.00	4,000	160.00

For British travelers here is how the pound sterling was exchanged for the Thai Baht at press time.

THE BAHT & THE BRITISH POUND

Baht	£	Baht	£
2	.05	368	8
4.5	.10	414	9
11.5	.25	460	10
23	.50	690	15
34.5	.75	920	20
46	1	1,150	25
92	2	1,380	30
138	3	1,610	35
184	4	1,840	40
230	5	2,300	50
322	7	4,600	100

2. WHEN TO GO—CLIMATE, HOLIDAYS & EVENTS

CLIMATE Thailand has two distinct climates; the humid south is tropical, and the humid north is a tropical savanna. There are three distinct seasons (except in the more temperate south). The hot season lasts from March to May, temperatures averaging in the upper 90s Fahrenheit (mid-30s Celsius). The rainy season lasts from June to October; the average temperature 84° F (29°C) with 90% humidity. The cool season, from November through February, has temperatures from the high 70s to low 80s Fahrenheit (26°C).

In the north, particularly in the hills around Chiang Mai, temperatures can go down to the low 60s (16°C). The southern half of the country, particularly the southern Malay Peninsula, has intermittent showers year-round, and daily ones during the monsoon (temperatures average in the low 80s [30°C]). However, Thailand's monsoon isn't as imposing as in other Asian countries—you can actually travel around the country in some comfort.

HOLIDAYS Many holidays are based on the Thai lunar calendar; check with TAT for the current year's schedule and see Chapter 11, "Exploring Northern Thailand," for festivals and events specific to that region.

The national holidays besides our New Year's Eve and New Year's Day (there is also the Buddhist new year's water-throwing festival Songkran, each April 12–14, and the Chinese New Year, late January/early February) are: Magha Puja, in February, celebrating the day the Buddha preached his doctrines; Chakri Day, April 6, commemorating the founding of the Chakri dynasty (the reigning dynasty); Coronation Day, on May 5, honoring the coronation of His Majesty King Bhumibol in 1950; Visakha Puja, in mid-May, marking the birth, enlightenment, and death of the

Buddha; Asalha Puja, in July, signaling the beginning of the Rains' Retreat and the 3-month period of meditation for all Buddhist monks; August 12, marking the birthday of Her Majesty the Queen and also Mothers' Day; Thot Kathin, in October, during which monks are presented with new robes; Chulalongkorn Day, on October 23, honoring the country's favorite king; Loy Krathong, in early November, one of Thailand's greatest holidays, honoring the water spirit and serving as a day to wash away sins committed during the previous year; December 5, marking His Majesty the King's birthday and Fathers' Day; and December 10, Constitution Day, recognizing Thailand's first constitution in 1932.

There are many more holidays celebrated by local people of various regions; check with TAT or see specific chapters for regional information and local schedules.

THAILAND CALENDAR OF EVENTS

FEBRUARY

☐ **Flower Festival,** Chiang Mai. Parades and exhibits (first weekend).

APRIL

☐ **Pattaya Festival,** Pattaya. Arts, fireworks, beauty pageant (first week).
☐ **International Kite Festival,** Bangkok. Contest and displays (third week).

MAY

☐ **Royal Plowing Festival,** nationwide. Demonstrations, Royal blessings to mark the commencement of the rice-planting cycle (first week).

SEPTEMBER/OCTOBER

☐ **Boat Races,** in Phichit and in Nan Province. Races, country fairs, parades to mark the end of the rains (first week of each month).

OCTOBER

☐ **Vegetarian Festival,** Phuket. Chinese religious festival with parades, temple ceremonies, athletic competitions (second week for nine days).

NOVEMBER

☐ **Elephant Roundup,** Surin, Northeast. Elephant parades, demonstrations, cultural performances (third weekend).

3. HEALTH, INSURANCE & OTHER CONCERNS

HEALTH You shouldn't have any health problems; however, it's best to be aware of potential problems associated with travel to exotic lands. First, consult with your doctor regarding his/her recommendation on immunizations and inoculations (though none are legally required for entrance into Thailand), at least one month prior to departure. Malaria, Japanese encephalitis, typhoid, and hepatitis A are endemic to some rural parts of Thailand and some prophylaxis may be recommended. You can also call the Centers for Disease Control and Prevention (tel. 404/332-4559) or order the current edition of their book *Health Information for International Travel.*

Health Tips Above all, do not drink the tap water, even in Bangkok where the Municipal Authority purifies it. Make sure water is boiled or bottled, and that boiled water has been used to make ice cubes. Avoid salads and fresh dairy products, including ice cream. Don't eat unpeeled fruit or vegetables, except at the larger hotels and restaurants, and even there, inquire whether fresh food is washed with purified water. We love to eat street food, but exercise caution; check to see if oil and ingredients look fresh, and never eat anything raw prepared at a street stand, especially seafood.

Don't swim in freshwater streams or pools (other than chlorinated hotel pools), as they are probably contaminated. Avoid the ocean near the outlets of sewage pipes and freshwater streams, because of contaminated water (especially around Pattaya) and the poisonous sea snakes that inhabit these areas. Be especially careful of coral reefs (such as those along Phuket), jellyfish, and sea urchins, and treat all cuts or stings immediately by washing and applying an antibiotic cream. Ear infections are a common problem, so dry your ears thoroughly.

Avoid sunstroke or heat exhaustion by exercising caution about physical activity. Thailand's slower pace of life is dictated by the hot and humid weather. Drink lots of liquid to avoid dehydration; inexpensive bottled water is widely sold. Avoid excessive exposure to the sun, use a strong sunscreen, and wear a hat for protection. Restricting alcohol consumption and eating lightly will help acclimatization. Diarrhea is to be expected in the adjustment to a new cuisine and climate. If it persists beyond 48 hours or is accompanied by fever or dehydration, consult a doctor.

The **Medical Service** (tel. 252-5040) at the American Embassy is extremely knowledgeable about local maladies and can refer you to local physicians or hospitals for appropriate treatment.

SEX Every day you're in Thailand, in any part of the country, you will see foreigners enjoying the company of Thai women and men. Although prostitution is illegal, it is as much a product of the tourism industry as superb hotels and stunning beaches.

To many, the Thai sense of morality may seem contradictory and confusing. As devout followers of Buddhism, Thais should theoretically eschew lust as a worldly sin. Yet, Thai men openly frequent brothels after marriage, while condemning the prostitutes who work there. In poor, uneducated, rural families, where sons are counted on as farm labor, sex has become an unfortunate income-earning occupation for daughters. Yet girls sent to the big cities as CSWs (the official term is "commercial sex worker") can quietly retire, return to their villages, and even get married. Thai society tends to ignore the men employed as CSWs; although homosexuality is not condoned, most turn a blind eye to it and the more blatant transvestism seen in the major cities.

Stemming from a legacy of royal patronage and social acceptance, the oldest profession has been part of Thailand's economy for centuries, although, until the 1930s, the majority of CSWs were foreign. Today this burgeoning industry is still publicly ignored, at a time when the estimated 800,000 Thai-born CSWs (with an additional 70,000 working in Japan) outnumber schoolteachers by at least 30%.

Despite these numbers, there are not enough CSWs to satisfy demand. The growth in tourist arrivals has meant a tremendous increase in new clientele. Increased rural employment opportunities and education have created a shortage of willing workers. Because clients are insisting on younger and younger CSWs in the foolhardy belief that children will be AIDS-free, Thailand currently has the world's largest child sex industry. Many traders who promise parents urban employment opportunities (such as domestic service, dishwashing, or housekeeping work) then enslave male and female children in sex clubs and massage parlors.

Since sex has become a standard stop on the tourist itinerary, Thailand has had to aggressively develop research and education programs on the subject of AIDS. The largest nongovernmental organization in Thailand, the PDA or Population and

Community Development Agency, has enlarged the scope of their rural development programs from family planning and cottage-industry schemes, to distributing condoms and running informational seminars for CSWs. Even the royal family is in on it: Her Royal Highness Princess Chulaporn Walailuke, founder of the Chulaporn Research Institute and an internationally known activist, sponsored the 1990 International Global AIDS Conference in Bangkok, and continues to be active.

As elsewhere, when it comes to AIDS prevention, education and practice are still worlds aparts. According to EMPOWER, an activist group founded by Bangkok's CSWs to provide education and health care, CSWs connot convince most of their clients to wear condoms. Government statistics estimate as many as 400,000 carry the AIDS virus, equal to approximately 50% of the CSW population.

INSURANCE Check your insurance policy before departure to make sure that overseas medical treatment, hospitalization, and medical evacuation are fully covered. Contact your own insurance company (or any membership organization such as AAA) to see if they can provide a rider to cover trip cancellation, baggage insurance, and any uncovered medical expenses. Make arrangements with someone at home who will assume financial responsibility for your medical care or can wire transfer funds to you in case of emergency.

Several travel insurance and assistance companies offer short-term policies to cover trip cancellation costs, medical bills, medical transporation, and baggage insurance. International SOS Assistance, Inc., Eight Neshaminy Interplex, Suite 207, Trevose, PA 19053 (tel. toll free 800/523-8930), or at P.O. Box 466, Place Bonaventure, Montreal, Quebec H5A 1C1 (tel. 514/874-7674), provides emergency evacuation services to members for a small fee (an air-ambulance evacuation with accompanying medical personnel can run as high as $25,000), plus other coverage at reasonable rates. Two recommended companies who issue temporary policies (fees are based on amount of coverage and duration of trip) are Healthcare Global, c/o Wallach & Company, Inc., Middleburg, VA. (tel. toll free 800/237-6615); and Travel Guard Internationale, c/o Transamerica Premier Insurance Co., 1100 Center Point Dr., Stevens Point, WI 54481-9970 (tel. toll free 800/782-5151). Travmed, issued by the International Travelers Assistance Association of Baltimore (tel. toll free 800/732-5309), is another policy with a low deductible and good coverage.

4. WHAT TO PACK

CLOTHING Light, casual clothing is your best defense against the heat. Breathable cotton or linen is far preferable to synthetics (hotels usually offer inexpensive, prompt laundry service). Thai society is relatively formal; count on wearing modest styles (no strapless blouses or shorts, for example), especially if you are touring wats (temples) or other religious or royal monuments. Since you are often required to remove your shoes in religious buildings, we suggest easy-to-remove footwear, such as sandals or slip-on shoes. At the beaches, nudity is illegal and offensive to local residents.

Men should generally wear long pants, though longer shorts are acceptable in beach communities. Pressed cotton pants, shirt, and tie (a jacket is optional, depending on the formality of the meeting) are appropriate for business and government meetings, a coat and tie is proper for evening engagements. Women should refrain from short or revealing clothing; casual skirts or dresses are appropriate for evening. Though it's very fashionable, we try to avoid wearing too much black; it's considered, at least among the more traditional Thais, an unlucky color. During the winter, bring a light sweater; during the monsoon, bring an umbrella.

OTHER ITEMS Travelers who wear eyeglasses or contact lenses should carry an extra pair. If you're traveling outside the big cities, a small flashlight will come in handy during occasional power blackouts. Low budget travelers should bring a towel and soap with them, as the cheapest hostels will not provide them, and may need a sleeping bag in rural areas during the cool season. Many common nonprescription medications and toiletries are widely available, but we always carry our favorite sun block and mosquito repellent with us. You may also want to carry premoistened towelettes, effective for cleaning your hands before dining and refreshing in the heat.

5. ALTERNATIVE/SPECIALTY TRAVEL

EDUCATIONAL/STUDY TRAVEL The Thai language is very difficult for most foreigners to learn. However, several institutions offer courses to resident expatriates and long-term visitors. One of the most successful programs is at the **AUA Language Center,** 179 Rajdamri Rd., Bangkok 10330 (tel. 02/252-8170 or 02/252-8395), where 5-week terms (classes given five days a week) begin year-round. Rates vary according to programs, but both the Natural Approach and Structural Approach to teaching languages, as well as reading and writing, are offered to students. Another popular language school with on-site dorm accommodations (at the YWCA) is the **Siri Pattana Language School,** c/o Bangkok YWCA, 13 Sathorn Tai Rd., 10120 Bangkok (tel. 02/213-12060. Contact the TAT for more information about language study in other regions of Thailand.

Thai cuisine is so fine and sophisticated that cooking is also a popular study topic. The fanciest and best-known program is the **Thai Cooking School** at the Oriental Hotel, 48 Oriental Ave., Bangkok 10500 (tel. 02/236-0400 or 02/236-0420), a 5-day course ($500 for four hours per day including lunch) which repeats every week. Students are given clearly printed recipes; bags of Thai spices and herbs; exciting demonstrations of chopping, cooking, arranging, and serving; and the opportunity to sample dishes assembled by a uniformed staff of sous-chefs who assist the able instructor. See "Attractions," in Chapter 12 for a recommended Chiang Mai chef who teaches in his home, or contact the TAT for other cooking school recommendations.

Last but not least, some travelers come to Thailand to study Buddhism. Depending on your interest, you might want to contact Wat Po, the monastery in Bangkok, where the traditional Thai massage and healing arts are taught. Bangkok's Wat Mahathat near the Grand Palace is the home of the **Mahu Chulalongkorn Buddhist University.** Those interested in meditation and theology may want to spend time at **Suan Mokkh,** a monastery and meditation center in Chaiya, Surat Thani (See Chapter 7, "Ko Samui & the Southeast Coast," for more information) are held monthly. Contact the TAT for more retreats ($24 including room and board) are held monthly. Contact the TAT for more specific information about Buddhist organizations.

Several museums, societies, universities, and colleges plan escorted educational Southeast Asia and Thailand tours for their members. Two of the largest institutions whose experts host tours are the **Smithsonian Institution,** Study Tours and Seminars, 1100 Jefferson Dr. SW, MRC702, Washington, DC 20560 (tel. 202/357-4700), and the **Asia Society,** Travel Department, 725 Park Ave., New York, NY 10021 (tel. 212/288-6400). Nonmembers can receive information about tours and pay the nominal membership fee with their reservations.

ADVENTURE/WILDERNESS International enthusiasm for trekking, the sport of walking escorted by local guides and porters, has inspired several tour operators in Northern Thailand to provide services to remote hill-tribe areas best visited on foot. In fact, many also offer Jeep, boat, and elephant-back treks to accommodate those unwilling or unable to walk. These trips have frequent departures and can be arranged after your arrival in Thailand (see Chapters 11, 12, and 13 for information about treks in Northern Thailand).

Some adventure travel specialists offer organized trips to Thailand that can be the centerpiece of your journey. Our favorite such company, and one we've had wonderful adventures with, is **Mountain Travel Sobek,** 6420 Fairmount Ave., El Cerrito, CA 94530 (tel. toll free 800/227-2384). In 1993, they offered a 16-day combination hike/elephant trek in the northern hills, with stops in Chiang Mai and Phrae, as well as extensions to Laos and Cambodia. ($2,590 land costs per person, from Bangkok, for two to six passengers).

Another adventure specialist we've had good experiences with is **Exodus Adventures,** 9 Weir Rd., London SW12 OLT, England, U.K. (tel. 081/675-5550; 081/673-0779). They offer a 17-day trip from Bangkok through central and northern Thailand, then to the beach (combining trekking, a rice-barge cruise, train, bus, and ferry). **Absolute Asia,** 155 W. 68th St., Suite 525, New York, NY 10023 (tel. 212/595-5782), runs several Thai trips (including sidetrips to Laos, adventure trekking, and leisurely beach holidays) throughout the year, on a group or privately arranged basis. Scuba-diving enthusiasts can organize their own PADI-certification course or scuba-diving trips through one of the many dive shops noted in Chapter 6 about Pattaya, or Chapter 8 about Phuket, both considered the best areas for diving.

6. GETTING THERE

Thailand is centrally located in Southeast Asia and functions as a hub city for many international carriers, making it exceptionally easy to reach. Most international air carriers fly to Bangkok. In addition, there is train service from Singapore and Malaysia, and freighter service from various Asian ports. Only privately owned cars (not rented autos) can be driven into the country along the Malaysian frontier.

THE MAJOR AIRLINES One of the most relaxing, yet exotic, ways to reach Thailand is on **Thai Airways International** (tel. toll free 800/426-5204), the country's international, gracious, and efficient airline. Thai flies daily from several U.S. cities via Los Angeles and Seoul to Bangkok.

In 1994 the Los Angeles–originating advance-purchase excursion fare was $1,150 round-trip, plus $75 more for one stopover in Seoul, Hong Kong, or Taipei. Business-class tickets run $2,270, with one stopover allowed for $75; first-class seats cost $5,000, with unlimited stopovers. Thai Airways also offers good-value air-and-land packages that combine discounted hotels and guided day trips with your airline ticket. Call Royal Orchid Holidays (tel. toll free 800/426-5204) for information.

Northwest Airlines (tel. toll free 800/447-4747) has daily flights from New York and the West Coast (Seattle, Los Angeles, or San Francisco) via Tokyo to Bangkok. The 1994 weekday advance-purchase fare from the West Coast was $1,020, or $1,320 from New York, round-trip, with one stopover allowed. Northwest's weekend flight ($100 surcharge) also allows one free stopover. Northwest flies daily from Montreal or Toronto to Bangkok via Detroit and Tokyo ($1,350 on a midweek advance-purchase excursion fare).

Canadian Airlines International (tel. toll free 800/426-7000) flies daily except Friday from Vancouver, B.C., or Toronto, to Bangkok via Tokyo. In 1994 the advance-purchase excursion fare was $1,132 U.S. round-trip from Vancouver, $1,323 U.S. from Toronto, with $43 U.S. for one stopover. Business-class tickets run $2,187 U.S. or $2,642 U.S., respectively, with one stopover allowed for an extra $43 U.S.; first-class seats cost $5,202 U.S. from either city, with unlimited stopovers. Contact Canandian Airlines or your travel agent about special connecting fares from Montreal and other Canadian cities.

United Airlines (tel. toll free 800/538-2929) is the largest carrier crossing the Pacific. United flies daily to Bangkok from Canada (Toronto or Vancouver via the U.S.) and from major U.S. cities via Tokyo (daily) or Taipei (several days a week). The 1994 weekday advance-purchase excursion fare from New York was $1,300 round-trip, with one stopover allowed. Tickets in business class run $3,812 from New York; first-class is $6,060, both fares include unlimited stopovers. United also offers Bangkok air-and-land packages; for information, call toll free 800/351-4200.

FROMMER'S SMART TRAVELER: AIRFARES

1. Shop all the airlines that fly to Thailand, asking about their lowest-priced fares and special excursions. Don't forget the Asian national carriers, such as Philippine Airlines, MAS, Garuda Indonesian, Korean Airlines, etc., who may offer special Bangkok fares combined with routing through their country's capital city.
2. Check the weekend travel section of your local newspaper, plus the Sunday editions of the *New York Times* and the *Los Angeles Times* for advertised discount fares and charter operators. London's *Time Out* is an excellent magazine that advertises many discount travel agencies.
3. Consult your travel agent about special round-the-world fares.
4. Call around to consolidators (discount air-ticket sellers who profit by buying unused seats in bulk from various airlines), and be prepared to leave on short notice. Some recommended consolidators: Council Charter (tel. toll free 800/223-7402) and Travac (tel. toll free 800/872-8800), in the U.S., or Flight Solutions (tel. 71/232-1864) and Trailfinders (tel. 71/938-3366) in London.

Delta Airlines (tel. toll free 800/241-4141) now flies four times weekly via Portland, Oregon, Taipei, and Seoul to Bangkok. Their midweek advance-purchase excursion fare in 1994 sold for $1,000 ($100 surcharge for weekend travel), including one free stopover in Taipei or Seoul, and up to two more stopovers at $75 each (including Tokyo for this fee). Business-class passengers would pay $2,952, first class $5,000, with both fares including free stopovers.

Travelers who prefer to make their stopovers in Europe should consider **KLM Royal Dutch Airlines** (tel. toll free 800/374-7747), which flies to Bangkok via Amsterdam, or **Finnair** (tel. toll free 800/950-5000), which flies via Helsinki. The transatlantic routing from North America is currently more expensive than the transpacific ones commonly used, but it's actually a faster and sometimes easier flight.

Flights from the U.K. Daily, nonstop flights from London to Bangkok are offered by British Airways (tel. 081/897-4000, in London).

BY TRAIN Train service on the State Railway of Thailand originates in Singapore, passes through Malaysia (stopping in Kuala Lumpur and Butterworth), and terminates in Bangkok. The 1994 fare ran about $150 for a first-class, air-conditioned sleeping berth. The entire 1,860km (1,160 mile) trip takes 31 hours, plus a 10-hour layover in Kuala Lumpur.

Orient Express Hotels (tel. toll free 800/524-2420) has launched a new luxury train, the *Eastern & Oriental Express*. Once weekly it rolls along 1,200 miles of track between Singapore and Bangkok in 41 hours. Stops are made in Kuala Lumpur and Penang, Malaysia, and at Surat Thani and Hua Hin in southern Thailand. Estimated all-inclusive cost for passengers on this nostalgic overnight journey, one steeped in elegance and feted with gourmet fare, is $390.

BY BUS There is limited private bus transportation between Singapore or Malaysia and Hat Yai in southern Thailand. See "Hat Yai & Songhkla" in Chapter 7, "Ko Samui & the Southeast Coast" for more information.

BY SHIP A few international cruise companies sail to Thailand, docking near Pattaya. The Ocean Pearl Lines, with four to six annual departures to Asian ports and Bangkok, is one of the best known. Contact your travel agent for current schedules and informtion.

PACKAGE TOURS Several tour operators within Thailand offer package tours (usually by bus) originating in Bangkok and including any resort, cultural, or historical destination which interests you. World Travel Service Ltd., 1053 Charoen Krung Rd., 10500 Bangkok (tel. 02/233-5900), is one of the oldest. An American company that specializes in Thailand is Absolute Asia, 155 W. 68th St., Suite 525, New York, NY 10023 (tel. toll free 800/736-8187 or 212/595-5782 in the U.S.). Contact both companies directly or inquire through your travel agent for information.

7. GETTING AROUND

Travel within Thailand is extremely efficient and cheap. If your time is short, fly. But if you have the time to take in the countryside, travel by bus, train, or private car.

BY PLANE Other than to Ko Samui, all domestic flights are on **Thai Airways** (part of Thai Airways International), with Bangkok as its hub. Flights connect Bangkok and 25 domestic cities, including Chiang Mai, Chiang Rai, Mae Hong Son, Phitsanulok, Loei, Surat Thani, and Phuket. There are also connecting flights between many of these cities.

In 1989, Bangkok Airways began flying to Ko Samui from Bangkok daily, and between Phuket and Ko Samui. Children under the age of 12 years old travel at half the posted rate; infants travel at 10% of the normal fare. Flights from Bangkok to any location within Thailand are less than an hour. See below for typical (1994) one-way fares.

Route	One-Way Fare	Daily Flights
Bangkok to Chiang Mai	1,650B ($66)	10
Chiang Mai to Phitsanulok	650B ($26)	3
Bangkok to Surat Thani	2,040B ($81)	2
Bangkok to Phuket	2,400B ($96)	10
Chiang Mai to Mae Hong Son	345B ($13.80)	4

Thai Airways also sells a "Discover Thailand" airpass enabling you to fly to four cities within Thailand, as long as it's purchased in conjunction with an international ticket, outside of Thailand. The four-city pass costs $219 and is valid for 60 days from the first date of domestic travel (a date that must be confirmed at time of purchase).

BY TRAIN Excellent, comfortable train service runs throughout the country with a full range of service available. The **State Railway of Thailand** (tel. 223-7010 or 223-7020) organizes routes along four separate lines, all starting and ending in Bangkok. The Southern Line stops at Kanchanaburi, the River Kwai Bridge, Hua Hin, and Surat Thani (Ko Samui stop), with international service continuing to Kuala Lumpur and Singapore; the Northern Line stops at Don Muang, Bang Pa-In, Ayutthaya, Lopburi, Phitsanulok, Lampang, Lamphum, and Chiang Mai; the Northeastern Line stops at Don Muang (the airport), Ayutthaya, Surin, and ultimately, Nong Khai, near the Laotian border; and the Eastern Line runs to Aranyaprathet, near the Cambodian border.

There are three categories of trains (in order of speed and comfort): express, rapid, and ordinary. In most cases, only rapid and express trains have sleeping berths; express trains also offer first-class compartments. The express surcharge is 30B ($1.20), 20B (80¢) for a rapid, and 50B ($2) for a second-class, air-conditioned coach. The first-class, air-conditioned, double-cabin sleeping berth surcharge is 250B ($10) per person. The second-class surcharge for an air-conditioned berth is 250B ($10) for a lower berth, 200B ($8) for an upper berth, per person. Children between the ages of 3 and 12, and less than 150cm (59 inches) travel half price. See Chapter 3, "Introducing Bangkok: Departing," for more information.

Typical one-way, private air-conditioned train fares (as of 1994) and average travel time to these destinations are shown in the table.

Route	One-Way Fare [2nd Class]	Time
Bangkok to Chiang Mai	470B ($18.80)	10 hours
Bangkok to Phitsanulok	190B ($7.60)	6 hours

| Chiang Mai to Phitsanulok | 98B ($3.90) | 6 hours |
| Bangkok to Surat Thani | 350B ($14) | 11 hours |

BY BUS Buses are the cheapest transportation to the farthest and most remote destinations in the country. Options abound, but the major choices are public or private, air-conditioned or non-air-conditioned. Most travelers use the private, air-conditioned buses. Ideally, buses are best for short excursions; expect to pay a minimum of 50B ($2) for a one-way ticket. Longer-haul buses are an excellent value (usually less than $1 per hour of travel), but their slowness can be a real liability. See Chapter 3, "Introducing Bangkok: Departing," for information.

BY TAXI OR TUK-TUK The more expensive, private cars affiliated with hotels and travel agents post their rates, but you'll have to negotiate with public sedan taxis and tuk-tuk (motorized three-wheel rickshaw) drivers. If you don't know the correct fare, ask a shop owner, hotelier, or restaurateur what you should expect to pay for your destination and negotiate accordingly. Most taxi fares will average from 50B ($2) in the provincial town, to 125B ($5) within Bangkok, depending on route, distance, traffic, condition of the car, and mood of the driver. Tuk-tuks cost about 35% less. In the provincial areas, small pickup trucks fitted with bench seats (called song tao, but also sometimes tuk-tuks) usually cruise the main streets offering group-ride taxi service at cheap, set fees. With taxis or tuk-tuks, always remember to agree on your fare before engaging a driver or you will almost certainly overpay. Tipping in not expected.

BY CAR Renting a car is a snap in Thailand, although we recommend hiring a driver to minimize the aggravation of driving in chaotic traffic. Among the many car-rental agencies, **Avis** (tel. 255-5300 in Bangkok or toll free 800/331-1212 in the U.S.) and **Hertz** (tel. 253-6251 in Bangkok or toll free 800/654-3131 in the U.S.) have offices around the country with representatives in Bangkok and the major destinations. Many smaller, local agencies rent cars for less, but some don't have full insurance coverage or chauffeur service. Gas costs about 15B (60¢) per liter ($2.40 per gallon). See Chapter 3, "Introducing Bangkok: Departing," for more information.

BY FERRY There is regular hydrofoil service between Bangkok-Pattaya, Bangkok–Hua Hin/Cha-Am and Surat Thanii–Ko Samui. There is regular ferry service between the mainland and the islands of the Andaman Sea, including Phuket and the islands of the Gulf of Siam, including Ko Samet and Ko Samui. See the relevant chapters for ferry information and see Chapter 3, "Introducing Bangkok: Departing," for more information about hydrofoils and inter-Thai ships.

HITCHHIKING Public transportation by air, train, and bus is so reasonably priced, frequent, and convenient, that we never found a need to hitchhike. We also never saw any hitchhikers, though it isn't prohibited.

SUGGESTED ITINERARIES

The following itineraries are based on only the highlights of the country and are geared for the general-interest traveler. Those with special interests can modify these basic plans, but should contact the TAT for further information about topics of interest.

IF YOU HAVE 1 WEEK

Days 1–3: Begin in Bangkok, with a day trip to Ayutthaya, Phimai, or Kanchanaburi.
Days 4–5: Fly to Chiang Mai, with day trips to Lamphun, Lampang, and Chiang Rai.
Days 6–7: Fly or take train or bus to Phitsanulok, with day trips to Sukhothai and Si Satchanalai; or after returning to Bangkok, fly to Phuket.
Day 7: Return to Bangkok.

IF YOU HAVE 2 WEEKS

Days 1–8: Follow the itinerary above.
Days 9–10: Fly to Phitsanulok, with day trips to Sukhothai and Si Satchanalai.

Days 11–13: Fly, via Bangkok, to Phuket or to Surat Thani and take the ferry to Ko Samui or fly via Bangkok to Ko Samui.
Day 14: Return to Bangkok.

IF YOU HAVE 3 WEEKS

Three weeks is enough time to indulge your specific interests. Follow the 2-week itinerary above, and if you're interested in the hill-tribe cultures of northern Thailand, allow time for Chiang Mai's excellent museums, an extra four days for a trek from Chiang Mai to the Golden Triangle area near Chiang Rai, plus another two days to visit Mae Hong Son in the northwest. From Mae Hong Son, you can fly via Chiang Mai to Phitsanulok, then relax at a beach.

If you're interested in the less-touristed, recently opened historical region called the Northeast (Isan), follow the 2-week itinerary up to Phitsanulok; fly from there to Khon Kaen or Ubon Ratchathani via Bangkok, hire a car and spend a week exploring this little-known, but fascinating, area. After that, a 3-day rest at the beach will be very welcome.

FAST FACTS: THAILAND

American Express The American Express agent in Thailand is Sea Tours Company, with offices in Bangkok, Phuket, and Chiang Mai. See "Fast Facts" in those chapters for further information.

Banks Most hotels will change foreign currency, but banks and money changers offer better rates. Official banking hours are Monday to Friday 8:30am to 3:30pm. Major cities have foreign-exchange banks and money changers, which are open daily until as late as 10pm for exchange.

All charge a commission (usually 5B or 20¢) and government stamp tax (3B or 12¢) per traveler's check. It's essential to have your passport for cashing traveler's checks, as a photocopy will often not suffice. Carry baht and some cash dollars when traveling to more remote areas.

Business Hours Government offices (including branch post offices) are open Monday to Friday 8:30am to 4:30pm, with a lunch break between noon and 1pm. Businesses are generally open 8am to 5pm. Shops often stay open from 8am until 7pm or later, seven days a week. Department stores are generally open 10am–7pm.

Camera & Film Kodak has a plant in the region and Kodak and Fuji film prices are about the same as at home. Expect to pay 120B ($4.80) for a 36 exposure roll of Kodak print film. The light is very bright, so an ultraviolet or sky-light filter and lower-speed film (ASA 25-100) are advisable. Keep your film in a cool place. When flying, it's a good idea to have your film inspected by hand rather than passing it through an X-ray machine. (The FILMSAFE signs on X-ray machines don't account for the cumulative effect of many passes.) One-hour processing centers are nearly everywhere and are cheaper than in the States.

Climate See "When to Go," above in this chapter.

Crime See "Safety," below.

Currency See "Information, Entry Requirements & Money," above in this chapter.

Customs Tourists are allowed to enter the country with one liter of alcohol and 200 cigarettes (or 250 grams of cigars or smoking tobacco) per adult, duty free. Cars (with a cash or bank guarantee, vehicle registration, and proper driver's license), photographic equipment (one still, video, or movie camera, plus five rolls of still film or three rolls of 8mm or 16mm motion-picture film), and "professional instruments" (typewriter, personal computer, etc.) are allowed, provided they are taken out on departure. (The film rule is not strictly enforced.) All items must be declared. Certain plants are restricted for import; contact the Department of Agriculture (tel. 02/579-1581) in Bangkok for particulars.

Firearms and ammunition can only be brought in with a permit from the Police Department or local registration office.

Documents Required   See "Information, Entry Requirements & Money,"
above in this chapter.

Driving Rules   See "Getting Around," above in this chapter.

Drug Laws   All kinds of narcotics (including hemp, opium, cocaine, morphine,
heroin) are illegal throughout Thailand.

Drugstores   There are excellent drugstores stocked with many brand name
medications and toiletries throughout the country. Pharmacists often speak some English.

Electricity   All outlets—except in some luxury hotels—are 220 volts, 50 cycles,
AC. If you use a 110-volt hair dryer, electric shaver, or battery charger for a computer, bring a transformer and adapter.

Embassies and Consulates   The U.S. Embassy, 95 Wireless Rd. (tel. 252-
5040), is open for consular services Monday through Friday from 7:30 to 10am and
noon to 4:30pm. There are regional consular offices in Songhkla, Chiang Mai, and
Udon. The British Embassy, 1031 Ploenchit Rd., off Wireless Rd. (tel. 253-0191-99;
fax 255-8619), is open Monday to Thursday from 8 to 11am and 1 to 3:30pm and
Friday 8am to noon. The Canadian Embassy, 11th floor, Boonmitr Building, 138
Silom Rd. (tel. 237-4126; fax 236-6463), is open Monday to Thursday 8am to
12:30pm and 1:30 to 4:30pm. The Australian Embassy, 37 S. Sathorn Rd. (tel 287-
2680), is open Monday to Friday 9:30am to 12:30pm and 1:30 to 4:20pm. The
New Zealand Embassy, 93 Wireless Rd. (tel. 251-8165), is open Monday to Friday
8am to noon and 1 to 4:15pm, consular hours are 8am to noon.

Most embassies will deal with emergency situations on a 24-hour basis. If you
are seriously injured or ill, do not hesitate to call your embassy for assistance.

Emergencies   Throughout the country, the emergency number is 191 for police or medical assistance, or 1699 for the Tourist Police. Do not expect many English speakers at these numbers outside the major tourist areas. You should also
contact your embassy or consulate, the Tourist Police, or the local Tourist Authority
of Thailand (TAT) office.

Etiquette   Disrespect for the royal family and religious figures will cause great
offense. Women should never touch a monk; to give one something, put the object
down and let him pick it up. Great respect is also shown to parents and elders.

Thais consider the soles of the feet unclean; pointing your toes or the soles of
your feet at someone is considered impolite. When you enter a temple, remove your
shoes and be sure not to point your toes at the Buddha. Sit down and fold your
legs to the side. Be careful not to cross your legs, especially during an official government visit. Do not climb on or pose in front of a Buddhist figure. Shoes should
be removed when entering a private home, or any Buddhist or Islamic shrines. It is
an insult to touch someone on the head, the highest spiritual point of the body.
Avoid pats on the head or back.

On an official or business call, coffee or tea will probably be served. Wait until
your host invites you to drink (usually just before the visit is to end) before touching
your cup or glass. When eating with others, do not fill your plate with food. Take a
small amount (a few bites at most) or your host may think you a glutton.

A public display of anger is absolutely taboo. It is very rude and ineffective for
Westerners to respond with anger or raised voices to private problems. Above all,
find a way for your rival to save face. Be insistent, but smile and remain calm. Public affection, with the possible exception of hand-holding should be kept to a minimum.

A lovely Thai greeting is the *wai* (pronounced *why*): Place your palms together,
raise the tips of your index fingers to eye level, and make a subtle bow from the
waist while bending your knees. The wai honors a person's presence and is done
with all but children and service people. Don't be surprised if you are addressed by
your first name—such as Mr. John or Ms. Kyle—which is normal etiquette and is
not informal.

Even though this is a tropical country and you've probably come in search of the
ultimate beach experience, it is offensive to the Thais to see tourists go shirtless and
even wear shorts, except at the beach. It is particularly forbidden for men or women
to wear shorts in temples.

Gasoline   See "Getting Around," above in this chapter.

Hitchhiking   See "Getting Around," above in this chapter.

Holidays   See "When To Go," above in this chapter.

Information   See "Information, Entry Requirements & Money," above in this chapter.

Language   Thai is the official language, derived from such diverse sources as Mon, Khmer, Sanskrit, and Pali. Hill-tribe people speak many different dialects, with roots spreading as far as Tibet, China, Laos, and Burma. Thai script is a modified form of Mon and Khmer, which in turn was influenced by Sri Lankan writing styles. English is spoken in the major cities in most hotels, restaurants, and shops, and is the second language of the professional class. Thai people welcome those who attempt to speak their language. *The Thai Phrasebook*, published by Lonely Planet Publications, is a useful guide for everyday phrases available in the United States and in many Thai bookstores.

Laundry   Most hotels have laundry service at very reasonable prices except at the pricey hotels where rates can be exorbitant. You'll find a laundry and a dry cleaner in nearly every town. There are few coin-operated laundries in the main cities.

Mail   You can use poste restante as an address anywhere in the country. For those unfamiliar with this service, it is comparable to General Delivery in the United States, whereby you can receive mail addressed to you, care of Poste Restante, GPO, Name of City. You need either a valid passport or ID card, must sign a receipt, and pay 1B (4¢) per letter received. Hours of operation are the same as the post office. Airmail postcards to the United States cost 10B (40¢); first-class letters cost 15B (60¢) per 5 grams (rates to Europe are about the same). An express sticker will speed up delivery for an additional 20B (80¢). Air parcel post costs 480B ($19.20) per kilogram ($8.77 per pound). Surface or sea parcel post costs 160B ($6.40) for 1 kilogram ($2.90 per pound, 3 or 4 months for delivery). International Express Mail (EMS) costs 300B ($12) for 250 grams ($21.80 per pound), delivery guaranteed within four days. See individual chapters for local post offices and their hours.

Shipping by air freight is expensive. DHL Thailand, 501/111 Nang Linchee Rd., Ratchada-Pisek Intersection, Yannawa, Bangkok (tel. 286-7209), and Federal Express, which ships through Transport and Freight Forwarding Internatinal Co., CCT Building, 10th floor, 109 Surawong Rd., Bangkok (tel. 235-8602), the major international delivery services, have their main dispatching offices in Bangkok, though they deliver throughout the country. A 2-pound package costs about $48, not including any applicable duties.

Maps   The TAT gives out excellent regional and city maps at their information offices. For specific map recommendations, see "Orientation" in each region.

Newspapers and Magazines   There are two domestic English-language dailies, the *Bangkok Post* and *the Nation*, distributed in the morning in the capital and later in the day around the country. Both cover the domestic political scene, as well as international news from AP, UPI, and Reuters wire services, and cost 12B (48¢). You'll also find up-to-date schedules of cultural events and movies. Both the *Asian Wall Street Journal* and *International Herald Tribune* are available Monday to Friday on their day of publication in Bangkok (in the provinces a day or two later). *Time*, *Newsweek*, the *Economist*, *Asiaweek*, and the *Far Eastern Economic Review* are sold at newsstands in the international hotels, as well as in bookstores in all the major cities.

Passports   See "Information, Entry Requirements & Money," above in this chapter.

Pets   Animals brought by plane are allowed with a permit for entry, which can be obtained at the airport. If pets are brought in by boat, one must apply in advance to the Department of Livestock Development (tel. 02/251-5136) in Bangkok. In any case, all animals must have proper vaccination certificates. Be advised that the United States has quarantine restrictions on animals returning from Thailand. (Also see "Information, Entry Requirements & Money," above).

Police   The Tourist Police, with offices in every city (see specific chapters), speak English (and other foreign languages), are open 24 hours. You should call them in an emergency rather than the regular police at 191 because there is no guarantee that the regular police operator will speak English.

Radio and TV American and British television shows are broadcast in Thai; local FM stations sometimes simulcast English-language sound tracks for selected programs, such as English-language news. Large hotels show fairly recent films on their own video sysems (VDO) and video-rental shops are all over the country. There is English-language programming on certain AM and FM radio stations throughout the country. Foreign radio networks such as American Armed Forces Radio and the BBC can also be received in Thailand. Check the local newspaper for frequencies.

Rest Rooms Many restaurants and all hotels above the budget level will have Western toilets. Small towns, shop rest rooms, restaurants, and budget hotels will have an Asian toilet (a hole in the ground with foot pads on either side). They are usually clean but difficult for the disabled. Near the toilet is a water bucket or sink with a small ladle. The water is for flushing and cleaning the toilet. There may be some toilet paper, but it's best to carry your own supply. Dispose of it in the wastebasket provided. In some lodgings you may find an Asian shower—a square sink and a ladle. Pour (cold) water over yourself, soap up, and rinse.

Safety Serious crime in Thailand is scarce; petty crime such as purse snatching or pickpocketing is not. Particular care should be taken by those traveling overland (especially on overnight buses and trains) in remote parts of the country and near the Burmese and Laotian borders, as local bandits or rebel groups sometimes rob travelers.

Beware of credit-card scams; never leave your cards with others for safekeeping (such as during a trek). If you don't want to carry them, put them in the hotel safe. Keep all other valuables in the hotel safe. Pay particular attention to your things, especially purses and wallets, on public transportation. Use extra caution on buses and trains.

A special warning: Be wary of strangers who offer to guide you (particularly in Bangkok), take you to any shop (especially jewelry shops), or buy you food or drink. This is most likely to occur near a tourist sight, and you will find it hard to resist a con man's friendly greeting and concern. Be warned that this kind of forward behavior is simply not normal for the average Thai. There are rare exceptions, but most likely these new friends will try to swindle you in some way. This often takes the form of trying to persuade you to buy "high quality" jewelry or gems (usually worthless) at "bargain" prices. Also, beware of anyone inviting you to their home, then offering to show you a famous Thai card game. You *will* lose. If you are approached about such schemes, call the Tourist Police immediately.

For those who contemplate bringing a "companion" to their hotel room, be advised of the danger of food or drink laced with sleeping potions. There are many incidents, with victims waking up two days later to find their valuables gone.

Taxes and Service Charges Hotels charge a 7% government tax and typically add a 10% service charge; hotel restaurants add 8.25% government tax. Smaller hotels quote the price inclusive of these charges.

Telephone, Telex, and Fax Major hotels in Bangkok, Pattaya, Phuket, Chiang Mai, and the provincial capitals have international direct-dial, long-distance service, and in-house fax transmission. Hotels charge a surcharge on local and long-distance calls, which can add up to 50% in some cases. Credit-card or collect calls are better value, but most hotels also add a hefty service charge for them to your bill.

There are Overseas Telegraph and Telephone offices (also called OCO or Overseas Call Office) open 24 hours throughout the country for long-distance international calls and telex and fax service. You cannot make domestic long-distance calls from overseas call offices, but you'll find certain shops offering domestic long-distance calls at prices only slightly higher than the official rate. International calls can take up to an hour to place (normally it's only a few minutes). The cost of a person-to-person call to the United States is 250B ($10) for three minutes; station-to-station calls are 200B ($8) for three minutes, 60B ($2.40) per additional minute. Collect or credit-card calls can be made without an extra fee. You can utilize the "HOME COUNTRY DI-RECT" service of AT&T, Sprint, or MCI from most hotels and from special phones in the airports and some train stations. This allows you to dial a special number for your long-distance service and charge the call to your calling card. Hotel surcharges still apply, but the overall cost will generally be less than if you dial direct. The access code for AT&T's USA DIRECT is 011-999-11111; for Sprint Express, 0012-99-13877; for MCI's CALL USA, 001-999-12001. These numbers may change, so check with your carrier before you depart.

Local calls can be made from any red public pay telephone. Calls cost 1B (4¢) for three minutes, with additional 1B coins needed after hearing multiple beeps on the line; private pay phones can cost up to 5B (20¢) in hotel lobbies or shops.

Time Zones   Bangkok and all of Thailand are seven hours later than GMT (Greenwich mean time). During winter months, this means that Bangkok is exactly seven hours ahead of London, 12 hours ahead of New York, 15 hours ahead of Los Angeles. Daylight saving time will add one hour to these figures.

Tipping   If a service charge is not added to your restaurant check, a 10% to 15% tip is appropriate. In small noodle shops, a 10B (40¢) tip may be added if the service is particularly good. Airport or hotel porters expect tips of 20B (80¢) per bag. Tipping taxi drivers is not expected. Carry small bills, as many cab drivers either don't have (or won't admit having) small change.

Tourist Offices   See "Information, Entry Requirements & Money," above in this chapter as well as specific city chapters.

Visas   See "Information, Entry Requirements & Money," above in this chapter.

Water   Don't drink the tap water, even in the major hotels. Most hotels provide bottled water in the bathroom; use it for brushing your teeth as well as drinking. Most restaurants serve bottled or boiled water and ice made from boiled water, but always ask to be sure.

INTRODUCING BANGKOK

Bangkok is an ancient and a modern city, with a network of *klongs* (canals) and the Floating Market, the Temple of the Emerald Buddha, and the Grand Palace, as well as golden *wats* (temples), museums, and regal monuments. It's the financial capital of one of the fastest-growing economies in the world, and a megalopolis suffering from some of the worst air and water-pollution on Earth. Surrounding the city are legendary Thai, Chinese, and Indian markets that rival anything on the Asian continent. Outside this core are new high-rise neighborhoods, more Wild West boom towns than manicured suburbs, where most of the city's six million inhabitants reside. Though not exactly a microcosm of all of Southeast Asia, Bangkok is definitely the region's most exotic and at the same time, out of control, capital city. For many first-time visitors it's an assault on the senses.

Bangkok has probably the greatest concentration of luxury hotels of any city in the world, and, as the capital of sumptuous Thai cuisine, some of the best dining options. Even in a city choked by cars and pollution, frenetic building and a pace that challenges New York, you'll likely encounter the uniquely Thai tradition of fine, friendly service. And with the exception of Chiang Mai, Bangkok offers unrivaled shopping for Southeast Asian handicrafts, antiques, silk, and jewels. For nightlife, there are no exceptions—One Night in Bangkok still delivers.

Bangkok is the third capital of the Kingdom of Siam, established after the destruction of the second capital at Ayutthaya by the Burmese in 1767. King Taksin retreated south to Thonburi, where he spent the next 15 years rebuilding the capital, while continuously fighting the Burmese. To complete the rejuvenation process, Taksin handed the royal reins to his most powerful general, Chao Phrya Chakri (Rama I), thus beginning the (current) Chakri dynasty.

One of Rama I's first acts in 1782 was to move the capital across the river to the quiet trading village of Bangkok (Village of the Wild Plums). He had klongs dug to make his city a more defensible island and began a building program that recognized but eventually surpassed Ayutthaya's legacy. He also enacted a series of laws, called the *Tra Sam Duang*, or Law of the Three Seals, incorporating administrative and economic aspects of both the Sukhothai (the first capital) and Ayutthaya empires' guiding principles. The new capital, called Krung Thep or City of Angels by its inhabitants, flourished.

1. ORIENTATION

Vintage 19th-century photographs of Bangkok show vivid images of life on the Chao Phraya River, bustling with bobbing vessels that ranged from the humblest rowboat to elaborate royal barges. Built along the banks of the broad, S-shaped

WHAT'S SPECIAL ABOUT BANGKOK

Architectural Highlights

The Grand Palace, a fascinating complex of royal buildings and temples, surrounded by garuda figures and Naga snake guardians.

Wat Arun, a Khmer-style prang decorated in cracked tiles and porcelain that casts its slender, towering shadow over the Chao Phraya River.

The turn-of-the-century Writers Wing in the deluxe Oriental Hotel, with its colonial charm and legacy of literary guests.

The gingerbread Victorian, 81-room, golden teak Vimanmek Palace built for King Chulalongkorn the Great, Rama V.

The stunning blend of contemporary comfort, superb Asian art, and classic Thai architecture on view at the Jim Thompson House.

The late Princess Chumbhot's five traditional Thai houses, lovely gardens, private klong (canal), and collection of Thai art and antiquities now open to the public as Suan Pakkard Palace.

Activities

An adventurous, self-guided *klong* (canal) tour by river taxi through Bangkok's floating suburbs.

A walk through the fascinating markets, shophouses, and traditional street life of old Chinatown.

Sampling and dining from the dozens of steam carts and Thai snack food vendors housed in department store food malls.

After Dark

One night in Patpong's sex clubs, cabarets, massage parlors, and bustling Night Market for unrivaled entertainment and shopping bargains.

A romantic moonlit cruise on the Chao Phraya River, the perfect venue for Thai cuisine and dancing.

Religious Shrines

Wat Po's reclining Buddha and its famous School of Thai Healing Massage.

The beloved jade Emerald Buddha housed in the royal Wat Phra Kaeo.

---

river, the city spread inland through a network of klongs (canals) that rivaled the intricacy—though never the elegance—of Venice.

As Bangkok became more densely populated and developed, more and more of the klongs were filled in to create broad thoroughfares. Cars, buses, motorcycles, and tuk-tuks (motorized three-wheeler rickshaws) followed, and today, the resultant rush-hour traffic jams are so horrendous (commuters spend on average, 40 working days per year waiting in traffic!) that the best way to travel around the city is, once again, via the river.

ARRIVING

The capital's central location makes it both the region's and the country's major transportation hub. Bangkok has three bus stations, a centrally located train station, and a huge, modernized airport that is seemingly close (but maddeningly far and getting farther in the dense traffic). Plan on an hour-long ride from the airport into the city, and at least that long from one end to the other. Within the city, taxis and tuk-tuks (*samlors*) cruise the broad avenues and provide inexpensive, reliable transportation. The Bangkok of the next millenium promises an elevated light railway or a monorail to help alleviate the traffic problems.

BY PLANE

Bangkok is a major hub for air travel in Southeast Asia, with more than 70 airlines providing service. All international and domestic flights come and go from **Don**

Muang International Airport, which is 22km (14 miles) north of the heart of the city. International and domestic flights arrive at different terminals, a short (1km [⁶⁄₁₀ mile]) walk or a free shuttle ride apart.

THE AIRPORT Travelers arriving at the international terminal will find a wide range of services awaiting them, available 24 hours unless otherwise noted: free luggage carts at the arrival gates; luggage storage for 20B (80¢) per day with a three-month maximum; currency exchange banks with the same rates as in-town banks; a post office with overseas telephone service; an Airport Information Booth and a Tourist Authority of Thailand (TAT) booth, open 8:30am to 4:30pm (tel. 523-8972); a Thai Hotel Association desk which will assist you in finding available accommodations; restaurants, serving both Thai and international food; and the first-class Amari Airport Hotel (see "Accommodations" in Chapter 4), a short walk or free shuttle ride away.

The domestic terminal offers most of these services, though on a more limited schedule: luggage storage, for 20B (80¢) a day, 14-day limit, is open 6am to 11pm; a post office in the departure wing with overseas telephone service; a foreign exchange bank; and the Hotel Association desk, all open 24 hours; a cafeteria-style coffee shop open 6:30am to 11pm.

The airport provides free shuttle service between the international and domestic terminals, with buses every 10 minutes. If you have light luggage, you might find it more enjoyable (and sometimes faster) to walk. For general airport information, call 535-1111. For information about arriving or departing domestic flights call 535-2081, 535-1253 or 523-6121; for international flights, 535-1254. Passengers on domestic flights pay 20B (80¢) departure tax, while those on international flights pay 200B ($8). Children under 2 years are exempt.

Getting to and from the Airport Most of the larger hotels will pick up guests if requested in advance, at a typical charge of 450B ($18). You can easily arrange a private sedan to your hotel at the Thai Airways Limousine desk, found just opposite the exit from Customs at Counter 7. A comfortable four-passenger car with English-speaking driver costs 500B ($20); a Mercedes-Benz "VIP" car costs 750B ($30). To arrange a pickup in the metropolitan area, call 533-6208. Thai Airways Limousine also has a minivan that stops at every passenger's hotel, for 100B ($4) per person.

Public taxis are a better value than the Thai Airways limos, though a compromise in comfort. The fare is determined by a fixed schedule and varies with the distance from the airport, averaging 250B ($10) to most hotels in central Bangkok. There is a "Public Taxi Queue" inside the international terminal (turn left out of Customs and walk toward the "Meeting Area") where you are told the fare and assigned to a taxi. At the domestic terminal, you'll find it just outside the front door. The dispatcher will give you a card that specifies the fare and provides a check against possible price gouging. Most legal taxi drivers speak some English. Don't let one take you to the wrong hotel, where the driver may get a kickback.

Public buses no. 4, 29, 10, and 13 run between Bangkok's main streets and the airport for 6B to 20B (30¢ to 80¢), a tiresome journey we wouldn't recommend.

The **Airport Express Train** runs between the central Hua Lampong Railroad Station (tel. 223-7461) and the Don Muang station near the airport six times daily. For 125B ($5) you can save lots of hassle with their 35-minute express train and 15-minute air-conditioned shuttle van direct to your terminal. Tickets can be purchased at Hua Lampong, track 12; Thai Airways Limousine Counter, no. 7, in the International Arrivals Hall; or at Thai's counter in the Arrivals Hall of the domestic terminal.

BY TRAIN

You can travel by train from Singapore, via Kuala Lumpur and Butterworth, Malaysia, to Bangkok. Passengers arrive at **Hua Lampong Railroad Station,** east of Chinatown at the intersection of Rama IV Road and Krung Kasem Road (tel. 223-7461 or 223-7010). An information booth is open Monday through Friday from

THAILAND

★ Bangkok

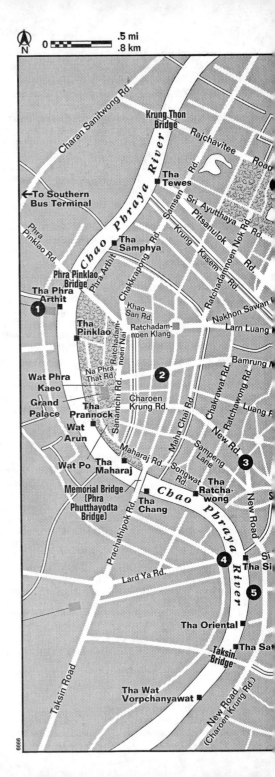

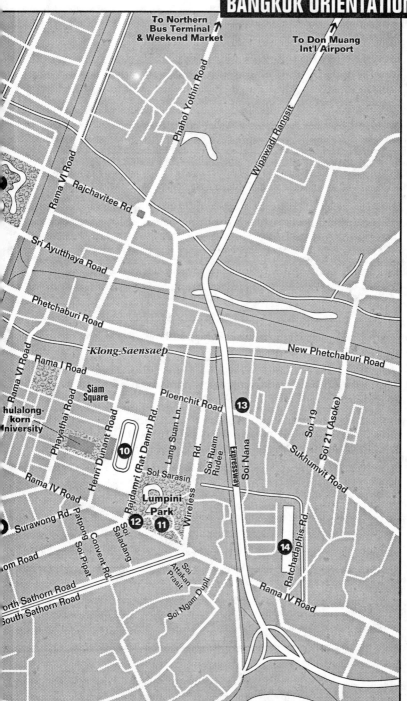

BANGKOK ORIENTATION

To Northern
Bus Terminal
& Weekend Market

To Don Muang
Int'l Airport

Phahol Yothin Road

Wipawadi Rangsit

Rama VI Road

Rajchavitee Rd.

Sri Ayutthaya Road

Phetchaburi Road

Klong-Saensaep

New Phetchaburi Road

Rama VI Road

Rama I Road

Siam
Square

Ploenchit Road

Phayathai Road

Soi 19

Soi 21 (Asoke)

Chulalong-
korn
University

Henri Dunant Road

Rajdamri (Rat Damri) Rd.

Lang Suan Ln.

Soi Ruam
Rudee

Soi Nana

Sukhumvit Road

10

13

Rama IV Road

Soi Sarasin

Lumpini
Park

11

Wireless Rd.

Expressway

Ratchadaphis Rd.

Surawong Rd.

Patpong

Soi
Saladang

12

14

om Road

Convent Rd.

Soi Pipat

Soi
Attakan
Prasit

orth Sathorn Road

South Sathorn Road

Soi Ngam Dupli

Rama IV Road

River Taxi Pier

8:30am to 6pm, and on Saturday, Sunday, and holidays from 8:30am to noon. Taxis and tuk-tuks wait at the station. For more information about train travel, see "Departing," below.

BY BUS

Passengers arriving by bus will find themselves at one of Bangkok's three bus stations, depending on the area of the country they've come from. For information on bus travel, see "Departing," below.

TOURIST INFORMATION

The **Tourist Authority of Thailand** (TAT) offers thorough and accurate information about all aspects of traveling in Thailand. They have a counter in the international terminal of Don Muang airport (tel. 523-8972), open daily 8:30am to 4:30pm. Their main office is at 372 Bamrung Muang Rd., (tel. 02/226-0060 or 02/226-0085) east of the palace area, open daily 8:30am to 4:30pm. They also can provide you with a variety of excellent brochures and maps. You can also call the information numbers for assistance. If you have problems, call the Tourist Police (tel. 225-7758 or 221-6206, section 4).

Travel tip: Save yourself a long journey to the TAT by starting at your hotel's front desk. We've found hotel concierges and reception clerks to be extremely knowledgeable and helpful in providing basic information for tourists.

CITY LAYOUT

MAIN ARTERIES & STREETS

Bangkok's most significant axis is still the **Chao Phraya River,** which meanders on a north-south line through the heart of the city and divides Bangkok from Thonburi on the western bank. Along its eastern bank are most of the major tourist sites including, from north to south, the National Museum and National Theater, the Grand Palace and Wat Phra Kaeo (repository of the Emerald Buddha), the Reclining Buddha at Wat Po, the Khmer-style complex of Wat Arun on the Thonburi side, the city's historic Chinatown, the golden trio of luxury hotels (the Oriental, Shangri-La, and Royal Orchid), and the River City Shopping Complex.

The river is spanned by four major bridges. The **Krung Thon Bridge** crosses at the northern end of the city, with its major artery, Ratchawithi Road, leading east to the Dusit Zoo, Vimanmek Palace, Chiralada Royal Palace, Wat Benchamabophit (the Marble Temple) off Rama V Road, the Victory Monument, and off Sri Ayutthaya Road, Suan Pakkard Palace. On the Thonburi side of the **Phra Pinklao Bridge,** along Klong Bangkok Noi, are the Royal Barges. Ratchadamnoen Klang Road crosses the bridge close to the National Museum and Theater on the Bangkok side, continuing east past the Democracy Monument and becoming Phetchaburi (and later New Phetchaburi) Road.

Running parallel to the south of Phetchaburi Road is **Rama I Road,** one of the city's most important avenues, which runs east and eventually becomes Ploenchit Road and, ultimately, Sukhumvit Road. Jim Thompson's House is off Rama I, along Klong Mahanak. **Siam Square and Mah Boon Krong Center (MBK),** two of Bangkok's largest shopping malls, are along Rama I, as are the Royal Bangkok Sports Club (and race track), several foreign embassies, some of the city's largest office buildings, and several of Bangkok's best hotels including the Hilton (on Wireless or Wittayn Road) and the Regent (on Rajdamri). **Sukhumvit Road** is also home to many excellent restaurants and shopping arcades.

The **Memorial Bridge** leads north from Thonburi directly into Chinatown, Sampeng Lane, and many specialized markets, one of the most richly ethnic neighborhoods. The southernmost of the major crossings is **Taksin (or Sathorn) Bridge,** crossing from Thonburi east over to the Bangkok side just south of the Shangri-La Hotel. This street is Sathorn Road and intersects with Rama IV Road at

Lumpini Park. Running parallel, to the north of Sathorn, are Silom Road and Surawong Road, both important for shopping, restaurants, hotels, and evening entertainment (including notorious Patpong, home to Bangkok's wild sex-club scene). **Rama IV Road,** which begins as Charoen Krung Road in Chinatown, leads east past the Golden Buddha at Wat Traimit, Hua Lampong Railroad Station, the Red Cross Snake Farm, and several hotels, including the deluxe Dusit Thani.

FINDING AN ADDRESS

Good luck! Street numbers follow Western conventions, to a point, in that even-numbered addresses are on one side of the street and odd-numbered on the opposite side. Most addresses are subdivided by a / symbol, as in 123/4 Silom Road, which is a variation on sequential numbering that accounts for new construction. Be aware that 123 and 124 Silom Road will be on opposite sides of the street, but not necessarily close to each other. You'll find the term **Soi** frequently in addresses. A soi is a small lane off a major street. So, 45 Soi 23 Sukhumvit (sometimes written 45 Soi Sukhumvit 23), is found at number 45 on Soi 23, a lane which runs perpendicular to Sukhumvit Road. Even-numbered sois will be on the north side, and odd-numbered on the south side, though Soi 21 and Soi 20 may be far apart.

It's also a good idea to ask the staff at your hotel to write the address of your destination in Thai, to assist taxi drivers. Many do not speak English, or if they do, may not understand your pronunciation of a street address. Most hotels have a "taxi card" with their address in Thai to assist guests.

NEIGHBORHOODS IN BRIEF

We've divided the city into several neighborhoods and organized hotels and dining options within these categories. The distinctions are broad and somewhat imprecise but our categories should help you organize the city during your stay.

Historic Bangkok—Near the Grand Palace   This area, the site of the original Bangkok capital, lay within the confines of Rattanakosin Island, created as a defense measure by King Rama I. A klong, now called Klong Ong Ang, was dug from a point at a bend in the Chao Phraya River (near what is now the Memorial Bridge), running north, then turning east near Wat Saket, where it became Klong Banglamphu, and rejoined the river north of the Phra Pinklao Bridge. The area includes a majority of the tourists sites, beginning with Wat Po, the Grand Palace and Wat Phra Kaeo, then continuing north to the Dusit Zoo and Vimanmek Palace Museum. There are numerous historic wats, the National Museum, and the National Theater and Library. There are only a handful of first-class and moderate hotels in this area, but their proximity to the sites makes it an attractive area to stay in. Low-budget travelers will find an especially rich choice of guest houses and cheap hotels.

On the River   Though the Chao Phraya River runs far beyond the city limits of Bangkok, this area roughly contains Bangkok's grand riverside hotels. We also include other hotels in this category, as well as the River City Shopping Complex, and some other smaller shopping malls.

The Business District   The Business District is bounded by Rama IV Road on the east, Chinatown on the north, New Road (near the river) on the west, and South Sathorn Road on the south. Silom Road and Surawong Road run east-west through the center. As its name implies, many banks and businesses have offices in this area, as well as a number of embassies, many shops and malls, and the famous Patpong nightlife area. Good restaurants and high-quality hotels abound.

The Shopping/Embassy Area   This includes the neigborhoods on either side of the thoroughfare called Rama I Road on its western end, then Ploenchit Road as it runs east and crosses Rajdamri Road, and finally, Sukhumvit Road as it crosses under the airport freeway. Here are several deluxe hotels, many first-class and moderate hotels, numerous shopping complexes, the newer office buildings, most of the Western embassies, and a large concentration of the expatriate community.

Chinatown Once home to the majority of Bangkok's Chinese citizens, Chinatown is still a unique enclave located north of the river (which bends to run east-west here), west of the business area and east of the Grand Palace area. There are few hotels, but it is rich in ethnic character. We strongly recommend a visit.

Thonburi This area on the west bank of the Chao Phraya was Siam's capital until the reign of Rama I and still remains a quiet and fairly unchanged collection of neighborhoods, where few tourists ever venture. You'll find some wonderful wats in one of our favorite walking tours (see "Walking Tours" in Chapter 5).

There are countless other neighborhoods in the Bangkok area, but few contain the same concentration of tourist sites.

STREET MAPS

There are three excellent Bangkok maps. The first is "Latest Tour's Guide to Bangkok and Thailand"—affectionately called "The Bus Map." It costs 60B ($2.40) and is available at most bookstores, though the TAT sells it for less at their main office. The "Bangkok Thailand Guide Map," by Discovery Map, is a slightly more up-to-date version of the Bus Map and also costs 60B ($2.40). The third map we enthusiastically recommend is Nancy Chandler's "Map of Bangkok"—alias "The Market Map and Much More." Nancy, a graphic designer who lived in Bangkok for 19 years, uses her keen eye for quality and value (not to mention the bizarre) to fashion a colorful guide focused on Bangkok's rich markets, shopping opportunities, and sightseeing highlights. The map costs 110B ($4.40) and is available at most bookstores.

Most hotels will provide Bangkok guides with simple maps to their guests free for the asking.

2. GETTING AROUND

Getting around Bangkok is an experience to be forgotten, unless you are clever. The traffic, already legendary is getting worse. Driving through the narrow streets of Chinatown during the business day is like waiting to exit a crowded parking lot. Although certain major thoroughfares are reminiscent of the broad boulevards of European capitals (and, in fact, were patterned after them), the Chao Phraya River is the fastest thoroughfare of all. Almost all sites and tourist services are located near the river and are easily reached from other river points by the excellent and inexpensive Chao Phraya Express Boat system. Taxis are still a relative bargain and the best alternative on land; open-air tuk-tuks are recommended only for short trips, as they expose you to heavy doses of auto fumes.

Most of the main streets are one-way and getting around requires some thought. Plot your route carefully and decide whether river, klong, or land transportation is better. If you're near the river and traveling during daylight hours, it's no contest. Hop on a boat. The most arduous taxi ride will be from the Sukhumvit area to the palace area at almost any time of day, a journey that can stretch to well over an hour.

BY PUBLIC BUS Unfortunately, the very cheap (4B [16¢]), frequent, and fairly fast public bus system must be used with care because of pickpockets, purse slashers, and other petty criminals who take advantage of the densely crowded conditions. If you prefer the public bus, take the air-conditioned ones for a few baht extra; keep your possessions in front of you, carry only what you can afford to lose, and stay away from the back door where most thieves operate. The Bus Map (Latest Tour's Guide to Bangkok) provides route information.

BY MINIBUS Until the government supplies the promised fleet of new air-conditioned public buses, the private sector has taken mass transit into their own hands with several fleets of air-conditioned, express service minibuses. They ply all the major thoroughfares, stopping at main intersections only during rush hours. The green and red/white ones cost 3.50B (14¢); the blue/white and pale green ones cost 2.50B (10¢); the pink/red ones offer pay mobilephones and cost 15B (60¢).

BY FERRY & LONG-TAIL BOAT   We're unabashed fans of travel on the Chao Phraya River. It's an efficient, inexpensive, and fairly tranquil way to get around and provides a remarkable window on local life. Branching off from the river is the ancient network of klongs, most of which are serviced by the basic long-tail boats (*hang yao*).

The **Chao Phraya Express Company** (tel. 222-5330) operates a system of ferries that run up and down the river, stopping at the many piers (*tha* in Thai) on both sides of the river. Cross-river ferries carry passengers back and forth across the river from almost every express-boat pier, though often from a separate landing. Most tourists will board the express boats near the Oriental Hotel, at the pier just south of the hotel or at the Tha Siphya Pier, just south of the Royal Orchid Sheraton. There are numerous other piers (many of which charge a 1B entrance fee), though most are hard to find: Ask your hotel desk for guidance, ask on the street, or look for small signs pointing the way to express-boat piers.

Express boats are long white boats with a pointed bow and a large number near the front. They carry the Chao Phraya Express logo on the side, and have bench seats and open sides. Don't confuse these with the smaller, cross-river ferries, distinguished by their squatter shape and rounded bow.

Boats pull up and pause for a fleeting moment, so boarding passengers must step lively. Fares are based on distance. The onboard ticket taker will ask your destination and charge between 4B and 10B (20¢ to 40¢) for the trip, the best deal in town. To exit, move to the back of the boat and be ready to hop off. As on any public conveyance in Bangkok, keep a close hand on your belongings. Cross-river ferries will usually cost 2B to 3B (8¢ to 12¢). Both express boats and ferries operate daily between the hours of 6am and 6pm, with boats arriving every 10 minutes or so.

Long-tail boats provide ferry-like transportation through the inland klongs on the Thonburi side, leaving when full from the Tha Ratchawong, Tha Thien, Tha Chang, and Tha Maharaj piers. Allow an hour to ride on one, just to see the fascinating neighborhoods across the river. The fare should be 5B to 10B (20¢ to 40¢). Get off at any stop and take another boat back.

Those looking for adventure or those staying in the Shopping/Embassy Area, should try the system of long-tail boat taxis operating on Klong Mahanak, which runs parallel to and between Phetchaburi Road and Rama I/Ploenchit/Sukhumvit Road. You can board at most major cross-streets (such as Rajdamri, Wireless, or Soi Asoke #21) and ride to the western end, near Wat Saket and the Democracy Monument.

The government has joined what began as a private venture, adding new, larger "River Buses" which ply the length of this major east-west klong, also known as Saensaep, or "deep pain." The name doesn't reflect the service, which is efficient and incredibly easier and faster than taxis. If you're heading all the way west to Wat Saket, you may have to transfer to a smaller, shallow-draft boat at the Krung Kasem road intersection. Fares run from 7B to 15B (28¢ to 60¢) depending on distance, and include transfers. This is definitely an adventure, as the klong's appearance and odor can get pretty funky, especially in the hot season. But it's cheap, quick, fun, and a terrific way to meet people.

BY TAXI   Since the government revolutionized the taxi industry by requiring drivers to have and use meters, traveling around Bangkok has not been the same! Great! Except we found it impossible to hail a "taxi meter" (as they're known by their rooftop signs) with a driver who knew where he was going. It seems all the long-standing professional drivers who speak some tourist English are sticking with their unmetered taxis (they actually will insist on a higher fare than a meter would read) till the bitter end, and only rural immigrants seeking work will drive with meters. Soon enough the situation will improve, and taxis are still comfortable, mostly air-conditioned, and extremely cheap. The flag fall is 35B ($1.40) and goes up, very slowly, by time and distance; it's difficult to reach 100B ($4) in a cross-city trip. Tipping is not expected, though certainly welcome from tourists.

Hotels, of course, offer private luxury cars, like Mercedes-Benz, if you request a "taxi" from the concierge. Rates run approximately double the taxi fare, or about 400B ($16) per hour.

BY CAR If you can afford it, we recommend hiring a car for some parts of your Bangkok experience, as it will be more efficient and comfortable than finding taxis particularly for shoppers. The best, and most expensive, cars for hire are provided at the major hotels. These will be fancier cars, like Volvos or high-end Japanese cars, the drivers will speak English, and the price will start at 250B ($10) for almost any trip. They can be hired with driver by the hour for about 400B ($16) per hour with a 3-hour minimum. The day rate will range from 2,000B ($80) to 3,000B ($120) for a 9-hour day, with 200km (120 miles) included. You can arrange this through your hotel's transportation desk or through a travel agent. Sea Tours (tel. 251-4862) and World Travel (tel. 233-5900) are two companies that can also arrange English-speaking guides to lead you on a customized tour at similar rates. Avis and Hertz also offer chauffeured cars, but at the highest rates.

BY TUK-TUK As used to be with taxis, to get about by three-wheeled, motor-driven tuk-tuk (known formally as the samlor), you'll have to negotiate your fare. Expect to pay 40B to 100B ($1.60 to $4) for a given trip. The advantage of the tuk-tuk is their maneuverability in heavy traffic; the disadvantage is exposure to auto fumes (and worse, Bangkok's air!) They're great for short trips or for trips at nonpeak hours, when you're less likely to get stuck in a jam. Tipping is not expected.

ON FOOT It's easy and safe to walk around Bangkok, though you'll find the traffic congestion generates so much pollution that you'll limit your walking to certain neighborhoods and smaller streets. We've suggested walking tours for areas that are easily toured by foot (see "Walking Tours" in Chapter 5).

FAST FACTS: BANGKOK

American Express The American Express agent in Bangkok is Sea Tours Company, in the Siam Center, Suite 413–414, Fourth floor, 965 Rama I Rd., Bangkok 10330, between Henri Dunant and Phyathai roads (tel. 251-4862). Hours are Monday to Friday 8:30am to 4:30pm; Saturday 8:30am to 11:30pm. You must bring your passport for all transactions. American Express also operates a 24-hour telephone service for lost cards and traveler's checks: 273-0022. *Note:* This office does not cash traveler's checks except in case of emergency.

Area Code The area code for Bangkok and vicinity is 02. The Thailand country code is 66.

Babysitters Most hotels can arrange a babysitter, but all require some advance notice.

Banking Many American banks maintain offices in Bangkok, including Bank of America, next door to the Hilton at 2/2 Wireless Rd. (tel. 251-6333); Chase Manhattan, at 965 Rama I Rd. in the Siam Center (tel. 252-1141); and Citibank, at 127 S. Sathorn Rd. (tel. 213-2442). However, an American customer of one of these banks cannot use these as branches of the domestic bank; to access personal funds from an American account will require making special arrangements before leaving the States.

Americans with bank cash cards that are part of the *CIRRUS Network* can withdraw Thai money from their accounts at a number of cash machines located around town. Some convenient locations: The Royal Orchid Exchange Office, opposite the Royal Orchid Sheraton on Siphya Road; all Robinson Department Stores; Patpong Exchange Office, 3 Patpong Rd. Before you leave home, you will need to establish a four-digit PIN code on your account.

Bookstores You'll find a number of bookstores offering a wide variety of English-language books. One of our favorites for their extensive selection of books on Thailand and Asia is Asia Books, with stores at 21 Sukhumvit Rd. (between Soi 15 and 17, tel. 252-7277), on the ground and third floor of the Landmark Plaza Building (tel. 252-5839) on Sukhumvit Road at Soi 4, on the third floor of Thaniya Plaza (tel. 231-2106) on Silom Road, second floor of Times Square (tel. 250-0162), and in the Peninsula Plaza mall near the Regent Hotel on Ramri Road, south of Rama I Road (tel. 253-9786). All are open daily 10am to 8 or 9pm. You'll find a good selection of English-language paperbacks at D.K. Bookshops, 244-6 Siam Sq. on Rama I Road (tel. 251-6335). The Bookseller Co. Ltd., 81 Patpong Rd. (tel. 233-1717), off Silom Road, also has a fine selection of English-language books, magazines, and cards, and is open daily 9am to midnight. Almost every international-class hotel has a newsstand, with papers and a few books.

Business Hours   See Chapter 2.

Car Rentals   See "Getting Around" in this chapter.

Climate   See "When to Go" in Chapter 2.

Courier Services   Bangkok is serviced by most major international courier services, including Federal Express (tel. 367-3222), DHL Worldwide Express (tel. 207-8407), and United Parcel Service (tel. 513-1109). A 2-pound package would cost $48 (plus duty, if any) to ship to the United States by Federal Express and would take at least two days.

Credit Cards   Most hotels and larger restaurants take credit cards, though smaller guest houses and local restaurants will not. Smaller establishments that do take credit cards usually only accept MasterCard or VISA. For lost credit cards, call: American Express, 253-0990; Diners Club, 235-7305; MasterCard and VISA, 252-2212. Some hotels add a surcharge of 3% to 5% for credit-card charges. The credit-card companies do not recognize this practice and will refund the surcharge if notified.

Currency   See "Information, Entry Requirements & Money" in Chapter 2.

Currency Exchange   Most banks will exchange foreign currency Monday to Friday 8:30am to 3:30pm. Exchange booths affiliated with the major banks are found in all tourist areas, open daily from as early as 7am to as late as 9pm.

Dentist and Doctors   Thailand has an excellent medical care system. Most medical personnel speak English and many were trained in the United States. Most of the better hotels have doctors and/or nurses on staff or on call who can treat minor maladies. Check first with your concierge for assistance, then contact your country's consulate if you need further help. U.S. citizens can call the U.S. Embassy Medical Unit (tel. 252-5040), open Monday to Friday 7:30am to 4:30pm for a list of recommended physicians and dentists.

Drugstores   Bangkok has a great many drugstores, though the drugs dispensed may differ widely in quality. Always check the expiration date, before purchasing. Among the better outlets are the British Dispensary, 109 Sukhumvit Rd., near Soi 5 (tel. 252-8056), and also on the corner of New Road and Oriental Lane (tel. 234-0174); and the Phuket Dispensary, 383 Sukhumvit Rd., Soi 21 (tel. 252-9179). For additional recommendations, call the medical unit of your embassy or ask the concierge at your hotel.

Embassies and Consulates   See "Fast Facts: Thailand" in Chapter 2.

Emergencies   In any emergency, first call Bangkok's Tourist Police—dial 1699 or 221-6206 or 281-5051. Someone there will speak English. (The local emergency number is 191, but operators speak little English.) In case of fire, call 199 or 281-1544. Ambulance service is handled by private hospitals; call 251-0415 or 253-0250. The central emergency number for the police hospital (where accident victims are often taken) is 252-8111.

Eyeglasses   You'll find optical shops in all the major shopping areas of the city, most of which can provide replacement glasses within 24 hours at reasonable prices. For eye problems, try the Bangkok Eye Clinic at 430/35 Siam Sq. on Rama I Road, between Phyathai and Henri Dunant roads (tel. 253-1917), or the Rutnin Eye Hospital, 80 Soi 21, Sukhumvit Road (tel. 258-0442).

Hairdressers and Barbers   The locally recommended hairdressers cut both women's and men's hair. Among them is: The Best, in the Nai Lert Park Building, at 87 Sukhumvit Rd., near Soi 5 (tel. 251-1358) and also at Soi 21, Sukhumvit Road (tel. 258-3621). Most of the international hotels also have haircutting services. Although manicures, pedicures, body waxing, and facials are a very inexpensive treat in Bangkok, more complicated processes such as hair coloring and permanent waves should wait until your return home.

Holidays   See "When to Go" in Chapter 2.

Hospitals   All hospitals listed here offer 24-hour emergency room care and ambulance service. Be advised that you may need your passport and a deposit of up to 20,000B ($800) before you are admitted. Bills must be settled before you leave. Your domestic medical insurance policy will probably not be accepted for payment, though major credit cards are. Among the best hospitals with English-speaking staff are Bumrungrat Medical Center and Hospital, 33 Soi 3, Sukhumvit Road (tel. 253-0259); Bangkok Nursing Home, 9 Convent Rd., between Silom and Sathorn roads, south of Rama IV Road (tel. 233-2610). The public and busy Chulalongkorn Hospital (tel. 252-8181) and Ramathipodi University Hospital (tel. 246-0024) are leading teaching and research facilities and are located on Rama IV Road. The Bangkok General Hospital, which is the public hospital (and known for treating coronary problems), is off New Phetchaburi Road, at 2 Soi Soonvijai 7 (tel. 318-0066).

Hot Lines   There is a volunteer Hot Line (tel. 277-7699 or 277-8811) for those in emotional distress. The Samaritans of Bangkok, a nonsectarian group of volunteers, offer English-language counseling (tel. 236-7465 or 249-9977). Alcoholics Anonymous has several groups in town. One chapter meets at the Holy Redeemer Church, 123/19 Ruam Rudee, off Wireless Road, (tel. 256-6578 or 256-6305) several times a week.

Information   See "Information, Entry Requirements & Money" in Chapter 2.

Laundry and Dry Cleaning   Most hotels offer good, inexpensive laundry and dry-cleaning services. Locals recommend the dry cleaners in the Dusit Thani Hotel shopping arcade or the Erawan Dry Cleaners in the basement of the Landmark of Bangkok. For laundry, try Ochin Laundry, 18/6 Soi 23, Sukhumvit Road (tel. 258-4235). They also do cleaning.

Libraries   The American University Alumni (AUA) runs a free public library at 179 Rajdamri Rd. (tel. 252-8170), open to foreigners and residents Monday to Friday 8:30am to 8pm, and Saturday 9am to 1pm. The National Library, on Samsen Road (tel. 281-0263), is open daily 9:30am to 7:30pm. The Siam Society at 131 Soi 21, Sukhumvit Road (tel. 258-3494), operates a library concentrating on history, art, and culture but is open to members only. The Neilson Hays Library, at 195 Surawong Rd. (tel. 233-1731), is a subscriber-supported lending institution open Monday to Friday 9:30am to 4pm. The British Council, 428 Siam Sq., Soi 2, Rama I Road (tel. 252-6136), has a library and information services open Tuesday to Friday 10am to 7:30pm, Saturday to 5pm.

Lost Property   If you have lost anything or had your valuables stolen, call the Tourist Police, Crime Suppression Division, Vorachak Road (tel. 225-7758 or 221-6206, ext. 4). We have heard several reports of lost items being returned to the appropriate consulate by taxi drivers or bus attendants. Call the consular services section of your embassy to check.

Luggage Storage   Both the domestic and international terminal of Don Muang airport offer luggage storage for 25B ($1) a day 7am to 10pm in the domestic terminal, 24 hours a day in the international terminal. Most hotels will allow you to store luggage while away on trips in the countryside.

Mail   See "Fast Facts: Thailand" for rates. If shipping a parcel from Bangkok, take advantage of the Packing Service offered by the GPO; open Monday to Friday 8am to 4:30pm, Saturday to Sunday and holidays 9am to noon. Small cardboard packing cartons costs 5B to 17B (20¢ to 70¢); they pack things for you, with an enormous 5B (20¢) service charge!

Newspapers and Magazines   *Where* and *Look East* are slick monthly English-language magazines distributed free. Both emphasize events and features about Bangkok, with lesser coverage of other Thai cities and provinces. See "Fast Facts: Thailand" in Chapter 2 for more information.

Photographic Needs   See "Fast Facts: Thailand" in Chapter 2 for general information. In Bangkok, fast photo-processing labs offering adequate quality at low prices abound; ask your concierge at your hotel for a local suggestion. If your camera needs repair, inquire at the concierge's desk in your hotel for a reputable shop. The Silom Road shops which sell major brand cameras also provide repair service

Police Call the Tourist Police (tel. 1699 or 221-6206-10), open 24 hours, for assistance.

Post Office The General Post Office (GPO) is on New Road, between the Oriental and Sheraton Royal Orchid hotels (tel. 233-1050). Telegraph and telephone service are available in the north end of the building. GPO hours are Monday to Friday 8am to 8pm, Saturday to Sunday and holidays 8am to 1pm.

Radio and TV You can listen to English-language programming on Radio Thailand at 97 on the FM band daily 6am to midnight. Classical music can be heard on FM 101.5 daily 9:30am to 11:30pm, presented by Chulalongkorn University.

Television channels include 3, 5, 7, 9 and 11, which offer some English-language programming. Check the *Bangkok Post* or *the Nation* for listings. It's a rare hotel that doesn't offer in-house cable TV (VDO in Thai) and English-language movies.

Religious Services For English-language Catholic services, contact the Holy Redeemer Roman Catholic Church, 123/19 Soi Ruam Rudee 5, off Wireless Road (tel. 256-6305) or the 19th-century Assumption Cathedral, 23 Oriental Lane (east of the Oriental Hotel, tel. 234-8556). Anglican, Episcopal, and Eumenical services are held at Christ Church, at 11 Convent Rd., between Silom (at Patpong) and Sathorn roads (tel. 234-3634). There are Jewish services at the Jewish Association of Thailand, Soi Sai Pan 2, off Soi 22, Sukhumvit Road (tel. 258-2195), and at the Bossotel Inn. For those who are kosher, contact the Jewish Association for food recommendations.

Rest Rooms Except at temples and tourist sights, public toilets are a rarity in Bangkok, but you'll find no difficulty using restaurant or hotel rest rooms.

Safety In general, Bangkok is a safe city. There are specific areas, however, where pickpocketing and bag snatching are problems. The Bangkok public buses are infamous for skilled and ingenious pickpockets. If you must ride the public buses, pay very close attention to your belongings at all times, keeping valuable possessions in front of you (don't keep a wallet, for example, in a back pocket).

It's advisable to keep all important documents, including your passport and valuable jewelry, in your hotel's safe-deposit box. Carry a photocopy of your passport. Be careful with credit cards; destroy carbons and keep all receipts. Be suspicious of any prolonged period when your credit card is away from you. See "Fast Facts: Thailand" in Chapter 2 for additional safety tips.

Shoe Repairs Break that heel descending Wat Arun? There are many shoe-repair shops along New Road and lower Silom Road, near the Oriental, and along Sukhumvit Road. Try Siam Bootery, at 292-4 Sukhumvit Rd. (tel. 251-6862). Most department stores and shopping malls have a Mr. Minit counter for shoe repairs. Better yet, ask your concierge to arrange the repair.

Taxes See "Fast Facts: Thailand" in Chapter 2.

Taxis See "Getting Around" in this chapter.

Telephone, Telegrams, and Telex The main government telephone office occupies a separate building on the grounds of the GPO (General Post Office) on New Road between the Oriental and Sheraton hotels and is open 24 hours, 7 days a week. This office is for international calls. The procedure for making a call is as follows: Book your call by filling out a form at one of the desks, specifying the telephone number you wish to call and an approximate length of your call; take the form to the cashier and pay; wait until you are called to a booth. Beware of the hotel surcharges on international calls, usually 25% to 40% (check with the operator before dialing). A credit-card or collect call placed from your room also carries a service charge, often 160B ($6.40). See "Fast Facts: Thailand" in Chapter 2 for rates and additional information. Don't miss the free public phone booths in both the departure lounge and baggage claim area of the domestic terminal of the airport.

There are also blue or the newer silver long-distance telephones in strategic places throughout Bangkok (such as at the airport), used for domestic long-distance calls, at rates from 6B to 18B (25¢ to 75¢) per minute. You will need a pile of 5B coins and can observe your running total on the meter, putting in more coins as needed. For information within the Bangkok metropolitan area, dial 13; for the provinces, 183.

Telegraph services are offered in the telephone and telegraph office of the GPO, open 24 hours a day, every day, including fax service and telegram restante service. The same service (except for telegram restante) are offered at the telephone and telegraph offices at Don Muang airport. A fax to the United States costs about 350B ($14) and must be prepared on the official form. Every hotel offers normal fax service, as well.

Transit Info   Call the following for schedule information and reservations. Thai Airways International; international reservations 280-0070, domestic reservations 233-3810, airport flight information at 535-2081. Bangkok Airways, tel. 229-3456. For air-conditioned buses to the North, tel. 279-4484; to the South, tel. 435-1199. For train information, Hua Lampong Railroad Station at 223-7461 or 223-7010. For general information, Tourist Authority of Thailand at 226-0060 or 226-0072.

3. DEPARTING

TRAVEL AGENTS   Bangkok has an array of travel agencies that provide everything from local tours to cut-rate international airline tickets. **Sea Tours** (tel. 251-4862) and **World Travel Service** (tel. 233-5900) have branch offices in nearly every major hotel and offer a full range of travel services, including booking international and domestic airline tickets, arranging hotels and tours at other destinations in Thailand, and organizing tours of Bangkok, both customized and packaged. They can also provide a car with driver for your stay in Bangkok.

Where Travel Service, 27 Ngam Dupli, Rama IV Road (tel. 286-7274 or 287-1438, fax 02/287-1439), opposite the Malaysia Hotel, is a reputable bucket shop (discount travel center) we have used since 1981 with good results. Open Monday to Friday 9am to 5pm, Saturday until noon. Cheap tickets have their drawbacks. The tickets are usually highly restricted, with severe penalties for cancellation or changes. Check the conditions that apply to any discounted ticket before purchasing.

Be very careful of storefront bucket shops, particularly in the Khao San Road area. There have been several instances of ticket agencies disappearing, leaving customers holding worthless tickets. Check the airline's reservation roster to confirm your seat before paying, or you might find that your ticket is worthless.

AIRLINE TICKET OFFICES   Bangkok has become a major hub for airline travel in Southeast Asia, with over 70 airlines offering connections. Domestic service is provided primarily by Thai Airways, serving numerous cities throughout the

READERS RECOMMEND

Beware of Bucket Shops.   *"You may wish to note the continuing problem of ticket scams (particularly on Khao San Road); per this article from the* Nation: *'. . . By all accounts the "agency" has been doing a roaring trade, prices have been at rock bottom level for the last three weeks, effectively building up a short term swell in trade and boosting their "cash only" intake well above its normal level. Then, without warning, the agent vanished leaving in his wake a group of tourists who had paid over their savings in return for the promise of airline tickets to destinations all over the world. . . . The instance of fraud on tourists would seem to be something of a trend.'"*—Lemuel Morgan, Vice Consul, British Embassy.

country. Rapidly growing Bangkok Airways, is the sole carrier flying between Bangkok and Ko Samui, with connections on to Phuket and daily service to Hua Hin. As of 1993, Bangkok Airways was planning service from Bangkok to Trat.

Here are a few useful airline addresses and telephone numbers:

- Thai Airways (domestic), 6 Larn Luang Rd. (tel. 280-0070)
- Thai Airways International, 485 Silom Rd. (tel. 233-3810); airport office (tel. 535-2081)
- Bangkok Airways, 140 Pacific Place Building, Sukhumvit Road (tel. 253-4014 or 229-3465)
- United Airlines, on 9th floor of Regent House, Rajdomri Road (tel. 253-0558)
- Delta Airlines, on 7th floor of Patpong Building, 1 Surawong Rd. (tel. 237-6838)
- British Airlines, on 2nd floor of Charn Issara Tower, 942/81 Rama IV Rd. (tel. 236-0038)
- Garuda Indonesia Airways, 27th floor, Lumpini Tower, 116B Rama IV Rd. (tel. 285-6470)
- Pakistan International Airlines, 52 Suawong Rd. (tel 234-2961)
- Qantas Airways, Charn Issara Tower, 942/51 Rama IV Rd. (tel. 237-6269)
- Singapore Airlines, on 12th floor of Silom Center Building, 2 Silom Rd. (tel. 236-0440)
- Canadian Airlines International, 6th floor, Maneeya Center, 518/5 Ploenchit Rd. (tel. 251-4521)
- Continental Airlines, 4th floor, Charn Issara Tower, 924/126 Rama IV Rd. (tel. 237-6145)
- Northwest Airlines, 4th floor, The Peninsula Plaza, 153 Rajdamri Rd. (tel. 254-0789)

TRAVEL BY TRAIN   The Thai rail network is extremely well organized, connecting Bangkok with major cities throughout the country. All trains to and from the capital stop at Hua Lampong Railroad Station, at the intersection of Rama IV and Krung Kasem roads. Contact the reservation and information office (tel. 233-7010) for current schedules and fares, open weekdays 8:30am to 6pm, weekends and holidays 8:30am to noon. Some travel agents also provide reservation service. Reservations can be made up to three months in advance of travel and should be made as early as possible during the peak season (particularly for a sleeper on the overnight trains to Chiang Mai or the southern resorts).

The train station has a money-exchange booth open daily from 8am to 6:30pm. The luggage storage room (20B or 80¢) for each piece is open daily from 4am to 10:30pm. An information booth is open Monday through Friday from 8:30am to 6pm, and on Saturday, Sunday, and holidays from 8:30am to noon. As the station is centrally located, a metered taxi will cost no more than 100B ($4) to most hotels; a tuk-tuk will be no more than 70B ($2.80).

Warning: On trains, pay close attention to your possessions. Thievery is common on overnight trips.

TRAVEL BY BUS   Thailand has a very efficient and inexpensive bus system, highly recommended for budget travelers and short-haul trips. There are differences other than temperature between air-conditioned and non-air-conditioned buses: air-conditioned buses cost more but are significantly more comfortable, make fewer stops, and therefore, offer a shorter trip. There are also fancier, more comfortable VIP buses, operated by private companies, which offer even more comfortable seats, serve sodas and snacks, and sometimes torture you with overloud Thai disco music or videos.

There are three bus stations, each serving a different part of the country. All air-conditioned public buses to the southern peninsula depart from the Southern Bus Terminal on Charansanitwong Road, west of the river over the Phra Pinklao Bridge from the Democracy Monument (tel. 435-1199 or 435-1200). Service to the east coast (including Pattaya) originates at the Eastern Bus Terminal, on Sukhumvit Road past Soi 63 (tel. 392-9227 or 391-9829); to the northern, northeast, and northwest areas from the Northern Bus Terminal, Phaholyothin Road, just west of the airport freeway near the Chatuchak Weekend Market (tel. 279-4484). To confuse matters further, some private companies have buses originating at their offices, some at the terminals. Consult the concierge or travel agent at your hotel for advice.

As all stations are far from most hotels, you should take a taxi or tuk-tuk, unless you've chosen a private bus company which provides a courtesy pick up from your hotel. Public buses also make easy connections to certain areas of town. Ask at the information counter at the bus terminal for public bus routes.

Warning: When traveling by long-distance bus, pay close attention to your possessions. Thievery is common, particularly on overnight buses when valuables are left in overhead racks.

TRAVEL BY CAR   We don't recommend driving yourself in Bangkok, but outside the city, it's an option for those willing to risk reorienting themselves to driving on the left side of the road. You can rent a car with or without driver through Avis, 2/ 12 Wireless Rd. (tel. 255-5300). All drivers are required to have an international driver's license. In 1994 self-drive rates started at 1300B ($52) per day or 7,800 ($312) per week for a Toyota Corolla or Nissan Sunny, plus modest (300B to 500B or $12 to $20) drop-off fees for one-way trips. A Volvo 740 GL with driver cost 2,700B ($108) per day, plus 5B (20¢) per kilometer over 200km, and 250B ($10) per hour beyond nine hours. There is also a living allowance charge for the driver on overnight trips. Prices include insurance.

Local tour operators can also arrange chauffeured cars, usually at lower rates, and many local car rental agencies rent self-drive cars. See "Getting Around," above, for more information.

DRIVING RULES:

1. Always drive on the left side of the road.
2. Maximum speed limit for cars inside a city limit is 60kmph (36 m.p.h.); outside a city limit, 80kmph (48 m.p.h.).
3. Give the right-of-way to vehicles coming from main roads.
4. There is no turning on a red light.
5. Slow down through school zones and around hospitals.
6. If involved in a traffic accident which causes injury or property damage, notify the police.
7. Never operate a vehicle if under the influence of drugs or alcohol.

CHAPTER 4

WHERE TO STAY & DINE IN BANGKOK

1. ACCOMMODATIONS
- **FROMMER'S SMART TRAVELER: HOTELS**

2. DINING

If you checked the annual surveys of the world's great hotels, you'd certainly find Bangkok well represented. Fortunately, the capital offers a rich variety of choices in all price categories, and, compared to similar facilities in Europe, even the most expensive, truly grand hotels are good value. Dining is one of the country's greatest attractions, and in Bangkok visitors will find everything from a superb Thai banquet, to gourmet French fare or even a pepperoni pizza.

1. ACCOMMODATIONS

Given the tremendous traffic problems and the size of the city, we suggest you read the "Orientation" section of Chapter 3 carefully before selecting a hotel. Choose the location of your hotel based on how you plan to spend your time in Bangkok (tourists will have a different orientation from business travelers). Unfortunately, few of Bangkok's world-renowned hotels are located in the heart of the sightseeing zone, near the Royal Palace. Yet, each part of the city has its own appeal for first-time visitors.

Accommodation listings are organized by price range within each area of the city and are then listed alphabetically. The star and dollar symbols indicate our special favorites or what we consider to be best-value choices. In the high season (December through February), you must make reservations well in advance for the very expensive and expensive hotels, and even for the popular guest houses, or you may find yourself with no room at the inn. During the low season nearly all hotels offer discounts from 25% to 60%, making travel at that time a real bargain.

Note: Unless otherwise noted, the prices listed are subject to 7% government tax and 10% service charge.

As we went to press in the spring of 1994, three new deluxe hotels were under various stages of construction, all on Bangkok's most prized real estate, the banks of the Chao Phraya River. However, these new palaces will be on the Thonburi side, accessible by bridge and possibly private boat to Bangkok's major sites. From north to south, they are the Chao Phraya Sofitel Bangkok, bound to be a culinary as well as an architectural landmark for the prestigious French chain; the Ritz Carlton, on a site opposite the Oriental, and likely to rival its venerable competition with top-notch service; and the stately Peninsula, breaking ground across from the Shangri-La, and certain to excel in old-world style and grandeur.

ON THE RIVER

This is one of our favorite areas. The river hotels have the priceless view of, and easy access to, the fascinating Chao Phraya River. View and access don't come cheaply, so expect to pay the highest prices at the three centrally located facilities. For less money, you can go up or down river, and soon, across river, to hotels that are less convenient but provide their own boat transportation. There are also two lower-priced choices for budget travelers.

VERY EXPENSIVE

THE MENAM HOTEL RIVERSIDE, 2074 New Rd., Yannawa, Bangkok 10120. Tel. 02/289-1148. Fax 02/291-9400, Telex 87423TH. 688 rms, 39 suites. A/C MINIBAR TV TEL **Directions:** 3km (1.8 miles) south of Sathom Bridge.

$ Rates: 5,100B ($204) single; 5,450 ($218) double; suite from 8,400B ($336). AE, DC, MC, V.

For a large hotel the Menam offers a fair amount of charm with an unpretentious, comfortable air. The good news is its riverside venue; the less good news it that it's downriver from areas where most tourists will roam. This leaves the traveler with lengthy bus or taxi trips to the major tourist attractions. However, if you're adventuresome enough to try the riverboats (and we recommend that you do), the location can work to your advantage. The hotel offers hourly shuttle boats to either the Oriental Hotel or River City Shopping Center or you can walk a block up New Road and hop on the Chao Phraya Express Boats to go almost anywhere on the river. (See "Getting Around" in Chapter 3).

The hotel is popular with tour groups, drawn by its relatively reasonable (for the riverfront) prices. Deluxe river-view rooms are nicely appointed, with colorful Chinese murals for headboards and marble-tiled bathrooms. The style and view set them well apart from the less appealing (but 10% cheaper) city-view standard rooms, which feel a bit worn down by the steady stream of tour groups, and are not such good value. The pool is large, though screened from the river by the Riverview Terrace Barbecue. As with any major hotel, you must book at least one month in advance for high-season travel.

Dining/Entertainment: The Chinese luncheon buffet at Menam Tien is very popular; our Saudi Arabian friends raved about the evening seafood buffet at the Riverside Terrace Barbecue. Classic French fare is offered at La Brasserie. In addition to standard fare, the 24-hour coffee shop has a Japanese Corner, offering a wide array of Japanese foods at lunch and dinner.

Services: 24-hour room service, concierge, limousine service, babysitting, laundry service.

Facilities: Swimming pool, health club, business center, beauty salon and barbershop, shopping arcade.

THE ORIENTAL, 48 Oriental Ave., Bangkok 10500. Tel. 02/236-0400. Fax 02/236-1937, Telex 82997 ORIENTAL TH. 394 rms, including 34 suites. A/C MINIBAR TV TEL **Directions:** On the riverfront off New Road.

$ Rates: 7,200B–8,700B ($288–$348) River Wing single, 8,700B ($348) Garden Wing single; 7,500B–9,200B ($300–$368) River Wing double, 9,200B ($368) Garden Wing double; suite from 10,800B ($432). AE, DC, EU, MC, V.

Cited by publications too numerous to list and favored by honeymooners to CEOs, the Oriental has long belonged to the pantheon of the world's best hotels. Its history goes back to the 1860s when the original hotel, no longer standing, was established by two Danish sea captains soon after King Fama IV (Mongkut) reopened Siam to world trade. The hotel has since built three new buildings—the first in 1876; the larger and more modern pair in 1958 and 1976—which have withstood occupation by Japanese and American troops and played host to a glittering roster of Thai and international dignitaries, celebrities, and malcontents (chiefly, writers) such as Joseph Conrad, Somerset Maugham, and Noël Coward. Jim Thompson, of Thai silk trade fame, even served briefly as the hotel's proprietor.

It would be inaccurate to describe the Oriental merely as a hotel, as it offers the kind of facilities that lead some to spend their Bangkok stay exclusively within the confines of its properties (not that we suggest you do this). There is the Thai Cooking School; the *Oriental Queen I* and *II* make daily river runs up the Chao Phraya;

the nearby shopping arcade offers a fine selection of shops; in-house restaurants have a wide range of quality options; there's a nightly classical dance concert; and daily cultural programs with lectures and demonstrations covering a wide swath of Thai culture. These activities and facilities are in addition to those normally found at other top hotels.

Not to rest on its considerable laurels, the hotel has undergone an overall upgrade. We visited each wing, the new library, and three restaurants and were impressed by the tastefully redecorated interior. However, it's the level of service that distinguishes the Oriental from the other riverfront hotels. Time and again, we hear from travelers about some particular nicety that made their stay remarkable with only an odd complaint from those who'd been treated as "second-class citizens." Whether such service justifies the price is up to your wallet, but as far as we're concerned, if you can afford it, you'll not come away disappointed.

Even with increased competition and a complaint or two, the Oriental remains very popular, so we suggest that you make a reservation as far in advance as possible.

Dining/Entertainment: There are many food options but among them we highly recommend the Normandie (see "Dining," below), high tea in the Author's Lounge (if you can't afford to stay here it's the next best thing; daily 3:30 to 6pm), the Bamboo Bar, the healthy breakfast buffet on the Veranday, and the Terrace's evening barbecue. The China House, is a wonderful building with a fantastically expensive (by no means universally admired) Cantonese menu. Equally regarded for its high prices and less than perfect food is Lord Jim's, the Oriental's seafood outlet.

Services: 24-hour room service, concierge, complimentary welcome fruit basket, limousine service, babysitting, house doctor, laundry service.

Facilities: No-smoking floors, two swimming pools, health club, tennis-and-squash courts, beauty-and-fitness spa, business center, cooking school, beauty salon and barbershop, shopping arcade, tour boat for daily excursions to Ayutthaya and the Summer Palace.

ROYAL ORCHID SHERATON HOTEL & TOWERS, 2 Captain Bush Lane, Siphya Rd., Bangkok 10500. Tel. 02/234-5599 or toll free 800/325-3535 in the U.S. Fax 02/236-8320. Telex 84492 ROYORCH TH. 771 rms, including 70 suites. A/C MINIBAR TV TEL **Directions:** Next to River City Mall.

$ Rates: 5,300B–5,500B ($212–$220) single or double, 6,700B ($268) Tower single or double; suite from 9,000B ($360). Extra person 600B ($24), 950B ($38) in Tower. AE, DC, EU, MC, V.

The Royal Orchid, like its downriver neighbors the Oriental and Shangri-La, overlooks the magnificent Chao Phraya, offering the best view of all the major riverfront inns. It's ideal as a base for shopping or sightseeing. The rooms are spacious, pastel hued, and trimmed with warm teakwood, lending a refined and distinctly Thai ambience to your stay.

Some may disagree, but we think the Royal Orchid feels like a fancy, but not luxurious, group hotel. Perhaps it's due to the enormous number of guests crowding its too small lobby or maybe it's that just slightly less well-maintained hallway or the mediocre service and food in the coffee shop, but if you're in search of the ultimate, you might go elsewhere.

The Sheraton Towers, a hotel within a hotel on the 26th through 28th floors (with its own check-in desk and express elevator), offers more ornate decor and a higher level of service for a premium; Tower suites, for example, have personal fax machines in the sitting room, and all rooms are manned by 24-hour butlers on call to attend to individual needs.

Dining/Entertainment: Befitting such a complex, the Royal Orchid boasts eight major food outlets including such cuisines as Japanese, Indian, grill, Italian, Thai, and generic Wester (bravo for their kids' menu). We found the Thara Thong Thai restaurant the most attractive, both commanding a lovely view of the river and set in a gorgeous room resplendent with teak, bronze, and celadon. In the evening there is a low-key performance of Thai classical music. The Captain Bush Grill, on the same floor, is very popular with Western guests for its well-prepared prime rib.

THAILAND
★ Bangkok

Amari Airport Hotel 47
Amari Boulevard 45
Bangkok Center Hotel 11
Bangkok Christian Guesthouse 26
Bangkok YWCA 30
Bossotel Inn 14
City Lodge 41
Comfort Inn 44
Dusit Thani Hotel 27
Golden Dragon Hotel 46
Golden Horse Hotel 7
Grand China Princess Hotel 9
Grand Hyatt Erawan Bangkok 32
Happy Inn 37
Hilton International at Nai Lert Park 36
Holiday Inn Crowne Plaza 22
Hotel Majestic Palace 6
Krung Kasem Sri Krung Hotel 10
Le Meridien President 35
Lek Guesthouse 3
The Mandarin Bangkok 23
Manhattan Hotel 43
Manohra Hotel 15
The Menam 20
The Montien 24
Nith Charoen Hotel 4
Novotel Bangkok 33
The Oriental 18
P.S. Guesthouse 2
Peachy Guesthouse 1
The Regent, Bangkok 31
River View Guesthouse 12
Royal Garden Riverside 21
Royal Hotel 5
Royal Orchid Sheraton Hotel 13
Royal Princess Hotel 8
Ruamchitt Travelodge 39
Shangri-La Hotel 19
Siam Inter-Continental 34
The Somerset 42
The Sukhothai 28
Suriwongse Tower Inn 16
Swan Hotel 17
Tai-pan Hotel 40
Trinity City Hotel 25
Uncle Rey's Guesthouse 38
YMCA Collins House International 29

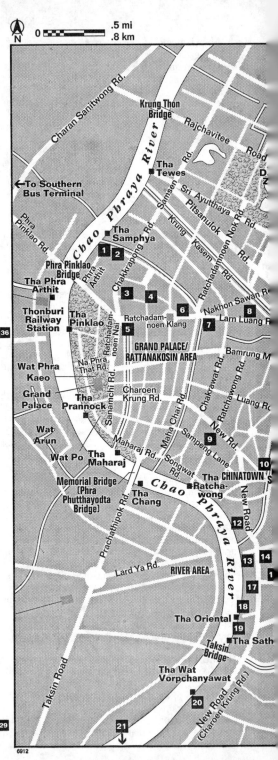

6912

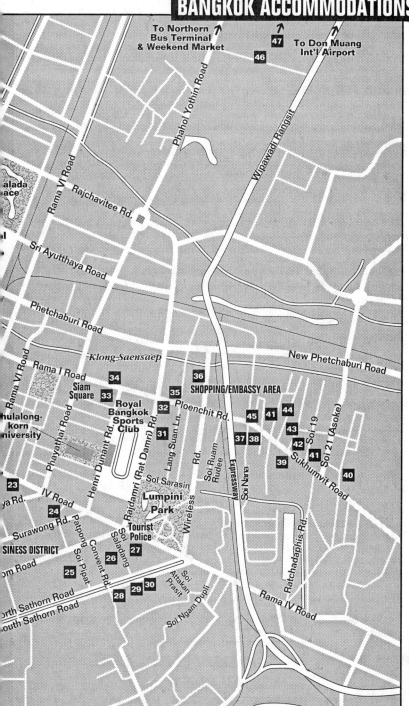

To Northern
Bus Terminal
& Weekend Market

47

To Don Muang
Int'l Airport

46

Wipawadi Rangsit

Phahol Yothin Road

Rama VI Road

Rajchavitee Rd.

Sri Ayutthaya Road

Phetchaburi Road

New Phetchaburi Road

Klong-Saensaep

Rama I Road

34

Siam
Square

33

Royal
Bangkok
Sports
Club

36

SHOPPING/EMBASSY AREA

35

32

Ploenchit Rd.

45 **41** **44**

Soi 19

Soi 21 (Asoke)

43

31

Lang Suan Ln.

37 **38**

42

41

Rama VI Road

Chulalong-
korn
University

Phayathai Road

Henri Dunant Rd.

Rajdamri (Rat Damri) Rd.

Soi Ruam
Rudee

Rd.

39

Sukhumvit Road

40

23

IV Road

ya Rd.

Soi Sarasin

Lumpini
Park

Soi Nana

Expressway

24

Surawong Rd.

Patpong

Soi Pipat

Convent Rd.

Soi
Saladang

Wireless

Tourist
Police

27

Ratchadaphis Rd.

SINESS DISTRICT

om Road

25

26

28 **29** **30**

Soi
Attakan
Prasit

Soi Ngam Dupli

rth Sathorn Road

outh Sathorn Road

Rama IV Road

alada
ace

al

Services: 24-hour room service, concierge, complimentary welcome tea (Tower only), house doctor, limousine service, babysitting, laundry service, jogging shuttle to Lumpini Park.

Facilities: No-smoking floors, swimming pool, health club, sauna, children's pool and playground, tennis courts, business center, beauty salon and barbershop, shopping arcade.

SHANGRI-LA HOTEL, 89 Soi Wat Suan Plu, New Rd., Bangkok 10500. **Tel. 02/236-7777** or toll free 800/359-5050 in the U.S. Fax 02/236-8579. Telex 84265 SHANGLA TH. 868 rms, including 60 suites. A/C MINIBAR TV TEL **Directions:** Adjacent to Sathorn Bridge, with access off New Road at south end of Silom Road.

$ Rates: 5,400B–6,800B ($216–$272) single, 6,000B–7,400B ($240–$296) double, 7,500B–8,200B ($300–$328) Krung Thep Wing; suite from 9,600B ($384). AE, DC, MC, V.

Ⓢ The glitzy Shangri-La, on the banks of the Chao Phraya, is getting bigger and better. Cast in the mold of this chain's other prestigious Asian hotels, it boasts acres of polished marble, a jungle of tropical plants and flowers, and two towers that offer breathtaking views of the river. Though thoroughly modern, the opulence of the Shangri-La hearkens back to the august hotel palaces of the late 19th century.

All rooms command a view of the river and are decorated with lush carpeting, teak furniture and marble baths; amenities include flowers, slippers, hair dryer, safe, and a tea-and-coffee maker. The views are terrific from the higher floor, deluxe rooms, and most either have a balcony or a small sitting room, making them closer to junior suites. We think these are a particularly good value for on-the-river upscale accommodations, especially in comparison to the higher-priced Horizon Floor. Don't mistake this for the Oriental; but for such an enormous place, the level of service and facilities is surprisingly good.

The superluxurious Krung Thep Wing adds another 17-story, riverview tower to the grounds, as well as a restaurant, riverside swimming pool, and breakfast lounge. After passing through the flower-filled atrium signifying the Krung Thep's own entry, guests register in their superlarge rooms, surrounded by colorful Thai paintings and meters of glistening Thai silk. Deluxe features include a separate shower stall, twin sinks, and bidets in the huge marble bathrooms. Small balconies overlook the Sathorn Bridge and busy Chao Phraya River. The full-size, one bedroom junior suites (12,000B/$480), with a dining area and 1½ baths, are particularly good value for families. Larger suites include private fax machines, Jacuzzis, living rooms, and even more opulent Chinese decor.

We'd suggest the livelier main building for tourists, groups and families, and the quieter Krung Thep Wing for those seeking a respite from Bangkok's busy byways, or just a sojourn in luxury. The only complaint we've ever received about the Krung Thep Wing is noise from other rooms. The solution—change rooms!

Dining/Entertainment: Extravagance means 11 separate dining facilities, including the riverside Coffee Garden and Menam Terrace (which offers a nightly barbecue dinner); popular Shang Palace for Chinese food (see Section 1 of Chapter 5), and one of Bangkok's prettiest settings for Thai cuisine, Sala Thip (see Section 1 of Chapter 5), housed in two teakwood pavilions sitting right by the active riverside. The new Club Restaurant has nightly music. The hotel's river cruiser, the *Ayutthaya Princess*, motors up the Chao Phraya to Ayutthaya daily and makes a 3-hour dinner cruise on Sunday.

Services: Concierge, 24-hour room service, house doctor, limousine service, helicopter transfer, babysitting, laundry service.

Facilities: No-smoking floor, two swimming pools, health club, tennis courts, squash courts, business center, beauty salon and barbershop, shopping arcade.

EXPENSIVE

ROYAL GARDEN RIVERSIDE, 257/1-3 Charoen Nakhorn Rd., Thonburi, Bangkok 10600. Tel. 02/476-0021. Fax 02/476-1120. 394 rms, 26 suites. A/C

FROMMER'S SMART TRAVELER: HOTELS

1. Although many hotels belong to international reservations networks (like Utell and SRS), it's often possible to improve upon the published rates at the larger hotels by reserving your room through a Bangkok travel agent. (We recommend several in the "Orientation" section of Chapter 3.) Lower rates often include airport transfers and continental breakfast.
2. Ask your local travel agent about savings through combining your hotel reservation with your air ticket (through Thai Airways packages, for example).
3. In the off-season months, hotels will lower their rates if asked, or will at least include breakfast, an item that can save a considerable amount of money. It might seem odd to haggle in the lobby of a superior hotel, but it's possible to reduce your room rate by as much as 25% to 60%, especially in the months March through September. Another approach is to bargain over the phone, when you won't feel as vulnerable as you might in the lobby with your baggage.
4. If possible, avoid major holiday periods (see "When to go" in Chapter 2), unless you are interested in a particular festival. Rooms are more difficult to find, and often more costly, in these periods.
5. For excursions outside of Bangkok, you can often save money by booking a hotel through a Bangkok travel agent. Call your selected hotel for their rates, then compare with the rates available through the travel agent in your hotel or through one of the recommended agents in this book.
6. Compare prices between "twin room" rates and "single" room rates. Singles will include a standard double-size bed, and twin rates are sometimes higher in the budget hotels.
7. The real money savers are the best of the hotels in the "Moderate" or "Budget" categories, which may have most of the basic comforts but will lack a large hotel's small luxuries.

MINIBAR TV TEL **Directions:** On the Thonburi side of the Chao Phraya River, near the Krung Thep Bridge, 15 minutes by boat from River City.
$ Rates: 4,300B–4,800B ($172–$192) single; 4,800B–5,000B ($192–$200) double; from 6,000B ($240) suite. AE, DC, MC, V.
This city resort is the newest of the river-front hotels, a luxuriously sprawling complex on the banks of the Chao Phraya a few miles downstream from its nearest competition. You can leave the urban jangle of Bangkok behind as you board the hotel boat at River City for the short ride. The three wings of the hotel surround a large swimming pool set in a garden by the river. The marble-clad lobby is dramatic and soaring. Rooms are comfortable and modern, with pale cream walls and pink-and-blue fabrics, tastefully decorated and fully equipped with all the amenities. If you don't mind the boat ride (and we don't), it's a good choice. Boats go to and from River City every half hour, from early to late.

Dining/Entertainment: They go for the big international name—Trader Vic's Polynesian Restaurant and Benihana Japanese-American Steak House, as well as their own Garden Café (Thai and international cuisine), the Rice Mill Chinese Restaurant, and the Market Restaurant for beef and seafood.

Services: 24-hour service, concierge, limousine service, babysitting (arranged with advance notice).

Facilities: Swimming pool, tennis courts, health club, business center, beauty salon and barbershop, shopping arcade.

MODERATE

BOSSOTEL INN, 55/8-9 Soi Charoen Krung 42/1 New Rd., Bangkok 10500. Tel. 02/235-8001. Fax 02/237-3225. 39 rms, 7 minisuites. A/C MINIBAR TV TEL **Directions:** Off New Road, on Soi 42, to Shangri-La Hotel.
$ Rates: 1,075B–1,350B ($843–$54) single; 1,350B–1,600B ($54–$64) double. AE, MC, V.

⑤ Situated in the shadow of Bangkok's giants in the hotel world, this is one of those places that escape most budget travelers. It's not on the water and there isn't a view to speak of, but the spiffy, renovated new wing, in particular, warrants consideration.

Many of the guests are long-term visitors, and interestingly, quite a few are Orthodox Jews in the jewelry trade. This explains why, on our last visit, we discovered that the lobby restaurant served the only kosher food in Bangkok. The large rooms are Spartan, but up-to-date; facilities include a small business center and laundry service. The Bossotel's renovated wing (behind the slick glass entrance) is a better value than the older wing above the restaurant.

We'll let readers Ted and Dee Slosek from Pleasanton, California speak: "We had a delightful stay at the Bossotel. The room was spacious, clean, and comfortable—a good value for the price and only a few steps away from the Shangri-La and the Chao Phraya River. We found the staff to be pleasant, cordial, efficient, and helpful. The friendly greetings, care, and service we experienced here stood above any other of our entire stay in Bangkok."

INEXPENSIVE

RIVER VIEW GUEST HOUSE, 768 Soi Panurangsri, Songvad Rd., Sanjao Tosuekong, Taladnoi, Bangkok 10100. Tel. 02/234-5429. Fax 02/236-6199. 44 rms. **Directions:** 500 meters southeast of railroad station, between the intersection of Songwat and New roads, and the river.

$ Rates (including tax and service): 255B ($10.20) single with fan; 515B ($20.60) double with fan; 770B ($30.80) single or double with A/C. MC, V.

As you might gather from the address, this special place deep in the heart of Chinatown, only five minutes from the railroad station, and a stone's throw from the river, is difficult to find! We stayed there four days during out last visit and grew to love the views of the river and a neighboring Chinese temple, but we're not sure we could find it again. Half of this guest house's appeal is the friendly staff; the other half is wandering through the neighboring sois, lanes, and labyrinthine alleys, asking everyone to point the way. There's a lot of variety in the quality, upkeep, and views from each room, so look first if you're lucky enough to arrive when there's more than one room open. However, breakfast in the eighth floor restaurant, overlooking temples and the busy Chao Phraya, is truly special for everyone. How can you find it? Arrange with the airport taxi desk to explain the address to your driver, or have someone write it out for you in Thai; then, as soon as you get there, grab one of the River View Guest House business cards and keep it with you.

SWAN HOTEL, 31 Coi Charoen Krung 36, New Rd., Bangkok 10500. Tel. 02/234-8594. 72 rms. TEL **Directions:** Off New Road.

$ Rates (including tax and service): 425B ($17) single with fan, 650B ($26) single with A/C; 550B ($22) double with fan, 775B ($31) double with A/C. No credit cards.

Many budget travelers have discovered the Swan, which sits on the banks of the Chao Phraya River in the shadow of the aristocratic Oriental. The pool is large, there is a left luggage and laundry service and only 10 spacious guest rooms are without air-conditioning—all have toilets and showers, but with limited hot-water hours. Our only gripe, and it remains after visiting the Swan for many years, is that many of the rooms are clean but worn and shabby. Look first before committing to a room, and check out the rear wing. If it meets your standard, you've found one of the few acceptable low-cost accommodations smack in the middle of Bangkok's Gold Coast.

HISTORIC BANGKOK: NEAR THE GRAND PALACE

Since our last visit, one new Chinatown hotel and several renovations have made staying in this part of town a real possibility. Most of the major tourist sights are located here, making sightseeing by foot a pleasure and taxi rides mercifully short.

There are fewer restaurant choices than in other areas, but enough to satisfy most people. For budget travelers, the widest range of low-price accommodations are found in this area.

EXPENSIVE

GRAND CHINA PRINCESS HOTEL, 215 Yaowaraj Rd., Samphantawon-gse, Bangkok 10100. Tel. 02/224-9977. Fax 02/224-7999. 133 rms, 22 suites. A/C MINIBAR TV TEL **Directions:** Corner of Ratchawong Road, just south of New Road.

$ Rates: 2,280B–2,400B ($91.20–$96) single; 2,520B–2,640B ($100.80–$105.60) double; from 6,000B ($240) suite. Extra bed 550B ($22). AE, DC, MC, V.

The hotel we, and many tourists, have been waiting for—luxurious yet affordable, close to many attractions, and only a 5-minute walk from Ratchawong pier and the Chao Phraya ferry system. Built amid the bustling shop houses and businesses of colorful Chinatown, the Grand China Princess begins 10 stories above a shopping arcade and Chinese restaurant. Rooms are modern, yet gracefully Oriental and very comfortable, with the amenities found in much more expensive hotels. The suites are especially roomy, and decorated in muted tones of rose and gray. The 25th floor features Bangkok's first revolving lounge, with spectacular views over the city and Chao Phraya River. Other facilities include a coffee shop, whose lavish buffet breakfast (200B/$8) is a real bargain; a fitness center; a business center; and a Chinese banquet restaurant.

ROYAL PRINCESS HOTEL, 269 Larn Luang Rd., Bangkok 10100. Tel. 02/ 281-3088. Fax 02/280-1314. Telex TH 87688 PRINCES. 165 rms, 5 suites. A/C MINIBAR TV TEL **Directions:** East of Wat Saket.

$ Rates: 3,900B–4,300B ($156–$172) single; 4,300–4,700B ($172–$188) double; from 7,800B ($312) suite; 4,800B–5,100B ($192–$188) Princess Club. Extra bed 700B ($28). AE, DC, MC, V.

At long last, there's a new first-class hotel near the Grand Palace in the Raanakosin Island area, and it's great. Completed in 1989, this gem more than lives up to the high standards of the Thai-owned Dusit Thani Hotels and Resorts family. Its proximity to government offices brings a steady flow of official visitors (including major movers and shakers on lunch break), but we recommend it highly to tourists interested in the sights of old Bangkok.

Public spaces are wall-to-wall marble, and bustle with activity, yet the scale is intimate. Rooms are very tastefully appointed in muted blues and grays; marble bathrooms are fully stocked with amenities. Higher-priced deluxe rooms have balconies overlooking the tropically landscaped pool, while the superior room of the same style looks out over the neighborhood. It's a 10-minute taxi ride to either the Grand Palace or Vimanmek Palace, and though the area lacks a diversity of dining, the original flavor of this old neighborhood more than compensates.

Dining/Entertainment: Food service is a plethora of rices, starting with the superb Cantonese cuisine of the Empress Restaurant (see "Dining, below). The Mikado offers fine Japanese cuisine in a garden setting, with Piccolo providing Italian specialties. The Princess Café serves both Asian and Western food, with a sumptuous Thai buffet available at lunch.

Services: 24-hour room service, concierge, turndown service, limousine service, babysitting, laundry.

Facilities: Swimming pool, business center, exercise room.

MODERATE

GOLDEN HORSE HOTEL, 5/1-2 Damrongrok Rd., Bangkok 10100 Tel. 02/ 280-1920. Fax 02/280-3404. 130 rms. A/C MINIBAR TV TEL **Directions:** North side of Klong Mahanak near Wat Saket.

$ Rates: 1,350B ($54) single; 1,550B ($62) double. MC, V.

This small hotel is conveniently located just one block from the main Thai Airways International office and near the city's major tourist attractions. Because of its popularity with economy-minded tourists and small groups, the busy staff is helpful and ready to answer any questions. Minibars and televisions grace every nondescript room, all simply furnished but well maintained. Higher-floor, south-facing rooms even have a view of nearby Wat Saket, the golden chedi on the mount.

The attractive marble lobby has seating areas and newspapers for guests, as well as a large restaurant serving moderately priced Thai food, some Chinese and continental favorites.

HOTEL MAJESTIC PALACE, 97 Ratchadamnoen Ave., Bangkok 10200. Tel. 02/280-5610. Fax 02/280-0965. 60 rms, 5 suites. A/C MINIBAR TV TEL **Directions:** Near the Democracy Monument.

$ Rates: 1,680B ($67.20) single; 2,150B ($86) double; 3,600B ($144) junior suite. MC, V.

Bangkok's oldest hotel, built by King Rama V over 80 years ago in a grand Thai interpretation of colonial Victorian, has been recently renovated to its former glory. The high-ceilinged marble lobby, with bay windows and a shrine to his Highness, remind you that this property is still in the hands of the royal family.

The new management team have outfitted the pastel-toned, compact rooms with carved teak headboards, pink marble bathrooms with hair dryers, a cozy seating area, and sepia photos of old Bangkok. The corner junior suites have a writing desk, larger sitting areas, and overlook Bangkok's Champs-Elysées. (Request an avenue-facing room for the view and size. Double-glazed windows blunt the traffic noise).

It's not as flashy or convenience filled as many of the new hotels, but the Majestic Palace has a mature elegance that will please old Asia hands, those on sentimental journeys, and those who just admire a good renovation.

Dining/Entertainment: The glass-enclosed Milady Room Café looks out onto the avenue and serves moderately priced Thai, Chinese, and continental cuisine.

Services: Room service, concierge, limousine service, laundry.

ROYAL HOTEL, 2 Ratchadamnoen Rd., Bangkok 10200. Tel 02/222-9111. Fax 02/224-2083. Telex 84252 ROYALHO TH. 130 rms. A/C MINIBAR TV TEL **Directions:** 2 blocks east of National Museum.

$ Rates: 1,150B ($46) single; 1,560B ($62.40) double. AE, MC, V.

The venerable Royal, near Thammasat University and a 5-minute walk from the Royal Palace, is perfect for budget-minded sightseers. The glitzy lobby, with polished marble floors, chandeliers, and massive modern white Corinthian columns was a field hospital during the May 1991 Democracy demonstrations. Now it's again abuzz with guests from around the world. The simpler old wing's large staircase and other architectural details date from the art deco era. Other aspects of the Royal hearken back to the 1950s, so that the overall effect is an architectural pastiche that would make Robert Venturi proud. Clean, kitschy (pink, ruffled polyester Chinese bedspreads) doubles in the old wing have high ceilings and are quite spacious. Request a room that faces away from the noisy street.

The less descript new wing has comfortable, already-worn rooms which are usually presold to group tours. Many overlook the small pool. Other facilities include a multinational cuisine restaurant, an inexpensive 24-hour coffee shop, a tour desk, and several shops. The reception desk will arrange babysitters.

BUDGET

LEK GUESTHOUSE, 125-127 Khao San Rd., Banglamphu, Bangkok 10200. Tel. 02/281-2775. 20 rms (all with bath). **Directions:** Near Chakkra Phong Road.

IMPRESSIONS

From the very beginning I was charmed by Bangkok.... I like its polite, gentle, handsome people, its temples, flowers and canals, the relaxed and peaceful rhythm of life here.
—S. J. PERLMAN, *WESTWARD HA!*

$ Rates (including tax and service): 100B ($4) single; 175B ($7) double. No credit cards.

What distinguishes the Lek from the others in a row of guest houses is that it's slightly more dependable than its neighbors. The accommodations are as basic as can be—small partitions, all with fans—but most guests we spoke with felt that the proprietor and family work hard to make guests feel at home. The house has a safe for storing valuables, a simple roof terrace, free luggage storage for guests that have checked out, laundry facilities, and a few balconies. For a quiet night, request a room away from the street.

NITH CHAROEN HOTEL, 183 Khao San Rd., Banglamphu, Bangkok 10200. Tel. 02/281-9872. 25 rms. **Directions:** Between Chakkra Phong and Tanao roads.

$ Rates (including tax and service): 385B ($15.40) single/double. No credit cards.

Set back from busy Khao San Road, this well-maintained guest house is a good choice if you're willing to pay a higher price for a quieter and cleaner place. We liked it for the fresh coat of paint and the friendly staff. All rooms even have a simple cold-water Asian bath, as well as a toilet and shower.

PEACHY GUESTHOUSE, 10 Phra Arthit Rd., Banglamphu, Bangkok 10200. Tel. 02/281-6471. 35 rms. **Directions:** 1 block form Phra Arthit Express Boat pier.

$ Rates (including tax and service): 110B ($4.40) single with fan; 155B ($6.20) double with fan. No credit cards.

This large, comfortable guest house is one of our favorites for the price. Rooms are stacked in a U-shaped block around a courtyard where breakfast and snacks are served. Large, bright rooms are spartan but clean, most with ceiling fans. Communal toilets and cold-water showers on each floor are kept very clean. Peachy also has a funky lounge on each floor where fellow travelers can hang out. This place is popular with a budget crowd more mature than that found in the Khao San Road guest houses—Peace Corps and UNICEF workers, as well as families.

P.S. GUESTHOUSE, 9 Phra Sumeru Rd., Chanasongkram Pranakorn, Bangkok 10200. Tel. 02/282-3832. 50 rms. **Directions:** 2 blocks from Tha Phra Arthit Express Boat pier.

$ Rates (including tax and service): 110B ($4.40) single; 165B ($6.60) double. No credit cards.

Another in the "Spartan but clean" category. The small rooms barely give you walking space around the twin beds, but there are fans, screened windows, and washed linens for each, as well as scrubbed-clean toilets and cold showers down the hall. Rooms start on the second floor, above the simple Evergreen Restaurant. You'll find the higher floors to be quieter. The extra perk here is the Washy Mashy Laundromat across the street, where a full load costs only 85B ($3.40) if you do it, 115B ($4.60) if they do.

THE BUSINESS DISTRICT

This area is good for business travelers whose appointments are concentrated in nearby office buildings and banks. There is a wide range of good choices in the upper and middle-price categories as well as some good values in the inexpensive range. It's an easy taxi ride to the river area and a half to 1-hour trip to the Palace area (depending on time of day).

VERY EXPENSIVE

DUSIT THANI, Rama IV Rd., Bangkok 10500. Tel. 02/236-0450. Fax 02/236-6400. Telex TH 81170. 487 rms, 33 suites. A/C MINIBAR TV TEL **Directions:** At corner of Silom Road opposite Lumpini Park.

$ Rates: 6,300B ($252) single or double; Landmark deluxe rooms. 8,000B ($320) single or double. Extra bed 1,200B ($48). AE, DC, MC, V.

⭐ Gurgling lobby fountains, exotic flower displays, and a poolside waterfall cascading through dense foliage make this top-rated hotel a welcome retreat at the end of a day's sightseeing. Dusit Thani literally means "a town in heaven." Luxurious, well-lit rooms are adorned with Thai arts and architectural details, and use traditional materials such as mudmee silk and teakwood. The Landmark Tower rooms are extremely large and include butler service, complimentary daily fresh fruit, flowers, and English-language newspapers, bathrobes, hair dryers, slippers, large baths and separate massage showers, with complimentary breakfast and drinks available to guests in the Landmark Lounge.

Dining/Entertainment: Among the hotel's nine restaurants, the Mayflower and the Benjarong are ranked among the finest restaurants in Bangkok (see "Dining," below). The top-floor French-cuisine Tiara Restaurant has a sensational view over the city. The popular Pavilion Coffeeshop, with fine international buffets and "light" cuisine, and Chinatown Restaurant are lesser-priced establishments. There is also a steak house, a Vietnamese restaurant, as well as Japanese eateries, the latter two especially popular with businesspeople. Bubbles Videotheque draws a high-class local crowd as well as hotel guests.

Services: 24-hour room service, concierge, house doctor, limousine service, babysitting, laundry/valet.

Facilities: Business center, fitness center, tennis-and-squash courts, swimming pool, shopping arcade, barbershop, beauty salon.

THE MONTIEN, 54 Surawong Rd., Bangkok 10500. Tel. 02/233-7060. Fax 02/236-5219. Telex TH 81160. 500 rms, including 40 suites. A/C MINIBAR TV TEL **Directions:** Near Patpong.

$ Rates: 4,800B–6,720B ($192–$269) single; 5,280B–7,200B ($211–$288) double; suite from 9,600B ($384). AE, DC, MC, V.

Like many of the first-class tourist hotels that are attempting to break into the business market in Bangkok, the Montien is really two facilities in one. The first is directed at its traditional market, mainly Australian groups, who occupy the lower floors of one of the Montien's two wings with their dark teak hallways and bright, pleasant rooms. The other wing has been thoroughly upgraded and renamed the Executive Club. In this part of the hotel, dark teak has given way to bleached wood, granite, and matching gray carpet. The elegantly furnished Executive Club commons, adjoining the business center, serves complimentary continental breakfast and, in the evening, free drinks. The new decor and near-Patpong location have, apparently, lured Japanese businesspeople to the Montien. Whether the additional tariff justifies doubling the standard room rates is up to you, but we were impressed with the fine facilities and services in the newly upgraded wing. Unique in Bangkok is the Montien's Montientong Theater, where Thai and international plays are produced. And if that's not enough to sway you, how about the 20 in-house fortune-tellers who offer their prognostications from the mezzanine level for approximately 350B ($14) per reading and are widely consulted by Bangkok residents.

Dining/Entertainment: The Montien has an in-house bakery and good French and Chinese outlets. Our favorite is the Jade Garden Cantonese restaurant.

Services: 24-hour room service, concierge, complimentary welcome tea, house doctor, limousine service, babysitting, laundry service, fortune-telling.

Facilities: Swimming pool, health club, tennis club, business center, beauty salon and barbershop, shopping arcade, theater.

THE SUKHOTHAI, 13/3 Sathorn Rd., Bangkok 10120. Tel. 02/287-0222. Fax 02/287-4980. 146 rms, 76 suites. A/C MINIBAR TV TEL **Directions:** South of Rama IV Road next to the YMCA.

$ Rates: 5,200B–6,600B ($208–$264) single or double; form 9,000B ($360) suite. Extra bed 700B ($28). AE, DC, MC, V.

The stunning new Sukhothai, a property of the prestigious Beaufort Group from Singapore, brings unexpected luxury to a noisy, busy locale better known for the neighboring low-budget YWCA and YMCA hostels. Nonetheless, once you've left Sathorn Road behind for one of the Sukhothai's five white pavilions, peace reigns supreme. The hotel's Thai minimalist aesthetic bathes visitors in a welcome, if studied, serenity. Every design element contributes to a heightened sense of drama throughout. The broad, colonnaded public spaces are decorated with mud- and olive-toned silk panels, woven to fit this unique space. Bronze metalwork is brushed a dull black, so as not to clash with the redbrick stupas and sculpture which quietly accent black-tiled wading pools. Terra-cotta friezes, stupa-shaped wall sconces, and celadon ceramics and tiles evoke memories of the ancient kingdom of Sukhothai. The work of master designer Ed Tuttle (maestro of Phuket's Amanpuri and Bali's Amandari resorts), it is truly beautiful.

Guest-room pavilions overlook lotus ponds inspired by the gardens of the Sukhothai era. Teak and cinnabar-accented rooms strive for the latest in luxury: reclining chaises, butler service, electronic "Do Not Disturb" signs and automatic doorbell override, two full-size teak closets, separate shower stall in granite bathrooms, personal fax machines installed on request, and terraces with the Garden Suites. Though gorgeous design is the Sukhothai's most obvious attribute, guests command its excellent service and assured sense of privacy.

Dining/Entertainment: There are many stylish dining venues. The less formal Colonnade (is coffee shop a wild misnomer?) is most popular at Sunday brunch, when local jazz bands play while guests cruise the deluxe international buffet (500B/$20). The exterior Terrazzo serves nuova Italiana under big Japanese umbrellas by the pool; formal French fare is dished up at lunch (Monday to Friday only) or dinner (nightly) in La Noppamas's elegant silver and beige dining room. Celadon is the gourmet Thai restaurant, housed in a pavilion perched above a water garden.

Services: Room service, 24-hour butler service, concierge, house doctor, limousine service, babysitting, laundry.

Facilities: Olympic-size swimming pool, health club, two squash courts one tennis court, business center, Guerlain beauty salon, upscale shopping arcade.

EXPENSIVE

HOLIDAY INN CROWNE PLAZA, 981 Silom Rd., Bangkok 10500. Tel. 02/238-4300. Fax 02/238-5289. Telex 82998 HIBKK TH. 726 rms, including 28 suites. A/C MINIBAR TV TEL **Directions:** On Silom Road 1 block above New Road.
$ **Rates:** 3,800 ($152) Plaza Tower single; 4,300B–4,800B ($172–$192) Crowne Tower single; 4,300B ($172) Plaza Tower double; 4,800B–5,300B ($192–$211) Crowne Tower double; 5,275B–6,000B ($211–$240) Executive Club floors; suite from 7,200B ($288). Extra person 600B ($24) Children under 19 years stay free in parents' room. AE, DC, MC, V.

If you've never been to a Holiday Inn outside the United States, you're in for a shock. The surprise is the near spectacular quality of these properties, where the level of luxury and service may represent the best of the entire chain. The entrance to the gleaming white marble lobby is on the second floor, isolated from the street noise and traffic of busy Silom Road (the hotel is only a short walk from the Shangri-La and Oriental). The lobby links the Holiday Inn's two towers.

Rooms in the Plaza Tower represent an excellent value. The most distinctive aspect of their design are the oversized porthole windows, which, framed by heavy drapery, look out over the city. Although the rooms are less spacious than those in the Crowne Tower, the high ceilings make the space feel quite large. A soothing gray-and-white color scheme and the quality amenities give the impression of living in deluxe accommodations at a standard-room price.

The Crowne Tower offers up-to-date, high-end quarters, worthy of nearly any hotel in Bangkok. Our deluxe king room had a large, walk-in closet, a marble bathroom with a glassed-in corner shower (and separate bath) and all of the amenities one associates with the best in town. Although few rooms have a genuine river view, the upper floor rooms do command a fine panorama from their angled bay windows.

Managing its solid facilities is a genuinely helpful staff.

Dining/Entertainment: One of Bangkok's better breakfast buffets is served in the Window on Silom Restaurant. In the afternoon, the hotel serves a lovely high tea in the Orchid Lounge. The Thai Pavillion and the mogul cuisine Tandoor serve

66 • WHERE TO STAY & DINE IN BANGKOK

lunch and dinner, which can be followed by an evening drink at the Cheers Pub (see "Evening Entertainment" in Chapter 5).

Services: 24-hour room service, concierge, complimentary welcome tea, limousine service, babysitting, laundry service.

Facilities: Swimming pool, health club, tennis courts, business center, beauty salon and barbershop, shopping arcade.

THE MANDARIN BANGKOK, 662 Rama IV Rd., Bangkok 10120. Tel. 234-1390. Fax 02/237-1620. Telex TH87689. 400 rms. A/C MINIBAR TV TEL **Directions:** East Si Phraya Road.

$ Rates: 3,200B–3,700B ($128–$148) single; 3,500B–4,000B ($140–$160) double; 6,600B–9,000B ($264–$360) suite. Extra bed 480B ($19.20). AE, DC, MC, V.

The Mandarin, a property of the Dutch Golden Tulip Hotels Group, is a glitzy, full-service hotel, perhaps better known in Bangkok for its nightclub (wildly popular with locals on weekends) than for its rooms. The lively lobby combines velvet-upholstered reproductions of Asian and European antiques with polished-brass doors and glittering chandeliers. All accommodations are clean, modern, and spacious, done in a luminous white-and-gray color scheme. Rates vary with size and decor, but all rooms are good value.

The pool is small, often shrouded in shade, and noisy from the nearby traffic. However, double-pane windows, to cut down on street noise inside the hotel make its convenient location bearable.

Dining/Entertainment: The Mandarin is home of the queen of the Bangkok cocktail lounges, the Mandarina. Next door is the Nile Night Club, handling much of the overflow from the Mandarina. These clubs and the 24-hour Coffee Shop (also with live bands!) are open nightly, but the real action takes place on the weekends.

Services: 24-hour room service, concierge, limousine service, babysitting (with some notice), laundry service.

Facilities: Small swimming pool, business center, beauty salon and barbershop, shopping arcade.

MODERATE

MANOHRA HOTEL, 412 Surawong Rd., Bangkok 10500. Tel. 02/234-5070. Fax 02/237-7662. Telex TH 82114. 242 rms, 8 suites. A/C MINIBAR TV TEL **Directions:** Between New Road and Mahesak Road.

$ Rates: 2,650B–2,900B ($106–$116) single or double; from 4,800B ($192) suite. Rollaway bed 600N ($24). AE, DC, MC, V.

The bright and fetching Manohra Hotel, a 5-minute walk from the Oriental (hotel) and the Chao Phraya River, is a modern, quiet oasis with a pleasant coffee shop overlooking this busy street. The glass-and-stone-sheathed lobby faces a small indoor swimming pool, contributing to the glitzy appearance of the public spaces. Guest rooms, on the other hand, are rather dimly lit and tend to be smaller than those in other first-class hotels. However, they have a full range of amenities and are often booked by European tours.

TRINITY CITY HOTEL, 425 Silom Rd., Bangkok 10500. Tel. 02/231-5050. Fax 02/231-5417. 110 rms, 4 suites. A/C MINIBAR TV TEL **Directions:** 2 blocks east of Silom Road on Soi 5.

$ Rates: 2,500 ($100) single; 2,800B ($112) double; 3,200 ($128) suite. Extra bed 350B ($14). AE, MC, V.

At the quiet end of "Can't Keep Your Money" Lane (famous among Bangkokians for its many and various bargains), you'll find the most pleasant small midpriced hotel in town. It has the marble lobby and tastefully furnished rooms of a large hotel, with the intimacy of a smaller European establishment. The staff is charming, friendly, and helpful. The 24-hour coffee shop has good food and service at very reasonable prices; there's a supermarket a few doors up and several nearby restaurants. The rooftop swimming pool in an adjacent tower, fitness center, beauty shop, massage and sauna, and easy access to both the Silom Road business-and-shopping activity and the river, make this top of the class for both comfort and convenience.

INEXPENSIVE

BANGKOK CHRISTIAN GUESTHOUSE, 123 Saladaeng, Soi 2, Convent Rd., Bangkok 10500. Tel. 02/233-6303. Fax 02/237-1742. 30 rms. A/C TEL

Directions: 1 block east of Silom Road off the corner of Convent Road.

$ Rates (including breakfast): 770B ($30.80) single; 1,150B ($46) double. Extra person 350B ($14). No credit cards.

This tranquil two-story guest house, originally a Presbyterian missionary residence, was converted into a lodge in the late 1960s, operated by the Church of Christ in Thailand. Large recently refurbished rooms are simple but spotless. The nicest rooms are on the second floor overlooking the large lawn with its seating area, goldfish pond, and teak pavilion. There's a grandma-style lounge and library, a cheap restaurant where you must reserve lunch or dinner, and a friendly young staff. There's a definite Christian atmosphere here and it's so comfy, in fact, that it's usually booked four to six weeks in advance.

BANGKOK YWCA, 13 Sathorn Tai Rd., Bangkok 10120. Tel. 02/286-3310. 46 rms (10 with shared bath). A/C Directions: A short walk South of Rama IV Road.

$ Rates (including tax and service): 680B ($27.20) single; 820B ($32.80) double. Rooms with common shower, 50B ($2) less. No credit cards.

⑤ The venerable YWCA has come of age since our last stay, by offering its clean, simple rooms to women, men, and couples. It would be hard, it not impossible, to top this Y for value. There is a nice pool, beauty salon, tour desk, and common TV lounge. In addition, there's a canteen/snack bar and a cozy, very popular full-service restaurant where two can dine for less than 225B ($9). Did we forget to mention the YWCA Cooking School or the Sri Pattana Thai Language School? A solid value for short, or long-term visitors.

YMCA COLLINS HOUSE INTERNATIONAL, 27 S. Sathorn Rd., Bangkok 10120. Tel. 02/287-1900. Fax 02/297-1966. Telex 72185 BYMCA TH. 258 rms. A/C TV TEL Directions: A short walk south of Rama IV Road.

$ Rates (plus 11% tax; no service charge): 1,300B–1,600B ($52–$63) single; 1,450B–2,000B ($58–$80) double; 2,800B ($112) suite. AE, MC, V.

★ This is a good value in the moderate-price range, with no compromise in comfort. Imagine a modern, nine-story hotel with sparkling, homey rooms with private showers, a 75-foot swimming pool, and multiethnic restaurant service, all tucked into a quiet lane off Sathorn Road, near the Dusit Thani Hotel and business district. We love staying here and met the nicest people; both staff and clientele are very friendly. The Y's front desk offers copy, fax, telex, and secretarial services. Our friends Joan and David claim that the Rossukon Restaurant has the most delicious and varied buffet in town, at a bargain price.

A new wing contains a gym and second restaurant, as well as 120 more deluxe rooms featuring TV, minibar, and full bathtubs, though at higher prices. Families should note that this YMCA even has suites—a Bangkok best buy.

SURIWONGSE TOWER INN, Executive House Building, 410/3-4 Suriwong Rd., Bangrak, Bangkok 10500. Tel. 02/235-1206. Fax 02/237-1482. 80 rms. A/C MINIBAR TV TEL Directions: Between New Road and Mahesak Road.

$ Rates: 1,450B–1,700B ($58–$68) single; 1,500B–1,800B ($60–$72) double; from 4,000B ($160) suite. Extra bed 250B ($10). AE, MC, V.

This establishment is difficult to find because it comprises the 14th to 18th floors of the modern Executive House condominium tower, in a cul-de-sac off of noisy Suriwong Road. Don't be put off—it's a good value for families who will make use of its oversize rooms (formerly apartments), with their small balconies (great Chao Phraya views), well-kept bathrooms, and simple, eclectic international modern furnishings. That each room offers its unique, odd leatherette armchair, or wall-to-wall carpeting, flower-print bed linens, parquet floors, or mirrored bar area only contributes to the residential feeling exuded here. Although worn in a homey way, the Suriwongse Tower is well-maintained, with a nice staff and a small coffee shop on the ground floor.

SHOPPING/EMBASSY AREA

This is a wide-ranging area, covering the hotels on either side of Sukhumvit/Ploenchit/Rama I Road. Many of the major shopping centers and stores are here, as well as the Sukhumvit shopping area, which is popular with the expatriate community. Many businesses have spread into office towers in the area, so business travelers may also find it convenient. The river is not so far away, but the taxi ride to the Palace area can be over one hour at peak traffic times.

VERY EXPENSIVE

GRAND HYATT ERAWAN BANGKOK, 494 Rajdamri Rd., Bangkok 10330. Tel. 02/254-1234. Fax 02/253-5856. Telex 20975 HYAT BKKTH. 362 rms, 38 suites. A/C MINIBAR TV TEL **Directions:** Corner of Rama I Road.

$ **Rates:** 5,900B–6,500B ($236–$260) single or double; 7,200B ($288) Regency Club single or double; from 9,000B ($360) suite. Extra bed 700B ($28). AE, DC, MC, V.

A grand hotel has risen anew at the site of Bangkok's famed Erawan shrine, the bustling, open-air temple dedicated to the four-headed Brahma, Tan Thao Mahaprom. Beyond the portal guarded by two bronze Erawans, dozens of banyan trees dapple the light pouring into a four-story atrium lobby. The air is filled with the sounds of waterfalls and gurgling goldfish ponds. Modeled after the residential gardens of a Thai mansion, it's just part of the grandness at the aptly named new Hyatt.

Although it aims to lure expense-account business travelers (the brochure even claims that the hotel's proximity to the shrine may bring luck in business!), the Hyatt Erawan is a luxurious choice for all travelers. The works of dozens of contemporary Thai artists grace hallways and spacious rooms, where earth-toned silks, celadon accessories, antique-finish furnishings, parquet floors, Oriental rugs, large bathrooms, and city views abound. The three Regency Club levels feature a lounge for continental breakfast, day-long coffee and tea service, cocktails, butler service, and private entertainment units with a library of CDs and videos. Suites include additional amenities such as pantries for entertaining, Jacuzzis, a sauna with built-in TV, and in the Presidential Suite—a baby grand piano!

In addition to the facilities one expects from a five-star hotel, there is a delightful fifth-floor pool terrace, where a waterfall tumbles down a rocky wall into a full-size hot tub. The teak Sala Thai surrounded by fountains is used for cocktails, and the casual, fan-cooled café services pool guests and health-club members.

Dining/Entertainment: The pleasant lobby restaurant features a grand buffet at breakfast, lunch, and dinner, as well as a continental à la carte menu and a high tea. Spasso is the Hyatt's trendy Italian bistro cum jazz bar, a popular local hangout. The stunning high-style Deco Chinese Restaurant is a gourmand's delight and worthy of a special trip. The basement shopping arcade features a pastry-and-cappuccino parlor.

Services: 24-hour room service, concierge, limousine service, house doctor, babysitting, laundry.

Facilities: Swimming pool, large health club with jogging track, tennis-and-squash courts, business center, beauty salon and barbershop, rooftop heliport, shopping arcade.

HILTON INTERNATIONAL AT NAI LERT PARK, 2 Wireless Rd., Bangkok 10330. Tel. 02/253-0123. Fax 02/253-6509. Telex 72206 HILBKK TH. 306 rms, 37 suites. A/C MINIBAR TV TEL **Directions:** Between Ploenchit Road and New Phetchaburi Road.

$ Rates: 5,300B–5,800B ($212–$232) single; 5,900B–6,600B ($236–$264) double; from 10,800B ($432) suite. Garden room 600B ($24) extra. Executive Floor 6,600B ($264) single; 7,200B ($288) double. Extra person 1,200B ($48). AE, DC, MC, V.

★ Set in lushly landscaped Nai Lert Park, near the British and American embassies, this tropical paradise is something of a mixed blessing—you will sleep far from the madding crowd, but you may find the taxi ride to the river or tourist sights a minor nuisance (though the brave will ride the convenient klong boat to the Grand Palace Area). However, after a long day of business or sightseeing, returning to the peaceful tranquility of the Hilton has the very comfortable feeling of returning home. The airy atrium lobby, distinctly Thai modern in design, is at once elegant and friendly. With its classic teak pavilion and open garden views, it ranks as one of the great public spaces in Bangkok.

The spacious guest rooms all have bougainvillea-draped balconies, the most preferred (and expensive) of which overlook the free-form pool and parklike grounds. Handsome Thai cotton prints cover the comfortable rattan armchairs. All-marble bathrooms feature not one but two bathrobes (one light cotton, one heavier terry cloth), slippers, and hair dryers. Fruit baskets greet all newcomers, and treats of candy, Thai sweets, sushi, or cakes arrive unexpectedly at your door.

The fifth floor is dedicated to busy executives who don't mind the premium price for amenities such as complimentary continental breakfast, drinks served in the private lounge, and 24-hour butler service. The Hilton's professional and friendly staff is a decided plus on all floors, and especially accommodating and friendly to our energetic toddler. The Hilton offers periodic special-rate weekends, which include rooms and meal packages at a very attractive price.

Dining/Entertainment: Food service is outstanding and very good value. The so-called "coffee shop," Suan Saranrom, is really a grand dining area overlooking the garden. Though serving both Thai and continental dishes, it has, for many years, been voted the best Thai restaurant in a Bangkok hotel. (It also serves up the champion breakfast buffet in all of Thailand.) The elegant Ma Maison offers excellent French cuisine (see "Dining," below). Genji, the Japanese restaurant (also included in "Dining," below), a cozy lobby bar, and an evening poolside grill complete the offerings. On Sunday, the sumptuous brunch buffet includes pool privileges for kids (who are entertained by clowns) and parents alike.

Services: 24-hour room service, concierge, limousine service, house doctor, babysitting, laundry service.

Facilities: World-class swimming pool, fitness center with tennis-and-squash courts, business center, beauty salon and barbershop, shopping arcade.

LE MERIDIEN PRESIDENT, 135/26 Gaysorn Rd., Bangkok 10330. Tel. 02/253-0444, or toll free 800/543-4300. Fax 02/253-7565. Telex TH 81194. 373 rms. A/C MINIBAR TV TEL **Directions:** Near intersection of Rama I Road and Rajadamri Road.

$ Rates: 3,600B–4,600B ($144–$184) single; 4,100–5,400B ($164–$202) double; from 4,100B–6,600 ($264) suite. AE, DC, MC, V.

Part of the Meridien chain, this group-tour-oriented hotel has undergone extensive renovation. The gray marble lobby now has a welcoming and homey ambience (a far cry from some Bangkok hotels with their impressive, though cold, decor). The newer suites are more sumptuously appointed than in the compact attractive rooms, with pale paneling, tasteful pastel furnishings, and the usual panoply of luxury amenities. As in other Meridien hotels, many of the guests are French, and the renowned Gallic culinary sophistication may explain why the dining rooms here are among the top choices in Bangkok.

Dining/Entertainment: The Fireplace Grill is considered one of Bangkok's best Western dining rooms. Cappuccino rates as one of Bangkok's better coffee shops; desserts are excellent.

Services: 24-hour room service, concierge, complimentary welcome tea, house doctor, limousine service, babysitting, laundry service.

Facilities: Swimming pool, health club, business center, beauty salon and barbershop, shopping arcade.

NOVOTEL BANGKOK, Soi 6, Siam Sq., Bangkok 10330. Tel. 02/255-
6888. Fax 02/255-1824. Telex TH 22780. 429 rms, including 36 suites. A/C
MINIBAR TV TEL **Directions:** In Siam Square off Rama I Road.

$ **Rates:** 4,900B ($196) single; 5,400B ($216) double; 6,200B ($249) deluxe; suite from
7,000B ($283). Extra bed 600B ($24). AE, DC, MC, V.

This is a slickly built high-rise hotel set in the midst of the Siam Square shopping
area. It's elegant and opulent, representing one of this French chain's best inns. The
grand entrance was designed with a mountain of granite and marble and expansive
glass walls. The interior is a play of gray stone complemented by soft pink leather-
upholstered sofas and chairs, pastel tones which carry over into guest quarters,
where the rooms are spacious and fully equipped. Among our favorite facilities are
the 18th-floor no-smoking suites and the full-featured business center that overlooks
the hotel's kidney-shaped pool. Novotel's fitness center is totally slick, reminding us
of the brilliant chrome-and-mirror motif of the Vertical Club in Manhattan.

The location isn't ideal for vising Bangkok's traditional tourist sites, but if you're
in town on business or don't mind centering yourself in one of Bangkok's better
shopping areas, the Novotel is a fine choice.

Dining/Entertainment: The Pastel Lounge serves a delicious continental breakfast and afternoon tea; in the evening there is an oh-too-elegant string quartet.
Chinese, Thai, seafood, and Western food are available in the hotel's other dining
outlets.

Services: 24-hour room service, concierge, house doctor, limousine service,
babysitting, laundry service.

Facilities: No-smoking floor, swimming pool, health club, business center, bakery, beauty salon, barbershop.

THE REGENT, BANGKOK, 155 Rajdamri Rd., Bangkok 10330. Tel. 02/
251-6127. Fax 02/253-9195. Telex 20004 REGBKK TH. 400 rms. A/C MINIBAR TV
TEL **Directions:** South of Rama I Road.

$ **Rates:** 5,400–7,800B ($216–$312) single/double; suite from 9,600B ($384). AE, DC,
MC, V.

★ The starkly modern Regent of Bangkok feels like home to all who have
sampled this chain's other deluxe accommodations in the United States or
Asia. The impeccable service begins at the front desk, where guests are
greeted, then whisked off to complete check-in in their own room. Complimentary
Chinese tea soon follows, joining the fruit basket and box of chocolates.

An air of luxury pervades each room, with amenities such as cotton robes, slippers, a scale, and umbrella tucked in a plush carpeted dressing area off the tiled
bath. Cool pastel-upholstered couches and armchairs invite windowside seating, especially if your room overlooks the verdant Royal Bangkok Sport Club, and racetrack.
The cavernous lobby, with its high ceilings decorated with colorful frescoes and a
vast mural depicting 200 years of Bangkok history, constantly hums with activity
and is always colorfully decorated for the festival of the season.

For visiting royalty (this hotel is rated No. 1 for security by the U.S. Embassy) or
the high-dollar executive, the ninth-floor Rajdamri Suite is one of the most elegant in
town. Private dining/conference room, huge sitting room with silk couches, seven
bedrooms with Khmer and Thai antiquities, and a manorial library (with a tape
player and music cassettes) provide even more than you would expect for 43,000B
($1,720) a night. The more affordable executive suites have a roomy dining area and
executive work desk, plus many of the same amenities. The seven recently built Cabana Rooms and single Cabana Suite, each with private patio, overlook the

---

IMPRESSIONS

*Bangkok has been so loved because it is the expression of Thais themselves, of their
lightheartedness, their love of beauty, their reverence for tradition, their sense of
freedom, their extravagance, their devotion to their creeds—to characteristics that are
constant and continuing in themselves.*
—ALEC WAUGH, BANGKOK STORY OF A CITY, 1987

landscaped pool area and evoke a nouvelle grandeur with colonial era overtones.

Dining/Entertainment: We found the lobby dining area a bit too exposed for a casual dinner, but it's great for tea, at 180B ($7.20), accompanied by the sounds of a string quartet from the balcony above. La Brasserie's indoor booths and outdoor café tables are better for relaxed dining. The international cuisine buffet lunch (360B, $14.40) is very popular in this upscale shopping district. The informal Spice Market is one of the finest Thai restaurants in the city (see "Dining," below). The Regent Grill is the Regnet's premier spot for continental fare, featuring California cuisine in an L.A.-slick setting. The intimate Bar, decorated with the watercolors of Thai artist Suchart Wongthong, offers evening piano music.

Services: 24-hour room service, complimentary welcome tea, concierge, house clinic, limousine service, eight-seat "office bus" with phone and fax, babysitting, laundry/valet, complimentary shoeshine and necktie cleaning.

Facilities: Pool and health club with sauna, business center, beauty slaon and barbershop, gourmet bakery and deli, shopping arcade.

SIAM INTER-CONTINENTAL, 967 Rama I Rd., Bangkok 10330. Tel. 02/ 253-0355. Fax 02/253-2275. Telex TH 81155 SIAMINT. 400 rms. A/C MINIBAR TV TEL **Directions:** Opposite Siam Square.

$ Rates: 4,000B–5,200B ($160–$208) single; 4,300B–5,500B ($172–$220) double; suite from 8,400B ($336). AE, DC, MC, V.

Set in 26 acres of parkland—part of the Srapatum Royal Palace estate—the Siam Inter-Continental is an island of calm in frenetic Bangkok. A gracious driveway leads to a massive Eero Saarinen—inspired, clamshell-shaped lobby, which overlooks the well-landscaped grounds. As might be imagined with such enormous property, it offers some of the best outdoor sports facilities of any hotel in Bangkok. Groomed jogging trails, lit tennis courts, and golf (minicourse and driving range) are among the more popular facilities. The hotel's small playground is also popular with children.

A 1993 renovation has spruced up the rooms and public spaces of the sprawling ranch-style complex. Pastel carpets and dark Chinese-style furniture provide a rich, pleasing ambience. The Club Inter-Continental Wing is the two-story equivalent of an "Executive" floor, with slightly smarter furnishings and free breakfast and drinks in the private lounge. The least expensive, "standard" rooms in the one contemporary Tower Wing had not been renovated as of our visit.

Dining/Entertainment: The all-you-can-eat buffet lunch at Similan, the Inter-Continental's Thai and seafood restaurant, is good value at 375B ($15).

Services: 24-hour room service, concierge, complimentary welcome tea, house doctor, limousine service, babysitting, laundry service.

Facilities: Swimming pool, sports center, business center, beauty salon, barbershop, shopping arcade, and bakery.

EXPENSIVE

THE AMARI BOULEVARD, 2 Soi 5, Sukhumvit Rd., Bangkok 10110. Tel. 02/255-2930. Fax 02/255-2950. Telex TH 84033 AMARIBV 300 rms, 15 suites. A/C MINIBAR TV TEL **Directions:** North of Sukhumvit Road, on Soi 5.

$ Rates: 3,300B–4,500B ($132–$180) single; 3,600–5,000B ($144–$200) double; suite from 6,600B ($264). Extra bed 600B ($24). AE, DC, EU, MC, V.

Since the completion of a glass-and-steel tower that seems to lean back against the original hotel, the modern Boulevard appears more elegant than ever. The glamorous Krung Thep Wing adds 137 spacious rooms in contemporary muted tones, featuring full-granite bathrooms and terrific city views. The larger corner deluxe rooms are especially striking, with separate shower stalls, two seating areas, and a desk. The original wing, with mahogany-paneled hallways and attractive balconied rooms, is now sold at the lowest prices and is an even better value. When we stayed there, the links between the original building, with its small pool and restaurant, and the new wing, with its coffee shop and common lobby but separate elevators, remained confusing. Yet, despite the erratic service, when rooms are discounted 40% to 60% in the low season, this is a very good value.

Dining/Entertainment: The Peppermill Restaurant serves an array of international cuisine, including Thai, Japanese, and vegetarian dishes. In addition, there is a 24-hour bar serving snacks.

Services: 24-hour room service, concierge, limousine service, babysitting, laundry, complimentary fruit basket.

Facilities: Swimming pool, health club, business center, beauty salon and barbershop, shopping arcade.

THE SOMERSET, 10 Soi 15, Sukhumvit Rd., Bangkok 10110. Tel. 02/254-8500. Fax 02/254-8534. Telex 72361 SOMRSET TH. 76 rms, 5 suites. A/C MINIBAR TV TEL **Directions:** 1 block north of Sukhumvit Road.

$ **Rates:** 2,900B ($116) single; 3,200B ($128) double; 5,400B ($216) suite. AE, DC, MC, V.

It's surprising to find a Best Western affiliate on a quiet lane off Sukhumvit Road, but don't be misled by any chain stereotypes, for this is a fine little hotel. Lobby and rooms are tastefully done with lots of marble and cool pastels. The 24-hour business center, eager-to-please service, and the small, intimate scale make this a good business traveler's choice in this price range in the Sukhumvit area.

Dining/Entertainment: The Kensington Café is an above-average coffee shop serving a variety of international dishes.

Services: 24-hour room service, concierge, limousine service, babysitting (with notice), laundry service.

Facilities: Swimming pool, health club, business center.

TAI-PAN HOTEL, 25 Sukhumvit Road, Soi 23, Bangkok 10110. Tel. 02/260-9888. Fax 02/259-7908. Telex 20540 TAIPAN TH. 139 rms, 11 suites. A/C MINIBAR TV TEL **Directions:** 1 block north of Sukhumvit Road on Soi 23.

$ **Rates:** 2,900B–3,400B ($116–$136) single; 3,100B–3,600B ($124–$144) double; from 6,000B ($240) suite. Extra bed 600B ($24). AE, DC, MC, V.

Known by shoppers for the excellent luncheon buffet at its coffee shop, Tai-Pan is within walking distance of Rasi Sayam, L'Arcadia, and several other boutiques. Opened in 1991, this modern white tower rises above a quiet soi in a neighborhood that's perfect for shoppers, decorators, and those in the fashion industry. The attentive staff and the bright, carpeted rooms with comfortable seating areas and city views guarantee a pleasant stay. With all the facilities you'd expect from a more expensive hotel, this is a good value.

Dining/Entertainment: Excellent coffee shop with bargain buffet breakfasts and lunches. Great Thai and continental food.

Services: 24-hour room service, limousine service, babysitting, laundry.

Facilities: Small swimming pool, exercise room, business.

MODERATE

MANHATTAN HOTEL, 13 Soi 15, Sukhumvit Rd., Bangkok 10110. Tel. 02/255-0166. Fax 02/255-3481. Telex TH 87272. 200 rms, 3 suites. A/C MINIBAR TV TEL **Directions:** Just north of Sukhumvit Road near Ambassador Hotel.

$ **Rates:** 1,450B ($58) single; 1,700B ($68) double. AE, DC, MC, V.

⑤ We New Yorkers are loath to put you in a hotel of this name, especially one with an inexpensive coffee shop (a favorite with Swedish friends who spent all week here) named the Broadway. But this modern high-rise is surprisingly attractive with rooms that are spacious and quietly tasteful. Plus, it has features you'd pay more for elsewhere—pool, friendly lobby bar, nightclub with live bands, and their own Four Seasons Restaurant! A very good value for this neighborhood—and even busier since its rave review in the *New York Times*!

INEXPENSIVE

CITY LODGE, Soi 9, Sukhumvit Rd., Bangkok 10110. Tel. 02/253-7705. Fax 02/255-4667. 28 rms. A/C MINIBAR TV TEL **Directions:** Corner of Sukhumvit and Soi 9.

$ Rates: 1,140B ($45.60) single or double. MC, V.

Budget watchers will do well by the two small, spiffy City Lodges. Both the newer lodge on Soi 9, and its nearby cousin, the older, 35-room City Lodge on Soi 19 (tel. 02/254-4783; fax 02/255-7340), provide clean, super-compact rooms with simple, modern decor. Each has a pleasant coffee shop (facing the bustle on Sukhumvit Road at Soi 9; serving Italian fare on Soi 19), a small but friendly staff, and privileges at the rooftop swimming pool at the more deluxe Amari Boulevard Hotel on Soi 5. All three belong to the Amari Hotels and Resorts Group. No frills here, but still a lot of comfort for your money.

COMFORT INN, 153/11-14 Soi 11, Sukhumvit Rd., Bangkok 10110. Tel. 02/251-0745. Fax 02/254-3562. Telex 22418 COMFORT TH. 36 rms. A/C MINIBAR TV TEL **Directions:** North of Sukhumvit Road opposite Swiss Park Hotel.

$ Rates: 1,250B ($50) single or double. MC, V.

This small hotel has clean, compact rooms, very simply furnished but with a warm, homey feel. The friendly staff and quiet but convenient location on Soi Chaiyod really make it worth it. A 5% discount is offered for stays of a week or longer; 10% for a month or more.

RUAMCHITT TRAVELODGE, 11/1 Soi 10, Sukhumvit Rd., Bangkok 10110. Tel. 02/251-0284. Fax 02/25-1372 72 rms. A/C TV TEL **Directions:** Near end of Soi 10, South of Sukhumvit Road.

$ Rates (including breakfast): 1,375B ($55) single; 1,500B ($60) double. Extra person 300B ($12). Student and senior citizen discounts available. AE, MC, V.

A scrubbed-clean, matter-of-fact hotel that has large, simply furnished rooms with refrigerators and sparkling new all-tile bathrooms, is a real find in this popular neighborhood. The atmosphere is quiet and friendly, with a lobby coffee shop that seems made for lounging.

BUDGET

HAPPY INN, Soi 4, 20/1 Sukhumvit Rd., Nanatai, Bangkok 10110. Tel. 02/252-6508. Fax 02/255-6794. 10 rms. A/C TV TEL **Directions:** South of Sukhumvit, beyond the Rajah Hotel.

$ Rates (including tax and service): 600B ($24) single/double. No credit cards.

The name seems to match the place, and, although the rooms are plain and simple, the staff was all smiles with a fair command of English. The basics are here—air-conditioning, shower, TV, minifridge, twin beds—but nothing extra, not even an elevator. Still, if everything's full, you'll find it a neighborhood of cheap food stalls.

UNCLE REY'S GUESTHOUSE, 7/10 Soi 4, Sukhumvit Rd., Bangkok 10110. Tel. 02/252-5565. 24 rms. A/C TEL **Directions:** Cul-de-sac off Soi 4, opposite Nana Hotel.

$ Rates (including tax and service): 400B–500B ($16–$20) single/double. No credit cards.

Its convenient and quiet location makes this family-run inn a good value. Decent-sized rooms are simply furnished but include an armoire and small writing desk. Each is quaintly named. Attached bathrooms include a bathtub with Danish shower. The cheaper rooms give you a good workout on the way up the two or three flights of stairs.

AIRPORT AREA

Don Muang International Airport is so far from the center of Bangkok that we recommend staying in the area only if you have connecting flights and want to avoid the time and expense of a taxi to a city hotel.

AMARI AIRPORT HOTEL, 333 Choet Wudhakat Rd., Don Muang, Bangkok 10210. Tel. 02/566-1020. Fax 02/566-1941. Telex TH 87424 AMARIAP 434 rms. A/C MINIBAR TV TEL **Directions:** Across the highway from the international terminal.

$ Rates: 3,900B–5,000B ($156–$200) single; 4,000B–5,400B ($160–$216) suite. Extra person/bed 950B ($34). AE, MC, V.

This is the fanciest, the closest, and, if budget is not a concern, the best, of all choices near the airport. It's connected by a 533-foot overpass to the international terminal, from which you can take a free shuttle to the domestic terminal about half mile away. There is also a free shuttle bus to and from the airport. It's a short walk to the Don Muang railroad station, where many, but not all, trains to and from the north stop en route to and from Bangkok's Hua Lampong station. For those wanting to pop into the city, there's a 60B ($2.40) shuttle bus that runs regularly to Ploenchit Road in the heart of Bangkok's shopping district.

But the Airport Hotel is so comfortable that you may not want to go anywhere. It's got all the facilities you'd expect from a first-class hotel, including a top security Ladies Floor, plus that recurring aeronautical theme, played out in the Cockpit Lounge, Le Bel-Air Grill, Airbridge Café, and Zeppelin Coffee Shop (open 24 hours). Flight arrival and departure information scrolls across monitors in the lobby. Spacious deluxe rooms are decorated in soothing pastel colors and, best yet, the windows are soundproof. Although expensive, this hotel tries to give you your money's worth, especially on the new premium-rate Executive Floor.

Note: Transit passengers waiting for a flight will appreciate the hotel's 3-hour ministay package. For 550B ($22) single or 600B ($24) twin room (inclusive of tax and service charge), guests can use a room, the pool, health club, and other hotel facilities. The offer is strictly limited to a 3-hour period, daily 8am to 6pm.

GOLDEN DRAGON HOTEL, 20/21 Ngarm Wongwan Rd., Bangkok 11000. Tel. 02/589-5141. Fax 02/589-8305. Telex 82133 NGDTEL TH. 120 rms. A/C TV TEL **Directions:** 10km (6 miles) or 15 minutes south of Don Muang International Airport.

$ Rates (including tax and service): 1,150B ($46) single; 1,400B ($56) double. AE, MC, V.

For travelers-in-transit, this is the best, relatively inexpensive alternative to the luxurious but pricey Airport Hotel. Rooms are simple but clean, though the Hardest-Mattress-in-Thailand Award must go to this establishment. There is a pool and basic restaurant and, best of all, only a 15 to 20 minute drive to the airport.

RAILROAD STATION AREA

As with most cities, the area around the train station is not what you would call idyllic. If you're in Bangkok more than one night, take a tuk-tuk or taxi to a recommended hotel in another part of town, or contact the information booth in the terminal (open Monday through Friday from 8:30am to 6pm; to noon all other days and holidays) for advice.

BANGKOK CENTER HOTEL, 328 Rama IV Rd., Bangkok 10500. Tel. 02/238-4848. Fax 02/235-1780. Telex 72067 BACENHO TH. 250 rms. A/C MINIBAR TV TEL **Directions:** 2 blocks east of the Hua Lampong Railroad Station.

$ Rates (including service, plus 7% tax): 1,600B ($64) single; 1,600B–1,800B ($64–$72) double. Extra bed 300B ($12). AE, DC, MC, V.

It's a basic businessperson's hotel—plain, functional, and set back from the busy, clamorous thoroughfare. Rooms are simple, convenient, and comfortable. There's a lunchtime buffet in the scenic rooftop ballroom and a popular Chinese restaurant (open daily 11am to 2pm and 6 to 10pm) downstairs. Night owls can sample the Centre Club Disco or the 24-hour coffee shop.

KRUNG KASEM SRI KRUNG HOTEL, 1860 Krung Kasem Rd., Bangkok 10100. Tel. 02/225-0132. Fax 02/225-4702. 129 rms (all with bath). A/C TV TEL **Directions:** Across the street from Hua Lampong Railroad Station.

$ Rates (including tax and service): 600B ($24) single; 650B ($26) double; 1,075B ($43) triple. No credit cards.

Just across the klong from Hua Lampong station, this is the best nearby budget choice for cross-country train travelers. The quieter, back-facing rooms have small balconies and a city view, air-conditioning, private toilet, and Asian shower, as well as a high standard of cleanliness. Each of its seven floors has a luggage locker, handy for storage during an upcountry expedition. Business travelers and neighborhood vendors like the Valentine Coffee Shop's inexpensive Thai/Chinese fare.

2. DINING

Thai food is among the finest cuisines in Southeast Asia, and some would argue, in the world. Bangkok offers a delightful variety of Thai restaurants, ranging from simple noodle stands to elegant dining rooms offering "palace" cuisine. It's so reasonably priced that in the fanciest Thai restaurant, you'll have a hard time spending more than $30 for two! If you find the task of ordering daunting, see "Food & Drink" in Chapter 1.

The city also offers a spectacular array of fine European, Chinese, and other Asian dining spots, generally more expensive than those catering to locals (up to $130 for two in the top hotels), but still a bargain compared to back home. You'll even find the familiar "fast-food" outlets with familiar prices—McDonald's, Kentucky Fried Chicken, Burger King, Pizza Hut, Dunkin' Donuts—plus inexpensive Thai-style fast-food, on the street or in the shopping malls.

We've organized this section first by neighborhood, then by cuisine, listed alphabetically. Under "Specialty Dining," below, we recommend the few restaurants that offer Thai classical dance performances. Though not the ultimate in Thai cuisine, the dinner cruises on the Chao Phraya River are also a special treat. Reservations, if necessary, are noted throughout the section.

ON THE RIVER

ASIAN CUISINES

HIMALI CHA CHA RESTAURANT, 1229/11 New Rd. Tel. 235-1569.
   Cuisine: INDIAN. **Directions:** On a side street off New Road, corner of Surawong.
$ **Prices:** Appetizers 50B–150B ($2–$6); main courses 50B–200B ($2–$8). MC, V. (300B/$12 minimum for credit cards).
   Open: Lunch daily 11am–3:30pm; dinner daily 6–10:30pm.
Cha Cha, the graying chef and proprietor, was on Lord Mountbatten's staff in India. He then cooked for the diplomatic corps in Laos and after that country's fall, came to Bangkok to open this restaurant in 1980. You'll find him in attendance at the cash register nightly. House specialties include three *darbesh* curry, vegetable *kofta* curry, and *palak paneer*, all extremely flavorful and well prepared. The Indian *thali* plates are our favorites. Two people can taste this sampling of seven dishes with bread and rice for 425B ($17) for the vegetarian thali and 550B ($22) with meat. Vegetarians will enjoy the wide selection of meatless offerings. All who dine here will enjoy the friendly atmosphere.

SALA THIP, in Shangri-La Hotel, 89 Soi Wat Suan Plu. Tel. 236-7777.
   Cuisine: THAI. **Reservations:** Recommended. **Directions:** Overlooking Chao Phraya River, adjacent to Sathorn Bridge.
$ **Prices:** Appetizers 110B–175B ($4.40–$7); main courses 150B–400B ($6–$16). AE, DC, MC, V.
   Open: Dinner Mon–Sat 6–10:30pm; high-season Sun buffet dinner 6–10:30pm.
Located on the river terrace of the Shangri-La Hotel, Sala Thip is arguably Bangkok's most romantic Thai restaurant. Classic music and traditional cuisine are superbly presented under one of two aged, carved-teak pavilions perched over a lotus pond, or at outdoor tables that overlook the Chao Phraya. (For those who crave a less humid environment, we suggest reserving a table in one of the air-conditioned

dining rooms.) Although the food may not inspire aficionados, it is skillfully prepared by one of the few woman chefs in town. We find the airy spring rolls, *kuai tiao phad thai* (broad rice noodles), and roast duck with vegetables achieve divine heights in this wonderful setting.

THANYING, 10 Pramuan Rd. Tel. 236-4361.
> **Cuisine:** THAI. **Reservations:** Recommended. **Directions:** 1½ blocks south of Silom Road behind the Holiday Inn Crowne Plaza.
> **$ Prices:** Appetizers 85B–145B ($3.40–$5.80); main courses 180B–425B ($7.20–$17). AE, MC, V.
> **Open:** Daily 11am–11pm.

Even by our first visit in 1987, the stately Thanying had, for many years, been an old-world restaurant favored by petty royalty and an aging wealthy class. Excellent imperial cuisine from the recipes of King Rama VII's time was artfully presented and slowly savored by the gracious, but fast disappearing, social elite. As Bangkok's market economy took off and created rich young tigers, Thanying fell out of favor. Too fussy. Too old-fashioned. Too slow. Now, those bored with too casual, too new, and too fast restaurants, have become an appreciative clientele. Traditional favorites include red curry with roast duck, fried chicken in pandanus leaves, fresh fish with tamarind and mango sauce, and the fluffy, delicately-spiced catfish salad. A slightly more casual branch at the too new World Trade Center shopping complex on Rajdamri Road has helped revive this classic dining room's popularity with the young.

WESTERN

THE NORMANDIE, in the Oriental Hotel, 48 Oriental Ave. Tel. 236-0400.
> **Cuisine:** FRENCH. **Reservations:** Required. **Directions:** Off New Road, overlooking the river.
> **$ Prices:** Appetizers 375B–1,025B ($15–$41); main courses 575B–1,450B ($23–$58); menu degustation 2,500B ($100). AE, DC, MC, V.
> **Open:** Lunch daily noon–2:30pm; dinner daily 7–10pm.

★ The Normandie represents the apex of formal dining in Thailand, both in price and quality. Set atop the renowned Oriental, with commanding panoramic views of Thonburi and the Chao Phraya River, this ultraelegant hotel dining room has recently emerged from a 25,000,000 baht renovation decked out in stunning champagne-colored silk and gold brocade. In keeping with our more modest times, two excellent-value fixed-price lunches (500B/$20 and 575B/$23) have been added to a new menu with lower prices overall. At our visit, the superb menu degustation began with prawns served on a bed of watercress, and included a risotto with red snapper and clams, a melt-in-your-mouth lamb with mushrooms and basil, assorted imported cheeses, a chocolate mousse, and a refreshing chilled fruit soup with ice cream. The chef's so-called menu découvert (30B/$152) also features a variety of wines by the glass, selected to enhance the fine seasonal cuisine.

We found the service a bit on the formal side, but this is only a minor quibble in what is obviously a superior culinary event. Reservations are a must, as the dining room is relatively small.

HISTORIC BANGKOK—
NEAR THE GRAND PALACE

THAI

KALOANG HOME KITCHEN, 2 Sri Ayutthaya Rd. Tel. 281-9228.
> **Cuisine:** THAI. **Reservations:** Required for boat tables only. **Directions:** North of National Library, overlooking the Chao Phraya River.
> **$ Prices:** Main courses 60B–300B ($2.40–$12). AE, MC, V.
> **Open:** Daily 11am–11pm.

For ambience alone, the Kaloang Home Kitchen has become John's favorite Thai restaurant in Bangkok. Some might find the atmosphere funky (strange for a place that sometimes requires men to wear a sport coat!), but we think that this riverside café, overlooking the Royal Yacht Pier and adjoining a lovely residential neighborhood, is about as sublimely Thai as can be found in the capital.

We supped on *yam paduk fu*, a salad of roasted catfish whipped into a foam and crisply (and deliciously) fried, horseshoe crab curry with pineapple and coconut, sam lee fish with mango, and chicken marinated in an unknown (to us) Thai liquor. In fact, some of the best food we sampled didn't appear on the menu, so inquire about daily specials.

You'll get a taste of the ambience when you approach the pier on which Kaloang Home Kitchen resides—street vendors selling quick-fried banana and grilled squid line the narrow entrance to the restaurant. When you arrive, you'll face two separate dining areas. The first is a covered wooden pier set with simple outdoor furniture, while adjacent is a retired wooden boat that hosts about 10 small tables. We just loved sitting at the head of the boat, commanding a vista of the quiet river and taking in a cool breeze. Nearby, kids play in the water, swimming next to the royal family's private boats, while across the way are several lovely colonial-style villas. If you have the patience to hunt this one down, don't miss this off-the-beaten-tourist-track experience.

TAKIANG, 62 Charkphatdiphong Rd. Tel. 281-2837.
   Cuisine: THAI. **Reservations:** Recommended for large groups. **Directions:** Near TAT office and Ratchadamnoen Road.
$ Prices: 50B–110B ($2–$4.40). No credit cards.
   Open: Lunch daily 11am–2pm; dinner daily 4–11pm.

The atmosphere at Takiang (the Lamps) is almost better than the excellent Thai fare. Behind a nondescript facade with only a Thai name on the sign beneath the canopy, you'll find a cozy teak-trimmed series of rooms lit by the warm glow of dozens of table lamps, chandeliers, wall sconces, and overhead fixtures. Amid the gentle Thai tunes of the resident pianist, specials like steamed seafood in coconut curry, fish or shrimp *tom yam* soups, ground beef- and tomato-filled omelets, and light, crispy, stuffed chicken wings, will send you happily to the nearby (10-minute cab ride) palace area. The place is a little hard to find, so ask for help at the Thai Airways office around the corner at 6 Larn Luang Rd.

CHINESE

THE EMPRESS, Royal Princess Hotel, 269 Larn Luang Rd. Tel. 281-3088.
   Cuisine: CHINESE. **Reservations:** Recommended. **Directions:** West of Krung Kasem Road.
$ Prices: Appetizers 115B–215B ($4.60–$8.60); main courses 115B–1,000B ($4.60–$40). AE, DC, MC, V.
   Open: Lunch daily 11:30am–2:30pm; dinner daily 6–10:30pm.

This hotel eatery augments the Bangkok Chinese cuisine scene with two strengths—dim sum and gourmet Cantonese. The high-style mint-and-jade padded banquettes are jammed at lunch with government officials, upscale tourists, and local businesspeople, all savoring a selection from the 20 or so dim sum choices. The fresh steamed, fried, and boiled morsels (mostly seafood) provide an inexpensive midday break. Former prime minister Chatichai Choonhaven prefers a Cantonese banquet menu at lunch, including the tart abalone salad; bird's-nest, chicken, and black mushroom soup; and the whole steamed fish of the day. Even the lesser-priced fare is delicious and artfully presented. We liked the tender, moist, tea-leaf smoked duck, steamed bean curd stuffed with minced prawns, and sautéed seasonal vegetables with crabmeat sauce. This is one restaurant where you can't go wrong.

MARIA RESTAURANT, 50-52 Building 4, Ratchadamnoen Rd. Tel. 221-5211.
   Cuisine: CHINESE/JAPANESE. **Directions:** Near Wat Saket in the Chalerm Thai Theater Building.

THAILAND

★ Bangkok

 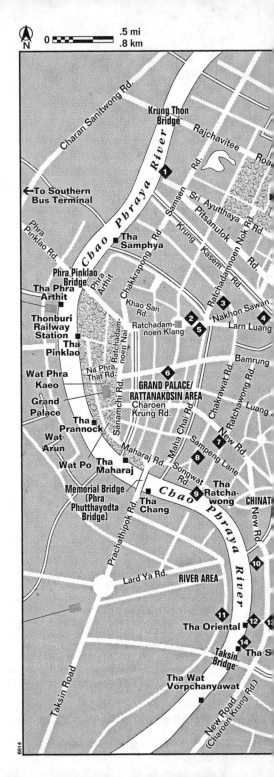

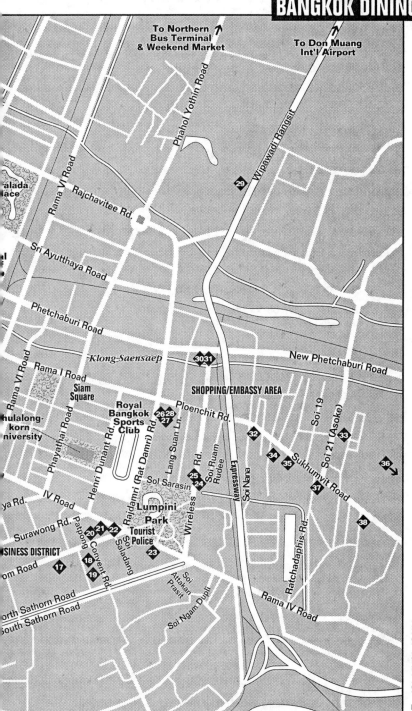

BANGKOK DINING

To Northern ↗
Bus Terminal
& Weekend Market

To Don Muang ↗
Int'l Airport

Rama VI Road

Rajchavitee Rd.

Phahol Yothin Road

Wipawadi Rangsit

alada
ace

Sri Ayutthaya Road

Phetchaburi Road

Klong-Saensaep

New Phetchaburi Road

Rama VI Road

Rama I Road

Siam
Square

Royal
Bangkok
Sports
Club

Ploenchit Rd.

SHOPPING/EMBASSY AREA

Soi 19

Chulalong-
korn
University

Phayathai Road

Henri Dunant Rd.

Lang Suan Ln.

Rajdamri (Rat Damri) Rd.

Soi 21 (Asoke)

Sukhumvit Road

Soi Ruam Rudee

Rd.

Soi Sarasin

Lumpini
Park

Tourist
Police

Wireless

Expressway

Soi Nana

IV Road

ya Rd.

Surawong Rd.

Patpong

Convent Rd.

Soi
Saladang

Ratchadaphis Rd.

BUSINESS DISTRICT

om Road

om Road

orth Sathorn Road

South Sathorn Road

Soi
Attakan
Prasit

Soi Ngam Duplì

Rama IV Road

River Taxi Pier ■

$ Prices: Appetizers 40B–75B ($1.60–$3). No credit cards.
Open: Lunch daily 11am–2pm.

For a super lunchtime bargain, we suggest a stop at the Maria Restaurant, a local favorite where tasty dim sum appetizers are brought to your table on a rolling cart and served in bamboo steamers. The single dining room is cavernous and clean, though a tad on the dark and dingy side. You'll likely be the only tourists in a sea of government workers, but if large and noisy isn't too jolting, the Maria will certainly deliver on authentic Chinese fare.

MAJESTIC HOUSE, in the Hotel Majestic Palace, 97 Ratchadamnoen Rd. Tel. 280-5610.
   Cuisine: INTERNATIONAL. **Directions:** Near the Democracy Monument.
$ Prices: Appetizers 75B–145B ($3–$5.50); main courses 75B–300B ($3–$12). MC, V.
   Open: Daily 7am–2am.

Here is one restaurant that is bound to accommodate nearly anyone's tastes. Imagine a single dining room that offers hamburgers, *tom yum kung*, chicken with cashews, and spaghetti bolognese all in a spacious, air-conditioned haven overlooking one of Bangkok's busiest thoroughfares. Speaking of thorough fare, we were not only impressed with the breadth of the menu but were equally delighted to find good quality cuisine. The Chinese dishes were by far the most impressive and are well recommended. We wouldn't go out of our way to eat here, but if you have a hungry crew with diverse tastes, you'll have a hard time finding a better dining alternative.

WESTERN CUISINE

KANIT RESTAURANT, 68 Ti Thong Rd. Tel. 222-1020.
   Cuisine: CONTINENTAL. **Reservations:** Recommended dinner. **Directions:** West of Wat Suthat.
$ Prices: Appetizers 105B–300B ($4.20–$12); main courses 200B–575B ($8–$23). AE, DC, V.
   Open: Mon–Sat 11am–11pm.

We discovered this refined and relaxed eatery on a hot afternoon while mapping out our Bangkok's Wat Walking Tour. The shaded facade and cold drinks list beckoned us, and inside we found an ambitious menu that includes French and Italian specialties, a fine wine list with lots of California varietals, a wide sampling of snacks, teas, and coffee, and a moody, dark wood interior.

Among the better dishes that we tried are Pizza Gulf of Siam with shrimp, mussels, and clams; rib-eye steak with coriander seeds and fresh Brazilian red pepper sauce; and spaghetti with prawns and herb butter. Desserts are French inspired; there is a long list of coffees and teas; and service is efficient and friendly.

THE BUSINESS DISTRICT

THAI

BANANA LEAF, Basement Level, Silom Complex, Silom Rd. Tel. 231-3124.
   Cuisine: THAI. **Reservations:** Not required. **Directions:** Basement level of shopping mall.
$ Prices: Appetizers 55B–75B ($2.20–$3); main courses 60B–180B ($2.40–$7.20). No credit cards.
   Open: Daily 11:30am–9:30pm.

If you're ready to drop from shopping around Silom Road, you can't beat this clean, brightly lit place for fast, good, and inexpensive Thai food. Decor is not its strong suit, but authentically spiced delicacies like baked crab with glass noodles and spicy beef salad more than compensate for the ambience. In the evenings, Banana Leaf is packed with locals who stop for a quick bite on their way to the mall or the movie theaters.

BENJARONG, Dusit Thani Hotel, Rama IV Rd. Tel. 236-0450.
   Cuisine: THAI. **Reservations:** Recommended. **Directions:** Corner of Silom Road.

$ **Prices:** Appetizers 100B–265B ($4–$10.60); main courses 120B–550B ($4.80–$22). AE, MC, V.
Open: Dinner daily 6–10:30pm.

This classy dining room, names for the exquisite five-color pottery once reserved exclusively for the use of royalty, is one of the few places where you'll want to dress up. Benjarong prides itself on offering the five basic flavors of Thai cuisine (salty, bitter, hot, sweet, and sour) in traditional "royal" dishes. The illustrated menu encouraged us to start with the unusual *kratai chom suan*, delicate cakes of jellied pork; followed by *gung pao nam pla wan*, grilled lobster with tamarind sauce; *pro ram long song*, an unusual beef tenderloin, baked and served with morning-glory greens (one of Kyle's favorites) and a peanut/coconut/curry paste; and *mee krob chao wang*, crisp-fried vermicelli with bean curd, decorated with a papaya bean sprout "daisy" that was the most artistically presented dish of all. The *kong wan* is an ornate selection of typical Thai desserts, light but odd, sweet, and very satisfying.

BUSSARACUM, 35 Soi Pipat 2, off Convent Rd. Tel. 235-8915.
   Cuisine: THAI. **Reservations:** Recommended. **Directions:** Between Silom and Sathorn roads.
$ **Prices:** Appetizers 50B–200B ($2–$8); main courses 95B–240B ($3.80–$9.60). AE, DC, MC, V.
   Open: Lunch daily 11:30am–2pm; dinner daily 5:30–10:30pm.

This is a traditional favorite for Thais hosting foreigners because of the fine food and the classical royal decor.

At this tranquil, teak-paneled sanctuary with linen tablecloths the Thai menu changes monthly. Their *rhoom* (minced pork and shrimp in egg-net wrapping) was the favorite appetizer of King Rama II. The *saengwa* (cold shrimp salad served in a squash gourd) is an unusual dish that complements their noteworthy *tom yam soup* and *gaeng kari gai hang* (special chicken curry). Allow the helpful staff to make suggestions, and finish the meal with *bauloy sarm see*, a dessert of taro and pumpkin in coconut milk.

SHANGARILA, 154/4-5 Silom Rd. Tel. 234-9147.
   Cuisine: CHINESE. **Reservations:** Recommended for large parties. **Directions:** South of Rama IV Road.
$ **Prices:** Appetizers 25B–220B ($1–$8.80); main courses 60B–700B ($2.40–$28). AE, DC, MC, V.

Shangarila is a glitzy, crowded, Shanghai-style restaurant. The decor is bright and splashy, with a carp pond taking up part of the downstairs room. The fine food is inexpensive, well prepared, and more interesting than at many casual Chinese eateries.

The traditional beggar's chicken is stuffed with mushrooms and baked in a thick clay coating. Peking duck, peppery Shanghai dumpling soup, and the fresh seafood dishes (especially crab) are among our favorites. The crisp mille-feuille-style Shanghai spring rolls are light as air.

The Grand Shangarila, with its 15 chandeliers on the ground floor, is a larger version of the original, with the same menu, at 58/4-9 Thaniya Rd., in Thaniya Plaza, off Silom Road (tel. 234-0861).

SILVER PALACE, 5 Soi Pipat, Silom Rd. Tel. 235-5118.
   Cuisine: CHINESE. **Reservations:** Recommended. **Directions:** Just east of Silom Road on Soi Pipat.

READERS RECOMMEND

Green Mango, Surawong Road, Bangkok. *"We found a wonderful restaurant right across from the Tawana Ramada called the Green Mango. It is in a house with a garden and bills itself as featuring classical Thai cuisine. We had dinner there a couple of nights, spending about $24 for two including tips, drinks, more food than we could eat, and dessert. It is a peaceful oasis in the middle of a noisy part of town, and the food is inspired and service excellent. Also, they have their own herb garden which they were delighted to show us"*—John D. Connelly, Chicago, Ill.

$ Prices: Appetizers 150B–300B ($6–$12); main courses 150B–600B ($6–$24). AE, DC, MC, V.

Open: Dim sum lunch daily 11am–2pm; dinner daily 6–10pm.

Edith Tai's Silver Palace is one of Bangkok's slickest Hong Kong–style restaurants. It's warm, elegant dining room is furnished with lovely Chinese bentwood chairs. The basic menu is diverse and imaginative, with exotic seasonal specials changing often. The duck, seafood, and shark's-fin choices are extensive and delicious. Favorites include braised duck with *eight-jewel* (vegetables and condiments) rice, a large and truly succulent whole roast pig (sometimes devoured by as few as three diners), subtly flavored prawns, asparagus with crabmeat in a light sauce, and tender fried duck in steamed ginger. Some complex dishes, such as the excellent Peking duck, *phu thew chang*, and other shark's-fin specialties, require advance notice. Mrs. Tai personally lends a gracious touch to the service.

OTHER ASIAN CUISINES

KIKUSUI, 133 Pan Rd., Silom. Tel. 234-6687.

Cuisine: JAPANESE. **Directions:** East of Silom Road.

$ Prices: Appetizers 145B–280B ($5.80–$11.20); main courses 95B–700B ($3.80–$28). AE, MC, V.

This small Japanese country inn off busy Silom Road is very simple, with the focus solely on the food. The expert sushi chefs work only with the freshest fish: fish roe and yellowtail tuna imported from Japan, as well as Thai abalone, snapper, and tuna. Sushi platters of 10 artfully arranged pieces cost from 275B to 600B ($11 to $24), depending on the selected fish. Kikisui also specializes in grilled fish (we especially like the eel) and in beef shabu-shabu (traditional stew).

LE CAM-LY, 2nd Floor, no. 1 Patpong Building, Soi Patpong 1-2, Surawong Rd. Tel. 234-0290.

Cuisine: VIETNAMESE. **Reservations:** Recommended at dinner. **Directions:** Corner of Surawong Road and Patpong 1 Road, south of Rama IV Road.

$ Prices: Appetizers 80B–125B ($3.20–$5). AE, DC, MC, V.

Open: Lunch daily 11:30am–2pm; dinner daily 6–10pm.

This is a sister restaurant of the popular Le Dalat (see "Shopping/Embassy Area," below), serving similarly excellent food, concentrating on small dishes, though lacking the lovely garden setting. The restaurant is slightly more businesslike, as befits its neighborhood. We love the *bi guon* (spring rolls with herbs and pork), as well as the *sala* pork ribs and noodles.

WESTERN

BOBBY'S ARMS PUB & RESTAURANT, 114/1-2 Silom Rd. Tel. 233-6828.

Cuisine: BRITISH. **Directions:** Patpong 2 car park, between Silom and Surawong roads.

$ Prices: Appetizers 60B–180B ($2.40–$7.20); main courses 120B–350B ($4.80–$14). AE, DC, MC, V.

Open: Daily 11am–1am; Sun Dixieland music 8–11pm.

Anglo-food-philes will enjoy this boisterous British pub with its lunch special, draft beer, and typical pub offerings of fish-and-chips, shepherd's pie, roast beef with Yorkshire pudding, and steak-and-kidney pie. Other less pubish offerings will also satisfy the carnivores among us. Sunday evenings are popular for the Dixieland band, while quieter singers and musicians entertain the largely expat crowd on other nights.

SHOPPING/EMBASSY AREA

THAI

CABBAGES & CONDOMS, 10 Soi 12, Sukhumvit Rd. Tel. 251-5552.

Cuisine: THAI. **Reservations:** Recommended for dinner. **Directions:** ½km (³⁄₁₀ mile) south of Sukhumvit Road.

$ **Prices:** Appetizers 55B–80B ($2.20–$3.20); main courses 95B–210B ($3.80–$8.40). AE, MC, V.
Open: Daily 11am–10pm.

This may be the only restaurant in the world where population control is the theme, but that's only natural, since it's affiliated with the Population Development Association (PDA) in Thailand. Have a drink in the Vasectomy Bar, then take a seat in the Condom Room. Don't be misled by the whimsical theme elements—this is a very popular eatery serving excellent food. Try the *yam tung yang*, a/k/a condom salad (prawns and chicken on Shanghai noodles), or the *chaw muang* (chicken and onions steamed in dough), or perhaps the *sam lee dad deao* (deep-fried cotton fish in a spicy sauce). Don't leave without information about the work of the PDA, and make a donation if you like their approach.

LEMONGRASS RESTAURANT, 5/1 Sukhumvit, Soi 24. Tel. 258-8637.

Cuisine: THAI. **Reservations:** Required for dinner. **Directions:** Off Sukhumvit Road.
$ **Prices:** Appetizers 30B–100B ($1.20–$4); main courses 100B–450B ($4–$18); set menus 450B–1,200B ($18–$48). AE, DC, MC, V.
Open: Lunch daily 11am–2pm; dinner daily 6–11pm.

The Lemongrass, located in a converted Thai house decorated in a homey pastiche of Asian styles, runs a kitchen that turns out consistently delicious food, although to our tastes, in recent years, the food has been overly tailored to an enthusiastic foreign clientele. Offsetting this, we found the staff helpful and knowledgeable, and most waiters speak enough English to guide you through the menu of Thai classics.

Among our favorite dishes are *gai yang pak panang* (a richly sauced, grilled chicken on coconut sticks), chili-stuffed pork, a sumptuous lemongrass chicken, Burmese-style pork curry, and *tom yang kung* (a spicy, sweet-and-sour broth flavored with large fresh shrimp and ginger shoots). Many of the dishes we sampled were tasty, but the spices and ingredients were a bit bland.

SPICE MARKET, The Regent, Bangkok, 155 Rajdamri Rd. Tel. 251-6127.

Cuisine: THAI. **Reservations:** Recommended. **Directions:** South of Rama I Road.
$ **Prices:** Appetizers 85B–250B ($3.40–$10); main courses 125B–500B ($5–$20). AE, CB, DC, EU, MC, V.
Open: Lunch daily 11;30am–2:30pm; dinner daily 6:30–11pm.

⭐ Many contend that the Spice Market is the city's finest pure Thai restaurant. The theatrical decor reflects the name: burlap spice sacks, ceramic pots, and glass jars set in dark-wood cabinets around the dining area playfully re-create the mercantile feel of a traditional Thai shop house. The food is artfully presented, authentically spiced, and supremely delicious. The menu's "chilli rating" guarantees that spices are tempered to your palate. Among the better dishes are *khao tang na tung* (deep-fried crispy rice with minced-pork dip), *kaeng phed-ped* (duck curry with fried swordfish), *kai hor bai-toey* (deep-fried chicken), *pla dook thord foo* (deep-fried catfish), and *pla jaramet sarm rod* (a whole pomfret in a spicy sweet-and-sour sauce). The adventurous might want to try the traditional Thai herbal potions, available here (as in local herb shops) for those seeking qualities like long life and potent sexuality. It's a special place to entertain, though slightly pricey by local standards.

SUDA RESTAURANT, 6-6/1 Soi 4, Sukhumvit Rd. Tel. 252-2597.

Cuisine: THAI. **Directions:** 1 block south of Sukhumvit Road.
$ **Prices:** Main courses 35B–150B ($1.40–$6). No credit cards.
Open: Daily 11am–midnight.

$ This is one of those basic restaurants where the food is all that matters. With out style, the place has its own charm—it's an open-air, high-ceilinged room with overhead fans cooling the local crowd (mostly Thais and expats) that spills out onto the sidewalk. The food is good, solid, well-prepared Thai cuisine with Chinese overtones. We started with a big bowl of tom yam kai (coconut-milk soup with chicken), then moved on to the grilled yellowfin tuna with cashew nuts and roasted curry paste and fried squid with vegetables over rice. You could also dive into the fried fish with three-flavor sauce. In the bang-for-the-baht sweepstakes, Suda could just be the winner.

OTHER ASIAN CUISINES

THE CHINESE RESTAURANT, Grand Hyatt Erawan, 494 Rajdamri Rd. Tel. 254-1234.

Cuisine: CHINESE. **Reservations:** Recommended. **Directions:** Corner of Ploenchit Road.

$ **Prices:** Appetizers 50B–100B ($2–$4); main courses 145B–1,800B ($4.80–$72). AE, DC, MC, V.

Open: Lunch daily 11:30am–2:30pm; dinner daily 6–10:30pm.

Style and substance are harmoniously wed in this ultraelegant, ultragourmet Cantonese restaurant. Three of Hong Kong's best known chefs were lured to the Erawan and given free reign to delight customers with the likes of exotic shark's-fin dumpling soup (delicate shreds of shark's fin in a rich broth), delicious pigeon and ham steamed in lotus leaves (moist and a bit salty), scallop and bean curd soufflé (delightfully light and subtle), and crispy chicken and shrimp dipped in tangy lemon sauce. Of course, we also sampled many of their lighter-than-air dim sum, including some imaginative vegetable-and-seafood combinations wrapped in seaweed, instead of the typical rice flour pastry. A delightful gastronomic experience in a high-style Shanghai deco-inspired dining room. A real treat!

GENJI RESTAURANT, in the Hilton International, 2 Wireless Rd. Tel. 253-0123.

Cuisine: JAPANESE. **Reservations:** Recommended; required for a tatami room. **Directions:** A short walk north of Ploenchit Road.

$ **Prices:** Appetizers 60B–300B ($2.40–$12); main courses 85B–1,000B ($3.40–$40); set dinners 700B–2,000B ($28–$80). AE, DC, MC, V.

Open: Lunch daily noon–2:30pm; dinner 6:30–10:30pm.

To our tastes, one of the best Japanese restaurants in Bangkok is located in a great hotel that caters to a large Japanese clientele. If you go to Genji for lunch you'll likely discover a room full of Japanese businesspeople, a good sign for sushi eaters. Lunch served from the set menu is not only delicious but also a great value. For as little as 180B ($7.20) you can have a complete meal. The Executive Special Lunch, more than thrice the price, is also an excellent value for an extremely well-prepared and -presented five-course meal. The sushi, something that we always question in warm-water locations, is either imported from Japan or utterly fresh from the morning market.

At dinner there are both set menus as well as an enormous selection of à la carte dishes. Aside from the excellent sushi, sashimi, and *makizushi*, we sampled several robust hot-pot concoctions with a rich broth, fresh vegetables, and a variety of fish and seafood (you can also find a Kobe beef shabu-shabu at the high end of the price range). A lengthy list of grilled meat and fish as well as a multitude of noodle dishes round out the menu. We would be remiss if we didn't mention the highly imaginative Japanese drink menu with 12 separate cocktails made with sake. What can you say about a samurai rock?

LE DALAT, 47/1 Soi 23, Sukhumvit Rd. Tel. 258-4192.

Cuisine: VIETNAMESE/FRENCH. **Reservations:** Recommended at dinner. **Directions:** About half mile north of Sukhumvit Road.

$ **Prices:** Main courses 100B–135B ($4–$5.40). AE, DC, MC, V.

Open: Lunch daily 11am–2:30pm; dinner daily 6–10pm.

We appreciate Le Dalat both for the fine food and for the lovely garden setting. The restaurant is casual, understated, and quietly elegant, with excellent food prepared by Vietnamese-trained Thai chefs. We enjoyed the *bi guon* (spring rolls with herbs and pork), followed by *chao tom* (pounded shrimp laced on ground sugarcane in a basket of fresh noodles), and *cha ra* (fresh filet of grilled fish). In nice weather, you'll enjoy dining in the gracefully landscaped outdoor garden.

MA MAISON, in Hilton International, 2 Wireless Rd. Tel. 253-0123.

Cuisine: CONTINENTAL. **Reservations:** Recommended at lunch; required at dinner.

Directions: In Nai Lert Park.

$ **Prices:** Appetizers 125B–350B ($5–$14); main courses 450B–1,050B ($18–$42); menu degustation 1,600B ($64); set menu 1,200B ($48). AE, DC, MC, V.

Open: Lunch daily noon–2:30pm; dinner daily 6:30–10:30pm.

⭐ If the *Bangkok Post* had polled us, we would have voted Ma Maison Bangkok's best continental restaurant. They didn't ask us, but other readers have come to the same conclusion. The food is superb, the service attentive but unpretentious, and the pastel-and-bleached-wood decor soothing and gracious. If you're on a budget and want to try Ma Maison, go for the fixed-price lunch for a very reasonable 650B ($26).

Although the menu has changed several times since we first visited it still retains its French orientation. One can enjoy a classic succulent sliced breast of duck with panfried reinette apples or oven-baked rack of lamb with rosemary sauce, among other highly imaginative dishes. For dessert we sampled several excellent fruit pastries, foregoing the tantalizingly creamy sweets. A fine wine list rounds out the menu, but be careful: the French varieties, in particular, are wildly expensive.

Apparently the king and queen, who rarely dine in public outside of state ceremonies, have graced the restaurant with their royal presence, as have many dignitaries. If it's good enough for them . . .

WESTERN

LE BANYAN, 59 Soi 8, Sukhumvit Rd. Tel. 252-5556. Fax 253-4560.

Cuisine: FRENCH. **Reservations:** Recommended. **Directions:** 1 block south of Sukhumvit Road.

$ **Prices:** Appetizers 200B–650B ($8–$26); main courses 300B–1,100B ($12–$44). AE, MC, V.

Open: Lunch Mon–Fri noon–2pm; dinner Mon–Sat 7–10pm.

⭐ In the same league as the top hotel French restaurants, this local favorite serves fine classic French fare on a quiet Sukhumvit soi. A spreading banyan tree on the edge of the gardenlike ground inspires the name. Dining rooms are warmly furnished, with sisal matting and white clapboard walls adorned with stunning Thai carvings, old photos, and prints of early Bangkok.

The cuisine is classically French, with Thai touches. The most popular house special is pressed duck for two: Baked duck is carved and pressed to yield juices that are combined with goose liver, shallots, wine, and Armagnac or calvados to make the sauce. The sliced meat is lightly sautéed, and when bathed in the sauce, creates a sensational dish. Other fine choices include a rack of lamb à la Provençale and salmon with lemongrass. All are served with seasonal vegetables and can be enjoyed with one of their reasonably priced wines. A friendly and capable staff help make this a memorable culinary evening.

L'OPERA, 53 Soi 39, Sukhumvit Rd. Tel. 258-5606.

Cuisine: ITALIAN. **Reservations:** Recommended at dinner. **Directions:** About half mile north of Sukhumvit Road.

$ **Prices:** Appetizers 120B–260B ($4.80–$10.40); main courses 120B–390B ($4.80–$15.60). AE, DC, MC, V.

⭐ The decor is so familiar—exposed brick walls, Chianti bottles covered with candle wax, checkered tablecloths, framed Italian photographs—you'll forget you're in Thailand. L'Opera serves wonderful pasta, veal, grilled meats, pizza, and local seafood prepared Italian style. The homemade gelatin and the Italian crooners' Muzak will only enhance that feeling that you're back home in your local Italian joint.

NEIL'S TAVERN, 58/4 Soi Ruam Rudee. Tel. 256-6874.

Cuisine: STEAK/SEAFOOD. **Reservations:** Required on weekends. **Directions:** Behind U.S. Embassy, off Ploenchit Road.

$ **Prices:** Appetizers 125B–300B ($5–$12); main courses 350B–1,000B ($14–$40). AE, DC, MC, V.

Open: Lunch Mon–Sat 11:30am–2pm; dinner daily 5:30–10:30pm.

For over two decades the expatriate community has relied on smartly decorated Neil's Tavern, behind the embassies on Wireless Road, for steak and seafood American style. Though the dress is casual, you'll find the place full of diplomats and businesspeople in jacket and tie. Nearly everything about Neil's will make an American in Bangkok feel at home. Surf-and-turf, charcoal-broiled filet (with burgundy sauce), and cobalt-blue Phuket lobster (the closest thing this side of Tonga to a Maine snapper, at about $32) are prepared in a style that's reminiscent of a similar establishment we visited in suburban Omaha—they've even gone so far as to import beef from the United States! Dinner includes salad, baked potato, garlic bread, and vegetable. For dessert try the chocolate cake.

THE REGENT GRILL, in the Regent, Bangkok, 155 Rajdamri Rd. Tel. 251-6127.

Cuisine: CONTINENTAL. **Reservations:** Recommended. **Directions:** South of Rama I Road.

$ **Prices:** Appetizers 150B–400B ($6–$16); main courses 300B–850B ($12–$34). AE, DC, MC, V.

Open: Lunch Mon–Fri noon–2:30pm; dinner 6:30–11pm.

The Regent Grill is a delightfully bright, cheerful space, with an equally sunny menu. Daily specials often combine Thai ingredients with those from Mexico or Italy. This cross-cultural dining experience originated at the Regent Beverly Wilshire in Los Angeles, a pedigree lends a certain "Californian cuisine" credibility to the Grill's inventive menu. At a recent lunch we had vegetable salad with a tart coriander dressing, creamy corn bisque with rock lobster, and grilled *plakapong* with caper mayonnaise. Dinner delights include lobster cream soup with lemongrass, angel hair pasta with Thai basil and tomato, and surf-and-turf (U.S. prime rib with a tiger prawn).

The dining room is best described as well landscaped—another Thai/California touch—and is a treat at lunch when the light pours in, bathing the slick decor in warm tones. The two-course set lunch is a very reasonable 450B ($22). At dinner, the mood is more serene, though no less attractive. As with almost all first-class Bangkok restaurants, watch out for surprisingly high wine prices; a bottle of average quality runs about 850B ($34).

SPASSO, Grand Hyatt Erawan, 494 Rajdamri Rd. Tel. 254-1234.

Cuisine: ITALIAN. **Reservations:** Recommended dinner. **Directions:** Corner of Ploenchit Road.

$ **Prices:** Appetizers 120B–265B ($4.80–$10.60); main courses 195B–525B ($7.80–$21). AE, DC, MC, V.

Open: Lunch daily 11:30am–2:30pm; dinner daily 6–10:30pm.

Since great word of mouth first drew us to this classy trattoria in the Erawan's arcade, we didn't mind finding a mobbed bar and jovial crowd waiting outside. That's because the popular, hip, young Spasso really pays off with surprisingly good food and even better company. After an authentic caponata (eggplant salad, here served with goat cheese) and minestrone, Ron tried the gnocchi with pesto sauce and John had the Thai-style fusili with chilies and shrimp. Thin-crust pizza fans will find a dozen combos, all made with fresh ingredients and baked in a brick oven. Ciao down before the local bands start at 9pm, when the dancing bodies make it hard to think about food.

VITO'S RISTORANTE, 20/2-3 Ruam Rudee Village. Tel. 251-9455.

Cuisine: ITALIAN. **Reservations:** Recommended. **Directions:** Behind the U.S. Embassy, off Ploenchit Road.

$ **Prices:** Appetizers 145B–435B ($5.80–$17.40); main courses 145B–500B ($5.80–$20). AE, MC, V.

Open: Lunch daily 11:30am–2:30pm; dinner daily 6–11pm.

Ebullient chef Gianni Favro greets newcomers to Vito's with genuine enthusiasm. He's justly proud of the trattoria-style display of delicious antipasti: mushrooms, baked eggplant, peppers, salads, olives, and other assorted appetizers. Although there are many fresh pastas, Gianni recommends his northern Italian specials such as scalloppine of veal, grilled meats or fish, and the particularly tasty frutta di mare made with excellent locally caught shrimp and lobster.

SEAFOOD

THE SEAFOOD MARKET & RESTAURANT, 388 Sukhumvit Rd. Tel. 258-0218.
   Cuisine: SEAFOOD. **Reservations:** Recommended for large parties. **Directions:** Corner of Soi Asoke (Soi 21).
$ **Prices:** Main courses approximately 225B–575B ($9–$23). AE, DC, MC, V.
   Open: Daily 11am–midnight.
The Seafood Restaurant is a cross between the consummate tourist restaurant and an American-style supermarket: low ceilings, long, cool fluorescent lighting, shopping carts, and checkout lines. Their three-story neon marquee proudly boasts "If it swims, we have it!" Below it, the open-air kitchen appears reckless and wild, outdoing even Benihana. Inside, you walk to the rear to choose your fish, fresh vegetables, or bounteous fruits (all sold by the pound), and select from the imported wine and liquor choices. Food consultants (not waiters) will tell you how your fish selection is best cooked (either grilled, steamed, or fried, with or without Thai seasoning). Though its spices are distinctly Thai, the Seafood Restaurant will please those who seek out the freshest foods and don't mind paying a premium for them.

CHINATOWN

There are few if any large Chinese restaurants in the Chinatown area other than in the hotels. Locals eat at small food stalls or tiny hole-in-the-wall places. We've listed a few restaurants which are part of our Chinatown walking tour, all on the fringes of the area.

ROYAL INDIAN RESTAURANT, 392/1 Chakraphet Rd. Tel. 221-6565.
   Cuisine: INDIAN. **Directions:** On small soi off Chakraphet Road, south of Sampeng Lane, on western edge of Chinatown.
$ **Prices:** Appetizers 6B–25B (25¢–$1); main courses 25B–60B ($1–$2.40). No credit cards.
   Open: Daily 9am–10pm.
You'll have to work at finding it, but it's worth the journey to this tiny, charming Indian restaurant. The northern Indian cuisine is well prepared and dirt cheap. Vegetarians will find solace in the few dozen dishes prepared just for them.

RA-BIENG RATCHAWONG, 292-8 Ratchawong Pier, Chinatown. Tel. 222-8679.
   Cuisine: THAI. **Directions:** By boat. Take the Chao Phraya Express boats to Ratchawong (also spelled Rajawongse) Pier, get off and walk to the left (north) end of the pier. On foot: Walk to the end of Ratchawong Road and enter restaurant on the right side of pier.
$ **Prices:** Appetizers 60B–180B ($2.40–$7.20); main courses 60B–215B ($2.40–$8.60). No credit cards.
   Open: Dinner daily 5pm–2am.
This is a simple Thai restaurant with a world-class view of the river. The decor is nothing fancy but the food is good and inexpensive. The English language is not normally part of the service (even with new management), so point, pray, and you'll be fine. We loved the steamed whole *garoupa* with chili sauce, but those with more sensitive palates should stick with milder dishes like mixed vegetables.

SIANG PING LOH, Grand China Princess Hotel, 8th Floor, 215 Yaowaraj Rd. Tel 224-9977.
   Cuisine: CHINESE. **Reservations:** Recommended. **Directions:** Corner of Rajawongse Road.
$ **Prices:** Appetizers 90B–200B ($3.60–$8); main courses 110B–1,600B ($4.40–$64). AE, DC, MC, V.
   Open: Lunch daily 11:30am–2:30pm; dinner daily 6:30–10:30pm.
At last, a high-quality mid-to-upscale restaurant in Chinatown. We've looked for years now for this type of establishment and it's here in the newly opened Grand China Princess. Dishes range across the spectrum of Cantonese, Szechuan, and Tae

Chew cuisines. The lotus carpet and dark furniture lend a lush, exotic air to the place. Downstairs, on the ground floor, the hotel is opening a tea/coffee bar, which will also offer traditional Chinese potions to the local trade and daring travelers.

SPECIALTY DINING

DINNER WITH THAI DANCE

SALA RIM NAAN, on the Thonburi side of the Chao Phraya River, opposite the Oriental Hotel. Tel. 437-6211.

    Cuisine: THAI. **Reservations:** Required. **Directions:** Take the free shuttle boat from the Oriental Hotel pier.

$ Prices: Buffet lunch 350B ($14); fixed-price dinner 950B ($38) adult, 800B ($32) children. AE, MC, V.

    Open: Daily lunch noon–2pm; dinner 7pm, performance 8:30pm.

As you would expect from the Oriental's Thai restaurant, this is one of Bangkok's special places. Guests sit on pillows at low tables in the glittering, bronze-trimmed, teak-and-marble main hall and dine on finely crafted Thai dishes (readers complain about the food, but everyone loves the ambience). In the evening, classical dancers from Bangkok's Department of Fine Arts perform a 1-hour show of royal dances of the Sukhothai and Ayutthaya periods, as well as various folk dances.

    Lunch is served buffet-style, with no dance performance, while dinner is a full-service affair. You can take the free shuttle from the dock behind the Authors' Wing of the Oriental Hotel, or ferry pick ups can be arranged from other hotels. Check with your concierge.

TUM NAK THAI, 131 Ratchadaphisek Rd. Tel. 274-6420.

    Cuisine: THAI/CHINESE. **Reservations:** Recommended for large groups. **Directions:** 2km (1.2 miles) north of New Phetchaburi Road on Ratchadaphisek Road, parallel to the airport freeway.

    Prices: Appetizers 50B–90B ($2–$3.60); main courses 75B–200B ($3–$8). AE, MC, V.

    Open: Daily 11am–11pm; dance performance 8–9:30pm.

Tum Nak Thai has long billed itself as the largest restaurant in the world, with tables for 3,000, and who are we to disagree. Roller-skating waiters with hand-held computers ferry orders to and from 33 far-flung dining pavilions (tell your host you want a table near the stage). Tum Nak Thai has a huge menu, with specialties from Thailand's major regions. The food is good but hardly Bangkok's best, though we enjoy the traditional dancing and the overall spectacle.

    In total defiance, the recently opened Royal Dragon Restaurant swept the 1994 "Guiness Book of World Records" title with 32,000 square meters of Chinese pagodas, Confucian temples, and boat-style seating for 5,000! If you enjoy this Thai-style extravaganza, try Chinese cuisine on roller skates and let us know what you think.

KOSHER

BOSSOTEL INN, 55/12-14, Soi Charoen Krung 42/1, New Rd. Tel. 235-8001.

    Cuisine: KOSHER. **Directions:** Off New Road, on the way to the Shangri-La Hotel.

$ Prices: Appetizers 45B–120B ($1.80–$4.80); main courses 60B–250B ($2.40–$10); buffet 250B ($10). AE, MC, V.

    Open: Dinner daily 6–9:30pm.

Where do Bangkok's finest five-star hotels turn when they're asked to cater a kosher wedding? The kosher kitchen of the Bossotel's plain, informal coffee shop (formerly

---

READERS RECOMMEND

Royal Dragon Restaurant *"I believe it's actually the largest restaurant in the world, located at the foot of the Bangna-Trad Expressway. A wonderful time when dining with friends. Everything you select is from live aquariums. Prices are quite reasonable, most of the staff is on roller skates. It's a good time and quite worth mentioning!"*—Tonya Mathis, Portland, Oreg.

the Tina Tower Inn Restaurant) handles all such requests, as well as turning out a nightly repast for the hotel's many Israeli guests. The food is prepared under the supervision of Rabbi Jeremy Mizrachi; multiethnic buffets range from barbecue to vegetarian, and from Israeli to Persian. Occasionally the spread includes Thai noodles or an Indian curry, but at our visit it offered a tasty tabbouleh salad, Israeli diced tomato-and-cucumber salad, rice pilaf, vegetable-and-spinach strudel, and an eggplant salad. As of early 1994, the Bossotel Inn served the only kosher food in Bangkok, although this may change soon (call the Jewish Association; see "Fast Facts: Bangkok" in Chapter 3 for information).

DINNER CRUISES ON THE CHAO PHRAYA

The two most widely recommended cruises are offered by **Loy Nava** (tel. 437-4032 or 233-4195) and **Sun Moon Shine Tour** (tel. 448-0211). Loy Nava's twice nightly cruises begin at the River City Pier between 6 and 8pm (in the high season only). Sun Moon's excursions run according to demand and are available for private charter. The boats are either lavishly converted rice barges or luxury vessels similar to those that travel up to Ayutthaya. Both companies offer a mixed Thai and Western buffet, and in some cases, there is music to accompany the meal.

A dinner cruise can be booked through **Sea Tours** (tel. 251-4862) or by any major hotel, while reservations on the Sun Moon Shine boats should be made directly with the company at their office at 603/1 Arun Amarin Rd. Your concierge can also make this booking. Each company charges approximately 720B ($28.80), including food and transfers.

HEALTH FOOD

We didn't find a single strictly vegetarian restaurant in Bangkok, so if you find one, please write to us. We recommend that you stick with Chinese, Indian, and Japanese restaurants, most of which offer choices of nonmeat appetizers and main courses. Another, more expensive option, is to dine at nearly any of the top hotels where you'll find "spa cuisine," "low fat," and "light" menus.

FAST-FOOD

The world may drive Japanese cars and watch videos on Japanese VCRs and TVs, but when it comes to fast-food, the Americans reign supreme. You'll feel right at home with the array of familiar menus; prices are comparable to those back home.

In the Siam Square shopping complex, and on Rama I Road between Phyathai and Henri Dunant roads, there is a long row of fast-food outlets. Among them: Kentucky Fried Chicken; McDonald's; A&W Family Restaurant; Pizza Hut, Shakey's, and Dunkin' Donuts. Several cinemas which screen American films are found in this area, so you can combine a movie with a Big Mac, side of fries, and a crispy apple turnover.

On Ploenchit Road, east of Sogo Department Store and the corner of Rajdamri Road, you'll find McDonald's, Pizza Hut, and Swenson's. In the Business District, you'll find Pizza Hut and McDonald's in the C.P. Tower, 313 Silom Rd. The World Trade Center boasts Mr. Donut and KFC. Most fast-food restaurants are open from 9 or 10am until 10pm weekdays, until 11pm or midnight on weekends.

For authentic Thai fast-food, try the Mah Boon Krong Food Center on the sixth floor of the MBK Shopping Center, at the corner of Rama I and Phyathai roads. This is our favorite Thai fast-food outlet, offering a vast trove of Thai and Chinese specialties at astonishingly low prices—$2 to $3 is a princely sum here. Most of the take-out food, packaged in Baggies, is destined for the modern, on-the-go Thai household—giving rise to the somewhat sexist name "the plastic housewife"—but there are also clean booths and tables for those who wish to dine "al shopping mall." One can order small amounts of food here, making MBK an ideal place for the single traveler or families who want to sample a wide variety of tastes.

The ordering system is unusual: Buy food coupons from the vendors; take each dish from one of the trays and pay with your coupons; cash in excess coupons for change. MBK is one of the best examples of how contemporary Thai families combine local and Western styles.

Lovers of traditional street food should note that on almost every corner in Bangkok, you'll find a food stand serving simple and inexpensive fare. You must be careful of what you eat and make your own judgement about the freshness of the food and the hygiene of the stand. We've survived (and even thrived on) freshly cooked, hot food, but as always—caveat eater!

HIGH TEA

In our opinion, the ritual of high tea is one of the greatest legacies of the British Empire. We love its civilized atmosphere, the opportunity to sample goodies between meals, and the cool and relaxing break it provides in a busy day. The Chinese insist that hot tea (which encourages perspiration) is the most cooling and revitalizing fluid on hot days. After reveling in the tea ceremonies at the following hotels, we couldn't agree more.

GRAND HYATT ERAWAN, Garden Lounge, 494 Rajdamri Rd. Tel. 254-1234.

Cuisine: HIGH TEA. **Reservations:** Not necessary. **Directions:** Corner of Ploenchit Road.

$ **Prices:** Snacks 55B–150B ($2.20–$6). AE, MC, V.

Open: High tea daily 2:30–7pm.

The Erawan's soaring colonnaded atrium, filled with trees and tinkling ponds, makes the Garden Lounge a popular shopper's halt at teatime. As a soothing, classical trio beckons all to enter, diners choose from several blends of tea (80B/$3.20) and an à la carte selection of muffins, scones, meat pies, sandwiches, and ice creams. We always feel guilty about taking a tea break when the sweets are part of a fixed package, but this is a particularly soothing and special place for a break.

HILTON INTERNATIONAL, Lobby Lounge, 2 Wireless Rd. Tel. 253-0123.

Cuisine: HIGH TEA. **Reservations:** Recommended on weekends. **Directions:** Between Ploenchit and New Phetchaburi roads.

$ **Prices:** High tea 175B ($7). AE, MC, V.

Open: High tea daily 2:30–5:30pm.

Our favorite high tea for its superb pastries and delicate tea sandwiches, the Hilton's elegant and intimate lounge is also the perfect place to snack and talk. Three-tiered silver servers bearing scones, pastries, and tea sandwiches are as proper as the bone china, linen, and chamber music performed by a classical trio. Excellent value, and a lovely way to while away the afternoon.

SHANGRI-LA HOTEL, Main Lobby, 89 Soi Wat Suan Plu. Tel. 236-7777.

Cuisine: HIGH TEA. **Reservations:** Not necessary. **Directions:** On the Chao Phraya River, with street access from the south end of Silom Road.

$ **Prices:** High Tea 250B ($10). AE, MC, V.

Open: High tea daily 3–6pm.

If a huge buffet of delectable pastries, candies, Thai sweets, puddings, cakes, crêpes, and tasty sandwiches on fresh-baked rolls doesn't faze you, rush to the opulent high tea spread at this comfortable, river-view lounge. One of the riverfront's better food values, an afternoon with the Shangri-La's string quartet provides welcome respite from the city's heat and congestion.

CHAPTER 5

WHAT TO SEE & DO IN BANGKOK

- **1. ATTRACTIONS**
- **• DID YOU KNOW . . . ?**
- **• WALKING TOUR: WAT'S WHAT**
- **• WALKING TOUR: THONBURI**
- **2. SPORTS & RECREATION**
- **3. SAVVY SHOPPING**
- **4. EVENING ENTERTAINMENT**
- **5. EASY EXCURSIONS FROM BANGKOK**

Few capitals in Southeast Asia have as much to offer as Bangkok. From its fascinating klongs to its incredible Buddhist wats, from a wide range of exotic sports (kick boxing, beetle fighting) to endless places to shop, Bangkok offers a bounty of sightseeing opportunities.

We've also included two walking tours in this chapter. Though the streets of Bangkok can get pretty congested, we've outlined areas that are easily toured by foot.

Bangkok's legendary nightlife is detailed in this chapter as well, along with plenty of information on several interesting day trips.

1. ATTRACTIONS

SUGGESTED ITINERARIES

IF YOU HAVE 1 DAY Tour the Grand Palace, Wat Phra Kaeo, and Wat Po and enjoy a massage (possibly on a walking tour). After lunch, hire a long-tail boat for a Thonburi klong tour. At night, enjoy a Thai dinner with a dance performance (see "Specialty Dining" in Chapter 4).

IF YOU HAVE 2 DAYS See above for your first day. On your second day in Bangkok, take a boat to Wat Arun, then tour the National Museum. Shop after lunch. After dinner, walk through the Patpong district.

IF YOU HAVE 3 DAYS See above for your first two days. On your third day, take our Thonburi walking tour in the morning, with stops for more shopping. In the afternoon, take a tour of the Jim Thompson's House museum.

IF YOU HAVE 5 DAYS OR MORE See above for the first three days. On your fourth day, take a boat trip to Ayutthaya and the Bang Pa-In Summer Palace. On your fifth day, hire a car or join a tour to the Floating Market at Damnoen Saduak. Visit Wang Suan Pakkard in the afternoon.

THE TOP ATTRACTIONS

BANGKOK'S WATERWAYS

The history of Bangkok was written on its waterways, which have always been the essential focus of the city's life. When the 18th-century capital was moved from Ayutthaya to Thonburi, and then across the river to Bangkok, King Rama I built a canal (now called Klong Ong Ang and Klong Banglamphu), which created Ratanakosin Island out of the large bend in the river, to strengthen the defensive position of the Grand Palace. Other klongs were added, which became the

THAILAND

★ Bangkok

Democracy Monument 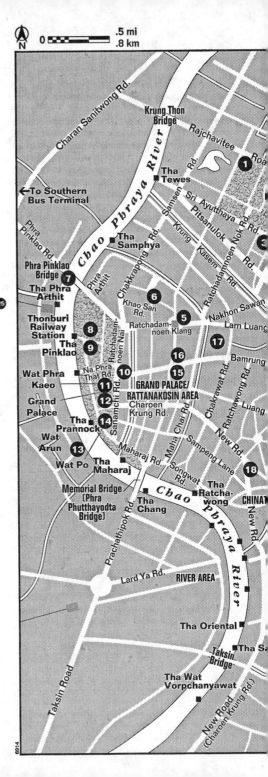 ⑤
Dusit Zoo ②
Giant Swing ⑯
The Grand Palace ⑫
Kamthieng House ㉖
Lak Muang ⑩
Lumpini Boxing Stadium ㉔
Lumpini Park ㉓
Magic Land ㉗
National Museum ⑧
Queen Sirikit Convention Center ㉕
Ratchadamnoen
  Boxing Stadium ①
Red Cross
  Snake Farm ㉒
Royal Bangkok
  Sports Club ㉑
Royal Barge Museum ⑦
Royal Turf Club ④
Jim Thompson House ⑲
Vimanmek Mansion ①
Wang Suan Pakkard ⑳
Wat Arun ⑬
Wat Benchamabophit ③
Wat Bovornivet ⑥
Wat Mahatat ⑨
Wat Phra Kaeo ⑪
Wat Po ⑭
Wat Saket ⑰
Wat Suthat ⑮
Wat Traimit ⑱

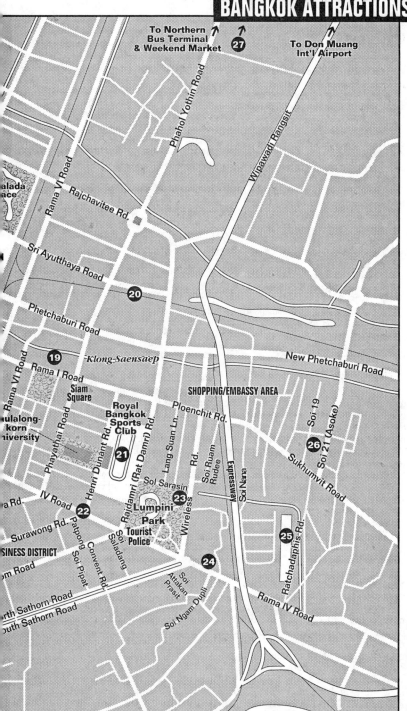

BANGKOK ATTRACTIONS

To Northern Bus Terminal & Weekend Market

27

To Don Muang Int'l Airport

Phahol Yothin Road

Wipawadi Rangsit

Rama VI Road

Rajchavitee Rd.

alada ace

Sri Ayutthaya Road

20

Phetchaburi Road

New Phetchaburi Road

19

Klong-Saensaep

Rama VI Road

Rama I Road

Siam Square

SHOPPING/EMBASSY AREA

Soi 19

Soi 21 (Asoke)

ulalong-korn niversity

Royal Bangkok Sports Club

Ploenchit Rd.

Lang Suan Ln.

26

Sukhumvit Road

Phayathai Road

Henri Dunant Rd.

Rajdamri (Rat Damri) Rd.

21

Rd.

Soi Ruam Rudee

Expressway

Soi Nana

IV Road

22

Soi Sarasin

23

Lumpini Park

Tourist Police

Wireless

25

Ratchadaphis Rd.

Surawong Rd.

Patpong

Soi Saladang

Convent Rd.

Soi Pipat

BUSINESS DISTRICT

m Road

rth Sathorn Road

uth Sathorn Road

24

Soi Attakan Prasit

Soi Ngam Dupli

Rama IV Road

River Taxi Pier ■

? DID YOU KNOW . . .?

- The full name of the capital city is "Krung Thep, Maha Nakorn, Amorn Ratanakosindra, Mahindrayudhya, Mahadilokpop Noparatana Rajdhani, Burirom, Udom Rajnivet Mahastan, Amorn Pimarn Avatarn Satit, Sakkatuttiya Vishnukarm Prasit," which translates as "The city of gods, the great city, the residence of the Emerald Buddha, the impregnable city (of Ayutthaya) of God Indra, the grand capital of the world endowed with nine precious gems, the happy city, abounding in enormous palaces which resemble the heavenly abode where reigns the reincarnated God, a city given by Indra and built by Vishnukarm."
- Five hundred new vehicles were purchased in Bangkok every hour during 1992.
- The island of Ko Samui ships more than two million coconuts to Bangkok each month.
- The Oriental Hotel has been voted the "Best Hotel in the World" by *Institutional Investors* for 10 years in a row.

boulevards and avenues of the city. Boats were the primary means of transportation, with horse-drawn travel reserved for royalty.

As Ayutthaya was before it, Bangkok came to be known as the "Venice of the East," but sadly, many of these klongs have been paved over in the last decade or so. But the magnificent Chao Phraya River (which means River of Kings) continues to cut through the heart of the city, separating the early capital of Thonburi from today's Bangkok. On the Thonburi side, the klongs still branch off into a network of arteries which are relatively unchanged as the centers of neighborhood life.

Boats of all sizes and shapes ply the Chao Phraya River day and night. Ferries run up, down, and across the river, carrying commuters to work, kids to school, and saffron-robed monks to temple. Strangely elegant rice barges pull mountains of rice, gravel, sand, lumber, vegetables, and the countless families who make them their homes.

The strangest, most frequently seen boat on the river is the *hang yao*, or long-tailed water taxi, a long, thin, graceful vessel, powered by an automobile engine connected by a long, exposed shaft (tail) to the propeller. The exposed engine is balanced on a fulcrum mount, and muscular boatmen move the entire motor and shaft assembly to steer the boat—an amazing feat of strength and balance, especially at 30 knots. These water taxis carry passengers throughout the maze of klongs and are a vital element in supplying fresh food from upriver farms and fresh fish from coastal villages to Bangkok.

For an intimate glimpse of traditional Thai life, we urge you to explore the waterways. You'll see people using the river to bathe, wash their clothes, and even brush their teeth at water's edge (a habit not recommended to Westerners). Floating kitchens in sampans serve rice and noodles to customers in other boats. Men dance across carpets of logs floating to lumber mills. Wooden houses on stilts spread back from the banks of the river and klongs, each with its own spirit house perfumed with incense and decked out with flowers and other offerings.

There are several approaches to touring the klongs. Both Sea Tours and World Travel offer standard group tours: The basic Canal Tour is organized around a so-called "Floating Market" in Thonburi, but it's become very touristy and crowded. Instead, take either a rice barge cruise or a canal tour that is devoted to just that. Some tours explore the canals north of the city on the west bank, where the mark of urban sprawl is less visible.

Better yet, charter a long-tail hang yao for about 300B to 400B ($12 to $16) an hour—expect to negotiate the price. You'll find boats for hire at any pier, or you can organize it through your hotel concierge. Beware of independent boat operators that offer to take you to the nearby Thonburi Floating Market or to souvenir or gem shops. Take your time and explore Klong Bangkok Noi and Klong Bangkok Yai, with a stop at the Royal Barge Museum on the way back.

A more leisurely way to see the klongs (our favorite) is to travel on the local long-tail taxis that depart from almost every Chao Phraya Express Boat pier. Try the Ratchawong (also spelled Rajawongse) Pier, where you can climb into any long-tail boat that is filling up and ride up Klong Bangkok Yai, across the river in Thonburi. The fare is a paltry 5B (20¢) and you can ride until you want to turn back, then get off and catch the next boat back. We enjoyed a stop at the spectacular temple complex of Wat Pak-Nam. Ask the driver to point it out and wander among the myriad buildings of the wat. You'll see few Westerners here. Try this serendipitous approach and enjoy the rich window into life on the banks of Bangkok's klongs. It's a unique experience.

If you've got the time, take a day to visit the more original floating market at Damnoen Saduak, about 80km (48 miles) southwest of Bangkok in Ratchaburi Province. (See "Easy Excursions from Bangkok," below.)

THE GRAND PALACE, near the river on Na Phra Rd. near Sanam Luang. Tel. 222-8181, ext. 40.

One of King Rama I's earliest accomplishments was to move the capital from Thonburi to a more defensible site on the opposite bank of the Chao Phraya. He chose the center of the Chinese community, which was then moved south to Sampeng, the current Chinatown. The capital was built in the exact image of the destroyed capital of Ayutthaya. The construction of the Grand Palace and Wat Phra Kaeo were the first phase of his grand goal, though both were added to and rebuilt in subsequent reigns.

The palace as it appears today was greatly influenced by Western architecture, including colonial and Victorian motifs. Anna—tutor to the son of Rama IV and the central figure in the story *The King and I*—lived here. The royal family moved to Chitlada Palace after the death of King Ananda in 1946, but it was here, in 1981, that General Chitpatima attempted to overthrow the government in an unsuccessful coup.

As you enter the palace gate, built in the 1780s, you'll see the Pavilion for Holy Water, where priests swore loyalty to the royal family and purified themselves with water from Thailand's four main rivers. Nearby is a lacquered-wood structure called the Arporn Phimok Prasad (Disrobing Pavilion), built so the king could conveniently mount his palanquin for royal elephant precessions (most of the time it served as a kind of elephant parking lot).

Also nearby is the Chakri Maha Prasad, designed as a royal residence for Rama IV by Western architects to commemorate the century of the Chakri dynasty. The king's advisors urged him to use Thai motifs to demonstrate his independence from growing Western influence: The Thai, temple-style roof rests physically and symbolically on top of an imperial Victorian building. This Thai-Victorian building contains the ashes of royal family members on the third floor, the throne room and reception hall on the main floor, and a collection of weapons on the ground floor.

The whitewashed stone building nearby now serves as the Funeral Hall, though it was originally the residence of Rama I and Rama II. The corpse of a deceased royal figure is kept in this building for a year before it's cremated in a nearby field. On the four corners of the roof are garuda figures ("vehicles" for the Hindu god Rama) symbolizing the king, who is thought to be a reincarnation of Rama. The garden was rebuilt under Rama IV in the 1860s, and the highlight here is a section that reproduces the landscape of a Thai mountain-and-woods fable. This structure was used as a ceremonial place for Thai princes to cut the top knot of their hair in a coming-of-age ritual.

The Grand Palace also has a harem, the Forbidden Quarters (no one other than the king was allowed to enter), where the king's wives lived. Close by is the Amarin Vinichai Prasad or the Coronation Hall, built by Rama I and added to by subsequent kings. Today this building is used, like the palace in general, for royal coronations, weddings, and state events only, and it is here that the king makes his most grand appearance.

Admission: 125B ($5). Price includes Wat Phra Kaeo, as well as admission to the Vimanmek Palace (near the National Assembly) and to the Coin Pavilion. The ticket booth is on the north side of the complex.

Open: Daily 8:30am–noon and 1–3:30pm; most individual buildings are closed to the public except for special days proclaimed by the king. **Directions:** Take the Chao Phraya Express Boat to the Tha Chang Pier, then walk east and south.

WAT PHRA KAEO, in the Grand Palace complex. Tel. 222-8181, ext. 40.

Probably no Thai shrine is as revered as Wat Phra Kaeo, or as it is commonly known, the Temple of the Emerald Buddha. It sits within the grounds of the Grand Palace, surrounded by walls over a mile long, with some of the finest examples of Buddhist sculpture, architecture, painting, and decorative craft in the country.

Central to the wat is the Emerald Buddha itself, a rather small, dark statue, a little over two feet high, made of green jade ("emerald" in Thai refers to intense green color only, not to the specific stone) that sits atop a huge gold altar. This very revered image was first discovered inside a *chedi* (a pointed, dome-shaped stupa housing a Buddha relic) in Chiang Rai when a bolt of lightning struck the monument in 1434. Some historians believe that the Buddha was sculpted around that time, attibuting it to the Chiang Saen school; others believe that it was produced in Sri Lanka. The reigning king of Chiang Mai, at the time the most powerful state in the north, tried to bring the Buddha to his city, but on three separate occasions the elephant that was to transport the statue stopped at the same spot at a crossroads in Lampang. Never one to cross the determined spirit of the Buddha, the king built a monumental wat at that spot in Lampang, where it remained for 32 years.

A more dogged monarch, King Tiloka, insisted that the Emerald Buddha be brought to Chiang Mai. There it was placed in a chedi at Wat Chedi Lunang until 1552, when the new ruler of Chiang Mai, King Chaichettha took the peripatetic Buddha to Luang Prabang. Some 12 years later, the statue was moved again, this time to Vientiane, Laos, where it stayed for 214 years, until Rama I brought it back to his capital at Thonburi after his successful campaign in Laos. In 1784, when the capital was moved across the river to Bangkok, Rama I installed the precious figure in its present shrine, where it's been displayed ever since.

The Buddha, like all others in Thailand, is covered in a seasonal cloak, changed three times a year to correspond to the summer, winter, and rainy months. The changing of the robes is an important ritual, performed by the king, who also sprinkles water over the monks and well-wishers to bring good fortune during the upcoming season.

The Emerald Buddha is housed in an equally magnificent *ubosoth*, used by monks for important religious rituals. The interior walls are decorated with late Ayutthaya–style murals depicting the life of the Buddha, steps to enlightenment, and the Buddhist cosmology of the Worlds of Desire, Form, and Nonform. The cycle begins with the birth of the Buddha, which can be seen in the middle of the left wall as you enter the sanctuary, and the story continues counterclockwise. Also note the exquisite inlaid mother-of-pearl work on the door panels.

The surrounding portico of the ubosoth is an example of masterful Thai craftsmanship. On the perimeter are 12 open pavilions, built during the reign of Rama I. The portico galleries across from the ubosoth contain painted murals depicting stories from the *Ramakien*, the Thai version of the Hindu epic *Ramayana*.

Subsequent kings built more monuments and restored or embellished existing structures. Among the most interesting of these are the three pagodas to the immediate north of the ubosoth, representing the changing centers of Buddhist influence: The first, to the west, is Phra Si Ratana Chedi, a 19th-century Sri Lankan–style stupa housing ashes of the Buddha; in the middle is the library, or Phra Mondop, built in Thai style by Rama I, known for its excellently crafted Ayutthaya-style mother-of-pearl doors, bookcases containing the *Tripitaka* (sacred Buddist manuscripts), human- and dragon-headed *nagas* (snakes), and statues of Rama kings; and to the east is the Royal Pantheon, built in Khmer style during the 19th century—it's

---

IMPRESSIONS

The royal Wat is not a wat but a city of wats; . . . there are structures made of tiles and encrusted with strange tile flowers . . . and small ones, rows of them, that look like the prizes in a shooting gallery at a village fair in the country of the gods.
—SOMERSET MAUGHAM, THE GENTLEMAN IN THE PARLOUR, 1930

open to the public in October for one day to commemorate the dynasty of the first Rama kings. To the immediate north of the library is a model of Angkor Wat, the most sacred of all Cambodian shrines, constructed by King Mongkut as a reminder that the neighboring state was under the dominion of Thailand. To the west of the ubosoth, near the entry gate, is a black stone statue of a hermit, considered a patron of medicine, before whom relatives of the ill and infirm pay homage and make offerings of joss sticks, fruit, flowers, and candles.

Scattered around the complex are statues of elephants, thought to represent independence and power. Thai kings went to battle atop elephants, and it is customary for parents to walk their children around an elephant three times to bring them strength. Rub the head of an elephant statue for good luck (and notice how smooth it is from millions of superstitious palms).

Admission: Included in the Grand Palace fee, 125B ($5).

Open: Daily 8:30am–noon and 1–3:30pm. **Directions:** Chao Phraya Express Boat to Tha Chang Pier, then walk east and south.

WAT PO, Maharat Rd., near the river. Tel. 222-0933.

Wat Po, the Temple of the Reclining Buddha (also called Wat Phra Chetuphon), was built by Rama I in the 16th century and is the oldest and largest Buddhist temple in Bangkok. The compound is divided into two sections by Chetuphon Road, a 15-minute walk south of the Grand Palace entrance. The northern area contains the most important monuments, and the southern portion is where resident monks live.

Most people go straight to the enormous Reclining Buddha in the northern section. It's more than 140 feet long by 50 feet high and was built during the mid-19th-century reign of Rama III. The statue is brick, covered with layers of lacquer, plaster, and always-flaking gold leaf; the feet are inlaid with mother-of-pearl illustrations of 108 "auspicious" signs of the Buddha.

Outside, the grounds contains 91 chedis, four viharns (halls), and a bot (the central shrine in a Buddhist temple). Most impressive, aside from the Reclining Buddha, are the four main chedis dedicated to the first four Rama kings and, nearby, the library. It's among the most photogenic of all the wats in Bangkok.

Of all of the major temples in Bangkok, Wat Po is one of the most active. The temple is considered Thailand's first public university, with many of the monuments that explain principles of art, religion, science, and literature. Visitors still drop 1-satang coins in 108 bronze bowls—corresponding to the 108 auspicious signs of the Buddha—for good fortune and to help the monks keep up the wat.

Visitors are encouraged to learn about traditional Thai massage and medicine at the Traditional Medical Practitioners Association center. Alghough we enjoyed a fabulously restorative Thai medical massage here—90B ($3.60) for 30 minutes, 150B ($6) for an hour—those with sensitive muscles may prefer to abstain and watch instead.

Admission: 10B (40¢).

Open: Daily 8am–5pm; massages offered until 6pm. **Directions:** About half mile south of the Grand Palace.

WAT ARUN, west bank of the Chao Phraya, opposite Tha Thien Pier.

The 260-foot-high, Khmer-inspired tower, the centerpiece of the "Temple of Dawn," rises majestically from the banks of the Chao Phraya, across from Wat Po.

IMPRESSIONS

At daybreak went to see one of the large pagodas of Bangkok. They are ornamented in a barbaric style of gorgeousness; hideous figures of every sort are stuck around them.
—Sir John Bowring, 1857

Bangkok is stuck as thick with pagodas as a duff with plums.
—Crosbie Garstin, *The Dragon and the Lotus*, 1928

This religious complex served as the royal chapel during King Taksin's reign (1809–24), when Thonburi was the capital of Thailand.

The original tower was only 50 feet high, but was expanded during the rule of Rama III (1824–51) to its current height. The exterior is decorated with flower and other decorative motifs made of ceramic shards donated to the monastery by local people, at the request of Rama III. At the base of the complex are Chinese stone statues, once used as ballast in trading ships, gifts from Chinese merchants.

You can climb the central prang, but be warned: The steps are treacherously large and steep, and are even more precarious on the descent. If you go up, notice the caryatids and the Hindu gods atop the three-headed elephants. The view of the river, Wat Po, and Grand Palace is well worth the climb. Be sure to walk around back of the tower to the monk's living quarters, a tranquil world far from the bustle of Bangkok's busy streets. Despite its name, we suggest a late-afternoon visit.

Admission: 5B (20¢).

Open: Daily 8am–5:30pm. **Directions:** Take a water taxi from Tha Tien Pier (near Wat Po) or cross the Phra Pinklao Bridge and follow the river south on Arun Amarin Rd.

THE NATIONAL MUSEUM, Na Phra That Rd. Tel. 224-1333.

The National Museum, a short (15-minute) walk north of the Grand Palace and the Temple of the Emerald Buddha, is the country's central treasury of art and archeology (32 branches are located throughout the provinces). Some of the buildings are themselves works of art.

The current museum was built as part of the Grand Palace complex when the capital of Siam was moved from Thonburi to Bangkok in 1782. It was called the Palace to the Front and was the home of the Wang Na—the Prince of the Palace to the Front, who was then the brother of Rama I, the deputy king, and his appointed successor. (He died before Rama I.) There was also a Prince of the Palace of the Rear. The position of princely successor was eventually abolished and the Wang Na buildings became space for the museum. Thammasat University, the College of Dramatic Arts, and the National Theater were also built on the royal grounds, along with additional museum buildings.

To see the entire collection (which we recommend), plan on at least three hours, starting with the Thai History and the Prehistoric Galleries in the first building. If you're rushed, go straight to the Red House behind it, a traditional 18th-century Thai building that was originally the living quarters of Princess Sri Sudarak, sister of King Rama I. It is furnished in period style, with many pieces originally owned by the princess.

Another essential stop is the Phutthaisawan Chapel, built in 1787 to house the Buddhist figure Phra Buddhasihing, brought here from its original home in Chiang Mai. It's an exquisite example of Buddhist temple architecture.

From the chapel, work your way back through the main building of the royal palace to see the gold jewelry, some from the royal collections, and the Thai ceramics, including many pieces in the five-color bencharong style. The Old Transportation Room contains ivory carvings, elephant chairs, and royal palanquins. There are also rooms of royal emblems and insignia, stone carvings, wood carvings, costumes, textiles, musical instruments, and Buddhist religious artifacts.

We loved the collection of royal funeral chariots, but connoisseurs of fine art and sculpture will spend most of their time in the newer galleries at the rear of the museum compound. Gallery after gallery is filled with both Thai and Pre-Thai sculpture (including some excellent Mon work) and Hindu and Buddhist images from the provinces.

Admission: 25B ($1).

Open: Wed–Sun 9am–4pm. English-language tours: Thai Art and Culture, Tues 9:30am; Pre-Thai and Thai Art, Thurs 9:30am (call the museum or TAT or check newspaper for current schedule). **Directions:** About half mile north of Grand Palace.

MORE ATTRACTIONS

JIM THOMPSON'S HOUSE, Soi Kasemsan 2. Tel. 215-0122.

Jim Thompson was a New York architect who served in the OSS in Thailand during World War II and afterward settled in Bangkok. He single-handedly revived Thailand's silk industry, employing Thai Muslims as skilled silkweavers and building up a thriving industry. After expanding his sales to international markets, Mr. Thompson mysteriously disappeared while vacationing in the Cameron Highlands of Malaysia in 1967. Dispite extensive investigations, his disappearance has never been resolved.

Thompson's legacy is substantial, both as an entrepreneur and collector. Thompson's traditionally Thai house contains a sumptuous display of Khmer sculpture, Chinese porcelain, Burmese carving (especially a 17th-century teak Buddha), and antique Thai scroll paintings.

Thompson's training as an architect paid off handsomely, if his house is any measure of his skill. It comprises six linked teak and theng (harder than teak) wood houses from northern Thailand that were rebuilt according to Thai architectural principles, but with Western additions (such as a staircase and window screens). In some rooms the floor is made of Italian marble, but the panels are pegged teak. The house slopes toward the center to help stabilize the structure (the originals were built on stilts without foundations). The nearby, busy klong and landscaped garden make a lovely spot, especially on a hot day.

You can buy silk from the Jim Thompson Company retail shop at the intersection of Surawong and Rama IV roads (see "Savvy Shopping," below).

Admission: 125B ($5), 40B, ($1.60) students. Profits support local charities.

Open: Mon–Sat 9am–7:30pm. **Directions:** On a small soi off Rama I Rd. opposite the National Stadium.

WANG SUAN PAKKARD, 352 Sri Ayutthaya Rd. Tel. 245-4934.

One of our favorite places in Bangkok is Wang Suan Pakkard, or Palace of the Cabbage Garden. This nontouristy site was the home of Princess Chumbhot of Nagara Svarga. Five 19th-century teak houses were moved from Chiang Mai in 1952 and rebuilt in a garden on a private klong, separated by a high wall from the tumult of Bangkok's streets. The Lacquer Pavilion (actually an Ayutthaya house, moved here in 1958) was a birthday present from the prince to the princess.

Princess Chumbnot was an avid art collector and one of the country's most dedicated archeologists—credited with having partly financed the excavations at Ban Chiang I in 1967. There is an entire room of objects from that site, including pottery and jewelry, surpassed only by the prehistoric findings exhibited at the National Museum. The balance of the collection is diverse, with Khmer sculpture, ivory boxes, perfume bottles, nielloware, and wonderful prints by European artists depicting their image of Siamese people before the country opened to the Western world. There is a fabulous Buddha head from Ayutthaya, as well as a royal barge. Be sure to ask to see the pavilion housing the princess's collection of Thai and Chinese ceramics—it's exquisite.

The gift shop at Wang Suan Pakkard offers ceramics, some real and some reproductions, though prices are quite reasonable.

Admission: 60B ($2.40), including material for self-guided tour of grounds and collections.

Open: Mon–Sat 9am–4pm. **Directions:** East of Phyathai Rd.

VIMANMEK MANSION MUSEUM, 193/2 Rajchavitee Rd., Dusit. Tel. 281-6880.

Built in 1901 by King Chulalongkorn the Great (Rama V) as the Celestial Residence, this large, beautiful, golden teakwood mansion was only recently restored and reopened by Queen Sirikit as a private museum with a collection of the royal family's memorabilia. An intriguing and informative hour-long tour takes you though a series of apartments and rooms (81 in all) in what is said to be the largest teak building in the world. The original Abhisek Dusit Throne Hall houses a display of Thai handicrafts, and nine other buildings north of the mansion display photographs, clocks, fabrics, royal carriages, and other regalia. Classical dance and martial art demonstrations are given daily at 10:30am and 2pm.

Admission: 75B ($3); 125B ($5) with a ticket to the Grand Palace and Wat Phra Kaeo.

Open: Daily 9:30am–4pm. **Directions:** Opposite the Dusit Zoo, north of the National Assembly Building.

THE ROYAL BARGES, on Klong Bangkok Noi, north of the Phra Pinklao Bridge, Thonburi. Tel. 424-0004.

If you've hired a long-tail boat on the Chao Phraya, stop by this unique museum housing the royal barges. These elaborately decorated sailing vessels, rowed by up to 60 men, are used by the royal family on state occasions or for high religious ceremonies. The king's barge, the *Suphanahong*, is decorated with red-and-gold carvings of fearsome mythological beasts, like the Garuda or the dragon on the bow and stern. If you can't make it to the royal barges, there is a smaller display of barges at the National Museum, near Wat Phra Kaeo.

Admission: 15B (60¢).

Open: Daily 8:30am–4:30pm. **Directions:** Take a taxi over the Phra Pinklao Bridge or hire a boat from the Tha Maharaj Pier or any other Express Boat pier.

WAT MAHATHAT, Na Phra That Rd. Tel. 221-5999.

This temple, still much used as a Buddhist center of meditation and study, is known for the overwhelming amulet, talisman, and traditional medicine market on the periphery of the temple grounds. Each Sunday hundreds of worshipers squat on the ground, magnifying glasses in hand, studying tiny images of the Buddha, hoping to find the one that brings good fortune. (The newer amulet market is part of Wat Ratchanada, off the intersection of Mahachai Road and Ratchadamnoen Klang Road, across from the Golden Mount at Wat Saket.)

Wat Mahathat itself is one of Bangkok's oldest shrines, built to house a relic of the Buddha. Inside is a center for Vipassana Meditation at Buddhist University, which offers some programs in English. Inquire at the wat's "Section 5" for more information.

Admission: Free.

Open: Daily 9am–5pm. **Directions:** Na Prathat Rd., near Sanam Luang Park, between the Grand Palace and the National Museum.

LAK MUANG [City Pillar Shrine], Sanam Chai Rd.

The "City Pillar," northeast of the Grand Palace complex, near the Defense Department Building, is a diminutive though delightful shrine, said to be inhabited by the spirit that protects Bangkok. Rama I placed a stone pillar—perhaps hearkening back to the Hindu custom of installing a *lingam* (phallic symbol) at the center of Shiva temples, to mark the site of the city's guardian soul. Lak Muang was recently renovated, and though it isn't on most tourist itineraries, many locals pay tribute to the shrine. Often Thai classical dancing is performed (a little before noon) to amuse the spirit.

Admission: Free.

Open: Mon–Fri 8:30am–4:30pm. **Directions:** About a quarter mile northeast of the Grand Palace on the southeast corner of Sanam Luang.

WAT BENCHAMABOPHIT, Sri Ayutthaya Rd. Tel. 281-2501.

Wat Benchamabophit (the Marble Wat) is an early 20th-century temple designed by the half brother of Rama V, and is the most modern of Bangkok's royal wats. Unlike the older complexes, there is no truly monumental viharn or chedi dominat-

---

IMPRESSIONS

And then I think of Siam, which by the almost miraculous cunning of its rulers escaped enslavement by the West, only to become through liberty and propensity hardly more than a fun-fair mirror reflective of the U.S.A.
—NORMAN LEWIS, THE CHANGING SKY, 1959

ing the grounds. Many smaller buildings reflect a melding of European materials and designs with traditional Thai religious architecture. The courtyards are made of polished Carrara marble. Walk inside the compound, beyond the main bot, to view the many Buddhas that represent various regional styles. During the early mornings, monks chant in the main chapel, sometimes so intensely that it seems as if the temple is going to lift off.

Admission: 10B (40¢)
Open: Daily 8am–5pm. **Directions:** South of the Assembly Building near Chitralada Palace.

WAT BOVORNIVET, Phra Sumein Rd.

Although few visitors bother to come to this quiet retreat opposite the old town wall, we find it rewarding. You can wander along the paths between the monks' quarters and the waterways, used by the king for water purification experiments. Many kings were monks here, including Prince Mongkut (later King Rama IV), who served as abbot here for 14 years. Of the two Buddhas inside the bot, the smaller one in front was cast in bronze in Sukhothai in 1257 to celebrate the country's liberation from Khmer rule. Several murals depict farangs in Thailand—the English at a horse race, American missionaries, Germans prospecting for minerals.

Admission: Free.
Open: 8am–5pm. **Directions:** North of Ratchadamnoen Klang Rd. near the Democracy Monument.

WAT SUTHAT [The Giant Swing], Sao Chingcha Sq. Tel. 222-0280.

The huge teak arch in front is all that remains of an original giant swing, which was used until 1932 to thank Shiva for a bountiful rice harvest and to ask for the god's blessing on the next. The minister of rice, accompanied by hundreds of Brahman court astrologers, would lead a parade around the city walls to the temple precinct. Teams of men would ride the swing on arcs as high as 82 feet in the air, trying to grab a bag of silver coins witih their teeth. The swing ceremony has been discontinued, but the thanksgiving festival is still celebrated in mid-December after the rice harvest.

The temple is among the oldest and largest in Bangkok and was built by Rama I—he carved one of the viharn's doors. It houses a beautiful 14th-century Phra Buddha Shakyamuni that was brought from Sukhothai. The wall paintings for which it is known were done during Rama III's reign. Outside the viharn stand many Chinese pagodas, bronze horses, and figures of Chinese soldiers.

Admission: 10B (40¢).
Open: Daily 9am–5pm. **Directions:** Near the intersection of Bamrung Muang Rd. and Ti Thong Rd.

KAMTHIENG HOUSE [The Siam Society], 131 Soi Asoke. Tel. 258-3491.

The 19th-century Kamthieng House, on the grounds of the Siam Society Headquarters, is a rice farmer's teak house transplanted from the banks of Chiang Mai's Ping River. Its collection, organized with financial help from the Asia and Rockefeller foundations, is oriented toward ethnographic objects illustrating the culture of everyday life.

Many agricultural and domestic items (we liked the woven fish baskets and terracotta pots) are on display, but we were drawn most to the exhibit about the Chao Vieng, or city dwellers from the northern Lan Na Thai Kingdom. If you plan to trek through this area, you will particularly enjoy this small but informative collection. We also enjoyed walking through the grounds, which are landscaped like a northern Thai garden.

The Siam Society also supports an excellent library and gallery, at the same location, concentrating on regional culture. They also publish scholarly texts on Thai culture.

Admission: 40B ($1.60); students free.
Open: Tues–Sat 9am–noon and 1–5pm. **Directions:** North of Sukhumvit on Soi 21.

WAT TRAIMIT, Traimit Rd.

Wat Traimit (Temple of the Golden Buddha) houses one of the most astonishing Buddhas—10 feet high, weighing over 5 tons, and said to be cast of solid gold. This powerful image has such a reflective, polished finish that its edges seem to disappear. The seated statue was supposed to have been cast during the Sukhothai period, though it looks strangely robotic.

Its story is as fantastic as its appearance. During a storm not long ago, water soaked a large stucco Buddha (believed to be from Ayutthaya) that was being temporarily stored. The stucco cracked and pieces flaked away, revealing gold underneath. The protective exterior is thought to have been applied to disguise the Buddha during the Burmese invasions of the 18th century. Pieces of the stucco are on display in a case to the left.

Admission: 10B (40¢).

Open: Daily 9am–5pm. **Directions:** At intersection of Krung Kasem and Charoen Krung (a continuation of Rama IV, near the train station), walk southwest on Traimit Rd. and look for a school with a playground. The wat is up a flight of stairs overlooking the school.

WAT SAKET, Ratchadamnoen Klang and Boripihat Rds.

Also known as the Golden Mount, Wat Saket is easily recognized as the huge white stucco stupa near the pier for Bangkok's east-west klong ferry. Begun in the late 18th century during the reign of Rama I, this temple is most interesting for the vista of old Rattanakosin offered from its stucco "hill" (a breathtaking, but short, walk uphill). The golden chedi is open to visitors and contains some relics of the Buddha.

Admission: Free.

Open: All day for the view; chedi, 9am–5pm.

RED CROSS SNAKE FARM, 1871 Rama IV Rd. Tel. 252-0161.

For a short, entertaining, and enlightening show, stop by the Thai Red Cross Snake Farm (the Queen Saovabha Memorial Institute) in the heart of Bangkok opposite the Montien Hotel. Established in 1923, the farm was the second facility of its type in the world (the first was in Brazil). There are slide shows and snake-handling demonstrations weekdays at 10:30am and 2pm; on weekends and holidays at 10:30am.

You can also watch the handlers work with deadly cobras, and you'll cringe when they handle the equally menacing banded kraits and green pit vipers. They also demonstrate venom milking—the venom is stockpiled as an antidote for those bitten by ominous serpents. The Thai Red Cross sells medical guides and will also inoculate you against such maladies as typhoid, cholera, and smallpox in their clinic, weekdays.

Admission: 100B ($4).

Open: Daily 8:30am–4:30pm. **Directions:** At the corner of Rama IV Rd. and Henry Dunant.

DUSIT ZOO, Rama V and Ratchawithi Rds. Tel. 281-0000.

The Dusit Zoo (also called Khao Din Wana) is in a lovely park between the Chitralada Royal Palace and the National Assembly. Besides admiring the many indigenous Asian animals (including royal white elephants), you can rent paddleboats on the pond. Children love riding the elephants while tired parents sit at one of the zoo's cafés under broad shade trees.

Admission: 10B (40¢).

Open: Daily 8am–6pm.

QUEEN SIRIKIT NATIONAL CONVENTION CENTER, Ratchadaphisek Rd., off of Rama IV Rd. Tel. 229-3000.

The stunning QSNCC (as it's popularly known), christened in August 1991, is the venue for many new exhibits and art shows open to the public. At our visit, an International Travel Show (with interesting photo exhibits highlighting different provinces of Thailand) was followed by a huge Philatelic Exhibition. Keep an eye on the *Bangkok Post* or the *Nation* calendar of events to see what's happening. The

QSNCC has also become the pivotal point for Bangkok's fastest-growing neighborhood.
Admission: Free.
Open: Call for the schedule of each show. **Directions:** Just south of Sukhumvit Rd. at Soi 21.

WALKING TOURS

We've designed two interesting walking tours that avoid some of Bangkok's noise, traffic, and pollution problems and explore older neighborhoods via smaller back streets (sois).

Even though any walking trip will become a hot experience, keep in mind that you'll be entering religious buildings and will need to dress modestly (in other words, no tank tops or shorts). Also, carry bottled water and small baht bills or change to use for contributions at the wats (10B, about 40¢, is appropriate).

The directions for these routes are sometimes complicated, but don't hesitate to ask the locals if you lose your way.

WALKING TOUR — WAT'S WHAT

Start: Wat Saket.
Finish: Maharaj Pier.
Time: Approximately 2 hours, not including tours of Wat Po, the Grand Palace complex, shopping, or snack stops.
Best Times: Weekend or weekdays in the cooler early morning.
Worst Times: Midday heat and late afternoon (the Grand Palace closes at 3:30pm).

Our Wat's What tour is designed to serve as an introduction to many of Bangkok's best-known Buddhist shrines. The walk is centered in Rattanakosin or "old Bangkok," that is, the original part of the city, although many of the buildings and neighborhoods are anything but old. What you'll find is a view, some shopping, excellent sightseeing, good food, a dose of exercise, and, if you're up for it, a traditional herbal massage.

The tour begins at:

1. Wat Saket along Thanon Boriphat, which runs parallel to Mahachai on the other side of one of the city's older klongs (in fact, if you take a klong boat, get out at the Wat Saket stop). Thanon Boriphat is lined with woodworking shops and lumber yards, and the curious will, like us, stick their heads into the shops to garner a view of wood-carvers and craftspeople fashioning intricately worked architectural elements. The stairs at Wat Saket (also known as the Golden Mount, built in the late 18th century during Rama I's reign) wind around the base of the massive structure and lead up to the top. There is a 5B (20¢) admission fee, ostensibly for a chance to look out over the city (the relics inside are of little aesthetic or spiritual importance), and in our case, to map out the balance of the walking tour. Proceed to the windows on your left as you enter the observatory room. Immediately in front and below is Wat Ratchanada; to the right are the four pillars of the Democracy Monument; farther away and to the left are Wat Suthat and the Giant Swing; and even more distant are the spires of the Grand Palace and Wat Po.

After descending the winding staircase and ramp, find your way back out to Thanon Boriphat and turn right, crossing over Klong Mahanak; veer left, turn left (crossing over the klong again), and proceed straight to:

2. Wat Ratchanada (The Temple of the Metal Castle). Prior to crossing the street, pay attention to vehicles; the jog from Wat Saket should take about five minutes. This may be your first Buddhist wat, so explore but don't dawdle, as there are many more (and more interesting) wats to discover.

REFUELING STOP Stop in for a snack at the **3. Majestic House** in the Majestic Hotel, deliciously cheap dim sum at the Maria Restaurant, or funky Thai at Methavalai Sorn Daeng, opposite the Democracy Monument. All can be found on Ratchadamnoen Road.

Walk west (left) as you exit the wat on:

4. **Ratchadamnoen Road,** the Champs-Elysées of Bangkok (it really was patterned after Paris' most famous boulevard!). The buildings along this long stretch of road, built in the 1920–30s, were the first major integration of contemporary European city planning and architecture in Bangkok, a previously haphazard sprawl of klongs, bridges, and roads; you can be the judge of which system works better.
   Pay a visit to the:

5. **Democracy Monument,** built to honor the establishment of the modern Thai form of parliamentary monarchy (which these days is under some strain). We like this spot for picture taking; if there's a group of visiting school kids check out the shutter-bug scene.
   There's an enormous traffic circle that revolves around the Democracy Monument; navigate this (if you can) and backtrack a bit up Ratchadamnoen Road and turn right on Dinso Road (which quickly becomes Ti Thong Road) to see the:

6. **local shops;** gold vendors, food stalls, bakeries and florists, Buddhist religious supplies, and discount tapes are all on sale here.
   Ease on down Dinso Road/Ti Thong: Your goal is:

7. **Wat Suthat** and the **Golden Swing,** located about three blocks down from Ratchadamnoen Road, at the corner of Bamrung Muang Road.
   Take some time to explore:

8. **Wat Suthat,** built over a 27-year period during the reign of Rama III (1824–51); the complex is a wonderful and typical cacophony of colors, smells, shapes, and textures found in the city's most intriguing temple grounds.

REFUELING STOP Near the Giant Swing and Wat Suthat, is the **9. Kanit Restaurant** where East meets West on your palate and everyone goes home happy. It's located just across the street from the west gate.

Continue several blocks along Ti Thong Road, making a right turn on Ratchabophit Road to:

10. **Wat Ratchabophit.** The road leading down to the wat is another good one for shops, with a noisy school and a legion of uniformed students. The temple is elaborately decorated and nicely maintained: Walk in and explore the inner sanctum. Pay particular attention to the mother-of-pearl inlaid door and the hand-painted tiles in this European-influenced complex (it may remind some of the Marble Wat).
    Continue along Ratchabophit Road until it dead-ends into a klong. Cross over the footbridge, and on your right is a:

11. **venerated pig** (sculpture, that is) occupying a prominent position atop a rock tableau.
    The street opposite this porcine beauty is Saranrom Road; take it to:

12. **Watratpradit** which will be on your left, behind a fairly discreet gate. This certainly isn't a well-known place, but you can be among the wat cognoscenti in saying that you've been there, too: Check it out! It's full of neighborhood life, and kids play wild games of Ping-Pong.
    After demonstrating your paddle proficiency, exit on Saranrom and turn left, continuing for a few blocks; this will cleverly deposit you at the rear of the Grand Palace on Sanam Chai Road. Ah ha, but that is for later; our goal is Wat Po, so turn left on Sanam Chai (we suggest walking on the cooler, garden

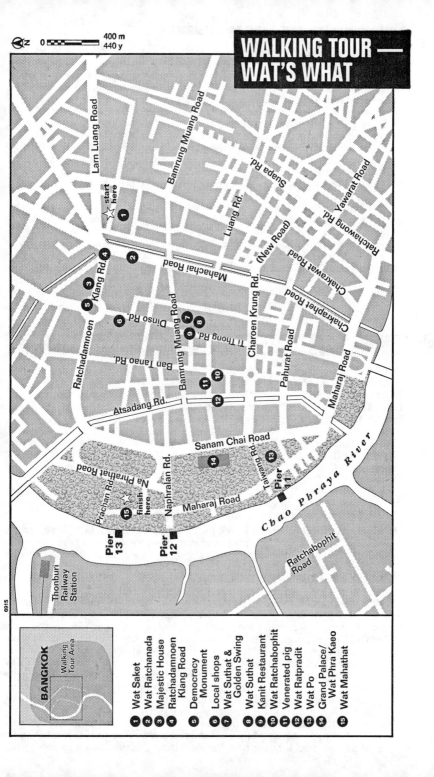

WALKING TOUR —
WAT'S WHAT

z

0 [ ] 400 m
440 y

start here
1

BANGKOK

Walking Tour Area

1 Wat Saket
2 Wat Ratchanada
3 Majestic House
4 Ratchadamnoen Klang Road
5 Democracy Monument
6 Local shops
7 Wat Suthat & Golden Swing
8 Wat Suthat
9 Kanit Restaurant
10 Wat Ratchabophit
11 Venerated pig
12 Wat Ratpradit
13 Wat Po
14 Grand Palace/ Wat Phra Kaeo
15 Wat Mahathat

Lam Luang Road

Bamrung Muang Road

Suphen Rd.

Luang Rd.

Mahachai Road

Charoen Krung Rd. (New Road)

Yawarat Road

Ratchawong Rd.

Chakrawat Road

Chakraphet Road

Klang Rd.

Dinso Rd.

Bamrung Muang Road

Ti Thong Rd.

Ban Tanao Rd.

Ratchadamnoen

Atsadang Rd.

Pahurat Road

Maharaj Road

Sanam Chai Road

Taiwang Rd.

Pier 11

Na Phratlan Rd.

Prachan Rd.

finish here

Maharaj Road

Pier 13

Pier 12

Thonburi Railway Station

Chao Phraya River

Ratchabophit Road

6915

side), continuing for several blocks, make a right on Chetuphon Road, and, voilà, you'll be at:

13. **Wat Po**—this will take about 15 minutes from Watratpradit. We won't bore you with details about Wat Po (you can get those in other sections of this guide), but this is the much ballyhooed stop for those in need of a good herbal massage, Thai style (open daily 8am to 5pm; 90B [$3.60] per half hour). Oh, don't miss the bottoms of the feet of the reclining Buddha (you'll see what we mean when you circumnavigate the wat's most famous attraction).

   After exiting Wat Po, work your way to Maharat Road, running parallel to the Chao Phraya, turn right and, if you have time, enter the gates to the Grand Palace (we suggest allocating a good two hours to the:

14. **Grand Palace/Wat Phra Kaeo complex;** open daily 8:30 to 11:30am and 1 to 3:30pm; admission 125B ($5).

   Continue north along Maharat Road to Bangkok's most thriving street market for amulets and other chotchkas; we particularly like the Tha Chang fruit and vegetable market on the pier of the same name. The final stop is:

15. **Wat Mahathat** located on the Phra That Road, which runs parallel to Maharat. To find it, turn right on Na Phra Lan Road and veer left on Na Phra That; Wat Mahathat will be a little farther on, abutting the vast green known as the Pramane Ground or Sanam Luang (at the right time of year, April or so, you may see some mean kite flying/fighting here). This is one of Bangkok's oldest wats and of vast educational significance, as it contains the country's leading Buddhist teaching center; open daily 9am to 5pm.

WALKING TOUR — THONBURI

Start: Tha Saphan Phut Express Boat Pier.
Finish: Tha Tien Express Pier, opposite Wat Arun, near Wat Po.
Time: Allow approximately 2½ hours, not including an exploration of Wat Arun.
Best Times: Early morning or late afternoon.
Worst Times: Midday.

This tour starts with a walk over the river to a fascinating wat, circles a Portuguese Catholic church, continues through an old local neighborhood into an impressive wat complex, across a klong by small boat, and ends at the soaring Wat Arun, Temple of Dawn.

   From the Tha Saphan Express Boat Pier, near the Pak Klong Talaat Market in Chinatown, walk over the upriver side of the:

1. **Memorial Bridge.** Pause in the middle and look upriver (northwest), where you will see the "high" points of your journey—the soaring points of chedis, the elegant peaks of temple rooftops, and the cross of the Church of Santa Cruz.

   At the far side of the bridge, walk down the steps and continue to the right on the curved drive, past several food shops, across one small lane (Thanon Thesaban Soi 1), and then after another short walk turn right into:

2. **Wat Prayunrawonsawat** (Wat Prayun), a complex of temples and buildings built during the reign of Rama III by a powerful local family. It is totally dominated by the immense (55 foot) chedi, but look first to your right as you enter to find Turtle Mount, a gnarled grotto of small shrines and stupas that rises out of the small pond. As you circle the mount (Buddhists go clockwise) you'll see the hundreds of turtles that give this grotto its name. You can buy bread (10B/40¢) or papaya (20B/80¢) to feed the little beasties, but don't forget to get a stick to put the food on, as the turtles have developed a taste for tourist fingers. Enter the temples reverently, after removing your shoes. Near the temple shop, you can leave a donation toward a new temple roof.

   Continue straight through the temple complex, past the giant chedi on your right, then turn right as you pass through the gate, after passing a small graveyard on your left. Turn left onto the small street (Thanon Thesaban Soi 1), then

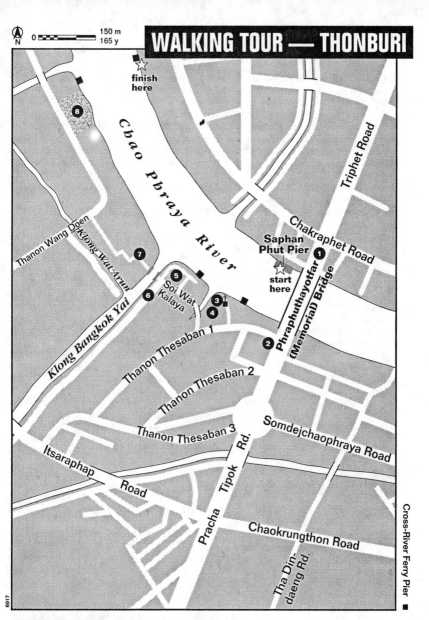

WALKING TOUR — THONBURI

0 ——— 150 m
——— 165 y
N

finish here ☆

Chao Phraya River

Triphet Road

Chakraphet Road

Saphan Phut Pier ❶

Phraphuthayotfar (Memorial) Bridge

start here ☆

Thanon Wang Doen

Klong Wat Arun

❼

❺

Soi Wat Kalaya ❻ ❸ ❹

Klong Bangkok Yai

❷

Thanon Thesaban 1

Thanon Thesaban 2

Thanon Thesaban 3

Somdejchaophraya Road

Pracha Tipok Rd.

Itsaraphap Road

Chaokrungthon Road

Tha Din-daeng Rd.

Cross-River Ferry Pier ■

6917

BANGKOK

Thonburi Area

❶ Memorial Bridge
❷ Wat Prayunrawonsawat
❸ Church of Santa Cruz
❹ Portuguese neighborhood
❺ Wat Kalaya Namit
❻ Klong Bangkok Yai
❼ Buddhist compound
❽ Wat Arun

cross the street and turn right into a small walkway past the parking lot and walk toward:

3. **Church of Santa Cruz,** also known as the Temple of Chinese Monk's Quarters, for reasons unknown. The original church was established on this site by the Portuguese community during the reign of King Taksin (1767–82) and was named after a crosslike piece of wood that washed ashore at the site. The first Portuguese came to Thailand in the 16th century as part of their exploration effort in Southeast Asia. Eventually, a minor colony developed here, though there is little Portuguese presence today. The present church was built in the early 20th century with an interior incorporating both Western and Chinese elements. Unfortunately, the doors are only open for daily masses (only delivered in Thai). Sunday masses are held at 6am, 8:30am, and 5pm; other days at 6am and 7pm (tel. 465-0930 or 466-7009.)

Explore the labyrinth of walks through the:

4. **Portuguese neighborhood** adjacent to the church and admire the fine wooden houses there. Please respect the privacy of the residents, who are not accustomed to tourists in their neighborhoods. Most of the paths here end at a small klong, but there is a route that will lead back to a small street from which you can continue the tour. Kudos to those who find it, but most will want to retrace their steps to the church and then to Thanon Thesaban Soi 1, where you turn right onto that street and right again on the first street, Soi Wat Kalaya, and continue until you come to:

5. **Wat Kalaya Namit.** This is a complex of decaying buildings, the largest of which contains a huge (90 foot) seated Buddha in the subduing Mara pose. The statue is sometimes lit only by a feeble fluorescent light, but wait for your eyes to adjust and you'll find it very impressive and moving. You can purchase candles for the altar from the desk on the right. As always, remove your shoes and show proper reverence for the worshipers. Beggars outside the door will approach you as you enter and exit.

Walk to the river and inspect the rice barges that are home to the people who work them. For a short detour, turn right on the walkway, and you'll come to another interesting neighborhood and a cross-river ferry dock. To continue the tour, turn left at the river and walk until it turns through a series of homes and shops that specialize in recycling cooking-oil cans. Next to these shops runs:

6. **Klong Bangkok Yai,** where you'll soon come to a small dock where you can hail a small long-tail boat to cross the klong. The fare should be 2B but you'll be charged 5B (20¢). (You can also reach the dock by returning to the street from Wat Kalaya Namit and walking until it dead-ends at the klong.)

After crossing the klong, you'll find a:

7. **Buddhist compound.** Turn left before the temples and walk past the school buildings up to the main road. Novice monks may try to practice English with you as you pass their quarters. Turn right past the school, then left at a white wall (behind which sits Vichai Prasit Fortress), then right again at the Klong Wat Arun. Walk until this small lane joins the larger street, Thanon Wang Doen, and follow it as it curves to the right and leads to the walls of:

8. **Wat Arun** with its recognizable mosaicked chedi. Turn right into the Wat Arun complex and make your way past monk's quarters to the river, for refreshments, and the main entrance to the wat.

The cross-river ferry dock is found on the upriver side of Wat Arun, where you can connect to the Tha Thien Express Boat stop. Cross over and return to your hotel, or walk from Tha Thien Pier inland to Wat Po and the Grand Palace. If you're going straight to the Grand Palace, take an upriver boat to Tha Chang Pier, one stop away.

ORGANIZED TOURS

There are numerous travel agencies offering local tours. Two of the largest are **Sea Tours** (tel. 251-4862) and **World Travel Service** (tel. 233-5900), both have branch offices in nearly every international hotel and can arrange custom tours as well as offering the standard packages.

Typical tours and rates include: Temples Tour, 550B ($22); Royal Grand Palace and Emerald Buddha Temple Tour, 600B ($24); Floating Market Tour, 475B ($19); Boat and Barge Cruise, 650B ($26); Jim Thompson House and Suan Pakkard Palace, 600B ($24); River Kwai Tour, 950B ($38); and the Oriental Queen Ayutthaya Tour, 1,300B ($52); Rose Garden, Thai Village and Show, 475B ($19); Damnoen Saduak Floating Market and Rose Garden, 1,000B ($40). Some of these tours have a two-person minimum. Children under 12 pay half price on most tours.

See "Bangkok Waterways," above, for information on boat tours.

Two of our favorite aspects of Thai culture—Bangkok's waterways and Thai cuisine—are combined in this imaginative tour organized on request by **Asian Overland Adventures/The Thai House,** a local travel company. Participants take a 1-hour cruise by long-tail boat deep into Bangkok's back klongs, then arrive at a traditional Thai teak house where ingredients have been assembled for a basic cooking class. After a day of studying, watching, chopping, and sampling class efforts, you're transported by boat 22km (13 miles) back to the city. The fee in 1993 was 1,850B ($74), with a two-person minimum. Contact the Thai House reservation office (tel. 280-0740; fax 662/280-0741) for information on week-long cooking classes and homestay programs.

2. SPORTS & RECREATION

SPECTATOR SPORTS

COCK, BEETLE & FISH FIGHTING These are the spectator sports of Thailand's gamblers, rarely viewed by tourists. Besides battling cocks, Siamese fighting fish and large-horned beetles are the dueling pugs in these bouts. At some markets, you can buy the animals. Also, children train crickets for fighting and arrange bets. Check the marketplaces, especially the Chatuchak Weekend Market, for some of these illicit goings-on.

HORSE RACING Few other cities in the world offer easier access to horse racing. There are two elegant tracks in the heart of town, with racing starting each Sunday at 12:10pm on an alternating schedule. The private Royal Bangkok Sports Club ocupies a prime spot on Henri Dunant Road, opposite Chulalongkorn Univeristy, north of Rama IV Road (tel. 251-0181). The Royal Turf Club is located just south of Chitralada Royal Palace on Phitsanulok Road. At our visit admission to each was 125B ($5) and betting began at 50B ($2) on a win-place basis only.

KITE FIGHTING A favorite Bangkok sport is kite fighting, a team event with sponsors and prizes. The sport is seasonal, extending from February through April, and is held in the city's main parks. Even if you aren't part of a team, you can buy a colorful *chula* "male" or *pukpao* "female" kite and just send it flying into the sky. The two major sites are Sanam Luang (Pramane Grounds) just north of Wat Phra Kaeo, and Lumpini Park, at Rama IV and Rajdamri roads.

T'AI CHI Though t'ai chi is actually Chinese, this stretching and exercise regimen is practiced in Thailand by Chinese and Thai alike. You'll have to get up early in the morning to watch (or participate). Lumpini Park, at the intersection of Rama IV and Wireless roads, is a center of t'ai chi.

THAI BOXING We are big fans of Thai boxing and heartily recommend it to either boxing fans or travelers with an interest in genuine Thai culture. It's a combination of karate and Western boxing, in which boxers (who wear Western-style gloves) are allowed to kick their opponents as well, even in the head.

There are two major stadia for boxing: Lumpini Stadium, on Rama IV, east of the park of the same name (tel. 280-4550 or 252-8765), and Rajdamnern Stadium, on Ratchadamnoen Nok Road (tel. 281-4205 or 281-0879), near the TAT office.

Admission ranges form 175B ($7) to 1,200B ($48). Bouts begin at 5pm at Rajdamnern and 6pm at Lumpini and go well into the evening. There are fights at one or the other every night of the week. Call the TAT office (tel. 280-1305) or the stadium for the current schedule.

RECREATION

GOLF   Golfing in Thailand has rapidly come of age. Japanese and Thai investors have brought in world-class designers to build stunning new courses, many of them a short drive from the heart of Bangkok. Greens fees range form 1,000B ($40) on weekdays to 2,500B ($100) on weekends. Clubs can be rented from 400B ($16). The sport is wildly popular, so reservations should be made well in advance. Some courses require a deposit in advance of the play date. Ask your hotel concierge to help arrange your game.

Navatanee Golf Course, site of the 1975 World Cup, is a top-rated course designed by famous designer Robert Trent Jones. It is in the eastern suburb of Bangkapi, at 22 Mu 1, Sukhaphibarn 2 Road (tel. 376-1031 or 376-1034). Rose Garden Gold Course is close to the Rose Garden cultural center, so the family can enjoy that experience while others tee off. It is located on the way to Nakhon Pathom, 45 minutes southwest of town (tel. 253-0295). Krung Thep Kritha, also known as Huamak Golf Course, is a challenging course, located about a half-hour east of Bangkok, at 516 Krung Thep Kritha Rd., Hua Mak, Bangkapi (tel. 374-0491).

TENNIS   While several of the international hotels have their own tennis courts, others can enjoy the game at two convenient tennis centers. Central Tennis Club, Soi Attakarnprasit, off South Sathorn Road (tel. 286-7202 or 391-8824), charges 50B ($2) per hour from 7am to 6pm; 90B ($3.60) 6 to 10pm. Sawadii Soi Sawadii, Sukhumvit Road between Sois 29 and 31 (tel. 258-4502), charges 60B ($2.40) from 7am to 6pm, 100B ($4) 6 to 11pm.

3. SAVVY SHOPPING

It may not have Hong Kong's or Singapore's reputation for shopping, but Bangkok will dazzle you with markets ranging from primitive to ultrachic. Even the most world-weary shopper will find unusual, high-quality goods at extremely reasonable prices.

THE SHOPPING SCENE

The TAT publishes the *Thailand Shopping Guide*, which offers sound advice on what to purchase and which markets to visit. A commission reviews a vast number of shops in Bangkok and only recognizes those that operate on a high standard with fair trading practices. If you do encounter problems with merchants, you can contact the Tourist Police (tel. 221-6206).

Great Shopping Areas & Markets   There are many shopping areas in Bangkok: plan your itinerary with a map (we recommend Nancy Chanler's *The Market Map and Much More*). One of the main issues in planning your shopping routes is traffic. Try to concentrate in one area, say Sukhumvit Road, and spend your day exploring those streets, leaving another area for another day.

Most major hotels have shopping arcades, in many cases with respectable, quality shops, though their prices are often much higher than those in less upscale neighborhoods. The best arcades, in our opinion, are those at the Oriental (don't miss the diminutive stall with the model Thai and Chinese ships; one of our favorites!) and Regent hotels. Similarly priced quality goods are at the high-end malls, particularly at River City, next to the Royal Orchid Sheraton. The World Trade Center, Sogo, Charn Issara Tower, Peninsula Plaza, and Central have displaced Siam Square and the nearby Mah Boon Krong Center as the city's leading malls; all of these are centrally located in Bangkok's shopping district.

Specific streets or areas are also known for excellent shopping. Among these are the **Chinatown streets,** off and on Sampeng Lane, where one finds the so-called Thieves Market, the Pahurat cloth market, and a million and one notions stands; the compact **Bangrak Market,** behind the Shangri-La Hotel; **Sukhumvit Road** with its upscale antiques and handicrafts shops as well as bookstores; **Silom and Surawong roads,** between the Oriental and Lumpini Park; **Thewet Market,** the wholesale flower outlet off Samsen Road; and the huge weekend market at **Chatuchak Park.**

It used to be that Charoen Krung (New Road) and the smaller outlet roads near the Oriental were lined with antique shops (see "Shopping A to Z," below). There are still a few in this congested area, although some of the finest shops have moved to the notable **River City shopping mall,** creating Bangkok's greatest concentration of high-end antiques galleries. In this great sampling of Thai antiques, you're certain to find something to your taste; however, the River City shops are, like the Monogram stores, among the most expensive in the city.

Prices We've quoted prices in U.S. dollars, as is the custom in many, if not most, upmarket shops. Remember that nearly all shops will negotiate, so don't be shy. If they don't want to haggle, they'll politely inform you that their prices are fixed. Go get 'em!

SHOPPING A TO Z
ANTIQUES

Take note: Certain items, such as Buddha images and antiques, cannot be taken out of Thailand legally, and Thai Customs is extremely vigilant on this point. Also, there are many well-crafted, fake antiques sold at prices equal to the original; if you plan to buy an expensive item, make sure the dealer is reputable and will be willing to take the object back (and return your money) if you discover that it's not the genuine article.

L'ARCADIA, 12/2 Soi Sukhumvit 23. Tel. 259-9595.

This is a little gem of a shop with very good antique furniture (mostly from Myanmar/Burma), crafts, carved teak architectural ornaments, and older folk-art pieces. We particularly admired an early 20th-century Burmese four-poster bed, surely a striking centerpiece for any bedroom, it cost 28,000 ($1,120).

THE FINE ARTS, Sukhothai Hotel, Shop no. 4, 13/3 S. Sathorn Rd. Tel. 287-0222.

An expensive but fine collection of terra-cotta pieces, Buddhist statuary, woven fabrics from the region, and one-of-a-kind objects grace the shelves of this small boutique in the ultrastylish Sukhothai Hotel. One of the shop's distinctive offerings is a collection of folk-art religious posters on cloth from Cambodia (about $250); another is the line of terra-cotta reproductions of Sukhothai era art and architectural elements (beautiful 18-by-24-inch tiles for $880) created by decorators to grace the hotel. Open daily 10am to 6pm.

THE GOLDEN TRIANGLE, Room 301, River City, 23 Yotha Rd. Tel. 237-0077.

This shop is quite unlike anything else in River City, if not in all of Bangkok, and is chiefly known for its excellent quality hill-tribe artifacts. This simply decorated gallery carries antique textiles and hill-tribe clothing and jewelry, reminding us more of the fine shops in Chiang Mai than most outlets in Bangkok. Silver jewelry from 20 to 100 years old, clothing made from authentic hill-tribe textiles, trading beads, and various musical instruments are among the highlights. Although there are many high-priced items, canny shoppers might be tempted by hand-embroidered fabric samples for $45 to $80; cast-brass souvenir bells go for $44 to $86; and large antique bells for $140. These quintessentially northern crafts on diplay are part of a private collection of antiques culled by Ms. Sumiko Chotikavan, the shop's keenly qualified owner. One of the best in Thailand. Open daily 11am to 7pm.

READERS RECOMMEND

Shopping Tip: "*A note of caution about buying goods to be shipped home, based on our experience with buying rattan from Manila Furniture in Sukhumvit Road. We selected items from Manila's 'catalogue'. . . agreed on a price for the furniture and, separately, a price for shipping and insurance. When we got home we received a letter from the shipping company demanding 100 pounds sterling for ocean-freight charges because the furniture had been sent Freight on Board. Looking again at our receipt we saw it had the letters FOB written on it. These letters meant nothing to us at the time we bought the furniture so we had disregarded them—much to our cost. To give Manila Furniture their due, the furniture was made exactly how we wanted it and of good quality, but having paid twice for shipping it was no cheaper than buying it in London.*"—Philip M. Bates, London, U.K.

THE HEIGHT, Suite 354, River City, 23 Yotha Rd. Tel. 237-0077, ext. 354.

Also known as Piak Padungsiriseth (for its owner), the Height is best for its excellent old mutmee silk, pottery, and statuary. Khun Piak also makes intricate miniature boats to order. For good quality, older silk, you can't do much better than this specialty boutique. Open daily 10am to 6:30pm.

MONOGRAM I AND II, in the Oriental Hotel and the Oriental Arcade. Tel. 236-0400.

These are the oldest and, if Elizabeth Taylor and the Reagans are to be believed, once were the finest antiques shops in Bangkok. On our last visit we found some gorgeously carved wooden sculptures and finely embroidered Burmese tapestries (*kalaga*), but the prices are as high as anywhere in Bangkok. Open daily 9am to 8pm.

NEOLD COLLECTION, 149/2-3 Surawong Rd. Tel. 235-8352.

A fine selectioin of new and old objects, including recently made paintings, shell hill-tribe belts ($150), 19th-century Chinese puppets ($650), and a small offering of furniture and finely crafted silver boxes. Only the rarest items may have difficulty leaving the country. Open Monday to Friday 10am to 8:30pm, Saturday 10am to 6pm.

Branch showroom at the Regent Bangkok, 155 Rajdamri Rd. (tel. 250-0737).

THE OLD TIME, River City Mall, 23 Yotha Rd., Suite 404-405. Tel. 237-0077.

The Old Time is one of those places that gets better the longer you browse. Khmer stone sculptures are found mixed with impressive 18th-century furniture. When we last visited our eyes were drawn to several 60- to 70-year-old baskets ($190), exquisite early 20th-century musical instruments ($770), and betel-nut sets over 100 years old ($192). Open daily 10:30am to 7pm.

PENG SENG, 942/1-3 Rama IV Rd., corner of Surawong Rd. Tel. 236-8010.

After encountering so many fakes, it's a wonder to find anything genuine in the world of Thai antiques. We are hardly expert enough to judge, but those in the know assure us that the objects sold at Peng Seng are genuine. Located near Jim Thompson's, Peng Seng's two stories are filled with Thai and Chinese sculptures and pottery. An antique teapot or celadon bowl may cost over $1,500, but then again you could pay $27,000 for a 3-foot-high Khmer stone sculpture. Among the more affordable objects that appealed to us were a series of Burmese carved wooden temple figures, two feet high and $2,700. Peng Seng exports nearly all of the objects for sale, and can usually arrange the necessary papers for antiques. Not to be overlooked is the store's excellent selection of art books for sale. Open Monday to Saturday 9am to 6:30pm.

SHOPPING ALONG SUKHUMVIT ROAD

Soi Ekamai
Soi Charoen Suk
Soi Thong Lor
Soi Akkapat
Soi Klang
Soi Promsri
Soi Prommitr
Soi Prompong
Soi Prompong
To Eastern Bus Terminal
SUKHUMVIT ROAD
Soi Aree
Ratchadaphisek Rd.
To New Phetchaburi Road
Soi Asoke
SUKHUMVIT ROAD
Soi Nana

Asia Books 3 4
Elite Used Books 13
Gifted Hands 11
H.M. Factory Thai Silk 18
Home Made Thai Silk 17

Homespun Creations
Nandakwang 9
Italy Furniture 12
L'Arcadia 7
Manila Furniture 13

Mengrai Kilns 2
Nana Hotel—street vendor stalls near 1
Pastorius Accessory Shop 10
Patches 15

Private Collection 16
Rasi Sayam 6
Shinawatra 8
Thai Celadon House 5

SAOWTHAI IKAT, Room 438-440, The River City Shopping Complex, Yotha Rd. Tel. 237-0077, ext 438.

We like to recommend Saowthai Ikat for those who prize examples of older woven fabrics; this may be the best shop for textiles in all of Bangkok. In particular, they maintain a great selection of Lao and Cambodian "antique" silk. They also have a store in Room 308 at the Thaniya Plaza, 52 Silom Rd. Open daily 10:30am to 7pm.

BOOKS

Bangkok is blessed with a great many bookstores, many of which carry English-language books.

ASIA BOOKS, 2nd floor, Peninsula Plaza, Rajdamri Rd. Tel. 253-9786.

With branches at 221 Sukhumvit Rd. (tel. 252-7277), in the Landmark Plaza (tel. 252-5456) and in the Thaniya Plaza (tel. 231-2106), Asia Books is one of Bangkok's best for phrase books, cultural guides, and publications about Asia. Open daily 10am to 8pm.

ELITE USED BOOKS, 593/5 Sukhumvit Rd., near Soi 331. Tel. 258-0221.

They advertise that they carry over 39,000 volumes and we're not going to argue. This used bookstore stocks English, French, Japanese, and German titles, but the majority are in our mother tongue. They take good used books in for trade or will buy your books at a very low rate. Open daily 9am to 9pm.

BRONZE & NICKEL

Most of the major handicrafts, silk, or jewelry shops also carry bronze (or bronze and nickel alloy) flatware. We love the handmade quality and weight of these Thai-designed sets, but be warned that our set has tarnished after repeated cleaning in the dishwasher. Decorative pieces can be coated with silicon, but it renders it unusable for dining. We purchased a complete set for 12 at Uthai's Gems, including every possible implement, for $150.

THAI HOME INDUSTRIES, 35 Oriental Lane, near Oriental Plaza. Tel. 234-1736.

This is one of the better outlets for Thai souvenirs and especially bronzeware (ignore the surly sales staff). There are many different sets available at the Thai Home Industries Shop for about $150 to $200. Be aware that such sets weigh up to 50 pounds and will have to be shipped home; expect to pay an additional $65 for postage.

SIAM BRONZE FACTORY, 1250 New Rd. Tel. 234-9436.

This is one of Bangkok's larger outlets for complete bronzeware table settings. Be sure to inquire whether they'll pack and ship merchandise before buying as it may add up to $75, depending on the style and number of place settings you buy.

CERAMICS

We aren't big fans of bencharong, especially the brightly colored variety, but we do enjoy celadon with the best of them and the Thai designs and quality has improved steadily over the years.

PRASART COLLECTION, Peninsula Plaza, 2nd floor, 153 Rajdamri Rd. Tel. 253-9772.

This boutique features copies of antique items from the collection at their museum. We're generally not wild about bencharong porcelain, but even we liked Prasart's blue and white and other muted color combinations. Open daily Monday to Saturday noon to 6:30pm.

THAI CELADON HOUSE, 8/6-8 Ratchadaphisek Rd., Sukhumvit Rd., off Soi Asoke (16). Tel. 254-6033.
The Thai Celadon House displays and sells some of the most attractive celadon ceramics in the city. The factory is in Chiang Mai; here is a showroom where you can order and a seconds shop with slightly imperfect goods. Open Monday to Saturday 8:30am to 5:30pm.

CLOTHING

Bangkok is internationally known for its designer look-alike fashions, clothing with famous labels that is "knocked off" at substantially lower prices than the original. Less known are the small, independent designers with their own Thai fashions that look good in Asia and back home. We found the quality of construction to vary from shoddy to outstanding, so give a careful once over to seams and material. If you're in the market for high fashion at medium to top-end prices, we suggest heading straight to the Charn Issara Tower for everything from knockoff Matsuda ($35 for a dress shirt) to exquisite bespoke tailoring.
If you only want to buy lengths of silk or cotton, see the "Silk & Cotton" section, later in this chapter.

ART'S TAILOR, 62/15-16 Thaniya, Silom Rd. Tel. 236-7966.
This well-regarded tailor shop is primarily for men and carries a full line of wool and cotton fabrics for suits, pants, and shirts. It typically takes about three weeks for a suit to be altered. Open Monday to Saturday 8:30am to 5pm.

CHOISY, 9/25 Surawong Rd. Tel. 233-7794.
This small French-owned and -operated boutique, featuring ready-to-wear and custom clothing, is popular within the expat/diplomatic community; fashions tend to appeal to an older, more conservative clientele. We appreciate Choisy's selections of silk clothing, which is made with thinner, less stiff fabrics than found in most Bangkok shops. Off-the-rack fashions include a simple white silk blouse for $50; a midcalf length skirt for $110; and miniskirts for $80. There is a thriving tailoring business upstairs with well-made custom clothing. Choisy is located next door to Jim Thompson. Open Monday to Saturday 10am to 6:30pm.

JIMMY'S FASHIONS, New Trocadere Hotel Arcade, 343 Surawong Rd. Tel. 235-8786.
Unlike most of the top tailors in Bangkok, Jimmy's works with both men and women and enjoys a good reputation within the expatriate community. Open Monday to Saturday 10am to 8pm.

NORIKO, 566 Ploenchit Rd. Tel. 251-7712.
This ready-to-wear clothing boutique carries some of the best tailored fashions in Bangkok. Our enthusiasm for the clothing not only extends to its contemporary design but also to its materials: the most attractive mutmee silk and ikat cotton we found in Bangkok. Noriko offers a full line of formal and casual skirts (from $180 to $225), jackets (about $200), and tops ($120 and up), all of high quality and many in smallers sizes only. Open Monday to Saturday 9am to 6pm, Sunday 10am to 6pm.
There is also a branch at 919/1 Sukhumvit Rd. (tel. 258-7963).

PERRY'S THAI SILK CO., LTD., 60/6-7 Silom Rd. Tel. 235-3241.
This is a popular ready-to-wear as well as custom clothing boutique. Most outfits take a minimum of two to three days and Perry's maintains a large inventory of both English and Italian fabrics. In addition to the tailoring operation, Perry's carries a line of silk products including attractive appliqué pillows for about $12. Open Monday to Saturday 8:30am to 7pm.

VIPAVEE, 2nd Floor, Charn Issara Tower, 942/86 Rama IV Rd. Tel. 237-6154.
This off-the-rack and custom clothing boutique (formerly Rasee) represents the height of quality and fashion in this center of sartorial style. Viparee makes exquisite

suits and dresses of fine fabric with a typical suit selling for $400 to $600. Open daily 10am to 6pm.

RIVER MARK, Suite 238 or 246, River City, 23 Yotha Rd. Tel. 237-0077, ext. 238.

This and the Mark Collection (in suite 246) are the best outlets in Bangkok for made-to-order linen clothing. It will typically take two to three days to custom-make a dress or suit, but you can expect good quality tailoring and fine materials. River Mark also carries a large selection of cotton, silk, and wool, but head here for their large linen inventory. Open Monday to Saturday 10:30am to 8pm. There is another branch at 1287-9 New Rd., opposite Oriental Hotel (tel. 234-4453).

DEPARTMENT STORES & SHOPPING PLAZAS

Bangkok supports a mushrooming number of department store chains. The **Central** is the largest; its most accessible branches are on lower Silom Road, Ploenchit Road near the Le Méridien Président, and off the highway near the airport, next to the Hyatt. Similar to the Central chain is **Robinson's** (the most convenient branch is at the intersection of Rama IV and Silom), which, like Central, is best for buying staples such as socks, underwear, and other supplies.

We always enjoy browsing in the perpetually crowded **Thai Tokyu department store** in the Mah Boon Krong Center (where there is also the city's best food court); this is better for the spectacle of "how Bangkok shops" than for the merchandise. The Tokyo based **Sogo Shopping Center,** just up the road from the Regent, is Bangkok's newest and most upscale emporium; it features merchandise from both European and Asian fashion houses.

Among the city's many shopping arcades, malls, and plazas, our preference is for the **Thaniya Plaza** (Soi 4, Silom Road), the wonderful shops at the Charn Issara Tower, the Regent Hotel shopping arcade, the nearby Peninsula Plaza arcade, the River City antiques mall, and the venerable Oriental Hotel arcade.

DOLLS

BANGKOK DOLLS, 85 Soi Rajatapan (Soi Mohleng), Makkasan. Tel. 245-3008.

From the *New York Times* we found this far out of the way "factory" where intricately detailed figures are crafted. Traditional Thai dancers, hill-tribe figures, and playful images are the main products made and sold. Prices range from $15 to $100. It's best to call ahead, both to make sure that they're open and also for directions; plan on 45 to 60 minutes from the center of Bangkok. Shop open Monday to Saturday 10am to 5pm; factory open Monday to Saturday 8am to 5pm.

FURNITURE

It may not be practical for a few small pieces, but some sophisticated shoppers buy rooms full of well-crafted antique and newly made furniture and have them shipped back home. Teak and other hardwoods as well as wicker or rattan are the most popular material. Also stroll down Sukhumvit between Sois 43-47 for many other shops.

ITALY FURNITURE, 527-529 Sukhumvit Rd., between Sois 29 and 31. Tel. 258-4643.

This design and manufacturing outlet of quality wicker and rattan furniture sells and ships to all parts of the world. A typical rattan armchair set runs $480 to $1,120, while a side table costs $64, both without shipping. To ship a cubic meter (about two chairs and a table), expect to pay around $120. Open Monday to Saturday 10am to 7pm.

MANILA FURNITURE, 521 Sukhumvit Rd., near Soi 29. Tel. 258-2608.

Very similar and just down the street from Italy Furniture, Manila also sells a complete line of rattan. We priced a complete living room set including armchairs, table, and sofa for about $720, however you'll have to add almost twice that for packing and shipping. Like Italy, you can either pick styles from the floor or from their photo book. It typically takes about three weeks to complete an order and a minimum of one month (we say count on three or four months) to ship. Open Monday to Saturday 9am to 6:30pm.

GIFTS/SOUVENIRS

We couldn't fail to mention street vendors. They're hardly the most reliable purveyors of goods, but you can almost always count on them for delightful souvenirs—and if you're a good bargainer, you'll get the lowest price in Bangkok. The best stalls are along Silom Road, near the Silom Village, near the Nana Hotel off Sukhumvit, Soi 4, and in Chinatown. For many, the bustling Night Market in Patpong represents the best shopping for "counterfeit" goods in the city. Although we don't condone the purchase of counterfeit brand goods, a huge number of travelers head here to buy pirated audiotapes; most tapes are sold for about 50¢ to $1. If you buy videotapes (also in large supply), make sure that the video standard works with your machine; in most cases, you want NTSC (American standard VHS), not PAL, tapes.

HANDICRAFTS

If you shop carefully, you'll find that Bangkok has examples of Thailand's best crafts, equal to anything found in the far-flung regions of the country and at prices that are comparable to such places as Surin, Chiang Mai, and Chiang Rai.

CHITRALADA SHOP, Chitralada Palace. Tel. 281-1111.
The royal family, in their ongoing effort to encourage production of Thai handicrafts, sponsors several stores in Bangkok under the name of the Chitralada Support Foundation. The Chitralada Shop, as well as the Hill Tribe Foundation at the Srapatum Palace, sells standard-quality Thai and hill-tribe crafts at reasonable prices. Open Monday to Friday 9am to 4:30pm. There is also a branch in the Oriental Plaza.

GIFTED HANDS, 172/18 Sukhumvit Soi 23. Tel. 258-4010.
It's difficult to find but well worth the search. Gifted Hands is the shop of Cholada Hoover, a former art teacher who wanted to find a way to help her village. What she has done is to take traditional village silver jewelry design and her own glass beads and incorporated them with a more modern aesthetic. Ninety-eight percent pure silver-bead and silver-accented, polished coconut earrings begin at a very reasonable $8, while coconut-and-silver pins in animal shapes run $5 to $10. Gifted Hands also carries the nicest nielloware jewelry (with semiprecious stones) that we've found. You'll find Gifted Hands on the street with Jaspal's Residence II and on the same soi as Shinawatra; approaching from the south, it's the third 172 block on the right. As of our visit, they took cash only. Gifted Hands publishes a catalog and will ship. Open daily 8am to 6pm.

HOMESPUN CREATIONS NANDAKWANG, 108/3 Sukhumvit 23 Prasanmitr. Tel. 258-1962.
This is the place for textured cotton housewares and "soft goods." Homespun features beautifully hand-spun and woven cotton napkins and place mats in a

---

READERS RECOMMEND

Chatuchak Weekend Market. *"As I'm sure you know, it's a long (45-minute) taxi ride, but well worth it as the bargains were irresistible and prices a fraction of the already-low downtown prices. We shipped most of the stuff back by Federal Express which was expensive, but we were advised against using the local post office. Regardless of whether you make any purchases, I'd recommend the trip on Saturday or Sunday as a unique Bangkok experience."*
—Jeff Sharlach, New York, NY.

gorgeous array of colors. Napkin prices begin at a bargain 70¢, place mats start at $1.50, while bedspreads run about $58 for a double. Open Monday to Saturday 9am to 6pm; Sunday 10am to 5pm.

LOTUS, Parichart Court, The Bangkok Regent Hotel, 155-157 Rajdamri Rd. Tel. 250-0732.

This shop, perhaps more than any other in Bangkok, reflects the best of both Asian and European design sensibilities. With its branches at Bangkok's Sukhothai and the Amanpuri in Phuket, Lotus is the exclusive domain of upscale tourists from America, Europe, and Asia who are attracted to the new and old objects d'art collected by its European owners from Thailand, Burma, Indonesia, Tibet, and India. The exquisite, one-of-a-kind jewels and decorative objects are among the most attractive we've found anywhere in the country. Here one finds stingray-skin desk acessories, Indian ruby-encrusted animal sculpture, luscious cashmere shawls and silk scarves, silver boxes made with supreme craftsmanship, and textiles worthy of a museum. Prices are extremely high. Open Monday to Friday 10:30am to 8pm.

NARAYANA PHAND, 127 Rajdamri Rd., Pratumwan north of Gaysorn. Tel. 252-4670.

Our ace shopper, Victoria, suggests that this enormous handicraft emporium, partially funded by the government, is the ideal spot to work down that long list of souvenirs you need to buy before returning home. Not only is the breadth of goods impressive, but the quality/price relationship is a very acceptable level. Items that impressed us are: a variety of jewelry, betel-nut boxes ($39 to $54), bencharong pottery, wicker ware, a glittering, peridot pendant ($44), and a lacquer box ($80). Open daily 10am to 8pm.

PATCHES, 591/16 Sukhumvit Soi 33/1. Tel. 258-5057.

We like the idea of Patches more than the goods, which tend to be too traditionally early American in design and materials for our taste. Patches is the retail outlet for a women's self-help project started in the slums of Klongtoey by Catholic missionaries. Custom-made quilts of a decidedly non-Asian design (they look like what you might find in a rural American church sale!) are crafted by women from low-income families. There are a few Hmong-style products, but the main line of quilts, pillows, and table linens are of the early American variety. It generally takes about six weeks to finish a quilt, and they export to the United States. Prices are extremely reasonable. Open Monday to Saturday 8:30am to 5:30pm.

RASI SAYAM, 32 Sukhumvit Rd., Soi 23. Tel. 258-4195.

⭐ Founded by a North American, Jonathan Hayssen, Rasi Sayam is our favorite contemporary Thai handicrafts shop in Bangkok. Mr. Hayssen has located some of the country's best craftspeople and encouraged them to continue their manufacture of decorative and folk art by giving them an outlet for their work. To describe the crafts available for sale is to make an inventory of Thailand's best contemporarily produced work. Baskets, loom parts, bows, ceramics, lacquer ware, bells, wood carvings, textiles, and a myriad of other one-of-a-kind pieces are on display in the attractively designed shops. If you're in a rush and can only get to a couple of shops, keep this one at the top of your list. Rasi Sayam is totally reliable, and will ship by UPS air. Open Monday to Saturday 9am to 5:30pm.

JEWELRY

Again, the best advice is beware of touts! On your own, compare both quality and price at several stores before buying. We were told repeatedly by knowledgeable locals that nearly all jewelers who display their work in the best hotel shopping arcades produce fine-quality work at fair prices. Nearly all jewelry shops, even the most exclusive, negotiate, so be prepared to ask for a discount on the quoted price. We took the advice of William Warren, the *New York Times* correspondent, and read John Hoskin's *Buyer's Guide to Thai Gems* (Asia Books, 1988), an informative and entertaining book that even sophisticated shoppers will enjoy; it won't make you an instant expert, but you'll certainly have a better idea of what's on display in the city's reputable shops.

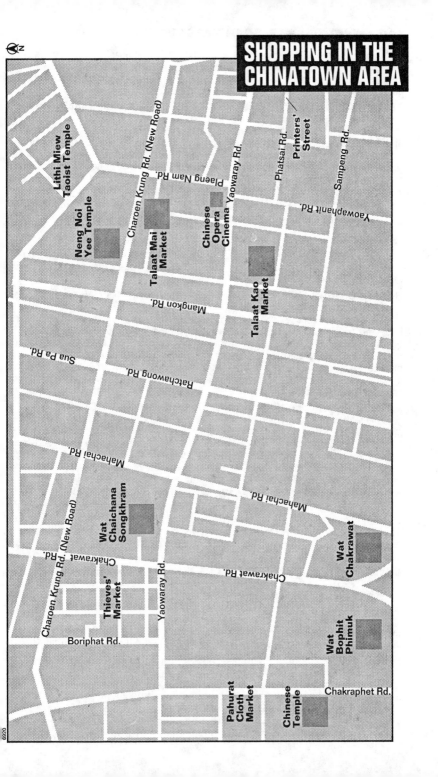

SHOPPING IN THE CHINATOWN AREA

N

Lithi Miew Taoist Temple

Neng Noi Yee Temple

Charoen Krung Rd. (New Road)

Plaeng Nam Rd.

Talaat Mai Market

Chinese Opera Cinema

Yaowaray Rd.

Phatsai Rd.

Printers' Street

Sampeng Rd.

Yaowaphanit Rd.

Mangkon Rd.

Talaat Kao Market

Sua Pa Rd.

Ratchawong Rd.

Mahachai Rd.

Mahachai Rd.

Charoen Krung Rd. (New Road)

Wat Chaichana Songkhram

Chakrawat Rd.

Wat Chakrawat

Thieves' Market

Yaowaray Rd.

Chakrawat Rd.

Wat Bophit Phimuk

Boriphat Rd.

Pahurat Cloth Market

Chinese Temple

Chakraphet Rd.

6920

If you're in town to explore the wholesale market, similar to New York's West 47th Street, head to Mahesak Road, just off Silom. Here you'll find Thai, Chinese, Iranian, Israeli, and Indian dealers, most of whom are engaged in the import and export of colored cut stones.

ASIAN INSTITUTE OF GEMOLOGICAL SCIENCES, 484 Ratchadaphisek Rd. Tel. 513-2112.

A number of quality gem and jewelry dealers offer a certificate of identification prepared by the AIGS, a professional agency that specializes in categorizing cut stones. A typical analysis takes one to two days and includes information about the cut, color, mineral content, and size of the free (unmounted) stones. If you intend to purchase expensive gems, and have the time, attend their three-hour courses or take advantage of this service. Their new headquarters is in the Rama Jewelry Mart (tel. 513-7044) at 987 on Silom Road near Mahesak Road.

BEE BIJOUR, Peninsula Plaza, 2nd Floor, 153 Rajdamri Rd. Tel. 252-1571.

One of the better manufacturers of fashionable costume jewelry made with semi-precious stones is Bee Bijour. Although their main business is tailored to the export market, this boutique displays lines sold to the local-and-tourist markets as well. Open daily 10am to 7:30pm.

BUALAAD JOAILLIER, 106-107 Peninsula Plaza, 153 Rajdamri Rd. Tel. 253-9760.

We were impressed by the fantastic stones (especially the Thai and Burmese rubies) and jewelry on display at this decidedly upmarket jewelry design house. The quality is superb and, unlike most of the jewelry stores in Bangkok, this one eschews the current trends, preferring to base its designs on traditional motifs. We were mesmerized by an emerald necklace that ran a cool $3,400; there are many lesser-priced goodies for sale, so don't worry about our pie-in-the-sky tastes. Open Monday to Saturday 11am to 6pm.

CABOCHON, Oriental Hotel Arcade, Oriental Ave. Tel. 236-6607.

This well-established reputable boutique displays brilliant sapphire pendants (for approximately $500) and quality ruby rings accented with diamonds for $460. As with the best shops, all of Cabochon's pieces are sold with certificates of authorization by AGIS gemologists with an offer of a refund. There is a new branch in the Dusit Thani Hotel, ground floor, Rama IV Road (tel. 233-4371). Open Monday to Friday 10am to 8pm, Saturday 10am to 6pm.

WORLD JEWELS TRADE CENTER, 987 Silom Rd. Tel. 233-8388.

This "Supermarket of Gems" is run by Mr. Ho, considered the doyen of the Bangkok gem industry, having started the Asian Institute of Gemological Sciences. This is not only a fine place to look at jewelry, but one of the best inventories of cut stones in town. Prices are reasonable. Open Monday to Friday 8:30am to 5pm and some Saturdays.

ROYAL ORCHID COLLECTION, 11 Soi Ruam Rudee, Ploenchit Rd. Tel. 255-2725.

This is a place to purchase inexpensive gifts for those great-aunts and grandmothers back home. Their line of contemporary costume jewelry is popular. However, the specialty is orchids and other exotic flowers that are plated with 24-karat gold and fashioned into simple jewelry. Our favorite items are a gold-plated flower petal necklace for $20 and a pin made of orchids for $16. Open Monday to Saturday 8:30am to 5pm.

TASTE JEWELERS, 292/3 Silom Rd. Tel. 234-7651.

If you love marcasite jewelry, we recommend a visit to Taste Jewelers. They have a wide variety of marcasite jewelry, some plain and others mixed with onyx and carnelian. Open Monday to Saturday 9am to 6pm.

TOK KWANG, 224/6 Silom Rd. Tel. 233-0658.

As soon as you enter you'll know you've come to a major, major jewelry store with quality and price to match. Tok Kwang has been in business since 1946 and has built a solid reputation for the best pearls in town. Most of their pearls come from Japan, but an increasing number are imported from Burma and Autstralia. A string of first-rate medium-size pearls ranges from $1,000 to $2,500. Tok Kwang also sells fine watches, diamonds, and gems. There are many more exotic varieties for prices that can only be described as astronomical. There is a second branch at the Regent Bangkok, 155 Rajdamri Rd. (tel. 250-0735). Open daily 10:30am to 7pm.

UTHAI'S GEMS, 28/7 Soi Ruam Rudee, Phoenchit Rd. Tel. 253-8582.
One of the most reliable jewelers in Bangkok is Uthai Daengrasmisopon. You'll be amazed at the number of Americans who stream in and out of his store and the number of repeat shoppers who make Uthai's their first stop on the Bangkok buying trail. Many come to buy from Uthai's enormous inventory of extremely well-priced, conservatively styled jewelry, but not a small number visit Uthai for custom work or repairs—generallly allow two to three days for simple items, longer for more complex work. We found lovely 1-karat sapphire kings in a 14-karat-gold setting for about $225; a comparable ruby ring runs about $800. Uthai sells princess rings for $130. We are impressed with the quality and value of Uthai's gold chains, handcrafted in 22-karat gold. Uthai also runs a mail-order business and has a good collection of bronzeware. Open daily 9:30am to 6pm.

YVES JOAILLIER, Charn Issara Tower, 3rd Floor, 942/83 Rama IV Rd. Tel. 233-3292.
⭐ We are unabashed fans of this boutique, arguably the most elegant in Bangkok for its exquisitely conceived designs and exceptional quality. Perhaps it's his French background or his eight years in Turkey, but for us, Yves Bernardeau's best designs incorporate the best of contemporary European design with ancient Mediterranean motifs. Accordingly the majority of his clients are from America and Europe, with the local Thai and expat community just beginning to accept his unique—for Bangkok—style. Our favorite pieces are banded gold, hammered in a matte finish and featuring sapphires or rubies. Yves is brilliant at made-to-order jewelry; expect three days for a ring, one to two weeks for a neckace. As for prices, we found his work competitive with the local market and an absolute bargain in contrast to American boutiques. Ruby earrings run about $1,500 while his Bali-imported goods, in silver, are considerably less (he also chooses the wonderful Indian and Balinese jewelry at Jim Thompson). All locally made jewelry with gems comes with AIGS certificates. If you're serious about buying jewelry in Bangkok, plan to stop here early. Open 10am to 7pm.

LEATHER GOODS, SHOES & BOOTS

Many people leave Bangkok wearing shoes and cowboy boots made from ostrich, elephant, snake, alligator, or other exotic leathers. Before planning to purchase any goods made from these skins, consult the U.S. Customs office for prohibited goods lest they be confiscated upon your return. There are many shops along New Road near the Oriental and in and around Patpong that also carry clothing (inspect those seams, clasps, and zippers), wallets (for about $14), and purses. Prices for boots range from $75 to $300.

CHAO PHRAYA BOOTERY, 116/3 Silom Rd. Tel. 234-1226.
This is another excellent outlet for shoes, boots, and a full range of leather accessories. In addition to having a large inventory, they do efficient custom work (cowboy boots only); expect to have a pair made within four to five days for approximately $170, depending on the leather. One of the better bargains was a leather knapsack for $168. Open daily 10am to 9pm.

PATOU, Indra Shopping Center, 95/250 Rajdamri Rd. Tel. 251-3971.
Many shoe stores, such as Patou, will custom-make footwear. They also sell locally produced Charles Jourdan and other high-fashion shoes.

MARKETS

PATPONG NIGHT MARKET, Patpong Soi 1.

Although Patpong has been famous for its bars, neon lights, girls, sex shows, girls, massage parlors, and girls since the Vietnam War, only in the last 10 years has it become a bona fide tourist attraction. Just as the film *Deep Throat* made it acceptable for "nice" people to go to porno movies, so has Patpong's Asian mystique and anything-goes sexuality become a standard stop on the "Bangkok By Night" bus tours. Then its proprietors (the land under Patpong's many lanes is privately owned) realized what profits could be made if Patpong became an attraction for the whole family! Thus, its bustling Night Market, the direct result of closing thoses lanes to traffic, began renting out tables to vendors of everything faux: Every sound and picture pirated, every leather good stampled with someone's initials, every Hard Rock Café T-shirt, and every handicraft or cotton clothing available to sell, sell, sell . . . Not cheap, not original, but lively. Open daily after sundown; between Silom and Suriwong roads.

WEEKEND MARKET, Chatuchak Park.

If you're in Bangkok on a weekend, don't miss the Weekend Market, off the Airport Highway (up to an hour away in traffic), which covers a vast area with rows of stalls selling everything—fresh crabs and seafood, dried seafood, chilis piled high in great baskets and other vegetables, blue vases and other pottery, live fish that are scooped from tanks, live chicks, orchids, clothers, foods of all sorts, and a host of strange exotic items you won't know what to call. It's a great way to introduce yourself to the exotic sights, flavors, and colors of Thai life. On our last trip, the fastest moving fashion item for the tourist trade was a patchwork mutmee silk baseball jacket; we bought one for about $20 and saw them on the streets in New York selling for over $80. Open Saturday and Sunday.

PAK KLONG TALAAT, along the Chao Phraya on Luk Luang.

Pak Klong Talaat (also called the Talaat Taywait) is home to Bangkok's cut-flower market. Huge bushels of cut flowers and vegetables arrive nightly; buyers from around the city shop in the very early morning hours. If you're wandering around the city after midnight looking for an offbeat attraction, stop by and choose from baskets of orchids, lotus, jasmine, marigolds, and many more. You'll pay about $2 for a lovely bunch of orchids. You can also watch the flower vendors threading leis and assembling the huge, colorful, intricately patterned funeral wreaths. Open 24 hours. The market is located near the Memorial Bridge, on Chakrapatch Road.

SILK & COTTON

Besides those places listed below, there are also very good silk outlets in the international hotel shopping arcades. If you're looking for ready-to-wear or custom clothing, see "Clothing," above.

DESIGN THAI, 304 Silom Rd. Tel. 235-1553.

Design Thai is a deliberate imitation of Jim Thompson, in both style and merchandise (even the building is similar). Like the high-priced original, they stock a wide range of fabrics and accessories including silk slippers ($20), jewelry boxes (from $12 to $18), a good selection of purses, and a fuddy-duddy selection of ready-to-wear clothes. Our favorite item: brightly colored stuffed cotton water buffalo for $8. Open daily 9am to 7pm.

READERS RECOMMEND

Venus Jewelers, Bangkok. "*Venus Jewelers, located down the street from the American Embassy, does a lot of business with the U.S. Military and enjoys an excellent reputation, as evidenced by the huge number of business cards left by Admirals, Generals, and personnel of lower ranks. They have excellent service and a wide range of precious stones and settings.*"
—Melissa Lockman, Duncannon, Pa.

H. M. FACTORY THAI SILK, 45 Promchai, Sukhumvit 39. Tel. 258-8766.

This is a lovely place to visit and a good place to watch mutmee silk in the weaving stage. Silk weavers buy raw material from Isan and spin and weave clothing and upholstery-grade fabric in the private garden/home. The majority of plain, patterned, and mutmee silk is available for sale by lengths, although there is a modest selection of clothing. One-ply mutmee runs about $16 a yard, while two-ply costs about twice that amount. This workshop may be hard to find, so keep your eye out for a sign (it's located on a side street off of the soi).

MOTIF, 296/7-8 Silom Rd. Tel. 237-8454.

This silk-and-cotton emporium stocks a large selection of quality fabric as well as off-the-rack clothing for women. Many people come here for tailoring; expect a 2-to-3-day turnaround for custom work. Motif also has a housewares/gift section that includes hardwood boxes and desk accessories, lacquer ware, and our favorite, good quality celadon dishes. Open Monday to Saturday 9am to 7pm; Sunday 9am to 6pm during high season only.

Branches in River City (tel. 237-0077, ext. 220) and at the Ambassador Hotel at 8 Sukhumvit Rd. (tel. 254-0444, ext. 1147).

SHINAWATRA, 94 Sukhumvit Rd., Soi 23. Tel. 258-0295.

We've visited many of this chain's branch stores but only learned on our last trip that this outlet, the largest of all, is supplied by its own factory. There is an enorous selection of both silk and cotton (particularly in wonderful solid colors), rivaling all including Jim Thompson for variety. (*Note:* We suggest buying upholstery-grade silk elsewhere.) One-ply, plain silk runs $18 to $22 a yard, while two-ply costs $22 to $25 a yard. There is a small selection of ready-made clothes, such as silk bathrobes for about $180 and silk ties for about $15. Although it's not a specialty, Shinawatra stocks a small line of handicrafts including doll, crocodile purses, and teak goodies as well as operating a jewelry counter. Open Monday to Saturday 8:30am to 6pm.

JIM THOMPSON THAI SILK COMPANY, 9 Surawong Rd. Tel. 234-4900.

It's nearly impossible to mention silk in Thailand without referring in some way to Jim Thompson (see Jim Thompson's House in "Attractions," above), the legendary American who reestablished the modern Thai industry of silk weaving. Even if you don't visit his company's elegant shop, most competitors will compare their workmanship and prices with his goods. For top-drawer goods, including finely woven cotton, Thompson's is the place—but expect to pay for the quality and know that the styles are ultra-, ultraconservative. This may sound like heresy, but we have a hard time recommending the purchase of silk or cotton clothing. Instead, we suggest buying either silk or cotton by the yard (upholstery-grade silk, for example, runs about $44 a yard), or even better, well-designed and crafted jewelry from India, Indonesia, and Thailand. We also like the large variety of picture frames, place mats, and napkins, made of cotton or silk; prices start at $8. Open daily 9am to 9pm.

SILVER

CHAI LAI, Floor 1, Peninsula Plaza, Rajdamri Rd. Tel. 252-1538.

This is a great store for hill-tribe and older Thai jewelry at reasonable to high prices. We particularly admired such objects as gold-bead earrings with rubies for about $315 to $415; 40-year-old rings with five different varieties of blue stones; antique ruby earrings, approximately 50 years old, for $940; and a carnelian-and-silver key ring for $125. Open Monday to Saturday 11am to 6pm.

CHARTERED GEMS LTD., 292 Silom Rd. Tel. 233-9320.

We came here looking for jewelry and discovered their nicely made silver products. The best values that we found in silver were a tea strainer ($80), a pair of candlesticks for $110, and a $62 salt-and-pepper set with a tray. Will negotiate. Open Monday to Saturday 9:30am to 7:30pm.

4. EVENING ENTERTAINMENT

Bangkok has one of the liveliest nightlife scenes in all Asia, with a range of cultural and hedonistic activities that should satisfy anyone. Most visitors won't leave without a stroll down Patpong; the famous sex strip, and Night Market, with myriad vendors and two blocks of bars and clubs.

At the other end of the spectrum are the programs of Thai classical dance and music, whose subtle movements and unusual rhythms challenge the most devoted fans. For those who want to venture deep into all aspects of local culture, here's a small sample of the evening's physical, intellectual, and cultural highlights.

Both the *Bangkok Post* and *The Nation* offer daily listings of cultural events and performance schedules. The TAT (tel. 280-1305) will also provide schedule information. Your hotel concierge should also be able to guide you toward the evening of your choice, particularly with tips on the latest clubs.

THE PERFORMING ARTS

Tourism funds most of the venues for Thai classical performing artists. Although one of the large shopping malls or international hotels often sponsors a cultural show, most travelers experience the Thai classical performing arts at a commercially staged dance show accompanying a Thai banquet. Several hotels and restaurants offer this program, an easy and enjoyable way to sample Thai culture. Generally there is a fixed-menu dinner of Thai favorites accompanied by a small orchestra, followed by a dance performance. Combined, you won't get the best food or the best dance, but we encourage every visitor to see at least one dance performance. (See "Specialty Dining" in Chapter 4 for specific recommendations.)

For a different experience, visit the **Erawan Shirne** at the corner of Rajdamri and Ploenchit roads (near the Grand Hyatt Erawan Bangkok and Sogo Department Store). In front of the large, white marble Hindu altar to the god Shiva, you'll often find musicians and beautifully costumed dancers, sent to amuse Shiva by a thankful worshiper, performing.

There are two major theaters for Thai and international performances, the National Theater and the Thai Cultural Center. The **National Theater,** 1 Na Phra That Rd. (tel. 224-1342), presents demonstrations of Thai classical dancing and music by performers from the School of Music and Dance in Bangkok, which are generally superior to those at the tourist restaurants and hotels. There are also performances by visiting ballet and theatrical companies. Call the TAT or the box office for the current schedule.

The **Thailand Cultural Center,** Ratchadaphisek Road, Huai Khwang (tel. 245-7711), is the newest and largest performance center in town, offering a wide variety of programs. The Bangkok Symphony performs during its short summer season. Other local and visiting companies also present theater and dance here. Call for the current schedule.

THE CLUB & MUSIC SCENE

There are dozens of music clubs (primarily for modern jazz), dance clubs and discos (for dancing and watching), and sex clubs (for watching, not touching).

JAZZ CLUBS

BLUES-JAZZ, Soi 53, Sukhumvit Rd. Tel. 258-7747.
This little spot offers a dose of jazz fusion every evening except Sunday after 9pm.

BROWN SUGAR, 231/20 Sarasin Rd., opposite Lumpini Park. Tel. 250-0103.

This is a cozy and sometimes too popular bar and restaurant where the Brown Sugar Jazz Band swings every night, except for Sunday, from 9pm to 1am. (On Sunday, a country band kicks in.) They also serve lunch and dinner. Open Monday to Saturday 11am to 1am, Sunday 5pm to 1am.

ROUND MIDNIGHT PUB, 106/12 Soi Lang Suan. Tel. 251-0652.

Off Ploenchit Road, north of Lumpini Park, is a club which reminded us a bit of Santa Fe, with vines added for a tropical touch. Nightly until 9:30pm, there's a supply of American and European music with videos, then comes a live band mixing cool pop, soul, and funk with jazz. Popular with expats.

SAXOPHONE, 3/8 Phyathai Rd.

On the traffic roundabout, at the south corner of the Victory Monument, Saxophone remains a popular club. A bright and lively nightspot (open till 3am) where you can savor all the jazz standards.

DANCE CLUBS/DISCOS

BUBBLES, at the Dusit Thani Hotel, Rama IV Rd. Tel. 236-0400.

This pricey place in one of the city's top hotels attracts an older expat crowd mixed with high-fashion young yuppies known as "Tuppies" from Bangkok's growing middle class. It's a dead zone during the week, but jumping on Friday and Saturday nights.

Admission: Cover and two drinks, 350B–400B ($14–$16).

NASA SPACEADROME, 999 Ramkamhaeng Rd., Klongton, Klongtoey. Tel. 314-4024.

This long-lived hot spot is way out of town near the eastern suburb of Huamark (taxi required). The decor matches the name, with extraterrestrial motifs throughout. NASA Spaceadrome's au courant Western music mix and stage shows draw hordes of young Thais looking for action.

Admission: Sun–Thurs 225B ($9), Fri–Sat 300B ($12), including two drinks.

ROME CLUB, 90-96 Soi 4, Silom Rd. (Patpong 2). Tel. 233-8836.

This is our favorite (we're in our midthirties) and one of the most popular discos for cosmopolitan Thais, expats, and visiting Westerners. Most of the local clientele is young, some straight, some gay, and everyone has a fine time. The marble dance floor is surrounded by video monitors and the usual array of moving lights. The Rome's quieter coffee bar across the street provides a welcome respite from the pulsing disco beat and is its own scene for those who hate the music.

Admission: Weekdays 125B ($5), including two drinks; weekends 275B ($11), including two drinks.

THE NILE CLUB, Mandarin Hotel, 662 Rama IV Rd. Tel. 238-0230.

More of a nightclub than a disco, this is an extremely popular Asian-style dance club, where local party animals enjoy the live Thai singers and dance bands. Try it for a very typical Thai evening experience.

Admission: Sun–Thurs 175B ($7), Fri–Sat 325B ($13).

ZAZA PARTY HOUSE, in the basement of the Shangri-La Hotel, 89 Soi Wat Suan Plu. Tel. 236-7777.

⭐ This is the current hot favorite among the Thai teenage and college crowd. The DJs spin good disco/rap/classic tunes, the beat emphasized by the "body sonic" system that drives the bass notes through the floor and up into your body. It's a fun place to dance or watch the scene in stylish New Mexican/Keith Haring–style surroundings. Open daily 9am to 2am (later is hotter).

Admission: 500B ($20), which includes 2 drinks.

SEX CLUBS

While the 1985 hit song "One Night in Bangkok" was actually about chess (from the musical, *Chess*) the song celebrated the naughtiest aspect of life in Bangkok. Since the 1960s—and particularly since the Vietnam War—Bangkok has served as the sin capital of Asia, with sex clubs, bars, massage parlors, and prostitutes concentrated in Patpong and the so-called Soi Cowboy districts. Recent acknowledgements by the Thai government of the startling increase in HIV-positive cases has toned down some of the sex-club scene, while some vendors have shifted their focus to younger and younger merchandise.

Patpong Road is perpendicular to Silom and Surawong roads and its two sois (lands) have long hosted an international sex-street fair. A popular addition is the Night Market that has sprung up on Patpong Road 1. You'll find Midwestern families combing a sea of vendors selling everything counterfeit, from ersatz designer jeans to the latest in knockoff designer luggage to cassettes of recent pop music. This market in consumer goods has undercut the impact of the once all-too-obvious market in flesh, so you may be disappointed (or not) in Bangkok's famous sex strip. Soi Cowboy—between Soi 21 and Soi 23 off Sukhumvit Road—is a less concentrated version of Patpong. There are V.D. clinics in both areas, as well as many pharmacies.

It's nearly impossible to wander Patpong without a hawker approaching you with a laminated menu card, displaying the evening program at one of the numerous sex clubs. These shows are usually upstairs, sometimes above a "go-go" bar, and, though they vary a bit, usually consist of the following: "Woman smokes cigarette. Woman and razor blades. Woman opens Coke bottle. Woman and Ping-Pong balls. Woman uses chopsticks. Woman and live fish." The shows tend to be pretty routine in style, though if you've never seen one (and you probably haven't), this is the place.

Warning: Some of these shows are aboveboard, charging only for drinks. But some are simply classic clip joints, where you'll be hit with an enormous bill when you leave. You should ask and ask again whether there is a cover or "show" charge before you go in. These fees can also be hidden in drink charges, where a bottle of Scotch might cost 2,500B ($100). If you're presented with an exorbitant tab when leaving, insist on calling the Tourist Police. If this doesn't work, pay up and report the problem to the Tourist Police at their booth at the end of Patpong Road 2.

At our most recent visit, the club hawkers were having a tough time tearing people away from Night Market bargains, signifying a change in public opinion which may help eliminate Bangkok's abusive sex trade.

For those who are interested in catching the act (and smart enough not to catch AIDS), try the **Limelight Bar,** the extremely loud rock scene at **Goldfingers, Lipstick,** and the better-costumed, more upscale **King's Castle III.** At all of these go-go bars, located on Patpong Soi I, you're only charged for drinks, which range from 65B to 90B ($2.60 to $3.60) for a beer. Patpong Soi II now boasts mainly massage and "Turkish bath" parlors and is a seedier proposition (no pun intended) altogether.

THE BAR SCENE

Bangkok has a large, varied bar scene. Budget watchers should drink local beer; imported liquor is expensive.

THE BAMBOO BAR, at the Oriental Hotel, 48 Oriental Ave. Tel. 236-0400.

The Bamboo Bar, off the lobby of this legendary hotel, is a tastefully low-key rendezvous for older, well-to-do world travelers. After 10am, you'll enjoy live music and singers. On Monday, a Dixieland band performs. Don't forget to stroll over to the riverside terrace.

BOBBY'S ARMS, 114/1-2 Silom Rd. at Soi Patpong 2. Tel. 233-6828.

This is a popular pub for both local and visiting Anglophile and pubophiles, serving solid English food and a lively banter of expat gossip. On Sunday from 8 to 11pm, a Dixieland band plays, while quieter singers and musicians entertain Friday and Saturday nights.

CHEERS PUB, Holiday Inn Crowne Plaza Hotel, 981 Silom Rd. Tel. 238-4300.

This is one of our favorite bars-in-a-hotel. The regular crowd of airline crews, tourists, expats, and Thais from the nearby business district gives it a local and cheerful ambience. On our visit, a Filipino band was doing great covers of popular Western music.

HARD ROCK CAFE, 424/3-6 Soi 11, Siam Sq. Tel. 251-0792.

Yes, even here. This branch of the original chain should be filled with cheerful Tuppies and curious expats sitting at its guitar-shaped bar. After all, "Hard Rock Bangkok" T-shirts have already been sold in Thailand for years.

SPASSO, GRAND HYATT ERAWAN, 494 Rajdamri Rd. Tel. 254-1234.

Somewhere between a raucously loud, upscale Italian restaurant, a discotheque with no dance floor, and a bar with live music lies Spasso. It's fun, nightly after 9pm, when the local pop bands begin their set, and the bar's somewhat of a pick-up scene before then. Of course, people waiting for tables also hang out at the long, intimately lit bar, making it a cozy and lively place.

GAY BARS

Bangkok has an active gay-bar circuit. You'll find some of the raunchier clubs in the Patpong area, including male striptease shows. We always tell our gay friends to start at the popular **Rome Club** (see "Dance Clubs/Discos," above) on Patpong Road 2, find company at their coffee bar and ask about the current favorite. At our visit, it was the **Super A Cocktail Lounge,** on Soi Anumanrachaton, along with nearby **Harvey's Garden,** which draws the expat gay crowd and upscale locals.

Warning: AIDS continues to spread at an alarming rate among male and female commercial sex workers.

MASSAGE PARLORS/ADULT ENTERTAINMENT

For a traditional, medical massage, head for the school at Wat Po (see "Attractions," above); otherwise visit the health club at the hotel. "Traditional" or "healing" massages will cost from 250B to 400B ($10 to $16) per hour, except at Wat Po, where the rate is a bargain 100B ($4) per hour.

Bangkok has hundreds of "modern" or "physical" massage parlors, which are heavily advertised, and offer something not meant to relax your limbs. Physical massage usually involves the masseuse using her entire body, thoroughly oiled to massage the customer, a "body-body" massage. If one wishes, a "sandwich," with two masseuses, can also be ordered.

Nearly all massage parlors are organized along the same lines. Guests enter the lobby where there is a coffee shop/bar and several waiting rooms where young Thai women wearing numbers pinned to their blouses sit on bleachers. Guests examine the women through a window and select their masseuse. Both guest and masseuse take a room in the building and typically spend between one and two hours on a massage. Rates for a physical massage start at about 500B ($20).

A Word of Warning Although many of Bangkok's activities are semi-illicit, drugs, personal safety, and AIDS are a real concern. Marijuana and other controlled substances are easily available, but are not tolerated by the local authorities. The police frequently clamp down on both sellers and buyers, and ignorance is not an accepted legal defense. Western embassies report numerous cases of tourists who are drugged in their hotel room by the girl of the night, waking two days later to find all their valuables gone. There are a shocking number of stories about young Western travelers found dead in their hotel rooms (42 Americans in 1992) from unexplained causes. We urge caution in your dealings with strangers. The incidence of AIDS among Thailand's commercial sex workers is alarmingly high. If you must use their services, take proper precautions. Wear condoms.

READERS RECOMMEND

Telephone Bar, Bangkok. *"The Rome Club Disco seems to attract a very young straight crowd (maybe it was just the night we were there), the Rome Bar across the street was dead, but a place called Telephone (next door) was lively. Kind of cute actually: they had dozens of little phones around the bar identified with large numbers so you could presumably call someone you thought might be fun to talk with."*—Jeff Sharlach, New York, N.Y.

MORE ENTERTAINMENT

Movie Theaters   There are movie theaters at nearly all of the shopping centers and malls (such as Siam Square) in the city. Most of the main cinemas show recently released English-language films, some dubbed, others with subtitles. You'll find listings in the daily English-language newspapers; ask your concierge to call and determine whether the film is being shown in English. (The Thai action/romance films are also fun to see.) For classic films in English, try American University Alumni Language Center, 179 Rajdamri Rd. (tel. 252-8170); and the British Council, 428 Siam Square, Soi 2 (tel. 252-6136).

Night River Cruises   A few local boat companies offer night dinner cruises on the river. We can't vouch for the food (and can almost vouch for its mediocrity), but the experience can be a relaxing and entertaining view of the city across the water. Ask your concierge to arrange a cruise through one of many tour operators.

Classes, Lectures, etc.   There are several Western groups that offer cultural programs and film series. These are geared to expatriate nationals living in Bangkok, but tourists can also enjoy them.

Among the groups are **Alliance Française,** 29 Sathorn Rd. (tel. 213-2122), which offers a continuing program of French cultural events, including films, concerts, and lectures. There is also a French-language bookstore and a library. Their new branch is located at Ramkamhaeng Huamark (tel. 300-4425).

The **American University Alumni Association,** 179 Rajdamri Rd. (tel. 252-8170), presents lectures, courses, and a film series. They also have a library. The **British Council**, 428 Siam Sq., Soi 2, Rama I Road (tel. 252-6136), offers lectures and programs on art, music, dance, and drama. Call for information or check the newspapers for schedules. You'll find German classes, film programs, lectures, and a library at the **Goethe Institut Bangkok,** 18/1 Soi Attakarnprasit, South Sathorn Road (tel. 286-9002).

5. EASY EXCURSIONS FROM BANGKOK

There are plenty of easy day trips from Bangkok. Favorites include various cruises along the Chao Phraya to the more distant klongs and to the ancient capital of Ayutthaya, north of Bangkok, with a stop at the Bang Pa-In Summer Palace. There's also a floating market south of Bangkok that is still a bit more authentic than the one in town. Culture buffs should explore the Thailand-in-miniature Ancient City, the Rose Garden's performance arts show, and the world's tallest chedi at Nakhon Pathom. For those interested in a good wildlife show, there's the Samutprakarn Crocodile Farm and the Elephant Grounds. Kids will enjoy most of these, but if they are restless, head for one of the splashy, nearby water parks.

Ayutthaya, the Kingdom of Siam's second capital (after Sukhothai but before Bangkok), is a historical site that's commonly visited as a day trip, but may entice history, art, and architecture buffs into an overnight stay. Kanchanaburi is a jungle-clad village on the banks of the famous River Kwai, which can be seen on a long day trip, but is better enjoyed as an overnight excursion. Lopburi is an ancient Buddhist city with a few interesting sites, often visited as an overnight stop on the way to touring the Northeast.

EASY 1-DAY EXCURSIONS

RIVER DAY TRIPS Several river tours venture outside Bangkok. The *Oriental Queen,* a luxurious cruise boat operated by the Oriental Hotel (tel. 236-0400), leaves the Oriental Pier every day at 8am for Ayutthaya (see "Ayutthaya and Bang Pa-In," below, for more information about Ayutthaya). Buses meet the boat in Ayutthaya for tours of the city ruins and the lovely Bang Pa-In Summer Palace. At 5pm, the buses leave for the 2-hour return trip to Bangkok. You can also travel up by bus and return by boat. Cost is 950B ($38) per person, including lunch, tour, and full transportation.

The *Ayutthaya Princess* (tel. 255-9200) leaves at 8am daily from the Shangri-La Hotel for a trip which also includes stops at several interesting wats. Price is 1,000B ($40) with lunch.

A cheaper excursion to Ayutthaya is offered by the **Chao Phraya Express Company** (tel. 222-5330). Boats leave the Maharaj Pier (off Maharat Road, north of the Grand Palace) at 8am Sunday. The Chao Phraya Express Boat tour covers the Thai Folk Arts and Handicraft Center, the Bang Pa-In Summer Palace in Ayutthaya, and the Pai Lom Temple, a sanctuary for open-bill storks (the best time to visit is from December to June). The unguided, all-day excursion is very popular with locals and costs 225B to 300B ($9 to $12) per person, meals not included.

For a shorter and easier river trip, take the Chao Phraya Express Boats (you can catch it at the Thai Chang Pier) all the way up to Nonthaburi, about a half hour beyond the northern edge of Bangkok. You'll get the feeling of a smaller town, with its markets and gardens, and you can tour the colorful Klong Om.

FLOATING MARKET AT DAMNOEN SADUAK The Floating Market at Damnoen Saduak, Ratchaburi, is about 40 minutes south of Nakhon Pathom, so you can either combine the two sites into a 1-day trip or stop at Nakhon Pathom en route to Kanchanaburi. Some tours combine the Floating Market with a visit to the Rose Garden (see below). If you choose to go via organized tour, such as World Travel Service, expect to pay about 1,000B ($40).

At a real floating market, food vendors sell their goods from small boats to local folk in other boats or in klong-side homes. There are some floating markets in Bangkok that have been commercialized and touristized beyond the point of interest. Some will tout this market as more "authentic" than that in Bangkok: Forget it. This version is about as precise a duplicate as you could imagine; however, don't let that dissuade you from going. We love this place (it's great for photographers), and you will too as long as you resist the urge to buy anything. Goods are sold at this pressurized souvenir supermarket at up to five or six times their normal Bangkok prices!!

To do it on your own, take a bus to Damnoen Saduak from the Southern Bus Terminal on Charansanitwong Road (trip time: two hours; 75B [$3]). Buses leave every 30 minutes starting at 6am. Leave early, since market activity peaks between 8 and 10am. From the Damnoen Saduak station, walk along the canal or take a

---

IMPRESSIONS

As Calcutta smells of death and Bombay of money, Bangkok smells of sex, but this sexual aroma is mingled wtih the sharper whiffs of death and money.
—PAUL THEROUX, *THE GREAT RAILWAY BAZAAR,* 1975

water taxi for 18B (72¢) to the floating market. You can also rent a nonmotorized wooden boat for about 150B ($46) per half hour and explore it more fully. As always, negotiate the price (and do it with gusto; this can be a rip-off activity) with the driver before you leave.

THE ANCIENT CITY [MUANG BORAN] This remarkable museum is a giant scale model of Thailand, with the country's major landmarks built full-scale or in miniature and spread over 200 acres. It has been built over the last 20 years by a local millionaire who has played out on a grand scale his obsession with Thai history.

Because it's far from the heart of Bangkok, the Ancient City is best visited by organized tour, though you can certainly go on your own. It's at kilometer 33 on the old Sukhumvit Highway in Samut Prakan Province. For more information, contact the **Ancient City Co.,** on Ratchadamnoen Road in Bangkok (tel. 226-1936 or 224-1057); ask them for public bus route information.

All travel agents offer package tours that combine the Rose Garden with other attractions in the area, such as the Crocodile Farm or the huge Buddhist chedi in nearby Nakhon Pathom.

Admission to the Ancient City is 60B ($2.50). It's open daily from 8:30am to 5pm.

CROCODILE FARM Only 3km (2 miles) from the Ancient City you'll find the Samutprakatn Crocodile Farm and Zoo, at kilometer 30 on the Old Sukhumvit Highway (tel. 387-1166 or 387-0020). The world's largest, it has more than 40,000 snappers, both fresh- and saltwater. At the hourly show, handlers wrestle the crocs in murky ponds. A great outing for families!

Admission is 250B ($10) for adults, 125B ($5) for children. It's open daily from 8am to 6pm; feeding takes place from 4:30 to 5:30pm.

ROSE GARDEN COUNTRY RESORT Besides its rose garden, this attractive if somewhat touristy resort is known for its all-in-one show of Thai culture that includes Thai classical and folk dancing, Thai boxing, sword fighting, and cock fighting—a convenient way for visitors with limited time to digest some canned Thai culture. It's located 32km (20 miles) west of Bangkok on the way to Nakhon Pathom on Highway 4 (tel. 253-0295).

Surprisingly, the resort's restaurant is very appealing and not expensive. It overlooks the Nakhon Chaisri River, dotted with islands of water hyacinth. The *tom yam kung* and the green curry will set your taste buds afire. The pad thai noodles are good, as is the strange-looking but very tasty, spicy *pla krob salad* (dried fish with tamarind sauce).

Admission is 15B (60¢) for the grounds; 200B ($8) for the show. It's open daily from 8am to 6pm; the cultural show is at 3pm. Buses depart from the Southern Bus Terminal.

SAMPHRAN ELEPHANT GROUND & ZOO On one of our previous visits, this was called a crocodile farm, but now the **Samphran Elephant Ground and Zoo** (tel. 284-1873) has evolved into a new species. Located one kilometer (6/10 mile) north of the Rose Garden Country Resort in Yannowa (30km from the city), this 22-acre complex offers a lush gardenlike environment, an entertaining elephant show, plus its original thousands of crocodiles, including the world's largest white crocodile.

Admission is 225B ($9). The zoo is open daily from 9am to 6pm; crocodile wrestling shows—12:45 and 2:40pm; elephant show times—1:45 and 3:30pm; additional shows on Saturday, Sunday, and holidays at 10:30am.

NAKHON PATHOM En route to Kanchanaburi—about 60km (37 miles) west of Bangkok—the chedi of Nakhon Pathom's Phra Pathom soars like a golden bell into the sky (it's actually made of orange tiles brought from China). It's the world's tallest Buddhist monument (413 feet), and marks the spot where Buddhism was introduced to Thailand 2,300 years ago, making it one of the holiest shrines in the country. It was rebuilt at least twice: during the Khmer era, and in the 19th century by King Mongkut, who visited the site when he was studying Buddhism. Take the walk all the way around the central chedi and observe the many smaller shrines and their reclining and seated Buddhas.

Air-conditioned buses leave frequently for Nakhon Pathom beginning at 6am from the Southern Bus Terminal (trip time: one hour; 35B [$1.40]); for additional information, contact the station at 435-1199. You can also combine a day trip to Nakhon Pathom with an early morning stop at the Damnoen Saduak Floating Market, or with a visit to the nearby Rose Garden and Samphran Elephant Grounds.

WATER PARKS If the heat and the kids have gotten to you, consider a trip to one of two water parks. The closest is **Siam Park (Suan Siam),** 101 Sukhapibarn 2 Rd., Bangkapi, (tel. 517-0075), a 30-minute drive east of town (or an hour on bus no. 26 or 27 from the Victory Monument). It's a large complex of water slides (try the Super Spiral—about one-quarter mile long), enormous swimming pools with artificial surf, waterfalls, landscaped gardens, playgrounds, beer garden, and more. There is a fishing farm on the way, which the kids might also enjoy.

Admission is 225B ($9) adults, 120B ($4.80) children, including rides. Siam Park is open Monday through Friday from 10am to 11pm and Saturday and Sunday from 9am to 11pm.

Ocean World is located at Bang Saen, a beach resort on the way to Pattaya. It, too, has all the water slides you could ask for, plus pools galore, rides, restaurants, and a nearby beach. It's a 1½-hour bus ride, either on public buses from the Eastern Bus Station on Sukhumvit Road, or on special tour buses arranged through the tour operator at your hotel. Call the Ocean World office in Bangkok (tel. 399-0508) for more information.

Ocean World charges 100B ($4) for adults, 50B ($2) for children. It's open Monday through Friday from 10am to 5:30pm and Saturday and Sunday from 9:30am to 6pm.

AYUTTHAYA & BANG PA-IN

76km (47 miles) NW of Bangkok

GETTING THERE By Train Trains depart 20 times daily from Bangkok starting at 4:30am (trip time: 1½ hours; 25B [$1] third class).

By Bus Twenty-five buses leave from the Northern Bus Terminal in Bangkok (trip time: 1½ hours; 58B [$2.30]).

By Boat Tours to Ayutthaya leave from the Oriental Hotel (tel. 236-0400), Shangri-La Hotel (tel. 236-7777), or River City pier daily at approximately 8am (and include a stop at Bang Pa-In). Day trips include a cruise on the Chao Phraya and return by air-conditioned coach or vice versa (trip time: all day; 1,100B [$44]). At our visit Mekhala, a converted rice barge, sailed daily from the Menam Hotel, for an overnight cruise/tour of Ayutthaya (trip time: 1½ days; 4,800B [$192] double, includes meals, accommodations, guide, and fee).

A much cheaper, self-guided boat trip can be had each Saturday at 8am, when the **Chao Phraya Express Co.** (tel. 225-3002) offers service from the Maharat Pier to Ayutthaya. Return is via Bang Pa-In. History buffs may resent all the young Thais who come along just for an outing—we loved it.

SPECIAL EVENTS There is a week-long festival at the end of January, including elephant-training demonstrations and handicrafts fair.

AYUTTHAYA

Ayutthaya is one of Thailand's great historical highlights. Most people take the day tour from Bangkok and are allowed about three hours at the sites, but if you relish visiting archeological ruins, Ayutthaya justifies an overnight stay.

For 417 years (postdating Sukhothai and predating Thonburi/Bangkok), from its establishment in 1350 by King U-Thong, Ayutthaya was Thailand's capital and home to 33 kings of various dynasties. At its zenith and until the mid-18th century, Ayutthaya was a vast, majestic city with three palaces and 400 splendid temples on an island threaded with 35 miles of canals—a city that mightily impressed European visitors (for a depiction of Westerners in the ancient city, see the Ayutthaya-era murals in Phetchaburi).

Traces of two major foreign settlements can still be seen. Religious objects, coins, porcelain, clay pipes, and skeletons of the Portuguese (who arrived during Rama II's reign in 1511) are at the Settlement's memorial building. The Japanese memorial is a recently erected inscribed stone and a hall and gate.

There is something hauntingly sad about Ayutthaya. In 1756, after a 15-month siege, it was destroyed by the Burmese; today every temple testifies to the hatred that drives humans to rampant and wanton destruction. Here stands a row of headless Buddhas, there a head lies caught in the roots of a tree. Some temples are still being rescued from the jungle, and more are undergoing careful excavation.

We think you'll find the architecture of Ayutthaya fascinating, especially if you've traveled around Thailand (and Myanmar) and absorbed the many important foreign influences. For those who've traveled to the Northeast, you'll recognize the Khmer influence in the design of many of the ancient wats in Ayutthaya, particularly the use of the cactus-shaped *prang* (tower). For those who've visited Sukhothai, you're certain to notice the similarity of buildings from that magnificent site. And if you've just arrived and have confined your stay to Bangkok, you might connect with the riverside Wat Arun, an 18th-century structure that was built in the so-called Ayutthaya style, which is a melding of Sukhothai Buddhist influences with Hindu-inspired Khmer style.

ORIENTATION

City Layout   The town is encircled by water with the perimeters defined by the Chao Phraya on the southern and western sides, the Lopburi River to the north, and the Pasak to the east. The main ferry pier is located on the east side of town, just opposite the train station. The Bangkok bus makes its last stop at the station adjacent to the Siam Commercial Bank Building, off Chao Prom Road in the downtown area (there is another stop prior to this that lets travelers off near the bridge). Buses from Phitsanulok stop 5km (3 miles) north of town; you'll need to take a 10B (40¢) local bus into the center.

Getting Around   Once at Ayutthaya, a minibus from the train station into town will cost about 20B (80¢). You can also hire a minibus for about 700B ($28) per day. Better yet, hire a long-tail or other boat to see the city the leisurely way for about 85B ($3.40) per hour. There is regular minibus service between Ayutthaya and Bang Pa-In, departing from Chao Prom Market on the road of the same name (trip time: 50 minutes; 65B [$2.60]).

WHAT TO SEE & DO

AYUTTHAYA HISTORICAL STUDY CENTER, Rojana Rd. Tel. 245-5124.
Established in 1990 to serve as an educational resource for students, scholars, and the public, the center presents displays of the ancient city including models of the palace and the port area and reconstructions of ships and architectural elements as well as a fine selection of historical objects. There is an interesting section about the presence of foreigners in Ayutthaya. Start here for an overview of the area.

IMPRESSIONS

I stood in admiration of the strong great city, seated upon an island round which flowed a river three times the size of the Seine. There rode ships from France, England, Holland, China, and Japan.
—ABBE DE CHOISY, 1687 (ABOUT AYUTTHAYA)

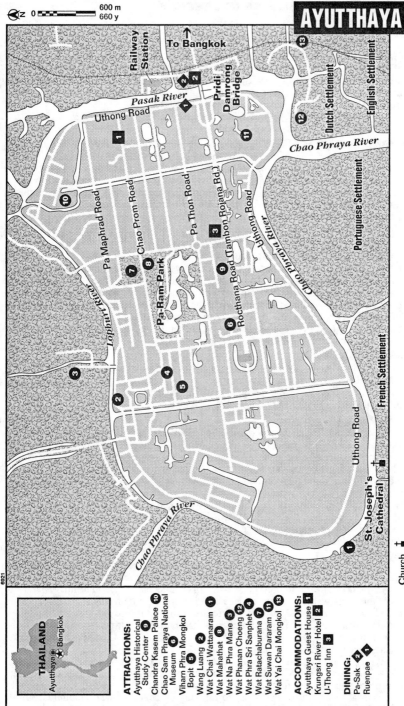

AYUTTHAYA

0   600 m
     660 y

To Bangkok

Railway Station

Pridi Damrong Bridge

Pasak River

Uthong Road

Chao Phraya River

Dutch Settlement

English Settlement

Portuguese Settlement

Pa Maphrad Road

Chao Prom Road

Pa Thon Road

Rocthana Road (Tambon, Rojana Rd.)

Uthong Road

Pa-Ram Park

Lopburi River

Chao Phraya River

French Settlement

Uthong Road

Chao Phraya River

St. Joseph's Cathedral

Church ✝

THAILAND
Ayutthaya ★ Bangkok

ATTRACTIONS:
Ayutthaya Historical Study Center ⑨
Chandra Kasem Palace ⑩
Chao Sam Phraya National Museum ⑥
Viharn Phra Mongkol Bopit ⑤
Wang Luang ②
Wat Chai Wattanaram ①
Wat Mahathat ⑧
Wat Na Phra Mane ③
Wat Phanan Choeng ⑫
Wat Phra Sri Sanphet ④
Wat Ratachaburana ⑦
Wat Suwan Dararam ⑪
Wat Yai Chai Mongkol ⑬

ACCOMMODATIONS:
Ayutthaya Guest House ❶
Krungsri River Hotel ❷
U-Thong Inn ❸

DINING:
Pa-Sak ◆②
Ruenpae ◆①

Admission: 125B ($5).
Open: Wed–Fri 9am–4:30pm, Sat–Sun 9am–5pm.

CHAO SAM PHRAYA NATIONAL MUSEUM, Rojana Rd.

Located 1½ blocks west of the center (near the junction of Sri Sanphet Road) is the first of two National Museum branches in Ayutthaya. It houses impressive antique bronze Buddha images, carved panels, religious objects, and other local artifacts.

Admission: 15B (60¢).
Open: Wed–Sun 9am–noon, 1–4pm.

CHANDRA KASEM PALACE, northeast part of old city.

The other National Museum branch, the Chandra Kasem Palace, is a splendid building, built in 1577 by King Maha Thamaraja (the 17th Ayutthaya monarch) for his son, who became King Naresuan. It was destroyed but later restored by King Mongkut, who stayed there whenever he visited Ayutthaya. On display are exquisite gold artifacts, jewelry, carvings, Buddhas, and domestic and religious objects from the 13th and 17th centuries.

Admission: 15B (60¢).
Open: Wed–Sun 9am–noon, 1–4pm.

WIHARN PHRA MONGKOL BOPIT

Wiharn Phra Mongkol Bopit, seven blocks west of the Chandra Kasem Palace, is home to Thailand's largest seated bronze Buddha. It's housed in a somewhat cramped viharn, built in 1956 in the style of the original, which was destroyed in 1767. It was either brought from Sukhothai or copied from a Sukhothai Buddha and was erected here in 1615 by King Ekatosarot, in honor of his brother Naresuan, who, in the 16th century, drove the Burmese from Sukhothai into Burma, where they remained relatively peaceful for 160 years.

WANG LUANG

Wang Luang, the old royal palace, was destroyed by the Burmese. The foundations of the three main buildings can still be made out, and the visitor can only be impressed by the size of the compound. Wang Luang is located in the northwestern end of the ancient city, overlooking the Lopburi River.

THE WATS

Near the old royal palace stands **Wat Phra Sri Sanphet,** originally built in 1448 as the king's private chapel (the equivalent of the Wat Phra Kaeo, Temple of the Emerald Buddha, in Bangkok) and renovated in the 16th and 17th centuries. The 55-foot bronze standing Buddha was originally cast in 1500 during the reign of the ninth king, Ramathipodi, and covered with gold. In 1767, the Burmese tried to melt the gold, causing a fire that destroyed the image and the temple. What remains is a replica. Nearby are three Sri Lankan–style chedis, built during the 15th century to enshrine the ashes of three Ayutthaya kings.

To the east of the royal palace, the prang of **Wat Phra Ram** soars into the sky. Originally built in 1369 by King Ramesuen (second King of Ayutthaya), the complex is in ruins.

Opposite **Wat Mahathat** (ca. 1384) stands **Wat Ratachaburana,** built in 1424 and splendidly restored—the prangs and chedis have even retained some of their original stucco. In the two crypts, excavators found bronze Buddha images and votive tablets, as well as golden objects and jewelry, many of which are displayed in the Chao Sam Phraya Museum. There are also murals, rows of seated Buddhas, standing disciples, and Jataka (tales from the Buddha's former lives) scenes in the four niches, as well as a frieze of heavenly beings and some Chinese scenes. Both remain severely damaged despite restoration.

A very large, impressive Buddha is at **Wat Phanan Choeng,** a temple built in 1324, 26 years before King U-Thong founded Ayutthaya. The image is 62 feet high and more than 45 feet from knee to knee. Adjacent to it is a small Chinese temple, a memorial to a princess betrothed to the king of Thailand, who committed suicide when he failed to attend her arrival.

Wat Suwan Dararam, across the river, is visited by the present royal couple when they come to Ayutthaya. It was built by Rama I. The murals and door panels depict stories from the *Ramakien.*

Wat No Phra Mane, on the Lopburi side of the river, survived Ayutthaya's destruction and is worth visiting to see the black stone Buddha dating from the Dvaravati period, as well as the principal Buddha fully decorated in regal attire.

Back on the main site on the other side of the river, one chedi serves as a moving reminder of the role women have often played in Thai history (in a country where they were expected to serve alongside men in war). Only a chedi and statue remain of a temple built to commemorate Queen Suriyothai, who was killed when she intervened in a duel (fought on the backs of elephants) between her husband and a Burmese general.

Don't miss **Wat Yai Chai Mongkol,** a few minutes southeast of ancient Ayutthaya. It's a well-tended temple built by King U-Thong in 1357 for meditation. The massive pagoda was built in 1592 by King Naresuan after he defeated the Burmese by killing their crown prince in single-handed combat on elephants.

A short distance from the other main temple sites (on the other side of the Chao Phraya, west of the royal palace) is **Wat Chai Wattanaram,** which is still being restored. Roots and branches straggle around the many chedis and prangs. The overgrown complex has that haunted sense of tragedy about it—the essence of Ayutthaya.

Note: Some of the sites charge 10B (40¢) admission.

WHERE TO STAY

KRUNGSRI RIVER HOTEL, 27/2 Rojana Rd., Ayutthaya 13000. Tel. 035/ 242996. Fax 035/242996. 202 rms. A/C MINIBAR TV TEL **Directions:** Northeast side of Pridi Damrong Bridge.
$ Rates: 1,675B ($67) single; 1,900 ($76) double; 4,200B ($169) suite. MC, V.
The construction of this handsome luxury hotel, close by the train station, was nearing completion at our visit. We could already see the marble-floored lobby was cool and spacious. Rooms are uncluttered, clean, and crisp, with good-sized gray granite bathrooms. (A number will be reserved for nonsmokers.) With 24-hour room service, a friendly staff, and many facilities, it's obviously the area's top choice.

The Krungsri has a very good coffee shop now (see "Where to Dine" below) and will have both Chinese and Japanese restaurants. Facilities include an outdoor swimming pool, a health club with saunas, a small bowling alley, a snooker room, and a beauty salon.

U-THONG INN, 210 Rojana Rd., Ayutthaya 13000. Tel. 035/242236. 100 rms. A/C MINIBAR **Directions:** In the center of the Ancient City.
$ Rates: 900B ($36) single or double. MC, V.
The U-Thong Inn is among the best of a modest selection. It has neat, clean, carpeted rooms and a pool. The front-desk personnel are accommodating and the hotel provides laundry service. There's also a restaurant attached.

AYUTTHAYA GUEST HOUSE, 16/2 Chao Prom Rd., Ayutthaya 13000. Tel. 035/251468. 10 rms. **Directions:** A short walk north of the in-town bus station.
$ Rates: 60B ($2.40) single; 120B ($4.80) double. No credit cards.
This establishment is under the domain of Mr. Hong and family, and offers the best of the low-budget beds in Ayutthaya. There are bikes for rent, as well as a small inexpensive garden restaurant attached to the guest house.

WHERE TO DINE

For real budget dining, try the small food shops near the Hua-Raw and the Chao Prom markets or the informal restaurants across from the entrance to Wat Mahathat.

For a different experience try the following:

PASAK COFFEE SHOP, Krungsri River Hotel. Tel. 244333.
    Cuisine: THAI/CONTINENTAL. **Directions:** Northeast side of Pridi Damrong Bridge.
$ Prices: Appetizers 75B–115B ($3–$4.60); main courses 115B–200B ($4.60–$8). MC, V.
    Open: Daily 5am–11pm.
On the first floor of the area's best hotel, this bright and airy place has marble
floors and a menu more varied than that found in most coffee shops. Standard Thai
dishes are carefully prepared (and not too spicy!), and Western entrées include the
popular cheeseburger.

RUENPAE, north of Pridi Damrong Bridge. Tel. 251807.
    Cuisine: THAI/CHINESE. **Directions:** North of Ancient City.
$ Prices: Appetizers 45B–100B ($1.80–$4); main courses 65B–125B ($2.60–$5).
    Open: Daily 11am–10pm.
Ruenpae is a simple floating river-front restaurant. It offers a typical Thai/Chinese
menu, with such dishes as steamed fish in plum sauce, roast chicken with salt,
Nanking soy cake, grilled prawns, and beef with chili. A good place to enjoy a
pretty good meal after a long day of sightseeing.

BANG PA-IN

Only 61km (38 miles) north of Bangkok, this royal palace is usually combined with
Ayutthaya in a 1-day tour, although—in our view—the palace is not as interesting.
If you have a choice, spend your time exploring Ayutthaya fully.
    Originally the 17th-century temple and palace at Bang Pa-In were built by
Ayutthaya's King Prasat Thong. They were abandoned when Bangkok became the
capital until King Mongkut began returning occasionally in the mid-19th century.
His son King Chulalongkorn constructed the royal palace as it is seen today.
    The architectural style mixes Thai with strong European influences. The building
in the middle of the lake is the Phra Thinang Aisawan Thippa-At, an excellent example of classic Thai style. Behind it, in Versailles style, are the former king's apartments, which today serve as a hall for state ceremonies. The other building of note
is the Phra Thinang Wehat Chamrun, a Chinese-style building (open to the public)
where court members generally lived during the rainy and cool seasons. Also worth
visiting is the Phra Thinang Withun Thatsuna, an observatory on a small island that
affords a fine view of the countryside.
    While you're across the Chao Phraya, the Gothic-style Wat Nivet Thamaprawat
(built during King Chulalongkorn's reign) is worth seeing. Buses leave regularly from
Bangkok's Northern Bus Terminal (tel. 279-4484) and Ayutthaya's Chao Prom Market (Chao Prom Road), beginning at 6am, for Bang Pa-In. Admission is 35B ($1.40).
It's open daily 8:30am to 12:30pm and 1 to 3pm.

KANCHANABURI

128km (79 miles) W of Bangkok; 65km (40 miles) W of Nakhon Pathom

GETTING THERE By Train Two trains depart daily from Bangkok Noi (tel.
411-3102) Station in Bangkok; (trip time: 2½ hours; 70B [$2.80]).
    Special tourist trains leave on Saturday, Sunday, and holidays, stopping 40 min-
utes in Nakhon Pathom, and for 30 minutes at the River Kwai bridge. A minibus
will take you from Nam Tok Station to Khao Phang Waterfall round-trip. The train
continues on to Kanchanaburi for a 45-minute stop with an overnight at the River
Kwai Jungle House before returning to Bangkok. Trains leave in the early morning
and arrive back at Hua Lampong station the following evening, and a morning excursion to the Krasae Cave Bridge in 1994 costs 690B ($27.60) adults; 490B
($19.60) children. Reservations recommended. A 1-day version of this program is
also available for 340B ($13.50) adults, 290B ($11.50) children; similar programs
are offered to Erawan National Park. Contact the State Railway of Thailand (tel.

02/225-6964) for information on overnight train, tour, and accommodation packages starting at 750B ($30).

By Bus   Sixty nonair-conditioned buses depart daily from Bangkok's Southern Bus Station (tel. 411-0511; trip time, three hours 50B [$2]); 75 air-conditioned buses (tel. 414-4978) leave daily after 5:30am (trip time: 2½ hours; 90B [$3.60]).

By Car   Take Route 4 West from Bangkok.

ESSENTIALS   The **TAT** office is on Saeng Chuto Road (tel. 034/511200 or 512500); it's open daily 8:30am to 4:30pm. The telephone **area code** is 034. The **Tourist police** can be reached at tel. 512759. **Currency exchange** is available at banks Monday through Friday from 8:30am to 3pm. The **post office,** on Saeng Chuto Road, is open from 8:30am to 4:30pm, Monday through Friday; Saturday and Sunday 8:30am to noon; there are facilities for telegrams and overseas calls everyday from 8:30am to 10pm. **Laundry** and dry cleaning can be taken to "White and Clean," a short walk south of the TAT office. **Cars** can be rented for 1,350B ($54) per day from the helpful Ron at B.T. Travel (tel. 511967), on Saeng Chuto Road; this and the bus station are located around the corner from TAT.

SPECIAL EVENTS   The River Kwai Bridge Festival is a Sound and Light Demonstration (with fireworks donated by the Japanese government), cultural shows, special period train rides, and historical displays beginning at the end of November. There is a symbolic "bombing" of the bridge twice weekly (Saturday and Wednesday when we last visited).

Kanchanaburi stands at the junction where two tributaries—the Kwai Noi and the Kwai Yai—meet and form the Mae Khlong River. For most visitors, the town is indelibly marked by its famous bridge, spanning the Kwai River. A visit to this site is, for some, an emotional pilgrimage to honor the suffering and heroism of those who perished (and the few who survived) under their brutal Japanese overseers. And moving as the story is, we find the actual site a good bit less inspiring and would recommend it only for those who are really passionate about this chapter of World War II history.

The city, near the bridge over the Kwai, is surrounded by some spectacular scenery, particularly to the north and west of the town. Mountains rise in misty haze along the river; waterfalls abound as the jungle stretches away. You'll drive past fields of tapioca, tobacco, sugarcane, tamarind, mango, papaya, banana, and palm trees.

Kanchanaburi is a fine base for jumping off if you have a taste for exploring Thailand's natural areas. We wouldn't suggest you stick around town too long; it's pretty dull and overly commercial. In other words, come to Kanchanaburi for an overnight stay to explore the area's diverse scenery or to delve into River Kwai lore. As a day trip, it's not so thrilling even when combined with stops at the Damnoen Saduak floating market or the giant stupa at Nakhon Pathom.

WHAT TO SEE & DO

Before going to see the bridge itself, the main attraction, stop at the **JEATH museum,** adjacent to Wat Chaichumpol in town. Constructed of thatch and bamboo to resemble prisoners' barracks, it provides a sobering display of the suffering of the prisoners of war who built the bridge and the railroad.

The railway was built as a communication and supply link for the Japanese army in Burma. It replaced the sea route (via the Strait of Malacca) that had been closed by the Allies. The name "Jeath" is an acronym of the initials of those nationalities that built the railway—Japanese, English, American, Australian, Thai, and Hollanders.

The museum is filled with photographs, personal mementos, and newspaper accounts of their lives, recording the tortures the Japanese inflicted upon them—malnutrition, disease, and despair.

The Japanese originally calculated that it would take five to six years to complete the 425km (264 miles) track, but they reduced that figure to 18 months for the POWs. It was finished in a year. Some 16,000 Allied prisoners, mostly British, Australian, and American, died, but even more brutal was the fate of another 100,000 Burmese, Chinese, Indians, Indonesians, Malays, and Thais who were also killed under forced labor and buried in unmarked graves where they dropped. It's open daily 8:30am to 5pm. Admission is 25B ($1).

On Saeng Chuto Road in town, near the railroad station, you can stop by the **Kanchanaburi War Cemetery,** where every stone tells a story of a lost life. Many of the 6,982 graves are those of young men in their 20s and 30s who died far from home. Another cemetery, a few miles out of town contains close to 2,000 graves. Another 1,750 POWs lie buried at the **Chon-Kai War Cemetery,** once the site of a POW camp, and now a tranquil place on the banks of the Kwai Noi about 2km (1.2 miles) south of town.

The **Bridge over the River Kwai** is about 4½km (2½ miles) north of the town center. The bridge was brought from Java and assembled by POWs. It was bombed several times and rebuilt after the war, but the curved spans are the originals. You can walk across it, looking toward the mountains of Myanmar as you go. For some it's a nerve-racking experience: rickety railroad ties laid on an open grid allow you to see the water below. If you visit during the River Kwai Bridge Week (usually the end of November or the beginning of December), you can also see a son-et-lumière spectacle.

WHERE TO STAY

JOLLY FROG BACKPACKER'S, Mae Nam Kwai Rd., Kanchanaburi 71000. Tel. 034/514579.
$ Rates: 60B–110B ($2.40–$4.40) single; 110B–140B ($4.40–$5.60) double. No credit cards.
The Jolly Frog has remained a clean and friendly place, located in the tourist center of town. Some rooms have toilet facilities; all are fan cooled. The management can arrange treks and tours.

V. L. GUESTHOUSE, 18/11 Saeng Chuto Rd., Kanchanaburi 71000. Tel. 034/513546. 24 rms. A/C (in some rooms).
$ Rates: 150B ($6) single or double with fan and toilet; 300B ($12) single or double with A/C and hot-water shower. No credit cards.
This guest house, across from the pricier and dirty River Kwai Hotel, is a clean, fluorescent-lit hostel. The back-facing rooms are quieter, and there is a simple, cheap restaurant and laundry service. Toilets are of the flush Asian style.

Nearby Places To Stay

FELIX RIVER KWAI RESORT, 9/1 Moo 3 Thamakham, Kanchanaburi 71000. Tel. 034/515061. Fax 034/515086. Telex 79802 RIVKWAI TH. 235 rms. A/C MINIBAR TV TEL **Directions:** On the banks of the River Kwai.
$ Rates: 3,600–3,850B ($144–$154) single; 3,850B–4,000B ($154–$160) double; from 6,600B ($264) suite. Extra bed 600B ($24). Peak season surcharge (Dec 20–Jan 20) 600B ($24). Compulsory Gala Meals during River Kwai Bridge Week, Christmas, New Year's Day, Chinese New Year 600B–1,200B ($24–$48). AE, MC, V.
Built for, but no longer managed by, the Sheraton chain, the Felix is a long, low resort tucked into the dense undergrowth surrounding the river. Rooms are spacious and filled with amenities, offering mountain and river views. Some are reserved for nonsmokers; three others have been modified for the disabled. This is the most luxurious way to experience the River Kwai, and one sure to appeal to WWII veteran's groups looking for the comforts of home.
Dining/Entertainment: The "fern bar" coffee shop offers good continental, and some Thai dishes, in a very pleasant setting. The more formal Guilin Restaurant is for Chinese fare. There's also a relaxing piano bar, and a Karaoke Bar is promised for 1994.

Service: 24-hour room service, concierge, car rental, doctor on call, Thai massage, babysitting, laundry.

Facilities: Two swimming pools, work-out room, business center.

RIVER KWAI JUNGLE HOUSE, 378 Tharua, Thamaka, Kanchanaburi. Tel. 034/561052. Fax 034/561429. 15 rms. **Transportation:** Management will pick up from the Kanchanaburi train station.

$ Rates (with full board): 900B ($36) single; 1,800B double. V.

The "Ban Rim Kwae," about 25 miles west along the river from Kanchanaburi, is in a forest of mango, bamboo, and bougainvillea; turkeys and chickens peck at the dust; a couple of pet monkeys hang around for company. This primitive "hotel" is a traditional, floating resort. Rattan bungalows with fans and Asian toilets float on the river, overlooking a stretch of the famed railway. The hotel conducts cave exploration, at Tamka Sae, local treks, and rafting trips. You'll need a sense of adventure and flashlight as the grounds are poorly lit.

WHERE TO DINE

Note: If you're out touring the bridge at lunchtime, try the River Kwai Restaurant (tel. 512540) or Sai Yok (tel. 512702), both nearby, which serve Thai and some Chinese dishes. We also want to give special mention to the Aree Bakery (no phone), at 90-02 Prakjak Rd., two blocks from the riverside. Sgt. Maj. Tanom Lonmasuarapan and wife run an American-style ice-cream shop that also serves homemade fruit pies and breakfast: what a treat!

PAE-BANN NOUE, Song Kwai Rd. Tel. 512326.
   Cuisine: THAI.
$ Prices: Appetizers 20B–50B (80¢–$2); main courses 35B–70B ($1.40–$2.80). MC, V.
   Open: Daily 10am–midnight.

Highlights at this riverside eatery in town are shrimp with lemongrass, steamed whole fish on lemongrass and salted prune, beef with shredded eggplant and hot pepper, and rice noodles fried with pork, dried shrimp, and tomato sauce. Try the *kwai tiao pad thai*, a local variation on the famous noodle dish.

TONGNATE [Thong Nathee], Song Kwai Rd. Tel. 512944.
   Cuisine: THAI/SEAFOOD.
$ Prices: Appetizers 45B–60B ($1.80–$2.40); main courses 60B–145B ($2.40–$5.80). MC, V.

The Tongnate is a riverside restaurant with a floating dining pavilion. During the evening there is an entertaining floor show featuring a bevy of local singers. Although the food isn't great we suggest rice with chicken, garlic, and fresh pepper and fresh river poached fish in tomato sauce.

EASY EXCURSIONS

The surrounding area is widely known for its natural sites, especially the **Erawan Waterfall and National Park, Sai-Yok National Park,** and **La Wa Cave.** The best time to visit is during the rainy season (August to October) when the waterfalls are in full flood. There is bus service to nearly every major excursion destination in the area; however, if you so choose, rental cars are available in town from B. T. Travel (tel. 511967), on Saeng Chuto Road, for 1,350B ($54) per day.

Since **adventure tours** have become popular, this scenic area has begun capitalizing on its natural assets. The RSP Travel Center, 271/1 Saeng Chuto Rd. (tel. 512280), organizes local jungle treks and river-rafting trips. The V. N. Guesthouse (tel. 514831) at 44 Rong Heeb Oil 2 Rd., rents very basic rooms but also has good guides for budget hikes, elephant treks, and river trips. Check with the local TAT office for current rates and recommendations.

The **La Wa Cave** is about 75km (45 miles) from town along Route 323; **Sai-Yok National Park** is about 104km (62 miles) along the same route; its focal point is its waterfall, Sai Yok Yai, often celebrated in Thai song and verse. You can take a private boat to these two places from Pak Saeng Pier at Tam-Bon Tha-Saow. The round-trip will take about four hours and cost about 850B ($34). Buses to Sai Yok take about two hours and cost 32B ($1.30).

Just off route 323, but further away from town, are Dawadung Cave (110km, 68 miles), the Hin Dat Hot Springs (130km, 80 miles), and the remote three-tiered waterfall Pha Tat.

The most popular attraction is **Erawan Waterfall and National Park,** about 65km (40 miles) along Route 3199. The waterfall is 1¼ miles long and drops down seven tiers, creating a series of ponds and streams; it's a great bird-and-butterfly sanctuary and a popular camping spot for locals. Buses leave for Erawan from the bus terminal in Kanchanaburi on Saeng Chuto Road (tel. 511182), every 50 minutes from 8am to 4pm. The trip takes about 1½ hours and, with guide, costs 90B ($3.60). Buses to Sai Yok take about two hours and cost 60B ($2.40). The last bus returns to Kanchanaburi early.

Along Route 3086 (31 miles north) in the Bo Phloi area, you can watch sapphire mining. From the roadside you'll spy the wooden framework of a winch and people filling wheelbarrows with hard lumps of earth. After washing through the mud, they may find—if they're lucky—blue or black sapphires and earn a day's living. Travel another 50km (30 miles) or so north along the same route and you'll come to the 300-meter-long Than Lot Noi Cave and Traitrung Waterfall in Than Lot National Park.

We're interested in archeology and were mildly impressed by the **Ban Kao Neolithic Museum** and **Prasat Muang Singha,** a Khmer site that pales in comparison to those found in the Northeast (it's interesting if you don't plan to visit that region). The museum is open daily 8:30am to 5pm; 20B (80¢) admission fee; it's located about 45 minutes north of town.

LOPBURI

153km (95 miles) N of Bangkok; 98km (61 miles) NE of Ayutthaya

GETTING THERE By Train Frequent train service operates from Bangkok (trip time: 2½ hours; 95B [$3.80]).

By Bus Three nonair-conditioned buses and two air-conditioned buses per hour depart from Bangkok's Northern Bus Terminal (tel. 279-4484); trip time: 2¼ hours; 45B to 85B [$1.80 to $3.40]).

By Car Take the main highway, Route 1, north past Ayutthaya on Route 32, to Singburi, and turn southeast to Lopburi.

ESSENTIALS The telephone **area code** is 036.

From the 10th through the middle 13th century, Lopburi served as a satellite capital of the Khmer empire. With the rise of the Thai nation in Chiang Mai, and later in Sukhothai, the Khmer were driven out of Lopburi and the ancient city was reestablished as a second capital under the suzerainty of Ayutthaya. King Narai, who was the first Thai monarch to open the country to the West, collaborated with French architects in the 1660s to rebuild the city in a Thai-European mode. Today, Lopburi's few sites reflect these many presences: Hindu influenced Khmer-era temples, Buddhist influenced Sukhothai-Ayutthaya structures, and Jesuit-influenced European buildings. Many travelers make it their first overnight stop on the way to exploring the Northeast (try to time it with the annual October Banana Festival).

Like Ayutthaya, the old town is surrounded by water, principally, the Lopburi River on the southern and western perimeters. Just opposite the town gate, on the south side, is the train station. Nearly all of the major tourist sites are located within the old city.

WHAT TO SEE & DO

Phra Narai Ratchanivet Palace and **Somdet Phra Narai National Museum** are located on Sorasak Road, between Ratchadamnoen Road and Pratoo Chai Road. The palace was built during King Narai's reign over a period of 12 years beginning in 1666 and renovated by King Mongkut. Finds from the area as well as objects from the buildings within this complex are on display in the National Museum of Lopburi (also known as the Somdet Phra Narai National Museum). This facility was thought of as a reception grounds for both Thai and European emissaries, and the buildings reflect both a local and Western sensibility. For example, the Chantara Phisan Pavilion, built as a residence and reception hall for the King is designed in Thai style, while the Dusit Sawan Thanya Maha Prasat Building is an audience hall (where King Narai is thought to have recieved Chevalier de Chaumont, Louis XIV's ambassador) that incorporates both Thai and French architectural styles, as well as a fine throne and antique mirrors imported from France. The Phiman Mongkut Pavilion was King Mongkut's Lopburi residence, designed by a Frenchmen in the style popular in 19th-century Europe, and used today to house archeological finds from the area. His harem (so to speak) was housed in the nearby Phra Pratiep, where Thai folk arts are currently on view. The grounds are filled with fascinating structures, most in ruins, that are worth devoting a few hours to explore. Admission is 10B (40¢). It's open Wednesday to Sunday 8:30am to 4:30pm.

Vichayen House was built as a residence for Chevalier de Chaumont (see above) by King Narai. The estate is largely in ruins, though there is still evidence of a Catholic chapel, several residences for the ambassador and his entourage, as well as water tanks and other outbuildings. Admission is 25B ($1). It's open daily 8:30am to 4:30pm.

Wat Phra Sri Maha That, a shrine located one block behind the train station, was probably built in the early 1300s, during the Khmer period, and later rebuilt in the Sukhothai style, with additions made during the Ayutthaya era. One prang, Prang Prathan, is very finely decorated.

WHERE TO STAY & DINE

LOP BURI INN, 28/9 Narai Maharat Rd., Lopburi 15000. Tel. 036/ 412300. Fax 036/411917. 134 rms. A/C MINIBAR TEL **Directions:** In the center of the Ancient City.

$ Rates: 725B ($29) single, 900B–1,450B ($36–$58) double. MC, V.

This, the largest hotel in Lopburi, is also its most fully equipped and comfortable. Like most provincial hotels in popular stops, the Lop Buri Inn is often used by tour groups and consequently suffers from wear and less-than-perfect upkeep. Its location, however, is central to both sites and restaurants.

There are a series of typical Thai restaurants in the 200 block of Narai Maharat Road, all worth trying and of about equal quality: Maha Sarakham (226/7-10 Narai Maharat; tel. 411643); Bua Luang (229/129-32 Narai Maharat; tel. 411014); and Anodat (226/21 Narai Maharat; no phone).

CHAPTER 6

THE EAST COAST BEACHES

Thailand's beaches, along the Gulf of Thailand (also known as the Gulf of Siam), are world renowned for their clean white sand, palm groves, and warm water. Today, most areas are served by a sophisticated tourism infrastructure and indulgent accommodations. Although no sandy crescent is protected from the hotel developer's hand, there are still areas that are relatively undeveloped.

Pattaya, the oldest and most decadent of Thailand's southern resorts, lures people seeking a break from the big city because of its proximity to Bangkok (3½ hours by bus). It has suffered from what used to be its once positive image as the sex playground of Southeast Asia; AIDS, environmental pollution, and bad foreign publicity have contributed to the tremendous drop in tourism. The local government has been cleaning up Pattaya Bay and enacting strict new waste-management guidelines, even while development continues.

Ko Samet is the star of Rayong Province: a small island (protected by a national park) whose primitive bungalows create a very different feel from Pattaya's swinging hotels. It's easily reached by a 45-minute ferry ride from the tiny port of Ban Phe (4½ hours from Bangkok by bus); though isolated, it gets lots of crowds due to its popularity with Bangkok residents. East of Ban Phe, along the coast of the South China Sea, are several new resorts in Rayong Province. Several high-end Thai hoteliers have invested in beachfront property, expecting Rayong to be the next "hot" resort. The provincial capital of Chanthaburi is a commercial hub for the East Coast, but has little of interest to the tourist.

Ko Chang has earned a cult following among young budget tourists because its remote location has kept development to a minimum. Ninety-eight percent of the 500 hotel rooms on this huge island are coconut-wood bungalows with thatch roofs and shared toilets. It's far from Bangkok to the nondescript port of Trat (5 to 6 hours by bus), then another long ferry (2½ to 4 hours) to your desired port. But once there, it's easy to see what all the hype's about.

EN ROUTE TO PATTAYA: CHONBURI PROVINCE

Coastal Highway 3 eastbound is one of the fastest ways to get to the eastern beaches, though it's not particularly scenic. In between smoke-belching fish-canning factories and local manufacturing plants are salt fields, where spindly metallic windmills pump seawater from the Gulf of Thailand for processing. In this province, salt "mining" is beginning to overtake prawn farming as the most lucrative reuse of family-held rice paddies, since rice cultivation (due to water pollution and rising costs) is no longer profitable.

About 5km (3 miles) from Chonburi town or Amphur Muang is Angsila, a fishing village best known for another industry—bronze Buddha casting. Mr. Pinit Tonerat owns one factory where bronzes are cast using the lost-wax process. In a complex ritual to welcome the newborn image—after offerings, chanting, and prayers by monks—the figure is heated, the wax discarded, and the molten bronze is

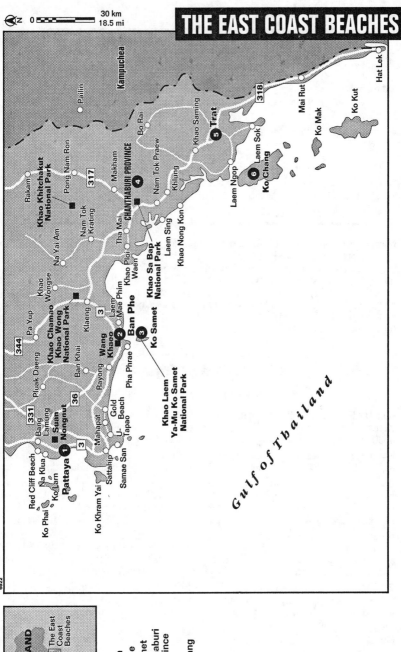

THE EAST COAST BEACHES

N   0   30 km
         18.5 mi

Hat Lek

Kampuchea

Ko Kut

Pailin

Mai Rut

Ko Mak

318

Bo Rai

Khao Saming

Ko Chang

Rakam

Khao Khitchakut
National Park

Pong Nam Ron

317

Makham

5 Trat

Laem Sok

6 Ko Chang

Laem Ngop

Na Yai Am

CHANTHABURI PROVINCE

4

Nam Tok Praew

Khiung

Nam Tok
Krating

Tha Mai

Laem Sing

Khao
Wongse

Khao Chamao
Khao Wong
National Park

Klaeng

Laem
Mae Phim

Khao Ploi
Waen

Khao Sa Bap
National Park

Khao Nong Kon

Pa Yup

3

Wang
Khaeo

2 Ban Phe

3 Ko Samet

Pluak Daeng

Ban Khai

Rayong

Pha Phrae

Khao Laem
Ya-Mu Ko Samet
National Park

344

331

Bang
Lamung

Suan
Nongnut

36

Mahapat

Gold
Beach

U-
Tapao

3

Pattaya 1

Red Cliff Beach

Na Klua

Ko Larn

Sattahip

Samae San

Ko Phai

Ko Khram Yai

Gulf of Thailand

THAILAND

The East
Coast
Beaches

1 Pattaya
2 Ban Phe
3 Ko Samet
4 Chanthaburi
    Province
5 Trat
6 Ko Chang

6922

WHAT'S SPECIAL ABOUT THE EAST COAST

Beaches

Ko Chang's Hat Sai Kaeo, a beautiful, unspoiled fine sand beach that stretches for 5km (3 miles) lined with pine trees.

Extra-challenging windsurfing off of Ko Samet's rocky northwest cape.

Excellent scuba diving and snorkeling off of Ko Si Chang and Sattahip, both outside of Pattaya.

After Dark

Pattaya has more bars, cabarets, massage parlors, and sex clubs than any other city except Bangkok.

Festivals

New Year's Eve festivities and fireworks every December 31 over Pattaya Bay.

poured in through the hollow base. Completed Buddhas may only be "rented" to their clients as the image is too sacred to have any material value.

Another point of interest for Thai tourists is Si Racha, a seaside resort 24km (15 miles) south of Chonburi, where fresh seafood and locally grown pineapple are popular souvenirs. There is daily ferry service (between 8:30am and 3pm, 50B [$2] one-way) to the island Ko Si Chang, known as an elegant 19th-century summer resort for the Thai elite. Pedicabs wait at the ferry pier to offer round-the-island 1-hour tours (about 125B [$5]).

1. PATTAYA

147km (91 miles) E of Bangkok

GETTING THERE By Plane The Pattaya International Airport is only open to charter flights from Europe and the Middle East. Bangkok Airways (tel. 038/603063) has four flights weekly from Bangkok (1,800B [$72]).

By Train Once a day trains leave from Bangkok's Hua Lampong station. Call 02/223-2762 in Bangkok or tel. 429285 in Pattaya for schedule information.

By Public Bus More than 50 buses a day leave from Bangkok's Eastern or Ekamai Bus Terminal (trip time: 2½ to 3½ hours; 75B [$3]), 25 buses a day leave from Bangkok's Northern or Morchit Bus Terminal (trip time: 3½ hours; 75B [$3]).

By Private Bus Major hotels or travel agencies often operate their own transport or can recommend private buses. Thai International Limousine Service (tel. 423140) has private car-and-driver service (trip time: 2½ hours; 1,800B [$72]), and a minibus three times daily (trip time: 3 hours; 225B [$9] one-way) to and from Bangkok's Don Muang airport; they will pick you up from your hotel in Pattaya.

By Taxi The concierge in our Bangkok hotel negotiated with a metered taxi driver to take us to a Pattaya resort, door to door, for 1,250B ($50). Traveling with a child and lots of luggage, this proved faster (2½ hours) and almost cheaper than the private minibus services.

By Car Take Highway 3 east from Bangkok.

Pattaya leaves two impressions. The first is from its legacy as Thailand's R-and-R capital for Vietnam-weary American troops: discos, massage parlors, transvestite clubs, bars with scantily clad Thai teens—all are conveniently jammed together along a beachfront strip. The other is as a sophisticated, international retreat of sprawling, manicured seaside gardens. Pattaya is sometimes a honky-tonk, other times elegant, but Bangkok residents (and tourists with little time) continue to make Pattaya their most favored weekend destination. For those who desire a more tranquil beach environment, we recommend heading south to Hua Hin Cha-Am.

ORIENTATION

ARRIVING   All buses use the terminal on North Pattaya and Sukhumvit roads, five minutes from the north end of Pattaya Beach Road.

INFORMATION   The **TAT** is midway along Pattaya Beach at 241/1 Beach Rd. (tel. 038/428750; fax 038/429113), and is open daily 8:30am to 4:30pm. The **Tourist Police** (tel. 429371), next door to the tourist office, is open 24 hours. (Both agencies will be moving to the corner of Beach Road and Soi 7 as part of Pattaya's beautification program.)

CITY LAYOUT   Pattaya is basically a long strip of hotels, bars, restaurants, travel agencies, and shops along Pattaya Beach Road, opposite a narrow beach overlooking Pattaya Bay. Central Pattaya (Pattaya Klang) Road bisects Pattaya Beach Road and the two parallel streets behind the strip, Pattaya II Road and Pattaya III Road. At both the far northern (Dusit Resort) and southern (Royal Cliff Beach Resort) ends of the strip are two bluffs. Due south is condo-lined Jomtien Beach, a 15-minute ride from town.

GETTING AROUND

BY MINIBUS OR SONG TAO   Song Tao, baht buses, or minibuses (actually open-bed trucks with wooden bench seats) cruise the major streets for passengers and are the best and cheapest form of transport. Fares within Pattaya should range from 10B to 30B (40¢ to $1.20); to far-flung beaches as Jomtien they're 30B to 85B ($1.20 to $3.40). Rates are fixed by the local governments, but most drivers will negotiate fiercely. Some hotels operate their own minibuses, but they charge much more for the same bumpy ride.

BY CAR   Avis, at the Royal Cliff (tel. 421421) or at the Dusit Resort (tel. 425611), is one of the many rental-car companies offering self-drive or chauffeured cars to explore the east coast. Self-drive rates are approximately $70 per day with insurance; a car and driver costs $160 including 200km (120 miles) free. Several popular destinations have fixed rates (Pattaya-Bangkok for $96; Pattaya-Trat for $144). VIA Rent a Car at 215/15 Pattaya II Road (tel. 426242) is a local company we liked. Their day rate for an insured, self-drive car is 900B ($36).

BY MOTORCYCLE   For those who dare brave the often drunk and reckless foreign drivers in downtown Pattaya, 150cc motorcycles rent for 250B ($10) a day without insurance (ask for a helmet!). Mopeds and larger motorcycles are available from many companies along the beach strip and Central Pattaya Road.

FAST FACTS: PATTAYA

Area Code   The area code for Pattaya is 038.

Banks   There are many independent money-changing booths; many bank exchanges (with better rates) stay open 24 hours.

Hospitals   The most recommended centers are Pattaya Memorial Hospital 328/1 Central, Pattaya Road. (tel. 429422), and Pattaya International Hospital, Soi 4 Beach Rd. (tel. 428374).

Post Office   The Post and Telegraph Office (tel. 429341) is between Beach Road and Pattaya II Road on Soi Post Office; open Monday through Friday 8:30am to 4:30pm, Saturday and Sunday and holidays 8:30am to noon.

Telephone/Telex/Fax   The Telecommunications Centre (tel. 429601) on South Pattaya Road is open 24 hours for overseas calls. Many travel agents will also book long-distance telephone calls.

WHAT TO SEE & DO

The town **beach,** along Pattaya Beach Road, is polluted and not recommended for swimming; the best choices for bathing are the north end of Pattaya Beach below the Dusit Resort, or Dong Than Beach at the north end of Jomtien Beach. The south end of Jomtien is for windsurfing and sailing; it is too heavily trafficked for swimming. Though huge condos and constant construction overwhelm the Jomtien beach community, for the moment it's still cleaner than Pattaya. Jomtien's narrow beaches are easily reached by minibus (the fare is 50B [$2]). If you are serious about finding a really great beach, move on to nearby Ko Samet; but for convenience, Jomtien is the best in the area.

For **water sports,** most people go to nearby islands where the seawater is cleaner. Dozens of boats will take you on a day cruise (about 350B [$14] per person), jetskiing or waterskiing (about 1,000B [$40] per hour), or parasailing (350B [$14] per flight). Local fishing and motor boats are usually moored on the central beach stretch, near the TAT. Several beach vendors offer Windsurfers, for rent at 450B ($18) per hour. Skilled windsurfers prefer to sail off of Jomtien Beach where there's less boat traffic; the best winds blow northeast from November to January. Contact any of the Beach Road travel agencies if you're interested in deep-sea fishing; packaged excursions usually cost 5,000B ($200) per day per boat, including fishing gear.

Snorkeling and **scuba diving** are popular because of Pattaya Bay's clear waters (20m to 25m average visibility), colorful coral reefs (including mushroom, lettuce, brain, and staghorn corals), and tropical fish (white- and black-tip sharks, stingrays, angelfish, and many others). Nearby Ko Larn, Ko Sak and Ko Kroh can be reached within 45 minutes by boat. There's also diving off of Ko Klung Badan, Ko Man Wichai, or Ko Rin, which are farther offshore. North of Pattaya is Ko Si Chang, once famous as the summer playground of foreign ambassadors to Siam during the 19th century. Here, and off Sattahip to the south, is even better diving, at depths up to 130 feet.

The most convenient of the good dive shops with PADI and NAUI certified instructors in the area are: Seafari Sports Center, at Soi 5, Beach Road (tel. 429253, fax 038/424708), is a PADI-certified school run by American expats Patti and Bill Burbridge. In nearby Jomtien, there's Mermaid's Dive School, Soi Mermaid (tel. 232219, fax 038/232221). Dave's Divers Den/The Professionals has relocated away from the beach to Moo 3, Pattaya-Naklua Road, Naklua (tel. 221860, fax 038/221618).

Check the certification, class schedules, equipment, itinerary, and fine print at each outfit before committing to a program. Most scuba day trips, including equipment for two dives, lunch, transportation, and dive master cost 1,500B to 2,000B ($60 to $80) depending on your destination. Snorkeling or island-hopping day trips begin at about 450B ($18), plus 150B ($6) to rent snorkel gear. Certification courses and night dives can also be arranged.

EXCURSIONS TO NEARBY ISLANDS

Ko Larn's main port is a long, sandy beach cove facing the mainland, just a 45-minute boat ride away. Dozens of seafood restaurants and snack bars line the beach. Bamboo Island and Ko Man Wichai, within an hour of Ko Larn, are largely uninhabited and perfect for the deserted tropical island crowd. Fishing boat and motor boat operators moored on the main part of Pattaya beach offer Ko Larn day trips for about 350B ($14) per person on a full boat, or about 1,500B ($60) for a privately chartered boat; it's 2,500B ($100) to Bamboo Island. There's lots of competition, so bargain. If you're too shy to organize this on your own, many of the beachside tour operators will sell you a ticket on their day-trip boats.

WAT KHAO PRAYAI, KHAO TAPPRAYA HILL

If you feel a need to rise above the earthly foibles of Pattaya, this small temple complex offers excellent vistas. Khao Prayai means "Great Buddha on the Hill," and a

32½-foot gold Buddha sits serenely surveying the western sea. There's also some history here—*tappraya* was the Ayutthaya-era title for "general," a name which evolved into Pattaya. The walk up Tappraya Hill will do wonders for the cardiovascular crowd. Another wat, on a neighboring rise, can also be visited. Admission is a suggested contribution of 10B (40¢). It's open daily 6am to 6pm. Take the minibus to Jomtien from the beach road and get off on top of the hill and walk up between dragonheaded columns.

PATTAYA PARK, 345 Jomtien Beach Rd., Jomtien. Tel. 442300.

Though we wouldn't normally recommend Pattaya as a place to take your kids, if you find yourself there with restless children, a day at Pattaya Park's playland could save you. It's a worn, but fun water park with a small Thai restaurant, network of pools, several water slides, a narrow, clean beach and many kinds of watersports equipment (windsurfing, catamarans, etc.) for rent.

Admission: 60B ($2.40) adults, 35B ($1.40) children under 120cm (4 feet).
Open: Daily 8:30am–6pm. **Directions:** Take the minibus to Jomtien to the Pattaya Park Hotel, 8km (5 miles) south of town.

MINI SIAM, 387 Sukhumvit Rd., North Pattaya City. Tel. 421628.

For those who don't have time to see all of Thailand's many wonders, this is a comprehensive tour of the highlights, all shown as miniature models (an example of scale: Bangkok's huge Grand Palace is waist high). Most of Thailand's famous structures, in meticulous detail, are included. Coming in 1995: Mini Europe, to thrill the Thai tourists who bring their kids here!

Admission: 250B ($10) adults, 125B ($5) children.
Open: Daily 9am–9pm. **Directions:** It's 14km (8.4 miles) north of Pattaya City, and can be reached by taxi (about 800B [$32] with wait) or by joining a local group tour.

WHERE TO STAY

Most of these establishments are on Pattaya Beach Road in the middle of the entertainment scene. However, the city's top resorts are blissfully isolated—perfect for a sun-and-fun getaway weekend.

All prices are exclusive of the 7% VAT and the 10% service charge and do not reflect the peak-season supplement (usually 600B to 1,000B [$24 to $40] per room per night) charged by many hotels from mid-December to mid-January. (If business is bad, these fees are often waived.) At this time, reservations are recommended at least two weeks in advance.

VERY EXPENSIVE

ROYAL CLIFF GRAND, Royal Cliff Bay, Pattaya City, 20260 Chonburi. Tel. 038/250421. Fax 038/250514. Telex 85904CLIFFGR TH. 187 rms, 15 suites. A/C MINIBAR TV TEL **Directions:** On cliff, south part of Pattaya Beach.
$ Rates: 4,300B–5,400B ($172–$216) single or double; from 10,800B ($432) suite. Extra bed 1,200B ($48). AE, DC, MC, V.

If stunning, columned public spaces with fountains, staircases, chandeliers, and acres of granite mean "Grand," then this newest addition to the fine Royal Cliff Beach Club Resort complex lives up to the name. Everything about the place is larger than life.

Spacious rooms in the contemporary, scallop-shaped tower have private VCRs and fax setups, as well as marble bathrooms with separate shower stall and twin sinks. They are elegantly appointed with classic furniture and coffered ceilings in tribute to the era of King Rama V, who inspired the Victoriana/Siam design. The Royal Club on the sixth floor boasts a private spa and sundeck, as well as seven Jacuzzis for its VIP and business guests. An impressive colonnaded lobby leads down to the scenic and excellent Grand Café, whose three-story picture windows overlook the huge free-form pool and richly opulent grounds.

Dining/Entertainment: The Grand Café offers terrific continental and Thai cuisine indoors in a towering sun room or outdoors on a patio overlooking the gardens. Both quality and service are first-rate and prices reasonable. Guests also have access (a pleasant walk) to the many facilities at the Royal Cliff and Royal Wing hotels (see below).

Services: 24-hour room service, concierge, limousine service, babysitting, house doctor, laundry.

Facilities: Swimming pool, health club, water sports, mini–golf course, business center, beauty salon and barbershop, shopping arcade, deli/bakery.

ROYAL WING, Royal Cliff Beach Resort, Pattaya City 20260, Chonburi. Tel. 038/250421. Fax 038/250511. Telex 85907 CLIFFEX TH. 84 executive suites, 2 presidential suites. A/C MINIBAR TV TEL **Directions:** On cliff, south of Pattaya Beach.

$ Rates: 7,700B ($308) suite; 27,500B ($1,100) Presidential Suite. AE, CB, DC, EC, MC, V.

The dazzling Royal Wing is treated both by guests and its capable Swiss management as a separate entity within the impressive Royal Cliff resort. The level of service here is more personal (butlers on call 24 hours!), and the rooms are more regally furnished, than anywhere else in town.

As opulent as Bangkok's Shangri-La, the Royal Wing is the pinnacle of Hong Kong–style glitz. The lobby is white marble, with lotus bud–capped columns combining Thai and Chinese influences. Each guest is catered to personally, with butlers unpacking your luggage on arrival and beach chaise longues reserved with your brass nameplate. The large, bright, quietly tasteful rooms—decorated throughout with teak and fine pastel Thai cottons—are spaced around the breadth of the cliff. For maximum privacy, each has two balconies, draped in fuchsia or orange bougainvillea, overlooking Pattaya Bay. The free-form swimming pool is crisscrossed by small bow bridges; waterfalls add an extra exotic touch. The beach is small but uncrowded and well maintained.

Dining/Entertainment: The hotel offers daytime or romantic evening poolside dining at La Ronde, an elegant lobby bar, and the Palm Terrace for breakfast or lighter fare. The Benjarong Restaurant, with peach-colored Thai-silk upholstery and polished bleached marble floors, serves French and continental fare with a hint of Thai. Guests can try the Thai Market or Seafood Market open-air pavilion (see "Where to Dine," below), as well as the facilities at the nearby Royal Cliff or Royal Cliff Grand.

Services: 24-hour room and butler service, concierge, limo, babysitting, house doctor, laundry, nonsmoking rooms.

Facilities: Pool, Cliff Club Spa (with sauna, steam bath, and two pools), water sports, mini–golf course, tennis courts, jogging track, business center, beauty salon, barbershop, shopping arcade, deli/bakery.

EXPENSIVE

ASIA PATTAYA BEACH HOTEL, Cliff Rd., Pattaya City 20260, Chonburi. Tel. 038/250602. Fax 038/250496. Telex 85902 ASIAPAT TH. 304 rms, 10 suites. A/C MINIBAR TV TEL **Directions:** On cliff above south end of beach; 3km (1.8 miles) south of town.

$ Rates: 2,300B ($92) single/double with mountain view; 2,900B ($116) single/double with water view; 5,200B ($208) family suite. AE, CB, DC, EC, MC, V.

The Asia Pattaya offers immaculate grounds, all heavily planted, and one of our favorate images, a topiary A-S-I-A in the middle of a circular driveway. The rooms are aging but well kept and have numerous amenities. Many are decorated with kitschy 1960s paneling or with leather-look furniture. The Dutch-owned Golden Tulip chain manages the resort in a friendly, homey way; European tour groups abound. The well-priced rooms and two-bedroom family suites are a good value if you're looking for a well-groomed private beach, tranquillity, and relative seclusion.

Dining/Entertainment: The open-air Cliff Top Restaurant offers great views and good continental or typical Thai fare. The Neptune Disco has a popular DJ nightly, with a pretty good selection of European hits and, often, a live band.

Service: 24-hour room service, concierge, limousine service, babysitting (with notice), laundry service.
Facilities: Swimming pool, 9-hole golf course, shopping arcade.

DUSIT RESORT, 240/2 Pattaya Beach Rd., Pattaya City 20150, Chonburi. Tel. 038/425611. Fax 038/428239. Telex TH 85917. 474 rms, 26 suites. A/C MINIBAR TV TEL **Directions:** North end of Pattaya Beach.
$ Rates: 2,250B–3,150B ($90–$126) single/double with garden view; 3,750B ($150) single/double with sea view; 6,550B ($262) single/double Landmark rooms; from 7,200B ($288) suite. Extra bed 700B ($28). AE, DC, MC, V.

This beautifully landscaped resort offers fresh air, water sports, a good health club, and some nightlife (far from the seamier side of Pattaya). Straddling a bluff on the north end of the main beach, the Dusit has two pools and sun decks, access to two small but well-kept sandy beach coves, several dining outlets, a small shopping arcade, and newly reduced rates, making it a great value!

Most of the balconied rooms overlook Pattaya Bay, but the best values are the garden view–priced rooms in Wing B, which face manicured lawns, hibiscus beds, and and side view of the sea. Tastefully modern rooms trimmed in stained woods offer all-marble bathrooms, hair dryers, and personal bathrobes. Landmark deluxe rooms have large bathrooms with separate bath and shower stalls, plus outdoor showers on their large balconies, as well as comfortable and luxurious sitting areas. We loved the Landmark Honeymoon Suite (12,000B [$480]), whose huge bathroom features a raised oval Jacuzzi tub overlooking the sea, a green silk fainting couch (what do they expect?), and a walk-in shower the size of many budget hotel rooms. If only the service matched the high-quality facilities!

Dining/Entertainment: The Dusit has several dining options, including the Empress for panoramic views and gourmet Chinese food, as well as the slow, but poolside Bay. There is an okay coffee shop and delightful lobby lounge, the latter serving evening drinks with live musical accompaniment.

Services: 24-hour room service, concierge, limousine service, babysitting, laundry service, and nonsmoking rooms.

Facilities: Two outdoor swimming pools, water sports, health club (open 7am–11pm) with daily aerobic classes, sauna rooms with TV sets, pool tables, tennis courts, squash courts, shopping arcade, a beauty salon, and a barbershop.

ROYAL CLIFF BEACH RESORT, Royal Cliff Bay, Pattaya City 20260, Chonburi. Tel. 038/250421. Fax 038/250511. Telex 85907 CLIFFEX TH. 383 rms, 423 minisuites, 127 suites. A/C MINIBAR TV TEL **Directions:** On cliff, above south end of Pattaya Beach.
$ Rates: 3,100B ($124) single or double; 4,100B ($164) minisuite; from 6,000B ($240) two-bedroom suite. AE, DC, EC, MC, V.

⭐ This is Pattaya's top family-resort selection, at the southern end of town on the same garden property as the more exclusive Royal Wing and Royal Cliff Grand. It was built and upgraded in phases: the Royal Cliff Terrace building houses four terraced stories of suites with patios; the nine-story sea-view hotel tower houses most of the guest rooms, including huge, perfect-for-families two-bedroom suites. Most rooms have bay views, as well as bleached wood and pastel decor; all offer spacious living quarters and terraces. If you tire of the lushly planted grounds, there's an elevator from the precipice down to the sandy beach, which is relatively clean but by most standards disappointingly small. Go for the pools, the grounds, the health club, not for the beach. The hotel has a staff of more than 1,500 waiting to serve. We found it a friendly, luxurious, and relaxing place.

Dining/Entertainment: There is an indoor/outdoor poolside coffee shop (delightful for a grand American or Thai-style buffet breakfast), as well as snack bars by the sea, in the gardens, and by the Cliff Club pool. For the evening, there's a piano bar off the lobby (for people watching) and one in the open-air Thai Market pavilion. Restaurants include the stately up-country Grill Room, the Thai Market/Seafood Market (see "Where to Dine," below). Guests are also welcome at the exclusive Royal Wing's formal Benjarong Restaurant and the poolside La Ronde.

Services: 24-hour room service, concierge, fruit basket in suites, house doctor, limousine service, babysitting, laundry service.

Facilities: Outdoor swimming pool, Cliff Club spa (with jogging track, sauna, steam bath, and two pools), water sports, mini–golf course, tennis courts, squash courts, jogging track, business center, beauty salons, barbershop, shopping arcade, deli/bakery.

THE ROYAL CRUISE HOTEL, 499 N. Pattaya Beach Rd., Pattaya City 20260, Chonburi. Tel. 038/424242. Fax 02/236-2361 (Bangkok). Telex 84204 A-ONE TH. 176 rms, 24 suites. A/C MINIBAR TV TEL **Directions:** Midbeach, near Soi 2.

$ Rates: 2,150B–2,600B ($86–$104) single or double; suite from 3,400B ($136). Extra bed 500B ($20). AE, DC, MC, V.

Into cruise mode? Like the idea of a huge white cruise ship berthed among thatched-roof bars and T-shirt stalls? If the answer is yes, try an art deco–style, sea-view cabin at this ultrathemed, boat-shaped hotel. Nine decks include deco signage, glass-lamp bases filled with sand and coral, and hallways with portholes. There's a Le Bateau coffee shop, a nice pool and kid's playground, and a tiny weight-room/minispa. Fun place—and you don't get seasick.

INEXPENSIVE

FLIPPER LODGE MOTEL, 520/1 Soi 8, Pattaya Beach Rd., Pattaya City 20260, Chonburi. Tel. 038/426401. Fax 038/426403. 126 rms. A/C MINIBAR TV TEL **Directions:** Midbeach strip, off Soi 8.

$ Rates: 850B ($34) single/double with garden view; 950B ($38) single/double with sea view; 1,800 ($72) suites. AE, MC, V.

The best thing about the Flipper Lodge is the life-size statue of Flipper the dolphin gracing the lobby; the second best is the price, making this the fave budget choice in the middle of the beach strip. The decor is basic, but the older rooms are clean and the new ones look great; their sea-view rooms (with that great view) can't be beat. After you take a swim in their short pool (under Flipper's watchful gaze) you can proceed to the attractive open-air coffee shop for some pretty good Thai and continental fare.

NAUTICAL INN, 10/10 Pattaya Beach Rd., Pattaya City 20150, Chonburi. Tel. 038/428110. Fax 038/428116. 80 rms, 2 suites. A/C MINIBAR TV TEL **Directions:** Between Soi 11 and Soi 12.

$ Rates (including tax and service): 1,000B ($44) single/double with garden view; 1,500B ($60) single/double with sea view. AE, MC, V.

The Nautical Inn is a good budget choice on the beach strip. It's a relatively new, though Spartan, facility set well back from the road. Plain tower rooms are worn, but all have sea views, while the garden-view rooms surround a respectable pool. If you're staying two days or more, ask for their special reduced rates. The daily published rates are often discounted up to 50% in the low season.

NEARBY PLACES TO STAY

Expensive

ROYAL JOMTIEN RESORT, 408 Moo 12, Jomtien Beach Rd., Pattaya City, Chonburi. Tel. 038/231350. Fax 038/231369. Telex 85934 ROYAL TH. 400 rms. A/C MINIBAR TV TEL **Directions:** North end of Jomtien Beach.

$ Rates: 2,900B–3,200B ($116–$128) single; 2,000B–2,400B ($120–$136) double; from 8,400B ($336) suite. Extra bed 600B ($24). AE, MC, V.

Amid a cluster of contemporary condos, this newly built 16-story tower has some of the nicest rooms along Jomtien Beach. Most feature sea views, are set back from the busy road, and are refreshingly quiet. With lots of print fabrics, rattan-accented furnishings, and well-appointed if compact bathrooms, they are very pleasant. The lobby overlooks a good-sized pool and a landscaped sitting area. And if you've arrived in the rainy season, you can select a video to watch in your room, hit the fitness center, or head down to the eight-lane bowling alley! There is a too-formal, but convenient and varied menu, coffee shop off the lobby.

Services: 24-hour room service, taxi service, babysitting, laundry.

Facilities: Swimming pool, health club, snooker, business center.

SUGAR PALM BEACH HOTEL, 45/16 Moo 12, Sugar Palm Beach, Jomtien, 20260 Chonburi. Tel. 038/231386. Fax 038/231889. 32 rms. A/C TEL **Directions:** North end of Jomtien Beach, just northwest of Jomtien Plaza Condos, on boardwalk.

$ Rates: 950B ($38) single/double; 1,450B ($58) single/double with sea view. AE, MC, V.

Our favorite lower-priced choice for a purely casual, beachy hotel, this place faces the quiet, clean Sugar Palm Beach and its gently lapping surf—far from the crowds on noisy Jomtien Beach Road. The simple rooms are spotless, though only two have ocean views. The Style Restaurant next door offers open-air dining on the beach, with good food and cheap prices (an American breakfast is only 80B [$3.20]).

SURF HOUSE INTERNATIONAL, 75 Jomtien Beach Rd., Jomtien, 20260 Chonburi. Tel. 038/231025. 36 rms. A/C MINIBAR TV TEL **Directions:** East end of Jomtien Beach.

$ Rates (including tax and service): 720B–810B ($28.80–$32.40) single/double. Extra bed 125B ($5). AE, EC, MC, V.

Like most Jomtien accommodations, the Surf House seems to attract a younger, more beach-loving crowd than that which frequents the Pattaya hotels. Rooms are simple and clean, with private baths, and most have balconies and water views—request a seaside room on the top floor for a good panorama of the windsurfers. Because the Surf House is separated from the beach by the busy road, we consider it a second choice to the Sugar Palm Beach Hotel.

WHERE TO DINE

EXPENSIVE

THAI MARKET/SEAFOOD MARKET, Royal Cliff Resort Hotel, Cliff Rd. Tel. 250421.

Cuisine: THAI/SEAFOOD. **Directions:** South end of Pattaya Beach.

$ Prices: Thai appetizers 175B–400B ($7–$16); seafood sold by weight, average portions 300B–700B ($12–$28); Thai buffet 625B ($25). AE, DC, MC, V.

Open: Daily 6–10:30pm.

If you've been tempted by the aromas from those tin-and-wood pushcarts parked near the beachside bars, you'll find a hygiene-guaranteed forum to sample everything right here, in this twin-sided "market." On one side of the open-air pavilion you'll find shrimp balls; *garoupa* steamed in banana leaves; beef, chicken, and pork satay; and many other grilled, fried, and boiled Thai standards.

On the other side of the tropical bamboo bar are lobster, crab, prawn, shellfish, and many locally caught fish, all displayed on ice for your choosing. Fresh salads and fruit round out the menu, a perfect finale for fitness buffs here on retreat.

MODERATE

DOLF RIKS, 463/77 Sri Nakorn Center, North Pattaya. Tel. 428269.

Cuisine: INDONESIAN/EUROPEAN. **Reservations:** Recommended during high season. **Directions:** 1 block north of Soi 1.

$ Prices: Appetizers 60B–300B ($2.40–$12); main courses 250B–450B ($10–$18); fixed-price "tourist special" 400B ($16). AE, DC, MC, V.

Open: Daily 11am–midnight.

Dolf Riks is an Indonesian-born Dutch restaurateur who's also a bit of a character. His restaurant is Pattaya's oldest and remains something of a legend; it specializes in Indonesian and European dishes. Although Dolf's menu changes with his whims, he normally serves a delicious Indonesian Rijstaffel (good, but very different from what we eat in Jakarta!), as well as continental favorites. His regulars prefer the seafood in a wine-drenched broth, the Spanish garlic soup, and his fragrant ramekin Madras, an oven-baked curry ragoût.

HAFEN STUBL, Nipa Lodge Hotel, Pattaya Beach Rd. Tel. 428195
Cuisine: GERMAN. **Reservations:** Not necessary. **Directions:** Corner of Pattaya Klang Road.
$ Prices: Appetizers 60B–145B ($2.40–$5.80); main courses 75B–200B ($3–$8). MC, V.
Open: Daily 11:30am–10pm.

If you've been longing for the taste of schnitzel and wurst, try this pocket of Germany on the beach. Thai girls in Heidi wardrobe serve cold steins of Anarist on tap (a new German beer), followed by platters of stout Teutonic fare. We enjoyed it as a break from Thai food, and for the convivial pubby atmosphere.

PIC KITCHEN, Soi 5, between Beach Rd. and Pattaya Rd. Tel. 428387.
Cuisine: THAI. **Directions:** 2 blocks north of Beach Road.
$ Prices: Appetizers 85B–150B ($3.40–$6); main courses 100B–275B ($4–11). AE, DC, MC, V.
Open: Daily 8am–midnight.

PIC stands for Pattaya International Clinic, the medical center located directly across from the restaurant (no relation). In several lovely classic teak pavilions you can dine in air-conditioned comfort, sit on floor cushions Thai style, or sit in an outdoor courtyard . This is the only restaurant we ate in twice! Our favorite dishes include deep-fried crab claws, spring rolls, spicy eggplant salad, mixed fried vegetables with oyster sauce, fried chicken with cashews, and steamed white snapper on a bed of vegetables, with ginger and salted prunes. Each night from 7pm to 1am there's a live jazz show free of charge.

INEXPENSIVE

NANG NUAL, 123/24-25 Moo 12, So. Jomtien Beach Rd., Jomtien. Tel. 231548.
Cuisine: THAI/SEAFOOD. **Directions:** Midbeach in Jomtien.
$ Prices: Appetizers 60B–140B ($2.40–$5.60); main courses 60B–300B ($2.40–$12). AE, CB, MC, V.
Open: Mon–Fri 8am–11pm, Sat–Sun 6am–11pm.

Nang Nual is an excellent breakfast, lunch, or dinner choice in Jomtien Beach. A Thai restaurant specializing in seafood, it is a favorite choice of Bangkok friends. A cheery, fluorescent-lit, blue-and-white interior is the setting for steamed butterfish with Chinese lime sauce or the sumptuous seasonal grilled seafood combination. Our combination had grilled prawn, a whole local lobster, and fresh crab; it varies with the catch. Diners can choose their meal from fish tanks out front.

READERS RECOMMEND

Mermaid's Rest, Jomtien Beach, Pattaya. *"There is a fairly new Mermaid's Rest in Jomtien Beach, with the all-famous Texas BBQ. It's a bit more upscale, with reasonable prices and a nice layout. You can receive a 40% discount if you dive with Mermaid's Dive School (PADI)—I had a great experience."—* Tonya Mathis, Portland, Oreg.

EVENING ENTERTAINMENT

Open-air and topless bars, sex shows, and massage parlors abound on Pattaya Beach Road. Most of the pick-up action takes place in the clusters of outdoor bars of Soi 8 or around Soi 14–17. At the raunchier go-go bars in Pattayaland (south-beach strip), topless women dance on an island bar. Each wears a number and is available "after the show" for a fee. Sometimes, exuberant drinkers less than delicately place money on the bodies of their favorite dancers, demanding more. There's always more available in Pattaya, but there's other evening entertainment as well.

Warning: AIDS continues to spread at an alarming rate in Thailand.

NIGHTCLUBS/CABARET SHOWS Pattaya is well known for its wildly costumed and choreographed transvestite song-and-dance revues. The **Tiffany Club** (tel. 421700) and **Alcazar Cabaret** (tel. 428746), two of the most popular nightclubs, are both on Pattaya Second Road, in the northern part of Pattaya. At both clubs, three shows nightly (about an hour each) feature coy fan-waving boys in flowing silk gowns and traditional Thai costumes performing untraditional dances. Some would say "Don't miss it!" Admission is 475B ($19) or 575B ($23) for a VIP seat at Tiffany, including one drink. Here again, liquor costs can mount up quickly. Many prefer Alcazar, about 100B ($4) cheaper.

GAY BARS Pattayaland, Sois 1, 2, and 3 (in southern Pattaya), like Soi Cowboy and Patpong in Bangkok, have many clubs catering to a gay crowd. **A Friend, Cockpit,** and **Boys Boys Boys** are some of many in Pattayaland, Soi 3, also known as "Boys Town" to locals. Ask for the latest tips at the Ambiance Hotel (tel. 424099) on Soi 3. In addition, there are several gay escort services advertised in local giveaway brochures and magazines.

DISCOS **Disco Duck,** in the Little Duck Pattaya Resort Hotel on Central Road (tel. 428104), is much admired by visiting Thai teenagers and "Tuppies," particularly on weekends. **Marina Disco,** in the Regent Marina Hotel (tel. 428105), offers live music most weekends to a mixed Thai and foreign young adult crowd in their 20s and 30s. Both have free entry and are open from 9pm to 2am. **Palladium,** on Pattaya Second Road (tel. 424933), outshines all the other discos with its vast, polished metal dance floor and hyperkinetic lighting grid. Admission is generally 250B ($10), including two drinks, higher if a well-known live band is performing (open nightly 9pm to 3am). Very popular with Thais, it also features one of the few traditional Thai massage parlors, where gentle but penetrating therapeutic massage costs 250B ($10) per hour (open daily noon to midnight).

ADULT ENTERTAINMENT Examples of the go-go flesh trade abound in bars along Pattayaland, Soi 1, where Thai beer and a look costs about 125B ($5), though the girls work off commission and encourage clients to buy rounds for everyone. A classier act and higher prices prevail at any of the new **Karaoke sing-along/hostess clubs** scattered along Pattaya Second and Third roads. Liquor is sold: 2,000B ($80) for a bottle of Mekhong and two setups is almost the minimum.

Warning: The police frequently clamp down on drug sellers and buyers in these venues; ignorance of the law is not an accepted defense in Thailand.

Most of Pattaya's "physical" massage parlors are on Pattaya Second Road in northern Pattaya. Typically, dozens of girls with numbered signs wait to be selected by clients, who are then whisked away to private massage rooms.

Repeat warning: Police frequently clamp down on drug sellers and buyers in these massage parlors.

All-night companionship is easy to come by, though payments to club owners, security guards, etc., mount up. Beware of "companions" bearing drinks laced with "knockout" drugs; watch your wallet; wear a condom.

SHOPPING

For sex-joke T-shirts and postcards, you can try the dozens of small souvenir stands tucked in between the open-air bars along Pattaya Beach Road. Branch stores of well known Thai silk shops and jewelers (none cheaper or better than that found in Bangkok or Chiang Mai) are located on Pattaya Second and Third roads. But for good, clean fun, try **Mike Shopping Mall,** a modern five-story mall on Pattaya Beach Road near Soi 11.

EN ROUTE TO BAN PHE

Rayong Province stretches east along the Gulf of Siam from Pattaya and its ever-mushrooming satellite resorts to the agricultural villages of Chanthaburi. To foreigners, the once-sleepy island of Ko Samet, reached by ferry from the fishing village of Ban Phe, is Rayong's greatest attraction.

Most Thai drivers heading east through Rayong leap at the chance to double back through Pattaya City, head up Sukhumvit Road, and hop onto the colorless Highway 36, the quick through route to Rayong city. We prefer the meandering coast road.

The warm waters of the Gulf of Thailand support more fishing villages than any other region in Thailand. Each night, hundreds of brightly painted, low-slung trawlers fish for squid, crab, lobsters, oysters, and other fish. The twinkling of lights offshore is one of the unexpected pleasures of seaview accommodations anywhere on the east coast. When you arrive at Ban Phe's pier, you can inspect these trawlers, some of which are converted to tourist ferries, for the voyage to Ko Samet, during the day.

---

2. BAN PHE & KO SAMET

220km (137 miles) E of Bangkok via Highway 3, or
185km (115 miles) via Highway 3, and the Pattaya bypass.

GETTING TO BAN PHE By Bus Fifteen air-conditioned buses a day leave from Bangkok's Eastern or Ekamai Bus Terminal direct to Ban Phe (trip time 3½ hours; 100B [$4]). 20 buses a day leave from Bangkok's Eastern Terminal to Rayong (trip time: 3 hours; 95B [3.80]), then minibuses from Rayong's clock tower to the Ban Phe pier (trip time: 40 minutes; 40B [$1.60]). Several buses a day leave from Pattaya to Ban Phe (trip time: 1 hour; 50B [$2]). Contact Wattana Tours, Pattaya, tel. 018/422607. The Bangkok-bound air-conditioned buses are very popular, particularly on weekends and holidays; reserve your return seat at the Ban Phe pier bus stop immediately on arrival.

By Private Bus

From Bangkok Many travel agencies operate their own transport—it's the easiest way to go. S. T. Travel has a minibus leaving from its office at 102 Rambutri Rd., (at Khaosan Road), Banglamphu, daily at 8am (trip time 3½ hours; 240B [$9.60]). Call them in Bangkok (tel. 02/281-3662 or 282-7312) or in Ban Phe (tel. 01/212-8641) for schedule information and reservations.

From Pattaya Malibu Travel (tel. 038/423180) or Ville Travel (tel. 038/427292) operate four minivans daily from varous hotels (trip time: 50 minutes; 175B [$7]). Contact Malibu Travel (tel. 01/211-7654) or Samet Ocean Tours (tel. 038/613300) in Ban Phe for schedules and information.

To/From Trat and Ko Chang The S. T. Travel minibus leaving Bangkok daily to Ban Phe continues on to Trat and Laem Ngop, the port for ferries to Ko Chang (trip time: 2 hours; 240B [$9.60]). Call S. T. in Bangkok (tel. 02/281-3662 or 282-7312), in Ban Phe (tel. 01/212-8641), or in Trat (tel. 039/511597 or 01/212-8014) for schedule information and reservations.

By Car Take Highway 3 east from Bangkok along the longer, more scenic coastal route (about 3½ to 4 hours), or the quicker route: via Highway 3 east to Pattaya, then Highway 36 to Rayong, then the coastal Highway 3 to Ban Phe (about 3 hours).

GETTING TO KO SAMET By Ferry During the high season, ferries leave Ban Phe pier for the main port every half hour (trip time: 40 minutes; 40B [$1.60]). You must catch a song-tao boat (about 25B [$1]) to other beaches, and pay the 25B ($1) park entrance fee. Several travel agents on the Ban Phe pier sell their own boats to Wong Duan and other beaches. These leave three to six times daily from 8:30am to 6pm (depending on destination, trip time: 40 to 120 minutes; 40B to 110B [$1.60 to $4.40]). On weekends, it's possible to charter your own fishing boat for 800B to 1,500B ($32 to $60), depending on the number of passengers and destination.

Ban Phe is 35km (22 miles) east of Rayong city, along Sukhumvit Highway, which was being widened during our last visit. As you turn south toward the Gulf of Siam, you'll pass through a bustling village to the seaside main street, dominated by the large pier and its colorful fishing boats destined for Ko Samet.

Ko Samet (also called Ko Kaeo Phitsadan) first became popular with Thais from the poetry of Sunthon Phu, a venerated 19th-century author and Rayong native who set his best-known epic on this "tropical island paradise." Fortunately, despite its appeal to Thais and foreigners, a shortage of potable water kept rampant commerce and tourism at bay for many years. In 1981, Samet became part of the six-island Khao Laem Ya–Samet National Park, a designation meant to preserve its relatively undeveloped status. Since then, small-scale construction has boomed, and there are more than 50 licensed bungalow hotels with more than 1,500 rooms on the 6km (3.6 miles) long island. In 1990, a TAT-sponsored effort to close the national park to overnight visitors met with such fierce resistance that four days later Samet was reopened, for business as usual. Until inadequate water supplies, waste treatment, and garbage disposal are dealt with, the TAT is encouraging visitors to go to the still-lovely Samet for day trips only.

ESSENTIALS Orientation Ban Phe has three streets: The coast road features the ferry pier at the east end of a C-shaped cove; the second road runs westbound and has the town's open-air market; the third inland road runs eastbound. Buses stop in front of everything; everything is within easy walking distance.

Information The nearest TAT office is about 12km west on the highway to Rayong (tel. 038/655420; fax 038/655422). The temporary office of the **Tourist Police** is at the Pines Beach Hotel, Ban Phe (tel. 038/651636).

Fast Facts The **area code** is 038, though radio phones (widely used) work on 01, and have eight-digit numbers. (There are very few long-distance phones available on Ko Samet.) The **post** and **telegraph office** is on Highway 3, 2km (1.2 miles) east of the pier. A bank minivan parks at the pier daily 9am–4pm for **currency exchange;** bring plenty of cash to Ko Samet. If you get stranded, the Nual Napa Hotel opposite the pier has 45 OK rooms with private toilets, which cost 200B ($8) with fan, 500B ($20) with air-conditioning, single or double (tel. 038/651668).

WHAT TO SEE & DO

The small island's northern half is triangular, with a long tail leading to the south that looks somewhat like a kite. Most of the beaches are on the east coast of the tail; although Ko Samet's only about 1km (⁶/₁₀ mile) wide, it has a rocky spine and there are five paths that connect the two coasts.

Passengers alight from the ferry at Hat Sai Kaeo (Diamond Beach on the northeast cape), which is linked by a dirt path to 10 other small beach developments. Most day-trippers take the regular ferry and then hike the shoreline path between beaches.

Windsurfing is particularly popular with weekenders from Bangkok. The island's best is said to be north of Hat Sai Kaeo, around the cape which bulges out of Samet's east side. The rocky north coast is even more challenging, with strong currents and sometimes erratic winds caused by the deep channel between the island and the mainland. Windsurfers are available at most guesthouses for 90B to 150B ($3.60 to $5) per hour, without instruction. The most developed east-coast beach cove is the closest and dirtiest, just south of the jetty at Ao Thian or Candlelight Beach. Heading south, Ao Tubtim, Ao Cho, and Ao Taiwan (*ao* means bay) are popular bays with smaller bungalow villages. Wong Duan is a U-shaped cove that's very popular with foreigners; antienvironmentalists can rent mopeds here to cruise the island's dirt paths (for about 750B [$30] per day). Samet's southern, narrow kit tail has calm waters, good for swimming and snorkeling.

Up north on the west coast, is Ao Phrao (Paradise Beach), the most isolated cove on the island, Aficionados prefer snorkeling off the rocky west coast where coral reefs have escaped the damage caused by frequent ferries. The western coastline is mostly uninhabited; the easiest access is by sea.

WHERE TO STAY IN KO SAMET

Vong Deaun Resort offers a wide range of accommodations that can be booked in Bangkok, at 359/9-11 Ekamai Complex, Sukhumvit 63 Prakhanong (tel. 02/392-0879, fax 662/391-9571). If you don't book one of the few bungalow complexes with a telephone before your arrival, never fear. Several travel agents, enterprising fishermen, teenage girls, and others hover at the Ban Phe pier with photo albums showing off their rooms to rent. Accommodations are similarly primitive around the island; note that rates are higher than at other "undeveloped" island resorts because food and water must be imported from the mainland.

There are also many independent bungalows on Ao Wai, Hat Sai Kaeo (the longest sandy strip and the island's main port), and Ao Cho, as well as many under-10-room complexes scattered around the shoreline. Rates go as low as 125B ($5) for a thatch A-frame with a sleeping platform and shared Asian toilet but no mosquito netting, and as high as 750B ($30) for a fan-cooled, screened window bungalow with linens and a private toilet. Most bungalows have their own dining areas for inexpensive, fresh seafood (don't miss the locally caught squid and cuttle fish which are barbecued on skewers) and standard Thai rice and noodle dishes.

MALIBU GARDEN RESORT, 77 Wong Duan Beach, Samet Island, Ban Phe, 121160 Rayong. Tel. 01/321-0345 or 01/211-7654 in Ban Phe.
$ Rates (including tax and service): 600B ($24) single or double. V.
These clean concrete bungalows with tin roofs are clustered right on the beach, surrounding a much more picturesque thatch dining pavilion where light meals are served. Rooms have fans, cold-water showers, curtains, and a modicum of decor.

VONGDUERN VILLAS, Wong Duan Beach, Samet Island, 22 Moo 4 Pae, 121160 Rayong. Tel. 01/321-0789 or 038/613300 in Rayong.
$ Rates (including tax and service: 1,100B–1,400B ($44–$56) single or double; VIP suite from 3,500B ($140) single or double. V.
Simple, solid wood bungalows with air-conditioning and private hot water showers vary in price according to view and size of room. There are also elaborate VIP bungalows (perhaps the only ones on the island) with carpeting, TV, VCR with a private video collection, intrabungalow phone, and minibar—quite a change from what the average visitor to Ko Samet is seeking.

AO KIU NA NOK VILLAS, c/o Samed Travel Service, Ban Phe, 121160 Rayong. Tel. 01/321-1371.
$ Rates (including tax and service): 800B ($32) single or double with fan; 2,000B ($80) single or double with A/C. No credit cards.
The broad sandy cove of Ao Kiu Na Nok is near the southern tip of the Ko Samet kite tail, and therefore much less busy than other beaches. These fan-cooled, simple bungalows have private bathrooms, but only cold water. Pricier bungalows are more substantially built and have hot water, but all are well located on the beach. Over the holidays from mid-December to mid-January, Samed Travel says they will charge a 300B ($12) per room per night supplement.

EN ROUTE TO CHANTHABURI: RAYONG PROVINCE

If you have lots of time to kill in Ban Phe, the **Thai House Museum** and **Suan Son Botanical Gardens** are about 2km (1.2 miles) east of the ferry pier. Run by the private Sawet-Sobha Foundation, this odd collection of ceramics and a few pieces of furniture are placed around three traditional Thai teak houses on a landscaped piece of property. We say—only for old house buffs (open Friday to Tuesday 8am to 4pm; admission 60B [$2.40])!

The long, tree-shaded coastline east of Rayong has several small public beaches and isolated resort properties, with more under development. Just 7km (4.2 miles) east of Ban Phe is the bustling Suan Sum Park, a pine-and-palm-lined, narrow sand beach filled with Thai day-trippers and Thai Guides (national version of Boy Scouts) camping groups. There are dozens of food stalls, picnic tables with cars pulled up nearby, vendors renting inner tubes, modestly clad kids learning to swim, and lots of general hubbub.

From the headland at Wang Kaeo along the stretch of tranquil beach to Laem Mae Phim are several deluxe condo complexes and luxury hotels. We enjoyed a very relaxing stay during our most recent trip at the excellent **Palmeraie Princess** (weekday rates from 1,400B [$56], weekends from 1,700B [$68]), and we highly recommend it to those traveling by car.

As you get farther from the city, mango, coconut, and durian are under cultivation, though the provincial government has begun encouraging rubber plantations as an alternate industry. The old women in tight, flowery sarongs will squat below sun umbrellas to peddle dried squid or grilled octopus and grilled chicken to Bangkok's "Benz families" (those who drive Mercedes-Benz).

3. CHANTHABURI PROVINCE

Travelers heading east to the undeveloped, stunning, wooded isles of Mu Ko Chang National Park (see "Trat & Ko Chang," below) will pass through Chanthaburi province and its capital city, Muang Chan. This region is known for its gem mines (a lucrative export industry) and tropical fruit production. Durian, custard apple, longan, and rambutan are grown in large plantations, but small family farms are much in evidence. Don't be startled by the roadside 26-foot-high durian sculpture, or the many watermelon and fruit stands alongside the highway.

Muang Chan is a large city built on both sides of the Chanthaburi River. In central Taksin Park, there's a statue of King Taksin on horseback, surrounded by sword-brandishing troops, to commemorate his victory over Burmese invaders in 1767, after the fall of Ayutthaya. The city's main avenue is Tha Chalab Road. The taxi stand and bus station (to Trat or Bangkok) are just west of the Chanthaburi Hotel on this street; both flank the central produce and Night Market.

WHAT TO SEE & DO

Most of the area's attractions appeal to Thai tourists seeking the great outdoors: parks, natural sights, and beaches.

PARKS & PUBLIC BEACHES The 42,000-acre **Namtok Philu National Park,** very popular because King Rama V and his wife Queen Sunatha are said to have visited its pretty waterfall, is served by frequent shared taxis (truck taxis or song tao) from the Chanthaburi town market.

Laem Sadet is the best of the nearby beaches, and it's about 35km (22 miles) southwest of the city. From the rocky cape which forms a picturesque lagoon at Khung Krabane, the pine-shaded coastline has a long, but narrow, sand beach running south for several kilometers. Resort developers are bound to come soon, since the only commercial activities at present are prawn farms and fish-drying cottage industries. Laem Sadet and closer beach destinations can also be reached by shared taxis or public buses.

GEM SHOPPING In case you were intrigued by our mention of the local gem industry, remember: the best quality gemstones found here are sent to Bangkok for sale. Unless you are an expert, don't expect to find bargains on Gems Street (in Chanthaburi near the central market), or in any of the many jewelers' shops. For the curious, blue and black sapphires are mined near Wat Khao Ploy Wan, about 15km (9 miles) east of the city. Rubies are mined farther east in Trat and over the Cambodian border. Northeast of Chanthaburi in Nong Bon, and due east of town at Bo Rai (both in Trat province), are the major ruby markets. Each morning, gem sales take place at Bo Rai's central Hua Tung market; and each afternoon at the Khlong Yo Market. The market at Nong Bon (on Route 3299) takes place all day.

A NEARBY ATTRACTION **Oasis Sea World**, 48/2 Moo 5 Tambon Paknam, Amphur Ramsing, Chanthaburi (tel. 039/312567), is Thailand's largest dolphinarium. Partially open at our visit, there were 65 dolphins (some humpback and some Irrawaddi dolphins) housed in more than 25 acres of developed seashore. Feeding and playtime are fun to watch, but the dolphins are trained to do tricks for an audience. The construction of an aviary, swimming pool, water slides, and waterfall are on the agenda. Oasis Sea World is open daily from 8am to 5pm; admission is 60B ($2.40) for adults, 30B ($1.20) for children. To get there, take Highway 3 east to Trat city, turn south at the Laem Sing exit and follow the signs.

WHERE TO STAY & DINE

There is no reason to spend the night, but if you must . . .

THE EASTERN HOTEL, 899 Cha Laeb Rd., Chanthaburi 2200. Tel. 039/ 312218. 142 rms. A/C TEL **Directions:** Across from Taksin Park, 4 km (2½ miles) southeast of town market.

$ Rates: 600B ($24) single or double. MC, V.

Reputedly the best hotel in town before the new K. P. Grand (35/1 Trirat Rd., tel. 039/313878; rooms from 1600B [$64]) opened, this worn and aging structure is right in the middle of Chantaburi's depressing red-light district. There is actually a pleasant lobby bakery, a cheerful coffee shop mobbed with locals, a dimly lit bar (also mobbed), a loud and seedy nightclub (also mobbed) filled with besequinned young songbirds, and poorly kept but (sort of) clean rooms. Don't let the front desk hustle you into a windowless room; they're no cheaper than the cityview rooms.

THE CHAI LEE HOTEL, 106 Kwang Rd., Chanthaburi 2200. Tel. 039/ 311075. 66 rms. TEL **Directions:** In the central market.

$ Rates (including tax and service): 125B–175B ($5–$8) single or double. No credit cards.

These are very simple accommodations, recommended by a Canadian couple we met who became stranded overnight when trying to take a bus from Ayutthaya to Trat for a holiday on Ko Si Chang. Swept clean, fan-cooled rooms have a private shower inside; choose a back-facing room to avoid the bustle of the Night Market.

EN ROUTE TO TRAT

The Sukhumvit Highway (Highway 3) east from Chanthaburi to Trat is just 70km (42 miles) of two-lane blacktop wending through relatively undeveloped terrain. At the 31km market, two lion statues mark the turnoff for Laem Sing, a cape jutting into the Gulf of Siam that's said to resemble a resting lion. On a hill above are the remnants of a fortress built by King Rama III. Below Laem Sing, the pier is lined with seafood restaurants and fishing boats and the new Oasis Sea World is nearby, all hoping to appeal to the many traveling Thais.

Along the road you'll see leafy green vines tightly wound around slender poles—it's those small, fiery chilis the Thais love to cook with. Old women in straw hats and brightly patterned sarongs sell bamboo tubes stuffed with sticky rice steamed in coconut milk; these semisweet, chewy cylinders make great road snacks.

4. TRAT & KO CHANG

400km (249 miles) E of Bangkok

GETTING TO TRAT By Plane As of 1994, Trat's only airfield was the property of the Thai Air Force. However, long-term provincial plans call for the development of direct flights from Bangkok, so check with the TAT before you buy a bus ticket.

By Bus Eight air-conditioned buses a day leave from Bangkok's Eastern or Ekamai Bus Terminal (trip time: 5 to 6 hours; 175B [$7]); eight buses a day from Pattaya's Bus Terminal (trip time: 3½ hours; 125B [$5]).

By Private Bus

To/From Bangkok A few travel agencies operate their own transport—it's the easiest way to go because you're delivered direct to the Ko Chang ferries. S. T. Travel has a minibus leaving from its office at 102 Rambutri Rd. (at Khaosan Road), Banglamphu, daily at 8am (trip time: 6 hours; 250B; [$10]). Call them in Bangkok (tel. 02/281-3662 or 282-7312) or in Trat (tel. 039/511597 or 01/212-8014) for information and reservations.

To/From Ban Phe and Ko Samet The daily S. T. Travel minibus to Ban Phe continues on to Trat and Laem Ngop (trip time: 2 hours; 200B [$8]). Call S. T. in Bangkok (tel. 02/281-3662 or 282-7312), in Ban Phe (tel. 01/212-8641), or in Trat (tel. 039/511597 or 01/212-8014) for schedule information and reservations.

By Car Take Highway 3 east from Bangkok to Chonburi, then Highway 344 southeast to Klaeng (bypassing Pattaya and Rayong), then the coastal Highway 3 east through Chanthaburi and south to Trat (about 5 to 6 hours).

GETTING TO LAEM NGOP There is a constant stream of shared truck taxis (called minibuses or song tao) departing from Trat's central market, next to the bus terminal (trip time: 30 minutes; 40B [$1.60]); a private truck taxi costs about 200B ($8). Laem Ngop is a tiny village of shops selling shrimp paste and fish sauce, with a long pier housing dozens of fishing boats. Son Jan Restaurant just south of the pier is the best place to wait for a boat, have a Thai snack, or a cool drink. The helpful S. T. Travel desk in front books a private minivan to Bangkok (see "Getting to Trat," above) and rooms on the island (see "Where to Stay & Dine," below).

GETTING TO KO CHANG By Ferry You have to take a ferry from Laem Ngop to any of Mu Ko Chang National Park's many islands. Study this section, ask more questions at the Trad Tourist Information Desk (see below), and know where you want to go before you get to the pier. Boys from the passenger boats (none too helpful) solicit tourists to go to their assigned Ko Chang beaches (the fishermen/captains have divided up service to the main island and the park's smaller islands). However, at our visit, ferries to the most popular beaches on Ko Chang left at noon or 3pm (give or take an hour), according to demand and the captain's frame of mind (trip time: 2 to 4 horus; 50B to 250B [$2 to $10] depending on destination). Remain calm and you'll find the right boat.

Trat's dramatic, wooded landscape crests at the Khao Bantat Range, which separates Thailand's easternmost province from neighboring Cambodia. This region thrives on agriculture (primarily rubber and chili plantations), fish farming, and fishing. Gem mining is a troublesome occupation in the eastern hills, where miners pay license fees to Khmer Rouge guerrillas so they can gather rubies in peace. (See "Gem Shopping," in "Chanthaburi Province," above).

Foreigners and Thai tourists are advised not to travel south of the capital, Muang Trat, after dark because of security problems. Navy battle ships moored off Laem Ngop are a reminder of the region's troubled past (every January 13, the Thai

Navy honors those killed in the 19th-century war with France over Cambodian territory) and of its troubled present (ships patrol the coast to monitor activity along the Cambodian border).

Trat Province is the gateway to the tranquil, unspoilt beaches of Mu Ko Chang National Park, 52 heavily wooded islands, most accessible by ferry from the cape at Laem Ngop. If no phone or power lines, no discos or video bars, no beach vendors or mopeds sound like tropical paradise, this is your kind of place. It's naturally pure, scenically beautiful, and very, very quiet.

ESSENTIALS **Orientation**   Arriving visitors will find themselves in the center of Trat, at the air-conditioned bus terminal on main street or Sukhumvit Road. Next door is the central open-air market. Shared taxis going west to Chanthaburi or east to Laem Ngop leave from the market throughout the day. Everything is within easy walking distance.

Information   The very helpful Trad Tourist Information Desk is in the bus terminal (tel. 039/511052), open daily 6am to 11:30pm. Ban Phe has the nearest Tourist Police (tel. 038/651636).

Fast Facts   The **area code** is 039, though radio phones (widely used) work on 01, and have eight-digit phone numbers. Trat **banks** are only open weekdays from 8:30am to 3:30pm. However, a bank minivan parks at the Laem Ngop pier daily from 9am to 4pm for currency exchange. No facilities exist on Ko Chang. If you get stranded, the **Muang Trad Hotel**, at 4 Sukhumvit Rd., (tel. 039/511091), one block south of the bus terminal, has 144 rooms with private toilet and Asian mandi (ladle shower), which cost 175B ($7) single, 225B ($9) double with fan; 300B ($12) single, 600B ($24) double with air-conditioning. They accept MasterCard and VISA credit cards and have the nicest Thai coffee shop in town (open 6:30am to 9:30pm).

MALARIA ALERT   Malaria is endemic to the heavily forested islands of Mu Ko Chang National Park and the jungle-covered foothills of Trat province. Several strains discovered are resistant to all known medical prophylaxis. The only protection you have is to avoid getting bitten. Make sure to purchase insect repellent, preferably one with a high DEET content, in Trat (available at all pharmacies) before proceeding to the islands. Note: Be sure to consult your physician before you make this trip.

WHAT TO SEE & DO IN KO CHANG

Ko Chang, Thailand's second-largest island after Phuket, is the anchor of the 52-island Mu Ko Chang National Park. Thickly forested hills rise from its many rocky bays, forming a swaying hump reminiscent of a sleeping elephant (*chang* means elephant). Accommodations are primitive; budget tourists come for the beaches and the cleanest Mediterranean-blue waters this side of Greece. Pineapple and coconut palms dominate the landscape, with a few scattered fishing villages (established before the island was declared a national park) containing most of the sparse population. Cambodia can easily be seen from the eastern shore, site of a small naval base and the national park office. The Park Service has opened some dormitory-and-camping space; contact their Bangkok headquarters (tel 02/579-5269) for reservations and information. Most of the island's development, including a dirt road which stretches around the northern coast, and the few pickups which ply it carrying construction materials, are near Thaan Ma Yom pier.

Only a few pristine sand beaches, with newly built thatch bungalows tucked into the treeline, dot its western-and-southern shores. The best beaches are on the west coast, a 1½- to 2½-hour boat ride from Laem Ngop. Hat Sai Khao (White Sand Beach) is the closest of the western beaches, with the majority of Ko Chang's bungalow housing set in a narrow ribbon along its kilometer-long, fine sand beach. Twenty minutes by boat farther south is Hat Khlong Phrao, with a pier at its north end to serve some bungalows, an inland canal and fishing settlement in the middle, and one full-service resort and numerous bungalows to the south. This broad, palm-lined cove is one of Ko Chang's prettiest. Since housing is limited, boat captains help direct travelers to the available bungalows by hailing dugouts to come pick you up.

The best skin diving or snorkeling is around the small islands off Ko Chang's south coast, such as Ko Khlum, Ko Whai (a particularly beautiful island), Ko Phrao (near some wrecks of Thai naval ships), Ko Ngam, and Ko Lao Ya. All of these islands, except Ko Khlum, have some bungalows, but ferry service is erratic, infrequent, and expensive. Ko Lao Ya is the best organized for tourists, with a telephone and a fine resort (see "Where to Stay & Dine," below). Hat Bang Bao is a small cove on the island's southwest corner (within day-trip distance of these islands), whose mixed sand and coral coast supports a few bungalows.

WHERE TO STAY & DINE

As of 1994, there were only two "full-service" (even this is an exaggeration) hotels in the Mu Ko Chang National Park. Elsewhere, accommodations consist of simple thatch huts and A-frames, most without telephones to accept reservations. Transportation is the biggest problem. Beaches are serviced only by select ferries—it's almost impossible to move from one beach to another without returning to Laem Ngop. The only boats to Laem Ngop return from Ko Chang in the morning, so there's a chance (especially in the high season between mid-December and mid-January) that you'll end up on a great beach with no available bungalows and sleep outdoors overnight.

You can minimize the aura of adventurous unpredictability by checking with travel agents at the Laem Ngop pier or asking your boat captain what's happening at the various beaches. A reminder: Take precautions against mosquitoes, as malaria is endemic to this area. Hungry sand flies are also a big problem!

KO CHANG RESORT, 39 Moo 8, Ko Chang, Trat 23120 Tel. 01/211-5193 or 039/597028 in Trat. Fax 02/277-0975 (in Bangkok). 70 rms. A/C MINIBAR TV **Directions:** Hat Khlong Phrao, 2 hours by ferry.
$ Rates: 2,000B–2,500B ($80–$100) single/double. Extra person 400B ($16). MC, V.
With hot water, minibars, and even VCRs with Thai-dubbed American B pictures, this resort stands out as the most comfortable and expensive housing on the islands. You can choose between freestanding bungalows (two sizes) and slightly more modern, attached rooms in a two-story hotel block. The best value is found in four more expensive, front bungalows, priced the same as our no-view hotel room, but with delightful verandas and sea views. All rooms are cool and comfortably furnished with minimal decor and pastel tile floors, but cleaning is wildly sporadic.

The beach is superb, with rows of coconut palms marching down to the clear, shallow warm waters. It's a great spot for sitting (there are canvas deck chairs and no hawkers) or swimming (there are very few boats and only mild currents). The outdoor dining patio, tended by an amiable staff, serves up typical, but mediocre, Thai fare and a few continental dishes. We found their strong suit was grilled seafood from local waters.

LAO YA ISLAND RESORT, Ko Lao Ya, Trat 23120 Tel. 039/512552 or 02/ 391-1588 in Bangkok. Fax 66-039/512552. A/C MINIBAR **Directions:** Ko Lao Ya, 4 hours by ferry.
$ Rates: 1,250B ($50) single/double; 1,600B ($64) single with half board, 2,000B ($80) double with half board. MC, V.
This is the only lodging on this tiny island, making it a destination for those seeking obscure and far-off places. Bungalows have fully functioning air-conditioning, hot-water private showers, full bathrooms, and comfortable bedrooms. They're finished in burnished coconut wood and furnished with some style in tropical rattan. Our German friends claim the kitchen turns out the best food they ate on their entire trip. It's a good thing too, because the half-board is compulsory over the holiday season and there's nowhere else to eat!

Lao Ya is comparably good value, and ideal for those seeking a tranquil vacation. The beach is lovely but rocky, however, swimming is safe and easy. The marine park's best snorkeling is found in these waters, a real plus if you're so inclined.

SUNSET BUNGALOWS, Hat Bang Bao, Ko Chang, Trat 23120. Tel. 01/ 212-8014; or c/o A. D. Tours tel. 039/511597 (in Laem Ngop). 19 rms (none with bath).

$ Rates (including tax and service): 150B ($6) single; 250B ($10) double. No credit cards.

These are typical of the island's primitive accommodations, and worth mentioning only because of their phone. Fifteen simple, thatch and wood-slat huts are set along the pretty sand beach lining this narrow cove; four rooms are contained in one house. There is a communal cold-water shower and Asian toilets; there are no fans or screened windows, but mosquito netting is provided. The Sunset management also encourages camping on their grounds, making it a busy place during the high season. Check the A. D. Tours desk just south of the Laem Ngop pier for room availability before you hop in the Hat Bang Bao ferry.

On these and other beaches mentioned above, there are several clusters of anonymous, primitive thatch and coconut-wood A-frames, all without phone, private shower, or toilet, or any hot water. Few have fans or window screens, but proprietors will usually provide mosquito netting over the mattresses. Prices range from 150B to 300B ($6 to $12). Write to us with any discoveries.

CHAPTER 7

KO SAMUI & THE SOUTHEAST COAST

Thailand's slim Malay Peninsula extends 1,250km (777 miles) south from Bangkok to the Malaysia border at Sungai Kolok. Just as the beach resort of Phuket in the Andaman Sea dominates the list of west coast pleasures, so Ko Samui, a more laid-back, traditionally Thai resort island in the Gulf of Siam, dominates the east.

Heading south from Bangkok, we first reach the twin beach resorts of Hua Hin Cha-Am. The once-elegant retreat of royalty is blossoming with a flashy nouveau grandeur designed to appeal to Bangkok's elite. Well-priced luxury resorts and family-oriented cabana hotels provide a getaway for tourists, too.

From Hua Hin, it's a slow crawl on the busy highway to Chumphon, a region renowned for its pineapple crops that is trying to recuperate from a devastating hurricane in 1989. Following the quiet coast road to Surat Thani, we arrive at the ferries for increasingly popular Ko Samui, a coconut-studded isle sure to please the most demanding tropical-paradise seeker.

South of Surat Thani the pleasures are more cerebral. We head inland to the ancient Buddhist center of Nakhon Si Thammarat, then continue onto the predominantly Muslim villages farther south, ending up at the Malaysian border.

1. HUA HIN/CHA-AM

Hua Hin is 240km (140 miles) S of Bangkok; 223km (138 miles) N of Chumphon

GETTING THERE **By Plane** Bangkok Airways (tel. 02/229-3456) flies twice daily to Hua Hin (trip time: 30 minutes; 1,000B [$40]) from Don Muang airport.

By Train Ten trains leave daily from Bangkok (trip time: 3½ hours special express, 4½ hours rapid; 250B [$10] for air-conditioned special express), continuing south to Surat Thani. Two trains leave daily to and from Kanchanaburi (trip time: 6 hours; 60B [$2.40] in third class).

By Bus Twenty-two air-conditioned buses depart daily from Bangkok's Southern Bus Terminal (trip time: 3 hours; 115B [$4.60]). Fifteen buses leave daily to Chumphon (trip time 3 hours; 75B [$3]). There are many buses daily to Suran Thani (trip time: 10 hours; 125B [$5]).

By Car Take Route 35, the Thonburi-Paktho Highway (when we last took this, it was totally torn up and due for resurfacing; the trip took over 5 hours!). Allow 2 to 4 hours, depending on traffic.

WHAT SPECIAL ABOUT KO SAMUI & THE SOUTHEAST COAST

Beaches

Choeng Mon Bay, golden Chaweng, and rock-studded Lamai are some of Ko Samui's most scenic, palm-fringed beaches.

Natural Spectacles

Ko Samui's monkeys are trained to climb trees and harvest coconuts. Mu Ko Angthong (Golden Bowl) Marine Park's large, golden saltwater pool, mysteriously replenished from an undiscovered outlet to the sea.

Religious Shrines

Wat Mahatat in Nakhon Si Thammarat has housed a relic of the Buddha in its gold chedi since the 9th century.

The Suan Mokkhabalarama Monastery, known worldwide for teaching the elemental principles and practices of Buddhism.

Wat Phrayai's gold-tiled Big Buddha towers 83 feet above Ko Samui's north coast.

Narathiwat's Phra Buddha Taksin Ming Mongkol is one of the tallest, seated bronze Buddhas in Thailand.

Architectural Highlights

Hua Hin's fully restored colonial/Victorian/art deco–style Hotel Sofitel Central, with its wonderful lobby and eccentric topiary garden, was a major location for the film *The Killing Fields*. Phetchaburi's Khao Wang Hill and its wats decorated with Ayutthaya-era murals.

Regional Food/Drink

Southern Thailand's spicy coconut milk and red chili "yellow curry" dishes are best sampled near the Malaysia border.

Chaiya is known nationwide for its special salted eggs which are caked in mud and charred rice husks, then boxed to take home.

Surat Thani's oyster farms produce huge, firm-fleshed tilam oysters that shouldn't be missed.

Hat Yai's lively Hawkers Center (market) is a terrific venue for widely varied dining in a typical Night Market setting.

H ua Hin, developed in the 1920s, is actually Thailand's first beach resort, initially favored exclusively by the royal family (they still use the Klai Kangwon or "Far from Worries" Palace in the summer) and the upper crust of Bangkok society. In the 1940s and 1950s, and especially prior to the development of Pattaya in the mid-1960s, Hua Hin (and its sister resort of Cha-Am) changed dramatically as it became the most popular destination for middle-class Thai families commuting from Bangkok. Although its popularity declined with the ascendence of Phuket, Ko Samui, and Pattaya, recent renewal of the Hua Hin/Cha-Am resorts, with newly built grand hotels and luxurious high-rise condos, has created tourist interest in the area. If you're planning a visit, try to avoid the period from November to February, Hua Hin's rainy and windy season.

ESSENTIALS Orientation When Thais refer to "Hua Hin" they mean the 20km (12 miles) long strip extending from Hua Hin north to Cha-Am. Hua Hin is an older and more developed city, with great character, while the beachfront village of Cha-Am reminds us of a cheery, little Greek island town, or possibly a lesser destination along the New Jersey shore. Both are jammed with people and very densely commercialized. If you want to travel between the two, plan on taking a local bus, song tao, tuk-tuk, or taxi; the ride takes about 25 minutes and will run from 20B to 200B (80¢ to $8) depending on the mode of transport.

THE SOUTHEAST COAST

0   60 km
    37 mi

① Hua Hin/Cha Am
② Chumphon
Ko Tao
Ranong   Lang Suan
Ko Phangnghan
Ko Ta
Luang   ③ Ko Samui
Chaiya
Gulf of Thailand
④ Surat Thani
Phanom   Sichon
Tha Sala
Phrasaeng
Thung Yai   ⑤ Nakhon Si Thammarat
Klong Thom   Hua Sai
Huai Yot
Ko Lanta Yai   Phatthalung
Trang   Sathing Pra
Ko Li Bong
Thung Wa   ⑥ Songkhla
Hat Yai ⑦   Pattani
⑧
Ko Tarutao
Narathiwat
Andaman Sea
MALAYSIA
Sungai Kolok

Route 4
401
4009
401
4014
305
Route 4
Route 4

THAILAND
★ Bangkok
The Southeast Coast

① Hua Hin/Cha Am
② Chumphon
③ Ko Samui
④ Surat Thani
⑤ Nakhon Si Thammarat
⑥ Songkhla
⑦ Hat Yai
⑧ Pattani

Both villages are small and can be walked, although many visitors try an outing by *samlor*, a human-powered pedicab. Most of the larger resorts offer complimentary scheduled minivan shuttles into town. Buses and trains arrive in Hua Hin (the bus station is at the Sri Phetchkasem Hotel on Srasong Road; the nonair-conditioned bus station is near Chatachai Market; the Railway Station is near the post office on Damneonkasem Road).

Information   The **Tourism Authority of Thailand (TAT)** (tel. 032/471006; fax 032/471502) is at 500/51 Phetkasem Rd., halfway up the coastal route linking Hua Hin and Cha-Am. Though inconvenient, they are very helpful and are open daily from 8:30am to 4:30pm.

Fast Facts   The **telephone code** for the area is 032. The **police** (tel. 511027) can be found on Damneonkasem Road. The **Hua Hin Hospital** (tel. 511743) is 4km (2½ miles) out of town on Petchkasem Road. The **post office** and overseas telephone office are also on Petchkasem Road (in Cha-Am the Bangkok Bank is open daily 9am to 8pm along the main road). Most **shops** are open daily from 9am to 10pm; the Night Market is open from 6pm to 12am. **Minibuses** are available for rent opposite the Chatchai Market on Petchkasem Road. Avis operates a **car-rental counter** at the Royal Garden Resort (tel. 511881) in Hua Hin and the Dusit in Cha-Am (tel. 520008). A number of hotels offer **tours** in and around the area; **Western Tours** (tel. 512560) is an independent tour company located in Hua Hin at 11 Damneonkasem Rd. (Hua Hin's main street).

WHAT TO SEE & DO

Most people come here to sit on an evergreen-lined beach or revel in the luxury of an august resort complex, but there are a few diversions that might appeal to you. The most compelling of these is a day trip to **Phetchaburi**—60km (37 miles) north—one of Thailand's oldest towns and a repository of several Ayutthaya-era artifacts and structures (see "Easy Excursions," below).

For tee totalers there is the **Royal Hua Hin Golf Course** (tel. 511099), Thailand's first, having opened in 1924. Recently upgraded like the Sofitel Central, it features wild topiary figures along the fairways. It's open daily 6am to 6pm; clubs are available for rent.

Just 2km (1.2 miles) south of the Cha-Am Regent, down an unmarked road leading to the Rama VI Army Base, is one of the country's most sublime palaces, designed by King Mongkut and completed in 1924. Known as the **Maruekkhathayawan** (or **Mrigadoyavan**) **Palace** (Palace of Love and Hope), it is entirely made of teak and is more an open-air pavilion than a traditional European-designed structure. The palace fell into a state of disrepair and has, for several years, been under renovation. For those familiar with the Thai Victorian–style Sofitel Central, the palace appears to have been designed and built in an entirely similar manner. There are English-language brochures, and it's easy enough to navigate by yourself. Admission is free but donations are requested. It's open daily 8am to 4pm.

Water-sports enthusiasts should note that hotel owners are discouraging guests from renting fun-looking, minispeedboats (scooters) because of safety and pollution. There have been a number of accidents both with boat drivers and swimmers (who are inadvertently run over by inexperienced drivers). Scooters not only spew fumes and excess fuel into the water, but many tourists have been ripped off in gasoline or "lost or damaged" parts schemes involving credit-card deposits. Another pollution source are the ubiquitous ponies that schlepp up and down the beach; they are for hire (but keep in mind that other people swim and laze on the same stretch of sand)! Minispeedboats run 300B ($12) per hour; you can take a water taxi from Cha-Am to Hua Hin for about 180B ($7.20).

WHERE TO STAY

Note that every hotel in the "Expensive" category charges an additional peak-season supplement of 500B to 800B ($20 to $40) per room between mid-December and late January. Conversely, hotels in every price range offer substantial discounts in the low season.

HUA HIN

Expensive

ROYAL GARDEN RESORT, 107/1 Petchkasem Beach Rd., Hua Hin 77110. Tel. 032/511881. Fax 032/512422. Telex 78309 ROGAHUA TH. 217 rms, 5 suites. A/C MINIBAR TV TEL

$ Rates: 3,600B–3,800B ($144–$152) single or double; from 8,875B ($355) suite; 600B ($24) extra person. Supplement Dec 12–Jan 10 500B ($20). AE, DC, MC, V.

The extremely well-outfitted and maintained Royal Garden Resort is best suited for those in search of beach-and-sports activities. Singles and families are here throughout the year, lured principally by the ponds, pools, boats, golf, tennis, and other racket sports as well as the pet elephant and junglelike grounds leading out to the calm sea. The hotel is relatively convenient, with complimentary shuttle service into town and to its sister establishment, the more traditional Thai-style Royal Garden Village. Deluxe rooms are the best choice; large, amenity filled, and facing the sea. The fourth floor is for nonsmokers; there are several connecting rooms for families.

Dining/Entertainment: The Nautilus Lounge (very clubby) overlooks the pool and is open from 10pm to 1am. The Garden is a cheery coffee shop with a mixed international and Thai menu. On the beach lawn is the Italian Pavilion Restaurant; open daily 10am to 11pm.

Services: Concierge, babysitting, house doctor, laundry service, Avis car rental.

Facilities: Pool, tennis courts, beauty and barber shop, shopping arcade, golf, zoo, fitness center, playground.

ROYAL GARDEN VILLAGE, 43/1 Petchkasem Beach Rd., Hua Hin 77110. Tel. 032/520250. Fax 032/520259. Telex 78314 ROGAVIL TH. 162 rms. A/C MINIBAR TV TEL

$ Rates: 3,800B–4,300B ($152–$172) single or double; 11,000B ($440) Village suite; 700B ($28) extra bed. Supplement Dec 20–Jan 10 500B ($20). AE, DC, MC, V.

A series of elegantly designed Thai-style pavilions make up the structure of the lobby and the public facilities at this "village" away from the town center, off the main road. A lovely Kaliga tapestry hangs prominently in the lobby, which is tastefully decorated with ornately carved teak wooden lanterns, warm wood floors, and furniture with rose-colored cushions. A series of teak pavilions each houses 12 guest rooms. Consistent with the lobby, rooms are furnished in Thai style with teak-and-rattan furniture. Superior rooms have a garden view and deluxe rooms overlook the sand and sea. The hotel's sense of tasteful serenity is marred slightly by a seven-story concrete apartment-condo that abuts one side of the property, but otherwise it is a decidedly romantic setting.

Dining/Entertainment: Suan Luang is a Thai restaurant serving lunch and dinner with an elegant, cool green carpet and rattan furniture. The outdoor Rim Nam Restaurant serves European and seafood dinners only, and there is a pool bar for snacks and drinks.

Services: 24-hour room service, concierge, limousine service, babysitting, house doctor, laundry, complimentary welcome tea, and a fruit basket and flowers in all rooms.

Facilities: Swimming pool and children's pool, bicycles, tennis, waterskiing, parasailing, sailing lessons (four types of boats), windsurfing, jogging track, shopping arcade, Jacuzzi, playground 18-hole golf course nearby.

HOTEL SOFITEL CENTRAL, 1 Damneonkasem Rd., P.O. Box 31, Hua Hin Prachuabkirikhan 77110. Tel. 032/512021, or 800/221-4542 in the U.S. Fax 032/511014. Telex 78313 CETRAC TH. 146 rms, 8 suites. A/C MINIBAR TV TEL

$ Rates: 3,400B–4,400B ($136–$177) single/double; 7,200B ($288) suite. Extra person 600B ($24). Supplement Dec 12–Feb 25 600B ($24). AE, DC, MC, V.

The Sofitel Central, once known as the Railway Hotel, was the place to stay in the 1920s. With the revival of Hua Hin as a tourist destination and the renewed interest in this architectural gem in the mid-1980s (it served as the French Embassy in the film *The Killing Fields*), this restored and rebuilt hotel is not only a wonderful place to stay but a must-see stop on any tour of the area. If for no other reason, go to see the well-landscaped grounds including a 60-year-old, eccentric topiary garden gone wild; huge elephants, bears, rhinos, and birds are on display in a manner that would make Edward Scissorhands scratch his head in wonder. The menagerie gives way to gracious parklike grounds with an orchid and butterfly farm, wide lawns, flowering trees, and elegantly planned shrubbery. Suites are spacious and are decorated with dark fans and marble bath, richly furnished teak floors, and sitting rooms with chandeliers. Superior rooms have high ceilings and the same quality and taste as the suites.

And across the driveway is the unusual Villa Wing, with 42 bedrooms tucked into one and two-unit seaside bungalows reminiscent of an Adirondacks campground. Built in the 1950s, these are regulation forest-green and stone-gray cabins with verandas, small kitchens, cotton-covered wooden furniture, and an authentically casual and rustic feel. At 3,350B ($134) for one bedroom or 4,800B ($192) for a family-style two-bedroom, they are a terrific value; perfect for those who want privacy and a "country cabin" feeling. The Villa Wing also has its own small pool, beach access, a small playground, and a Thai restaurant with once-weekly classical dance performances.

Dining/Entertainment: The Satchmo Jazz Club, the nostalgic Railway Room (done with appropriate decor), an all-purpose coffee shop serving ice cream, and the excellent Palm Seafood Restaurant (see "Where to Dine"), set in a converted greenhouse with terrific views of the sea and lots of plants are the main dining venues. The kids will like the poolside snack bar with bananas for sale to feed the elephants, while the parents will appreciate the Museum, a coffee-and-tea corner with a display case of original china and other chotchkas.

Services: 24-hour room service, concierge, limousine service, babysitting, laundry, complimentary welcome tea.

Facilities: Three pools, tennis courts, daily craft and language lessons, billiards room, beauty and barber shop, shopping arcade, watersports, putting green, miniature golf.

Moderate/Budget

Most of the lower-priced accommodations in Hua Hin are located in the teeming back streets between Petchkasem Road and the beach. At night the area turns into an expat and tourist party zone: Expect noise.

FRESH INN HOTEL, 132 Naratdamri Rd., Hua Hin Prachuabkirikhan 77110. Tel. 032/511389. 29 rms. A/C MINIBAR TV TEL
$ Rates: 780B ($31.20) single; 840B ($33.60) double. No credit cards.
This clean inn opened in 1990 as an adjunct to Lo Stivale, an Italian restaurant that is connected via the lobby. Rooms are furnished in basic fashion and, though it's not a fancy place, the Fresh Inn represents good value for its near-to-beach and fishing-pier location. The popular restaurant, open daily 5pm to 10pm, is intimate and, unlike the rooms, stylish. We sampled several well-prepared main dishes including *bruschette al pomodoro*, spaghetti with tomato sauce and seafood, several kinds of pizza, salad, and chicken breast with lemon.

JED PEE NONG HOTEL, 13/7 Damneonkasem Rd., Hua Hin, Prachuabkirikhan 77110. Tel. 032/512381. 25 rms. MINIBAR **Directions:** On Main Street, near the town beach.
$ Rates: 480B ($19.20) single or double with fan; 600B ($24) single with A/C; 600B ($39) double with A/C. No credit cards.
This recently-built hotel with a Chinese flair is located less than 100 meters from the Sofitel Central's elegant driveway. It's so clean and well-kept that it's a good choice. A

bevy of family or local workers maintain the tiny garden filled with songbirds and fountains, a small pool, and the simple balconied rooms. Many rooms are carpeted and have air-conditioning. The higher-priced rooms have more decor and hug the pool, cabana style. There's also a Thai seafood restaurant off the lobby and laundry service.

PARICHART GUEST HOUSE, 162/6 Naratdamri Rd., Hua Hin, Prachuabkirikhan, 77110 Tel. 032/513863. 9 rms.

$ Rates: 420B ($16.80) single or double with fan, 550B–675B ($22–$27) single or double with A/C. No credit cards.

Among the low-priced alternatives along busy Naratdamri Road, we like this place. Newly built, and run by a friendly young woman, it's a modern "barefoot" guest house with white-tile floors and small, clean rooms.

CHA-AM

Very Expensive

DUSIT RESORT AND POLO CLUB, 1349 Petchkasem Rd., Cha-Am, 76120 Petchaburi. Tel. 032/520009. Fax 032/520296. Telex 78302 DRCPOLO TH. 298 rms, 10 suites. A/C/ MINIBAR TV TEL

$ Rates: 4,300B–4,900B ($172–$196) single or double; 8,500B ($336) Landmark double; from 13,000B ($520) suite. Extra person 700B ($28). Supplement (Dec 2–Jan 20) 700B ($28) per room, 1,200B ($48) per suite. AE, DC, MC, V.

Intended for the country's wealthy elite and the well-heeled foreign tourist, the Dusit combines the amenities and facilities of the best international deluxe resorts with an English country and polo club theme.

The grandly elegant marble lobby features bronze horses, plush carpets, and seating areas with hunting-and-riding oil paintings hung throughout. Hall doors have polo mallet handles; each public area follows suit with "horsey" artwork and decor. The staff is gracious and professional.

Guest rooms are large with oversized marble bathrooms. A range of toiletries, hair dryer, bathrobe and slippers, twice daily chamber service, and personal full-size writing desk are other luxuries. Room rates vary with the view, although every room's balcony faces out over the lushly landscaped pool (we think it's the largest in Thailand) and the tranquil Gulf of Thailand. Landmark rooms are actually suites, with a very elegant living room (with its own Victorian fainting couch), a full pantry area, a dressing room off the huge bathroom, and even finer decor. The Princess Suite is absolutely worthy of royalty.

For all its air of formality, the resort is also great for those who prefer swimsuits and T-shirts to riding jodhpurs. Families will find a great beach with calm, shallow water, a kiddie pool, water-sports instruction, daily demonstrations of Thai arts and crafts, and a mini–golf course.

Dining/Entertainment: Of the Dusit's excellent catering facilities, the Palm Court coffee shop has the best location, in a huge glass pavilion jutting out over a lotus pond, surrounded by the swimming pool and bougainvillea beds. It's open for breakfast, lunch, or dinner, serving Thai (excellent range of Thai breakfasts), continental, and casual snack food. The elegant Ascot Grill Rooms (see "Where to Dine," below) and the Rim Talay seaside dining pavilion (for seafood barbecues) are open in the evenings.

Other options include a lively outdoor Italian restaurant, the San Marco and the more formal and pricey Bencharong, a fine Thai restaurant set in a teak pavilion on the grounds. By day, The Polo Lounge is a comfortable leather-and-tapestry library; after 9pm it becomes a jazz bar with nightly live entertainment.

Services: 24-hour room service, concierge, limousine service, babysitting, house doctor, laundry, complimentary welcome fruit basket, Avis car rental.

Facilities: Fantastic outdoor pool and Jacuzzi; the Polo Club with horseback riding, weight rooms, squash courts, Ping-Pong, billiards, sauna and aerobics classes, tennis courts, and all water sports; business center, beauty/barber shop, shopping arcade, golf and minigolf, sauna.

Moderate/Budget

BEACH GARDEN RESORT, 949/21 Petchkasem Rd., Cha-Am, Phetchaburi 76120. Tel. 032/471350-1. Fax 032/471291. A/C MINIBAR TV TEL
$ Rates: 2,100B–2,800B ($85–$112) single or double. No credit cards.
Located at the southern periphery of Cha-Am is this moderately priced resort favored by European groups. The main attraction is the long, sandy beach—it's clean and wide—that abuts the hotel. Facilities include an outdoor pool, two tennis courts, minigolf, and windsurfing gear. Standard rooms have no TV, while superior rooms have all the amenities and are on high floors with views. Between the Beach Garden and its splashy neighbor, the Regent Cha-Am (unaffiliated with the Regent International chain), are a number of fun discos and restaurants. Just south of the resort's beach is the Family Shop, a seafood/Thai restaurant where they barbecue whole fish in foil (see "Where to Dine," below).

KAEN-CHAN HOTEL, 241/3 Cha-Am Beach Rd., Cha-Am, Phetchaburi 76120. Tel. 032/471314. Fax 032/47153. 48 rms. A/C MINIBAR TV TEL
$ Rates: 1,450B–1,800B ($58–$72) single or double. Extra roll-away bed 250B ($10). MC, V.
The Cha-Am beachfront Kaen-Chan, near the corner of Narathip Road, is very clean and tastefully designed. Bright rooms have bamboo furniture and a small seating area. Superior rooms have a view of the sea, but are over the quay and quite noisy, especially in the evening. The building has an elevator and a small pool on the rooftop.

THE CHA-AM METHAVALAI HOTEL, 220 Ruamchit Rd., Cha-Am, Phetchaburi 76120. Tel. 032/471028. Fax 032/471590. Telex 22158 METHA TH. 118 rms. A/C MINIBAR TV TEL
$ Rates: 2,500B–$3,000B ($100–$120) single or double. Extra person 300B ($12). Peak-season supplement (Dec 20–Jan 20). AE, DC, MC, V.
This four-story terraced hotel, at the north end of the beach, is distinguished with its overflowing purple-and-white bougainvillea on every level. Deluxe rooms are enormously long and lead to a flower-decorated balcony, but we think that the superior rooms are the better value (they, too, have balconies). The hotel has all of the amenities of the larger resorts and is ready to negotiate rates in the off-season.

WHERE TO DINE

Most people are likely to eat in the hotel (which is fine in Hua Hin or Cha-Am since both towns have few culinary high points), but for those who wish to venture out, we've found a few places worth sampling.

HUA HIN

BAN TUPPEE KAOW, 7 Napkehard St., Hua Hin. Tel. 512210.
Cuisine: THAI
$ Prices: Main courses 125B–200B ($5–$8)
Open: Daily 11am–midnight.
Located a 35B to 60B ($1.40 to $2.40) samlor ride from the town center, this northern seaside, two story greenhouse was built in the 1920s and, since then, has been only occasionally maintained. Pom, a wonderfully hospitable young man from Bangkok, is the host at Ban Tuppee Kaow (house of the Crystal Ladle). Specialties include lemongrass shrimp with baby coconut and an intricately wrapped chicken that Pom claims only his mother can manage. As for beverages, order the tropical leaf ice "tea"; we have no idea what it's made from but it's greatly refreshing.

MEEKARUNA SEAFOOD, 26/1 Naratdamri Rd. near the fishing pier, Hua Hin. Tel. 511932.

Cuisine: SEAFOOD.
$ Prices: Appetizers 60B–125B ($2.40–$5); main courses 100B–450B ($4–$8). MC, V.
Open: Daily 9am–11pm.

This small family-run restaurant serves fresh fish in a dining pavilion across the street or outdoors at tables overlooking the main fishing pier in Hua Hin. The menu is in English (with photographs) and we found the lack of hype—compared to the other fish places with their hustling touts—refreshing. Among the many good dishes, we recommend steamed pomfret with plum sauce, charcoal-grilled shrimp, and the fried vegetable combination with seafood. Wear bug repellent!

PALM SEAFOOD PAVILION, Hotel Sofitel Central, 1 Damneonkasem Rd. Tel. 512021
Cuisine: CONTINENTAL. **Reservations:** Recommended. **Directions:** On waterfront end of Main Street.
$ Prices: Appetizers 120B–350B ($4.80–$14); main courses 120B–500B ($4.80–$20). AE, DC, MC, V.
Open: Lunch daily noon–2:30pm; dinner daily 6–10:30pm.

Dining within this plant-filled crystal pavilion is a very romantic way to start your holiday. Attentive but discreet service, beautiful table settings and linen, soothing classical music, and excellent, elegantly prepared food all contribute in pleasing harmony. The light, homemade canneloni or tender steaks are for those who don't like seafood; we dove into a salmon consommé with tiny mushroom ravioli, fresh barracuda with fruit curry sauce, and a steamed cottonfish served with creamed spinach. As if that wasn't enough, we splurged on a fluffy baked Alaska and an apple charlotte drizzled with kirsch.

SANG THAI SEAFOOD RESTAURANT, Naratdamri Rd., Hua Hin. Tel. 512144.
Cuisine: SEAFOOD.
$ Prices: Appetizers 75B–100B ($3–$4); main courses 70B–400B ($2.80–$16). AE, DC, MC, V.
Open: Daily 9am–10pm.

The Sang Thai is on the busy Hua Hin fishing pier, with open-air dining (next to fishing boats docked in front). Popular with locals and tourists, it also has a photomenu in English. Among the recommended main dishes are shrimp with fried asparagus, fried crab with chili paste, bean cake with fried vegetables, grilled pomfret, lobster, and charcoal-grilled prawns. Often there are seafood tours (young guys offering up to a 10% discount, roping people into the restaurant). It's really an okay place, but try to avoid visiting when a tour group shows up or you might find service and cuisine below expectation.

CHA-AM

THE ASCOT, Dusit Resort and Polo Club, 1349 Petchkasem Rd., Cha-Am. Tel. 280480.
Cuisine: CONTINENTAL. **Reservations:** Recommended.
$ Prices: Appetizers 155B–400B ($6.20–$16); main courses 400B–720B ($16–$28.80). AE, DC, MC, V.
Open: Daily 6:30–10pm.

For a taste of Hua Hin's high society, and a good meal in a striking setting, visit the Dusit Resort's premier restaurant. Linen, candlelight, and crystal are juxtaposed against the grand view of dramatically lit lotus ponds, palms, and crazy frangipani trees planted throughout the pool area. The nightly chef's complimentary appetizer can be followed by fresh asparagus with prosciutto, soups (such as boullibaisse), or salads. U.S. prime sirloin, New Zealand lamb chops, or medallion of veal are among the expertly prepared main dishes cooked to your liking. Kyle sampled the delicious seafood special, which featured grilled *pla kapong* (a tender white fish), locally caught scallops, and huge prawns with a ginger hollandaise sauce. Dress is formal.

"FAMILY SHOP" RESTAURANT, on the beach, Cha-Am. No phone.
Cuisine: THAI.

$ Prices: 95B–120B ($3.80–$4.80). No credit cards.
Open: Daily 8:30am–9pm.

This family-run, rattan hut is just south of the Beach Garden Resort in Cha-Am. Dining by the sea is supremely rustic in this ultracasual setting. Although the menu is limited, the barbecued whole fish wrapped in foil is definitely worth sampling. If you're sunbathing on this part of the beach, the Family Shop is an ideal barefoot snack house for those between-meal cravings.

EASY EXCURSIONS

KHAO SAM ROI YOD NATIONAL PARK

Dramatic limestone caves, wondrous birds, beaches, and rarely seen mammals highlight this national park, located 20km (12.5 miles) south of Hua Hin. Bird watching is best done from December through March. There are well-marked trails leading up to Khao Daeng and Khao Chalomfang; bungalows are available for overnights at Tham Phraya Nakhon Cave as well as the park headquarters.

PHETCHABURI

Phetchaburi, one of the country's oldest towns, possibly dating from the same period as Ayutthaya and Kanchanaburi, is thought to have been first settled during the Dvaravati period. After the rise of the Thai nation, it served as an important royal military city and was home to several princes who were groomed for ascendance to the throne.

The most prominent geographic feature of the town is a series of hills. Khao Wang, on which there are two monasteries (one from the Ayutthaya period), a royal palace built in 1860 by King Mongkut, and many lesser shrines and administrative buildings, is the most significant. We suggest starting your tour here, as there is a spectacular view of the town and its important historic monuments. Khao Want can be visited via a walkway or, as most people do it, a tram; open daily 8am to 5:30pm, admission 30B ($1.20). The Phra Nakhon Khiri National Museum, at the top of the hill on Khiri Rataya Road, is open daily from 9am to 4pm, admission 25B ($1).

If you decide to visit Phetchaburi directly from Bangkok—perhaps on your way to Hua Hin or points south—there are direct air-conditioned buses (travel time two hours; 50B [$2]) departing from the Southern Bus Terminal as well as daily trains.

Accommodations are few; you'd best move on to Cha-Am, a mere 45-minute drive south. For food, we found a delightful local stop called Nam Tien (tel. 425121) at the intersection of Surin Lu Chai and Na Mai Street, about four blocks from Wat Mahatat. Perpetually busy, totally funky and cheap and with great food, the specialties are fried fish (*plajalamite tod pla*), *giao moo ra* (pork dumpling soup), and very refined noodles (a speciality and a meal in itself). Open daily 7am to 7pm.

Phetchaburi's Wats

Back down in the busy streets of central Phetchaburi are several superb wats, two of which—Wat Yai Suwannaram and Wat Ko Keo Suttharam—are decorated with unique murals reputed to be the only surviving paintings from the Ayutthaya era (ending in 1767) in all of Thailand.

Wat Yai Suwannaram, where the murals in the *bot* date from the latter years of the 17th century (but bear a striking resemblance to contemporary folk painting by Rev. Howard Finster of rural Georgia), is nearly always bypassed by tour groups. You'll have to ask for directions, and once there, you'll wave to track down somebody with a key to let you in. They'll know what you're looking for when you show up! Be sure to check out the other buildings in the complex, especially the elaborately decorated and windowless viharn.

The other wat with miraculous paintings is **Wat Ko Keo Suttharam,** also built in the 17th century, but with murals from the 1730s. These are far more representational and, of some interest to Westerners, there are several panels depicting the arrival in the Ayutthaya court of European courtesans and diplomats (including a Jesuit dressed in Buddhist garb). As with Suwannaram, you'll have to locate an abbot—or somebody with keys— to gain access to the bot.

If you want to tour a fine all-purpose wat, enter the compound of **Wat Mahatat.** When we visited, there were roving musicians banging out a Buddhist beat and chanting tunes. The most arresting structure is the five-tiered prang immediately behind the central hall; each level represents an offering made according to the precepts of Thayani Buddhism.

Another favorite wat, particularly for fans of Khmer architecture, is **Wat Kamphaeng Laeng,** thought to have been built as a Brahmanistic shrine; like many such temples in the Northeast of Thailand, it was renovated by Buddhists to serve their very different theological traditions. Each prang, which once honored a different Hindu deity, was replaced in the renovation by Buddhist imagery. Unlike the brick-and-stucco construction of Thai buildings, this complex was originally built of carved sandstone, but in the renovation its appearance was greatly altered.

Phraram Ratchaniwet

This European-style palace was built during a 7-year period, culminating in 1916, as a rainy-season retreat for Rama V. In 1918, Rama VI designated it a venue for state visits, and it must have impressed foreign dignitaries who thought Thailand was unaware of Western architectural fashion. The exterior is a jumble of post-Victorian/ central European baroque style, but don't let that or the army-base location put you off, for the interior is exquisite. It is also exquisitely empty, awaiting the funds to convert it into a museum. Phraram Ratchaniwet is open to the public, but it's located in a military base, so you'd best inquire about its hours (we tried, failed, but eventually cajoled them into opening it up and got it).

2. CHUMPHON

463km (287 miles) S of Bangkok; 193km (120 miles) N of Surat Thani

GETTING THERE By Train Six trains leave daily from Bangkok (trip time: 7½ hours) en route to Surat Thani.

By Bus Four ordinary (120B [$4.80]) and five air-conditioned (240B [$9.60]) buses leave daily (trip time: 7 hours) from Bankok's Southern Bus Terminal.

By Car Take Highway 4 south from Bangkok (about a 5-hour drive).

ESSENTIALS Information The Chumphon Travel Service (tel. 077/501880; fax 077/502479) is at 66/1 Thatapoa Rd., next door to the Thatapoa Hote.

Fast Facts The telephone area code is 0977. The **police** can be reached by telephone at 511505. The **hospital** is on Phisit Phayaban Road (tel. 511180). Currency can be exchanged at **banks** (open Monday to Friday 8:30am to 3:30pm) located on both Paraminthara Mankha and Saladaeng roads. The **post** and **telegraph office** is on Paraminthara Mankha Road (tel. 511013). Luggage can be stored at the **railroad station** for 20B (80¢) per day and is accessible 24 hours (Trirat Road; tel 511103). **Motorcycle taxis** and **rickshaws** to town can be hired at the railroad station for about 20B (80¢); **taxis** are available behind the market.

C humphon was nearly devastated by Typhoon Gay when it hit the coast of Thai land in 1989. The northern end of town and many outer lying villages were flattened, yet the surrounding hills, denuded of their once fertile fruit trees, are now making a slow comeback. The plains on the western side of the province are still extremely fertile, with coconuts, mangosteens, durians, rambutans, bananas, and pineapple plantations. The government has instituted a craftsmaking scheme to help local economies until all can resume the traditional agricultural trade. Perhaps because of the typhoon's deforestation, Chumphon today is a dusty, buggy town (bring moist towelettes for cooling off and mosquito repellent) with little of interest for most travelers. However—island explorers and divers take note—Chumphon has been selected as one of the country's target development sites for underwater sports and may one day boast of this unique appeal.

WHAT TO SEE & DO

In 1990 it was decided that Chumphon would be protected for its coral reefs, fishing grounds, and beaches. Since then the government and local diving clubs have identified many small islands and beaches for protection including Ko Ngam, and Ko Langka Chiu. Several of these, such as Ko Langka Chiu, are inhabited by thousands of swallows whose saliva-glued twig nests are collected to produce a culinary delicacy, bird's nest. Hin Pae, Ngam Yai and Noi, and Lak Ngam can be reached via the dock at Al Thung Wua Laen (in the proximity of the Chumphon Cabana Resort), about 12km (7 miles) north of Chumphon. The others are connected by boat at the dock leading out from the Chumphon River estuary, located to the south of town at the end of Route 4001, or farther south at the Tako estuary, off Route 41, at Arunothai Beach in the direction of Surat Thani.

If you want somewhat of a party scene consider visiting Ko Tao (ironic that it's a revelers' spot; like Ko Tarutao, Ko Tao served as a Devil's Island for political prisoners) or Ko Matra; both have bungalows and are popular destinations for both Thai and Western tourists. Boats depart twice weekly from Tha Saphan Tha Yang, 7km (4 miles) from Chumphon (trip time: 5 hours; 240B [$9.60]).

WHERE TO STAY

IN CHUMPHON

JANSOM CHUMPHON, 188/65-66 Saladaeng Rd., off Krom Luang Chumphon Rd., Chumphon 86000. Tel. 077/502502. Fax 077/821821. 139 rms, 1 suite. A/C MINIBAR TV TEL

$ Rates: 780B ($31.20) single, 960B ($38.40) deluxe single; 840B ($33.60) double, 1,080B ($43.20) deluxe double; 2,900 ($116) suite; 250B ($10) extra bed. MC, V.

The Jansom, like its cousin in Ranong, is both the newest and best hotel in town. Guest rooms are lacking in style but are clean and equipped with modern amenities. There is a good-quality coffee shop/restaurant on the lobby floor and the location, across from the Ocean Department Store in Chumphon center, couldn't be better. The hotel operates the Town Disco (open 9pm to 1am), which may bother some light sleepers, and has a massage parlor, a perfect combination for late-night entertainment.

THATAPOA HOTEL, 66/1 Thatapoa Rd., Chumphon 86000. Tel. 077/ 511479. Fax 077/502479. 80 rms. A/C TEL

$ Rates: 700B ($28) with hot water, TV, and A/C; 480B ($19.20) with A/C only; 300B ($12) with cold water and fan. MC, V.

Until the Jansom opened this was Chumphon's best lodging. Now it stands as number two and badly in need of maintenance. There are many different kinds of rooms available with different prices, a 24-hour restaurant, and a central location, near the bus station.

OUT OF TOWN

CHUMPHON CABANA RESORT, Thung Wua Laen Beach, Tambon Saphli 86000. Tel. 077/501990, or 02/281-1234 in Bangkok. 40 bungalows.

$ Rates: One bungalow (2 bedrooms and toilets) at 960B ($38.40); 20 bungalows at 720B ($28.80); 10 bungalows at 600B ($24); 2 bungalows at 360B (14.40). MC, V (plus 5% charge).

The Chumphon Cabana overlooks a picturesque bay flanked by mountains on one side and a very quiet, nearly private, beach on the other, about 12km (7 miles) north of Chumphon. The sand isn't perfectly white and a small amount of trash abides, but for a mainland beach it's relatively clean and fairly wide. The guest facilities have a pleasing layout, with groomed plantings around each bungalow.

Amenities are few: Rooms have fans, but there is no hot water; there is a TV, English-language lending library, and phone in the lobby (for international calls). The 720B bungalows are little houses with tiled floors and stucco walls, real beds, writing table, seating area inside, and patio outside with chairs and a small table. The 600B bungalows are made of wood in a mock log-cabin style. The restaurant is pretty good (open daily from 6am to 1pm), serving roast fish with chili, chicken curry, and fried curried crab.

For many guests the main activity is scuba diving. Boats cost 2,200B ($87) per day for a 16-person boat, 3,500B ($140) per day for a 25-person boat, and 5,500 ($220) per day for a 40-person boat. Saturday and Sunday are recommended for single divers (we know not why). There is a dive shop just off the lobby.

WHERE TO DINE

KANDA RESTAURANT, 252/12 Paraminthara Mankha Rd. Tel. 511707.
  Cuisine: THAI/WESTERN.
$ Prices: Appetizers 10B–120B (40¢–$4.80); main courses 40B–180B ($1.60–$7.20). No credit cards.
  Open: Daily 7am–6pm.
This very clean café near the post office has baked goods displayed in the window and sports seven small tables inside, where the friendly staff serves only breakfast, lunch, and tea. Menus are in Thai, so you'll have to point to others eating the American breakfast with eggs and sausage or the Thai breakfast with our favorite khao tom. There are also afternoon tea and snacks, with sandwiches, ice cream, banana muffins, and whole cakes, or luncheon salads, Thai pizza, and coffee.

RIN GARDEN, 118 Krom Luang Chumphon Rd. Tel. 511531.
  Cuisine: THAI.
$ Prices: Main courses 40B–120B ($1.60–$4.80). MC, V.
  Open: Daily 10am–10pm.
This open-air restaurant is a popular local joint with fine food. Among our favorites are seafood hot pot, a shrimp casserole with noodles, *pla ka phon khao* (extra crispy fried fish), and *tod man pla* served with ground peanuts. Your gracious host Khun Surin will gladly make suggestions. To find it, we suggest asking for "Suan Rin" looking out for a shiny brass Thai lettered sign flanked by a row of evergreens. (If you're coming here after dusk, remember to bring mosquito repellent.)

3. KO SAMUI

644km (400 miles) S of Bangkok to Surat Thani;
84km (52 miles) E from Surat Thani to Ko Samui

GETTING THERE Getting to Ko Samui is simpler than it appears; there are just too many choices. There's a flight direct to the island and one to the mainland; several bus and train options to Surat Thani (the nearest mainland town to the various piers); a hydrofoil from a canal in south Surat Thani; express ferries from Thathon, another port 5km (3 miles) south of town; and car-ferries from Donsak, 70km (43 miles) south of Surat Thani. Our choices: the nonstop Bangkok–Ko Samui flight if you can afford it, and the overnight train with express ferry package if you can't.

By Plane to Ko Samui Nine flights depart daily from Bangkok on Bangkok Airways (trip time: 70 minutes; 2,500B [$100]); two flights daily from Phuket (trip time: 45 minutes; 1,450B [$58]); Ko Samui Airport is a small private airfield (they charge an additional 125B [$5] airport tax) on the northeast side of the island. Contact Bangkok Airways for information: The local office is on the pier at Nathon, Ko Samui (tel. 077/421196); their Bangkok office is at Ratchadaphisek Road (tel. 02/229-3456).

By Plane to Surat Thani Three flights leave daily from Bangkok to Surat Thani on Thai Airways (trip time: 70 minutes; 2,040B [$82]); one flight daily from

Phuket (trip time: 30 minutes; 480B [$19]); two flights a week from Chiang Mai (trip time: 2 hours; 2,400B [$96]). Airport transfers to the pier (a 30-minute drive) are included in the price of one-way tickets.

By Train Eight trains leave daily from Bangkok's Hua Lampong station on Surat Thani (trip time: 13 hour; second-class sleeper 555B [$22.20], second-class seat 364B [$14.56]). One train departs daily from Butterworth Station in Penang, Malaysia (call 02/223-3762 in Bangkok for international train information).

In 1991, the **State Railway of Thailand** (tel. 02/233-7010) excursion train departed Bangkok daily at 6:30pm; the special fare of 849B ($34) included rail, bus transfer, and boat service. The Songserm Travel Company offers a similar package which meets the express ferry; call their Bangkok office (tel. 02/250-0768) or Surat Thani office (tel. 077/272928) for information.

By Bus Four air-conditioned buses leave daily from Bangkok's Southern Bus Terminal (trip time: 10 hours; 360B [$14.40]); four air-conditioned buses daily from Phuket (trip time: 5 hours; 100B [$4]); four minivans daily from Phuket (trip time: 4 hours; 185B [$7.40]). The boat companies provide minibus transfers from the Surat Thani Bus Terminal to the piers.

By Express Boat This is the most efficient way to get to Ko Samui from Surat Thani. Two boats leave daily (at our last visit, 8am and 2:30pm, with an additional boat in high season [November to May]) at the Songserm express boat pier (trip time: 2½ hours; 125B [$5]). Call Songserm's Bangkok or Surat Thani office for information. From Ko Samui's pier, Nathon, minitrucks eagerly await the new load of holiday makers.

By Car Ferry Two car ferries leave daily (at our visit, 6:20am, 7:15am) from the pier in Donsak (trip time: 2 hours and 20 minutes; 60B [$2.40] per passenger, 215B [$8.60] for a car and driver). If you've got a car, get to the ferry at least an hour before departure to get on line; contact the Panthip Ferry Company (tel. 077/272230) or Samui Tours (tel. 077/421092) for information. Ko Samui's Tong Yang car ferry jetty is 4 miles south of Nathon.

By High Speed Boat Island Jet has one boat daily at 8am from Ban Don Sak, about an hour's bus ride from Surat Thani; contact Phangan Ferry Co. (tel. 077/286461; fax 077/282713).

The island of Samui lies 84km (52 miles) off Thailand's east coast in the Gulf of Siam, also called the Gulf of Thailand, near the mainland commercial town of Surat Thani. Since the 1850s, Samui has been visited by Chinese merchants sailing from Hainan Island in the South China Sea to trade coconuts and cotton, the island's two most profitable products.

Ko Samui's coconuts are among Southeast Asia's most coveted, principally for their flavor. More than two million coconuts a month are shipped to Bangkok. Much of the fruit is made into coconut oil, a process that involves scraping the meat out of the shell, drying it, and pressing it to produce a sweet oil. To assist farmers with Samui's indigenous breed of tall palm trees, monkeys are trained to climb them, shake off the ripe coconuts, and gather them for their master. (See "Surat Thani," below, for information about visiting a monkey training school.)

That Ko Samui is both isolated (until 1988 there was no air service to the island) and agriculturally rich has made it a relatively late entry in Thailand's robust tourist derby. Although Ko Samui has been invaded by resort developers, it retains much of its village charm. Visitors can watch fishers and farmers leading lives their ancestors led a century ago.

For a while longer, Ko Samui will remain an idyllic tropical retreat with little traffic, clean warm water, and fine sand beaches, each with a network of simple bungalows that range from primitive to luxurious and a smattering of hotels.

The high season on Samui for tourists is from mid-December to mid-January. January to April has the best weather, before its gets hot. October through mid-December are the wettest months, with November bringing extreme rains and fierce winds which make the east side of the island rough for swimming. Some years, the island's west side is buffeted by summer monsoons from the mainland.

ORIENTATION

Information   The **Tourist Police** office south of the pier in Nathon (tel. 077/421281) is open 24 hours. There's a **TAT Information Center** on the north end of the waterfront street in Nathon, left from the piers, near the post office (no telephone yet), open 8:30am to noon and 1 to 4:30pm Monday to Saturday. The Tourist Police are about 2km south on the road to Lamai (tel. 421281 and 421360; for emergencies call 1699, 24 hours). Also contact the TAT office, 5 Talad Mai Rd., Surat Thank (tel. 077/281828; fax 282828), near the Wang Tai Hotel (open daily 8:30am to 4:30pm).

Island Layout   Though Samui is the country's third-largest island, with a total area of 90 square miles, its entire coastline can be toured by car or motorcycle in about two hours. The island is hilly, densely forested, and rimmed with coconut palm plantations. The Ko Samui airport is in the northeast corner of the island. The hydrofoils, car ferry, and express boats arrive on the west coast, in or near (depending on the boat) Nathon, the side of most tourist services. With few exceptions, the island's paved roads follow the coastline. There's an excellent new Guide Map of Ko Samui, Ko Phangan, Ko Tao, and Marine National Park published by J.S. Printing, widely available for about 50B ($2).

   Most of Samui's fine beaches are on the north and east coasts. The long east coast stretch between Chaweng and Lamai beaches is the most popular destination for visitors and, consequently, where you'll find the greatest concentration of hotels and bungalows. The south coast is home to the island's small fishing fleet, dating back to the era of the China trade. The west coast has a few sandy strips, but the busy boat traffic lessens its surfside appeal.

GETTING AROUND

By Minitruck   Minitrucks (pickups outfitted with bench seats) are the easiest and most efficient way to get around the island. They advertise their destinations—to such beaches as Lamai, Chaweng, and Mai Nam—with colorfully painted signs. Though they originate in Nathon, most going north and clockwise as far as Chaweng, some south as far as Lamai, with an interchange necessary at a pavilion near Chaweng Noi for those wishing to proceed further in either direction. You can hail one anywhere along the round-island road. To visit a site off the beaten track (or one other than that painted on a truck's sign), ask the driver to make a detour. Check when your minitrucks stop running (usually around sundown). The cost is 15B to 30B (60¢ to $1.20) one-way.

By Motorcycle or Jeep   Ko Samui's roads are narrow, winding, poorly maintained, and not lit at night. In the island's first decade of tourism, more than 350 foreigners died in accidents. To improve this situation would be very costly, would inconvenience the locals who primarily use truck-taxis, and would change the island's undeveloped character. If you're compelled to drive, use extreme caution, obey the 60kmph (37 m.p.h.) speed limit, and wear a helmet.

   There are Avis rental offices in Thong Sai Bay at the Tongsai Bay Cottages (tel. 421451) and in Chaweng at the Imperial Samui Hotel (tel. 421390); self-drive Suzuki Jeeps rent for $60, and cars with driver for $135, per day. Mopeds, off-road motorcycles, and Jeeps rent in Nathon and the various beach communities for 185B ($7.40), 250B ($10), and 950B ($38, plus $9 per day insurance), respectively. Most Nathon rental agencies are on the waterfront, north of the pier.

By Taxi   There are no private taxis on the island, but many hotels offer minivan service to various destinations, at a hefty price. Many of the larger hotels will meet you at the ferry depots upon arrival, and many of the larger restaurants will pick you up and return you to your hotel in the evening.

FAST FACTS: KO SAMUI

Area Code   The telephone area code is 077.

Bookstores   There are small bookstores/lending libraries in Chaweng and Lamai beaches, and small shops on the second street in Nathon for bestsellers.

Currency Exchange   Several banks are located in Nathon near the ferry pier; branches are open daily 8am to 6pm.

Hospitals   Ko Samui Hospital is on the main road, 2km (1.2 miles) south of Nathon (tel. 421230). Muan Thai Clinic in Lamai offers 24-hour help (tel. 424219).

Laundry   Many villagers collect, wash, and deliver laundry for about 15B (60¢) per shirt, quite handy if you're in a budget bungalow, but irrelevant in the larger hotels.

Post Office   The Post and Telecommunications Office is at the northern end of the waterfront street, near the taxi stand for the northern beaches (tel. 421013). It's open Monday to Friday 8:30am to 4:30pm, Saturday to Sunday 8:30am to noon. They handle mail, faxes, telegrams, telexes, and money transfer.

Religious Services   There is a Catholic church 1km (⁶/₁₀ mile) north of Nathon, with an English-language mass Sunday at 8:30am.

Safety and Security   There's little crime on Ko Samui, but the helpful Tourist Police asked us to pass on some warnings: Drive very carefully, always obeying the 60kmph (37 m.p.h.) speed limit, and avoid driving at night; don't be tempted to purchase jewelry, especially from beach vendors who often sell poor-quality merchandise; don't leave valuables unattended. Put your passport, etc., in your hotel or bungalow's safe-deposit box.

Sun Gear   Many shops, particularly on the second street in Nathon, sell inexpensive beachwear, sunglasses, suntan lotion, and imported sunblocks up to SPF15 in strength. Mosquito repellent is necessary from October to January.

Telephone   The larger hotels have IDD long-distance service; in several beach communities the local market or pharmacy will have a metered long-distance phone. The Overseas Call Office is upstairs from the post office in Nathon. It's open Monday to Friday 7am to noon and 1 to 10pm, Saturday to Sunday 8:30am to noon.

Useful Telephone Numbers   Songserm Travel Center (tel. 077/421316 or 421319), express boat ticket agent/operator will confirm airline tickets and make reservations for destinations throughout Thailand. World Travel Service (tel. 077/421475) is another travel agency which can also obtain discounts on Samui hotels if you arrive without a reservation. Songserm and World Travel are on the waterfront road in Nathon.

WHAT TO SEE & DO

Local aquanauts agree that the best **scuba diving** is off Ko Tao, a small island north of Ko Phangan and Samui. Since conditions vary with the seasons, the cluster of tiny islands south of Samui or Mu Ko Angthong National Park are often better destinations. Follow the advice of a local dive shop. The best outfit is the Swiss International Dive Center, P.O. Box 33, Ko Samui, with an office in Lamai (tel. 420157 or 422478). A day of diving, with boat, equipment, and a divemaster, costs 1,800B ($72) for two dives. The 4-day training program includes simple bungalow accommodation plus PADI certification for 7,800B ($312).

Some of the best **snorkeling** off Ko Samui is found around this tiny, coconut-covered island off the north end of Chaweng Beach. Several shops along Chaweng Beach rent snorkeling gear for about 70B ($2.80) per day; a package including equipment for two people and a long-tail boat to take you out and around the island costs about 550B ($22) a day.

Although there's a cleared corral in every village round the island, once-weekly **buffalo fights** now take place only on holidays. This equitable sport, popular in south Thailand, pits male water buffalo against each other in a contest of locked horns. Endurance, chutzpah, and brute strength determine the winner; the loser usually lies down or runs away. (Buffalo rarely hurt one another, though fans have been trampled!) Authorities have tried to curb gambling, but the event is still festive;

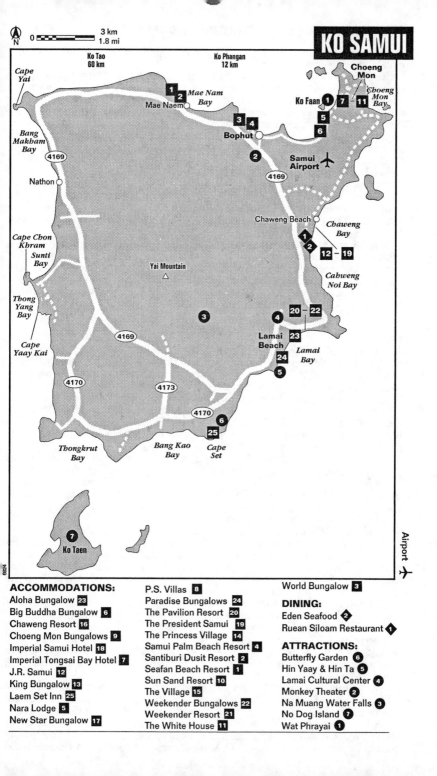

KO SAMUI

0   3 km
        1.8 mi

Ko Tao
60 km

Ko Phangan
12 km

Cape Yai

Bang Makham Bay

Nathon

Mae Nam Bay

Mae Naem

Bophut

Samui Airport

4169

Choeng Mon

Ko Faan

Choeng Mon Bay

Cape Chon Khram

Sunti Bay

Thong Yang Bay

Cape Yaay Kai

Yai Mountain

4169

4170

4173

4170

Chaweng Beach

Chaweng Bay

Cahweng Noi Bay

Lamai Beach

Lamai Bay

Thongkrut Bay

Bang Kao Bay

Cape Set

Ko Taen

Airport

ACCOMMODATIONS:

Aloha Bungalow **23**
Big Buddha Bungalow **6**
Chaweng Resort **16**
Choeng Mon Bungalows **9**
Imperial Samui Hotel **18**
Imperial Tongsai Bay Hotel **7**
J.R. Samui **12**
King Bungalow **13**
Laem Set Inn **25**
Nara Lodge **5**
New Star Bungalow **17**

P.S. Villas **8**
Paradise Bungalows **24**
The Pavilion Resort **20**
The President Samui **19**
The Princess Village **14**
Samui Palm Beach Resort **4**
Santiburi Dusit Resort **2**
Seafan Beach Resort **1**
Sun Sand Resort **10**
The Village **15**
Weekender Bungalows **22**
Weekender Resort **21**
The White House **11**

World Bungalow **3**

DINING:

Eden Seafood **2**
Ruean Siloam Restaurant **1**

ATTRACTIONS:

Butterfly Garden **6**
Hin Yaay & Hin Ta **5**
Lamai Cultural Center **4**
Monkey Theater **2**
Na Muang Water Falls **3**
No Dog Island **7**
Wat Phrayai **1**

shamans are called in to rile up the bulls, ribbons are hung around their necks, and buffalo horns are decorated with gold leaf.

If you've been on Samui long enough, a trip to downtown **Nathon** seems pretty exciting. The waterfront street has dozens of travel agents, T-shirt shops, minimalls filled with budget cotton sportswear, postcard and paperback bookstalls, and a traditional Thai massage parlor, open 24 hours. The second street has many souvenir shops, some food stalls, some dive shops, and local businesses. On Nathon's third inland street are a morning market, motorcycle repair shops, a Chinese temple, and, in the alley leading to the temple, a brothel with a sign written in Thai that warns, "If the door is closed, don't knock."

We have two favorite restaurants for ferry-boat waiting; both open daily 8am to 9pm. **Koh Gaew,** on the waterfront next the Songserm Travel office, is a simple, casual Thai restaurant with the usual Formica tables and fluorescent lighting (no phone). Its large variety of noodle-and-rice dishes (main courses cost 35B to 70B [$1.60 to $2.80]) made with locally caught seafood makes it very popular with Thai families vacationing on Samui.

The **Sunse House Restaurant** at 328/4 Moo 39 (tel. 421547), on the south end of town, has a large veranda looking west over the water. It's ideal for breakfast, snacks, or a sunset drink. The staff is gracious and the delicious fare is clean and fresh, cheap, and varied with many Thai noodle dishes, European favorites, a hearty American breakfast, and vegetarian specials (main courses cost 40B to 60B [$1.60 to $2.40]). The fruit shakes are especially good.

SIGHTS

The gold-tiled **Wat Phrayai** (Big Buddha), more than 80 feet tall, sits atop Ko Faan (Barking Deer Island), a small islet connected to shore by a dirt causeway almost 1,000 feet long. This Buddha and the polychrome Buddhas around its periphery were built in 1970; there's a fund-raising drive at present to renovate the small Wat Phrayai and its statuary. Though of little historic value, it's an imposing presence on the northeast coast and is one of the Samui's primary landmarks. Parking lot souvenir shops sell shells, beads, and locally made handicrafts at modest (and negotiable) prices. It's open all day; 10B (40¢) contribution recommended. It's easy to reach, just hop on any minitruck going to Big Buddha Beach.

Ko Samui's famed **Wonderful Rocks,** the most important of which are the sexually suggestive **Hin Yaay & Hin Ta** (Grandmother and Grandfather Stones), so-called because a vulva-like cleft is near the huge phallic one. They are located at the far southern end of Lamai Beach. Walk about an hour south of Chaweng Beach, or take any minitruck to Lamai Beach and get off at Paradise Bungalows.

The **Ban Lamai Cultural Center** is dedicated to preserving and exhibiting the arts and crafts of Chao Samui, the traditional folklife of the island's original inhabitants. The small museum displays tools, pottery, and glass recovered from shipwrecks off the coast, and Nang Talung, the tooled and painted buffalo-hide puppets used in traditional Thai shadow plays. It's open daily 8am to 4pm; admission is free. The museum is in the compound of Wat Lamai, on the north end of Lamai town, where the road is farthest from the beach.

The **Samui Monkey Theater** is in Bophut, near where the main road diverges south toward Chaweng. There are elephant shows and rides, cultural exhibits and performances, and monkeys at work. Monkey shows last about an hour and a half and begin at 10:30am, 2pm, and 4pm. (We didn't much like seeing animals dressed up and put through paces, but kids seem to find them a lot of fun.) Open from 9am to 5pm daily. Adults are charged 150B ($6); children under 12 are 100B ($4); kids 5 and under are free.

The **Samui Butterfly Garden** is at Natian, on the southern coast near Cape Set, and it should prove fascinating for both adults and kids. A couple of acres of well-landscaped hillside with a cascading stream and meandering walks are enclosed under blue plastic netting to provide a habitat. There's also a bee house and a very good insection collection with large and unusual species, as well as live demonstrations of butterfly metamorphoses. (Only the intrepid, well shod, and clothed should pick their way up to the top of the hill, being careful of thorns and slippery palm fronds, for some fair views and cool breezes.) There are various pavilions for snacks, a rock garden, and a restaurant, but we suggest you mosey on down the hillside to the Laem Set Inn for a really fine meal. By the way, we don't recommend the 150B ($6) glass-bottom boat tour to Ko Ang-wang, as the boat is a noisy smoke belcher and a 1½ tour is a bit rushed. Instead you might consider taking your snorkel and mask on a privately chartered fishing boat at Bang Kao for about 200B to 300B ($8 to $12) or rent a peddle boat with glass viewers for a couple hundred baht.

NA MUANG WATERFALLS & THE SOUTHERN COAST

The main island road forks at Ban Hua Thanon. At the village of Ban Thurian, the road climbs north past Na Muang Falls, a pleasant waterfall once visited by many kings of the Chakri dynasty. After the rainy season ends in December, it reaches a height of almost 100 feet and a width of about 66 feet. Na Muang is a steamy 5km (3-mile) walk from the coast road and makes for a nice bath and picnic stop.

NO DOG ISLAND

The modest port of Thongkrut on the southwest corner of Samui has long-tail boats and fishing boats (about 125B [$5] round-trip) to nearby No Dog Island (Ko Taen). No Dog Island apparently earned its name because no dog could survive on it (or, as popular legend has it, boat passengers became sick as dogs on windy days). There's a primitive bungalow and snack café along the east coast beach.

WHERE TO STAY & DINE

Ko Samui's bungalows are a bit different than the ones seen elsewhere in Thailand. Often less than 200B ($8) nightly, they're made from palm, rattan, and bamboo in a simple A-frame shape, with no interior bathroom or air-conditioning. After Ko Samui was "discovered" in 1987, several of the earliest bungalow complexes began plowing their profits back into real estate and building more modern concrete and tin cottages out back. These more costly units often include a cold-water shower, toilet, and, in some cases, air-conditioning, but because they lack that Robinson Crusoe charm, they're not automatically better. Don't be surprised if you go to rent a bungalow and are offered a veritable patchwork of huts in many styles and prices; it often pays to check into a more expensive unit and wait until a cheaper one becomes available. Most complexes have an open-air restaurant reception area, where simple, inexpensive Thai and continental meals are served and guests can use the phone.

Every habitable cove on Ko Samui has at least one bungalow complex and snack café, but each community has a different personality. We'll look at the most popular beaches, circling the island clockwise from the busy pier at Nathon. Don't forget to add 11% tax and 10% service charge to all accommodations listed below unless otherwise noted.

MAE NAM BAY

Mae Nam Beach is 12km (7½ miles) from the ferry pier, at the midpoint of Samui's north shore, facing nearby Ko Phangan. The beach is on a par with Lamai but narrower; it's long, coarse sand and shaded by trees. This bay is often spared the fierce winds that whip during the stormy months, making it popular during the winter. **Ban Mae Nam,** the commercial center, is just east of the resort and has several restaurants, laundries, shops, a medical clinic, and a gas station.

Mae Nam is relatively isolated; recent development is restricted to the wooded area near the coast, about ½km (3/10 mile) inland from the main road. The unpaved routes between small bungalow complexes create a far more tranquil ambience than elsewhere on the island. The Palarn Inn, Homebay, and Harry's Guesthouse are typical of what's available: all very simple with small snack bars, screened windows, common toilets, and no phones. However, there are two great resorts perfectly suited to isolationists:

SANTIBURI DUSIT RESORT, 12/12 Moo 1, Mae Nam Beach, Ko Samui 84330, Surat Thani. Tel. 077/425031-8. Fax 077/425040. 59 pavilions, 18 suites. A/C MINIBAR TV TEL **Directions:** On Mae Nam Beach.

$ Rates: 7,800B–8,400B ($313–$336) single or double; 11,400B–22,800B ($456–$1,152) suite. AE, DC, MC, V.

The latest in luxury, this tranquil resort—the name means peaceful town—is a village of palatial pavilions informally arrayed around the largest swimming pool on the island (an oval over 150 feet long), with a small river winding through its lush tropical gardens to the long, clean beach. Modeled after a mountain retreat built by King Rama IV over a century ago, strongly influenced by Western neoclassical architecture, yet distinctly Thai, it evokes that earlier era without neglecting modern comfort and convenience. Guests are welcomed by the sounds of splashing water and a relaxed but attentive staff in a cool, intimate lobby that opens out onto the spacious compound. Rooms are large, light, and inviting, with the special warmth of naturel teak, traditionally styled furniture, handwoven fabrics, and other distinctive Asian touches; the bathrooms are especially large.

Dining/Entertainment: Of the three major restaurants, we were most taken with the lovely Sala Thai, which served us one of the best banquets of classical Thai cuisine we've found on Samui, all in a most congenial environment.

Services: 24-hour room service, concierge, babysitting, laundry.

Facilities: Swimming pool, children's pool, tennis-and-squash courts, fitness center, sailing, and windsurfing.

SEAFAN BEACH RESORT, Mae Nam Beach, Ko Samui 84140, Surat Thani. Tel. 077/421350. Fax 077/425350. Telex 84419 VIEWTR TH (in Bangkok). 35 suites. A/C MINIBAR **Directions:** West end of beach.

$ Rates: 2,500B ($100) single; 2,600 ($104) double. Extra person 1,100B ($44). AE, DC, MC, V.

With a spirit of low-key elegance, these deluxe beach-style bungalows are tucked into eight acres of landscaped grounds fronting the bay. Each "primitive" rattan and coconut-wood house has two queen-size beds, an extra rattan daybed, a bamboo makeup table, hair dryer, bathrobe and slippers, pastel-cotton seating area, and a large, all-tile bathroom. Each has a terrace and is spaced far enough from its neighbors to ensure privacy, but the front beach-view bungalows (the same rate) really stand out. A small pool with kiddy pool and a snack bar overlook the beach. The nearby restaurant features Thai, continental, and several seafood specialties. Rates include attentive service, use of windsurfing boards, snorkeling gear, and other water-sports activities. The Seafan is a find for those seeking simple tranquillity.

BOPHUT BEACH

This beach, on the north coast just east of Mae Nam, is one of the island's fastest developing areas. Unfortunately, the main circle road runs very close to the shore all along the sandy stretch. The presence of many small Thai restaurants, businesses, shops, and taxis creates a busier pace than is evident at other, more removed beaches.

Bophut's very long, now-crowded sand beach narrows considerably in the monsoon season, but the water remains fairly calm year-round. At present, some of the myriad cheap bungalows and hippy compounds are being replaced by upscale accommodations. We recommend:

SAMUI PALM BEACH RESORT, 175/3 Thaveerat-Pakdee Rd., Bophut Beach, Ko Samui 84140, Surat Thani. Tel. 077/425494. Fax 077/425358. 50 rms. A/C MINIBAR TEL **Directions:** Center of beach strip.

$ Rates: 1,950B–3,000B ($78–$120) single/double. AE, V.

These attractively built, modern, minihouses are spaced apart from one another along a boardwalk facing the sea. Each has a large porch with comfortable furniture,

polished hardwood floors, a seating area, and tiled bathrooms with hot-water showers. Big picture windows and louvered ventilation windows with screens and curtains
add a bit of luxury. Now, a small pool, beachside restaurant, and 20 smaller bungalows with the same amenities, but limited sea views, have been added. All are attractive, but we prefer the relative privacy of the older, freestanding bungalows.

**WORLD RESORT BUNGALOW, Bophut Beach, Ko Samui 84140, Surat
Thani. Tel. 077/425355-6.** Fax 077/425355. 32 rms. A/C **Directions:** Center of
beach strip.
$ Rates: 550B ($24) single/double with fan; 900B ($36) single/double with A/C.
MC, V.
This is a large compound of simple, wood-paneled bungalows facing each other
around a well-kept garden. The communal lawn area and beachfront are well maintained by a friendly staff. Kudos to the much-respected Mr. Pinyo Sritongkul,
World's friendly owner, who organized the planting of 1,200 trees along Samui's
north coast road in a conservation drive to celebrate Mother's Day! Rates are based
on the use of fan or air-conditioning, as all simply furnished rooms come equipped
with both. There's a pleasant, seaside café and good pool. A special discount is offered to return visitors. (When the governor of Surat Thani Province visits Ko Samui
he stays at the World.)

BIG BUDDHA BEACH

Big Buddha Beach is a more recently developed cove (east of Bophut, on the north
coast) that is becoming popular with young, low-budget families. There is a fairly
clean, coarse sand beach (narrow in the monsoon months) and a calm, shallow
swimming bay. Some small hotels and many simple bungalows look out over Ko
Faan (also written Ko Farn), the island home of Samui's huge seated Buddha, which
is also the place to purchase seashells. Fishing boats and long-tail water taxis servic-
ing Ko Phanghan create some traffic, but it's very picturesque.

**BIG BUDDHA BUNGALOW, B34/1 Moo 4, Big Buddha Beach, Ko Samui
84140, Surat Thani. Tel. 077/425282.** 14 bungalows. **Directions:** East side
of beach near Nara Lodge.
$ Rates (including tax and service): 180B–250B ($7.20–$10) single or double. No credit
cards.
These coconut wood, split-log cabins are the best deal on this beach, and one
of the best on the island. They're large, with big porches, comfy furniture,
screened windows, fans, and private showers. Rates vary according to size,
and two rooms are air-conditioned, but all are near the well-swept beach, meticu-
lously clean, and face a large lawn. During our most recent visit we found new
owners busily cleaning up the place and planning changes. Let us know how you
find it.

**COMFORT RESORT NARA GARDEN, 88 Moo 4, Bophut, Ko Samui
84140, Surat Thani. Tel. 077/421364.** Fax 077/425292. 42 rms. A/C
MINIBAR TV TEL **Directions:** East end of beach.
$ Rates: 1,250B ($50) single/double. MC, V.
The recently remodeled Nara is one of the island's older inns, with attached rooms
as close to an American motel as you'll come in Ko Samui. A well-kept lawn leads
to an acceptable beach with gentle swimming. The Nara has a slightly suburban ambience that makes it especially comfortable for families.

THONG SAI BAY

Ko Samui juts out at the northeastern tip in a rough, irregular coastline. Bold rock
formations create private coves and protected swimming areas, though from mid-
October to mid-December the monsoon whips up the wind and waves, creating a
steep drop-off from the coarse sand beach and strong undertow. Thong Sai Bay is a
beautiful cove dominated by one resort; its privacy is a plus and a minus. While

exclusively tranquil, it's impossible to reach by cheap public transport, so getting there is tough unless you hire a car or taxi through the hotel.

IMPERIAL TONGSAI BAY HOTEL, Ban Plailaem, Bophut, Ko Samui 84140, Surat Thani. Tel. 077/421451. Fax 077/421462. Telex 69704 TONGSAI TH. 24 rms, 48 suites. A/C MINIBAR TV TEL **Directions:** Northeast tip of island; call for hotel pick up or charter private minitruck (about 250B [$10] from pier).

$ Rates: 4,000B–5,200B ($160–$208) single; 4,400B–$5,700B ($176–$228) double; 5,700B–12,000B ($228–$480) suite. AE, DC, MC, V.

Built amphitheatrically down a hillside, the white stucco, red-tile roofed bungalows and buildings remind one of the Mediterranean, though the palm and bougainvillea are pure Thai. Between the half-moon cove's rocky bookends, the coarse sand beach invites you to idle away the days. The free-form saltwater pool, landscaping (tended by 36 gardeners), tucked-away tennis courts, and myriad flowers delight the eye. Most guests admire the grounds and sunset from the spacious balconies of the three-story hotel wing or from the large, tiled patios of freestanding two-room bungalows. The imaginative "Rock suites," in which a natural rock outcropping has been incorporated into the split-level space à la Frank Lloyd Wright, command a premium price ($40 more per night), but are our favorite spaces. They're for a splurge; otherwise, they're very similar to the split-level "deluxe studios," also stocked with toiletries, hair dryer, bathrobes, slippers, fresh roses, a fruit basket, houseplants, lacy mosquito netting, and plush rattan furniture. "Deluxe suites" in either the bungalows or the hotel wing are equally charming, though only on one level.

Water sports are taught by enthusiastic young pool boys: windsurfing, snorkeling, sailing dinghies, canoes, and a catamaran or speedboat (the last two at additional charge) await you. Service, from the comfort-conscious front desk and to the amiable restaurant staff, is good. Advance reservations (up to three months) are a must from mid-December to February and in August. Our only caveat: The many steps between the hilltop reception area, the bungalows, and the beach challenge the elderly, but may thwart the disabled.

There's a pleasant poolside café for breakfast and lunch, and a more formal dining terrace which has a commanding view from the hill. Excellent continental and Thai fare is served; the Saturday evening Thai buffet with a classical and dance performance is worthy of an excursion if you have your own transport; expect to pay $25 and up per person. The hotel hosts thrice weekly welcome cocktail parties for guests.

CHOENG MON

At the southeast end of Thong Sai Beach, you'll come to a fairly formidable set of rocks (they can be climbed safely if you wear decent footwear). Just over these craggy cliffs is the find sand beach of Choeng Mon, a gracefully shaped crescent about half a mile long. Palm trees shading sunbathers reach right to the water's edge; swimming is excellent, with few rocks near the central shore. Across the way is Ko Fan Fa, a deserted island with an excellent beach. You can swim or, if the tides are right, walk there, but be careful of the rocks at low tide. Although Choeng Mon is as isolated as Thong Sai Bay, many small hotels and bungalows hidden in the hills have spawned a new public minitruck route to service this area.

SUN SAND RESORT, Choeng Mon Beach, Ko Samui 84140, Surat Thani. Tel. 077/421024. Fax 077/421322. 32 rms. A/C **Directions:** South tip of beach, on hill.

$ Rates: 1,150B ($46) single/double. MC, V.

This striking resort is composed of comfortable bungalows perched on a cliff with the most stunning views of Choeng Mon Bay. Our favorite large, wood-sided houses face southeast over the open sea, although north-facing ones overlook the sandy beach below. Each has a thatch lining, rattan furnishings, a clean, tiled bathroom with Danish shower and hot water, and a large deck with wooden rocking chairs. Because of the steep grade, houses are built on stilts and connected by an intricate series of boardwalks throughout the unlandscaped grounds. Closer to the water are a gazebo bar with gorgeous vistas, a sandy sunbathing shelf on a rocky plateau, and a concrete walkway leading over the coral coast to deeper water for swimming. The Sun Sand is popular with European tour operators, so early reservations are must.

CHOENG MON BUNGALOWS, 24/3 Choeng Mon Beach, Ko Samui 84140, Surat Thani. Tel. 077/425219. 26 rms. A/C MINIBAR **Directions:** Center of beach.

$ Rates (including tax and service): 125B–300B ($5–$12) single/double with fan; 425B–550B ($17–$22) single/double with A/C. MC, V.

If nothing else is available and Choeng Mon's seclusion sounds appealing, there are three classes of cheap bungalows here. Most are fan cooled, have toilets and cold-water showers inside, and screened windows. Rates rise as you move from the smallest thatch bungalows overlooking the simply planted lawn to larger ones facing the beach to the newest concrete bungalows with hot water and air-conditioning behind the beachside restaurant.

P.S. VILLAS, Choeng Mon Beach, Ko Samui 84140, Surat Thani. Tel 077/425160. 18 rms. **Directions:** North end of beach

$ Rates: 420B ($16.80) single/double; 660B ($26.40) with A/C. MC, V.

These spick-and-span bungalows are excellent value. The friendly staff maintains a large lawn, lots of flowering plants, and a seaview bamboo bar and dining pavilion. Large, attractively patterned thatch and rattan bungalows with bamboo porch furniture have three comfortable beds, fans, and cleanly tiled cold-water showers. Smaller, equally nice thatch bungalows with only two beds cost less. Good for families.

THE WHITE HOUSE, Choeng Mon Beach, Ko Samui 84140, Surat Thani. Tel. 077/425233. Fax 077/422382. 40 rms. A/C MINIBAR **Directions:** On Choeng Mon Beach.

$ Rates: 2,400B–2,900B ($96–$116) single or double. AE, MC, V.

This new resort in the graceful Ayutthaya style, built around a central garden with a lotus pond and swimming pool (neo-Ayutthaya!), was just about to open on our last visit. Knowing the resort's quality management team and seeing the graceful design assures us that the new White House will be a fine new addition. Check it out!

CHAWENG & CHAWENG NOI BAYS

Other than Lamai Beach, the two Chawengs (the main and south ["noi"] part) are the most popular destinations on Ko Samui, and generally draw a more upscale, clean-cut crowd. Nowadays there are a few families and an increasing number of European retirees scattered among the predominantly young travelers. The north or main bay was the first to be developed and is crowded at its north end with simple, budget bungalows whose cafés turn into an active nightlife scene; Chaweng Noi is more peaceful day or night. The distinctions blur if you enjoy walking along the beach; our selections in each area are within a half hour's walk of one another. The fine sand beach extends for about 3½ miles and is an ideal place to swim, windsurf, jog, or just sunbathe.

The main island circle road is ³⁄₁₀ to 1.8 miles inland from the beach, but there's a one-lane paved road closer to the beach with a number of supermarkets, restaurants, clubs, travel agents, photo shops, money exchanges, the Tourist Police, etc. Just inland from the rocky point that divides the two bays are a cluster of shops behind the First Bungalow. Here you'll find a cheap laundry, postcard and souvenir shop, motorbike rental shop (250B [$10] per day), and the Chaweng Library, a commercial book exchange where books in eight languages can be rented for 12B to 25B (50¢ to $1) until you've read them, with a 100B ($4) deposit; open daily 9am to 6pm.

Very Expensive

IMPERIAL SAMUI HOTEL, Ban Chaweng Noi, Ko Samui 84140, Surat Thani. Tel. 077/422020. Fax 077/422397. Telex 69702 INSAMUI TH. 155 rms. A/C MINIBAR TV TEL **Directions:** Middle of Chaweng Noi Beach.

$ Rates: 3,600B–6,000B ($144–$240) single; 5,280B–6,840B ($211–$274) double; suite from 5,800B ($235). AE, DC, MC, V.

This is one of the few luxury resorts on this vast coastline; like its sister at Thong Sai Bay, it is a member of the Thai-owned Imperial Hotel chain. The hotel's two wings are built up on a hill in a grove of coconut palms, overlooking idyllic Chaweng Noi. At our visit, two more wings, a second pool, and another indoor/outdoor restaurant were being constructed higher up the hillside; we imagine this additional capacity may make the Imperial too frantic when fully booked.

At our visit, every spacious, attached room had a sea view, lots of floral prints and rattan, large bathrooms with potted plants, and easy access (via steps) to the beach. Amenities include large balconies, cool tile floors that seem impervious to sand, and an odd-shaped saltwater swimming pool that looks ready to spill into the bay. We found the staff helpful but stressed by the regular arrival of large groups; the dining room suffered from the same pressures. If a local travel agent can get you a good rate here, it's a very pleasant resort.

Expensive

CHAWENG RESORT, Chaweng Beach, Ko Samui 84140, Surat Thani. Tel. 077/422378. 70 rms. A/C MINIBAR TV TEL **Directions:** Middle of Chaweng Beach.

$ Rates: 2,280B ($91.20) single; 2,520B ($100.80) double. Extra person 400B ($16). AE, DC, MC, V.

Like a quaint Florida resort development, the Chaweng Resort consists of two columns of freestanding bungalows, all alike, facing each other as they march down to the sea. Cottages are comfortable and spacious, with one queen-size bed, one single bed, a spotless bathroom, and personal safe in each. Grounds are nicely landscaped, with a medium-sized pool and Thai/continental restaurant overlooking the fine beach. A good family choice.

THE PRINCESS VILLAGE, P.O. Box 25, Chaweng Beach, Ko Samui 84140, Surat Thani. Tel. 077/422216. Fax 077/422382. 12 rms. A/C MINIBAR **Directions:** Middle of Chaweng Beach.

$ Rates: 2,300B ($92) single/double. AE, MC, V.

⭐ The most recent project of Thai architect Patcharee Smith is the surprisingly regal Princess Village. If you've wondered what sleeping in Jim Thompson's House or the Suan Pakkard Palace, both in Bangkok, might be like, here's your chance. Traditional teak houses from Ayutthaya have been restored and placed around a lushly planted garden. Several have sea views and each is on stilts above its own lotus pond; use-worn stairs lead up to a large veranda with roll-down bamboo screens.

Inside, you'll find a grand teak bed covered in embroidered silk or cotton and antique furniture and artwork worthy of the Ramas. Small, carved dressing tables and spacious bathrooms contain painted ceramics, silverware, a porcelain dish, a large khlong jar for water storage, or other Thai details amid the modern conveniences. Traditional shuttered windows on all sides have no screens, but lacy mosquito netting and a ceiling fan, combined with sea breezes, creates Thai-style ventilation. There is air-conditioning for skeptics. Currently, restaurant facilities are shared with the Village next door.

THE VILLAGE, P.O. Box 25, Chaweng Beach, Ko Samui 84140, Surat Thani. Tel. 077/422216. Fax 077/422382. 19 rms. **Directions:** Middle of Chaweng Beach.

$ Rates: 1,325B–1,450B ($53–$58) single/double with fan; 1,550B–2,300B ($62–$92) single, 1,650B–2,300B ($66–$92) double with A/C. Extra bed 250B ($10). AE, MC, V.

This bungalow compound is owned and operated by Thomas Andereggen, a Swiss hotel manager, and Patcharee Smith, a Thai architect who designed the hotel. Other than the two beach-view bungalows, each unit overlooks a humid jungle of tropical plants and has a large porch. The spacious interiors are scrubbed whitewash, with new wood furniture and cold-water private bathroom. The Village has three pluses a delightful garden (with a gazebo) leading to the beach; a Thai and continental restaurant/bar overlooking the beach; and a friendly staff.

Moderate

THE PRESIDENT SAMUI, 4/3 Moo 3, Chaweng Noi Beach, Ko Samui 84140, Surat Thani. Tel. 077/422256. 30 rms. **Directions:** North end of Chaweng Noi Beach.

$ Rates (including tax and service): 600B–850B ($24–$34) single/double with fan; 1,320B ($53) single/double with A/C. AE, MC, V.

It's very tough to get a room at this place (formerly called the Fair House) because it's got such terrific word-of-mouth on the low-budget grapevine. This popular budget spot offers simple but clean bungalows—on our favorite part of the beach—at unbeatable prices. The older cottages (nearer the beach) are small and cheaper, while newer, more substantially built ones are farther back, larger, and more expensive. Some have hot water; all have private facilities and fan cooling.

NEW STAR BUNGALOW, Chaweng Noi Beach, Ko Samui 84320, Surat Thani. Tel. 077/422407. Fax 077/422325. 50 rms. A/C **Directions:** North of Imperial Samui Hotel on Chaweng Noi.

$ Rates: 600B–840B ($24–$34) single/double with fan and cold water; 1,440B–2,160B ($58–$86) single/double with A/C, minibar and hot water. MC. V.

This is a new star on the housing scene, with a wide range of facilities clustered on Chaweng Noi. All are freestanding buildings with porches. Eight deluxe bungalows sit slightly up the hill with clear sea views, large rooms, air-conditioning, and charming stonework in the private bathrooms. Smaller, slightly cheaper, superior rooms with air-conditioning sit on the beach, but five rows deep, so that only the first row is really desirable (the best value). However, prices include one full-size bed and an alcove single bed, ideal for small families. Most of the rooms are air-conditioned now, but some are back from the beach and are small, with fans and twin beds.

Inexpensive

KING BUNGALOW [P. N. HUT], 12 Moo 2, Chaweng Beach, Ko Samui 84140, Surat Thani. Tel. 077/422304. 40 rms. **Directions:** Middle of Chaweng Beach.

$ Rates (including tax and service): 600B ($24) single/double with fan; 850B ($34) single, 1,200B ($48) double with A/C. No credit cards.

These simple bungalows are recently built, spacious, and comfortable, with fans and cold-water showers. Some older, smaller cottages are closer to the beach and cheaper, but lack window screens. The larger, higher-priced cottage has air-conditioning and is a better value only about 100 feet back from the beach.

J.R. BUNGALOW, 90/1 Chaweng Beach, Moo 2 Bophut, Ko Samui 84140, Surat Thani. Tel. 077/422258. Fax 077/422402. 40 rms. **Directions:** North end of Chaweng Beach.

$ Rates: 300B–1,200B ($12–$48) single/double. MC, V.

One of the better budget lodgings on Chaweng's north, more hippy stretch, J.R. is a typical collection of locally owned bungalows which have undergone several upgrades and expansions. Having started years ago with several small rattan, wood, and thatch bungalows on the beach (now the cheapest ones here), this compound grew inland, deep into the coconut groves, with concrete, stone, and tile bungalows. They're larger and neater, but all these bungalows have the same basic small porches, ceiling fans, and cold-water showers. The five-tiered rates vary according to size and view. There's a beachside restaurant/bar, with pretty good Thai food.

EDEN SEAFOOD, Chaweng Beach Road. Tel. 422375.

Cuisine: SEAFOOD. **Directions:** South end of Beach Road; call Eden for free pick up from hotel.

$ Prices: Appetizers 45B–95B ($1.80–$380); main courses 60B–200B ($3.80–$6). AE, MC, V.

Open: Daily 4pm–midnight.

From this pleasant group of thatch pavilions; some overlooking a winding creek from several levels, diners can choose from the freshest pomfret, red or white snapper, lobster, tiger prawns, mussels, or the catch of the day (priced per kilogram), or have anything from the à la carte menu. Fish is steamed, fried with sweet-and-sour sauce (the succulent fresh pineapple made this our favorite preparation), grilled, or poached with garlic and peppers (Kyle's preference). Don't forget the oysters, fresh from the famed farms of Surat Thani. The gracious staff proudly presents an extensive drink list which includes very sweet, Thai-produced red and Australian house wines for 35B ($1.50) a glass.

RUEN SAILOM RESTAURANT, The Princess Village, Chaweng Beach Rd. Tel. 422216.

$ Prices: Appetizers 40B–80B ($1.60–$3.20); main courses 50B–160B ($2–$6.50). AE, MC, V.

Some of our favorite Thai food on the entire east coast of Samui can be found at this lovely restaurant on the beach. You can have a quiet meal under the trees, inside under a transparent roof, or in the cozy interior. We put our gustatory selves into the hands of the very capable kitchen and enjoyed a meal of spring rolls, sauteed spicy shrimp, sauteed fish filets and vegetables in a mild garlic sauce, and broiled chicken in a piquant tomato curry.

LAMAI BAY

The long sand beach on Lamai Bay is comparable to Chaweng's, but the clientele is decidedly rowdier and more colorful, if not always younger. Though there are many bungalows, few are above the most primitive standard—they tend to attract those who want to retire from worldly cares. However, there's lots of new construction, most of it in the budget range, and the range of cafés, bars, discos, tourist services, and bungalows make Lamai the cheapest resort on the island.

The north end of the beach strip is known as Coral Cove, a rocky area where bungalows are built up on the hillside. South of here, along the inland lagoon where fishers moor their boats, there's a paved service road and beach access lane, both between the shoreline and the main island circle road. Public minitrucks cruise the inner service road and will deliver you to the "back door" of most of the beachfront bungalows. Lamai Noi is the quieter south end of the beach, somewhat removed from the fray by its autonomous network of inland service roads.

Everything you'll need is on the midbeach service road. The J & S Supermarket sells groceries, toiletries, and beach supplies and rents books (open daily 8am to 10pm). Dan Jeep and Motorbike rents Jeeps from 600B to 1,200B ($24 to $48) a day (250B [$10] a day). We definitely do not recommend mopeds or motorbikes as a form of transport, particularly around Lamai's crowded, often-washed-out dirt lanes. There's a bank exchange (open daily 10am to 7pm), a gas station, lots of restaurants and bars, and a few discos on a rowdy patch near the middle road (as yet unnamed) between the main highway and the beach road where you will also find Muang Thai Medical Service (tel. 424219).

Expensive

THE PAVILLION RESORT, Lamai Beach, Ko Samui 84140, Surat Thani. Tel. 077/424030. Fax 077/424420. 50 rms. A/C MINIBAR **Directions:** North end of Lamai Beach.

$ Rates (including tax and service): 1,920B ($77) single/double in hotel wing; 2,640B ($106) single/double bungalow. Extra person 400B ($16). AE, DC, MC, V.

One of Lamai's newcomers, these are attached rooms in a hotel block or Polynesian-style octagonal bungalows, all scattered throughout the beachfront grounds (limited sea views). Hotel rooms are nicely appointed, each with its own safe, and have good-sized patios for sunbathing. The larger bungalows have a campy primitive feel, as well as the comfort of a private bath and hot water. The pool and dining pavilion are right on the surf; combined with ground-floor hotel rooms, it makes a comfortable, easy access resort for the disabled. The proximity to Lamai's nightlife is a plus for most guests.

WEEKENDER RESORT, 124/19 Moo 3, Lamai Beach Rd., Ko Samui 84140, Surat Thani. Tel. 077/424429. Fax 077/424011. 70 rms. A/C MINIBAR TV TEL **Directions:** North part of Lamai Beach.
$ Rates: 1,560B ($62) single, 2,160B ($87) double in hotel wing; 1,800B–2,880B ($72–$115) bungalow room. Extra person 75B ($3). AE, MC, V.

The Thai-owned Weekender lodgings include this newly built resort; cheap, older "villas" north on Lamai Beach; even cheaper, roadside huts nearby; and a new three-story motel block of air-conditioned, full-amenity rooms with large verandas and side sea views with a pool and tennis court. The attractively decorated Thai-style bungalows (highest rates) have marble floors, seashell-studded cabinets, large bathrooms, and garden-facing porches. They're much better value than the plain, stucco-walled bungalows built farther inland. The ornately decorated, original dining/reception pavilion, with plaster murals of traditional Thai farm life and carved teak columns, is a very pleasant seaside breakfast venue.

Moderate

ALOHA BUNGALOW, 128 Lamai Beach, Ko Samui 84140, Surat Thani. Tel. 077/421478. Fax 077/424418 or 077/424419. 35 rms. A/C **Directions:** Middle of Lamai Beach.
$ Rates: 1,400B–2,200B ($57–$90) single; 1,700B–2,400B ($68–$96) double; 3,200B–3,600B ($129–$144) suite. AE, MC, V.

The name isn't new but the hotel, which is among the prettiest on Lamai Beach, is. The name should give you some idea of its American-style rooms with white walls, dusty rose carpet, and bright pastel curtains and bedspread. Besides the standard hotel rooms, there are simpler bungalows (or cottages) and several suites. The swimming pool is especially nice.

Inexpensive

PARADISE BUNGALOWS, Lamai Noi, Ko Samui 84140, Surat Thani. Tel. 077/424290. 37 rms. **Directions:** South end of Lamai Beach.
$ Rates (including tax and service): 125B ($55) single/double with common toilet; 480B ($19) single/double with private bathroom. No credit cards.

A nostalgic choice for us, since Kyle stayed here 10 years ago. Any bungalow compound that's still standing on this golden beach after so many years can't be bad. The oldest, simple, wood-and-thatch cabins on stilts have a wood platform bed, overhead light bulb, and access to cold-water toilets and showers out back. They're a bargain for their beachside location. The newer brick-and-concrete bungalows have their own cold-water plumbing. The grounds are plain but well swept, the café is still cheap and good, with steady reggae music, and the friendly staff maintains a safe for valuables (use it!).

WEEKENDER BUNGALOWS, c/o Weekender Supermarket, Lamai Beach Rd., Ko Samui 84140, Surat Thani. Tel. 077/424417. 47 rms. **Directions:** North end of beach road, opposite beach.
$ Rates: 250B ($10) single/double. No credit cards.

Like a military encampment, these four rows of no-view bungalows are the simplest of shelters, with a built-in bed, clean mattress and sheets, a fan, and a tiny stall with toilet and cold-water Danish shower. They're neatly kept and cheap; check in at the supermarket for information and keys. *Warning:* This can be a noisy place at night.

NOY BAR-B-Q, 124/59 Soi Noy, Lamai Beach. Tel. 077/424314.
Cuisine: SEAFOOD. **Directions:** Off middle of beach; follow the giant footprints up Soi Noy.
$ Prices: Main courses 95B–300B ($3.80–$12). MC, V.
Open: Daily 6pm–midnight.

Noy's space appears to be a cross between an airplane hangar and a Thai pavilion. Central tables cooled by industrial ceiling fans are set around a large, screened grill. Tables set outdoors are next to a Buddha-shrine. The steam from cooking prawns, lobster, squid, and fresh fish mixes with the shrine's incense to create a heady atmosphere. There are imported wines, and yes, barbecued meat is available, but that didn't deter us from the fresh seafood. The service is especially relaxed and friendly.

WILL WAIT RESTAURANT AND BAKERY, 124/12 Lamai Beach Rd. Tel. 424263.

Cuisine: CONTINENTAL. **Directions:** On access road, midbeach.

$ **Prices:** Main courses 30B–120B ($1.20–$4.80). No credit cards.

Open: Daily 7am–10pm.

Ⓢ A popular, casual hangout for burgers, sandwiches, and fairly cheap Thai food. Because of the large selection of rolls, bakery items, and fresh bread, there's a groggy breakfast crowd about 11am. We liked their distinctive pizza on a roll. At 7:30pm nightly, foreign travelers spinning travelers' tales gather for wine coolers and the evening video showing.

LAEM SET BAY

Laem Set is a small rocky cape on Samui's southeast coast whose dramatic scenery has prompted the construction of a few hotels on this nonbeach strip. The main island circle road is nearly 2km (1.2 miles) inland, but mototaxis (kids who will give you a ride on the back of their motorcycle for 25B [$1]) wait at the public minitruck junction to transport you out to the point. We love one resort here, but it's an eccentric choice.

LAEM SET INN, 110 Moo 2, Hua Thanon, Laem Set, Ko Samui 84310, Surat Thani. Tel. 077/424393. Fax 077/424394. 12 rms, 3 suites. **Directions:** See above, or call for pick up.

$ **Rates:** 1,500B ($60) single/double; 2,800B ($112) single/double bungalow; suite from 4,500B ($180). AE, MC, V.

★ This small, special resort is neither cheap nor for everyone, but if you want a cozy hideaway environment, you'll be satisfied. Kayaks, mountain bikes, and snorkel gear are available to explore this location's stunning scenery: The elevated pool seamlessly blends with the gulf, reflecting sea and sky from the pavilion restaurant, where gourmet fare and delicious Thai seafood are prepared fresh daily and served at lunch or supper.

The most exclusive accommodation is the private two-bedroom house, transplanted from a nearby island and converted to a suite decorated with hand-hewn furniture and natural, native grace ($410). The Ma-rat suites are two connected bedrooms ($340 for both bedrooms, $178 for one bedroom) and an open, eight-bed sleeping loft draped with mosquito netting that's perfect for a bevy of children. Large porches bookend the bedrooms and provide a magnificent perch for drinking in views beyond the pounding surf of No Dog Island. The basic screened-window, fan-cooled rooms are comfortable, but less charming than the thatch bungalows, which have beds canopied with mosquito netting and a large loft above. This boutique inn (it was built as a private club) has a handcrafted feel, far from the crowds, rustic and intimate. It's unique; an ideal getaway.

WEST COAST

From Laem Phang Ka, one of Samui's better beaches on the island's southwest tip, the main island circle road cuts inland, heading north past Ban Lipa Noi and the cutoff running west to the car-ferry jetty. Many Thai families stop for picnics at Hin Lat Falls, a rather uninteresting, littered site 2km (1.2 miles) south of Nathon that supplies the town with its drinking water.

EVENING ENTERTAINMENT

The beaches of Chaweng and Lamai have the island's widest variety of nightlife. If you haven't rented your own vehicle, or find it impossible to walk to the hot spots below, ask reception at your hotel or bungalow about the nightly "taxis" provided by young islanders, who cruise the beaches looking for party-going tourists and charge about 100B ($4) an hour to chauffeur you in their converted pickups.

CHAWENG BEACH

Nightlife here draws a more upscale crowd to the few bars and discos on Chaweng Beach Road. On our most recent visit, the **Reggae Pub** (with a halftone graphic of Bob Marley as its logo) was still the hottest, even after several seasons of Europeans toting home "Reggae Pub" T-shirts. The open-sided thatch disco, on a small lane one block inland, about midway up the beach road, not at all hard to find at night, is popular for island dancing to reggae and new European pop tunes. Sunday's the traditional Party Night, with cheap drinks, beer-drinking contests, etc. It's open nightly 9pm to 3am; no cover charge.

The **Green Mango** (far enough away from the Princess Village to not be heard) is another popular disco with an okay Thai food café and more Thai (thatch/bamboo/palm frond) decor. The music is Euro-pop; on Friday and Saturday Party Nights, the tequila goes for 25B ($1) a shot and live bands perform. It's open nightly 8pm to 3am; no cover charge.

During our most recent visit we enjoyed the **Club,** toward the north end of the beach. This more sedate place has an eclectic decor, delicious coconut shakes, and a sound level low enough to actually engage in conversation.

LAMAI BEACH

Lamai is the place for more raucous nightlife. On Lamai Beach Road, parallel to the beach, beginning just south of the Weekender Resort and continuing for about half a mile south, is a strip of Thai, continental, pizza, and seafood restaurants, all open-air, all pretty cheap, plus lots of bars and discos. Opportunities to meet young Thai women abound.

At the **Lamai Night Plaza,** opposite Soi Noy in the middle of this strip, a dozen or so open-air bars cluster back to back in a compound of Pattaya-style flesh and booze vendors. Beers cost 25B to 60B ($1 to $2.40), and the ever-popular Mae Khong whiskey and Coke is 25B ($1). Several bars also show video films. *Warning:* The girls make a commission off what you drink, so watch out or you'll end up buying everyone a round; guard your wallet; avoid the drug trade (heavily policed on this island); be wary of accepting drinks (often drugged) from a stranger. It's open nightly 6pm to 4am.

The scene is changing more rapidly here than elsewhere on the island, and you'll probably have to rely on your own reconnaissance when you arrive, as there will undoubtedly be new places. The **Bauhaus Pub,** which overlooks a crossroads, was making a big splash with banners all over the island and threatening to take top-club honors from the **Mix** (one big block north, across the main street). We didn't stick around long enough, but there's some possibility that partisans may have imbibed sufficiently to duke it out at the nearby **Thai Boxing Stadium;** always good for a night's entertainment.

EASY EXCURSIONS FROM KO SAMUI

Excursions to Ko Phangan or Mu Ko Angthong National Park are for those in search of the primitive, tropical Samui of yesteryear. Many day-trippers decide to stay longer.

KO PHANGAN

We, perhaps like you, are always looking for that island beyond the known resorts where life is like it used to be on . . . Bali . . . or Ko Samui . . . or Phuket . . . or wherever. Ko Phangan, easily visible from Samui and about two-thirds its size, with similar terrain and flora, does have beautiful beaches and inexpensive, primitive bungalows, but it's definitely not what we had in mind. Rather than paradise, it typifies an environmental nightmare of the nineties.

Ko Phangan is extremely popular with budget tourists; the misinformed, clean-cut kids, backpackers, and aging hippies come and find cheap beer, easy drugs, New Age massages, good junk food, and $4 bungalows just a Frisbee throw away from a white sand beach. Magic mushrooms are advertised alongside nightly showings of Cliffhanger and Zen Meditation workshops.

Most tourists head for the southwestern peninsula called **Haad Rin,** which has developed into a T-shirt and vegetarian restaurant village, replete with mopeds and VDO (big-screen video) bars. Word of the famous (or infamous) "Full Moon Party" reached us in Bangkok, and we might have gone if we could have gotten on a boat. On the east side of Haad Rin there is one of the most beautiful white powder beaches, arched in a gentle cove enclosed by rocky cliffs, that we've ever seen. It's covered with garbage. Plastic bags and discarded thongs, water bottles, dead coconut shells, food packaging, cigarette butts and boxes, plant matter, and myriad other fly-encrusted items are washed up from the liter-filled sea or tossed wholesale from the hillside bungalows down to the shore. No one pays enough rent to justify organized trash collection, and for generations (before the age of plastic) the Gulf of Siam was counted on to absorb all the islanders' waste. This pollution caused us to leave on the next ferry, but obviously wasn't a problem for the hundreds of foreigners left in our wake. Consider yourselves warned.

GETTING THERE   By Boat   Three big Songserm express boats a day leave Nathon pier in Ko Samui (9:40am, 10:40am, 4:30pm) for the port of Ko Phangan (trip time: 45 minutes; 75B [$3]). Dangerously overcrowded long-tail boats meet the Thong Sala ferries to shuttle travelers to Haad Rin (30 minutes; 25B [$1] away) or other beaches. Minitrucks go to the beaches which can be reached via the island's few unpaved roads. Two private fishing-boat ferries a day leave Bophut on Ko Samui at 1:30 and 3:30pm and go direct to Haad Rin Beach (trip time: 45 minutes; 90B [$3.60]); not recommended if you're prone to seasickness. Phangan Ferry Co. has daily service from Don Sak pier, Surat Thani (tel. 077/286461).

ESSENTIALS   There are very few phones on the island, so travel is serendipitous. **Thong Sala** is the port and largest settlement; there is a helpful travel agency selling tickets to Ko Tao to the right of the pier; a post office and overseas call office south of the pier on the first paved street; a **bank exchange** on the pier, open daily 9am to 6pm; and the good Beach Home Restaurant overlooking the harbor from the paved back street. The excellent *New Guide Map of Koh Samui, Koh Pha-ngan and Koh Tao*, published by JS Printing, notes many hiking trails and nature spots, it's sold in Surat Thani or on Ko Samui for 50B ($2).

Where to Stay & Dine

Most of Ko Phangan's development (primitive bungalows with their own electric generators and simple snack bars) is along the south coast facing Ko Samui. No one stays in the port of Thong Sala, on the southwest tip. Instead, moving east to parallel the south coast access road, we first get to **Ban Tai Beach,** a quiet, though not extraordinary, sand beach about 5km (3 miles) from Thong Sala, reachable by minitruck. The **Charm Beach Resort** offers decent sea-view bungalows for 50B to 300B ($2 to $12), the cheaper ones quite Spartan, the more expensive ones offering toilet, cold shower, and fan. **Green Peace** is another good inn, with acceptable accommodations for less than 100B ($4). Between Ban Tai and Haad Rin on the south coast there are many small, very isolated bungalows which can be reached by local long-tail boats from Thong Sala or Ban Tai itself. These beaches are narrow, but very quiet and clean. We liked the **Blue Hill Bungalows,** a collection of old Thai-style A-frames rising up the gentle hill above a pretty beach (120B to 200B [$5 to $8]).

Haad Rin is a narrow peninsula on the island's southeast tip, with a large number of bungalows on both the west and east sides and a footpath leading between them. The most attractive bungalows on the busier west side are **Coral Bungalows** (60B to 100B [$2.40; to $5]) about 550 yards north of the footpath, and the **Sunset Bay Resort** (60B to 300B [$2.40 to $12]), about 275 yards north. Both are more substantial and better maintained than their neighbors. The **Lighthouse Bungalows** on the very tip of the peninsula (reached by a boardwalk built out over the sea from the west beach) rent scenic-view huts for 75B to 250B ($3 to $10), but our English friends complained about the absence of service on the staff's part (not uncommon).

On the east side of Haad Rin, **Serenity Bungalows** sit serenely, high above the north end of the beach. Spartan bungalows with dramatic sea views cost 60B ($2.40) single or double with shared toilet, twice that with cold-water facilities. The 29 bungalow **Palita Lodge** (tel. 01/213-5445) with some private showers and toilets (125B to 450B [$5 to $17]) may be the best on the littered beach.

As Haad Rin gets unbearable, travelers are spreading out to other parts of the island. The **Bovy Resort** on Laem Son Beach, booked by the Bovy Market in Thong Sala, offers beachfront bungalows (75B [$3]) with a freshwater lake for swimming nearby. Haad Khuad Bay and Haad Naay Paan, both on the remote northeast corner of the island and accessible by private minitruck from Ban Tai (about 75B [$3]), are becoming the new hot spots.

OTHER EXCURSIONS

Tiny **Ko Tao** has been developed so recently that it skipped the slow-growth years of thatch shacks and candlelit meals and went straight to corrugated tin roofs and VDO bars. There are a few primitive bungalows on the west and south coasts, with most activity provided by the scuba tours which come from Ko Samui for the best coral diving in the area. Avoid Ko Tao in the stormy fall season, when the monsoon whips up and winds cloud the normally transparent seas. There's one boat daily from Ko Phangan's Thong Sala (2½ hours; 200B [$8]), and one boat daily from Ko Samui's Nathon pier (3½ hours; 250B [$10]).

Forty islands northwest of Ko Samui have recently been designated a national park. **Mu Ko Ang Thong National Marine Park** is known for its scenic beauty and rare coral reefs. Many of these islands are limestone rock towers (similar to Phangnga Bay off Phuket) once used by pirates marauding in the South Chinese Sea.

Ko Wua Ta Lap (Sleeping Cow Island), the largest of these, is home to the **National Park Headquarters,** where there are several dormitory bungalows sleeping 10 to 20 people (about 75B [$3] each), and some two-person tents (150B [$6] per night). These facilities can only be booked at the park's Bangkok office (tel. 02/579-0529), although visitors with their own camping gear can stay for free. The island has freshwater springs and a park service restaurant as well.

Mae Ko (Mother Island) is known both for its beach and Thale Noi, an inland saltwater lake that is mysteriously replenished through an undiscovered outlet to the sea. Known to the Thais as Ang Thong or Golden Bowl, this yellowish-green lagoon gave its name to the entire archipelago. The national marine park can be reached by day-excursion boats from Nathon pier run by Samui Holiday Tours. The 400B ($16) tariff includes round-trip cruise and lunch; overnighters can arrange to return on another day.

4. SURAT THANI

644 km (400 miles) S of Bangkok

GETTING THERE **By Plane** Two flights daily leave from Bangkok to Surat Thani on Thai Airways (trip time: 70 minutes; 2,040B [$82]). One flight daily leaves from Phuket (trip time: 30 minutes; 480B [$19]).

By Train Eight trains leave daily from Bangkok's Hua Lampong station to Surat Thani (trip time: 13 hours; second-class sleeper 555B [$22.20], second-class seat 364B [$14.56]). One train departs daily from Butterworth Station in Penang, Malaysia (call 02/223-3762 for information). The train station is very inconvenient, but minitrucks meet trains to transport you to town (tel. 311213).

By Bus Five air-conditioned buses leave daily from Bangkok's Southern Bus Terminal (trip time 11 hours; 350B [$14]; 420B [$17] for sleeper). Four air-conditioned buses leave daily from Phuket (trip time: 5 hours; 125B [$5]). Four minivans daily from Phuket (trip time: 4 hours; 225B [$9]). Call the Bangkok bus terminal (tel. 02/435-1199) or the Surat Thani Bus Terminal, on Kaset II Road a block east of the main road (tel. 272341), for information. Air-conditioned, more comfortable "VIP" buses are operated by private companies; call them directly (we like Krung Siam Tours, tel. 02/412-2828 in Bangkok, or tel. 278506 in Surat Thani).

By Car   Take Highway 4 south from Bangkok to Chumphon, then Highway 41 south direct to Surat Thani.

Surat Thani is believed to have been an important center of the Sumatra-based Srivijaya Empire in the 9th and 10th centuries. Today, it's known to foreigners as the gateway to beautiful Ko Samui and to Thais as a rich agricultural province.

The favorite food product is oysters, farmed in Ka Dae and the Tha Thanong Estuary (30km [18 miles] south of Amphur Muang, the capital town), where more than 16,000 acres are devoted to aquaculture. Fallow rice paddies now support young *hoi takram* or tilam oysters, which cling to bamboo poles submerged in brackish water. After two years they can be harvested; the summer months yield the best crop. We prefer the fleshy white tilam oysters, with their subtle taste, served in a number of Thai dishes.

In nearby Chaiya you'll pass boxes of roadside stalls piled high with cardboard boxes of another local treat, salted eggs. Chaiya's traditional recipe calls for eggs with a reddish yellow yolk, which are coated in a clay of water, salt, and earth from red anthills, then rolled in the ashes of rice husks. Boxed eggs have individual cooking directions, ensuring perfection of this celebrated dish.

Surat Thani's other famed product is the Rong Rian rambutan (*ngor* in Thai). The industry has blossomed since 1926, when a breed of the spine-covered fruit grown in Penang was transplanted here; now more than 125,000 acres of the Nasan district (40km [24 miles] south of town) are devoted to plantations. Each August (the harvest is August through October) a Rambutan Fair is held, with a parade of fruit-covered floats and performances by trained monkeys (see "What to See & Do," below, for information on monkey schools).

ORIENTATION

Information   For information about Surat Thani, Ko Samui, and Ko Phangan, contact the TAT office, 5 Talad Mai Rd., Surat Thani (tel. 077/281828 or 288818-9; fax 077/282828), down the street from the Wang Tai Hotel (open daily 8:30am to 4:30pm).

City Layout   The city of Surat Thani is built up along the south shore of the Tapi River. Talad Mai Road, two blocks south of it, is the city's main street, with the TAT office at its west end, and the bus station and central market at its east end. Frequent minitruck group taxis ply Talad Mai; prices are based on distance but rarely exceed 25B ($1).

Fast Facts   The **area code** is 077. **Currency exchanges** at the airport and train station maintain longer daily hours. The **Taksin Hospital** is at the north end of Talad Mai Road. (tel. 273239 or 273072). The **Tourist Police** and **Overseas Call Office** are together on the midstretch of Talad Mai Road at Chonkasean Road. The **Thai Airways** office is inconveniently located to the southeast at 3/27-38 Karoonrat Rd. (tel. 272610 or 273355).

WHAT TO SEE & DO

This pleasant town is little more than a transportation hub to Ko Samui and its less-developed satellite island, Ko Phangan. Those with an extra day or two (especially those with children) may want to organize a visit to a local Monkey Training Center, where monkeys are taught how to harvest ripe coconuts, or to Suan Mokkh Monastery, a renowned Buddhist retreat with meditation study programs in English.

At the **Monkey Training Center** Monkeys have been trained to harvest fruit

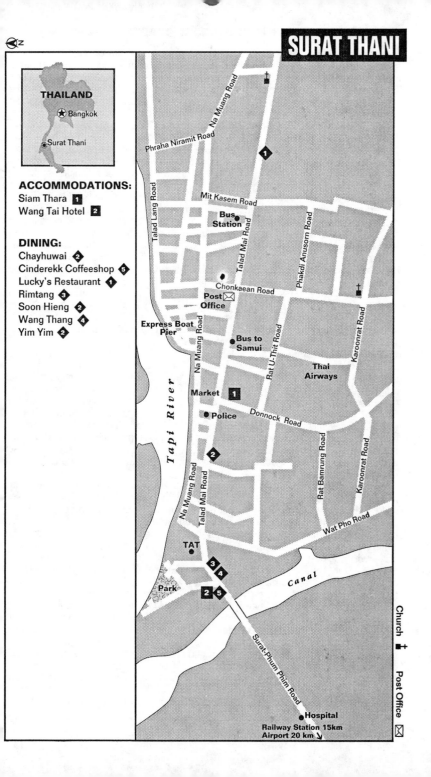

from south Thailand's particularly tall breed of coconut palm only since the 1950s. In that time, dozens of private schools have opened, each accepting up to about 50 monkeys per year. The Macaca nemestrina, or pig-tailed macaque (*ling kang* in Thai), is the only suitable breed; a farmer pays about 3,000B ($120) for a 1- to 3-year-old male, then another 3,000B for training the animal to eventually pick 800 coconuts a day.

We visited trainer Somphon Saekhow, of Kan Chanadit, Surat Thani (tel. 077/273378 or 282074), whose school is about a 25-minute drive south of Surat Thani town. The charming, smiling Mr. Somphon learned monkey training from his father (who studied with his father) and works with six monkeys at a time, for three to five months each. He usually teaches males, but will only train a female monkey for a female farmer/master. Gently calling each newcomer "loh" (son), he holds their skinny arms and shows them how to palm coconuts like a basketball player. Each is coaxed to handle coconuts themselves in two half-hour sessions per day. They are taught to distinguish ripe from unripe or rotten fruit, how to spin coconuts around their stems to break them off the tree, and how to pitch them into receptacles below. Mr. Somphon teaches his sons how to pick up coconuts and pass them to a master for husking, how to use teeth to tear handles into shells, even how to remove a master's shoes so he can nap. (They, of course, are trained to nap with their masters.)

Mr. Somphon accepts visitors by appointment only. Our 1-hour demonstration was arranged by the TAT; a car and driver and an English-speaking guide were provided by a local travel agent. The total cost was 3,000B ($120), steep for a twosome but manageable for a larger group, and the experience was magical. Call the TAT for assistance in making these arrangements.

Suan Mokkhabalarama (the Grove of the Power of Liberation, better known as Suan Mokkh) was founded by Bhuddhadasa Bhikku in 1932 and moved to this forest in Chaiya about 10 years later. The wooded, peaceful monastery/meditation center is dedicated to the study of Theravada Buddhism's original Pali scriptures and the personal study and practice of dharma (in brief, the ways and laws of Nature and Duty). Its abbot, Ajahn Buddhadasa, spent years traveling around Thailand teaching the elemental principles of the Buddha. His fame as a teacher spread, and his fluent English lured foreigners to Suan Mokkh to study under him. Today, many foreign monks and nuns continue the aging Ajahn's teachings in the simplest of settings, with no elaborate temple to contain their meditation and no Buddha images to pray to.

The first through 10th days of every month are dedicated to a 10-day Buddhist Meditation Course held at Suan Mokkh. The daily program typically includes a 4am wake-up and meditation session, breakfast, chores around the compound, lunch, private study, afternoon tea, an evening lecture, and evening meditation. The retreat has limited accommodations for visitors who are asked to "stay here as individuals committed to self-exploration." There are several rules of conduct. Applicants are accepted on a first-come basis; the 10-day course, dorm lodging, and meals cost 600B ($24) in 1994. Suan Mokkh accepts students at other times of the month free of charge, although beginners will find it awkward to fit into the self-motivated meditation routine. Write to them or the TAT Bangkok for information.

Suan Mokkh, Amphur Chaiya, Surat Thani 84110, is 50km (31 miles) north of Surat Thani on Highway 41 (tel. 431552); long-distance buses and minitrucks pass by the entrance throughout the day. On arrival, walk into the woods a short distance, then turn right to the Farang Dining Hall and Women's Dormitory. You can pick up a booklet with information about the monastery and its programs, and can usually find a Senior Monk or Coordinator to help you get settled. Suan Mokkh provides bedding, a sack for your possessions, and mosquito netting. Mosquito repellent is a necessity as malaria is endemic to the area. When you're there, don't forget to buy a box of salted eggs, a regional specialty sure to delight your Thai friends.

WHERE TO STAY

SIAM THARA, 1/144 Donnock Rd., Surat Thani 84000. Tel. 077/273740. 172 rms. A/C TEL **Directions:** Middle of town near bus station; corner of Talad Mai Road.

$ Rates: 475B ($19) single/double. MC, V.

Worn, but well-kept, rooms with dull beige and brown upholstery are good value, because of Siam Thara's central location, just a 2-block walk from the Samui Tours office (tel. 421221 for minivans to Donsak ferry pier) and a 5-minute tuk-tuk ride from the Songserm office (tel. 272928 for minivans to express boat pier). The lobby coffee shop becomes an evening nightclub from 8pm to 2am; high-floor rooms are quieter.

WANG TAI HOTEL, 1 Talad Mai Rd., Surat Thani 84000. Tel. 077/ 283020. Fax 077/281007. Telex 67408 WANG TAI TH. 238 rms. A/C TEL **Directions:** South side of town near TAT.

$ Rates: 660B–800B ($26–$32) single/double. Extra bed 175B ($7). AE, MC, V.

The best quality choice is a bit inconvenient, but only 25B ($1) by tuk-tuk from the bus terminal or ferry company offices. This new hotel tower features the Cinderell Coffeeshop, where acceptable Thai food and good salads are served at tables overlooking the Tapi River and a pleasant pool and sun deck. Spacious rooms are clean and comfortable (tels vary according to view).

WHERE TO DINE

We discussed locally farmed, succulent oysters in our introduction; they're served at most restaurants in town for as little as 8B (35¢) each. To sample this gustatory highlight, we recommend **Chayhuwai, Soon Hieng** (also try their crab salad), and **Yim Yim,** all in the middle of town, all specializing in Thai and Chinese cuisine.

Our favorite old place is in the north end of town—**Lucky's Restaurant** at 452/84-85 Talad Mai Rd. (tel. 273267). This large, busy establishment has a front, open-air dining room and an air-conditioned hall, both filled with locals enjoying the inexpensive, well-cooked food. Pork curry with coconut milk, ginger, and peppers is a spicy but tolerable brew, and deliciously tender. The *tom yam klung,* a shrimp soup with straw mushrooms, makes a good starter before their superb fried oyster omelet. Main dishes range from 45B to 145B ($1.80 to $5.80).

During our last visit we found the excellent new **Rimtang Steak and Seafood,** 14/6 Talad Mai Rd. (tel. 283850) near TAT and the Want Tai Hotel. Hours are daily from 10am to midnight. If you've got some extra baht to drop you might visit the nearby **Wang Thang Entertainment,** the most elegant place in town, with a huge coffee shop, cocktail lounge, karaoke bar, and gussied up Chinese restaurant— and prices to match.

5. NAKHON SI THAMMARAT

Nakhon Si Thammarat, one of the oldest cities in south Thailand, has long been its religious capital. Formerly known as Tamphonling, it was the center of Buddhism for the Malay peninsula during the Srivijaya Empire, about 1,200 years ago. At that time, records show that a relic of the Lord Buddha was transported from Sri Lanka to Hat Sai Kaeo, the Beach of Crystal Sand. Today, the ancient beachfront chedi built to house this relic is at Wat Mahatat, a site now 32km (20 miles) from the seaside. Tamphonling was an active port and a busy trading partner with other Asian nations. Many Indian merchants settled around the region and built Buddhist and Brahman Hindu temples.

By the late 13th century, Nakhon Si Thammarat (or Muang Nakhon), the dominant power in south Thailand, adopted the Sri Lankan school of Hinayana Buddhism. Because of Nakhon's spiritual influence, it was eventually adopted by the rulers at Sukhothai and became the country's official religion. Nakhon Si Thammarat came to be known as Muang Phra or Town of Monks.

At this point, facilities are still basic and few locals speak any English, making it very difficult to appreciate what the region has to offer. Nonetheless, if you're in the south, heading north to Ko Samui or west to Phuket, you should allow a few hours to see the city's most revered shrine, Wat Mahatat. For more information, contact the small TAT office at Wat Mahatat (tel. 075/346515); open Thursday to Tuesday 8:30am to 4pm.

WHAT TO SEE & DO

This is one of south Thailand's most revered shrines because the huge chedi at **Wat Mahatat** (or Wat Mahathat) is said to contain relics of the Buddha brought from Sri Lanka more than a millennium ago. The chedi is 250 feet tall with a a point decorated in sculpture and gold leaf. The wat's museum is composed of several small pavilions lined with dusty cupboards and old, carved woodwork, There are thousands of votive offerings, large and small Buddhas, porcelain, lacquer ware, jewelry, and other presents left at the shrine (open daily 8:30am to 4:30pm). Study the site plan at the main gate, opposite the TAT office, before you begin your tour. Outside the compound walls are several small food stalls and an open-air market selling local handicrafts and souvenirs. Donations (about 10B [40¢] for a candle, lotus bud, and incense offering) are gratefully accepted toward the restoration of the chedi.

Still a region noted for its **craftspeople,** Muang Nakhon offers a large variety of *niello* (silver oxidized a shiny blue black, much like polished hematite), repoussé, silver brass work, and woven straw products made from the superfine, locally cultivated liphao vine. Bronze and metalware designs are old-fashioned, but the workmanship is very high quality and prices are reasonable. Rice serving bowls, betel-nut boxes, serving pieces, and some traditional jewelry are available at several shops on Tha Chang Road. These stores also carry a small selection of woven pillboxes, handbags, evening purses, and decorative items, as well as some newly made shadow puppets (another cottage industry). The best shops have been designated by the TAT with their logo; most take credit cards and are open daily from 9am to 6pm. Tha Chang Road is parallel to, and two blocks west of, Ratchadmnoen Road. It dead-ends at the central market, near the bus terminal; walk south from there to see many shops.

Religious holidays are celebrated with fervor and often include performances of the traditional Nang Luang shadow-puppet plays. The Hae Pha Khun or **Homage Paying Ceremony** is one local event celebrated for three days in the third lunar month (usually February or March) to honor the relics of Buddha. The Prapheni Duan Sip or **Tenth Lunar Month Festival** (usually October) runs for 10 days from the waning of the moon. Locals make elaborate preparations to receive their *pret* (ancestors who were condemned to hell), who take a 15-day leave to visit the living.

WHERE TO STAY & DINE

If you have to spend the night here, you'll find the best hotels and restaurants near the train station, in a central but seedy part of town. Be careful, if walking around after dark.

THAI HOTEL, 1375 Ratchadamnoen Rd., Amphur Muang, Nakhon Si Thammarat 8000. Tel. 075/341511. Fax 075/341512. 251 rms. TEL **Directions:** 2 blocks from train station.

$ Rates: 200B ($8) single/double with fan; 400B ($16) single/double with A/C. AE, MC, V.

This is one of the few establishments where anyone speaks a little English. The helpful staff and tidy carpeted rooms (with writing desks and private baths) make it the best value in town. Their Thai Café (open nightly 6pm to 1:45am) is fun, with inexpensive Thai, Chinese, and a few continental dishes served in near darkness. On stage, songbirds in gold lamé, red sequins, and black satin entertain the local crowd. Quite a scene.

The **Montien Hotel**, next to the train station at 1506 Yommarat Rd. (tel. 075/ 341908), is another option with budget rooms at the same rates.

YELLOW CURRY HOUSE [GAENG SOM], 1467 Yommarat Rd. Tel. 341873.

Cuisine: THAI. **Directions:** 2 blocks from train station.

$ Prices: Main courses 20B–60B (80¢–$2.40). No credit cards.

Open: Daily 8:30am–9pm.

It's rare for us to cry "Stop Here!" just because there's a great Thai restaurant in town, but here we go. Gaeng Som (as the locals know it) serves fantastic, authentically spiced food. The delicious, hot (but not nuclear) yellow curry dishes, spiced with ginger, chili, and sliced bamboo, are made with mounds of fish, oysters, chicken, beef, or shrimp. The Yam Thai salad is a soothing grilled Japanese eggplant, trimmed with fried catfish, prawns, scallion, and green mango. We even liked the nonspicy vegetable platter of fresh bamboo shoots, mushrooms, carrots, corn, and quail eggs. Don't miss it.

EN ROUTE TO SONGHKLA

If you take Route 401 southwest from Nakhon Si Thammarat, at Hua Sai it joins the coast, becoming a two-lane blacktop wedged between the South China Sea and Songhkla Lake. Soon, dense groves of papaya, coconut palm, and cashew nut trees give way to flooded paddies. This was the rice bowl of the Malay Peninsula until skyrocketing land costs and diminishing yields forced rice farmers to sell their land to tiger prawn growers. The air is abuzz with small generators driving fans to aerate the water as the fish mature. In the evening, exposed fluorescent tubes illuminate the prawn pools so villagers can watch over their investment.

East of Phattalung town, in this region and neighboring Trang Province, are the remnants of the Sakai people, an aboriginal tribe whose hilltop habitats have slowly eroded with modern development. The few dozen Sakai who've been discovered in the jungle continue to hunt with blowpipes, chasing after gibbons, their sons in tow to learn these vital skills. Motivated by the difficulty of surviving on dwindling natural resources, Sakai youth have begun going to the nearby cities to find manual work. Soon their villages will give way to condominiums, and the traditional Sakai will become the object of tribal treks for tourists.

6. HAT YAI & SONGHKLA

1,013km (629 miles) S of Bangkok; 350km (217 miles) S of Surat Thani

GETTING THERE   By Plane   Four flights daily leave from Bangkok direct or via Phuket to Hat Yai on Thai Airways (trip times: 85 minutes/45 minutes respectively; 2,700B [$110] one-way from Bangkok). Call Thai Airways (tel. 245851) for information; their limo service from the airport costs 250B ($10) to Hat Yai and 400B ($16) to Songhkla, but there are minibuses to Hat Yai for 60B ($2.20) per person. Tradewinds Airlines from Singapore and MAS from Malaysia also service Hat Yai regularly.

By Train   Four trains depart daily from Bangkok's Hua Lampong station to Hat Yai (trip time: 16½ hours; second-class sleeper 670B [$26.80], second-class seat 375B [$15]). One train daily leaves from Butterworth, Malaysia, to Hat Yai (trip time: 5½ hours; 120B [$4.80]). Contact the Hat Yai Station on Thammanoonvithi Road (tel. 243705).

By Bus   Fourteen air-conditioned buses leave daily from Bangkok's Southern Bus Terminal (trip time: 14 hours; 480B [$19.80], 600B [$24] for sleeper). Four air-conditioned buses leave daily from Butterworth, Malaysia (trip time: 6 hours; 300B [$12]). Two air-conditioned buses leave daily from Singapore (trip time: 15 hours

500B [$20]). Call the Bangkok terminal (tel. 02/435-1199), the Hat Yai Bus Terminal (tel. 232789), Singapore Travel Service (tel. 245356), or Hat Yai Travel Service (tel. 244711) for information.

By Taxi   There are frequent group (six persons) taxis to and from several destinations in southern Thailand and northern Malaysia. Contact the TAT for schedules and information.

By Car   Take Highway 4 south from Bangkok to Chumphon, then Highway 41 south to Phattalung, then again Highway 4 south to Hat Yai.

Although it's one of the most popular destinations for foreign visitors to Thailand, most Western tourists never reach Hat Yai. But millions of Malaysian and Singapore visitors do, frequenting this rowdy, slightly sleazy, inexpensive, consumer-oriented playground, turning it into Thailand's most homogenous, pan-Asian city. We found Hat Yai's lively, melting-pot quality, reminiscent of the rough-edged Singapore of years gone by, to be its strongest appeal.

Hat Yai is a major transportation hub, so travelers exploring south Thailand or Malaysia may find themselves spending the night. If you do, don't miss the vibrant Night Market, the city's neon-lit venue for clothes and souvenir merchants, produce farmers and food vendors. The nearby Songhkla's natural beauties: an inland lake, a long broad beach, a smattering of wooded islands, and forested rolling hills endear it to the Thais; we found it made a relaxing, pleasant day trip.

ORIENTATION

INFORMATION   The **TAT** office is at 1/1 Soi 2 Niphat Uthit 3 Rd., a few kilometers southeast of the train station (tel. 074/243747 or 238518; fax 245986); open daily 8:30am to 4pm.

CITY LAYOUT   Hat Yai is a big city whose tourist services have been built in a compact column between the railroad tracks to the west and the curving Klongtoey on the east. Niphat Uthit Road, two blocks east of the train tracks, is one of the main streets; Niphat Uthit 2 Road and Niphat Uthit 3 Road, parallel it to the east, are the other major thoroughfares and home of the lively Night Market. The main east-west street is Thammanoonvithi, which runs from the train station east to the highway to Songhkla.

GETTING AROUND

Walking is the easiest means to reach most tourist sites in the city of Hat Yai or in the town of Songhkla. To travel between them, take a bus from the Hat Yai bus terminal (every half hour from 5am to 7:30pm; 12B [50¢]), or a minibus from the taxi stand at the Municipal Market, corner of Suppasanrangsan Road (every half hour from 5am to 8pm; 20B [80¢]). Both arrive in Songhkla near the central clock tower. Hat Yai's main thoroughfares are served by frequent minitruck taxis (here called tuk-tuks, even though they are large, bench-seat pickups); just hail one heading in your general direction (fare 5B [40¢]).

FAST FACTS: HAT YAI & SONGHKLA

   Area Code   The telephone area code is 074.

   Consulate   The Malaysian Consulate is at 4 Sukhum Rd. open Monday to Friday 8:30am to 4pm (tel. 31062 or 311104).

   Currency Exchange   There are several bank exchanges which maintain extended hours, usually daily 9am to 9pm. The airport bank is open daily 9am to 4am.

   Hospitals   The Songhklanagarind Hospital is at Prince of Songhkla University, at 17/1 Karn Chanawanich Rd. (tel. 212070).

Police   For theft, or loss of property, call the Tourist Police at 246733. For other problems, call the Hat Yai Police (tel. 243021) or the Songhkla Police (tel. 311011). In case of emergency, call 199.

Post Office   It's on Niphat Songkhro Road, two blocks north of the train station (tel. 243121).

Safety   We would have said Hat Yai was very safe after our enjoyable visit, but recently we've read about minor robberies (in the Night Market) and some unfortunate tourist/local drug-trade violence. Watch your valuables and stick to well-lit streets in the evening.

Telephone/Telex/Fax   The Overseas Call Office is on Phatkesan Road, on the north side of town (open daily 7am to midnight).

WHAT TO SEE & DO

HAT YAI

Hat Yai's **Night Market** is the city's most interesting attraction for Western tourists. It features the variety and vitality of a Singapore Hawkers Center or an Indonesian Pasar Malam more than the bargain-hunting frenzy of Chiang Mai's Night Bazaar. Most of the activity is centered on the north stretch of Niphat Uthit 3 Road, at the intersection of Pratchathipat Road, down to Niphat Uthit 2 Road, and up around the Regent Hotel and the small sois encircling it. There are a number of barbers and beauty parlors (open till 8:30pm); sidewalk vendors selling imitation "Locoste," "Dior," "Gucci," and other T-shirts; Chinese bakeries catering to the large, local Hokkien population; a Hawkers Center (market) with 30 different food stalls; the multistory, bargain-priced Ocean and Diana department stores (open 10am to 9:30pm); and myriad stalls of audio- and videotape dealers, dried shrimp and fish vendors, and housewives selling their dried sour plums, fresh durian, and luscious, moist raisins (45B [$1.80] per kilogram). Thai fruits are highly prized in Malaysia and Singapore, and these stalls are usually the most crowded.

The **Hawkers Center (market)** (everyone's fantasy of a clean, hygienic street-food extravaganza) opens about 6pm but comes to life after about 8:30pm. Each chef prepares their specialty in a chrome steam cart; roam from cart to cart, assembling a full meal, then settle in at anyone's table. We loved the crab-and-egg noodle soup (18B or 75¢), fried spring rolls (8B or 35¢ each), crisp-fried black-eyed pea cakes (four pieces for 6B or 25¢), steamed vegetable dumplings (six pieces for 35B or $1.40), taro root and rice noodle cakes (12B or 50¢ each), and vegetable egg foo yung (25B or $1). Many vendors sell sweets and condiments, particularly brightly colored jellies, stewed sweet corn and stewed fruits, and Chinese-style sugar donuts. Sample everything—you won't go wrong.

In front of the Hawkers Center (market) food stalls you'll find a Chinese Buddhist temple, **Wat Chu Chang,** where services are held in Mandarin. On the full moon night of the eighth lunar month, the **Moon Festival** is celebrated (October/November). During the festival's three nights, the city comes alive with lanterns and tables are set with beautifully displayed offerings for heroic ancestors. A parade and dragon dance, as well as fireworks are always part of the holiday.

Hat Yai's sleazy side is most apparent in its massage parlors, many nightclubs, and sing-along karaoke bars, which cater primarily to Asian tourists. The **Pink Lady,** in the Sukhontha Hotel on Pratchathipat Road, is popular for massages and other physical recreation (tel. 243999). The **Diana Club** in the Lee Gardens Hotel on Lee Pattana Road (tel. 234420), and the **Aladdin Club** in the Kosit Hotel at 199 Niphat Uthit 2 Rd. (tel. 244711), are popular choices for a drink or dinner accompanied by pretty Thai songbirds. All of these can be fun places, but watch your liquor bill because charges for booze (a small Singha beer costs 120B [$4.80]) and "escorts" can mount up quickly. As everywhere in Thailand, drugs are illegal— in Hat Yai you should definitely steer clear.

SONGHKLA

A day trip to Songhkla should include a visit to the Songhkla National Museum, the beach, and a fresh seafood lunch.

The **Songhkla National Museum** is housed in the well-restored home of Songhkla's former deputy governor on Platha Road. It was built in the Chinese style in 1878; red-tile pagoda roofs crown a two-story, teak-beamed house centered around a large courtyard. Because it hosted royalty while it was used as the State Hall for Nakhon Sim Thammarat province, the bed that King Rama V slept in is on display. On the ground floor are two framed flags from Siam—regal white elephants on a red field. The other dusty displays of local archeological finds are not of much interest. The museum is two blocks east of the clock tower and taxi stand. It is open Wednesday to Sunday 9am to noon and 1 to 4pm; admission is 10B (40¢). Across the street, you'll find a section of Songhkla's original fortified wall, built in 1839 under King Rama III.

There are many impressive wats in this town, once a distinguished merchant and maritime center. **Wat Matchimawat** on the Saiburi Road, built in the 16th century, includes a classic temple (to the left as you enter) in the style of Bangkok's royal Wat Phra Kaeo. The frescoes within are rumored to be painted by the same royal artists. There is another, newer pavilion housing a collection of votive offerings and relics from regional archeological sites. If the door isn't open (Wednesday through Sunday 9am to 4:30pm), ask the abbot for the key. The wat is about a 15-minute walk south, down Ramvithi Road, from the clock tower.

Laem Samila, 3km (1.8 miles) north of the Municipal Market on Ratchadamnoen Road, is the quintessential Asian beach. Thai, Malay, Singaporean, and Chinese tourists descend from minibuses with their cameras and children. They step off the beachside walkway to inspect the clean gold sand, climb on the bronze mermaid statue for photos, or look more closely at Cat and Rat (the nearer, hump-backed one) islands. If the weather's clear and seas are calm (usually from April to October), they may spread tatami mats on the sand for a picnic or allow their children to swim. Otherwise, it's straight to one of the seafood restaurants where fish, crab, and prawns can be selected for cooking.

Up above Samila is **Khao Noi Hill,** a forested slope whose foot is decorated in topiary animals and swings and whose peak (a hardy 45-minute walk) provides great views over land and sea.

Some visitors come solely to study at the **Institute for Southern Thai Studies,** part of Srinakharinwirot University (tel. 239899). This well-documented collection and research facility is housed in 24 modern Thai-style pavilions on wooded Ko Yo island, across the lake from the main town of Songhkla. At the roadside information building, pick up a site plan and brochure, then head up the steep hill to the first room of pottery and proceed through the collections of beads, cloth weaving, metal-work, religious displays, model boats, instruments, folk crafts, weapons, and household objects. If you're interested in the very old, traditional Thai Malay culture, you'll want to spend a few hours here. There's a cafeteria on the premises and nice gardens.

The museum is open daily 8:30am to 4:30pm; admission is 10B (40¢). It's 28km (17 miles; a 30-minute drive) from either Hat Yai or Songhkla; public buses to Ko Yo coast 10B (40¢) and group minitruck taxis cost 20B (80¢), a more convenient private taxi will cost about 1,000B ($40) for a half day.

WHERE TO STAY

Hat Yai has dozens of hotels, many not well suited to Western tastes. Here are a few convenient recommendations, plus two choices in Songhkla for those who want a peaceful retreat.

THE FLORIDA HOTEL, 8 Sripoovanart Rd., Hat Yai 90110. Tel. 074/ 234555. Fax 074/234553. Telex 62136 FLORIDA TH. 119 rms. A/C MINIBAR TV TEL **Directions:** South end of town between Niphat Uthit 2 and 3 roads.

$ Rates: 700B–1,000B ($28–$40) single/double. AE, MC, V.

We were surprised to find a hotel named Florida, and equally surprised at how nice it was. It's a first-class place with all the expected services, and large, comfortable, modern, and well-priced rooms. The staff is friendly and professional. The Florida has a popular outdoor restaurant and is fairly well located, about a 15-minute walk south of the train station.

LAEM THONG HOTEL, 46 Thammanoonvithi Rd., Hat Hai 90110. Tel. 074/244433. 133 rms. TEL **Directions:** 1½ blocks east of the train station.

$ Rates (including tax and service): 225B ($9) single/double with fan; 350B ($12) single/double with A/C. No credit cards.

This Chinese-run hotel is near the train station. Rooms are Spartan but clean, the dimly lit hallways seem reasonably safe, and the back-facing rooms are genuinely quiet. The air-conditioned rooms are more comfortable, with the luxurious addition of a minibar, seating area, and hot-water shower. Fan-cooled rooms only have cold water.

CATHAY GUEST HOUSE, 93/1 Niphat Uthit 2 Rd., Hat Yai 90110. Tel. 074/243815. 20 rms. **Directions:** 15 meters south of Thammanoonvithi Road.

$ Rates (including tax and service): 75B ($3) dorm bed; 150B ($6) single; 175B ($7) double. No credit cards.

The extensive bulletin board tells you that this is one crossroad for budget Asia travelers. It's a 2-block walk from the train station, offers travel services such as bus and train tickets and hotel bookings (for a small commission), and provides clean rooms with fan and private cold shower and toilet, at very cheap prices. Get to the Cathay at breakfast if you want a room; it's pretty much first come, first served.

SAMILA HOTEL, 1/11 Ratchadamnoen Rd., Songhkla 90000. Tel. 074/ 311310. Fax 074322448. Telex 64204 SAMILA TH. 70 rms. A/C MINIBAR TEL **Directions:** On beach, at north end of town.

$ Rates: 720B ($29) single; 850B ($34) double; suite from 1,800B ($72). AE, MC, V.

This feels a little like a faded Florida beach resort, and it's one of the things we like best. Rooms are comfortable, though worn, and all have balconies with ocean views. The small suites are well suited for families with a kitchenette and room dividers. There is a small pool and golf course and a host of fine seafood pavilions a brief walk away. In the winter monsoon, the sea is unfriendly and the beach somewhat dirty. Otherwise, it's a gentle blend of faded and fun.

HOLLAND HOUSE, 28/20 Ramvithi Rd., Songhkla 90000. Tel. 074/ 322736. 10 rms. **Directions:** Near the clock tower.

$ Rates: 150B–225B ($6–$9) single or double. No credit cards.

There's no Dutch flavor here, but we found a clean, well-maintained, homey guesthouse. Walk up the stairs past the inexpensive café and you'll find sunny, street-facing rooms. They can be noisy if you keep the windows open, but the back rooms have no view of Songhkla's sleepy small-town charm. The Holland House also has a few bicycles for rent (50B [$2]).

WHERE TO DINE

If our description of the Night Market's Hawkers Center didn't turn you on, there are many good conventional restaurants. The **Jae Lek Restaurant,** in the city center at 190/304 Niphat Uthit 2 Rd. (tel. 244466), has a collection of soccer trophies to complement the modern decor, but in this unlikely setting you'll find excellently prepared, authentic Thai fare, priced at 30B to 120B ($1.20 to $4.80) for main dishes. The pad thai are wrapped in a thin, delicious omelet pancake. Fried eggplant is served with squares of tempuraed spinach. The *tom yam* seafood and steamed fish in sour curry live up to the south's reputation for the spiciest food in the country. It's open daily 11am to 9pm.

We strongly recommend eating seafood in Songhkla, but if you don't want to stroll over to the beach, the pleasant coffee shop of the Pavilion Hotel is a good choice, within a block of the clock tower and a 5-minute walk of the museum, at

17 Platha Rd. It's moderately priced with a wide variety of Thai, Chinese, and continental dishes.

The **Nai Wan Restaurant** (tel. 311295) is one of half a dozen restaurants on Samila Beach offering local seafood, simply cooked, but deliciously fresh. Among the best choices are *pla klapong*, a fleshy white fish cooked in a red chili sauce with bits of pork; steamed crabs served plain but very tender; and fiery *tom yam* with shrimp in soothing coconut milk. Prices average 70B to 150B ($2.80 to $6) for seafood. Around the corner, the **Bourkaw Seafood** serves comparable meals at similar prices. For a take-home treat, buy the locally canned salt fish (broil or fry at home) or sea coconuts (sweet, candied palm fruit) from any of the local vendors.

7. SOUTH TO MALAYSIA: PATTANI, NARATHIWAT & SUNGAI KOLOK

From Bangkok: 1,055km (656 miles) S to Pattani;
1,149km (714 miles) S to Narathiwat; 1,215km (755 miles) S to Sungai Kolok

GETTING THERE   By Plane   Two flights a week leave from Hat Yai to Pattani; three flights a week, from Hat Yai to Narathiwat. Contact Thai Airways in Bangkok (tel. 02/280-0070), Hat Yai (tel. 074/245851), Pattani (tel. 073/394149), or Narathiwat (tel. 073/511595) for more information.

By Train   Two trains a day depart from Bangkok to Sungai Kolok (trip time: 20 hours; 550B [$22] second-class seat, 850B [$34] second-class sleeper).

By Bus   Four buses a day leave from Hat Yai to the border via Pattani (trip time: 1½ hours; 50B [$2]), Narathiwat (trip time: 3 hours; 80B [$3.20]), and Sungai Kolok (trip time: 4 hours; 110B [$4.40]).

By Taxi   Frequent group taxis (up to six persons) from Hat Yai to the border via Pattani (trip time: 1½ hours; 80B [$3.20]), and Narathiwat (trip time: 3 hours, 100B [$4]), and Sungai Kolok (trip time: 3½ hours; 160B [$6.40]).

By Car   Take Highway 4 south from Bangkok to Chumphon, then Highway 4/41 south to Hat Yai/Songhkla, then Route 42 south to Pattani, Narathiwat, and Sungai Kolok.

DEPARTING/ENTERING THAILAND   The Thai/Malay land border is open daily 5am to 9pm Thailand time or 6am to 10pm Malaysia time. Border officials have posted Immigration Act B.E.2522 (1979) identifying an "Alien with Hippy Characteristics," obviously not someone you want to be if you intend to enter either country. Travelers without a proper tourist visa will be required to prove assets of 10,000B ($400) before one can be issued.

ESSENTIALS   Area code is 073. The TAT **information office** and the local **Tourist Police** are at 13 Asia Road at the border crossing in Sungai Kolok, open daily 8:30am to 4:30pm (tel. 073/612126). Because border guards live next door, there is often someone helpful hanging out at the TAT after hours.

Thailand's southernmost territory, bordering the Malaysian state of Kalantan, is distinguished by a racial blend of Thai, Malay, and Chinese peoples (who settled here during its reign as a maritime power) and by a high percentage of Muslims. The only farang likely to pass through Pattani, Narathiwat, or Sungai Kolok are those traveling overland to or from Malaysia's east coast resorts. If you find yourself forced to overnight on this journey, Narathiwat provides the most pleasant interlude. We found it a charming little town, where life moves slowly and inhabitants are friendly to the few Westerners they encounter.

WHAT TO SEE & DO

Due south of Songhkla, past kilometers of coconut palm plantations and pine trees along the winding coastal Route 408, is the large town of **Pattani**. The small, orange-tiled, green-roofed, onion-dome **Central Mosque** is an attractive curiosity. Its arched stained-glass windows and two slender minarets distinguish it from an otherwise typical Thai townscape.

In central Pattani on Rattanaphram Road, you'll find a taxi stand and the main bus stop. Across the way, some older wooden houses on stilts are moored next to striped *korlae* (fishing boats) along the Pattani River.

Thirty kilometers (18 miles) south of town, near the Hat Yai–Sungai Kolok Railroad line, is the 300-year-old **Wat Chang Hai,** built to commemorate a monk who's said to have crossed the sea by foot, distilling salt from the water with every step. Everywhere you'll see fish farms, with large nets draped over raised platforms to control the amount of heat and sun the growing fish will receive.

The neighboring province of Yala is known for **Wat Khuha Phimuk** (Wat Na Tham), where a beautiful, 82-foot-long reclining Buddha from the Srivijaya Empire period (ca. A.D. 800–1000) is housed in a cave, 4km (2½ miles) outside the capital. There is also a village of the primitive Sakai people in the Ban Rae area. South of Yala, the small village of Ruso is typical of the region, with its many pale yellow, green-roofed mosques and rattan homes on stilts reminiscent of rural Malaysia or Indonesia.

The song of zebra doves (small gray cuckoos) emanates from ornate rattan cages overlooking the town's narrow lanes. Between January and August there are frequent competitions for best singer, prettiest singer, loudest singer, etc., all part of the south's Hokkien Chinese traditions

In town, pedicab drivers rule the roads, ringing their bicycle bells to signal availability. There are several taxi stands lining Narathiwat's main street, and all have vintage 1961 Mercedes-Benz taxis. A true mystery, as we saw dozens of aging sedans, but only in this part of Thailand. From the central area, a relaxing 15-minute walk north on the main street, Pichitbumrung, leads to **Narathat Beach**, a broad, fine sand stretch shaded by coconut trees, which define a public park, In the rainy season (July to December), the seas will likely be rough, but it's the Muslim sense of modesty that deters most visitors from having a swim.

Make sure to wander by the Ban Nara fishing village seen from the **Nara River bridge.** The naked young boys playing in the water, wiry elders polishing their striped, long-tail *korlae*, women with covered heads mending fishing nets, are rare views of a seemingly bygone rural life-style.

Narathiwat's other unexpected treat is at **Khao Kong Hill,** about 8km (5 miles) south of town, where the Phra Buddha Taksin Ming Mongkol, a 24 meter tall rotund Buddha, gazes serenely over the rice paddy. It's easy to charter a taxi for this excursion from town (about 200B [$8] including waiting time).

The 1961 Mercedes taxis plying the scenic coastal Route 4084 south of Narathiwat make it look like a scene from *American Graffiti*; at Route 4057 you must veer southeast for the journey to the border. The traditional fishing village of **Tak Bai** has a Muslim cemetery and old mosque, as well as a distinctly Asian feel sometimes missing in the more developed reaches of the country.

Huge teak logs line the road into **Sungai Kolok,** waiting for long-haul trucks to load them up for the journey south. In front of the high school we found a class of uniformed girls doing aerobics to "Wipe Out." Square blocks of markets filled with Chinese-made cotton clothing, bolts of batik, and fresh-picked Thai produce cater to the groups of Malaysian shoppers who come for the day. Neon lights, glistening chrome hotels, and air-conditioned private tour buses cater to the groups who come for the night. It's time to move on to Malaysia . . .

WHERE TO STAY & DINE

Narathiwat is our first choice, but we'll recommend a hotel in each of these towns in case you have to spend the night.

MY GARDENS HOTEL, 8/28 Charoen Prathet Rd., Amphur Muang 94000, Pattani. Tel. 073/348933. Fax 073/348200. 135 rms. A/C TEL **Directions:** North side of town, 2km (1.2 miles) from bus station at clock tower.

$ Rates (including tax and service): 480B ($19) single/double with fan; 550B ($22) single with A/C, 500B ($20) double with A/C. V.

My Garden is a contemporary high rise in the town center, with comfortable rooms and views over the quiet town and (in the distance) the scenic Pattani River. Their Chinese and Thai-style coffee shop is very popular with locals.

TAN YONG HOTEL, 16/1 Sopapisai Rd., Amphur Muang 96000, Narathiwat. Tel. 073/511477. Fax 073/511834. 84 rms. A/C MINIBAR TV TEL **Directions:** Town center, 2 blocks from bus stop.

$ Rates: 650B–750B ($26–$30) single/double. V.

This is a surprisingly fine hotel for such a small city. Large rooms are bright and comfortable; the staff speaks little English but try hard to please. There is a pool hall (open daily 9am to 2am), the Ladybird Ancient Massage Parlor, a barbershop, and an espresso bar off the lobby.

The Tan Yong Restaurant is the best in town, with a few continental and Chinese dishes to round out its terrific Thai menu. Locally raised duck (served grilled or cooked in a brown sauce) and fresh seafoods are popular, but oh so spicy! Avoid the mullet and *ka chad* vegetables in sour soup! There is a parade of lovely young girls in the wildest prom outfits belting out Thai love songs to the accompaniment of an electric synthesizer nightly, from 7:30pm. Don't miss this place.

GENTING HOTEL, 141 Asia Rd. 18, Sungai Kolok 96120, Narathiwat. Tel. 073/613231. 190 rms. A/C MINIBAR TV TEL **Directions:** 2 blocks from the border crossing.

$ Rates: 950B ($38) single; 1,050B ($42) double. MC, V.

Most of this border town's hotels do a brisk business by the hour. The modern, clean, and comfortable Genting has a pool, pool hall, massage parlor, and lively Chatvarin Restaurant, with a mixed Thai/continental/Chinese menu, plus live bands, to keep you occupied until the border reopens.

CHAPTER 8

SOUTHWESTERN THAILAND: THE BEACHES

Thailand's beaches, along the Andaman Sea, are world renowned for their clean white sand, coconut palm groves, and warm water. Less known are the glorious opportunities for exploring the underwater sea life and coral treasures, fine windsurfing and sailing, and the region's exquisitely simple seafood. For decades few but the brave and the hardy ventured to the often-primitive Thai beaches, but today most areas are served by a sophisticated tourist infrastructure and indulgent accommodations. Although no sandy crescent is protected from the hotel developer's hand, there are still areas that are realtively undeveloped.

1. RANONG & SURIN NATIONAL MARINE PARK

568km (352 miles) S of Bangkok; 117km (73 miles) S of Chumphon; 219km (136 miles) NW of Surat Thani; 412km (255 miles) N of Phuket

GETTING THERE By Plane There are no direct flights to Ranong. The closest airports are in Surat Thani or Phuket.

By Train From Bangkok take the train to Chumphon and from there a minibus or shared taxi to Ranong (trip time from Chumphon: 2 hours; 95B to 140B [$3.80 to $5.60]).

By Bus There are four air-conditioned buses daily from Bangkok (trip time: 7 hours; 350B [$14]), as well as several from Chumphon (trip time: 2 hours; 75B [$3]), Phuket (trip time: 5 hours; 250B [$10]), or Surat Thani (trip time: 3 hours; 85B to 120B [$3.40 to $4.80]).

By Car Travel south from Bangkok by Route 35 and 4 via Samut Sakhon, Phetchaburi, Pracaub, and Chumphon, or north on Route 4 from Phangnga and Phuket.

ESSENTIALS The **area code** is 077. The **police** can be reached at 812511 or 81099 and **Ranong Hospital** is on Kamlansap Road (tel. 821574). For a dentist or doctor check with the hotel. **Drugstores** can be found on Ruangrad Road. There is a Krung Thai Bank Ltd on the corner of Kamlungsab and Ruangrad roads (open Monday to Friday 8:30am to 3:30pm.) The **post office,** located at 328 Ruangrad Rd. (tel. 811185), is open Monday to Friday 8:30am to 4:30pm.

WHAT'S SPECIAL ABOUT SOUTHWESTERN THAILAND

Events/Festivals

The Phuket and Trang Vegetarian Festival (October) features arrow piercing and other religious events as well as parades and vegetarian food in Phuket's wats.

The Phuket International Marathon (July) attracts runners from all over Southeast Asia.

Hotels

The Amanpuri on Surin Beach in Phuket is one of the most elegant hotels in all of Southeast Asia.

People

Sea gypsies live on the islands off the coast of Phangnga as well as near Ko Pi Pi, Phuket, and Ko Lipe (Tarutao National Park).

Shopping

There are lovely shells for sale at markets in Phuket and at the various beach resorts.

Parks & Scenery

Similan National Park and Surin National Maritime Park are two island chains with pristine, white sand beaches and some of the best coral reefs in the world for snorkeling and diving.

Phangnga Bay has dramatic limestone karst outcroppings that are reminiscent of images in Chinese landscape painting.

Tarutao National Park is an archipelago largely undiscovered and unexplored, with wonderful beaches and undersea life.

Laundry and **dry cleaning, hairdressers** and **barbers,** and the *Bangkok Post*, can be found on Ruangrad Road or at the Jansom Thara Hotel. **Cars** can be rented through the Jansom Thara for about 2,500B ($100) per day. There is a local **bus** system in the town, and **motorbike taxis** (men with green vests) can be hired to take you to your destination. You can store your luggage at the hotel.

Situated on the Kra Isthmus, Ranong faces the Andaman Sea and borders the southern tip of Myanmar at Victoria Point, a village once famous for its ivory trade and now an important nexus for Thai-Burmese commerce. Many Thai nationals take the short boat excursion to Victoria Point on organized day trips. But foreigners are forbidden from crossing over. However it's another attraction that brings people to Ranong, namely its hot springs. The springs are located about a half mile east of the town center, just up the road from the Jansom Thara Hotel.

A growing number of travelers are discovering the islands off the coast of Ranong. The best known of these is Ko Surin, a national park which is distinguished by its fine coral reefs and relatively low level of development.

If you plan on visiting Ranong, keep in mind that it receives more rain than any other province in Thailand. The least amount of precipitation falls from November to April, while the same holds true from December through March on Ko Surin.

ORIENTATION

Information There is a TAT information office at the City Hall on Lu Wang Road (tel. 281828). Generally, you'll encounter very few people who speak more than a few words in English. Try to coax whatever information you need from the concierge at your hotel.

City Layout The town is easily walkable, but unless you like long strolls, you'll have to take a public bus or taxi to the hot springs. The main thoroughfare is Ruangrad Road; here you'll find an excellent market (don't forget to try the cashews

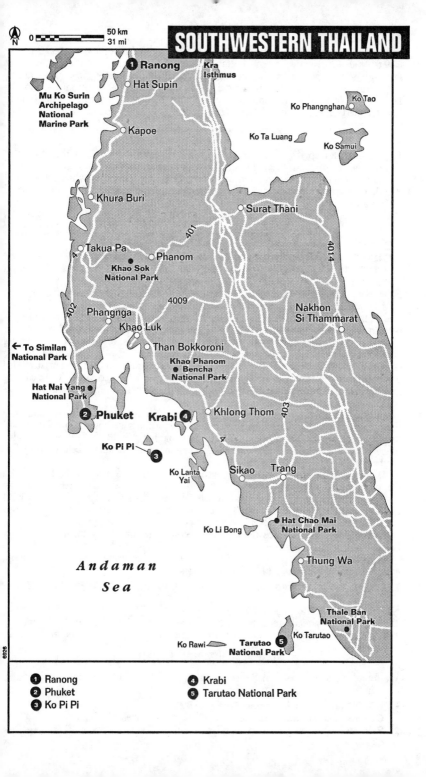

SOUTHWESTERN THAILAND

N
0   50 km
   31 mi

1 Ranong   Kra Isthmus

Hat Supin

Mu Ko Surin
Archipelago
National
Marine Park

Ko Tao

Ko Phangnghan

Kapoe

Ko Ta Luang

Ko Samui

Khura Buri

Surat Thani

401

4014

Takua Pa

Phanom

Khao Sok
National Park

4009

Nakhon
Si Thammarat

Phangnga

Khao Luk

← To Similan
National Park

Than Bokkoroni

402

Khao Phanom
Bencha
National Park

Hat Nai Yang
National Park

2 Phuket   Krabi **4**

Khlong Thom

403

Ko Pi Pi
3

Ko Lanta
Yai

Sikao   Trang

Hat Chao Mai
National Park

Ko Li Bong

*Andaman
Sea*

Thung Wa

Thale Ban
National Park

Ko Rawi

Tarutao
National Park   **5**

Ko Tarutao

6926

1 Ranong   **4** Krabi
2 Phuket   **5** Tarutao National Park
3 Ko Pi Pi

which are grown on a nearby island (125B [$5]), dried red dates and prunes, Burmese sweets, and a distinctive green vegetable called a *lieng* that finds its way in most shrimp-based soups, as well as the usual tourist facilities—bank, post, newsstands, drugstores, etc. The bus stop is located on the main road, just south of the Jansom Thara Hotel (it's set on the main road at the turnoff to the hot springs). The Ranong Pier, for the boats to Victoria Point, is south of town, a short bus ride away.

WHAT TO SEE & DO

The natural hot spring that attracts so many visitors is located within the Wat Tapotharam compound, located about 2km (1.2 miles) east of Ranong town center. The site is set in a lovely forested area, complete with pools (in which locals boil eggs!), trails, and thermal runoffs. The temperature of the water reaches 149°F (65°C) and is best appreciated in the pools at the Jansom Thara Hotel (they charge a nominal fee for those who wish to use the pools but aren't guests of the hotel).

WHERE TO STAY

JANSOM THARA, 2/10 Phetkasem Rd., Ranong 85000. Tel. 077/ 811511 or 821511. Fax 077/821821. Telex 68201 JSSPA TH. 206 rms, including 22 suites. A/C MINIBAR TV TEL
$ Rates: 1,200B ($48) standard single/double; 1,500B ($60) superior single/double; suite from 2,150B ($86). Extra roll-away bed 350B ($14). AE, MC, V.

The Jansom Thara is *the* hotel in Ranong, both because of its proximity and connection with the hot springs as well as the fact that it is a fully equipped resort. The main attractions are the sexually segregated thermal pools, and outdoor swimming pool, health/fitness club, and an in-house doctor who consults with those who've come to "take the waters." The rooms are nicely decorated and of decent size. Unfortunately, the lowest-price rooms are nearly always booked, so you'll likely end up in a superior room or junior suite. Even so, we think these rooms plus all of the facilities add up to pretty good value.

In addition to the usual facilities, the Jansom Thara also has its own massage parlor, offering traditional Bangkok-style services; a massage costs about 200B ($8) for one hour, or there is a body massage available for 1,200B ($48). The hotel also offers boat trips to Ko Surin (see "Easy Excursions from Ranong," below) from December to April on the weekends.

Dining/Entertainment: We enjoyed several wonderful meals in both the Palm Court as well as the Namtarm (see "Where to Dine," below), the latter sporting an evening show featuring a live band and local Thai girl singers. The Hills Cocktail Lounge is about as discreet as you can get: It's so dark that you can barely see your hand in front of you! The disco doesn't get going until after 10pm.

Services: Room service 6am to 2am, concierge, limo service, house doctor, laundry service, complimentary welcome drink.

Facilities: Outdoor pool, Jacuzzi with mineral-spring water, beauty/barber shop, gift/drugstore, and massage (4pm to midnight).

THE SPA INN, Phetkasem Rd., Ranong 85000. Tel. 077/411715. 70 rms. A/C TV TEL
$ Rates: 300B ($12) single; 700B ($28) double. MC, V.

This recently expanded inn is strategically located across the street from the Jansom Thara and, given its location, facilities, and price, stands as the best value in Ranong.

WHERE TO DINE

We found wonderful food in Ranong and suggest that you hit as many of our suggestions as possible during your stay.

KHUN NUNT, 35/3 Lu Wang Rd. Tel. 821910.
    Cuisine: THAI. **Directions:** Near the intersection of Chanra-U Road.
$ Prices: Appetizers 45B–70B ($1.80–$2.80) main courses 45B–350B ($1.80–$14). MC, V.

Open: Daily 9am–midnight.

If you have but one meal in Ranong, march directly to Khun Nunt Restaurant, located on the north side of town (about a 10-minute walk from the center, down the hill from the governor's office). This round, thatched, open-air pavilion with simple metal tables and chairs is a favorite lunch spot for government and hospital workers; we think it serves some of the best food in this part of the country. Venison is a specialty during the hunting season (September to December); it can be prepared barbecued-style or fried with garlic and pepper. *Tod man pla* is also very good and lobster is available, but the real star here is deep-fried soft-shell crabs in bread crumbs or with garlic and pepper. As prepared by Khun Nunt they are, bar none, the best we have ever sampled anywhere! That's right, anywhere. If you desire a taste of England as a complement to your meal, you can order a Guiness Stout.

NAMTARM CAFE, Jansom Thara Hotel. Tel. 811511.
  Cuisne: THAI/CHINESE/SEAFOOD.
$ Prices: Appetizers 45B–100B ($1.80–$4); main courses 60B–220B ($$2.40–$8.80). AE, MC, V.
  Open: Lunch daily 11am–2pm; dinner daily 5–10:30pm.

A cavernous dining club with elaborate stage lighting and a dance floor characterizes the Namtarm. Young local women sing Thai ballads and pop tunes to an always appreciative audience. The food is excellent with an emphasis on fish and seafood. Among the best dishes that we sampled are steamed white snapper smothered in thinly sliced ginger, soy sauce, and lemongrass; tofu chicken in a delicate broth; chicken with cashew nuts; a spicy *tod man pla*; oversized barbecued prawns; and steamed crab that was out of this world.

SOMBOON RESTAURANT, 231-233 Ruangrad Rd., Ranong. Tel. 811117.
  Cuisine: THAI/CHINESE/SEAFOOD.
$ Prices: Appetizers 60B–100B ($2.40–$4); main courses 60B–300B ($2.40–$12). MC, V.
  Open: Daily 11am–11pm.

This is a favorite downtown hangout both with the local business community as well as hip Thai rock and rollers. The atmosphere is casual and the food excellent. Among our favorites are steamed bass with Chinese sauce, fried prawn with vegetables, and squid fried with garlic, peppers, and onions. Our friend Victoria especially liked fried crab with curry and barbecued crab. The owner, Mrs. Naparpon, speaks very little English but is friendly and helpful with recommendations; the English-language menu helps considerably.

EASY EXCURSIONS FROM RANONG

An excursion to **Mu Ko Surin Archipelago National Marine Park** is for those who wish to lose the crowds on such popular beaches as Phuket, Krabi, or Ko Samui for the pristine sand and sea of a protected national park. Similar to Ko Similan, off the Phuket coast, Ko Surin is best appreciated for its fine sand beaches and exquisite coral reefs. There is little development on the main island (bungalows and tents are available through the National Parks Division) and literally no development on the surrounding three islets. An eight-person bungalow rents on Ko Surin for 2,000B ($80) per night, tents are about 100B ($4).

There are a number of different ways of experiencing Ko Surin. Boats leave from Ranong or the port of Ban Hin Lad in the Krura Buri district, about two hours south of the city. From Ranong the boat ride takes a shade over three hours, four to five hours from Ban Hin Lad. Most boats only operate from December through April and even then only on weekends, so if you do plan to go, contact the National Parks Division (tel. 02/579-5269) in Bangkok or the Tour and Transportation Department at the Jansom for the most up-to-date information. There are organized trips run by the Jansom Thara. For example, they offer a day excursion for 1,150B ($46), departing in the early morning and returning at about 7pm. If you decide to make it an overnight, expect to pay about 2,400B ($116) including transportation, accommodations, and food.

2. PHUKET

862km (534 miles) S of Bangkok; 176km (109 miles) N of Krabi;
87km (54 miles) N of Phangnga; 287km (178 miles) SW of Surat Thani

GETTING THERE By Plane Thai Airways flies 10 times daily from Bangkok
(trip time: 1 hour; 2,400B [$96]). Daily flight from Surat Thani (trip time: 45 min-
utes; 600B [$24]). Three flights weekly from Nakhon Si Thammarat via Surat Thani
(trip time: 2 hours; 850B [$34]). Twice daily from Hat Yai (trip time: 40 minutes;
950B [$38]). Four flights weekly from Chiang Mai (trip time: 2 hours; 4,200B
[$168]). Thai International also offers several flights a week to and from Singapore
and Kuala Lumpur. Malaysian Airline System offers limited service to and from
Kuala Lumpur; Bangkok Airways (tel. 212341) offers daily flights to and from Ko
Samui (trip time: 45 minutes; 1,300B [$52]).

By Bus Three air-conditioned buses leave daily from Bangkok (trip time 14
hours; 420B to 540B [$16.80 to $21.60]). Ten public buses daily depart from the
capital (trip time: 14 hours; 240B [$9.60]). Six buses daily leave from Surat Thani
(trip time: 6 hours; 90B to 200B [$3.60 to $8] buses, 6am to 6:30pm, 165B
[$6.60]). Seven buses daily leave from Hat Yai (trip time: 8 hours; 140B to 220B
[$5.60 to $8.80]). Nine buses daily leave from Nakhon Sim Thammarat (trip time: 8
hours; 120B [$4.80]). Eight buses leave daily from Trang (trip time: 6 hours; 90B to
180B [$3.60 to $7.20]). Three air-conditioned minibuses leave daily from Krabi (trip
time: 2½ hours; 200B [$8]). Six buses leave daily from Phangnga (trip time: 10½
hours; 45B [$1.80]). Nine buses leave daily from Ranong (trip time: 6 hours; 85B to
250B [$3.40 to $10]).

By Car Route 4 south from Bangkok leads directly to Phuket (trip time: 10
hours). There is shared taxi service to Phuket from Hat Yai (trip time: 6 hours;
300B [$12]); Surat Thani (trip time: 4 hours; 240B [$9.60]); Trang (trip time: 4
hours: 180B [$7.20]); Krabi (trip time: 3 hours; 180B [$7.20]); and Phangnga (trip
time: 2 hours; 100B [$4]).

SPECIAL EVENTS Phuket's **Vegetarian Festival** involves religious rites including fire walking, climbing razor-sharp ladders, and piercing the body with sharp
implements—all performed under hypnosis. The festival begins on the first day of
the ninth Chinese lunar month.

The festival's genesis relates to visiting Chinese performers who were brought in
to entertain Thai tin miners. Many of the actors were stricken with a disease that
forced them to stop performing. Several were convinced that those who had contracted the ailment were being punished for not practicing their traditional Taoist
rites and a remedy was proposed: For nine days and nights, the performers would
eat only vegetables and observe the religious rites they had neglected. The actors recovered and locals considered it a minor miracle.

Today the Vegetarian Festival is marked by a series of special events, some spectacular and magical. Strict observers eat only vegetarian food, often distributed by
the island's five Chinese temples (most tourists visit the two that are centered in
Phuket town). During the nine days, all participants wear only white.

We don't quite know what to make of Phuket. No other Thai destination has
changed so rapidly, and, unique to the megaresort destinations of the world, not
all to the bad. At its best, this island in the Andaman Sea is almost idyllic: It has
long sandy beaches (some with dunes), warm water, excellent snorkeling and scuba
diving off Ko Similan, ideal windsurfing conditions, mountains, and the best seafood
in all of Thailand. It's no surprise that for years Phuket has been Thailand's finest
resort destination.

But during the past decade the Thai government has granted economic incentives
to encourage developers to shape the island into an international-class resort. Hotels—

some of them enormous—are taking over every beach where once only a scattering of modest bungalows stood. As groups pour in from Singapore, Hong Kong, Germany, and Italy, out go the backpackers to nearby Krabi, Ko Pi Pi, or Ko Samui on the gulf.

But . . . some of the resorts are disarmingly attractive and elegant. The Miami Beach strip of concrete and steel is rarely seen on Phuket (although Patong Beach has sunk below the most honky-tonk beachside resort we've ever encountered). In its place are serene bays framed by tastefully designed retreats that are modeled after hillside villas or luxury bungalows. True, it's nearly impossible to find a totally secluded beach, but in its stead are extremely comfortable facilities with a high level of service—not a bad trade-off for those in search of all the luxuries. Yet we came away on our last trip feeling more comfortable on Krabi's beaches or those on the more remote islands in the Similan, Surin, or Tarutao chains. We had a strong sense that you could actually spend a week on Phuket and never really feel that you were in Thailand! If you're traveling with a family or looking for action, well why not: you need a break. Other than that, we suggest you consider other options first; think carefully before making plans to go.

The season on Phuket extends from September to March, with the four months between November and March being prime time. The monsoon strikes from April to August; during the period from late June through August, the so-called promotional season, many hotels and other establishments and services offer discounts up to 50%. During the monsoon season few people come to Phuket due to the perception that it rains all day and night, every day. It isn't so, and we think that for the more flexibly minded, it's an ideal time to make a visit.

ORIENTATION

ARRIVING By Plane Phuket International Airport is located on the northeast side of the island. Besides the fine vista, they have a luggage storage service open daily 8am to 8:30pm (25B [$1] per day per bag, 14-day maximum); a Phuket Tourist Business Association booth (open daily 9am to 7pm) where you can make hotel arrangements; a bus transport booth for bus, minibus, taxi, and limousine connections to Phuket, Patong, Kata, and Karon beaches, as well as runs to other parts of the island and Krabi and Phangnga; several banks (open daily 9am to 10pm); and Hertz and Avis rental-car booths.

By Bus or Car If you arrive by car or coach, you cross over to Phuket from the mainland at the northern tip of the island. The road inland from the airport passes Wat Phra Thong (Golden Buddha), the most sacred shrine on the island. It is here that a boy tethered his water buffalo to a post and mysteriously contracted a disease. The post, it was later discovered, was the top of a big, golden Buddha that was buried deep in the ground. For some reason, only the top of the image was excavated and a temple was built for it. Legend has it that those who tried to unearth the submerged portion were attacked by hornets and other insects. The buried Buddha is glazed with gold-leaf stucco to protect the solid-gold image beneath.

A few miles east is the Khao Phra Thaeo Wildlife Park, notable for Ton Sai falls, a lovely spot for a cool break on a blistering day. The park is home to a menagerie of birds and other fauna, as well as a variety of palm that is unique to the island. The road continues south to the middle of the island and, the largest town, Phuket.

INFORMATION The helpful **TAT office,** in the center of Phuket town at 73-75 Phuket Rd. (tel. 076/212213; fax 076/213582), is open daily 8:30am to 4:30pm. There is also a TAT desk at the airport (tel. 311110) which operates until the later of 4pm or after the last flight arrives; they dispense maps, brochures, and current data on available hotels.

A travel agency that we've found reliable with offices in Bangkok and in Phuket is **Seatran,** located at 1091/157 Metro Shopping Center, New Phetchaburi Road, Bangkok 10400 (tel. 02/253-5307); in Phuket: 6 Phangnga Rd., Amphur Muang, Phuket 83000 (tel. 076/211-809). **Sea Tours** (tel. 02/251-4862) operates several tours to Phuket as well as a full schedule of excursions to Phangnga and Ko Similan; their office in Phuket is located at 95/4 Phuket Rd. (tel. and fax 076/216979, open

Monday to Saturday 8:30am to 5pm). **Songserm Travel Center** has two locations: 5153 Satul Rd., Phuket Town, 8300 (tel. 076/222570-4; fax 076/214301); and 64/2 Rassada Shopping Center, Rassada Road (tel. 076/214272; fax 076/214301). We found that they offer the most complete range of services in the area, with a friendly and helpful staff. Hours are 7:30am to 10pm daily.

ISLAND LAYOUT   Phuket is Thailand's largest island, its terrain vast and varied. Wide, grassy plains give way to lush forests that are dense with mangroves, rubber, and palm trees.

The name "Phuket" is derived from the Malay "Bukit," meaning mountain, so it's appropriate that hills dominate much of the island, spilling their craggy rocks on the gentle beach coves below. From most high points you can see the enormous number of nearby islands and islets; among them, hourglass-shaped Ko Pi Pi, off the southern shore. In parts of the interior, open-pit mining for tin and other metals has scarred the land.

The town of Phuket, in the southeastern quarter, is the island's commercial-and-transportation nexus, with an active produce market. Most, if not all, local buses go to Phuket town (usually called "Phuket"). Because inland Phuket is often fiery hot and noisy with buzzing motorcycles, tourists usually head for the shore, where the blazing sun, fine white sand, and refreshing sea encourages a longer stay than most have planned.

Phuket's most attractive beaches are on the west coast, extending from Nai Harn, on the southern tip, to Bang Tao, about 30km (19 miles) north. Most bungalows and new resorts are in between, along the Kata, Kata Noi, Karon, Karon Noi, Patong, and Surin corridor. A coastal road linking most of these beaches has been completed. For now, travel between some of the beaches north of Patong requires a detour to the interior, although some stretches are navigable with four-wheel-drive vehicles.

In the northern and inland sections of the island, peasants still use basic tools and water buffalo to work the fields. In contrast, road crews tear up agricultural lanes along the perimeter of these centuries-old farms to create wide, modern thoroughfares for the tourist trade.

We've divided Phuket into four basic areas: the Southern Coast; Kata and Karon Beach; Patong Beach; and the Northwest Coast. For those in search of privacy, ranging from the elegant Amanpuri to tent camping, we suggest staying north of Patong, along the Northwest Coast, up as far as Nai Yang National Park.

GETTING AROUND

BY BUS   Many hotels and bungalows provide a van for those arriving from the airport for transfer to various points on the island; expect to pay 300B to 550B ($12 to $22). There is bus service from the airport to the Thai Airways office on Ranong Road in Phuket for 60B ($2.40). The public bus operates on an infrequent basis for 25B ($1).

Most routes pass through Phuket town and stop at the public market off Ranong Road near Bangkok Road, down from the Fountain traffic circle. Buses to Nai Harn Beach and Rawai Beach leave from Bangkok Road, around the corner. Fares to the most popular destinations range from 20B (80¢) to 30B ($1.20). Buses are typically scheduled to operate every 30 minutes, but usually run whenever there is a full load of passengers or produce. Be aware that most public buses cease operating at 6pm.

BY TUK-TUK   Within Phuket, tuk-tuks at 10B to 15B (40¢ to 60¢) for any in-town destination are an inexpensive mode of transportation. Tuk-tuks can also be hired for longer distances; a five-passenger tuk-tuk from Phuket to Patong, for example, costs 150B ($6).

BY JEEP   Rental Jeeps, for 2,000B ($80) a day, are also available on Rasada Road in Phuket and at the beaches and hotels.

BY CAR   Car rentals are available in Phuket at Pure Car Rental, opposite the Thavorn Hotel (tel. 211002), for about 2,000B ($80) a day, not including gasoline. There are additional car-rental outlets operating in most of the major hotels throughout the island, with Avis and Hertz dominating the field. Expect to pay approximately 2,500B ($100) per day for a Toyota Corolla with insurance and about 2,000B ($80) for a Jeep. You can contact either Avis (tel. 311358) or Hertz (tel. 311162) at the airport.

FAST FACTS: PHUKET

American Express   The American Express agent is Sea Tours, 95/4 Phuket Rd. (one block south of the TAT), Phuket (tel. 216979). They sell traveler's checks, replace lost ones, and also provide travel services. Open Monday to Friday 8:30am to 5pm, Saturday 8:30am to noon. For lost or stolen traveler's checks or cards, the 24-hour number in Bangkok is 02/273-0022.

Area Code   The telephone area code is 076 for Phuket.

Banks   Banks are located in Phuket (open 8:30am to 3:30pm), Patong, and at the airport. Most foreign exchange windows in Patong are open daily until 10pm. The airport bank is open daily, 9:30am until the arrival of the last flight of the day. Most hotels in other areas will change money, but at lower rates.

Bookstores   English-language books and magazines are available in the shopping arcade of most major hotels and at Patong International Books in Patong's New Shopping Arcade. Seng Ho Book on Suthat Road in Phuket (tel. 211396) has a small selection of English-language books.

Drugstores   Drugstores are located in Phuket and Patong and, with limited supplies, in major hotels around the island.

Emergencies   In case of emergency, call 199 for police; for ambulance service, call 212046 or 212115.

Eyeglasses   The best optician in the area is Better Vision Phuket, 10 Montri Rd., next to the Ocean Department Store (tel. 211705). They sell a stylish array of eyeglasses and sunglasses and can prepare a pair of prescription glasses in half an hour, for approximately 1,500B ($60). Open Monday to Saturday 9am to 9pm.

Hospitals   The expanding Phuket Adventist Mission Hospital (tel. 212386) serves Phuket and the surrounding area. The doctors speak English. It is located at 4/1 Thep Kasattri Rd., on the north side of town. There is also a 10-bed clinic at Patong (tel. 212386).

Post Office   The PTT is at the corner of Thalang Road and Montri Road (tel. 211020) in Phuket. Open Monday to Friday 8:30am to 4:30pm; Saturday, Sunday, and holidays 9am to noon.

Police   The Tourist Police, located next door to the tourist office (tel. 212468) is open daily 8:30am to 4:30pm. There is also a Tourist Police in Patong Beach (tel. 212213).

Telephone   The Overseas Telephone Office is around the corner from the PTT, on Phangnga Road near Phuket Road (tel. 216875), and is open 24 hours. For local and domestic calls, use any of the countless shops that advertise "Phone/Fax Service." Compare costs, as they may differ wildly. Directory assistance is 13.

Transit Info   Thai Airways (tel. 211195 or 212946, domestic; tel. 212400 or 212855, international) office is at 41/33 Montri Rd.

WHAT TO SEE & DO

Phuket is about going to the beach or nearby islands, so if you're looking for great historical or cultural sites, you might want to reconsider your travel plans. Backpackers and campers will want to head north to **Nai Yang National Park and Beach,** just a few miles from the airport. Those in search of an active party scene will find **Patong** ideal. The beaches south of Patong—namely **Karon** and **Kata**—attract a more sedate crowd, as well as those who enjoy fine swimming and diving.

Phuket Center Tour, on Rasada Road (tel. 212892), and Sun and Sand Tour, in the Pearl Hotel on Montri Road (tel. 211044), organize excursions around the island and are rental agents for boat companies. Magnum Travel Co. Ltd. in Phuket (tel. 381840) and Patong (tel. 321117; fax 321357), charters high-speed powerboats for cruising to the nearby islands and around Phuket; contact them for prices.

The **town of Phuket** is worth visiting, especially for those who've just arrived in Thailand for the first time. It will give you some sense of the vibrancy of even a small provincial town, with its open-air markets, interesting architecture, and busy street life. Even if you don't stay in Phuket, take a walk through the markets near Rasada Road or along side streets (with early 20th-century Sino-Portuguese architecture), visit the crocodile farm (tel. 211087) or Thai boxing stadium (at the south end of town on Phuket Road; events are on most Friday evenings), or stop at one of the two Chinese temples. At the intersection of Narisorn Road and Toh Sae Road is the **town hall,** a colonial-style estate that served as the French Embassy in the film, *The Killing Fields.*

If you have wheels and enjoy nature, we suggest visiting the compact **Ton Sai Waterfall Forest Park,** located in the north central region of the island. The turn-off is in the village of Thalang, and from there you'll pass through groves of rubber trees with workers tapping and rolling sheets of raw latex. We stopped in a field and watched a couple of older farmers rolling progressively thinner sheets and placing them on a line to dry. At the park there are snack bars, thatched picnic huts, and monkeys that may try to swipe your food or cameras!

There is a delightful 20-minute walk (remember to wear good shoes) up along the waterfall trail with a local guide (25B [$1]) who points out lizards, spiders, and other insects that blend in seamlessly into the surrounding forest. There are a large number of exotic birds and butterflies. Back at the trailhead is a small wildlife and nature exhibit (open Monday to Saturday 8am to 4:30pm) as well as a few cages containing white-handed gibbons. The park is open daily 6am to 6pm. Admission is free.

COOL FOR KIDS

A new company, Seatran Travel (6 Phangnga Rd., Phuket; tel. 076/211809, operates a fleet of high-speed **cruisers** that ply the waters around Phuket. Contact their office (Bangkok fax 02/249-0977) for the program.

Visit **Crocodile World and Elephant Land,** where kids get a chance to feed crocodiles (which is a sort of table-turning idea) and watch elephants riding tricycles. Conveniently located in Phuket on the south side of town on Chana Charoen Road. Daily show times are 11am to noon and 3:30 to 4:30 pm. Admission is 100B ($4).

Most kids will be perfectly bored by the flower aspect of **Phuket Orchid Garden and Thai Village** (tel. 214860), located on Thep Kassattri Rd., but will enjoy the show which features elephants, Thai boxing and sword fighting, and traditional Thai dancing and crafts. It's really a big tourist stop, but has a playground and four restaurants and a pretty decent show. Our shopper, Victoria, found the crafts for sale on the schlocky side, with preferences for the rubber-soled cushioned silk slippers, silk boxes, dolls, masks, and shell jewelry. Open daily 10am to 10pm; shows are at 11am and 5:30 pm. Admission is 275B ($11).

A traveling buddy suggested a visit to the **Phuket Butterfly Garden and Aquarium** (tel. 215616), about 2km (1.2 miles) from Phuket Town, where dozens of varieties of butterflies are cultivated in a huge covered garden. There's also an insect room featuring unusual specimens and 50 fish tanks with a wide variety of local sea life. It's open daily from 9am to 5pm. Admission is 100B ($4) for adults, 50B ($2) for children under 12.

And we have to admit **Tarzan's Jungle Bungee Jump** (tel. 231123), on the road to Patong beach, very nearly brought the Tarzan out in us. How's this for an excuse: we were too busy checking out restaurants and hotels for you that we just didn't have the time to jump off a 150-foot-tall tower into a jungle lagoon. What's your excuse?

EVENING ENTERTAINMENT

For many, this is the raison d'être of Patong Beach, if not all of Phuket. The liveliest part of the Patong beachfront road runs between the Patong Beach Hotel (at the corner of Patak Road) and the Holiday Inn. There are dozens of fresh seafood displays luring passersby to step in and dine (see "Where to Dine in Patong Beach,"

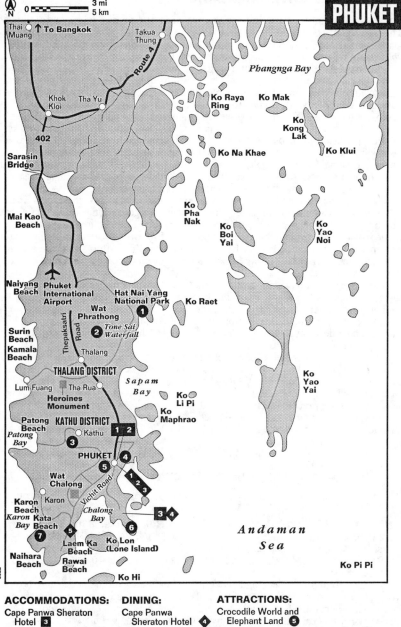

PHUKET

0 — 3 mi
0 — 5 km
N

To Bangkok

Thai Muang
Takua Thung
Route 4

Phangnga Bay

Khok Kloi
Tha Yu

402

Sarasin Bridge

Mai Kao Beach

Ko Raya Ring
Ko Mak

Ko Kong Lak

Ko Na Khae
Ko Klui

Ko Pha Nak

Ko Boi Yai
Ko Yao Noi

Naiyang Beach
Phuket International Airport
Hat Nai Yang National Park ❶
Ko Raet

Surin Beach
Kamala Beach

Wat Phrathong
Tone Sai Waterfall ❷

Thepaksatri Road

Thalang

Lum Fuang
Tha Rua

THALANG DISTRICT

Sapam Bay
Ko Li Pi
Ko Maphrao

Ko Yao Yai

Heroines Monument

Patong Beach
Patong Bay

KATHU DISTRICT
Kathu
❶ ❷

❸

PHUKET ❹
❺

❶ ❷ ❸

Wat Chalong

Vichit Road

Karon Beach
Karon Bay
Karon

Chalong Bay
❸ ❹

❻

Ko Lon (Lone Island)

Kata Beach
❺

❼

Andaman Sea

Laem Ka Beach
Naihara Beach
Rawai Beach
Ko Hi

Ko Pi Pi

6922

ACCOMMODATIONS:
Cape Panwa Sheraton Hotel ❸
Phuket Island Pavilion ❷
Phuket Merlin Hotel ❶

DINING:
Cape Panwa Sheraton Hotel ❹
Kan Eang II ❺
Khaw Yam ❶
Krua Thai ❷
Mee Sapam ❸

ATTRACTIONS:
Crocodile World and Elephant Land ❺
Marine Biological Research Center ❻
Nai Yang National Park ❶
Phuket Butterfly Garden and Aquarium ❹
Phuket Shooting Range & Riding Stable ❼
Tarzan's Bungee Jump ❸
Tone Sai Waterfall Forest Park ❷

below), hundreds of T-shirt and sunglass vendors and myriad tables and stalls of Thai souvenirs. you'll find yourself strolling down the road around parked mopeds just to avoid the pedestrian crush. Unlike the idle Greeks who enjoy an evening *volta* along the seaside, these people are here to shop!

The biggest concentration of nightclubs and bars is along Soi Bangla and continuing up Soi Sunset. You won't have any trouble finding them. Exstasy [sic] Ago-go [double sic] near the Expat Hotel, is one of the glitziest. Tin Mine '21 Discotheque in the new Royal Paradise Hotel is probably even a tad posher. We apologize to Rock Hard A-Go-Go, which commands the corner of Soi Bangla and Rat U-Thit Road, for confusing it with the smaller "Hard Rock Café," and pass on to you their claim to be one of the cleanest and most reputable clubs in the area. A beer will cost about 50B to 75B ($2 to $3) in most places. Drinks are often watered down and some are occasionally mickeyed. The "waitresses" earn part of their income on commission, so be warned. Need we remind you here of the importance of watching your wallet and the several benefits of the common condom?

Hard-drinking visitors from the Commonwealth countries favor the **Expat Rock 'n' Roll Bar,** a fun and loud place when it finally gets going. Others may notice the ubiquitous signs, on the model of Wall Drug, South Dakota, for such exotically named places as **Uncle Charlie's Boys for Men Bar,** located in a small gay bar enclave opposite the Patong Bayshore Hotel on Rat U-thit Road, the second road in from the beach. **Young Shark,** 3816 Si Nam Yen Rd., welcomes gays of any gender.

There are several bars with canned music and available girls which masquerade as discos. A cluster is located off Rat U-thit Road, near the Expat Rock 'n' Roll Hotel.

For action in the Kata/Karon area, the **Deep Sea Disco** in the posh Phuket Arcadia Hotel (tel. 381038) on Karon Beach is a cut above the rest; it's about a 15-minute taxi ride from Phuket. The cover charge is 300B ($12) which includes two drinks; open nightly 9pm to late.

Those willing to spend a lot for overnight escorts should check out the classy new branch of Bangkok's **Chamois Member Club,** in the slick new Metropole Hotel at 1 Soi Surin and Montri Road in Phuket town (tel. 214020). Temporary members can enjoy a drink and a feel nightly from 8pm to 1am. Not for those who need to ask the price; credit cards accepted.

If **movies** are your passion, the Alliance Française shows French films with English subtitles at the headquarters on 3 Pattana Rd., Soi 1 in Phuket; admission 25B ($1).

PHUKET TOWN

WHERE TO STAY

There are few who'll want to stay in town, but for those who do, we list a couple of the best.

PHUKET ISLAND PAVILION, 133 Satoon Rd., Phuket 83000. Tel. 076/ 215951. Fax 076/215951. 109 rms. A/C MINIBAR TV TEL **Directions:** 1km (about ⁶/₁₀ of a mile) north of downtown.

$ Rates: 1,200B ($48) single; 1,500B ($60) double; 5,000B–10,000B ($200–$400) suite. AE, MC, V.

If you like your hotels sleek and modern, this new curvilinear model may be for you. There's a neat spiral staircase, lots of pretty stone, and handsome chrome accents. The rooms are fashionably spare and quite comfortable. Some rooms have fine views; if you care, look before committing to a specific room.

PHUKET MERLIN HOTEL, 158/1 Jawaraj Rd., Phuket 83000. Tel. 076/ 212866. 180 rms. MINIBAR TV TEL **Directions:** North side of town, off Thungka Road.

$ Rates: 1,200B ($48) single; 1,440B ($57.60) double. AE, DC, MC, V.

This is the best of the in-town alternatives and, only a 10B (40¢) tuk-tuk ride from downtown. Compared to its rivals, the Merlin is serenity itself. The brick high-rise hotel sports clean, comfortable rooms, a pleasant coffee shop, and a snazzy wood and polished stone lobby. The hotel offers beachgoers a free shuttle bus four times daily to Patong Beach, where there is a companion hotel.

WHERE TO DINE

Phuket is known for its excellent and expensive seafood. The restaurants in town cater mostly to locals and serve inexpensive Thai and Chinese cuisine (as opposed to the mostly continental fare served in the resorts and associated towns).

KAW YAM, 5/72-73 Mae Luan Rd. Tel. 214201.
   Cuisine: CHINESE/THAI/SEAFOOD. **Directions:** Near the Phuket Merlin and Phuket Island Pavilion.
$ Prices: Appetizers 40B–60B ($1.60–$2.40); main courses 50B–130B ($2–$5.20). No credit cards.
   Open: Daily 7:30am–10pm.
Khun Nanta, Phuket Town's best cook for our money, has moved her restaurant a couple of blocks to larger quarters. You can savor culinary skill and nuance surrounded by Asian antiques and curios and shielded by a garden of potted plants from the busy street scene. Kaw Yam regulars recommend the ox tongue in tomato sauce. We liked the prawn with stir fried noodles so much we had it for lunch and dinner on the same day, just to make sure! The mixed vegetables are also special, and the fried rice is extraordinary (and they make it without MSG if asked).

KRUA THAI, 62/7 Rasada Center. Tel. 213479.
   Cuisine: THAI.
$ Prices: Appetizers 30B–60B ($1.20–$2.40); main courses 25B–85B ($1–$3.40). No credit cards.
   Open: Lunch and dinner daily 11am–10pm.
This casual, light, and airy restaurant, which opens onto the Phuket Shopping Center open-air market, serves some of the best Thai food in town. Among the better dishes we sampled were crispy smoked fish salad, fried crispy rice toast with pork and prawns topped with a coconut sauce, and the special lemon chicken.

MEE SAPAM, east side of highway, Ban Sapan. No phone.
   Cuisine: THAI. **Directions:** 8km (5 miles) north of Phuket town, on Route 402.
$ Prices: Appetizers 10B–20B (40¢–80¢); main courses 15B–25B (60¢–$1). No credit cards.
   Open: Daily 7am–10pm.
Perhaps the funkiest restaurant on the whole island, with birds flying in and the walls festooned with advertising posters, Mee Sapam serves a dish that is the most famous of all Phuket noodle specialties. The *mee* (noodles) are served with seafood, chicken, and gravy or, as *bak mee*, with squid, chicken, and vegetables. We also like their fried chicken, spring rolls with escargot, and curried chicken satay. The food is hot, hot, hot, so get psyched and drink plenty of cold beer. You can hire a tuk-tuk or taxi on the road for about 50B ($2) each way.

THE SOUTHERN COAST

Some of the island's earliest development began on its southern tip, from Cape Panwa, jutting out Phuket's southeast corner (and the jumping off point to Ko Pi Pi), traveling west along the southern coast to Chalong Bay, Rawai, and Nai Harn Beach. Chalong Bay is seven miles from Phuket and, like Rawai, has suffered from the past offshore tin mining. The beaches that once were wide and sandy now tend to be muddy and unattractive. Wat Chalang, on Chao Fa Road, is one of the island's most revered Buddhist sanctuaries; in 1876, its abbot defended the island against a miner's rebellion.

On the road to Rawai are a number of shops specializing in seashells and spirit houses. The beach at Rawai is not worth a visit, although many prefer to dine there (try the Me Klong Restaurant on Rawai, or for more upscale cuisine, Kan Eang II, see "Where to Stay & Dine," below).

There is frequent bus service (expect to pay about 20B [80¢] to all of the south coast destinations), and for those in a hurry, tuk-tuks will take you for about seven times the bus fare.

WHAT TO SEE & DO

PHUKET MARINE BIOLOGICAL CENTER, Sakdidej Rd., Cape Panwa. Tel. 391128.
The Phuket Marine Biological Center is on the very southeast tip of the island, about six miles south of Phuket town. It has a research facility, headed by Mr. Udom Bhatia, and the Phuket Aquarium, featuring indigenous sea life in glass tanks and exhibits about the cultivation and reintroduction of sea turtles into the Andaman Sea.
Admission: 25B ($1).
Open: Daily 8:30am–4pm.

WHERE TO STAY & DINE

Cape Panwa

CAPE PANWA HOTEL, 27 Moo 8, Sakdidej Rd., Phuket 83000. Tel. 076/ 391123 or toll free 800/325-3535 in the U.S. Fax 076/391177. Telex 69569 CAPANWA TH. 142 rms, 13 suites. A/C MINIBAR TV TEL
$ Rates: 3,840B ($154) single/double; suite from 8,760B ($350). Extra bed 400B ($16). AE, DC, MC, V.
This hotel is neither the fanciest or most up-to-date resort on Phuket, but we like the relatively small size and remote location. Most of the hotel's facilities (guest rooms, lobby, etc.) are perched up on the cape with a connection to the beach via lushly landscaped trails (steep) or an electric tram that shuttles guests up and down the hill. The private beach is small, but the setting is tranquil with a verdant lawn punctuated by lilting coconut palms and wooden chaise longues and hammocks (we wonder if the Sheraton carries coconut insurance!). Coconuts are for sale at 25B ($1). All guest rooms have a balcony, sea view, and modern amenities. A good value, especially for those who plan to move on to Ko Pi Pi (the hotel is five minutes from the pier).
   Dining/Entertainment: A faux-colonial-style building, Panwa House, is set among the palms and is a delightful venue for a nightly fixed-price Thai dinner (6:30 to 10pm). There is an English-style pub located in the Lighthouse (it really is one!); open 5pm to midnight. Top of the Reef is the continental dining room, while Café Andaman is the breakfast coffee shop.
   Services: In-house movies, 24-hour room service, concierge, complimentary welcome fruit basket, limousine service, babysitting, laundry service, shuttle bus to Phuket and Patong, boat to Ko Pi Pi.
   Facilities: Swimming pool, health club, nonsmoking floor, tennis courts, business center, beauty salon and barbershop, shopping arcade, game room, water sports.

Chalong Bay

KAN EANG II, 9/3 Chao Fa Rd., Chalong Bay. Tel. 216590.
   Cuisine: THAI/SEAFOOD. **Reservations:** Suggested for cabanas. **Directions:** 11km (7 miles) south of Phuket town.
$ Prices: Appetizers 40B–80B ($1.60–$3.20); main courses 50B–360B ($2–$14.40). AE, DC, MC, V.
   Open: Daily 10am–10pm.
Probably the best-known eatery on Phuket, Kan Eang II has a well-deserved reputation for its large selection of fresh fish and seafood, quality preparation, lovely setting, and friendly service (especially if you're there when the tour buses have departed). This outdoor, café-style restaurant with thatched cabanas and bayside tables is popular with locals and tourists alike; many come here for its picturesque view of Chalong Bay and the fishing-boat marina. We go for the food: grilled king prawns, deep-fried fish with chili sauce, fried Surat Thani oysters with garlic and pepper, and a wondrous soup

called Kan Eang Special Spicy Chicken Soup are among the many dishes that we've enjoyed. Fish is grilled over coconut husks, which imparts a delicate but noticeable flavor. We normally order by conducting a careful survey of the tanks to inspect what's still swimming; after that, choosing what to eat is a snap. It's rare to say a place is a "can't miss," but if Phuket has one, it has to be Kan Eang II.

Nai Harn Beach

PHUKET YACHT CLUB HOTEL & BEACH RESORT, 23/3 Vises Rd., Nai Harn Beach, Phuket 83130. Tel. 076/381156. Fax 076/381164. Telex 69532 YACHT TH. 100 rms, 8 suites, A/C MINIBAR TV TEL **Directions:** Above Nai Harn Beach, 18km (11 miles) south of Phuket.
$ Rates: 5,760B ($230.40) single; 6,480B ($259) double; suite from 8,640 ($345). Extra bed 600B ($24). Peak-season surcharge 600B ($24) per night per person. AE, DC, MC, V.

Prior to the opening of the Amanpuri, we considered the Phuket Yacht Club the best accommodations in Phuket, and we're happy to report that the quality is still there seven years after its opening (Executive Travel named it the third-best Overseas Hotel Resort in the world this year). Perched above the northern edge of Nai Harn and looking down at the public beach (now cleared of chockablock bungalows), the Phuket Yacht Club rivals nearly anything on the island. From its pagoda-style entryway to the terraced gardens overflowing with pink and white bougainvillea, it reeks of confident preeminence. All rooms view the beach, the Andaman Sea, and Promthep Cape from their landscaped, red tiled balconies. Newly redecorated guest rooms are spacious and decorated with cheerful fabrics and wicker furniture; most bathrooms have sunken tubs and are fully stocked with high-quality amenities. The Phuket Yacht Club has a pool, but be warned that it does not have its own, private beach. When we last visited, it was the weekend of the King's Regatta and the place was filled with the yachting set. Don't worry if you can't bring your luxury cruiser; just take along that blue blazer.

Dining/Entertainment: There are five dining venues at the Yacht Club. Among the most attractive are the Chart Room, a covered pavilion that overlooks the Andaman, serving Thai and continental cuisine; La Promenade, a beachside café for light snacks; and the Regatta Club, a cocktail-hour rendezvous with a delicious view of the cape.

Services: In-house movies, 24-hour room service, concierge, airport limousine service, babysitting, laundry service, shoe repair and cleaning.

Facilities: Swimming pool, fitness club, tennis courts, beauty salon and barbershop, shopping arcade.

JUNGLE BEACH RESORT, 11/3 Vises Rd., Ao Sane Beach, Phuket 83130. Tel. 076/214291. Fax 076/381108. 44 rms (3 without bath). A/C MINIBAR TV TEL **Directions:** Beyond the Phuket Yacht Club.
$ Rates: 500B–550B ($20–$22) single/double with fan; 1,450B ($58) single/double with A/C and hot water; suite from 1,800B ($72). Extra bed 250B ($10). AE, MC, V.

Half a mile beyond the Phuket Yacht Club along a dirt road is this bungalow compound, recently upgraded and now with a swimming pool. The bungalows are in a natural cove above Ao Sane Beach, but there is no access other than from Nai Harn. The setting is equatorial: Monkeys swoop down at night from the hills and climb the resort's trees; during the long rainy season, water cascades over the rocks. The bungalows are equipped in several configuratons, some with fans or air-conditioning, hot-and-cold water, and a large deck. It's pretty buggy at night, so bring repellent, but otherwise this is a comfortable, rustic alternative that's away from Phuket's hubbub. Phone ahead to arrange a transfer from the airport or town.

KATA & KARON BEACH

These are among the island's most attractive beaches, stretching from Kata to Karon, about 20km (12 miles) southwest of Phuket town and several miles north of Nai Harn. By day, the beaches resemble a kind of embryonic Saint-Tropez. Rows of rented beach chairs and umbrellas line the fine white sand—it's not completely packed, but the trend is unmistakable.

The two beaches are separated by a rocky promontory but are quite similar, in both ambience and development. A few primitive bungalows and an occasional behemoth (Club Med and the Arcadia Hotel, for instance) interrupt the long coastline. The most private of these beaches is Kata Noi, where the Kata Thani and a few lesser-priced guest houses are situated.

Despite their attractions, Kata and Karon highlight how the island is changing, most notably the local attitude. The people here are less friendly, more eager to cash in on tourism than in other less developed parts of Thailand. Most restaurants cater to the Western—particularly European, and especially Italian and German—palate. In the clubs, bars, and restaurants it's more likely that you'll hear Bon Jovi or Janet Jackson than Thai music (or eat fish-and-chips insted of *tod man pla*).

Both buses and tuk-tuks will take you to Kata and/or Karon; expect to pay about 20B (80¢) for the bus and 150B ($6) for a tuk-tuk.

WHERE TO STAY IN KATA BEACH

Expensive

THE BOATHOUSE INN, 114 Patak Rd., Kata Beach, Phuket 83000. Tel. 076/381557. Fax 076/381561. Telex 65 541 BOATINN TH. 36 rms. A/C MINIBAR TV TEL

$ Rates: 4,200B ($168) single; 4,320B ($173) double; suite from 8,400B ($336). Rollaway bed 500B ($20). Children under 12 free. High-season supplement 500B ($20). AE, DC, MC, V.

With its own beach at the south end of the quiet Kata Beach, this sister of the Phuket Yacht Club is a small but luxurious choice. All rooms face the sea, each with a terrace overlooking the huge Jacuzzi pool in the courtyard. Rooms are well appointed, the pool is small but beachside, and service attentive. The Boathouse boasts a high-style Thai and continental restaurant that guests have spoken of fondly. Although the room rates are about equal to those in the larger, megaresorts, we like the smaller, more intimate scale of the Boathouse. All in all, a good choice.

KATA BEACH CLUB MEDITERRANEE, 7/3 Patak Rd., Kata Beach, Phuket 83000. Tel. 076/330455-9 or 02/263-0108. Fax 076/330441-2. Telex 69526. 300 rms. A/C **Directions:** North end of Kata Beach.

$ Rates: 2,520B–4,800B ($100.80–$192) per adult, depending on season; children between 4 and 12 half price; children under 4, 300B–480B ($12–$19.20). AE, DC, MC, V.

Though there has been some recent renovation, the Club Med still suffers for lack of luxury. For example, all quarters contain two tiny bedrooms, divided by a rattan wall, with a shared bath and foyer; in other words, unless you pay a 20% premium, you'll share a room.

Set in its own sealed compound, Club Med commands an enormous and enviable piece of beachfront real estate. In typical Club Med fashion, the Kata Beach facility is so completely equipped that contact with the outside world is hardly required. A full range of water sports is available, and if you do feel compelled to wander off, various excursions around the island are offered. Special kudos for the food, including much locally caught Phuket seafood.

Among the many positive aspects of staying at this Club Med is its provision for children. There is the Mini-Club (open daily 9am to 9:30pm), which involves play groups, special classes for craftmaking, supervised activities, and babysitting (for kids under 4), all performed by people who are well versed in child care. Many vacationing parents leave their kids in the Mini-Club in the morning, eat lunch with them in the afternoon, and pick them up at the end of the day, leaving them to enjoy their holiday relatively unburdened by family demands. For teenagers there is an equivalent service called the Cadets Club. If you're looking for that type of facility, the Club Med might be just the place.

Services: Shuttle service, babysitting, laundry service, excursion boat.

Facilities: Swimming pool, health club, tennis courts, beauty salon and barber-shop, shopping arcade, game room, water sports, bowling, gymnasium, archery, vol-leyball court, soccer field.

KATA BEACH RESORT, 5/2 Patak Rd., Kata Beach, Phuket 83100. Tel. 076/381530. Fax 076/330128. Telex 69516 KATASEA TH. 200 rms. A/C MINIBAR TV TEL **Directions:** In the Kata Beach strip.

$ Rates: 3,000B–3,480B ($120–$139) single; 3,120B–3,720B ($125–$149) double; suite from 4,500B ($179). Extra bed 500B ($20). Peak-season supplement 600B ($24). AE, DC, MC, V.

As soon as you pull up to the soaring granite and marble lobby, you'll realize that you've arrived at the most formal facility in the Kata coast. The hotel is sparkingly clean, although we did detect a lingering odor of mildew in some of the guest rooms. Our inclination is to request the beach-view rooms in the central building; of course they're the higher-priced choice, but they really are lovely. All rooms are well and fully equipped and attractively decorated. This deluxe establishment is the glitziest accommodation in the area.

Dining/Entertainment: The Terrace has nightly seafood barbecues. Thai and continental food is served at the Orangerie Coffee Shop, while the Silk Road offers a range of Asian cuisine.

Serivces: In-house video, 24-hour room service, concierge, limousine service, laundry service, tailor and dressmaker.

Facilities: Swimming pools, health club and sauna, beauty salon and barber-shop, shopping arcade, water sports, business center, nursery and Children's Club.

KATA THANI AMARI HOTEL, Kata Noi Beach, Phuket 83100. Tel. 076/ 330417-24. Fax 076/330426. Telex 69516 KATHANI TH. 210 rms. A/C MINIBAR TV TEL **Directions:** North end of Kata Noi Beach.

$ Rates: 2,600B–5,000B ($104–$200) single; 3,100B–5,200B ($124–$208) double; 11,000B ($440) family suite. Extra bed 550B ($22). AE, DC, MC, V.

The Kata Thani is the dominant structure on lovely Kata Noi Beach and is a haven of quiet luxury. The top-end deluxe rooms are especially attractive, but even the standard ones are a good value, especially those with sea view. A wide, well-groomed lawn sur-rounds two sizable pools and leads to the graceful curve of the pristine cove.

Dining/Entertainment: There is a nightly poolside buffet. Breakfast and snacks are available at the coffee shop, while more elegant dining takes place in the Grill. The Rendezvous Cocktail Bar has music well into the night.

Services: 24-hour room service, concierge, limousine service, laundry serivce.

Facilities: Swimming pools, health club and sauna, tennis courts, beauty salon and barbershop, shopping arcade, water sports.

Moderate/Budget

KATANOI CLUB BUNGALOW, 3/25 Patak Rd., Kata Noi, Phuket 83100. Tel. 076/215832. 16 rms. **Directions:** South end of Kata Noi Beach.

$ Rates (including tax and service): 800B ($32) single/double. No credit cards.

These bungalows are more substantial than the old thatch ones that once lined Phuket's beach coves, and the price and location are right. Young owner Radhas Boreboon has constructed Thai-style bungalows around a large lawn, just 50 feet from the quiet south tip of this sandy beach cove. The guest quarters are very roomy, with ceiling fans and screened, shuttered windows. Each contains a small writing desk, armoire, and a tiled bathroom with cold-water shower. In front of the small snack bar and reception area is a windsurfing rental shop. This family offers several concrete bunkers with shared Asian toilet facilities for only 250B ($10) for two, but they're very grim. Instead, call Mr. Radhas early before he leaves his home to reserve one of these good-value lodgings.

MOUNTAIN BEACH RESORT, 4/7 Kata Noi Beach, Phuket 83100. Tel. 076/330565-6. Fax 076/330567. 33 rms. A/C TEL **Directions:** South end of Kata Noi Beach.

$ Rates (including tax and service): 1,250B–1,800B ($50–$72) single/double. Extra bed 250B ($10). High-season supplement 300B ($12). MC, V.

This is a very simple, three-story white stucco inn. Its major advantage is the location, directly across the street from what is arguably the quietest stretch of beach in the area. The facilities and services are modest, the price is moderate, but you'll be relatively isolated from the tourist throng. The Mountain Beach reminds us of our visits to Thailand years ago, before everything was so glitzy. Also, its recent complete renovation makes it especially enticing.

MARINA COTTAGE, 120 Patak Rd., Kata Karon Beach, Phuket 83000. Tel. 076/330625. Fax 076/330516. Telex 213604. 104 rms. A/C MINIBAR TV TEL **Directions:** On bluff at south end of Karon Beach road.

$ Rates: 2,040B–4,200B ($81.60–$$96) single or double bungalow; 1,440B ($57.60) single/double fan-cooled bungalow. Extra bed 200B ($8). Peak-season surcharge 300B ($12) per room per day. MC, V.

Simple cottages tucked in the woods above the cusp of Kata and Karon beaches are slightly more comfortable than older thatch bungalows nearby. Rates vary according to the view; all are a hike down to the rocky shore. Some rooms have air-conditioning. Our only gripe: The staff is less amiable than you should expect. The Marina Cottage is home to Marina Divers (tel. 381625), a PADI International Diving School, which conducts classes, rents equipment, and leads expeditions around the island reefs. The pleasant restaurant cottage serves good, inexpensive Thai food.

WHERE TO STAY IN KARON BEACH

Expensive

PHUKET ARCADIA HOTEL, 78/2 Patak Rd., Karon Beach, Phuket 83100. Tel. 076/396038. Fax 076/396136. Telex 69503 ARCADIA TH. 247 rms, 8 suites. A/C MINIBAR TV TEL **Directions:** Middle of Karon Beach road.

$ Rates: 3,720B–4,320B ($149–$173) single; 2,080B–4,500B ($163–$180) double; suite from 6,000B ($240). Extra bed 500B ($20). Peak-season supplement 800B ($32) per room per night. AE, DC, MC, V.

This modern, full-facility resort presents a massive presence on Karon Beach, and though we think it a pleasant place to stay, the Phuket Arcadia is expensive for a not-so-great beach area. Each room overlooks the beach and ocean; each is attractive but somewhat bland with standard bathroom amenities. The landscaping is a little stark, but the elevated pool and sun deck offer wonderful views of the bay. Kids (and travel writers) will like the courtesy tray of bananas to feed the hotel's pet elephant.

Dining/Entertainment: The hotel houses the Sand Dune café, with Thai, Chinese, and Western cuisine and a poolside snack bar. The Tai Kong restaurant, elevated above the road to amplify sea views, specializes in locally caught seafood and grilled meats; if it's too warm they have an indoor air-conditioned dining room. There's a lounge and disco.

Services: 24-hour room service, concierge, taxi service, babysitting, house doctor, bathrobes, hairdryers in room.

Facilities: Health club with sauna, large outdoor pool, tennis courts, putting greens, windsurfing, game room.

THAVORN PALM BEACH HOTEL, 128/10 Moo 3, Karon Beach, Phuket 83110. Tel. 076/381034. Fax 076/381037. 192 rms, 18 suites. A/C MINIBAR TV TEL **Directions:** In mid–Karon Beach area.

$ Rates: 4,300B ($172) single; 4,500B ($180) double; suite from 9,000B ($360). Extra bed 600B ($24). Peak-season supplement 500B ($20) per room per night. AE, DC, MC, V.

Most rooms have fine views and look over the Karon dunes. The decor is minimal, but pleasant, and there are four good pools and a kiddie pool (which for this money, there should be), along with a fitness center, tennis courts, and four restaurants. The beach is lovely, but it's across the busy beach road and the roar of the surf and the roar of the road are of equal volume.

Dining/Entertainment: The Thavorn has nine dining possibilities. Our favorite is the outdoor terrace venue called Sansai, which specializes in seafood; but there is certain to be a dining facility to your liking.

Services: 24-hour room service, concierge, taxi service, babysitting, house doctor, bathrobes, hairdryers in room.

Facilities: Health club, four outdoor pools, tennis courts, windsurfing, snooker room.

Moderate

SANDY INN, 102/12 Patak Rd., Karon Beach, Phuket 83100. Tel. 076/ 381935. Fax 076/381546. 12 rms (no hot water). A/C MINIBAR **Directions:** Down the road from the Karon Inn, south of Thavorn Hotel.

$ Rates: 800B ($32) single/double. No credit cards.

If you want a moderately priced room, don't care about a view, and don't mind a 5-minute walk to the beach, this is a good-value choice. Simple, clean, and cool, you'll share the same beach as those paying five times the price (admittedly, they do get hot water). There are cheap restaurants and laundry service nearby.

SAND RESORT, 53/7 Karon Beach, Phuket. Tel. 076/212901. Fax 076/ 216961. 32 rms. A/C MINIBAR **Directions:** Midbeach, next to the Karon Village Royal Wing.

$ Rates: 1,450B ($58) single; 1,600B ($64) double. Extra person 120B ($4.80). Peak-season supplement 250B ($10). MC, V (add 3% surcharge).

These very simple peaked-roof bungalows look out toward fields where water buffalo haven't yet been displaced by high-rise condos. Small clean rooms have attached showers, brightly striped bedspreads, and little verandas. There's not much else but an outdoor Thai, Chinese, and continental snack bar and a great, clean stretch of beach directly across the road. Overall, a good value.

Budget

JOR GUESTHOUSE, 102/11 Patak Rd., Karon Beach, Phuket 83100. Tel. 076/381546. 12 rms. **Directions:** Down the road from the Karon Inn and the Sunset Restaurant.

$ Rates: 300B ($12) single/double. No credit cards.

This is a simple guest house, with a cold-water shower in the room. Walls are thatch, fans are in the room, and it's near a busy road. Even though accommodations here are primitive, for Phuket this is reasonably well priced, but if you really want to save money, we suggest moving on south to Krabi.

WHERE TO DINE

Most people dine in their hotels, but if you want to go out for a bite head out to the unmarked street (Patak Road) leading away from the beach just south of the Thavorn, near the Karon Inn. Here you'll find a concentration of home-style restaurants that cater to a largely European crowd. The most venerable is **Sunset Soi Bangla** (tel. 396465) which feels like a summer camp. But the Thai chef has cooked in Europe and understands the taste buds of his clientele. A delicious mixed-seafood platter, with a beer and banana split is 300B ($12) per person.

Two other notables on Karon are **Sawadee,** on the beach strip, where barbecued seafood is the house specialty (don't miss the tiger prawns), and the restaurant at the **Marina Cottage,** up the hill at the south end of town.

RELAX BAY

This area is really a small cove on the far northern end of the vast Kata-Karon coastline.

Where to Stay

MERIDIEN PHUKET, 8/5 Tambol, Karon Noi, P.O. Box 277, Relax Bay, Phuket 83000. Tel. 076/340480-5 or toll free 800/543-4300 in the U.S. Fax

076/340479. Telex MERIHKT 69542 TH. 470 rms, 22 suites. A/C MINBAR TV TEL
Transportation: Relax Bay airport shuttle bus.
$ Rates: 4,080B–5,400B ($163–$216) single/double; suite from 10,800B ($432). Extra person 700B ($28). Peak-season surcharge, mid-Dec to mid-Jan, 400B ($16). AE, DC, EU, MC, V.

The Meridien Phuket is tucked away alone on secluded Relax Bay, with a lovely 600-yard beach and 40 acres of tropical greenery. This is one of the largest (if not verging on institutionally huge) resorts on the island, and during the high season it is almost always packed with European group vacationers. Although it sensitively combines Western and traditional Thai architecture, we think it's too massive in scale for its smallish, private location, and the beach is too hemmed in for extended seaside walks. One of the advantages to its U-shape layout is that it ensures that 80% of the rooms face the ocean. The modern furnishings in each room are of rattan and teak. Amenities include radio, personal safe, balcony with wooden sun-deck chairs, and a bathroom with hair dryer and clothesline.

Dining/Entertainment: The hotel houses the formal Le Phuket's, featuring gourmet French-inspired Thai cusine; Pakarang, overlooking the seawater lagoon, specializing in charcoal-grilled seafood; a French-style café serving Thai specialties; a poolside snack bar; a twice-daily barbecue; Portofino, an Italian venue with fresh pasta and pizza; and Ariake, a Japanese restaurant with sushi and other delicious dishes. Similan Lounge serves afternoon tea; Tonson Bar overlooks the sea. There is also a discotheque, and traditional Thai arts are performed in the open lobby. *Note:* when it's full, we've found the service at the food outlets both inefficient and slow.

Services: 24-hour room service, shuttle service (to Patong Beach, Phuket town, and the airport), concierge, house doctor, laundry service.

Facilities: Two swimming pools, 12,000-square-foot saltwater lagoon; seven-hole mini–golf course, putting green course, and driving range; two squash courts; four tennis courts; a fitness center; a variety of indoor games; yoga, aerobics, and jogging; plus scuba diving, snorkeling, windsurfing, canoeing, and fishing; a children's activity center.

PATONG BEACH

Patong has a proliferation of hotels and guest houses, and yes, the nightlife scene includes go-go girls and massage parlors. Unfortunately Patong has now strayed far into the realm of the tacky, and become a kind of soul brother to Pattaya or Tijuana. Despite pollution controls and water treatment, the beach is not terribly clean and there is often a funky smell. Even with this warning, many people love it and flock to the place for its action. Patong is hardly a virgin island paradise (as many people probably think based on glitzy hotel brochures), but it can be fun for those seeking a heady dose of action.

Public buses and tuk-tuks frequently shuttle passengers from Phuket to Patong for 20B (80¢) and 150B ($6), respectively; the distance is 20km (13 miles).

WHAT TO SEE & DO

You really don't want to do this in Patong Beach itself (for pretty obvious reasons), but a growing number of people come to Phuket for the fantastic diving off its coral reefs, and the majority of diving shops are located in Patong. These establishments offer everything from instruction and equipment rentals to individual chartering. Fantasea, Santana, and Ocean Diver are all on the beachfront strip and can arrange a full range of undersea adventures. The Phuket International Diving Center, based in the Coral Beach Hotel (tel. 321106), offers the same services. Of these, we've heard the best word about Fantasea Divers (tel. 076/321309; fax 076/321309), which offers trips to the Similan Islands (see "Easy Excursions from Phuket," below), Shark Point, Surin Islands (see "Ranong" above), Rajah Island, and Ko Pi Pi. They are an official PADI dive center that sponsors certification courses. Their 1-day tours, including two dives, cost 1,100B ($44); a 5-day Similan Island diving cruise runs 18,000 ($720) including food and most gear. They publish a listing of upcoming trips, so it would be wise to make a reservation as early as possible. Highly recommended.

WHERE TO STAY

Expensive

AMARI CORAL BEACH RESORT, 104 Moo 4, Patong Beach, Phuket 83150. Tel. 076/340106 or toll free 800/448-8355 in the U.S. Fax 076/340114. Telex TH 69527 CORALSL. 200 rms, 6 suites. A/C MINIBAR TV TEL **Directions:** Far south end of Patong Beach.

$ Rates: 3,100B–3,700B ($124–$148) single; 3,200B–4,000B ($128–$160) double; suite from 7,000B ($280). AE, DC, MC, V.

The tastefully renovated Coral Beach stands on the rocks high above Patong, its soaring lobby standing high above the din of Patong's congested strip. It's the only truly deluxe lodging in the area, with swimming pool, squash, badminton, and tennis courts. Rooms ae well furnished. Our main criticism: The swimming area immediately adjacent to the hotel is a small, rocky reef—fine for snorkeling—but for a sandy beach, you must walk down the hill to Patong or farther south to Relax Bay.

Dining/Entertainment: Although there are several dining alternatives, our favorite is La Gritta, an Italian seafood terrace restaurant that overlooks the broad bay. Great for a sunset drink; open 6 to 11pm.

Services: 24-hour room service, concierge, taxi service, babysitting.

Facilities: Jogging track, two swimming pools, tennis courts, badminton courts, squash, windsurfing, private beach with jetty. Also, South East Asia Divers offers dive services including a school.

DIAMOND CLIFF RESORT, 61/9 Kalim Beach, Patong, Phuket 83150. Tel. 076/340501. Fax 076/340507. Telex 69561 DICLIFF TH. 216 rms, 6 suites. A/C MINIBAR TV TEL **Directions:** Far south end, on the road to Kamala Beach.

$ Rates: 3,800B ($152) single; 4,400B–6,600B ($176–$264) double; suite from 9,000B ($360). Peak-season supplement 600B ($24). AE, DC, MC, V.

Located a 10-minute walk from the center of Patong Beach, the Diamond Cliff offers a level of luxury unrivaled in the area. The place is a gleaming, well-maintained, full-facility resort with rooms done in soothing sea greens and blues and light wood trim. All guest quarters command an ocean view and the grounds are attractively landscaped (they even have a boardwalk to Patong that winds through the rocky coastline). Our one caveat (other than the high price) is that the Diamond Cliff is for those who enjoy a view but don't require a beach on premises; they do operate a shuttle to a small private bit of sand across the bay, but for the money, we think you might want your own bit of sand.

Dining/Entertainment: A coffee shop, seafood café, a couple of bars, and a grill are pretty nice, but we loved the Kiko Japanese Restaurant, and in particular, their sushi bar; open daily 11am to 2pm and 7 to 11pm.

Services: 24-hour room service, concierge, taxi service, babysitting, car rental, house doctor.

Facilities: Health club, minigolf, swimming pool, scuba diving lessons, tennis courts, private beach, barber and beauty shop, shopping arcade, children's game room, sauna.

HOLIDAY INN, 86/11 Thaweewong Rd., Patong Beach, Phuket 83150. Tel. 076/340608 or toll free 800/HOLIDAY in U.S. and Canada. Fax 076/340435. Telex 695545 HIPHUKT TH. 280 rms, 17 suites. A/C MINIBAR TV TEL **Directions:** Patong Beach strip.

$ Rates: 3,240B ($129.60) single; 3,600B ($144) double; suite from 4,800B ($192). Extra person 600B ($24). Peak-season supplement 800B ($32). AE, DC, EU, MC, V.

The buildings at this Holiday Inn are modern, concrete blocks; guest rooms are furnished with rattan furniture and have balconies. The resort fronts the beach and offers water sports, including diving (they offer a special dive package with Fantasea Divers). This property has become especially popular with European groups, as is reflected in its restaurant offerings. Although there is little to distinguish it, the Holiday Inn is one of Patong's better accommodations.

Dining/Entertainment: The names give it away: The Riviera, the Pizzeria Restaurant, the Palm Court, the Sea Breeze, and Suan Nok (Thai restaurant).

Services: 24-hour room service, concierge, shuttle service, babysitting, house doctor, laundry service.

Facilities: Nonsmoking floors, AT&T Telephone Plus, swimming pool, tennis fitness club, water sports, laundry, game room, gym, sauna, golf driving range, barber and beauty shop, minizoo, diving center.

PHUKET CABANA HOTEL, 94 Thaweewong Rd., Patong Beach, Phuket 83150. Tel. 076/340138. Fax 076/340178. Telex 69544 CABANA TH. 80 rms. A/C MINIBAR TV TEL **Directions:** Middle of beach road.
$ Rates: 3,000B–5,000B ($120–$200) single/double; suite from 6,000B ($240). Extra bed 500B ($20). AE, DC, MC, V.

These Thai island cabins are closely packed but are quiet and have some character: exposed wood beams, dark lacquered bamboo, rattan wall coverings, and stone floors. Though crowded, the closeness of the beach, the seaside Aquatique Restaurant, the resident PADI-dive instructor, and the hotel's enticing pool make this one of Patong's better-value lodgings. Ask about their May to October discounts!

PATONG MERIN, 99/2 Moo 4, Patong Beach, Phuket 83150. Tel. 076/ 340037. Fax 076/340394. Telex TH 65522 MERLIN. 297 rms. A/C MINIBAR TV TEL **Directions:** On Patong strip at south end of town.
$ Rates: 2,640B ($129.60) single; 3,120B ($124.80) double. AE, DC, MC, V.

We've always been partial to this place (if we can say that about anyplace in Patong), maybe because of the hotel's Thai fishing motif. Who knows, but this venerable establishment is well maintained and has a particularly attractive center courtyard. All rooms have balconies, some of which overlook the three swimming pools (each with a pool bar) and a nicely manicured garden. The lobby is spacious and airy with comfortable, clubby rattan furniture.

Service: 24-hour room service, concierge, shuttle service, babysitting, house doctor, laundry service.

Facilities: Three swimming pools, fitness club, water sports, laundry, game room, gym, sauna, snooker, barber and beauty shop.

Moderate/Budget

During our most recent visit, we found the lower price accommodations near the beach noisy and tawdry. If you're looking for bargains, go up Soi Bangla away from the water to Soi Saen Sabai, where you'll find several small, new hotels.

ANDAMAN RESORTEL, 65/21-25 Soi Saen Sabai, Patong Beach, Phuket 83150. Tel. 076/340438. Fax 076/340847. 40 rms. A/C TV TEL **Directions:** Off Soi Bangla.
$ Rates: 1,200B ($48) single; 1,600B ($64) double. MC, V.

The most attractive of recent alternatives, the Andaman reflects warmth in a modern Thai style. The rooms are quite light with simple and comfortable furnishings.

SUMMER BREEZE PENSION, 96/1 Moo 4, Soi Saen Sabai, Patong Beach, Phuket 83150. Tel. 076/340464. Fax 076/340493. 32 rms. A/C TV TEL **Directions:** Off Soi Bangla.
$ Rates: 680B ($27) single; 780B ($31.20) double. MC, V.

Though it doesn't live up to its name, being rather stuffy, the Summer Breeze is still quite clean with plain and basic rooms. Continental breakfast is included.

WHERE TO DINE

Most restaurants line the seaside road (or run a block or two perpendicular to it), and though they have amazingly similar menus, there is some difference in price and quality. Although we suggest paying close attention to freshness and price, our strong nod goes toward ordering the island's incomparable seafood, especially our favorite, tiger prawns.

BAAN RIM PA, 100/7 Kalim Beach Rd. Tel. 340789.

> **Cuisine:** THAI. **Reservations:** Suggested. **Directions:** Across from the Diamond Cliff Hotel, on road to Kamala Beach.

$ **Prices:** Appetizers 85B–150B ($3.40–$6); main courses 95B–600B ($4–$24). AE, DC, MC, V.

> **Open:** Daily noon–midnight.

Are you interested in a sophisticated piano bar/restaurant that has served the likes of America's Cup skipper Dennis Connor, has a pianist, Tom Doyle, who entertained presidents in the U.S. Navy Band, and a chef, Chalee Amatyakul, who ran the Hotel Oriental's cooking school? If you can afford the tariff, you should be. You won't find many Thai restaurants with a more magnificent view, but then again you'll probably have a time unearthing one that charges so much for the pleasure. Baan Rim Pa is a lovely place, comfortably elegant with its deliciously simple wood interior, that serves a wide variety of well prepared and presented Thai specialities. We had a fine meal starting with *po pia thod* (a kind of fancy spring roll), followed by *tom ka gai paak tai* (chicken and coconut-milk soup), and finished with a spicy Panaeng ped. Dress is informal.

LAI MAI RESTAURANT, 86/15 Thaweewong Rd. Tel. 340460.

> **Cuisine:** THAI/WESTERN. **Directions:** On beach strip near the Holiday Inn.

$ **Prices:** Appetizers 60B–100B ($2.40–$4); main courses 75B–350B ($3–$14). MC, V.

> **Open:** Daily 7:30am–midnight.

Kyle was craving an American-style breakfast and that's when we discovered the Lai Mai, a sparkingly bright white sidewalk café with the friendliest staff in town. This ultracasual eatery serves several tasty Thai specialties, such as *pla sam rod* (deep fried fish with chili) and *yam nuea* (a salad of thinly sliced grilled beef), but it's the Western dishes—tenderloin with cognac or lobster in white sauce—that attract the crowds.

PATONG SEAFOOD, 98/2 Thaweewong Rd. Tel. 321247.

> **Cuisine:** SEAFOOD. **Directions:** Near the Safari Beach Hotel.

$ **Prices:** Appetizers 45B–145B ($1.80–$5.80); main courses 70B–250B ($2.80–$10). AE, MC, V.

> **Open:** Daily 9am–11pm.

Not to be confused with Baitong Seafood, Patong Seafood is typical of many open-air seaside eateries, with a casual ambience and a complete offering of undersea treasures on display for discerning diners to peruse. This basic restaurant serves a full range of locally caught Andaman specialties; among them are the much-heralded Phuket lobster, the scarcer tiger prawn, and a range of fish.

THE NORTHWEST COAST

PANSEA BEACH

Also known as Surin Beach, this area has coconut plantations, steep slopes leading down to the beach, and small, private coves dominated by two of the best hotels on the island.

Where to Stay & Dine

AMANPURI, Pansea Beach, Phuket 83110. Tel. 076/324333, or toll free 800/223-1588 in the U.S. Fax 076/324100. Telex 69529 AMANPURI TH. 40 rms, 3 suites. A/C MINIBAR TEL **Directions:** Next door to the Pansea.

$ **Rates:** 8,600B–11,800B ($344–$472) single/double; suite from 18,000B ($720). *Note:* 20%–40% discounts from May–Oct. AE, DC, MC, V.

This may be the most elegant hotel we have ever visited; so much so, that even now, months after visiting, we still think of the Amanpuri in reverential terms. Although the structures, all on a human scale, incorporate Thai decorative motifs, it is the overall design of the resort that reminds us most of a classical Greek temple complex. Picture an open-air pavilion fronted by a religious sculpture that opens to a pergola and beyond, a perfectly still reflecting pool. This in turns leads to a 40-foot-wide concrete stairway that plunges down a steep embankment to the sea. Why not the Aegean? Perhaps a temple to Poseidon. No, the open-air pavilion is the lobby, the sculpture is a standing Buddha, the reflecting pool is for swimming, the stairs lead to the beach, and the many lesser structures (guest rooms) are hidden in the dense coconut palm grounds.

As for the accommodations, we suggest foregoing the lesser priced—across the road—rooms and taking the so-called Superior Pavillion Suites (the higher priced of the normal rooms), which are integrated into the main part of the Amanpuri. All rooms, suites really, are designed in a traditional Thai-sala style, with teak and tile floors, sliding teak doors, and exquisite built-ins. We could wax enthusiastic for a while, but suffice to say, this is far and away the most sublime resort on Phuket.

Dining/Entertainment: Two restaurants (see below) and a bar make up the dining alternatives. In the evening there is a cultural performance including dance, live music, and sword fighting; we loved it.

Services: Room service (6am to midnight), concierge, complimentary airport taxi service, house doctor.

Facilities: Yacht, library (books and video), water-sports equipment and instruction, swimming pool, tennis-and-squash courts, gym, sauna, private beach, barber and beauty shop, and Lotus shop (see "Savvy Shopping," in Chapter 5).

PANSEA PHUKET BAY HOTEL, 118 Moo 3, Choeng Talay, Pansea Beach, Phuket 83110. Tel. 076/324017. Fax 076/324252. Telex 69522 PANSEA TH. 110 rms. A/C MINIBAR TV TEL **Directions:** Next door to the Amanpuri.
$ Rates: 4,000B–5,040B ($160–$202) single/double; suite from 7,200B ($288). AE, DC, MC, V.

The Pansea bungalows have been constructed in a manner that, if not a direct duplicate of the Amanpuri, certainly owes an architectural debt to that august neighbor. It, too, is located well above the beach, and its commands an excellent view as well as having its own private stretch of sand. We've probably had more enthusiastic mail about the Pansea than most any hotel in all of Thailand. On our last inspection we found it the most enticing accommodation on the island; it may not be as outwardly impressive as its extraordinary neighbor, but we have found a stay at the Pansea quiet, comfortably informal, and very relaxing.

THE RESTAURANT AMANPURI, Amanpuri Pansea Beach. Tel. 324333.
Cuisine: ITALIAN. **Reservations:** Required.
$ Prices: Appetizers 175B–426B ($7–$16); main courses 300B–1,325B ($12–$53). AE, MC, V.
Open: Dinner daily 7–10:30pm.
A stone-paved terrace facing west to the sea, flickering candlelight, whispering palms, fire liners, and a gamelan quartet create the ideal, if formal, ambience. And the food? Start with the full-flavored baked eggplant, then try the freshest of the locally caught seafood. The roast rack of lamb with spinach and goat cheese is presented with equal grace on exquisite china. The tiramisu is rich and fabulous, but the selection of sherbets homemade from local fruits is divine.

During the season, the Amanpuri also features a nightly (except Thursday) seafood barbecue. Candlelit talbes with linen and crystal are set right out on the private sand beach. Chefs grill the fruits of Phuket's waters under overhanging palms. It's all yours for 1,200B ($48) per person. An equally romantic choice.

THE TERRACE, Amanpuri Pansea Beach. Tel. 324333.
Cuisine: THAI. **Reservations:** Required.
$ Prices: Appetizers 175B–300B ($7–$12). AE, DC, MC, V.
Open: Lunch daily 11am–5pm; dinner 7–10:30pm.
Connoisseurs of fine design shouldn't miss the Amanpuri, Phuket's finest resort. From their terrace restaurant you can sample a variety of subtly spiced seafood, beef, and chicken, and noodle or rice dishes, all presented with artistically cut and shaped fruit or vegetable garnishes. Typical Thai ceramics and decor, and a view from wooded cliffs over the bay, create an aura of tropical splendor. Each day, six

dishes and a Thai dessert are packaged as a set menu; good value here at 525B ($21). Don't forget to visit their gallery of shops after you've eaten.

BANG THAO BAY

This area, set 22km (14 miles) west of Phuket town, is springing up resorts faster than anyone can imagine, with a major Sheraton slated to open later this year and, at about the same time, Pacific Islands Club resort. Our local intelligence tells us that there may be problems with the cleanliness of the water and the shoreline, as a number of tin dredges offshore have damaged the ecology during the past 20 years.

Where to Stay

DUSIT LAGUNA, 390 Srisoontorn Rd., Cherngtalay District, Phuket 83110. Tel. 076/324320. Fax 076/324174. Telex 69554 DLAGUNA TH. 226 rms, 7 suites. A/C MINIBAR TV TEL **Directions:** North of Surin Beach.

$ Rates: 5,000B ($200) single; 5,750B ($230) double; suite from 11,000B ($440). Extra bed 650B ($26). Peak-season supplement per night 1,000B ($40). AE, DC, MC, V.

The Dusit Laguna is a stylish, deluxe resort that faces a long, wide, white sand beach and is flanked by two lagoons. The well-landscaped gardens have a waterfall and a terrific pool. Rooms are tastefully decorated (they have mosquito nets as part of the decoration!) and have private balconies, tea and coffee makers, and large bathrooms. We suggest requesting the sea-view rooms. The facilities for kids are pretty good: a Kids Corner, open daily 10am to 8pm, for children 2 years old and up; babysitting; a playground; and computer games. The only complaint about the Laguna that we've heard relates to indifferent service.

Dining/Entertainment: The JunkCeylon fine dining room specializes in fresh seafood and meats; La Trattoria is a lunch-and-dinner venue for pizza, pasta, and other Italian dishes; the Ruenthai Restaurant, overlooking the South Lagoon, offers regional dishes from all over the country; Laguna Café has a view of the pool, waterfall, and gardens; there's also an al fresco barbecue terrace lounge that overlooks the water.

Services: 24-hour room service, concierge, shuttle service, babysitting, house doctor, laundry service.

Facilities: Windsurfing, waterskiing, sailing, diving; two pools, one designed for kids; golf course and putting greens; tennis court; and outdoor games, including giant chess; traditional Thai handicrafts classes.

NAI YANG BEACH

Nai Yang National Park is an expanse of haphazardly (and illegally) developed shoreline, framed by a dense forest of palms, casuarina, and other indigenous flora. It's good for those who want to leave the largest crowds behind, but be warned that it has become exceedingly popular with Thai campers. There are a few bungalows, but many people bring a tent.

Nai Yang was known in the past for its part in National Fish Species Multiplication Day, when the Phuket's Marine Biological Center released its crop of sea turtles back into the Andaman Sea. However in the past few years most turtles have been released in safer waters. The turtles weigh from 100 to 1,500 pounds and swim the waters around Phuket, but without protection from fishers. If not for the efforts of the Marine Biological Center, these creatures would probably be locally extinct. April 13, during the Songkran holiday, is the day when all animals are to be released, and activities are organized on this day.

Where to Stay

PEARL VILLAGE, Nai Yang Beach and National Park, P.O. Box 93, Phuket 83000. Tel. 076/327006. Fax 076/327338. Telex 65539 VILLAGE TH. 216 rms, 10 suites. A/C MINIBAR TV TEL **Directions:** 5 minutes south of the airport.

$ Rates: 3,250B–3,350B ($130–$134) single; 3,475B–3,850B ($139–$154) double; suite from 4,200B ($168). Extra bed 700B ($28). AE, DC, V.

Not as glitzy as some of Phuket's newest resorts, the Pearl Village nevertheless holds its own due to its location, facilities, and friendly feeling. Located on the periphery of the national park, the Pearl Village is relatively isolated from the ravages of over-development and, in comparison to other shorelines, it has a cleaner stretch of beach. The facilities are excellent, particularly for families (who can resist their elephant?); we really love their swimming pool with its powerful waterfall. As for friendliness, we appreciated the lack of an institutional sensibility and didn't feel overwhelmed by the size or scale of the place; it's a comfortable place to vacation. Special kudos go to the landscape architect and the gardening staff who maintain one of Phuket's lovliest grounds.

Our one caveat: The hotel is on the far north of the island (about 45 minutes from Phuket), so for those who need to be in the center of action, consider staying closer to Phuket town or Patong. But for those who care about their privacy, keep in mind that Michael Jackson, Prince Phillip, Michael J. Fox and King Gustav of Sweden are but a few of the luminaries who've stayed at the Pearl Village.

Dining/Entertainment: Among the several dining outlets are the Village Café, the Palm Court, and the lakefront Pae Thip. There are evening shows for kids, including magic, movies, and Thai dancing. There is a special tie-in with the Pearl in Phuket for a meal and evening shopping.

Services: 24-hour room service, concierge, shuttle service, babysitting, house doctor, laundry service.

Facilities: Windsurfing, fishing, two pools, one designed for kids, game room, barber and beauty shop, golf green, tennis courts, weight room, jogging track, horse-and-elephant riding, snooker, table tennis.

MAI KHAO BEACH

Like Nai Yang, Mai Khao is a marvelous beach on the northeastern shore that is even closer to the airport. It's Phuket's longest beach and is the site where a few sea turtles try to lay their eggs during December and January. Unfortunately their eggs are coveted by Thai and Chinese people, who eat them for the supposed life-sustaining power.

EASY EXCURSIONS FROM PHUKET

A few intrepid travelers make their way to Ko Surin from Phuket, via the port town of Ban Hin Lad in Krura Buri district (north of the island, on the mainland). For more information about this, see "Easy Excursions from Ranong," above.

PHANGNGA

The landscape of Phangnga presents a quintessentially Asian image, similar to Chinese scroll paintings of the Li River Valley (near Guilin), with flora-covered stone outcroppings rising majestically from tranquil water. On each formation there are craggy pinnacles with an occasional pine. Navigating around these huge rocks and through mangove swamps are solitary fishermen rowing out to the bay, presenting a visual cliché that if seen on a postcard would seem almost unbelievable.

These unique geologic forms are thought to have been created between 2 and 10 million years ago when tectonic plates pushed up layers of limestone and gave birth to the dramatic looking outcroppings with their caves and stalactites. Many people have seen this area on film, in particular the 1973 Bond classic, *The Man with the Golden Gun,* which gave rise to the name James Bond Island (Ko Tapu and Ko Pingan). Less well-known are the rock paintings on Ko Kian, dating from over 3,000 years ago.

There seem to be an endless stream of excursion boats, stinky and noisy, filled with day-trippers from Phuket slashing their way across this very much discovered waterway (it felt like taking the Jungle Cruise at Disneyland), so if you want to enjoy a visit here, we'd suggest you get up early and arrange your own tour at the pier, bypassing the quick and easy tour. Private boats for hire will take you to the usual spots, or as we'd suggest, to the less explored canals and backwaters of this exquisite bay. Fellow travelers Andrew and Trevor Davis from Sydney, Australia, had excellent luck with Mr. Kean, who operates a 6-hour boat trip for 200B ($8); you can book this tour or a private boat at the Rattanapong Hotel in the town of Phangnga. Many tours stop at the so-called **Fishing Village,** an ethnically Malay Muslim town called Ban Gi which is most known for its houses built on stilts. This "typical" fishing village now is just hype to get people to buy overpriced food and souvenirs; if you do stop here, walk past the shops to the far more interesting back of the town, where you can actually see the workings of the fishing trade.

Public buses travel from Phuket throughout the day to Phangnga (trip time: 1½ hours; 50B [$2]) over the 87km (54 miles) distance.

SIMILAN NATIONAL PARK

The nine islands that form the Similan archipelago are so pristine that they have been cited by diving authorities as among the best in the world for undersea exploration. We are hardly diving experts (in fact, we're decidedly amateur snorkelers) but we'd be hard put to find cleaner, clearer water than that around these utterly fantastic islands. The beaches that encircle all nine are fine, white sand bordered by lush forests that lead to rocky interiors. The only development is on Ko Muang (also known as Ko 4) which has a park's office and a few tents. Many people head to Ko 9 for its superb diving as well as interesting caves; we saw more varieties of brightly colored fish off Ko 9's coral reefs than in any snorkeling we've done anywhere!

The Similan archipelago is 80km (50 miles) northwest of Phuket. Excursion boats take both day-trippers (it's a long way but worth it) and campers to Similan daily for about 2,000B ($80) including food (it never stopped on our boat). Among the many, we had good luck with Songserm Travel, who have an office on Phuket at 64/2 Rasada Shopping Center, Rasada Road, Phuket (tel. 214272; fax 214301); the trip begins at 6:30am and returns you to Patong at about 7pm. Magnum operates high-speed boats to Similan on a private-charter basis, and Fantasea (see "What to See & Do," above, for details on both companies) runs excellent multiday dive trips to the Similans and beyond. Note that this trip is very much affected by weather conditions (both for travel and diving), so plan to visit from November to April (February and March are the best months) when the western monsoons are at their quietest. Under no circumstances should you fail to bring sunscreen with the highest possible rating; it's likely that the sun will be as hot and bright as you've ever encountered, and you can seriously burn within 10 minutes on the beach. We aren't kidding.

3. KO PI PI

40km (25 miles) SW of Phuket; 42km (26 miles) W of Krabi

GETTING THERE By Plane Thai Airways flies nine times daily from Bangkok (trip time: 1 hour; 2,400B [$96]) to Phuket, the closest airport (transfer to boat at Cape Panwa or take ferry from Krabi).

By Boat Boats depart twice daily from Krabi (trip time: 2 hours; 150B [$6]). Six boats leave daily from Phuket (trip time: 1¼ to 2 hours; 250B to 300B [$10 to $12]). One boat leaves daily to Lanta (trip time: 2 hours; 200B [$8]). One boat sails daily to Ao Nang (trip time: 2 hours; 200B [$8]).

By Bus Three air-conditioned buses leave daily from Bangkok (trip time: 14 hours; 350B to 500B [$14 to $20]) to Phuket. Eight public buses leave daily from the capital (trip time: 14 hours; 200B [$8]); transfer to boat at Cape Panwa or take ferry from Krabi.

ESSENTIALS There is no direct **telephone** service to Pi Pi as yet (there's bound to be soon), so all communications are via radio or cellular service. Most hotels either have such a phone or book through a Krabi-based office. A local cellular phone call runs 15B (60¢). There is a **police** office in addition to the marine police, near the landing at Ton Sai Bay. **Medical** needs may be met at the P. P. Health Office (no phone), located on the main street north of the port, near the View Point Trail; open Monday to Friday 8:30am to 4:30pm, closed Saturday Sunday, and holidays. Three nurses are on duty (there's no doctor), so most serious injuries are treated on Phuket. The clinic advised us to warn people about the sharp coral, rocks, and trees, as the majority of their work is patching people together after receiving a deep cut. T. P. Tours, on the trail to the View Point, has a paperback book exchange. There is one **bank** on the island, located on the east side of the bay, next the marine police office; they exchange currency daily 8:30am to 5pm. Most hotels will also **change money** at a lower rate. **Laundry service** is offered at Pi Pi Seafood (in town). There is a **Pi Pi Foto Fast** near Songserm Travel.

A quarter of a million tourists set foot on this once unvisited set of twin islets in the Andaman Sea last year, and it's beginning to show. The two Pi Pi's, Pi Pi Don and Pi Pi Le, are very close to one another, nearly everyone heads to Pi Pi Don for its sensational beaches and simple accommodations. Rocky Pi Pi Le is known for Viking Cave, crystalline water, psychedelic coral formations, and undersea life. The water between Phuket and Ko Pi Pi can be rough, forcing canceled boat trips, but don't despair: There's bound to be another boat that will shuttle you as soon as the sky clears. A trip to the Pi Pi's has become Phuket's most popular pastime, so there are tons of excursions you can join. The best time to visit is January to April, when the Andaman is tranquil and the weather ideal.

We like Ko Pi Pi, but find it most attractive on the far less-developed northeast coast. If you're in the mood to party, the area around Ton Sai Bay (where the boat docks) on up to Long Beach should be your destination; there are endless low-cost bungalows and pleasant beaches.

ORIENTATION

INFORMATION   There is no TAT office, but there are a number of travel agencies and boat companies in Ton Sai. The Songserm Travel Center has an office in Ton Sai, as well as Arida Tour (near the Ton Sai Village), and Andaman Moskito Shop; the latter books diving (they offer PADI certification training) and fishing trips.

ISLAND LAYOUT   Pi Pi Don, which most people refer to simply as Pi Pi, is an hourglass-shaped islet so thin in the middle it seems you could jump from one side of the island to the other. There are long beaches on both sides, but the deeper water is on the south and east coasts. About a 15-minute walk north from Pi Pi's fishing docks (where the excursion boats dock) is Long Beach, where there is fine swimming and innumerable bungalows. The town is likely not a place where you'll want to stay, but you might want to have your meals there.

The northern part of the island, and the long east coast, is far less built up, particularly around Laemthong Beach, where we prefer to stay.

GETTING AROUND

One of the best parts about staying on Pi Pi is that cars are not seen on the island. All travel is by boat. The unfortunate part is that these water taxis, long-tail boats, emit obnoxious odors and sounds that reverberate throughout the entire lower portion of the island.

BY BOAT   Long-tail boats may be hired all along the Ton Sai Bay waterfront, however, there is a main dock where they tend to congregate. There's a fairly standard rate that fluctuates according to season and demand. Expect to pay about 25B ($1) to go to Long Beach, about 400B to 500B ($16 to $20) for a 5-hour tour of the island (good for a whole boatload of people), and in excess of 1,200B ($48) to go to the northern end of the island. It's a good idea to ask long-staying travelers what the current rates are to avoid overpaying.

WHAT TO SEE & DO

The best place to begin your exploration of the island is along the **Mountain View Trail,** which starts at the back of the fishing village (Ton Sai) and continues up a marked path. The hike takes about 45 minutes to the top, but the vista is unforgettable. When the trail passes the water tanks, veer to the right for an easier path, or to the left for rock scrambling. We suggest doing this at the beginning or end of the day as it gets very hot; bring sunblock, a hat, and water. There is a thatched-hut snack bar atop the mountain.

Pi Pi Le is the most popular day trip on the island, and it's a fun excursion. Boats depart from the town and take you on a tour that includes stops at the Viking Cave, known for its swallows and their bird's nests, cave paintings with vessels that look like Viking ships (thus the name of the cavern), inland bays with dramatic rock formations, and small beaches for swimming and snorkeling. All of the above-mentioned travel agencies (and nearly all guesthouse/bungalows) book boat trips to Pi Pi Le. Expect to pay about 300B ($12) for a full-day trip. *Note:* Some of the Phuket-based day trips include stops at Pi Pi Le, obviating the need to book a separate excursion.

WHERE TO STAY

If you come in the off-season, there are bound to be heavily discounted room rates, so be sure to ask. We have not listed the multitude of Long Beach/Ao Nang bungalows, as they are virtually undifferentiated. Most bungalow complexes are built four or five deep on the beach and incorporate rattan and bamboo (old style) or prefab, 1950s tract house (A-frame, Swiss chalet, Levittown, or Thai-style) minibungalows (new style); Robert Venturi would be delighted. Among the better places are Pi Pi Andaman, Viking Village, and Pi Pi Island Village; expect to pay 250B to 600B ($10 to $24) for two. The following establishments are much better alternatives.

EXPENSIVE

PHI PHI PALM BEACH RESORT, Laemthong Beach, Ko Pi Pi. Tel. 076/ 214488 on Phi Phi or 076/214654 in Phuket. Fax 076/215090. 70 rms (all with shower). A/C MINIBAR **Directions:** At the north side of the island.
$ Rates: 3,800B ($152) single; 4,200B ($168) double; 7,600B ($304) family cottage. AE, MC, V.

This is far and away the best of the existing high-end resorts on the island, located on the far northern end of Pi Pi. The coconut palm–fringed beach is excellent and, on calm days, you can visit Bamboo Island, one of the best beaches in the region. The facilities, including the island's only freshwater swimming pool, are comparable to the midlevel resorts on Phuket, including tennis, windsurfing, scuba diving, sauna, jacuzzi, kiddie pool, game room, and two restaurants. Cottages include king-size beds, writing tables, and refrigerators. Larger family-style layouts with suitelike space are available. Lastly, how can you resist a place that has its own Chinese junk? The Palm Beach Resort has a booking office in Phuket at 196/1-3 Phuket Rd., Phuket 83000; contact them for reservations and transfer from Ton Sai harbor.

MODERATE/BUDGET

BAYVIEW RESORT, Laem Hin Beach, Ton Sai, Ko Pi Pi. Tel. 075/612964. Fax 075/620559. 30 bungalows (all with shower). A/C **Directions:** East end of Laem Hin Beach.
$ Rates: 1,600B ($65) single or double with A/C; 1,100B ($44) single or double with fan. No credit cards.

These recently constructed thatch-roofed bungalows offer comfort, seclusion, and sea breezes to augment the ceiling fan. The newest 10 units are more robustly constructed, with tile roofs and air-conditioning. An American breakfast is included.

MAPRAO RESORT, Maprao Ton Deao Beach, Ko Pi Pi. No phone. 21 rms (showers outside). **Directions:** 25B ($1) boat ride to east side of Ton Sai Bay.

$ Rates: 250B–350B ($10–$14) single/double. No credit cards.

We like this place more than any of the in-town accommodations or those on Long Beach. Its location, on Maprao Ton Deao (known as the "Beach with the Single Coconut Tree"), is thought to be the venue where the first palm arrived on the island. Maprao's beach is private and small, as well as being situated between the town and Long Beach, providing its residents with both access and isolation. The friendly Thai/Belgian management team ensures hospitality and good food. The thatch-constructed bungalows and restaurant/bar area have a comfortable, homey feel. A can't-miss place.

PI PI VIEWPOINT RESORT, Loh-Dalum Bay, Ko Pi Pi. Tel. 075/612193. 50 rms (all with shower). **Directions:** At the back of the town, at the base of the View Point Trail.

$ Rates: 900B ($36) single; 1,200B ($48) double. MC, V.

Arguably the most architecturally attractive buildings in an otherwise forget-it town. The Pi Pi Viewpoint is built of pine logs and rattan on a tiered site, lending a rustic touch. All rooms have double beds(!), fan, toilet, and shower, making them among the best equipped—and best value—in the lower part of the island. They have recently added another 30 more refined bungalows about 350 meters north.

WHERE TO DINE

Many people end up eating in their hotel/bungalow, but there are a scattering of eating establishments in town worth a visit.

GARLIC RESTAURANT, Ton Sai. No telephone.
Cuisine: INTERNATIONAL/SEAFOOD. **Directions:** 250 meters north of main road on road to View Point.
$ Prices: Appetizers 20B–40B (80¢–$1.60); main courses 40B–60B ($2.60–$2.40). No credit cards.
Open: Daily 7:30am–10pm.

During our last visit everyone we asked recommended this simple new eatery, and we happily concur. The service is friendly, and the portions more than generous. Garlic—who wouldn't like a restaurant with a name like this—has a pretty huge menu: 20 different sandwiches, a dozen soups and pastas, nine kinds of pancakes, and eight salads! In high season, when electricity is more reliable, they even have ice cream.

MR. JONG, Ton Sai. No phone.
Cuisine: WESTERN/THAI. **Directions:** On road to View Point.
$ Prices: Appetizers 35B–45B ($1.40–$1.80); main courses 45B–70B ($1.80–$2.80). No credit cards.
Open: Daily 8am–2pm and 6–9pm.

This is a pretty fair breakfast stop, advertising freshly ground coffee, espresso and cappuccino, and brown bread (none of which they had when we visited), but we were wild for their coconut-and-banana pancakes. At lunch and dinner, try the Thai red curry, *tom yam goong,* curried prawns in coconut, or seafood spaghetti.

MAMA RESTO, Ton Sai. Tel. 01/7230535.
Cuisine: WESTERN/THAI. **Directions:** In town on main street.
$ Prices: Appetizers 35B–200B ($1.40–$8); main courses 50B–200B ($2–$8). MC, V.
Open: Daily 8am–2pm and 6–11pm; closed Sept 15–Oct 15.

A true cross-cultural restaurant run by a Thai woman and her French husband, Mama's offers good, honest homemade food, well tailored to the international tourist market. This very casual space, with French pop playing in the background, serves mainly Thai specialties, but there are enough Western dishes to satisfy most palates. Among the best items on the menu are prawns with coconut-and-peanut sauce, pasta with seafood, sweet red curry with crabmeat, marlin or shark steak with mustard sauce (served with a baked potato), chicken curry coconut soup, and our usual favorite, *tod man pla* or *goong* with three sauces. For reasons unknown to us, Mama's also sells discount ferry tickets. Watch out for the high-price wine, but do go for their baked goods brought in daily from Phuket.

PIZZA HOUSE, Ton Sai. Tel. 612337.
    Cuisine: ITALIAN. **Directions:** On main road in town.
$ Prices: Main courses 50B–130B ($2–$5.20). No credit cards.
    Open: Daily 1–8pm.
Sometimes you just have to have a pizza, and the Pizza House answers that call. For spice fanatics, there's the Hot One with goat pepper and chili, and for wimps like us, the Vegetarian with fresh pineapple à la Australia.

4. KRABI

814km (505 miles) S of Bangkok; 165km (109 miles) E of Phuket;
42km (26 miles) E of Ko Pi Pi; 276km (171 miles) N of Satun;
211km (131 miles) SW of Surat Thani

GETTING THERE   Although the most efficient way to get to the Krabi area beaches is by bus from Phuket (assuming you're flying from Bangkok), we suggest taking a boat which gives you stopovers on Phuket and Ko Pi Pi and delivers you directly to Ao Nang. If you take an early morning flight, you'll have to spend a night on Phuket—we suggest staying in the Cape Panwa area, near to the Ko Pi Pi–bound boats—take the 8:30am boat to Pi Pi and stay over or connect with the afternoon boat to Ao Nang. It will certainly take longer and cost more than the airbus combination, but you'll get to sail on picturesque waters, take in Ko Pi Pi, and end up directly on Krabi's best beaches.

By Plane   Thai Airways flies nine times daily from Bangkok (trip time: 1 hour; 2,400B [$96]) to Phuket, the closest airport to Krabi. There is limousine service from the airport to Krabi for 1,800B ($72). Bangkok Airways has periodically served Krabi and may begin again.

By Boat   Twice daily trips leave from Ko Pi Pi (trip time 2 hours; 150B [$6]). There's one daily sailing to Lanta (trip time: 1 hour; 100B [$4]).

By Bus   Two air-conditioned buses leave daily from Bangkok (trip time: 13 hours; 400B [$16]) to Krabi. Three air-conditioned minibuses leave daily to Surat Thani (trip time: 2¾ hours; 300B [$12]). Three air-conditioned minibuses leave daily from Phuket (trip time: 20½ hours; 200B [$8]), as well as six air-conditioned buses (trip time: 2½ hours; 120B [$4.80]). Frequent service to Ao Nang and Rai Lai Beach (trip time: 30 minutes; 20B [80¢]).

ESSENTIALS   The telephone **area code** for Krabi is 075. There are several banks on U-Trakit Road, paralleling the waterfront (to the right as you alight from the ferry); hours are Monday to Friday 8:30am to 3:30pm. There is one **exchange bureau**, next to the Vieng Thong Hotel, that operates daily from 8:30am to 6pm. The **post office** and **police station** are located on U-Trakit Road, to the left as you leave the pier. There are two **banks** in Ao Nang, near the Phranang Inn, open daily for exchange; hours are 8am to 4:30pm.

The only reason to visit the town of Krabi is to connect with the frequent buses to Ao Nang and the farther flung beaches known as Rai Lai and Phra Nang, also referred to as Krabi Resort. These places have become the destinations of choice for those who've been displaced by the development on Phuket and Ko Pi Pi. Of course, they too are well developed but there is still a good feeling about this area. The lesser-known islands, such as Ko Lanta, Ko Pu, and Ko Hai are certainly in the process of becoming the latest and greatest, but most party people will find the Krabi beaches just fine. If you need quiet and tranquillity, we suggest heading farther south to Ko Tarutao and even farther out Ko Adang and Ko Rawi.

The best time to visit the Krabi area is December to April, with January and February the ideal months; the rainy season runs May to November, when it's wet nearly every day.

ORIENTATION

INFORMATION There is a newly established bureau of TAT on the north end of the esplanade along the river (open Monday to Friday 8am to 4:30pm, Saturday 8am to noon). Songserm Travel Center (tel. 075/612665; fax 6675/612318) is on 38 Kongka Rd., one block south of the esplanade. Leebi Travel (tel. 611150), on 3-7 Isara Rd., about 10½ blocks from the pier, books bus, train, and boat tickets.

CITY LAYOUT The only facts you need to know are that the boat docks at Chao Fah Pier on the Krabi River, is to the right, travel agents and banks are across U-Trakit Road, and the buses to Ao Nang are on the left.

WHAT TO SEE & DO

Krabi has a number of sites that were touted to us as required viewing, and we can reliably report that none of these were must sees. Stay on the beach and be happy.

Okay, here's one for the serious die-hards: the **Shell Cemetery,** otherwise known as Su San Hoi. It's 17km (11 miles) from town in Ban Laem Pho and struck us as one of those Ripley's Believe It or Not kind of places: is this a rare, 75-million-year-old petrified rock cliff composed of ancient seashells or is it a slab of parking lot that broke off from the shopping area above? The best part of the visit here is that it's on the way to Ao Nang Beach

WHERE TO STAY ON AO NANG, AO PHRA NANG & RAI LAI BEACH

VERY EXPENSIVE

DUSIT RAYAVADEE RESORT, 67 Moo 5, Susan Hoy Rd., Tambol Sai Thai, Amphur Muang, Krabi 81000. Tel. and fax 075/620630. 100 units. A/C MINIBAR TV TEL **Directions:** 30 minutes northwest of Krabi town by long-tail boat or 70 minutes from Phuket on the resort's own launch.

$ Rates: 9,600B–14,400B ($384–$576) pavilion; villas from 36,000B ($1,440). AE, DC, MC, V.

We hardly know where to begin praising this new resort, the finest we found on our last trip. The handsome two-story pavilions are large and luxurious, offering every modern convenience and utmost privacy—but what impresses us most is the impeccable way each is integrated into its beautiful environment, sparing every tree and natural feature possible. We're also immensely pleased with how this resort is cooperating with other locals to preserve the astonishing beauty of this very special place, where fantastic limestone cliffs tower over two of the most gorgeous beaches in the world. The staff is thoroughly professional yet relaxed, and the ambience is one of a peaceful village with paths meandering among lotus ponds and lovely landscaping. The sunsets at the big, beautiful round pool hovering over the ocean or on Railay Beach itself are sensational.

Dining/Entertainment: The Raya Dining Room serves a sumptuous breakfast and select international cuisine until midnight. The Krua Phranang serves traditional Thai cuisine and fresh seafood for lunch and dinner overlooking Phranang Beach in a setting made for romance. There's a bar at the pool and another cleverly concealed on a beach. Besides one handsome open-air lounge, there's another with air-conditioning and music.

Services: Personal host, room service, car rental, laundry service.

Facilities: Swimming pool, whirlpool, children's pool, 2 lighted tennis courts (in a beautiful setting), air-conditioned squash court, barber shop, beauty salon, boutique, fitness center (with good views), library, video library, massage and sauna, water sports center with facilities for sailing, scuba, snorkeling, and windsurfing.

MODERATE

KRABI RESORT, 53-57 Patthana Rd., Ao Nang Beach, Krabi 81000. Tel. 075/612161. Fax 075/612160. Telex 67201 TH SRIPONG. 87 rms, 3 suites. A/C MINIBAR TV TEL **Directions:** Overlooking beach at Ao Nang.
$ Rates: 1,089B–1,900B ($44–$76) single/double (including 10% service charge); suite from 4,250B ($170) (including service charge). MC, V.

Unlike other accommodations in the area, the Krabi Resort is a resort compound with two hotel buildings in addition to a full array of bungalows. The lobby is similar to a midrange Phuket resort, if scaled down a bit. Nicely maintained grounds with a swimming pool, an aviary, playground, tennis courts, and health club mark this as a fully equipped facility. We prefer the beach-facing thatched-roof bungalows with parquet floors to the more modern hotel buildings. In addition to the property in Ao Nang, the Krabi Resort also books 18 bungalows on Poda Island for 300B ($12); cold shower only and limited electrical service.

PHRA NANG INN HOTEL, 119 Ao Nang Beach, P.O. Box 25, Krabi 81000. Tel. 075/612173. Fax 075/612174. 41 rms. A/C MINIBAR TV **Directions:** Overlooking beach at Ao Nang–Rai Lai boat dock.
$ Rates: 1,550B ($62) single/double. DC, MC, V.

This is basically a group hotel that is rustically built with pine and palms. Shells are mixed into the stucco walls (clearly an aesthetic nod to the nearby Shell Cemetery) in the tiled rooms; beams are of coconut palm. The rooms form a U around a small pool, while the Phra Nang's restaurant (with a varied Thai/continental menu) overlooks Ao Nang Beach. A 30-room hotel wing is due in late 1994!

BUDGET

AO NANG VILLA, 125-127 U-Trakit Rd., Ao Nang Beach, Krabi 81000. Tel. 075/612431. 75 rms. A/C
$ Rates: 145B–300B ($5.80–$12) single; 500B ($20) double; 900B ($36) suite. MC, V.

The lesser-priced accommodations are traditional thatched bungalows, while the more expensive units are small prefab houses. Suites have air-conditioning. We like the pretty, open-air restaurant, open daily 7am to 11pm.

RAILEY VILLAGE BUNGALOWS, Rai Lai Beach, Krabi 81000. Tel. 075/ 612728. 47 bungalows. **Directions:** Midpoint on Rai Lai Beach.
$ Rates: 400B ($16) single or double. No credit cards.

The most attractive of the budget-class accommodations are in the middle of the beach, next to the well-hidden condominiums. These bungalows feature extra-firm beds, clean rooms, a fair restaurant (no booze served), and a small bookshop. (For faster service, alcohol, and VDO, go next door to the Sand Sea.)

EASY EXCURSIONS FROM KRABI

Longboats are available for hire to visit the various islands in the **Marine Park.** We were struck by the similarity of the limestone outcroppings that one sees at Ao Nang with those at Phangnga, 85km (53 miles) to the north. Although Phangnga is of equal appeal, the water and area around Ao Nang is considerably cleaner. Most people head to **Chicken** or **Poda Island** for swimming and sunbathing. The bay is also popular with sailors, several of whom anchored their boats off Poda Island when we visited. Few of the islands have bungalows, but you can set up tents for camping; Krabi Resort books the bungalows on Poda (see "Where to Stay," above). Expect to pay about 700B ($28) for a full day of longboat cruising or about 25B ($1) each way to Poda.

5. TARUTAO NATIONAL PARK

973km (603 miles) S of Bangkok; 30km (19 miles) W of Ban Pak Bara;
276km (171 miles) S of Krabi; 100km (62 miles) S of Trang

GETTING THERE   The jumping-off point for Tarutao is Ban Pak Bara, a port city roughly 100km (62 miles) south of Trang. Most buses bound for Satun and Trang stop in the hamlet of La Ngu, where you must transfer to song tao or motorcycle taxi to Pak Bara.

By Plane   Thai Airways flies three times daily from Bangkok (trip time: 1½ hours; 2,800B [$112]) to Hat Yai, the closest airport to Satun and Ban Pak Bara.

By Boat   Boats leave twice daily from Pak Bara (trip time 1½ hours; 200B [$8] round-trip); three times weekly from Ko Adang to Ko Tarutao with stops at Ko Kai and Ko Yang (trip time: 3 hours; 500B [$20] round-trip). There are treaties being negotiated between Malaysia and Thailand to permit boats to travel between Langkowi, Malaysia, and Tarutao.

By Bus   Three air-conditioned buses leave daily from Bangkok (trip time: 14 hours; 450B [$18]) to Trang. Frequent public buses leave from Trang to La Ngu, on the Satun orange bus (trip time: 2 hours; 40B [$1.60]). Song taos depart from La Ngu to Ban Pak Bara (trip time: 45 minutes; 25B [$1]). Frequent shared taxis leave from Satun (across from Bangkok Bank building) to La Ngu (trip time: 30 minutes; 50B [$2]). One bus daily (high season only) leaves from Hat Yai (in front of Plaza Market) directly to Ban Pak Bara (trip time: 2½ hours; 60B [$2.40]); shared taxi from Hat Yai (on Prathan Uthit Road near the President Hotel or post office) to La Ngu (trip time: 2 hours; 80B [$3.20]).

By Car   From Bangkok Route 4 south to Pettalung; west on Route 406 to Satun Province and northwest on Route 4073 at Chalung to Ban Pak Bara.

ESSENTIALS   There is limited telephone service on Tarutao; there are no banks or post offices. These services are best served in La Ngu (open Monday to Friday, 8:30am to 3:30pm), or better still, in Trang, Satun, or Hat Yai. Many people leave their packs and excess luggage at the ticket office in Pak Bara. There is a small shop on Tarutao which sells T-shirts and a few basic toiletries and food items. If you come off-season and charter a boat, plan on bringing your own food, as the island's few restaurants are closed.

The 51-island chain known as Tarutao National Park is located off of Thailand's far southwestern coast, only a few miles from the Malaysian border in the Strait of Malacca (leading out to the Indian Ocean). This fringe setting goes a long way toward explaining Tarutao's legacy. Originally settled by sea gypsies, it wasn't until 1939 that the main island received its first load of settlers. These pioneers were political detainees, enemies of the incipient Thai democracy, who were given the charge of constructing their own prison. More prisoners arrived and the facilities spread to other parts of the island. After the Japanese invasion of Thailand during World War II, the chain of command was broken to Tarutao and the prisoners and guards turned the place into a Devil's Island, preying on passing ships for booty. These feared pirates patrolled the Strait of Malacca until British troops, stationed in nearby Malaya, overcame the guerilla forces to return the island back to Thai peasants; they in turn established farms and plantations. The spirit of resistance continued well into the 1980s—and the battle is still being played out—between environmentalists and proponents of the national park, and factions of the local fishing industry. Some illegal trawlers have used destructive means (such as dynamiting coral reefs) to pursue their trade. As recent as 1981, illegal fishermen fired on park service workers in their offshore patrol boats.

Perhaps it's due to the chain's pioneering legacy or, more to the point, its Wild West behavior, but it has been spared the scars of industrial tourism. Due to the heroic efforts of both Thai and foreign workers, and especially Mr. Booruang Saison (the champion of Thailand's burgeoning national park system), the islands are protected for now, but there are plans to begin development. Currently there is a limit on the number of visitors to Tarutao at any one time (more than 10,000 travelers come to the chain annually), so it's important to check with the authorities to ensure that you'll be allowed to stay overnight.

Once there, you'll find islands the likes of which you thought disappeared decades ago. With only rough accommodations and facilities and few if any vehicles, life on Tarutao's islands is as primitive and pristine as exists in the country. Those in search of a quiet place, tranquil bays, long hiking trails, nearly deserted beaches, a seemingly endless number of islands, good snorkeling and diving, and cheap travel will think they've died and gone to heaven. Go now or forever hold your peace.

The season for travel to Tarutao and beyond is November through May. Monsoons dump rain during the balance of the year, severely hampering boat travel in the area.

ORIENTATION

INFORMATION The governing entity of the Tarutao archipelago is the National Park Division, Department of Forestry, Bang Khen, Bangkok (tel. 02/579-5269). There is a Tarutao National Park office in Pak Bara (tel. 074/711383) adjacent to the pier. Reservations may be made with either office; however, the local office has the most up-to-date information on the islands.

ISLAND LAYOUT The closest and largest island is called Tarutao, a lush and rocky place, that accounts for almost 180 square miles. The interior is covered half by rain forest and the balance by mangrove swamp, plains, and mountains. About 40km (25 miles) west are the archipelago's next two largest islands, Ko Adang and Ko Rawi; both of these are surrounded by many smaller islands, such as Ko Lipe, Ko Kra, Ko Jabang, and Ko Yang, all considered fine diving and snorkeling destinations due to their intact coral reefs.

All boats dock on the northern coast of Tarutao at Pante Bay. Here, in the island's main settlement, are the park headquarters, two small restaurants, visitor's center, sea turtle nursing ponds, tourist (tents and concrete-block bungalows) and government housing, the tourist police, and emergency services. To the south of Ao Pante are the island's two most popular beaches, Ao Jak and Ao Sone.

GETTING AROUND

Other than hiking, the only other means of transport is via long-tail boats. Most people pool their resources to hire a boat, especially for long-distance trips. We paid about 200B ($8) for 10 people to travel south to Ao Sone Beach.

In terms of getting between islands, be warned that the water between Tarutao and the far-flung destinations, such as Adang or Rawi, can be quite rough. The boats are small and frequently have problems navigating the seas. In some cases they will simply not run or will turn back after reaching open water. It's a good idea to plan on adding a few days to your itinerary if you intend to visit these areas. Even the two diminutive boats that shuttle people between Pak Bara and Tarutao are on the dodgy side, which is all the more obvious when the weather gets rough. Be prepared to improvise.

WHAT TO SEE & DO

PANTE BAY

There are several exhibits that are worth visiting at the park headquarters. The library and adjacent visitors center have interesting displays about the ecology and history of Tarutao, as well as books on the subject; open daily 8am to dusk. Nearby, to the left as you alight from the pier, are the **Sea Turtle Nursing Ponds.** Green, hawksbill, and Pacific Ridley turtles in various stages of growth (from two to seven years old) swim in shallow pools; try to visit during feeding time. This is part of the park's greater program to repopulate the ever-dwindling number of these species.

EXPLORING THE ISLAND

At low tide it's possible to walk a long way down the west coast of Tarutao. There are excellent and wide, sandy beaches with an amazing variety of marine life (sea horses, sand dollars, starfish, and hermit crabs galore) on or near the shoreline. We took a long-tail boat down to Ao Sone, 8km (5 miles) south of Pante, and hiked back on a trail that snakes through the interior of the island. There are mangrove swamps, rain forests, and a variety of other flora and some wild fauna to be seen on this 3- to 4-hour hike. There are small settlements on Ao Sane, on the southern tip of the island at An Taloh Udang (site of the penal colonies), and on the east coast at Al Taloh Wow (another former prison). Many people backpack to these places and set up camp.

For those who want a scenic overview, take the 15-minute hike up to **To Boo Cliff** that starts behind the library. It's especially nice at sunset. Intrepid travelers will enjoy a trip to **Crocodile Cave;** take a flashlight and expect to get wet wading through the mangrove swamps.

WHERE TO STAY & DINE

There are no guest houses, hotels, or other private housing alternatives on Tarutao. Your basic choice is camping in a tent (provided by the park for 75B [$3] per night or 25B [$1] for those with their own tent) or in four-person concrete bungalows; expect to pay 600B ($24).

There are two dining venues on Tarutao, both of which are located at Pante Bay. The first, the **Tarutao Co-op Café** is open daily from 7:30am to 5:30pm; it serves rice and curry dishes only. The **Tarutao Restaurant** serves a full menu of fresh fish and seafood, as well as other traditional Thai specialties; hours are 9am to 10pm. Both are open-air establishments, so bring your insect repellent at night.

EASY EXCURSIONS

Aside from exploring Tarutao, a few hardy souls make their way west to the many smaller islands in the archipelago. The most popular destination is **Adang,** and there is thrice weekly ferry service from Tarutao to Adang and the surrounding islands; the round-trip fare is 350B ($14). Most travelers to Adang-Rawi stop at **Ko Lipe,** a relatively flat island that has been settled by people known as Chao Le whose principle occupation is coconut farming. In addition to Ko Lipe, the islands of **Ko Kra, Ko Jabang,** and **Ko Yang** are also excellent places for snorkeling or diving because of their fine coral reefs. If you wish to stay on Adang, the boat docks at Laem Sone where there is a park headquarters office, as well as two bamboo longhouses, each sleeping four people; expect to pay 350B ($14). There is also a simple restaurant, adjacent to the accommodations.

CHAPTER 9

THE CENTRAL PLAINS

1. PHITSANULOK
• WHAT'S SPECIAL
  ABOUT THE CENTRAL
  PLAINS
2. SUKHOTHAI & SI
  SATCHANALAI
3. TAK & MAE SOT: THE
  MYANMAR BORDER

The vast Central Plains are known as the Great Rice Bowl of the country. This region, the source of Thailand's major crop, is also the source of the country's financial and cultural wealth. Washed by rivers, including the Chao Phraya, the land sweeps on with rice field after rice field, many hosting incredible archeological sites, including the nation's greatest wonder, Sukhothai. It's where you'll discover much traditional Thai culture, and where the Thai kingdom was first founded. Although Phitsanulok is the region's major commercial hub, with a variety of tourist facilities, travelers with limited time and an archeological bent should definitely stay in the hotels near the Sukhothai Historical Park.

---

1. PHITSANULOK

377km (234 miles) N of Bangkok; 93km (58 miles) SE of Sukhothai

GETTING THERE By Plane Two flights a day from Bangkok (flying time: 45 minutes; 920B [$36.80]); three flights daily from Chiang Mai via Nan (flying time: 2 hours; 650B [$26]). Taxis cost 25B to 55B ($1 to $2.20) into town from the airport. The Thai Airways office is at 209/26-28 Boromtrilokanart Rd. (tel. 258020), near the TAT.

By Train Three special diesel trains a day from Bangkok (trip time: 6 hours; 250B [$10] air-conditioned second-class seat). A sleeper is available, but should be reserved as early as possible; call Bangkok's **Hua Lampong Railroad Station** (tel. 02/223-0341, ext 4281) or the Phitsanulok Railway Station (tel. 055/251997).

By Bus Nineteen air-conditioned buses a day from Bangkok (trip time: 6 hours; 140B to 190B [$5.60 to $7.60]). Six buses a day from Chiang Mai (trip time: 6 hours; 98B [$3.95]). Contact Bangkok's Northern Bus Terminal (tel. 02/279-4484) or the Phitsanulok Bus Station (tel. 242430) for information. **Phitsanulok Yan Yon Tours** (tel. 258941 or 278-2063 in Bangkok) also runs several daily express VIP coaches (180B [$7.20]).

By Car Take Highway 11 north from Bangkok.

SPECIAL EVENTS The **Buddha Chinarat Festival** is held annually on the sixth day of the waxing moon in the third lunar month (usually late January or early February). Then, Phitsanulok's Wat Phra Sri Ratana Mahatat is packed with well-wishers, dancers, monks and abbots, children, and tourists, all converging on the temple grounds for a 6-day celebration.

The city of Phitsanulok is set on the banks of the Nan River and bisects Thailand's north and central provinces, in the country's fertile rice belt. If you're

WHAT'S SPECIAL ABOUT THE CENTRAL PLAINS

Ancient Monuments

Historic Sukhothai's magnificent temples and palace ruins.

The 39 elephant buttresses supporting Si Satchanalai's Wat Chang Lom.

Museums

Sukhothai's sculptural and architectural masterpieces in the Ramkamhaeng National Museum.

Sawanwaranayok National Museum's incomparable ceramics (especially celadon) collection.

Religious Shrines

In Phitsanulok, Wat Mahatat's stunning gold-and-black bot and the haloed Phra Buddha Chinarat bronze dating from 1357.

Architectural Highlights

The colorful, dilapidated houseboats moored along Song Kwai, Phitsanulok's Two River City.

Festivals

Loi Krathong (a harvest festival originated during the Sukhothai era), when banana-leaf boats with candles and offerings are launched in the city's rivers and fountains (late October/early November).

planning an all-encompassing tour of northern Thailand, Phitsanulok is roughly equidistant between Chiang Mai and Bangkok and is an ideal base for visiting Sukhothai and Si Satchanalai. Because of its strategic location, the city enjoys prosperity and some historic importance.

The area is surrounded by a seemingly endless array of rice paddies, their vivid green hue is delightful in the late spring. In winter, white-flowering tobacco and pink-flowering soybeans are planted in rotation. Rice barges, houseboats, and long-tail boats ply the Nan and Song Kwai rivers, which eventually connect to the Chao Phraya and feed into the Gulf of Siam.

Phitsanulok is the birthplace of King Naresuan (the Great) and his less famous brother, Prince Ekatosarot. The Ayutthaya king is legendary in Thai history for his gallant defense against the forces of the invading Burmese army during the 16th century. There are many paintings of Naresuan in hand-to-hand combat, on elephant back, with a Burmese crown prince. Other Ayutthaya kings used Phitsanulok as a staging and training ground for battles with the Burmese, and for 25 years it served as the capital of the Ayutthaya kingdom.

When most of the city burned in 1959, one of the only original buildings to survive was Wat Mahatat, Phitsanulok's most important site. Since then, concrete and steel have replaced carved teak and painted stucco. Today, the Nan River is the town's most picturesque asset, with houseboats moored to its banks and klongs lined with traditional housing. Tourism has become big business in Phitsanulok, but much has been lost in the process; the legendary Thai hospitality is now seen in fewer and fewer places.

ORIENTATION

INFORMATION The **TAT** office, at 209/7-8 Surasi Trade Center, off Boromtrilokanart Road (tel. 055/252742 or 252743; fax 55/252742), two blocks south of the Clock Tower, is open daily 8:30am to 4:30pm.

CITY LAYOUT The town is fairly compact, with the majority of services and sights for tourists concentrated along or near the east bank of the Nan River. The day market for housewares, Buddhist amulets, and knickknacks along the lower banks becomes a lively Night Market of food stalls each evening. A recently completed bridge links the two shores. Phyalithai Road, which runs perpendicular to the riverside Phuttabucha Road, leads directly to the Clock Tower, the town's most central landmark.

The other central artery is Boromtrilokanart Road, named after the 15th-century Ayutthaya king who lived and was crowned in Phitsanulok. This major commercial street begins along the lower banks of the river, angles to the middle of town, around the Clock Tower, and ends along the upper bank, near Wat Mahatat and its museum. The train bus stations are 2 ½ blocks east of the Clock Tower, near the Amarintr Nakorn Hotel, at Naresuan and Ekathosrod roads.

GETTING AROUND

BY SAMLOR (BICYCLE & MOTORIZED)   Bicycle trishaws (called samlors here) are common and cheap—about 75B ($3) per person for an hour-long ride in town. Motorized tuk-tuks (called taxis) are common near the bus and train stations. Fares have to be negotiated but should range from 15B to 25B (60¢ to $1) in town. Song tao (converted pickup trucks) are group taxis which leave from the bus or train station for nearby villages.

BY BUS   There is frequent (every half hour 6am to 6pm), inexpensive, local bus service to Sukhothai (trip time: 1 hour; 18B [75¢]). Note: The bus only runs to the modern town of Sukhothai. To reach the Sukhothai Historical Park (in Muang Kao or Old City), take a minibus (trip time: 20 minutes; 5B [20¢]) or a tuk-tuk 50B [$2]).

FAST FACTS: PHITSANULOK

Area Code   For the Phitsanulok region dial 055.

Currency Exchange   The most convenient bank is Bangkok Bank, one block from the Clock Tower (open daily 7am to 8pm).

Emergencies   The main police station (tel. 240199) is near the TAT, at the intersection of Naresuan and Boromtrilokanart roads. Dial 199 or 191 in emergencies.

Hospital   Roum Phaet Hospital (tel. 242574) on Boromtrilokanart Road, near the market, is the closest private facility.

Post Office   The General Post Office is on Phuttabucha Road, along the river just south of the houseboat restaurants.

Telephone/Telex/Fax   The Overseas Call Office is on the second floor of the post office; open daily 7am to 11pm.

WHAT TO SEE & DO

Other than leaving the city to visit the historical parks at Sukhothai or Si Satchanlai, there is only one major must-see in Phitsanulok—**Wat Phra Sri Ratana Mahatat (Wat Yai)**, one of the holiest and most beautiful Buddhist temples in the country. Located one block north of the Nan River bridge, you can pay homage to its brilliant late Sukhothai period Phra Buddha Chinarat. The power bronze image was cast in 1357 under the aegis of the Sukhothai king Mahatmmaracha; its most distinctive elements are the regal-looking halo and perfect expression of controlled tranquillity. (This image serves as a model for ideal representations of the Buddha in contemporary statue factories.)

The bot that houses this most revered of Buddhas is a prize example of traditional Thai architecture, with three eaves overlapping one another to emphasize the nave, and graceful black and gold columns. We enjoyed following the painted wall murals illustrating the life of the Buddha and the two painted *thammas* (pulpits) to the side. Be sure to examine the excellent late Ayuttaya period, mother-of-pearl inlaid doors leading into the chapel; similar to those in Bangkok's Royal Chapel, they were added in 1576 as a gift from King Borommakot of Ayutthaya.

Other than the main bot, the wat's most distinctive architectural aspect is the Khmer-style prang, rebuilt by King Boromtrilokanart. The gilding on the top half is probably recent, but it complements the Khmer temple decor. Notice also the Buddhist statuary; there is a small museum that houses a good collection of Sukhothai- and Ayutthaya-era Buddhas.

The wat is always packed with worshippers paying their respects, making offerings, and praying for a healthy mind and body. During the winter Buddha Chinarat Festival, it's transformed into a cultural circus!

Admission is a suggested contribution of 10B (40¢). It's open daily 6am to 6pm (during Buddha Chinarat Festival 6am to midnight); the museum is open Wednesday to Sunday 9am to 4pm.

PHITSANULOK'S OTHER SITES

From Wat Mahatat, you might want to stroll south along Phuttabucha Road, inspecting **Song Kwai,** the "Two River" city of semipermanently moored houseboats on the banks of the Nan River. From the east bank, near the Overseas Call Office, walk over the recently completed bridge to the other side to see the King Naresuan the Great Monument. It was built on the site of the Chandra Palace, where he was born in 1555. Nearby are the city and provincial government buildings. Farther south on the east bank is the day market with a panoply of everyday items and a smattering of hill-tribe crafts for sale at relatively low prices.

A samlor tour of the town (with driver) costs about 100B ($4) per person; stops include the fruit market (or the Night Market at night), the Clock Tower, the train station (an old British engine is on display), and the banks of the Nan River.

The **Buddha Casting Factory and Folklore Museum,** at 26/43 Wisutkasat Rd. (tel. 258715), is a kitschy treat for those who want to see how local artisans make a 40-foot-tall statue. The folk museum part isn't much, but will give you an accurate picture of Thai peasant life. The factory and museum are open daily 8:30am to 4:30pm; admission is free. From the train station, it's a 20-minute walk through the city, or you can catch bus no. 3.

Wat Chulamanee, south of Nakorn Sawan Highway, is the oldest temple in this Phitsanulok area and site of the original city. Like the prang at Wat Mahatat, this Khmer-built spire was rebuilt by King Boromtrilokanart after his instruction in the architecture of nearby Sukhothai. The wat, still an active monastery, was restored in the 1950s and is studied particularly for its fine laterite cactus-shaped prang and the elaborate stucco designs decorating the structure. The compound is open to the public daily from 6am to 7pm; 10B (40¢) is the suggested contribution. It's on Boromtrilokanart Road, and can be reached by bus no. 4 from the city bus stand, opposite the train station.

WHERE TO STAY

There are several acceptable moderate and inexpensive lodgings that offer more of a choice than anything in the surrounding towns other than Sukhothai—where we suggest you stay if you're touring the region. Most cater to large European tour groups so be sure to reserve ahead. Again, if the historical sights are your only interest and you can resist the hustle of the city, consider staying in Old or New Sukhothai.

MODERATE

AMARINTR NAKORN HOTEL, 3/1 Chaophrya Rd., Phitsanulok 65000.
Tel. 055/258588. Fax 055/258945. Telex 46253 AMARIN TH. 132 rms. A/C TV
TEL **Directions:** 1 block west of train station.
$ Rates (including tax and service): 580B ($23) single/double with TV; 450B ($18)
single/double without TV.
The tall white hotel, within sight of the train and bus stations, was built back in 1972. It's well preserved and still an acceptable choice for convenient lodging. I

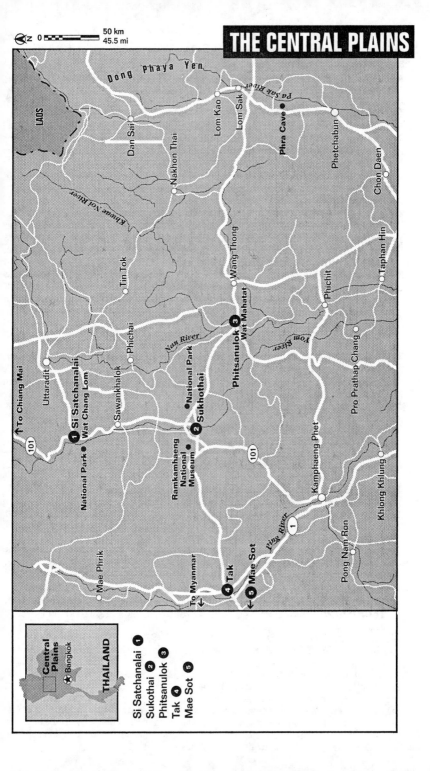

THE CENTRAL PLAINS

50 km
45.5 mi

Dong phaya Yen

LAOS

Pa Sak River

Lom Kao

Lom Sak

Dan Sai

Phra Cave

Nakhon Thai

Phetchabun

Chon Daen

Khwae Noi River

Tin Tok

Wang Thong

Phichai

Taphan Hin

Wat Mahatat

Phichit

Nan River

Phitsanulok ❸

Yom River

Pro Prathap Chang

National Park

Uttaradit

Si Satchanalai ❶ Wat Chang Lom

Sukhothai

Sawankhalok

National Park

↑ To Chiang Mai

101

National Park

Ramkamhaeng National Museum

101

Kamphaeng Phet

Khlong Khlung

Ping River

1

Mae Phrik

Tak ❹

Mae Sot ❺

To Myanmar ↓

Pong Nam Ron

← To Chiang Mai

Central Plains

THAILAND

★ Bangkok

Si Satchanalai ❶
Sukothai ❷
Phitsanulok ❸
Tak ❹
Mae Sot ❺

offers clean rooms; higher-priced ones have TV. There's a 24-hour coffee shop, Chinese restaurant, and a new barber and beauty parlor.

PAILYN HOTEL, 38 Boromtrilokanart Rd., Phutsanulok 65000. Tel. 055/ 252411. 212 rms. A/C MINIBAR TV TEL **Directions:** 3 long blocks north of clock tower.

$ Rates: 1,060B ($42.40) single; 1,648B ($65.90) double. Extra bed 200B ($8). AE, MC, V.

The Pailyn, one block from the river, is Phitsanulok's best-looking lodging, with a bright marble lobby that gives it panache. The rooms have textured wallpaper and rattan decor; they're clean and fairly quiet and priced according to size (though there are no double beds and the mattresses are very hard). Unfortunately, the staff is overworked by the many tour groups who come overnight. There is a coffee shop, a popular disco, sauna, massage parlor.

RAJAPRUK HOTEL, 99/9 Pha-Ong Dum Rd., Phitsanulok 65000. Tel. 055/258477. Fax 055/251395 or in Bangkok 02-229-4496. 101 rms. A/C TV TEL **Directions:** 1km (⅗ mile) northeast of clock tower, near bus terminal.

$ Rates: 800B ($32) single; 900B ($36) double; suites from 2,000B to 3,000B ($80 to $120). Extra bed 100B ($4). MC, V.

The Rajapruk is the only hotel in Phitsanulok with a swimming pool (small but clean). The hotel is a bit older and more worn than the Pailyn, yet the Spartan guest rooms are clean. The open-air Garden Bar is pleasant, and there's a coffee shop, Thai massage parlor, and boisterous disco.

INEXPENSIVE

THE GREENHOUSE, 11/12 Ekathosorot Rd., Phitsanulok 65000. No phone. 4 rms. **Directions:** 2km (1.2 miles) north of Wat Mahatat.

$ Rates (including tax and service): 70B ($2.80) single; 95B ($3.80) double. No credit cards.

Mr. Thoi and his delightful family keep very clean, simple rooms in this newly restored teak house in a quiet, residential neighborhood. The rooms' charm comes from teak floors and walls; a fan, screened windows, and linens come with each, and showers are nearby. Snacks and bicycles are available in the small yard. Mr. Thoi often waits at the train and bus stations for guests; otherwise take the no. 4 bus or a 15B (60¢) tuk-tuk to this guesthouse.

THE GUESTHOUSE HOTEL, 99/10 Pra-Ongdam Rd., Phitsanulok 65000. Tel. 055/259203. 40 rms. TEL **Directions:** Behind Rajapruk.

$ Rates (including tax and service): 214B ($8.60) single with fan, 279B ($11.15) with A/C; 236B ($9.40) double with fan, 321B ($12.85) with A/C. Extra bed free. No credit cards.

This appears to be a converted apartment building, located just outside the back door of the fancier Rajapruk Hotel (its owner). Rooms have simple linoleum floors, twin beds, a hot shower, and a fan. Though worn, they're clean. One of the town's best deals.

PHITSANULOK YOUTH HOSTEL, 38 Sanambin Rd., Phitsanulok 65000. Tel. 055/242060. 5 rms, 40 beds. **Directions:** 4km (2.4 miles) southeast of clock tower.

$ Rates (including tax and service): 180B–210B ($7.20–$8.40) single; 120B–140B ($4.80–$5.60) double; 40B ($1.60) bed in dorm. Nonmembers pay 40B ($1.60) extra per stay (not per night). No credit cards.

This hostel, known to locals as "No. 38," is distinguished by its owner, Mr. Sapachai, considered by his wards to be the most helpful, caring host in the country. It gets a great crowd of enthusiastic young travelers who overlook the Spartan lodgings for the enjoyment of making new friends. The five rooms in an old teak house hold two to eight persons each. A densely planted garden, cold shower, clean toilet, and breakfast are also available. The hostel is 1km (about ⅗ of a mile) from the airport. The no. 3 bus runs to the train or bus stations.

WHERE TO DINE

Be sure to try the local specialty, *khaew tak,* a sun-dried banana baked with honey—it's delicious. A small package costs 30B ($1.20) and is widely sold. If you want more solid food al fresco, head for the Night Market at Phuttabucha and Khun Phiren roads, along the river. *Alert:* Hygiene is questionable.

SONGKHEAW HOUSEBOAT RESTAURANT, 21 Phuttabucha Rd., Tel. 242167.

Cuisine: THAI/CHINESE. **Directions:** On Nan River.

$ Prices: Appetizers 25B–45B ($1–$1.80); main courses 45B–100B ($1.80–$4). No credit cards.

Open: Daily 11am–midnight.

This is one of many houseboats which serves Thai and Chinese cuisine; though mediocre, locals claim it has the best food. We had tasty *tom mon pla* (fried fish cake), grilled chicken, and a "light noodle" salad of glass noodles and seafood. Don't make the mistake of crossing over to the old, worn boats moored alongside; they pull out about 8:15pm and cruise the river.

COUNTRY ROAD, 20 Boromtrilokanart Rd. Tel. 242969.

Cuisine: THAI. **Directions:** 1 block east of Pailyn Hotel.

$ Prices: Main courses 40B–100B ($1.60–$4). No credit cards.

Open: Daily 8pm–midnight.

The wagon wheels and Christmas lights decorating the exterior proclaim "Cowboy!" to Thai passersby. Large steaks, pork chops, and chicken sizzle on the outdoor grill, while inside a three-piece country-and-western band performs. There are tree stump and cowhide barstools, suspended corncobs, longhorn steer skulls modified as light fixtures, and plenty of ol' fashioned friendliness. The menu's all in Thai but the gregarious waiters will follow you around while you point out your desired main course.

TOPLAND COFFEESHOP, 5th Floor, Topland Department Store. Tel. 252555.

Cuisine: INTERNATIONAL. **Directions:** Boromtrilokanart and Naresuan Rds.

$ Prices: Main courses 25B–95B ($1–$3.80). No credit cards.

Open: Daily 10am–midnight.

This place is terrific for kids—it's a huge, inexpensive department store with a wacky playground filled with rides and kids' games (fifth floor). On the fourth floor, next to the Bowling Alley, is a great coffee shop with an extensive menu of Chinese, Thai, European, and sukiyaki dishes. The active soda fountain offers dozens of desserts and floats; the general menu offers Fried Flora Army, Steamed Gannet Leg, and 18 Crown! The daylight skyline views are dimmed at night by the sequined pop singers who come out to entertain the crowd. Great place.

THE NIGHT MARKET

Pakbung Loy Fah is one of many large food stalls on the riverfront, but one of the few with a truck parked out front, especially a truck that says on its side: "The First in The World Flying Morning Glory." Okay, stay with us now . . . 1) A customer orders fried morning glory greens. 2) The chef puts them into a wok, and with a great show of pyrotechnics, quickly fries them. 3) The chef tosses them about 15 feet into the air to flip them, and turns his back to the stove. 4) A waiter grabs a platter, runs up the rolling stairs to the roof of his parked truck, and waits. 5) Suddenly the chef does a backhand toss, throwing the greens 15 meters over his head, and with a great leap, the waiter catches them! How can you resist an order! Fried morning glory is delicious and crisp, well worth the 30B ($1.20) price plus the 25B ($1) "show charge" the waiter will request.

The general sanitation here leaves a lot to be desired. It's a fun place to stroll, though, and freshly cooked food is cheap and edible. Don't be fooled by the Pak Bung Hern Faa a few stalls away. These upstarts have a taller truck, but we saw their chef/pitcher and waiter/catcher dump a plate of morning glory greens on a customer's head.

EVENING ENTERTAINMENT

Phitsanulok is a late-night town, with the usual set of Thai evening diversions, including discos, bars, nightclubs and a rather forlorn Night Market. Of the hotel discos, **Studio 54** at the Pailyn Hotel, **D. J. Music Hall** at the Amarintr Nakorn, and **Carina** at the Nanchao Hotel are the most popular. There's a one-drink minimum.

You can also take a samlor (bicycle rickshaw) tour of the town (see "What to See & Do," above). Samlor drivers wait outside the Pailyn and Amarintr Nakorn to make a deal.

---

2. SUKHOTHAI & SI SATCHANALAI

Sukhothai: 427km (265 miles) N of Bangkok; 58km (36 miles)
E of Phitsanulok. Si Satchanalai: 56km (35 miles) N of Sukhothai

GETTING THERE   By Plane   Phitsanulok has the nearest airport.

By Train   Phitsanulok has the nearest railroad station.

By Bus   Ten air-conditioned buses leave daily from Bangkok (trip time: 6 hours; 153B [$6.10]), departing from the **Northern Bus Terminal** (tel. 02/279-4484 or 278-2063).

By Local Bus   Hourly shuttle buses leave from Phitsanulok (trip time: 30 minutes; 20B [80¢]).

By Car   Take Singhawat Road east from Phitsanulok, then Highway 12.

ESSENTIALS   Orientation   Sukhothai Historical Park (or Muang Kao, Old City) is located 12km (7.5 miles) east of new Sukhothai. The modern town offers a few good hotels and useful services; it's built along the banks of the **Yom River** and is best traversed by tuk-tuk or samlor. Historic **Si Satchanalai** is built on the Yom 56km (35 miles) north of new Sukhothai, 17km (10.5 miles) south of Sawankhalok, the closest modern town to the historic site.

Information   Sukhothai has no TAT office; the closest one is in Phitsanulok (tel. 055/252742). Vaguely informative Tourist Information booths are located in the Sukhothai Historical Park.

Fast Facts   The region's **area code** is 055. There's **currency exchange** in the hotels or at **Bangkok Bank** during normal business hours. In a medical emergency, call the **Provincial Hospital** (tel. 611782 or 622701), on Jarod Vithithong Road.

SPECIAL EVENTS   Loi Krathong is a visually delightful, 3-day festival held on the full moon of the 12th lunar month (usually October/November) in honor of the water spirits. Around the country, crowds meet at ponds, klongs, rivers, and temple fountains to float small banana-leaf boats bearing candles, incense, a flower, and a coin. This is done as an offering and to wash away the previous year's sins. Since this festival dates from the Sukhothai era, celebrations (including a parade, fireworks, beauty pageant) are widespread throughout the province.

The emergence of Sukhothai (Dawn of Happiness) in 1238 as an independent political state signified not only the birth of a unified kingdom, but also of Thailand itself. It was here that Phor Khun Bangk Klang Hao became the first Thai monarch, as King Sri Indrathit, in what would become the country's most influential religious and cultural center. Today Sukhothai is a world-renowned historical site; it is to Thailand, what Borobudur is to Indonesia, or Angkor Wat is to Cambodia.

Si Satchanalai is another richly endowed legacy of the Sukhothai Kingdom, a city thought to have been built around the same time. The ancient city isn't in a fine state of repair; nevertheless, it is absolutely worth a detour.

If you're traveling from Phitsanulok, the drive takes you across wide plains where there are rice paddies, cotton fields, and mango-and-lemon groves. Though some peasants have purchased tractors (which locals call the "iron buffalo"), most still use traditional methods, water buffalo and manual plow.

The two main sites are the Sukhothai Historical Park and the Si Satchanalai Historical Park. In addition, there are numerous chedis and wats in the area, particularly in the hills around ancient Sukhothai; however, many guides will not take you because of their unpaved, sometimes treacherous, off-road locations.

SUKHOTHAI

In 1978 UNESCO named Sukhothai a target for preservation of world culture and heritage, along with Venice, Borobudur, Mohenjo-Daro, Carthage, and Nubia. In 1988, the Thai government, international and regional archeologists, and art historians completed the preservation of these magnificent monuments and an excellent museum in one large park.

HISTORICAL BACKGROUND Until the mid-13th century Sukhothai was a Khmer outpost, largely uninhabited by ethnic Thais. Fearful of military encroachment on their territory, two powerful Thai princes banded together to defeat the Khmer army. They then discouraged the Mongol Kublai Khan from attacking from Burma by founding the Kingdom of Sukhothai. During the next two centuries it expanded to Burma in the northwest, Cambodia in the east, and present-day Malaysia in the south. Since the 15th century, Thailand has never relinquished that land to a foreign power.

The Sukhothai Kingdom provided the foundations of Thai culture. The Buddhist religion was adapted from Sri Lanka, and to a lesser extent, Burma and India; Hinduism came from India; ancestor worship originated in China. The administrative system is thought to have derived from the Mongols. Social customs and the arts were strongly influenced by the Khmer (the written language, for example, was adapted from Khmer). Combined, these elements became distinctly Thai, and inspired new forms of religious temples, monuments, sculpture, and decoration.

Under King Ram Khamhaeng (Rama the Strong), the kingdom became a diplomatic and trading center, growing to 300,000 inhabitants within its 45-square-mile area. It was also a center of Buddhism, rivaled only by Nakhon Si Thammarat in the south; the Sukhothai Buddha is perhaps the best known of the era's artistic achievements. The walking figure, graceful in movement yet impassive in expression, is characteristic of the driving force of Buddhist Sukhothai faith. Seated Sukhothai Buddhas reflected the Enlightened One's victory over illusion, and are utterly transcendent, powerful images that no doubt created strong impressions on the animist hill tribes who were being absorbed into the kingdom.

Sukhothai's architecture incorporated both Khmer-style structures and Burmese-inspired Lanna Thai chedis and viharns. New evidence suggests that celadon (jade-green pottery) or Sawankholok ware, once though to have originated in China, was developed at Si Satchanalai, and is a purely Thai craft.

Eight monarchs of the Phra Ruang dynasty ruled Sukhothai, yet the kingdom began to wane as early as 1365 when it was overshadowed by the growing power of the Siam Kingdom at Ayutthaya. Within 50 years Sukhothai was another vassal state, its golden era exhausted. By the 18th century, the Ayutthaya rulers, who had maintained Sukhothai's most important monuments, moved south to establish their new capital at Bangkok. The once-glorious Sukhothai was abandoned to cultivation and grazing. A new commercial center was established, and the fate of the ancient capital was sealed for almost 200 years.

TOURING THE SITE You can reach Sukhothai and Si Satchanalai by taxi, private car, or bus (see "Getting There," above). Sukhothai offers several sightseeing options; early morning and evening bring fewer buses and groups; the site seems more serene and cooler. The historical park is open daily 6am to 6:30pm; admission is 25B ($1), free after 4:30pm. Don't forget comfortable shoes, a sun hat, and bottled water.

By Foot   Count on spending three to six hours visiting sites in and outside of the park. Start by exploring the museum, then buy a guidebook and map (the temples are well labeled). It's pleasant walking, with many soda and snack stalls en route.

By Tuk-tuk   Motorized trishaws can be hired in new Sukhothai for a round-trip to the park and a 3-hour tour. They seat two, are noisy but fun, and cost about 180B ($7.40) per person.

By Bicycle   These cost 25B ($1) per day. If you take the bus from town, be sure to bypass the stalls of inferior bicycles where the driver will try to deposit you. Wait and rent your bike from the food stalls on the main Sukhothai cross street, across from the museum entrance.

By Tram   Several beige trams wait in front of the museum to take visitors around. They circle the major sites (25B [$1]) in about a half hour, returning you to the museum entrance.

By Car   Most car and driver tours originate in Phitsanulok (see "Getting Around" in Phitsanulok for more information).

By Guided Tour   Sky Tour at 28-30 Prasertpong Rd. in Sukhothai (tel. 055/ 612237) is one company which offers guided private or group tours. A half-day trip costs 400B ($16) per person; a full-day trip including Sukhothai and Si Satchanalai costs 650B ($26) per person, with a two-person minimum.

SUKHOTHAI'S HIGHLIGHTS

A network of walls and moats defines the perfect rectangle that is the central city. (It is thought that the original moat connected Sukhothai with Si Satchanalai.) The Phitsanulok-Sukhothai highway runs right through the east or Kam Phang Hak Gate to the museum, a good beginning.

Ramkamhaeng National Museum

The museum houses a detailed model of the area, and an admirable display of Sukhothai and Si Satchanalai archeological finds largely culled from the private collection of the abbot of Wat Ratchathani. It is located in the center of the old city, opposite the historic park's pedestrian gate. Before exploring the site, stop here for maps and guidebooks. It's open Wednesday to Sunday 9am to noon and 1 to 4pm; admission is 10B (40¢). Closed on national holidays.

Wat Mahatat

Begin your exploration of the ancient city at the central area (five minutes' walk west of the museum). Wat Mahatat, part of the royal compound, is the most extraordinary monument in the park, a multichedi edifice that is dominated by a 14th-century lotus-bud tower and encircled by a moat. Surrounding its unique Sukhothai-style chedi are several smaller towers of Sri Lankan and Khmer influence and a grouping of Buddhist disciples in the adoration pose. An imposing cast-bronze seated Buddha used to be placed in front of the reliquary (this image, Phra Si Sakaya Muni, was removed in the 18th century to Bangkok's Wat Suthat). The viharn that housed this figure was built in 1362 by King Lithai. The small viharn to the south contains a fine Ayutthaya-era Buddha. Be sure to examine the large chedi: the lowest platform (south side of Wat Mahatat) and its excellent stucco sculpture, the crypt murals, and two elegant Sri Lankan–style stupas (equivalent to Thai chedi) at the southeast corner of the site. Some of the best architectural ornamentation to Sukhothai is found on the upper, eastern-facing levels of the niche pediments in the main reliquary tower. Dancing figures, Queen Maya giving birth to Prince Siddharta, and scenes from the life of Buddha are among the best-preserved details.

The Royal Palace

Between the museum and Wat Mahatat are the remains of the Royal Palace. Although this once-grand complex contained the throne and stone inscription of King

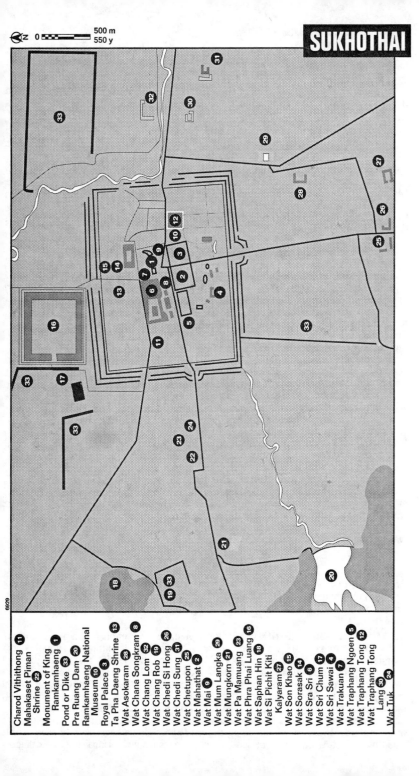

SUKHOTHAI

0   500 m
     550 y

Charod Vithithong 11
Mahakaset Piman
Shrine 22
Monument of King
Ramkamhaeng 1
Pond or Dike 33
Pra Ruang Dam 20
Ramkamhaeng National
Museum 10
Royal Palace 3
Ta Pha Daeng Shrine 13
Wat Asokaram 28
Wat Chana Songkram 8
Wat Chang Lom 32
Wat Chang Rob 19
Wat Chedi Si Hong 26
Wat Chedi Sung 31
Wat Chetupon 25
Wat Mahathat 2
Wat Mai 9
Wat Mum Langka 29
Wat Mungkorn 21
Wat Pa Mamuang 23
Wat Phra Phai Luang 16
Wat Saphan Hin 18
Wat Si Pichit Kiti
Kalyaram 27
Wat Son Khao 15
Wat Sorasak 14
Wat Sra Sri 6
Wat Sri Chum 17
Wat Sri Sawai 4
Wat Trakuan 7
Wat Traphang Ngoen 5
Wat Traphang Tong 12
Wat Traphang Tong
Lang 30
Wat Tuk 24

6929

Ram Kamhaeng (there is a copy in the Ramkamhaeng Museum; the original is in the National Museum in Bangkok), today it is a shambles.

Wat Sri Sawai

Southwest of the palace you'll come to the 12th-century Wat Sri Sawai, a Hindu shrine later converted to a Buddhist temple. The architecture is distinctly Khmer, with three Lopburi-style prangs commanding center stage. The viharns around the central prangs (cactus-shaped towers) are of more traditional Sukhothai design.

Other Monuments in the Park

Circling north, just west of Wat Mahatat, is **Wat Traphang Ngoen,** set in its own pond. Though little remains other than an attractive chedi, the vistas of the surrounding monuments are among the most superb in the park. North past Wat Mahatat, is **Wat Chana Songkram,** where there is a Sri Lankan–style stupa of note. Nearby is **Wat Sra Si,** with a Sri Lankan chedi and viharn set on a small island in Traphang Takuan pond. Take a moment to examine the stucco Buddha in the fore viharn.

SITES OUTSIDE THE HISTORICAL PARK

The remainder of monuments worth seeing are outside the historic central park, most to the north. You'll need to purchase another 25B ($1) ticket; the sites are open 8am to 4:30pm.

If you leave the park at the northern San Luang Gate and continue about 500 feet, you'll arrive at **Wat Phra Phai Luang,** similar to Wat Sri Sawai because of its three prangs. However, only the north tower still shows off its exquisite stucco decoration. This monument, originally a Hindu shrine, was once graced with a lingam, a phallic sculpture placed in Shiva temples. Conversion to a Buddhist sanctuary is evidenced by the mondop, a square building containing a Buddha image illustrating the four postures: sitting, standing, reclining, and walking.

One of the more astonishing and beautiful monuments in Sukhothai is found at **Wat Si Chum,** where there is a majestic 50-foot-tall seated Buddha, in the *mudra* (pose) of Subduing Mara (evil). When the narrow passageway to the top was open you could admire the 700-year-old slate reliefs within. Don't let fatigue deter you from seeing this celebrated image, still actively worshipped, but keep a hand on your bag. These isolated roads are one of the only places in northern Thailand where we've heard of purses being snatched.

About 550 yards away from Si Chum are the womblike brick remains of the Thuriang Kiln, where Sawankhalok ware was once produced. A few kilometers west, atop a 660-foot hill and visible from afar, is **Wat Saphan Hin.** It's well worth the steep, 5-minute climb to study the towering Phra Attaros Buddha, a 41-foot-tall figure, his right hand raised in the Dispelling Fear mudra, which towers above the wat's laterite remains.

SI SATCHANALAI

Ancient Si Satchanalai developed between the Yom River and the Khao Phra Si Valley, on more than 800 acres of land. The 228 acres contained within the old laterite ramparts and moats of the city wall are the focus of sightseeing in the historical park.

HISTORICAL BACKGROUND   Although a stone inscription found at Sukhothai refers to Si Satchanalai as a protectorate of King Ram Khamhaeng (possibly its founder), most historians believe that Rama I expanded a city that was built by Khmer settlers, and which was well established by the 13th century, or even earlier. During the Ayutthaya period the town was named Sawankhalok (now the nearest modern town) because of the area's highly prized product, it's famous celadon or ceramic Sawankhalok ware, which was exported throughout Asia. Si Satchanalai's riverside site was crucial to the development of the ceramics industry; there were literally over a thousand kilns operating along the river. These kilns have recently been excavated by a Thai-Australian team, led by archeologists from the University of Adelaide.

Their findings contradict the prevailing view that Chinese traders brought the method of producing celadon to Sukhothai in the 13th century. Instead they hypothesize that ceramic manufacture began over 1,000 years ago at Ban Ko Noi (there's a small site museum 6km [3.7 miles] north of Satchanalai), proving that it's an indigenous Thai art form. Don't miss the Sawanwaranoyok Museum's collection.

TOURING THE SITE Taking Route 101 north from Sukhothai through sugarcane and tobacco fields, one must cross the Yom River to enter the historical park's central city. The remains of the 22 monuments inside the old city rank well below those of Sukhothai in importance, yet the crumbling grandeur of the buildings and the relative isolation of the site add to its allure.

A taxi, private car, or guided tour are the best ways to see the spread-out sites of Si Satchanalai (see "Touring the Site" in Sukhothai, for more information). However, public buses to **Si Satchanalai** and **Sawankhalok** (25B [$1]) depart from the Sukhothai Hotel's bus stop every half hour, 6am to 6pm. From the park's pedestrian gate, you can tour the park on foot (one to two hours), or hire a bicycle (rented at the gate for 25B [$1] per day) and see monuments outside the walls as well. The historical park is open daily 8am to 5pm; admission is 25B ($1).

SI SATCHANALAI'S HIGHLIGHTS

The first two monuments that you'll encounter are the largest and most impressive in the city.

Wat Chang Lom This compound, to the right of the entrance, is distinctly Sri Lankan, with a characteristic stupa and 39 laterite elephant buttresses (it's unusual in Thailand to find so many elephant sculptures still intact). If you ascend the stairs, you can walk around the base of the stupas and admire the 19 Buddhas that are installed in niches above the terrace. The discovery of the Buddha's relics at the site during the reign of King Ram Khamhaeng prompted the construction of this temple, an event described in stone inscriptions found at Sukhothai. Enterprising locals have organized an elephant ride around the park (three passengers fit in the howdah, one rides the neck, and the mahout sits on the head). It costs 50B to 100B ($2 to $4) per person, depending on whether you choose a half-hour or hour-long trip.

Wat Chedi Chet Thaew Opposite it to the south, within sandstone walls, is Wat Chedi Chet Thaew. Like Wat Mahatat at Sukhothai, this wat is distinguished by a series of lotus-bud towers and rows of chedis thought to contain the remains of the royal family. The chedis are adorned with 33 Buddha images and other stucco decorative images, and some have traces of color.

OTHER MONUMENTS IN THE PARK

The balance of monuments within the ancient city walls can be inspected within an hour. **Wat Nan Phaya,** southeast of Chedi Chet Thaew, is known for the stucco bas-reliefs on the remains of a seven-room viharn. It is easily spotted by their tin-roof shelter. Nothing compares to **Wat Phra Si Rattana Mahatat,** located 1km (⁶/₁₀ mile) southeast of the bridge. The most prominent feature of this 13th-century temple is the Khmer-style prang, thought to date from the renovation of the original Sukhothai design made under the rule of the Ayutthaya king Borommakot in the 18th century. The exterior carving and sculpture are superb, in particular a walking Buddha done in relief. Some of the more delicate fragments of the wat, including very rare wooden doors, have been removed to the museum in Sukhothai.

OUTSIDE THE HISTORICAL PARK

Private transport will enable you to wander at will around the hundreds of archeological sites and kilns that dot the landscape; make sure to pick up the free brochure and site map given out at the park gate. **Wat Khao Phanom Ploeng,** a nearby hill topped by two wat compounds, offers an excellent vantage of the historic city from the top of its steep 112-step staircase.

Sawanwaranayok National Museum, Tambon Muang, Sawankhalok, a newly built museum, houses the superb collection of Sawankhalok pottery belonging to the late abbot of nearby Wat Sawankharam. Most of the ceramics (including, white, brown, underglaze black, and celadon pieces) are on the ground floor, but don't miss the sculpture upstairs. It's open Wednesday to Sunday 9am to noon and 1 to 4pm; admission is 10B (40¢). It's 3km (1.8 miles) beyond the historical park turnoff.

SHOPPING

The **Boonchew Antique Shop** in the Sukhothai Cultural Center, 2km (1.2 miles) east of the historical park at 214 Jarod Vithithong Rd. (tel. 612275), is the best shop for Sawankhalok ceramics and religious figures, some reputed to date from the 14th to 17th centuries. Prices reflect quality and presumed age: a celadon pedestal bowl cost 35,000B ($1,400); damaged but large, glazed ceramic temple tiles cost 15,000B ($600). Prices are somewhat better than in Bangkok, but the large selection is generally of lesser quality. Mr. Boonchew issues certificates of authenticity, but, of course, the risk is yours. (we never found any expert in Thailand who would authenticate items other than their own.)

On the village roads surrounding the Si Satchanalai Historial Park many women have set up bamboo tables filled with ceramic shards, "old" and new Buddhas, and other souvenirs. We figured some of these pottery shards might be old because farmers are constantly turning up pieces in their fields. Anything of real value would be sent to Bangkok immediately for sale, but bargain hunters will enjoy rummaging around.

WHERE TO STAY

PAILYN SUKHOTHAI HOTEL, 10 Moo 1, Jarod Vithithong Rd., Sukhothai 64210. Tel. 055/613310 or in Bangkok 2157110. Fax 055/613317 or in Bangkok 2155640. 238 rms. A/C TEL **Directions:** 4km (2.4 miles) east of historical park, 8km (4.8 miles) from the town center.
$ Rates: 800B–1,200B ($32–$48) single; 900B–1,400B ($32–$56) double; suites from 2,000B ($80). MC V.
This recently completed roadside resort is bright, modern, and the most luxurious Sukhothai has to offer. Beyond the rattan and granite lobby, an elevator leads to comfortable, carpeted rooms (4 story) built in a sextagonal wing encircling a small pool and sun deck. Rates vary according to room size and amenities; higher rates bring minibars and TVs. The suites are enormous but their bathrooms are surprisingly small. We preferred casual poolside dining to the more formal Thai/Chinese and continental restaurant, where burgers and ice cream are served.

NORTHERN PALACE HOTEL, 43 Singhawat Rd., Sukhothai 64000. Tel. 055/611193. Fax 055/612038. 67 rms. A/C MINIBAR TV TEL **Directions:** Center of town, around corner from bus stop.
$ Rates (including tax and service): 600B ($24) single; 650B ($26) double; 1,500B ($72) suite. MC. V.
This is a teriffic, recently renovated choice. Most of the street frontage is taken up by the 24-hour coffee shop (which becomes a nightclub with songbirds after dark), a popular venue for ice cream and snacks. The granite and chrome lobby is perky and small; rooms are plain, spotless, comfortable, and have small showers. With these amenities plus a small pool and airport minivan shuttle (100B [$4] to Phitsanulok) it's a good deal.

RAJTHANEE, 229 Jarod Vithithong., Sukhothai 64000. Tel. 055/611031. 62 rms. A/C TV TEL **Directions:** On west side of Yom River, 1km (6/10 mile) northwest of bus station.
$ Rates (including tax and service): 470B–780B ($18.80–$31.20) single/double. MC, V.
This acceptable new city lodging has guest rooms which are relatively clean; more expensive rooms have carpeting, a balcony, and TV, but even the cheapest rooms

are adequate. There's a Thai coffee shop and a fancier, second floor Krua Thai restaurant.

BAN THAI, 38 Pravet Nakhon Rd., Sukhothati 64000. Tel. 055/610163. 8 rms, 7 bungalows. **Directions:** On the west side of Yom River, 1km (⁶/₁₀ mile) northwest of bus station, 300 meters south of bridge.

$ Rates (including tax and service): Bungalows 120B ($4.80) single/double; rooms 60B– 80B ($2.40–$3.20) single/double. No credit cards.

This is our favorite budget choice in Sukhothai proper, partly because it's the only one with hot water (shower to share). It's conveniently located, scrupulously clean, and has a small, lushly planted garden with a Thai-style open pavilion where travelers of all ages sit around and swap stories. The A-frame teak bungalows with private toilets and cold-water baths are the best deal. But the rooms in the one-story modern house are nicely papered with coconut matting and have a few touches of Thai style.

THAI VILLAGE HOUSES, 214 Jarod Vithithong Rd., Muang Khao, Sukhothai 64000. Tel. 055/611049 or 612275. Fax 055/612583. 120 rms. A/C TEL **Directions:** 2km (1.2 miles) east of Sukhothai Historical Park.

$ Rates (including tax and service): 350B–500B ($14–$20) single/double; Suite 700B ($28). MC, V.

We applaud the old-style Thai Village Houses, set in gardens at the Sukhothai Cultural Center (a kind of minimall with souvenirs, handicrafts, and an "antiques" shop). The quarters are semiattached teak bungalows, attractive from the outside, clean and simple inside. Larger "suites" have a minibar and quaint charm. The Nam Khang garden restaurant is locally known for serving *hommok pao*, a curried fish soufflé made according to the traditional Sukhothai recipe. If you've come only for old Sukhothai and don't care to explore the new town, this is a great budget choice.

WHERE TO DINE

DONGTARN, Sukhothai Historical Park, Muang Khao. No phone.
   Cuisine: THAI. **Directions:** Across from Ramhamhaeng Museum.
$ Prices: Main courses 40B–100B ($1.60–$4). No credit cards.
   Open: Daily 10am–6pm.

This open-air café is located by the cool, tree-shaded entrance to the historical park. Thai and Chinese cuisine are served, as well as some continental dishes. It's a very convenient choice.

DREAM CAFE, 86/1 Singhawat Rd., Sukhothai. Tel. 612081
   Cuisine: INTERNATIONAL. **Directions:** Center of new city.
$ Prices: Appetizers 26B–80B ($1.40–$3.20); main courses 30B–95B ($1.20–$3.80). No credit cards.
   Open: Daily 10am–midnight.

We particularly like the Dream Café, the creation of Ms. Chaba Suwantmaykin, for its cozy teak and stucco decor, including an eclectic collection of ceramics, copper ware, memorabilia, glass, textiles, and old jewelry. Besides the huge menu of Thai dishes, including many of the Chaba family recipes, Dream also serves excellent European and Chinese dishes, good burgers, beer, and ice-cream sundaes. A small annex has opened across from Win Tours, right near the Night Market.

KHAN SAK RESTAURANT, Si Satchanalai Rd. No phone.
   Cuisine: THAI/CHINESE/CONTINENTAL. **Directions:** 1.2km (¾ mile) before entrance to Si Satchanalai Historical Park.
$ Prices: Appetizers 30B–50B ($1.20–$2); main courses 35B–180B ($1.40–$7.20). No credit cards.
   Open: Daily 9am–6pm.

This tree-shaded, wooden house near the banks of the Yom River and the archeological headquarters serves fairly good food in an attractive setting. The Wang Yom is a handicrafts center with a café attached, also on the park road. Both places seem designed to feed large groups. Thai snacks and sodas are sold in the park.

3. TAK & MAE SOT: THE MYANMAR BORDER

Tak: 426km (265 miles) NW of Bangkok;
138km (86 miles) W of Phitsanulok Mae Sot: 80km (50 miles) W of Tak

GETTING THERE By Plane Four flights a week depart to Tak (trip time: 35 minutes; 350B [$14]) and Mae Sot (trip time: 80 minutes; 550b [$22]) from Phitsanulok.

By Bus Eight buses leave daily from Bangkok (trip time 7 hours; 190B [$7.60]), from the **Northern Bus Terminal** (tel. 279-4484). Twelve buses daily from Phitsanulok to Tak (trip time: 3 hours; 30B [$1.20]). Five buses leave daily to Mae Sot (trip time: 5 hours; 50B [$2]). Local song tao (truck taxis) ply the Tak–Mae Sot road frequently

By Car Take Highway 1 north from Bangkok to Tak. From Phitsanulok, take Route 12 west to Tak, then Route 105 west to Mae Sot.

ESSENTIALS Orientation The city of Tak, built east of the pretty Mae Ping River, has a small central core between the riverside promenade and the busy Paholythin Highway, site of the town's picturesque lagoon. The bus station is on Mahadthai Bamroong Road; a few good hotels and useful services are nearby. The airport is 4km (2.4 miles) from town, best reached by the Thai Airways (tel. 512164) shuttle bus.

The tiny town of Mae Sot is built up around the Moei River, an ineffective border with Myanmar. The tiny airport is 2km (1.2 miles) east of town; contact Thai Airways (tel. 531730) for information.

Information Tak is scheduled to have a TAT office in late 1994; the closest one now is in Phitsanulok (tel. 055/252742). The region's **area code** is 055. There's **currency exchange** in the hotels or at banks during normal business hours.

SPECIAL EVENTS Every January, around the New Year, a **provincial festival** is held in Tak to honor King Taksin the Great. The streets around his shrine (on Taksin Road at the north side of town) fill with clothes, produce and food vendors, and stalls piled high with Thai sweets and cakes. Dancers, musicians, and monks come out to celebrate. The shrine is showered with floral wreaths and decked out in gold fabric to impress the Thais who come from afar to pay their respects.

Most travelers will never reach Tak Province, unless they're passing through on a Bangkok–Chiang Mai overland trip, or an east-west journey on the Asia Highway between Thailand's Northeast and Mae Sot at the Myanmar border. Tak is known to Thais for two attributes: the Bhumipol Dam, the country's largest, and for having the hottest weather in Thailand. In contrast, Mae Sot, in the nearby forested hills, is popular with vacationing Thais for its cool weather. The capital, Amphur Muang or Tak, is worth a stopover if you're traveling during the Taksin Festival (see above), when the King Taksin Shrine in the city center is showered with more than the usual incense, candles, and flower offerings.

WHAT TO SEE & DO

Other than the vigorous trading that goes on with Myanmar at the tiny border town of Mae Sot, there's not much to see in Tak. One spot we liked very much on the Asia Highway, 25km (15 miles) east of Tak, is the **Taksin Maharat (Krabak Yai) National Park,** known for having Thailand's largest tree. Once you've entered the park, the partially paved road goes uphill through forested terrain for a few kilometers, till it dead-ends in a large stand of bamboo. From here, it's a fun and rigorous 20-minute descent to a stream overshadowed by a huge Krabak tree. At our visit, this holy tree was draped in about 50 feet of greenish-gold winter clothes, and we guessed it would take 16 long-armed people to encircle it. Not a side trip for the disabled, or for those who've visited the redwoods in the American Sequoia National Park, but nonetheless a neat place.

MAE SOT

Although Mae Sot's border at Rim Moei is no closer to Myanmar than the northern towns of Mae Hong Son or Mae Sai, the recent (1990) establishment of Democratic Burma's government-in-exile nearby had created added tension and intrigue during our visit. We normally like border towns and their lively markets. However, there was something unusual in the Mercedes-Benz and two-story brick homes lining the village's main street.

We soon discovered the legal and illegal trade (particularly in Burmese jade bought by Hong Kong and Taiwanese dealers) is not to be believed! A border closing ordered by the Myanmar government in retaliation for the terrorist deaths of 33 Burmese citizens a few years ago was very short-lived because of the tremendous loss of income to this region. The *Bangkok Post* estimated that the first week cost merchants 150 million baht ($6 million)!

Despite the volume of hanky-panky, most visitors will only see bags of Thai-produced dried shrimp, cuttlefish, black fungus, soybean, and chickpea snacks traded for Burmese woven cotton blankets, lacquer-ware items, ruby jewelry (gems from Burma with Thai workmanship), newly made bronze Buddhas, cotton sarongs, and wicker ware. Goods can be paid for in Burmese kyat and Thai baht.

The border between Rim Moei (Mae Sot) and the easily seem Myawaddy, Myanmar, is open daily 8am to 5:30pm to citizens of Thailand and Myanmar only. A long-tail boat is used like a raft to float customers over the narrow Moei River for 5B (20¢). Although most of the traffic is heavily laden Burmese, Thais go over to shop for cheap, subsidized products in some of the shop houses.

WHERE TO STAY & DINE

If you're forced to spend the night, here are some ideas.

VIANG TAK HOTEL, 25/3 Mahadthai Bamroong Rd., Tak 63000. Tel. 055/ 511910. Fax 055/512169. 100 rms. A/C TEL **Directions:** 1 block south of bus station.

$ Rates (including tax and service): 450B–575B ($18–$23) single; 550B–700B ($22–$28) double. AE, DC, MC, V.

This is a surprisingly plush hotel for these prices, with an extremely helpful, polite staff. Large rooms are comfortable and spotless; higher-priced, "deluxe" ones boast a TV and minibar. The lobby bar has a pianist; the Romanee Night Club has nightly singers; and the excellent coffee shop, open 6am to midnight, is one of the town's hot spots. Its low-budget brother, the Viang Tak II (185 rooms) on the Mae Ping River at Jomphol Road (tel. 055/512507), has a simple, cold shower and fan rooms with no view for 180B ($7.20) single or double; larger, balconied ones overlooking the river, with air-conditioning and hot water cost 550B ($22).

MAE SOT HILLS HOTEL, 100 Asia Hwy., Mae Sot, Tak 63110. Tel. 055/ 532601. Telex 48214 MS HILL TH. 114 rms. A/C MINIBAR TV TEL **Directions:** 17km (10 miles) west of border.

$ Rates: 1,177B ($47) single; 1,530B ($61.20) double; suite from 2,590B ($103.60). MC, V.

This contemporary four-story hotel is built in two long wings fanning out from a glitzy atrium lobby. All comfortable rooms have modern amenities (suites also have work desks and a bar alcove) and nice views over the mist-shrouded, wooded hills. There's a popular coffee shop and supper club/disco. The Mae Sot also lures group tours, which favor its pool and tennis courts.

CHAPTER 10

EXPLORING THE NORTHEAST: THAILAND'S FRONTIER

The Northeast of Thailand, called Isan (*Ee*-saan) in Thai, accounts for roughly one-third of the country's land mass, yet until recently, only a few intrepid visitors, many of whom were aid workers in refugee and displaced-persons camps, made their way into the area. Bordered by Laos to the north and east (along the famed Mae Khong) and by Cambodia to the south, the region has long suffered political, military, and ethnic upheavals, stemming largely from the Vietnam War, and most recently from the ongoing civil war in Cambodia. The border skirmishes continue and refugees still inhabit camps and villages, but there is a growing sense that the politics in this part of Indochina are moving toward a more peaceful resolution; as they do, more and more tourists will visit what is arguably one of Thailand's final and most fascinating frontiers.

A trip to the Northeast is particularly recommended for those who have visited Thailand's better-known destinations, such as Chiang Mai, Mae Hong Son, or Chiang Rai, and who are looking for an adventure. The hotels are less luxurious and you might get lucky and find a menu in English, but what you'll discover are exciting archeological sites (mostly dating from the Khmer period), lovely river towns, finely made crafts, and fiery hot food: all this and few foreign visitors, inexpensive accommodations, surprisingly good roads, and friendly people. It's not surprising that the Northeast has become our favorite region in Thailand.

Much of the Northeast, particularly in the south, is a wide, infertile plain that is reminiscent of parts of Oklahoma and Texas. To the far east, as you approach the confluence of the Mae Khong and Moon rivers, the semifertile grasslands give way to arid, charred sandstone plateaus. The land has a primeval quality, as if an ocean had receded millions of years ago, leaving water-scarred ruts and ripples in the rock. (It's not surprising that paleontologists have found fossils and other evidence of prehistoric life.)

The northern and western sections of Isan are more fertile and mountainous (particularly around Loei), connecting that area with northern Thailand more than the Isan plains. Farms are organized on a much larger scale and the local economy is considerably richer than in the Southeast.

Although there are many new small-scale industrial enterprises cropping up in Isan, the economy of the area is primarily dependent on subsistence farming. After the crops are planted or harvested, many villagers produce handmade crafts,

WHAT'S SPECIAL ABOUT THE NORTHEAST

Events/Festivals

The Surin (November) and Chaiyaphum (January) Elephant Roundups are a regional highlight and fun for kids.

The longboat races on the Mae Khong during October in Nakhon Phanom.

In Phimai, during late October or early November, Lopburi-period stage performances and a play depicting scenes from the *Ramayana* are presented at the Sanctuary. The festival also includes boat racing, historical and cultural exhibitions, and a costume parade.

Archeology

Prasat Hin Phimai and Phanom Rung are the preeminent Khmer ruins outside of Angkor Wat in Cambodia. 4,000-year-old paintings at Pha Taem are fine neolithic works that cover cliffs overlooking the Mae Khong and Laos.

Museums

Ban Chiang has a magnificent exhibit of Bronze Age artifacts.

People

The Northeast is a refuge for people from Laos and Cambodians escaping the civil war; many reside in refugee and displaced-persons camps along the border areas near Pak Chom, Napho, Surin, and Buriram.

Religious Shrines

Nakhon Phanom has one of Thailand's most sacred Buddhist shrines, Phra That Phanom.

Shopping

Nong Khai's proximity to Laos makes it an important market for that country's finely crafted silver. Udon Thani is a center for some of the country's best basketmaking. Khon Kaen, Chaiyaphum, and Surin are centers for the production of handwoven silk.

Parks & Scenery

Long-tail boat rides up Mae Khong Valley from Chiang Khan. Khao Yai and Phu Kradung National Park and Phu Luang Wildlife Reserve.

especially silk and cotton, woven in the traditional mutmee or ikat pattern. High-quality silver work, ceramics, and basketry are also produced in Isan. The major growth anticipated in the Northeast is projected to come from the expansion of tourism in the next five years, especially if the borders with Cambodia and Laos become less restricted.

The weather in the Northeast is like the rest of Thailand. The cool season runs from November through February and is similar to summer in Southern California, with very warm days and cool nights. March to May is the dry season, which in the Northeast is considerably drier than in other sections of the country. The rains begin in earnest in June and there's nary a letup until October.

GETTING THERE

BY PLANE Thai Airways flies from Bangkok to Khorat, Udon Thani, Khon Kaen, Sakon Nakhon, and Ubon Ratchathani; Bangkok Airways flies to Loei. There are also flights between several of these destinations, and plans to expand the airport in Ubon to receive international flights. Flights are frequent and inexpensive, but you must make reservations as early as possible, particularly during the festival season. Thai Airways offers a special Discover Thailand program for $219 that includes four flight-segment coupons for any domestic flights within the country. Additional coupons may be purchased for $45 each and the tickets are valid for 60 days. This offer is good only if sold prior to arriving in Thailand, so you're advised to book it when making your international reservations.

BY TRAIN Express and rapid trains leave Bangkok for Khorat, Isan's transportation hub, several times a day. Sleeper cars for longer rides are available on certain trains, and should be reserved as early as possible. Purchase tickets and book sleepers at the Bangkok Hua Lampong Railroad Station (tel. 223-7010 or 223-7461) up to 90 days in advance.

BY BUS Dozens of private companies offer frequent, air-conditioned service to nearly every city in the Northeast from Bangkok; all depart from Bangkok's Northern Bus Terminal. There is also frequent service between nearly every major city in Isan and other northeastern cities, usually without a change of coach. The chart below will give you an idea of travel time:

MILEAGE CHART

City	Distance from Khorat	Hours by Bus
Bangkok	259km (161 miles)	3
Phimai	60km (37 miles)	1.5
Khon Kaen	190km (118 miles)	2.5
Udon Thani	305km (189 miles)	4
Loei	344km (213 miles)	5.5
Nong Khai	356km (221 miles)	5
Nakhon Phanom	481km (298 miles)	9
Ubon Ratchathani	370km (229 miles)	5
Surin	198km (123 miles)	3
Buriram	151km (94 miles)	2

GETTING AROUND

BY BUS There is frequent, inexpensive bus service between Khorat and other northeastern cities, although nonexpress routes or long detours—such as the Nong Khai–Nakhon Phanom route—often make these trips impossibly slow. There are also *song taos*, pickup trucks fitted with long bench seats, traveling the major routes throughout Isan. Song taos generally operate when the vehicle is filled; most short-distance runs cost 10B (40¢).

BY CAR One of the most difficult parts of travel in Isan is the lack of rental cars. There are no Hertz and Avis outlets, and most local agencies require the driver to return the car to the original rental office. In other words, rental cars are generally only available for those who can organize their travels on a round-trip basis.

We recommend renting a car with a driver, both for the driver's presumed knowledge of the area as well as the lack of proper insurance at most rental-car agencies (also, there are far fewer English-language signs both on the highway and especially in the cities). Local companies can arrange a car and driver for about 1,700B ($68) per day, depending on your destination. Most drivers will not speak English, so it's best to work out your itinerary with the agency before departing and update it at stops where someone—you hope—speaks English.

That said, the network of roads is uniformly good, largely a testament to the military requirements for an infrastructure that provides rapid access to the frontier border areas with Laos and Cambodia. As you approach these regions, don't be surprised to find military checkpoints, army bases, and elaborate radar and telecommunications centers along the roadways. All of this is very much part of life in a region that has been marked by war and guerrilla skirmishes for the past three decades.

Lastly, don't forget that Thailand operates on the British left-hand drive system.

BY BICYCLE OR MOTORCYCLE In several parts of the Northeast we recommend travel by bicycle, particularly along the Mae Khong from Chiang Khan to Si Chiang Mai and the area around Pha Taem, outside of Ubon. If you plan on using

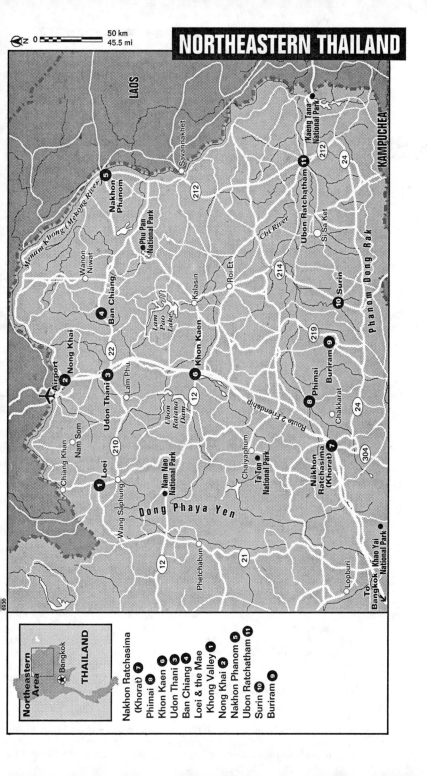

NORTHEASTERN THAILAND

0 ┅┅┅┅┅ 50 km
45.5 mi

LAOS

KAMPUCHEA

Menam Khong (Mekong River)

Savannakhiet

Nakhon Phanom **5**

Phu Pan National Park

Wanon Niwat

Ban Chiang **4**

Kalasin

Roi Et

Chi River

Kaeng Tana National Park

Ubon Ratchatham **11** (212) (24)

Si Sa Ket

Nong Khai **2**

Airport

Lam Pao Lake

Khon Kaen **6**

(214)

Surin **10**

Phanom Dong Rak

(22)

Udon Thani **3**

Lam Phu

Ubon Ratana Dam

(12)

(219)

Buriram **9**

Phimai **8**

Chakkarat

(24)

Chiang Khan

Nam Som

(210)

Loei **1**

Nam Nao National Park

Wang Saphung

Chaiyaphum

Ta Ton National Park

Route 2 Friendship

Nakhon Ratchasima (Khorat) **7**

(304)

Dong Phaya Yen

Phetchabun

(21)

Lopburi

Khao Yai National Park

(12)

To Bangkok

6930

THAILAND

★ Bangkok

Northeastern Area

Nakhon Ratchasima (Khorat) **7**
Phimai **8**
Khon Kaen **6**
Udon Thani **3**
Ban Chiang **4**
Loei & the Mae Khong Valley **1**
Nong Khai **2**
Nakhon Phanom **5**
Ubon Ratchatham **11**
Surin **10**
Buriram **9**

your bike as a means of transportation, bring your own from home (also bring spare parts and tools); however, if you intend to do short day trips or rides around town, you can rent low performance one- and three-speed bikes for about 50B ($2) a day.

Unlike the north, motorcycle rentals are fairly rare in Isan although they are beginning to crop up in the more densely touristed areas.

SUGGESTED ITINERARIES

Most tours of the Northeast divide the region into southern and northern routes, principally due to the enormous distances between cities and sights. Our suggestion is to pick only one of the two sections if you intend to travel for fewer than 10 days. The southern route is heavy on archeology while the northern itinerary features natural scenery, shopping, and some historical sites.

THE SOUTHERN ROUTE

IF YOU HAVE 3 DAYS

Day 1: Travel to Khorat and visit Phimai, Phanom Wan, and Ban Makah, returning to Khorat for an overnight; shop at the Night Market.
Day 2: Travel to Phanom Rung and Muang Tam and move on to Surin.
Day 3: Shop for silver and silk in the morning and visit the elephant village of Tha Klang in the evening, returning to Surin in the morning.

IF YOU HAVE 5 DAYS

Day 1–3: Take a plane, train, or bus to Khorat and follow the itinerary above.
Day 4: Travel to Ubon, making stops in Pha Taem, to see the cliff paintings and the organized overlooks along the Mae Khong and Moon River. (This trip can also be done in the reverse as both Ubon and Khorat have airports.)

THE NORTHERN ROUTE

IF YOU HAVE 3 DAYS

Day 1: Travel to Khorat and visit Phimai, Phanom Wan, and Ban Makah, continuing on to Khon Kaen for shopping and to Udon Thani for an overnight.
Day 2: Visit the Ban Chiang National Museum and excavation site (at presstime, they are closed Monday and Tuesday and on national holidays) and continue up to Nong Khai for an overnight.
Day 3: Shop for Laotian silver and crafts in the market and take an evening Mae Khong dinner cruise. Go back to Udon for return to Bangkok by plane.

IF YOU HAVE 5 DAYS

Day 1–3: Fly or take a train or bus to Khorat and follow the itinerary above.
Day 4: Hire a car or take the bus along the Mae Khong road to Si Chiang Mai, Pak Chom, and Kaeng Khut Khu rapids; overnight in Chiang Khang.
Day 5: Take a long-tail boat trip up the Mae Khong in the morning, returning to Chiang Khan and traveling south to Loei. Either return to Udon and on to Bangkok or transfer to Phitansulok.

COMPLETE TOURS OF THE NORTHEAST

IF YOU HAVE 10–14 DAYS

Basically the lines of this trip connect the two longer southern and northern itineraries. The trip should begin and end in Khorat and you can either head north toward Nong Khai (via Loei and the Mae Khong valley) or east toward Ubon. The connection point is

Nakhon Phanom: Either travel north from Ubon or east from Nong Khai or Udon to connect the two trips. If you have the time, plan on spending two days in Phu Kradung National Park outside of Loei and on taking a diversionary trip to Chaiyaphum.

1. NAKHON RATCHASIMA (KHORAT)

259km (160 miles) NE of Bangkok; 417km (259 miles) W of Buriram; 305km (189 miles) S of Udon Thani

GETTING THERE By Plane Eight flights per week leave from Bangkok (flying time: 45 minutes); 650B ($26) on Thai Airways.

By Train Khorat is well connected by rail to Bangkok and nearly all of the major destinations within the Northeast. Thirteen trains a day depart from Bangkok (trip time: 6 hours on ordinary train, 4 hours by express train, which is faster than flying, with trips to and from airports, air-conditioning, more comfort, and less cost; second-class ordinary 120B [$4,80], express 220B [$8.80]). Four trains leave daily from Udon Thani with a stop in Khon Kaen (trip time: 6 hours; 140B [$5.70]). Eight trains leave daily from Ubon Ratchathani, with stops in Si Saket, Surin, and Buriram (trip time: 6 hours; 200B [$8]).

By Bus There are air-conditioned buses departing from the Northern Bus Terminal (tel. 02/271-0101) in Bangkok on Paholyothin Road approximately every 15 minutes (trip time: 3 hours; 125B [$5]). Three buses leave daily from Chiang Mai (350B [$14]); four buses daily from Phitsanulok: 6 hours (210B [$8.40]). Hourly buses to Udon Thani (trip time: 3 hours; 130B [$5.30]). Three air-conditioned buses daily to Nong Khai (trip time: 4 hours; 200B [$8]). Seven air-conditioned buses daily to Ubon Ratchathani (trip time: 5 hours; 150B [$6]).

By Car The most direct road from Bangkok is along Route 1 to Saraburi, turning east on Route 2 into Khorat (trip time: 4 hours).

SPECIAL EVENTS There is a special fair held during New Year, and Khorat also commemorates the city's heroine, Tao Suranari (see "What to See & Do," below), in a 10-day fair during the end of March and the beginning of April. During this celebration there are expanded bazaars, parades, historic exhibitions, and cultural performances.

Nakhon Ratchasima, most frequently referred to as Khorat, isn't a wildly interesting city but makes a teriffic base for excursions to such highly recommended sites as Khao Yai National Park, Prasat Hin Phimai (see "Phimai," below), and other nearby Khmer ruins. In comparison with other Isan towns, it is considered the Bangkok of the Northeast due to its explosive growth and spread-out city plan. Before we visited Khorat we figured the constant references to it as the "Gateway to the Northeast" were just public relations hype. But, having toured much of the Northeast prior to our arrival, we now believe Khorat really is the Gateway to the Northeast.

What that simply means is that nearly all of the region's infrastructure emanates from Khorat. Train lines, bus routes, roads, communications, and shipping (via the deep-water port to the south) all go through Khorat. It has the largest number of new hotels in the area, and even the TAT office seems to have information that none of the other regional otuposts offer. All of this makes Khorat a great place to begin your exploration of the Northeast. Welcome to Khorat, Gateway to the Northeast.

ORIENTATION

Information The TAT office (tel. 044/243751; fax 044/243427) is located at 2102-2104 Mittraphap Rd. (the Friendship Highway), next to the Sima Thani Hotel on the west side of town. They publish a good map of the city (which also includes a Phimai plan), as well as maintaining up-to-date information about transport, jungle trekking programs, and hotel and restaurant listings. Hours are daily 8:30am to 4:30pm. Plan on taking a tuk-tuk or taxi to the office, as it is, unfortunately, on the periphery of the town.

City Layout   Khorat is a sprawl, with its commercial and industrial zones built concentrically around an older urban core. The central area, an east-west elongated rectangle, is roughly defined by Chromsurangyart Road to the south, Suranari Road to the north (the far northern boundary of Khorat is defined by the winding Lam Tha Khong River), the confluence of those two roads on the west, and Prajak Road to the east. Nearly all hotels, restaurants, markets, and tourists services are contained within this area, although the TAT office and the newest hotels are situated on the periphery. The distances between three or four blocks (as seen on the TAT map) may seem walkable, especially those within the central area, but, we found that in nearly all cases a tuk-tuk was required; the good news is that you'll pay no more than 20B to 50B (80¢ to $2) to get anywhere within the city.

The main bus station is located on the north side near Watmuang Lane, while the railway station is roughly midway between the TAT office and the central area off Mukkhamontri Road and requires a taxi or tuk-tuk to get into the center of Khorat. The airport is located south of town.

FAST FACTS: KHORAT

Area Code   The telephone code is 044.

Bookstores   The Klang Plaza Department Store on Assadang Road carries a small selection of English-language books.

Climate   June to October is the rainiest period, while November to February is the coolest and driest; March to May are hot-season months.

Currency Exchange   Khorat is a major commercial center with banks located all over the city. There are also three mobile exchange units (with changing locations; inquire at the TAT office) that operate outside of the normal Monday to Friday 8:30am to 4:30pm hours. There is a branch of the Krung Thai Bank on Mittraphap Road just north of the bus station, as well as the Siam Commercial Bank across from the train station.

Festivals or Special Events   There is a special longboat regatta held on the second weekend in October to celebrate the end of the Buddhist Rains Retreat. Sugar apples are available from June to September.

Hospitals   The Maharat Hospital (tel. 254990) is on Changphuak Road, north of Mittraphap.

Police   The Police Station (tel. 242010) is located on San-Pasit Road near the intersection with Chainarong Road. The emergency number is 191.

Post Office   The main branch of the post office (tel. 242004) is located on Assadang Road between Manat and Prajak. Open Monday to Friday 8:30am to 4:30pm, Saturday to Sunday 8:30am to noon.

Telephone/Telex/Fax   Overseas services are available at the main branch of the post office (see above), daily 8:30am to 11pm.

Transit Info   Thai Airways International (tel. 257211) maintains an office at 14 Manat Rd.

Travel Agents   Among the many in town is United Eastern Tour (tel. 213836; fax 258713) at 2098-2100 Mittraphap Rd. at Ampawan; they offer several package tours of Isan and can arrange for rental cars. Another creditable agency is Khorat Business (tel. 258631) on Buarong Road.

WHAT TO SEE & DO

There are a couple of minisites in Khorat that will appeal to those who have a proclivity toward completeness in their travels; otherwise we suggest straying from town for the more engaging excursions. A trip to Prasat Hin Phimai is an absolute requirement if you have any interest in archeology. Nature buffs will certainly enjoy a day trip, or longer, to Khao Yai National Park, while shoppers will decide for themselves about the quality of silk at famed Pak Thong Chai as well as the equally lauded pottery made in Dan Kwian village.

The genesis of Khorat dates back 600 years (postdating the classical Khmer period) to the unification of two villages into a larger provincial town. Little remains from this period other than pieces of city walls and gates as well as sections of a moat. The most highly regarded in-town site is the **Monument of Thao Suranari (Khun Ying Mo)**, located on Chumphon Road in front of the sandblasted Chumphon Gate and overlooking the town square. Although we think the statue is of little aesthetic interest, the story behind it merits retelling. During the reign of Rama III (19th century), Prince Anuwong of Vientiane led an invasion of Khorat, scoring an initial success with his rout of local forces; his intention was to establish a colony and enslave the local population. Khun Ying Mo, the wife of Khorat's deputy governor, enticed the invading Laotian army with alcohol. They became intoxicated and Khun Ying Mo and a band of women killed the Laotians, sending Prince Anuwong's army to defeat. It took about 100 years, but in 1934 a monument was built in her honor, and today it serves as a reminder (as if one is needed in this part of Thailand) that freedom needs to be defended.

The most interesting in-town Buddhist wat houses an image of Narayana, a sacred Hindu deity, at **Wat Phra Narai Maharat;** this testament to religious diversity can be found along Prajak Road, where you'll also find the **City Pillar.** Also in town is the **Maha Veeravong Museum,** on Ratchadamnoen Road just south of the intersection with Mahatthai Road, which has a small historical collection.

Wat Sala Loi is like none other. Modern in date and design, it's notable for its main chapel, which has been designed in the shape of a Chinese junk. The distinctive design has won it several architectural awards and is worth a look for those who relish the unusual. Wat Sala Loi is located on the far northwestern end of town along the Lam Tha Khong River.

WHERE TO STAY

ROYAL PRINCESS KHORAT, 1137 Suranarai Rd., Naimuang District, Khorat 30000. Tel. 044/256629. Fax 044/256601. 186 rms. A/C MINIBAR TV TEL **Directions:** Northeast of town, near stadium.

$ Rates: 1,650B–1,950B ($66–$78) single/double; suites from 5,000B ($200). Extra bed 500B ($20). AE, DC, MC, V.

The newest and best hotel in town, with a friendly and helpful staff, a little removed from the hubbub of this very busy city and yet convenient to transportation, it offers all the usual amenities plus the best pool in town, a tennis court, a business center, meeting rooms, boutiques, laundry and room service, a nightclub, and two restaurants. Its Empress Chinese Restaurant is probably the finest in Khorat.

SIMA THANI HOTEL, Mittraphap Rd., Friendship Hwy., Khorat 30000. Tel. 044/213100. Fax 044/213121. Telex 52509 SIMA TH. 135 rms, including 14 suites. A/C MINIBAR TV TEL **Directions:** Near the TAT office, west of town.

$ Rates (estimated): 2,100B–3,000B ($84–$120) single; 2,400B–3,600B ($96–$144) double; suite from 4,200B ($168). AE, DC, EC, MC, V.

A close second—just a little near the busy highway for our taste—its spacious five-story atrium lounge is especially handsome and inviting. The rooms are large and furnished with designs inspired by local heritage; the gray granite bathrooms are particularly attractive. There's a good pool, a fitness center with excellent saunas, two restaurants, a pub, and a bar.

MODERATE

CHOMSURANG HOTEL, 547 Mahatthai Rd., Khorat. Tel. 044/257088. 119 rms. A/C TV TEL **Directions:** Near the Night Market on Manat Road.

$ Rates: 650B ($26) single; 650B ($26) double. AE, MC, V.

Until the new upmarket hotels, the Chomsurang was Khorat's top accommodation. It is a fully featured hotel with a swimming pool, restaurant, and the typical niceties found in the city's better places. We found it a bit worn, with some fresh paint here and there indicating an effort at keeping up.

BUDGET

KING HOTEL, 1756 Mittraphap Rd., Khorat. Tel. 044/253360. 64 rms. TEL
   Directions: Far northwest edge of town, near the river.
$ Rates: 250B–400B ($10–$16) single; 400B–500B ($16–$20) double. MC, V.
This is for people who like living on the edge of town. The King Hotel is actually a good value, but the location is still pretty extreme and very little English is spoken. Some of the rooms, both single and double, have air-conditioning, and for that they are among the cheapest in the city.

KHORAT DOCTOR'S GUEST HOUSE, 78 Sueb Siri Rd., Khorat. Tel. 044/255846. 6 rms.
$ Rates: 80B ($3.20) single with fan; 120B ($4.80) double with fan; 250B ($10) double with A/C. No credit cards.
Okay, you thought the King Hotel had cheap air-conditioned rooms, well look again: The few who are lucky will find absolutely rock-bottom accommodations at this popular guest house. Services and facilities include hot-water showers, breakfast and dinner, and laundry service; as well as full guide services, the staff is friendly and speaks English. For the money you can't beat it.

WHERE TO DINE

LISA STEAKHOUSE, Jomsurangyard Rd. Tel. 242279.
   Cuisine: WESTERN/THAI/CHINESE. **Directions:** Across road from Wat Chaeng Nai, next to VIP Karaoki (not as shown on our most recent TAT map).
$ Prices: Sandwiches 30B–50B ($1.20–$2); steaks 80B–180B ($3.20–$7.20). MC, V.
   Open: Daily 11am–midnight.
If you can read Thai you may be able to make out the name; otherwise, find the vine-covered arbor and look through for the waterfall to find the most pleasant out-door restaurant around. You'll probably be hooked immediately just as we were and have to take a look at this lovely garden with goldfish ponds and water cascading down a very impressive facade of rocks. There's also a large Thai and Chinese menu, in Thai, but the friendly staff speaks some English.

THAWEEPHAN, Sueb Siri Rd. Tel. 257775.
   Cuisine: THAI/CHINESE. **Directions:** South of the rail lines and 1 big block east of Mittraphap Road; near the TAT office.
$ Prices: Appetizers 25B–60B ($1–$2.40); main courses 30B–180B ($1.20–$7.20). No credit cards.
   Open: Daily noon–11pm.
This is a typical Thai restaurant that is conveniently located near the TAT office. Thaweephan has a large menu that is augmented by mild but tasty Chinese dishes. Again, as with other places in Khorat, we suggest caution when ordering, as the staff speaks little English and our order came out differently than we anticipated; however, don't let that dissuade you from sampling some excellent Thai/Chinese dishes.

EVENING ENTERTAINMENT

If you're in need of a little nightlife, take a stroll along Jomsurangyard Road west from the center of town and check out the **Flyer Pub, Hot Station, Club Leo,** and **VIP Karaoke.**
   We spent a delightful evening at the Khorat **Night Market** where there are over 100 stands selling everything from cooking utensils, jeans, and nylons bags to a seemingly limitless amount of snack food—you can easily hop from one stand to an-other for an inexpensive meal. The dusk to dawn Night Market is open daily begin-ning from about 6 to 9pm, depending on the time of year, and is located on Manat

Road, running from Chumphon down to Mahatthai. During New Year's there is a wonderfully festive special Night Market that quadruples the size of the normal market and reminded us of an American state fair. Loads of fun.

EASY EXCURSIONS

PRASAT HIN PHANOM WAN & BAN MAKAH These two stops combine a Khmer historical stone castle with a small village, Ban Makah, that specializes in the manufacture of handmade knives. **Phanom Wan,** smaller and less restored than Phimai, is of architectural significance and still in use by monks. The main structure at Phanom Wan is decaying, and the long-term plan is to dismantle and reconstruct the main building on a new foundation; however, we were informed that this isn't imminent. The trip to Phanom Wan is best done by car or for those with lots of time; although Phanom Wan and Ban Makah are only 20km (12 miles) from Khorat in the direction of Phimai, there is limited bus service (the thrice-daily bus departs from Pratu Phonsaen, near the intersection of Mittraphap and Prajak in Khorat, but we suggest checking with TAT for the current schedule; 20B [80¢]). To get there by car, travel north on Route 2 for 11km (6½ miles) and take the turnoff for Phanom Wan; en route you'll pass through Ban Makah. Admission is 25B ($1). It's open daily from 8:30am to 6pm.

KHAO YAI NATIONAL PARK Khao Yai, located south of Pak Chom (southwest of Khorat), is Thailand's premier national park; it was selected recently as an ASEAN Natural Heritage Site and is now closed to overnight visitors. It is also the country's first national park—established in 1972—and spans four provinces. In it are a variety of ecological zones including marshlands, rain forests, limestone peaks, the Dongrak Range, and three different types of evergreen forests. Most people head to Khao Yai to see wildlife, which statistically abounds in greater numbers here than in other parks in Thailand; however, most of the more exotic fauna, such as tiger, hornbills, elephant, and leopard, are rarely seen by visitors. Still, there are plenty of gibbons, pigs, long-tailed monkeys, barking deer, and birds to satisfy most naturalists, and if you're lucky, you may see a larger mammal.

Among the highlights of Khao Yai National Park are hiking on 40km (29 miles) of trails, as well as visiting the white-handed gibbon meeting grounds around the **Heo Suwat Waterfall** (the waterfalls are at their peak from September to November), the bat-populated limestone cave at **Khao Rub Chang** (located at the periphery of the park), and in the late summer, the hornbills around **Nong Phak Chi.**

One way to visit the park is with a local travel company such as **Jungle Adventure,** 752/11 Kongvaksin Rd., Soi 3 (tel. 044/313836), which operates out of Pak Chom. Jungle Adventure offers trips into Khao Yai, including mountain hikes to see wrinkled lip bats, swimming, and hiking, as well as an evening "spotlight tour" that takes visitors by Jeep into areas that are known feeding grounds of nocturnal mammals. The price for such a tour is about 600B ($24).

For those whose passion is golf, the TAT operates a nine-hole course in a very attractive hillside setting in the park. Although we're not judges as to the quality of the course, we were informed by genuine golfers that it's less than ideal; the setting more than compensates for any deficiencies. Weekend greens fees are 210B ($8.40), caddies charge 100B ($4) for 18 holes, and club rentals run 250B ($10); hours are daily 6am to 6pm.

If you plan on visiting Khao Yai National Park during the cool season, remember to bring a sweater; temperatures drop below 50° in the evening.

There is frequent train and bus service to Pak Chom, with connecting buses to the park.

PAK THONG CHAI This village, located approximately 30km (18 miles) south of Khorat along Route 304, is known for its handwoven silk. In addition to the small factories and home shops where residents still engage in the craft of silk weaving, there are a handful of shops that carry a wide range of silk products. We found many fabrics and patterns very attractive though somewhat pricey. We were informed by professional buyers that much of the silk produced in Pak Thong Chai (as with other so-called silk villages) incorporates varying blends of polyester, so exercise caution if you intend to buy 100% silk.

Among the many shops we visited are the reputable Srithai Silk, 690/21-22 Sriphonrat Rd. (tel. 441151; fax 044/441899), with showroom at 333 Sueb Siri Rd. (tel. 441588), open daily 7am to 6pm; and Praneet Thai Silk, 96-97 Sriphonrat Rd. (tel. 441173).

DAN KWIAN VILLAGE The only reason to visit Dan Kwian is for the distinctive pottery that's produced by the descendants of the Mon tribespeople who settled here in the early 18th century. The style of the ceramics was not our taste, but we would heartily recommend a visit for anyone who wants to see how this unusual pottery is manufactured. This is especially interesting for those who intend to visit Ban Chiang's Bronze Age remains, among which are ceramic pots, made in a similar manner, that date back over 5,000 years.

Currently there are about 20 families engaged in the traditional manufacture of ceramic pots. The method is similar among them: Clay is gathered from the banks of the nearby Moon River during low water (between January and April); the clay is then built up, piece by piece, to form the basic shape; an assistant turns a wheel by hand, while the potter molds the shape; the pottery is then left to dry outdoors, placed in a wood-fired kiln, and stacked one on top other pieces. This "primitive" craft has largely disappeared though we found a former resident from Dan Kwian, who lives on the outskirts of Ban Chiang, who makes pots in an even more ancient fashion. A row of pottery stalls and workshops are located in this small town, and you're welcome to watch the entire process. Ask the TAT office in Khorat if any of the families are willing to have visitors in their workshops.

There is a competition during the Surin Elephant Roundup weekend in Dan Kwian for the largest pot.

Buses run every 20 minutes from Khorat's southern gate bus stop (Pratu Chainarong, near the intersection of Chainarong Road and Kamhaeng-Songkhram Road). Trip time is 30 minutes; fare is 5B (20¢).

EN ROUTE TO THE NORTH

We're delighted to find cities or towns that have largely escaped the stamp of group tourism, places that retain their identity and are still welcoming to foreign travelers. One such town is **Chaiyaphum,** located approximately midway between busy Khorat and Khon Kaen (take Route 202) but far enough off national Route 2 that it's largely overlooked.

One event that may put little Chaiyaphum on the map is the **Chaiyaphum Elephant Roundup** that takes place each year in February (contact the TAT for this year's date). This is meant to augment the Surin event on the elephant handlers circuit and has become increasingly popular.

Aside from the Dvaravati era (A.D. 6th–11th c.), Khmer-style sandstone sanctuary (with a carved bodhisattva) at Prang Ku (2km [1.2 miles] from the center; a bathing ritual takes place here on the first day of the full moon in April), most of our activity relates to exploring the streets and sois, seaching for examples of Chaiyaphum's most famous product, silk. Our local expert, Ms. Sandy Songuansri of the Phukhieo School (tel. 044/861505), informed us that the material woven in the Chaiyaphum area is made of 100% silk and is favored by the royal family. She advises visitors who wish to see the finest examples of weaving to visit people's houses instead of the shops and stands. Based on our experience with these things, you'll have to spend several hours searching out such people, but we're certain that you'll be rewarded with a memorable time—not to mention some exquisite silk.

If you end up spending the night, there is the **Lert Nimitra Hotel,** at 447 Nivetrat Rd. (tel. 044/811522), where rooms run 130B to 950B ($5.30 to $38), depending on fan or air-conditioned accommodations. Another alternative is **Yin's Guest House** (no phone), near the bus station. They will arrange inexpensive excursions to the natural scenery around Chaiyaphum as well as visits to silk-weaving establishments. Expect to pay 50B to 100B ($2 to $4) for dormitory rooms.

There are 20 regular and three air-conditioned buses daily that navigate the 119km (74 miles) distance from Khorat for 40B ($1.60) and 80B ($3.20) respectively.

Those interested in archeological digs may want to check out **Ban Prasat,** 45km (2.8 miles) north of Khorat on the way to Phimai, 2km (1.2 miles) left, off the main road. There are presently three pits, one dating back to about 3,000 years ago, with human skeletons, stone weapons, and ornaments of animal bones and shells. A second (about 1,600 to 1,800 years ago) also contains red-and-black pottery with incised decorations and gold wrist and ankle bracelets. The third (about 600 years ago) includes a kiln and pottery in both Khmer and contemporary styles, as well as weapons. If you go by bus, ask the conductor to let you off at the roadside pavilion, where you can catch a later bus to continue on to Phimai or return to Khorat.

2. PHIMAI

319km (197 miles) NE of Bangkok; 60km (37 miles) N of Khorat; 245km (152 miles) S of Udon Thani

GETTING THERE By Bus 24 buses a day leave from Khorat (trip time: 90 minutes; 25B [$1]).

By Car The most direct route is north on Route 2; take the eastbound Phimai turnoff.

ESSENTIALS The **area code** is 044. There is tourist **information** available at Bai-Teiy Restaurant (tel. 471725) on Chomsudasapet Road; open daily from 7am to midnight. One of the best ways to get around town is via bicycle; **bikes** are available for hire at Phimai Bike Rent (tel. 471725), near the ruins in the center of town. Both the Bangkok Bank and Thai Military Bank are located across the street from the entrance to the archeological site; the **banks** are open Monday to Friday 8:30am to 3pm.

SPECIAL EVENTS A celebration of dance, lights, and music honoring Phimai is held annually in late October or early November (contact the TAT for this year's date) as part of the Phimai Festival. Lopburi-period stage performances and a play depicting scenes from the *Ramayana* are presented at the Sanctuary. Other aspects of the festival include the Northeastern Boat Racing Championship, historical and cultural exhibitions, and a costume parade.

A long with Prasat Hin Phanom Rung, the completely restored ruins at Phimai are a highlight of any tour of the Northeast. In fact, because the site is in such a good state of repair, we would recommend beginning your tour of Khmer ruins here, so that you'll have a better idea of the original condition and design of lesser reconstructed/excavated archeological destinations.

WHAT TO SEE & DO

PHIMAI HISTORIC PARK [PRASAT HIN PHIMAI]. Tel. 471568.
Thailand's most well-known and best-restored Khmer site is Prasat Hin Phimai (Phimai), located 52km (30 miles; about 1½ hours by bus) northeast of Khorat. The stone sanctuary is built in the style, but certainly not the scale, of Angkor Wat in Cambodia and is thought to have been constructed during the reign of King Suriya Woraman I, who ruled the Khmer Empire from A.D. 1002 to 1050.

The Khmer people worshiped Hindu deities, in particular Brahma and Shiva, and consistent with Shiva worship, many of the *prasats* (cactus-shaped towers atop multistoried bases) contained phallic-shaped lingams in their central chambers; the most distinctive evidence of the Hindu origin of Phimai are the intricately carved sandstone lintels (many are on display in the outdoor museum) above the main doorways in the central prasats and *gopuras* (gate towers); images of a dancing

Shiva and Vishnu are among the most prominent. Yet much of Phimai, as it appears today, shows evidence of a Buddhist presence. After the decline of the Khmer Empire in Thailand, Phimai was rebuilt by Thai artisans and decorated with Mahayana Buddhist imagery; lingams were replaced by Buddhas and lintels depicting Hindu deities incorporated figures from the story of Buddhism, usually with the Buddhist figure positioned above the original Hindu deity. New buildings were added; in general, the lower, less-decorated structures were constructed after the 12th century by Thai architects.

The renovation of Phimai has turned what once was a moat surrounded site into a groomed lawn park with neatly trimmed trees; a rebuilt stone wall, overflowing with pink-and-white bougainvillea, encircles the site. A single *naga* bridge, with Anglo-style cobras, leads up to the main sanctuary. Massive sandstone columns form the entrance to the gallery. One very distinctive Khmer architectural motif is the balustrade window; archeologists believe that many of these windows contained other decorative elements that haven't survived. We found the well-proportioned, massive doorways particularly sublime.

Admission: 25B ($1).

Open: Daily 6am–6pm. **Bus:** From Khorat (travel time 1½ hours; 25B [$1]).

PHIMAI NATIONAL MUSEUM.

The handsome new building finished by the Fine Arts Department in 1993 is a major addition to this major site—and a must see. You'll pass it on your way to the ruin, but we suggest you save it until afterward, both to take a break from the sun and to better appreciate the experience. Downstairs are the superb archeological remains of Phimai, stone carvings, jewelry, and other artifacts which give a very good picture of the ancient city, its art, architecture, and culture. Upstairs contains artifacts of more recent origin, as well as displays that provide views of the social, economic, political, artistic, and cultural development of Northeast Thailand. Guided tours and books are available.

Outside, but within the compound, which has longer hours (8:30am to 4:30pm daily, no admission charge), you'll also find an open-air wing with a small collection of some of the finest carved lintels in the Northeast—some from other sites in Si Saket, Buriram, and Khorat.

Admission: 10B (40¢).

Open: Wed–Sun 9am–4pm.

WHERE TO STAY & DINE

If you've missed the bus on your way to Khorat or Khon Kaen or decide to spend the night in Phimai, there are two small, inexpensive inns: The **Old Phimai Guest House** (tel. 471918), in a teak mansion with dormitory beds and small fan-cooled rooms (100B to 225B [$4 to $9]), and the slightly more upscale **Phimai Hotel** (tel. 044/471306; fax 044/471940) with air-conditioned rooms that run 350B to 500B ($14 to $20). Their fan-cooled rooms are much cheaper. Both are within walking distance from the site on Haruthairom Road.

There are quite a few dining options in and around Phimai. Near the site is the **Bai-Teiy Restaurant** (tel. 471725), while the **Rim Moon Restaurant** (tel. 471692) and **Toiting** (no phone) are on the northern end of town, overlooking the Moon River. All are open daily for lunch and dinner. There is a **Night Market,** located near the southeast corner of the site, for extremely inexpensive food and casual dining; open nightly 6pm to midnight.

One of Phimai's most popular stops is a park known as Saingam or Banyon Trees Park. Nearby is the **Sai-ngam Restaurant** (tel. 471983), a tour-group stop. Our suggestion is to buy snacks in town or from the many stands in the park and enjoy a picnic out at the Banyan Trees Park; the park is within a 10-minute bicycle ride from the site.

3. KHON KAEN

449km (278 miles) NE of Bangkok; 190km (118 miles) N of Khorat;
115km (71 miles) S of Udon Thani

GETTING THERE By Plane   Three flights a day leave from Bangkok (flying time 55 minutes; 1,220B [$50] on Thai Airways). Three flights a week depart from Chiang Mai (flying time: 2 hours; 1,340B [$53.50]).

By Train   Khon Kaen is connected by rail to Bangkok via Khorat as well as Udon Thani, Nong Khai, and Sakon Nakhon. Five trains a day leave from Bangkok (trip time: 8 hours on rapid train, 7 hours by express train; second-class ordinary 300B [$12], express 340B [$13.60]). Seven trains depart daily from Udon Thani (trip time: 2 hours; 120B [$4.80]).

By Bus   Twenty air-conditioned buses a day leave from Bangkok (trip time: 6 hours; 240B [$9.60]). Thirty air-conditioned buses a day leave from Khorat (trip time: 2½ hours; 95B [$3.80]). Many buses depart daily from Udon Thani (trip time: 2 hours; 60B [$2.40]).

By Car   The most direct route from either Bangkok or Udon Thani is on Route 2.

ESSENTIALS   The **area code** is 043. The **TAT office** is on Prachasamosorn Road between Klangmuang and Langmuang roads. The **Tourist Police** share the same building and can be reached 24 hours a day at tel. 236937-8. The **Thai Airways** office (tel. 236523) is located at 183/6 Maliwan Rd. The **Khon Kaen Hospital** (tel. 236005) is on Si Chan Road; for **emergencies** dial 191. The **police** can be reached at 211162.

SPECIAL EVENTS   In December of each year is the **Khon Kaen Silk and Friendship Fair.** Silk weavers, large and small, from the surrounding area display their wares along with other locally manufactured handicrafts. In addition to the market there are other cultural performances and demonstrations.

For most travelers, Khon Kaen isn't much more than a transport hub, branching to the northwest to Loei, due north to Udon Thani (Ban Chiang) and Nong Khai, and northeast to Sakon Nakhon. The city's size and population rival Khorat's (though not its history) and nationally it's known for Khon Kaen University, the home of Channel 5 (one of the region's largest television stations), and for its gigantic branch of the Bank of Thailand. It's a pleasant, thriving city with a vibrant nightlife; however, we found little to recommend other than a very special shop and one excellent hotel. Better to move on, especially if you're on a tight program, than to try to fashion a tour, unless you're content with a look at local life. One exception to this is a visit to the silk village of Chonnabot.

The city is laid out in a simple grid system. The railway station is on the southwestern edge of town on Rueorom Road. The two main north-south boulevards are Na-Muang Road on the west and Klang Muang Road on the east, while Phimpasut Road forms a northern perimeter in the central section. The bus station is on Klang Muang, near Ammart Road.

WHAT TO SEE & DO

The Khon Kaen National Museum houses one of the better small collections in this area of the Northeast. Archeological finds from nearby sites are on display spanning the major periods of historic development. The most significant part of the collection focuses on the Dvaravati period, with a fine exhibit of carved stone markers. We also like the Ban Chiang–era artifacts. The museum is located in the Provincial Civil

Service Center, to the north of Khon Kaen's central district. Admission is 25B ($1). It's open Tuesday to Saturday 8:30am to 4:30pm.

In terms of shopping, the **Prathamakant Local Goods Center,** 81-85 Ruenrom Road (tel. 224080; fax 224736), is the number one handicrafts emporium in Khon Kaen, if not in this section of Isan. They stock an incredible selection of silk woven in Khorat, Chonnabot, Chaiyaphum, and other smaller villages at retail prices (600B to 3,000B [$24 to $120] per meter depending on quality and materials). We purchased lovely silver jewelry produced in Surin and Laos (about twice the cost of what we found in those locations but still cheaper by a quarter to a half from what's sold in Bangkok) and bought cotton weaves of various styles, especially mutmee or ikat; vests cost 360B ($14.40), ikat for pillows or tablecloths run 150B ($6) per meter. We also liked their selection of hill-tribe appliqué work, beadwork from Chiang Mai, and basketry. We had a hard time resisting their shirts and blouses made with panels of antique silk (660B [$26.40]). The staff speaks English. It's open daily 8am to 8:30pm. VISA and MasterCard are accepted.

WHERE TO STAY & DINE

Although there are coffee shop-style restaurants in the major hotels, we prefer dining al fresco at the **Khon Kaen Market,** off Klang Muang Road near the department store.

CHAROEN THANI PRINCESS, 260 Srichan Rd., Khon Kaen 40000. Tel. 043/220400. Fax 043/243220. 320 rms. A/C MINIBAR TV TEL **Directions:** Midway between train and bus stations, off Srichan and Na-Muang roads.

$ Rates: 1,850B–2,500B ($74–$100) single/double; suites from 5,000B ($200). Extra bed 500B ($20). AE, DC, MC, V.

This handsome 20-story hotel is by far the best hotel in town, as well as the tallest building. Facilities include a swimming pool, fitness center, business center, 24-hour room service, laundry service, bakery, drugstore, shops, meeting rooms, lobby lounge, Chinese restaurant, and coffee shop with international cuisine. Attractive, comfortable rooms have the expected amenities plus a room safe, international direct dial telephone, and color TV.

KAEN INN HOTEL, 56 Klang Muang Rd., Khon Kaen. Tel. 043/237744. 162 rms. A/C MINIBAR TV TEL **Directions:** At the intersection with Ammart Road near the National Bank of Thailand.

$ Rates: 960B ($38.40) single. AE, MC, V.

The Kaen Inn is a good quality, provincial hotel with fair service in a busy central location. Decor is standard as are the many facilities including a coffee shop, bar, and restaurant. The guest rooms are clean and well maintained.

KHON KAEN HOTEL, 43/3 Phimpasut Rd., Khon Kaen. Tel. 043/237711. 140 rms. A/C TEL **Directions:** Near the intersection with Na-Muang Road.

$ Rates: 750B ($30) single; 800B ($32) double. AE, MC, V.

The Khon Kaen Hotel is very popular with Thai businesspeople. Rooms are clean, worn, Spartanly furnished, and acceptable. The plus is a quieter location in an inner courtyard near a school.

EASY EXCURSIONS

About the only place that we'd recommend touring is to the silk-weaving village of **Chonnabot,** located southwest of the city. We felt that the quality of the silk, and the similar prices compared favorably with that in Pak Thong Chai (our Thai silk experts felt that it was of good quality, but not up to the standards of material from Chaiyaphum). Among the larger shops, with a wide selection of locally made silk and mutmee cotton, is **Ratree Thai Silk,** 246-248 Sriboonreung Rd. (tel. 286-054), where a 6-foot length of finely made silk runs 600B to 1,200B ($24 to $48).

To reach Chonnabot, take Route 2 south and turn on the 399km marker for an additional 12km (7 miles).

4. UDON THANI & BAN CHIANG

564km (350 miles) NE of Bangkok; 305km (189 miles) N of Khorat;
115km (71 miles) N of Khon Kaen; 51km (32 miles) S of Nong Khai;
152km (94 miles) E of Loei

GETTING THERE By Plane   One flight a day leaves from Bangkok (flying time: 55 minutes; 1,500B [$60] on Thai Airways). Three flights depart weekly from Sakon Kakhon (flying time: 45 minutes; 500B [$20] on Thai Airways).

By Train   Udon Thani is connected by rail to Bangkok via Khorat as well as to Nong Khai to the north. Five trains a day leave from Bangkok (trip time: 10 to 11 hours on rapid train, 8½ hours by express train; second-class ordinary 350B [$14], express 370B [$14.80]). Four trains leave daily from Khorat (trip time: 4½ hours; 210B [$8.50]).

By Bus   Ten air-conditioned buses a day leave from Bangkok (trip time: 9 hours; 275B [$11]). Twenty-six air-conditioned buses a day leave from Khorat (trip time: 4 hours; 130B [$5.30]). Many buses leave daily from Nong Khai (trip time: 45 minutes; 60B [$2.40]). There is one air-conditioned bus a day to Phitsanulok (trip time: 7 hours; 150B [$6]).

By Car   The most direct route from either Bangkok or Nong Khai is on Route 2 (Friendship Highway).

ESSENTIALS   The **area code** is 042. A small **TAT** office can be found in the government complex near the lake, about 100m off Phosi Road, near its intersection with Pohniyom Road. The **Thai Airways** office (tel. 243222) is located at 60 Makkang Rd. The **Udon Thani Hospital** (tel. 222572) is on Pho Niyom Road; the emergency number for the **police** is 222285. Most national **banks** have branch offices on Phosi Road.

CITY LAYOUT   The airport, train station, and bus depot are all located on the southeast end of town as are many tourist services. The main north-south artery is Phosi Road, which is the largest commercial strip in Udon. The hospital and U.S. consulate are located on the northeast side of town along Nong Phra Jak, an inland water park.

U don Thani, known simply as Udon, is a provincial center that once was the base for a large contingent of U.S. armed forces and their families, particularly during the Vietnam War. Today there are only a handful of American military advisors and a slightly larger number of retirees, who've either stayed or returned, from the more active days of the 1960s and 1970s. The most obvious reminder of American military presence in Udon, other than the small consulate, is the enormous air base that now serves both military and civilian sectors of the Thai air infrastructure. The only public access to this installation is when flying on a commercial airliner, so if you arrive by car, bus, or train you'll miss this unusual tourist site.

By far the most compelling reason to visit Udon is easy access to Thailand's premier Bronze Age excavation at Ban Chiang. This world-renowned archeological site has attracted interest from both scholars and travelers since its recent excavation dating back to the 1970s and was the subject of a traveling exhibition organized by the Smithsonian Institution in the 1980s. If you plan to visit Ban Chiang, make sure you're there between Wednesday and Sunday; it's closed on Monday, Tuesday, and national holidays.

WHAT TO SEE & DO

The city of Udon offers little to see for most travelers, as the main attractions, such as Ban Chiang or Wat Phra Buddha Baht Bua Bok, are located more than 50km (32 miles) out of town. Look for the "Made in Thailand" sign at 206-208 Phosi,

Meechai (tel. 222838), for the largest selection of souvenirs: the excellent local baskets, cloth, jewelry, and copies of Ban Chiang pottery.

WHERE TO STAY & DINE

If you crave an American meal, with real American food (it's good, really), try **T-J's.** The reason that T-J's works so well is that it's run by an honest to goodness American, T-J, who insists on turning out hamburgers and fries, among other specialties, your way. T-J's is located near the lake, on Nongsamrong Road, near the U.S. Consulate. By the way, T-J's seems to be a favored hangout for American expatriates, so if you want to check into the scene . . .

CHAROEN HOTEL, 549 Phosi Rd., Udon Thani. Tel. 042/248155. Fax 042/ 246126. 250 rms, including 25 suites. A/C MINIBAR TV TEL **Directions:** Near the train station.

$ Rates: 400B–720B ($16–$28.80) single; 480B–780B ($19.20–$31.20) double; suite from 840B ($33.60). Extra person 200B ($8). AE, DC, MC, V.

We're pleased to say that the service and management was much improved during our most recent visit, and we can now recommend this as undoubtedly the top accommodation in town. The rooms, quiet, clean, and modern, are equipped to varying degrees. Standard rooms have no TV or minibar, while deluxe accommodations have TVs but no minibar; junior suites have both. There is a pool in the front yard, immediately adjacent to the new 100-room addition that is completely kitted out and very modern. The best part of the hotel is the Poovieng Restaurant (see below), probably the best dining room in Udon. Rooms in the older wing are a better bargain, nice enough, and quieter.

UDON HOTEL, 81-89 Makkang Rd., Udon Thani. Tel. 042/248160. 190 rms. A/C MINIBAR TV TEL **Directions:** Near the intersection with Prajak Road, in the central area.

$ Rates: 360B–480B ($14.40–$19.20) single; 480B–900B ($19.20–$36) double. Extra person 200B ($8). MC, V.

The Udon is not as modern as the Charoen, but it's friendly and the facilities are similar; it has a new wing. Aside from the slightly worn rooms, the more downtown location makes it a noisier establishment. If you take one of the older rooms, avoid those facing the street.

POOVIENG RESTAURANT, in the Charoen Hotel, 549 Phosi Rd. Tel. 248155.

Cuisine: THAI/WESTERN. **Directions:** Near the train staton.

$ Prices: Appetizers 40B–80B ($1.60–$3.20); main courses 50B–220B ($2–$8.80). AE, DC, MC, V.

Open: Daily breakfast and lunch 6am–4pm; dinner 6pm–midnight.

We asked several residents to suggest a restaurant and they all came up with the Charoen Hotel, our hotel. We normally take dining in our hotel as a sign of exhaustion, but after pressing our friends, they insisted that the Poovieng Restaurant is the best dining room in Udon. We went, we dined, we agree.

As with most hotel restaurants that cater to a wide market, the Poovieng has something for everyone, but we suggest the Thai food. It's among the best-prepared cuisine we had in the entire Northeast, if not one of the top meals in Thailand. Among our favorites were *nua yam* (spicy beef salad with lemon), spring rolls, and *patgai* (basil chicken). In addition to these morsels, there is Chinese, Japanese, and Western food.

After our wonderful dinner, we returned for breakfast. John reports that he ate the best *khao tom* (with crab) ever—and he eats it everyday!—it was that good.

EASY EXCURSIONS

BAN CHIANG NATIONAL MUSEUM The tiny hamlet of Ban Chiang, a prehistoric village that dates back over 5,000 years, is located approximately 50km (31 miles) east of Udon, on the Sakon Nakhon highway. It is based upon the findings here that Thailand, and all of Southeast Asia, stakes it claim to historic and technological parity with its larger and more influential neighbors, China and India.

In the years 1974–75 the governmental Fine Arts Department, in conjunction with the University of Pennsylvania, led a major excavation of sites within the village. This in turn led to the startling discovery of ceramic vessels and metallic implements and tools, woven fabric, and human skeletons that date back to 3,600 B.C., placing a technologically advanced civilization in Northeast Thailand at the same time as those first established in other, previously considered more "developed," regions of Asia.

Although little is known about the people who inhabited the village, it is thought that they descended from the so-called Hoabinhians, Stone Age people who lived in Southeast Asia from 12,000 to 5,000 B.C. The settlement of Ban Chiang, based on the excavation, indicates three separate periods of development. The Early Period lasted for approximately 2,600 years, while the so-called Middle Period began in 1,000 B.C. and continued to 300 B.C. The Late Period extended through A.D. 200, after which Ban Chiang is thought to have been deserted.

Objects from these periods of development are on display at two separate museums in the town—they are across from one another on a common ground. The smaller, older museum (on your right as you enter) was founded in 1976 as a housing for the excavations conducted during the previous two years. The far more impressive collection is housed in the new wing (to your left as you enter) opened in 1986 and built by the Kennedy Foundation.

This museum is as interesting for its information on the processes of discovery, excavation, categorization, and reconstruction of the finds as it is about the early societies it details. We found it fascinating to read about the clues that contribute to the knowledge of this ancient culture: Analysis of snail remains help to establish seasonal and climatic conditions; rice in the pottery demonstrates agricultural techniques; dental studies determine diet and health. All of this is clearly described (in English and Thai) in an installation that was originally designed by the Smithsonian Institution for a traveling exhibition about Ban Chiang. The same exhibits have been permanently placed in the Ban Chiang Museum.

If you intend to return to Bangkok and wish to see a fine exhibition of Ban Chiang objects, plan an excursion to Wang Suan Pakkard (see "What to See & Do" in Bangkok in Chapter 5). This elegant palace was, until recently, the home of a Thai princess who was a benefactor of the excavations at Ban Chiang.

Admission is 25B ($1). The museum is open Wednesday to Sunday 8am to 4pm; closed all national holidays. To get there, take a Sakon Nakhon–bound bus or minivan (trip time: 20B [80¢]) from Muang Tong Market in Udon along Route 22, which will let you off on the main road, some 6km (4 miles) south of the site; take a tuk-tuk (20B [80¢]) to the museum. *Note:* Both the bus and minivan will often stop in the town, but ask before assuming, otherwise you may overshoot the town. If you plan on continuing your tour to Sakon Nakhon, remember to bring your luggage, as there's no need to return to Udon; you can pick up the eastbound bus on the main road.

BAN CHIANG EXCAVATION SITE   One of the archeological pits in Ban Chiang is open to the public. Though it's an obligatory stop—and you definitely should go—after seeing the museum, we felt it wasn't wildly interesting. The site itself is found within the grounds of Wat Pho Si Nai, a 5-minute walk from the museum. Admission is free with museum ticket. It's open every day, from dawn to dusk.

BAN KHAMOH & BAN PHU   If you admire the earthenware in the Ban Chiang Museum, you'll likely appreciate the ceramics produced Mr. Suewai Janjaroon, his wife Rien, and their fellow villagers in Ban Khamoh, located along the main road near Ban Chiang. These seven families have taken the ancient manufacture of clay vessels into the 20th century by reproducing Ban Chiang–era pottery for the Thai and tourist market. These pots have been known to be sold as "antiquities," yet the villagers consider their work as a revival of an ancient craft instead of fashioning fakes. (In fact, these pots are often the answer for those who feel that they must own part of Ban Chiang's precious legacy. There has been a huge problem with looting in the area, as residents were offered enormous amounts of money by dealers to "excavate" their fields and beyond for antiques that found their way to Japan, Europe, and America.)

Mr. Suewai is from Ban Dan Kwian (see "Khorat," above) and he combines those techniques with materials used over 3,000 years ago. For example, the clay is mixed with rice husks and textured with rough hemp. We saw pots fired by being placed on a bamboo rack, covered with dried rice shoots, and set ablaze—a bonfire in an open field.

Although the villagers in Khamoh produce pottery and decorate it with clay, it is in Ban Phu where these vessels are painted. Here you can see local craftspeople, such as Mr. Boonjong Lapo and his wife, decorate the pots in swirling geometric forms. These are then taken directly to the souvenir stands opposite the Ban Chiang Museum or sold to distributors in other parts of Thailand.

The larger, 3-foot-high decorated ceramics cost about 700B ($28), while the smaller souvenir-size pieces start at 60B ($2.40). Mr. Suewai can arrange shipping through a freight company in Chiang Mai, but we caution you that these are extremely fragile and may not make it though a long voyage home.

Ban Phu is the village that you pass through traveling from the main road to Ban Chiang, while Khamoh is but 3km (2 miles) west of Ban Phu. There are no shops in these villages; you'll have to ask for Suewai. He's usually found along the road, working on his pots.

WAT PHRA BUDDHA BAHT BUA BOK   Fifty kilometers (31 miles) northwest of Udon is a 1,200-acre park containing a shrine dedicated to the Holy Footprint and Relic of the Buddha that is under development as a historical park by the Fine Arts Department. These are contained within a 12-foot-high pagoda that is the subject of a festival in March when worshipers pay homage to Buddha. Prehistoric wall paintings—particularly those on Tham Wua and Tham Khon rocks—have also been found within the confines of the park. It's interesting that this area, as indicated by the later Buddhist presence, was also revered during the Dvaravati and Lopburi periods, and the painted geometric forms seen on the rocks may also contain some religious references.

The wat is built at the base of Khao Phu Phan, near Ban Phu, and can be reached either from Udon, Si Chiang Mai, or Nong Khai by bus.

---

5. LOEI & THE MAE KHONG VALLEY

520km (322 miles) NE of Bangkok; 344km (213 miles) N of Khorat;
206km (128 miles) NW of Khon Kaen; 202km (125 miles) W of Nong Khai;
269km (167 miles) NE of Phitsanulok

GETTING THERE By Plane   Bangkok Airways has three flights a week leave from Bangkok (flying time: 1 hour, 40 minutes; 2,120B [$85])

By Bus   Five air-conditioned buses a day leave from the Bangkok Northern Bus Terminal: 275B ($11). One air-conditioned bus and four normal buses a day leave from Phitsanulok (trip time: 4 hours; 75B [$3]). Many buses, song taos, and minivans leave from Chiang Khan: 75B ($3).

By Car   The most direct route from Khon Kaen is west on Route 12 and north on Route 201. From Udon, travel west on Route 210 and north on Route 201. From Nong Khai, travel west along the Mae Khong on Route 212.

ESSENTIALS   The **area code** is 042. The **Thai Airways office** (tel. 812344) is located at 191/1 Charoenrat Rd.; they rent air-conditioned vans with driver for about 2,400B ($96) a day. The **Loei Hospital** (tel. 811806) is on Loei–Chiang Khan Road; the emergency number for the **police** is 811254. Most national **banks**

have branch offices in town with normal operating hours (if you intend on traveling north to Chiang Khan change money in Loei as there are no other banks in the area).

As you enter Loei, you're likely to come across the following billboard, "Welcome to Loei, the Coldest Place in All Siam." This is a town with a sense of humor, which is a good thing since little else is happening. If ever there was a cow town in the Northeast it would have to be Loei. That said, we like it a lot.

When dividing up the different geographical zones within Thailand, one would have a hard time describing Loei as Northeastern. With its cool air, nearby mountains and rivers, and rich agriculture it would fall more naturally into the Northern or Central regions, yet Loei shares its relative isolation and sensibility more than its Isan neighbors than with the other, splashier parts of Thailand.

Not only do we like the place for its diminutive scale and friendly folks (don't expect anyone to speak a word of English), but it's a wonderful jumping-off point for two southern national parks, Phu Kradung and Phu Luang, as well as a gateway to the Mae Khong district, beginning at Chiang Khan and leading to Nong Khai. By the way, that coldest place in all Siam business is no joke; as your grandmother might say, "Take a sweater"—at least in the cool season.

There are really only a couple of streets that hold anything for travelers. The most important is Charoenrat Road, where you'll find, among other things, a bank, Night Market, hotels and restaurants, and shops open at night. Phitsanulok-bound buses depart from in front of the Phu Luang Hotel on Charoenrat. Perpendicular to it is Haisoke Road, another commericaly significant thoroughfare. Most of the official Loei is located across the Loei–Chiang Khan highway; here is where you'll find the Forestry Office where you may book rooms at Phu Kradung National Park.

WHERE TO STAY & DINE

We had a fine meal at the 200-foot-long **Night Market** just off Charoenrat Road. As usual, this is the cheapest dining in town, and Loei is no exception. The food stalls are set up about 6pm and finish around 11pm.

KING'S HOTEL, 1241 Haisoke Rd., Loei 42000. Tel. 042/811701. 46 rms. A/C TEL **Directions:** In the central area.

$ Rates: 200B ($8) single with fan; 350B ($14) single with A/C; 350B ($14) double with fan; 400B ($16) double with A/C. MC, V.

The King's is Loei's best hotel, but not by much. Accommodations are very basic with Spartanly furnished rooms and reasonably clean bathrooms; 30 rooms have air-conditioning. There's a small lobby with an attached coffee shop, but aside from that, there's little in the way of services and facilities. Still, the staff is friendly (though not English speaking) and the location is central.

PHU LUANG HOTEL, 55 Charoenrat Rd., Loei 42000. Tel. 042/811532. Fax 042/811532. 86 rms. A/C TEL **Directions:** In the central area.

$ Rates: 180B ($7.20) single with fan; 300B ($12) single with A/C; 210B ($8.40) double with fan; 350B ($14) double with A/C. No credit cards.

The Phu Luang runs a close second to the King's, but is just a tad less well run and less clean; nevertheless, it's an acceptable alternative. The best part of this place is that they've convinced the bus companies to stop right in front of the hotel, so it becomes Loei's grand meeting spot. Even late at night you'll often see a crowd outside of the hotel; don't worry, it's not a riot, it's just the bus coming to Loei. Forty guest rooms have air-conditioning.

SAVITA BAKERY, 137 Charoenrat Rd. Tel. 811526.
  Cuisine: WESTERN/THAI. **Directions:** In the central area.
$ Rates: Appetizers 35B–75B ($1.40–$3); main courses 50B–200B ($2–$8).
  Open: Daily 6am–10:30pm.

This is the only place for late-night snacks or early breakfast. At night, the cheery staff doles out Foremost ice cream by the bucket, while you can get a complete breakfast with eggs, sausage, toast, and jam for a mere 35B ($1.40). The Savita also has a complete and varied lunch-and-dinner menu, mostly serving Thai appetizers and main dishes.

EASY EXCURSIONS

PHU KRADUNG NATIONAL PARK   Phu Kradung may be Thailand's most dramatic, mountainous national park. To say mountainous is both descriptive and yet misleading. The whole park consists of a giant mountain (in girth not height; the summit is just under 4,000 feet) with a wide, heart-shaped plateau at the "peak." Upon reaching the high table summit, some 9km (5½ miles) from the Sithan trailhead and information station, there are 50km (31 miles) of hiking trails to explore, a tent village with basic facilities, waterfalls, sheer cliffs to admire, and numerous panoramic spots from which to gaze out over the nearby Phetchabun Mountains—from here you'll understand why Loei is referred to as the Province of a Sea of Mountains.

The name Phu Kradung means Bell Mountain, which connects with the Buddhist legend that the mountain once rang like a bell on a Sabbath day. Of course, the fact that it's bell shaped didn't hurt. Either way, the park is popular both with Thai and foreign travelers, especially from October to January, and even more so on weekends. Park rangers suggest visiting during weekdays and, if possible, in May and June—just at the beginning of the rainy season, when it's not too wet.

While there are rumored to be an enormous variety of mammals in the park, we saw few exotic breeds; however, we did see some glorious wildflower fields (best seen from February through May). Phu Kradung is one place in Thailand that actually has a fall season, only here it takes place during December. Whole stands of deciduous trees, including maple, oak, and beech, turn golden colors, reminding us of our New England roots. The park closes during the rainy season, from July through October.

The main place to stay is up top, Phu Kradung House, at the park headquarters. Down below, at Sithon, you can arrange for a porter to carry your bags. You'll also find restaurants, an information office, and a few bungalows. Up top accommodations are in tents—who said this was a laid-back place—with a simple Thai restaurant serving hot food (it gets cold up there). Reservations can be made in Bangkok with the National Park Divison, Forestry Department, 117/6 Paholyothin 7 (Soi Aree), Phyathai, Bangkok 10400 (tel. 02/271-3737 or 02/579-5269), or at the Administration and Service Office in Loei (tel. 800776 or 811700).

Phu Kradang National Park is located 82km (51 miles) south of Loei. To reach it, take Route 201 south and travel 8km (5 miles) west along Route 2019. Buses heading for Khon Kaen depart approximately every 30 minutes from Loei for 25B ($1); some minivans or buses go directly to the park while others stop along the main road where you'll have to flag a ride into the park.

PHU LUANG WILDLIFE RESERVE   Access to Phu Luang Wildlife Reserve is controlled by the Forestry Department to protect the many species of wildlife that live atop this wide plateau. The summit of Phu Luang is only about 500 feet higher than Phu Kradung, yet the ecology is more varied. In the reserve tropical flora gives way to deciduous and coniferous zones, which in turn host a wider array of fauna. There are reputed to be elephants and tigers within the bounds of the reserve, but it's unlikely that you'll see them as they shy away from human tourists.

The local branch of the Forestry Department organizes 3-day/2-night tours into Phu Luang, complete with admission, transport from Loei, guide, food, and tent fee for 950B ($38); contact the Administration and Service Office in Loei (tel. 800776 or 811700) for more information. There is normally a minimum number of people required for a group, so it's best to reserve space as early as possible.

PHRA THAT SISONGRAK   The history of Thailand and Laos isn't one marked by long periods of cooperation, but the mid-16th century was an exception. The two kingdoms were in a period of détente, and to commemorate that relationship, King Chakkaphat of Ayutthaya and King Chaichettha of Lan Xang constructed a 100-foot-tall brick-and-mortar stupa. This monument to international goodwill was built during a 3-year period (1560–63). Although the site isn't worth traveling far off the beaten path for—it's set 86km (53 miles) due west of Loei on the banks of the Moon River—it is a fine piece of Ayutthaya architecture that should be seen by those traveling west of Chiang Khan, along the river.

EN ROUTE TO NONG KHAI

ALONG THE MAE KHONG FROM CHIANG KAN THROUGH SI CHIANG MAI

This has become one of our favorite areas in Thailand. Almost totally unexploited and delightfully scenic, the northern perimeter of Isan runs along the famed Mae Khong, which divides the country with Laos. If we had our druthers, we'd traverse this route on bicycle, as this is arguably the best cycling route we've come across in Thailand. The terrain is relatively flat, the road is lightly trafficked and in a good state of repair, and there are a number of villages where you can stop for a quick drink or bite. A few guest houses in the area rent bicycles, though they are of the three-speed variety, and in general, are haphazardly maintained. At press time, several small companies still maintained that they were going to offer scheduled boat services between Chiang Khan down to Pak Chom; if this materializes, we'd heartily recommend the ride, as it follows some of the most interesting scenery in Isan. If you decide to travel here directly from Bangkok, there is daily overnight air-conditioned bus service to Chiang Khan (trip time: 10 hours; 390B [\$15.60]).

If you take the bus or song tao north from Loei (trip time: 45 minutes; 25B [\$1]) you'll reach the riverside town of Chiang Khan, opposite Sarakham, Laos. Here you'll find a guest house or two, a wat worth visiting, a couple of fun excursions, and about 150 expats who've discovered that life is pretty grand in a simple Thai border bown. The most highly recommended activity is cruising west (upriver) on the Mae Khong. The trip, motoring in long-tail boats, takes about three hours and traverses some of the most sublime scenery in all of the Northeast; boat trips should be booked by the owner of your guest house (or at the "Local Boats for Rent" sign at the intersection of Soi 10 and River Road), with a typical price of 200B (\$8) per person (prices fluctuate according to the time of year so don't be afraid to bargain). If, on your Mae Khong trip or any point on your travels, you take a swim in the river, be aware that each year many Thai residents drown due to the slyly swift currents. Stay close to the shore and make sure that you swim with someone else (or request that somebody keeps an eye out). By the way, we were told that the water is pretty clean.

The in-town site is called **Wat Sri Khun Muang** and is located adjacent to the town market. This shrine and place of worship is constructed in the Northern style and features walls constructed of glassy materials. Our favorite part of the wat are the guardian demons and lions situated in the main chapel area as well as the primitively painted murals of the life of the Buddha.

Five kilometers (3 miles) east of Chiang Khan is **Kaeng Khut Khu,** a particularly scenic Mae Khong overlook. There are more than 25 food stalls (try the som tam or pla yang) lining the shore, affording a fine vista and delicious lunch. The scene is reminiscent of a Mississippi River stop: lazy, wide, and muddy. There is song-tao service for 10B (40¢), tuk-tuk for 50B (\$2), but we suggest taking a 25-minute bike ride. For the height of luxury you can cruise downriver to KKK for about 125B (\$5) per person. If you have a desire to spend the night near the rapids, there is the Seeview Hut (no phone) where they have four bungalows that rent for 250B (\$10).

In-town accommodations at the **Suksumbun Hotel** (no phone) are better and some rooms have a river view. The Suksumbun has 15 fan-cooled rooms with sinks (toilet and bathing facilities are down the hall), 120B (\$4.80) for single or double; there is also a riverview dining area. Try the *larbs,* either larb moo or gai, *ya mut ya* (spicy noodles with sausage), and *play tot* (fried fish). Check out the three food outlets on Soi 9 where a complete meal can be had for only 25B (\$1); menus are in

English. The drink of choice is *mao lao*, literally "drunk on liquor," but it nearly always refers to Laotian whiskey which is both stronger and cheaper than the Thai variety. Remember to change money in Loei or Si Chiang Mai as there are no banks within Chiang Khan.

One kilometer (6/10 of a mile) west of town you'll find the new **Nong Sam Guesthouse** (which will soon have a telephone/fax), run by Noi and her British husband, Robert, where 10 bungalows set among spacious gardens on the riverbank rent for 80B ($3.20) single, 120B ($4.80) double. They serve breakfast every morning from 6:30 to 11:30am and dinner by arrangement, hire mountain bikes and canoes, and other nature tours. (Special minimal-impact, culture-sensitive, environment-friendly small-group tours can be arranged through **Green Pagodas;** contact Dr. Robert Mather, P.O. Box 7, Chiang Khan, Loei 42110; fax 042/821059.)

Highway 2186 continues along the Mae Khong passing through Pak Chom and Si Chiang Mai before arriving in Nong Khai. We enjoyed touring this area with its broad floodplains feeding the bordering Lao and Thai valleys. Lushly planted banana plantations, terraced fruit farms, manganese mines, and cotton-and-tomato fields reach deeply into the verdant valleys that intersect the Mae Khong basin. Farther inland are lovely waterfalls such as Nam Tok Than Thip (between Pak Chom and Si Chiang Mai), which are ideal picnic spots or just fun hiking stops.

Si Chiang Mai is situated opposite Vientiane, the capital of the Lao People's Democratic Republic, and is but 58km (36 miles) due west of Nong Khai. The town struck us, on our last vixit, as one of those perfect Thai backwaters that offers little to see and do—in the traditional sense—but is nearly idyllic in mood and sensibility. A trip to the bakery, watching Lao and Thai long-tail boats silently ply the Mae Khong, or taking a walk to a spring-roll factory is about the speed of things. We enjoyed lunch overlooking the river, with Vientiane (arguably the sleepiest capital city we've ever seen) in the background: It's a surrealistically serene setting. Try the candied tomatoes sold outside of the restaurants; they're scrumptious. During the dry season you can sunbathe on the beach or on one of the nearby islands (remember the water warning).

Outside of Si Chiang Mai is another Isan town called **Ban Phu** (not to be confused with the Ban Phu near Ban Chiang) where there are stone pinnacles similar to those in the Stone Forest in China's Yunnan Province. This is a worthwhile excursion, but accomplished more easily by car than bus. If you do bus it, take the coach directly to Ban Phu town via Thabo followed by the Nam Som–bound bus, getting off at Ban Tiew. After that you'll have to take a 4km (2½ mile) tuk-tuk ride to the park. Nearby is the restored 17th-century temple complex known as **Phrat That Bang Phuan,** thought to have been originally constructed around the same time as Phra That Phanom, between A.D. 500 and 1000. As with many shrines in Thailand, it is said to entomb relics of the Buddha, specifically his pelvis (this according to Urangkhathat legend). The lotus-bud–shaped central building is Lanna, referring to the Northern Thai mode of architecture; other buildings in the complex are influenced by Laotian styles.

If a stay in Si Chiang Mai sounds like the antidote to what ails you, proprietor Jean-Daniel Schranz runs **Tim Guest House** (tel. 042/451072; fax 042/451370), located on the quay but 200 yards from the bus stop on the main road. Single rooms range from 50B to 120B ($2 to $4.80) while doubles run a cool 80B to 140B ($1.60 to $5.60); there are dormitory rooms for a mere 40B ($1.60). There is even a 175B ($7) honeymoon suite which is just right for couples or families. They advertise an "experimental solar-heated shower" and "Francophone" management. How can you go wrong? They also rent bicycles, motorcycles, boats, and cars with driver. Bikes go for 50B ($2) per day; motorcycles cost 250B ($10). Expect to pay 500B ($20) for a car-and-driver excursion to Ban Phu. We dined at the three restaurants located about 200 yards east of Tim's and found them adequate and inexpensive.

Public transport from Chiang Khan to Nong Khai via Si Chiang Mai is somewhat involved. Take a song tao (trip time: 45 minutes; 25B [$1]) from Chiang Khan to Pak Chom and change to the green bus to Nong Khai (trip time: 3 to 4 hours; 60B [$2.40]). Alternatively, you can get a Thai Airways van from the office in

Loei for a tour of the area; expect to pay about 2,500B ($100) a day for an air-conditioned vehicle with driver.

6. NONG KHAI

615km (381 miles) NE of Bangkok; 51km (32 miles) N of Udon Thani;
356km (221 miles) N of Khorat; 202km (125 miles) E of Loei;
303km (188 miles) W of Nakhon Phanom

GETTING THERE By Plane   One flight a day leaves from Bangkok to Udon Thani (flying time: 55 minutes; 1,510B [$60.50] on Thai Airways).

By Train   Nong Khai is connect by rail to Bangkok via Khorat. Three trains a day depart from Bangkok (trip time: 11 hours on rapid train; second-class air-conditioned 550B [$12]).

By Bus   Five air-conditioned buses a day leave from Bangkok (trip time: 11 hours; 300B [$12]). Three air-conditioned buses a day leave from Khorat (trip time: 5 hours; 200B [$8]). Many buses daily from Udon Thani (trip time: 45 minutes; 80B [$3.20]). Seven daily nonair-conditioned buses to Loei stop in Si Chiang Mai (trip time: 1½ hours; 20B [80¢]), Pak Chom (trip time: 4½ hours; 70B [$2.80]), and with a change in Pak Chom, Chiang Khan (trip time: 7 hours; 100B [$4]).

By Car   The most direct route from either Bangkok or Udon Thani Khai is on Route 2 (Friendship Highway). Take Route 211 west to travel along the Mae Khong to Loei, via Si Chiang Mai, Pak Chom, and Chiang Khan.

ESSENTIALS   The **area code** is 042. The **Thai Airways office** (tel. 411530) is located at 453 Prajak Rd.; they operate a shuttle to and from the Udon Thani airport that departs two hours prior to departures for 150B ($6). The **Nong Khai Provincial Hosptial** (tel. 411504) is on Meechai Road; the emergency number for the **police** is 411020. Most national **banks** have branch offices on Phosi Road.

SPECIAL EVENTS   A **Rocket Festival,** on a lesser scale than that held in Yasothon in May, begins on the full moon in June. It's purpose is to appeal to the heavens as a reminder to bring plentiful rain in the upcoming season. The event takes place at Wat Pho Chai, the home of Nong Khai's most revered Buddha.

With the completion of the Friendship Bridge spanning the Mae Khong to Tha Dua, Laos, increased international commerce and travel will probably bring many changes to Nong Khai. On our last visit we found two big new hotels to prove we're not alone in our thinking. (We hope to see some easing in travel restrictions for foreigners in the near future, but they weren't yet evident.)

Nong Khai remains well worth a visit, retaining much of its small-town charm—you can still walk from one end to the other, though it's a 20-baht (80¢) tuk-tuk ride to the railway station and another 20 baht to the bridge—with the additional elements (and excitements) of a booming border town. Even if you're not crossing to Laos you can get a good view of it, get in some shopping, and make connections to the scenic Mae Khong basin and even the archeological site at Ban Chiang.

ORIENTATION

Information   Although there is no TAT office or municipal information booth, we found that the bulletin boards and maps at both the **Mut-mee Guest House** at 1111/4 Kaeworawut Rd. and **Sawasdee Guest House** at 402 Meechai Rd. offered all of the help you might need.

The best map of the town is available at the **Meeting Place,** a restaurant/bar at 1117 Soi Chuenchitt—sometimes known locally as Soi Si Chomchuen—(tel. 042/411327, ext. 217; fax 042/412644), managed by Australian Alan Patterson, who also offers guest rooms and motorcycles for rent, the latest information, and visa service.

The people at **Northeast Business & Travel** (tel. 412511; fax 411073) at 1105 Kwaeworawut Rd. book bus and train trips as well as offering excursions in and around Nong Khai. Mr. Thu-thu, a partner in the company, speaks excellent English and is well informed about travel to Laos.

City Layout   Nearly all tourist facilities and sites are located on three parallel streets running along the Mae Khong. The closest to the river is Rimkhong Road, and it's where you'll find the Immigration Office for Lao border crossings. Meechai Road is a commercial thoroughfare along which is the post office, Bangkok Bank at 374 Si Saket Rd., open Monday to Friday 8am to 8pm, and the hospital. The farthest of the three main roads is Prajak, on which you'll find Thai Airways, the air-conditioned and VIP bus terminals, and, near the regular bus station on the east side, Pochai Market. The train station is located on the western periphery of town.

No distance—with the exception of the train station—within town is beyond a long walk, or if you have luggage, a 10B (40¢) bicycle rickshaw or tuk-tuk ride.

WHAT TO SEE & DO

Shopping is a singularly significant activity in Nong Khai and is covered later in this section. The nearby excursions, such as a trip to Ban Chiang or Laos are also detailed in this chapter.

There is an interesting hybrid architectural style in Nong Khai. On the east side of town, along Meechai Road, are several mansions built in the early 20th century in what can best be described as French-Chinese colonial style.

There are a couple of in-town wats that are worth exploring, but the most unusual structure is located about 4 to 5km (3 miles) east of town at **Wat Khaek** on Route 212 (the Nakhon Phanom road). Here you'll find recently cast concrete Buddhas and other figures of enormous proportions inspired by an Indian guru who built his shrine in a lovely garden setting. New figures are being cast and the temple is adorned with Hindu and Buddhist motifs.

WHERE TO STAY

EXPENSIVE

HOLIDAY INN MEKONG ROYAL NONG KHAI, 222 Jommanee Beach, Nong Khai 43000. Tel. 042/420024. Fax 6642/421280. 208 rms. A/C TV TEL **Directions:** West of bridge, about a mile west of town.
$ Rates: 2,500B–3,100B ($100–$124) single/double; suites from 3,750B ($150). AE, DC, MC, V.

This handsome new high rise with a swimming pool and half a dozen restaurants beyond the bridge from town was completely full of happy Thais during our visit. We suppose they were excited about its States-like appearance. We'd recommend it only if you're planning to cross the bridge by auto or prefer its out-of-the-way location.

NONG KHAI GRAND HOTEL, 589 Moo 5, Nong Khai-Poanpisai Rd., Nong Khai 43000. Tel. 042/420033. Fax 042/412026. 126 rms. A/C MINIBAR TV TEL **Directions:** Just south of town on highway.
$ Rates: 1,600B–1,900B ($64–$76) single; 1,900B–2,150B ($76–$86) double; suites from 2,500B ($100). AE, DC, MC, V.

We were fortuante enough to stay here during our last visit and were immensely pleased with this lovely new hotel far enough off the main highway to be quiet, yet close enough to town for an easy walk. Facilities include a swimming pool, lobby lounge/music room, restaurant, café, rooftop grill, business center, meeting rooms, discotheque, massage parlor, snooker club, and jogging track. The big buffet lunch (150B) was the best meal we had.

MODERATE

PRAJAK BUNGALOWS, 1178 Prajak Rd., Nong Khai 43000. Tel. 042/ 412644. Fax 042/412644. 30 rms, all with hot-water shower. **Directions:** West side of town.

$ Rates: 180B ($7.20) single/double with fan; 450B–500B ($18–$20) single/double with A/C; 500B ($20) two-bedroom bungalow with fan. DC, MC, V.

A friendly English-speaking staff is the big plus here. The rooms, in various sizes and configurations, are clean and comfortable.

BUDGET

MUT-MEE GUEST HOUSE, 1111/4 Kaeworawut Rd., Nong Khai. No phone. 14 rms. **Directions:** ½ block from the waterfront next to Wat Haisok.

$ Rates: 110B ($4.40) single with fan; 140B ($5.60) double with fan. No credit cards.

This near-waterfront location guest house is favored by some travelers for its garden that overlooks the Mae Khong and beyond (to Laos) as well as for its proximity to Nong Khai's vibrant market and river activity. The rooms are more basic and higher priced than those at the Sawasdee, but the well-informed staff helps to compensate for any lack of comfort. The Mut-Mee rents bicycles; expect to pay 40B ($1.60) per day.

SAWASDEE GUEST HOUSE, 402 Meechai Rd., Nong Khai. Tel. 042/ 412502. 16 rms. A/C **Directions:** 1 block from the waterfront on the east side.

$ Rates: 90B ($3.60) single with fan; 300B ($12) single with A/C; 120B ($4.80) double with fan; 350B ($14) double with A/C and hot shower. No credit cards.

The oversize doors to this unassuming guest house lead to a spacious lobby with an eclectic selection of furniture. Wagon-wheel Western and traditional Thai with a curio cabinet make for an odd and satisfying mix. The lobby leads to an open courtyard where guests congregate after a long day of touring. The rooms (six have airconditioning) are clean and of guest house standard, but to our tastes this is the best-value accommodations in Nong Khai. One enthusiastic Australian father-and-son team who had been traveling for months proclaimed the Sawasdee the finest guesthouse in all of Thailand! There are bicycles for rent at nominal prices.

WHERE TO DINE

CHOR KOON RESTAURANT, 589 Moo 5, Nong Khai-Poanpisai Rd. Tel. 420033.

Cuisine: THAI/INTERNATIONAL. **Directions:** Nong Khai Grand Hotel, just south of town on highway.

$ Prices: Breakfast 75B–100B ($3–$4); lunch 150B ($6); dinner 180B ($7.20). AE, DC, MC, V.

We were disappointed during our last visit to find our favorate Vietnamese restaurant had become a nightclub, but we found compensation in our hotel, the Nong Khai Grand. There's an à la carte menu, of course, but we found their lavish buffet of Thai, Chinese, Japanese, Italian, and other specialties irresistible—and a good value.

FLOATING RESTAURANT, on the Mae Khong, near Wat Haisok. Tel. 412211.

Cuisine: THAI. **Directions:** Below Wat Haisok, connected by a stairway.

$ Prices: Appetizers 25B–50B ($1–$2); main courses 50B–90B ($2–$3.60). No credit cards.

Open: Daily 10am–10pm.

The main attraction here is dining on a boat that actually cruises up the Mae Khong. Among the many salads and curries are the *nun-on* (a variety of catfish) dishes such as nun-on and coconut curry. With a bottle of Kloster beer and chicken with cashews or mixed vegetables, a meal with a river cruise is a reasonable 150B ($6). The boat departs at 5pm daily and generally travels for about an hour; the fee is 40B ($1.60) whether you eat or not.

TADAN RESTAURANT, Rimkhong Rd. Tel. 411543
   Cuisine: THAI. **Directions:** Next to the Immigration Office, overlooking the Mae Khong.
$ Prices: Appetizers 25B–50B ($1–$2); main courses 40B–75B ($1.60–$3). No credit cards.
   Open: Daily 11am–10pm.
This riverside eatery is popular with both locals and travelers alike and serves very simple but tasty Thai cuisine. We had a delicious chicken with basil dish and what we judged to be a specialty, bubbling hot pot with meat and vegetables, for a pittance.

SHOPPING

This is a major activity in Nong Khai and shouldn't be ignored, although we were distressed on our last visit to discover much higher prices and reduced quality. The nexus of activity is the waterfront market on Rimkhong Road, just east of the Immigration Office. Although many crafts are on display, we prefer the Laotian silver work. Expect to pay abut 500B ($20) for a well-made silver bracelet and 1,200B ($48) for a long silver necklace with a handmade chain. (We found better goods and prices both in Nakhon Phanom and Ubon).

Among the shops that our ace shopper, Victorial Westhead, found and liked are: Porntip (302 Rimkhong Rd.) for Laotian silver boxes and finely crafted Loatian silver bracelets and necklaces; the shop at 923 Rimkhong Rd. for silver ball necklaces; no. 419 and no. 635 carry long Surin-style necklaces; one of the better shops is at the far eastern end on the north (river) side where they sell intricately woven baskets from Udon Thani (we bought several), but plan on paying about 900B ($36) for a small basket with a top.

Village Weaver Handicrafts (tel. 411236) on 786/1 Prajak Rd. (factory and showroom) and 1151 Soi Jittapunya Rd. (showroom only) began as a self-help project in 1982 and has flourished as a cooperative enterprise. The goal of the project is to provide a means by which local weavers can practice their art and remain in their home village while making a living. Weaving masters oversee villagers work to maintain quality and to introduce advanced techniques. The two shops—the Prajak Road location doubles as a factory and demonstration center—offer a wide selection of fabric, ready-to-wear clothing, and a variety of pillow covers, eyeglass cases, and other household items. Prices are fair; a 6-foot length of handwoven ikat cotton, for example, ranges from 200B to 500B ($8 to $20). Many products from this shop are featured in the Oxfam gift catalog.

Similar goods, though to our mind, not quite as well tailored, are produced at the shop known as House of E-San, located south of Nong Khai in Ban Nong Song Hong on the Udon highway. The shop is only a part of a complex that includes a series of small buildings where fabric is spun, dyed, woven, and cut, all on display for the interested shopper. We actually preferred their small collection of older weavings to the modern variety, but you'll find a large assortment of material and clothing for sale here at prices that are similar to those at Village Weaver Handicrafts. Nisa Chon, the gregarious proprietress of the establishment has a modest guest house on the premises (tel. 01/4100137). To get here, take a public bus to the checkpoint, approximately 12km (7½ miles) south of Nong Khai; the shop is located about 100 yards south of the guard station.

EASY EXCURSIONS

Aside from visiting Laos, the two most frequently requested excursions are to **Ban Phu** (with a side trip to Phra That Bang Phuan) and Ban Chiang. The former is a visit to a park with unique rock structures and is described in the section about Chiang Khan (see above). The archeologically significant finds at **Ban Chiang** can be explored from Nong Khai instead of the usual base in Udon Thani. Most travel agents book a 1-day excursion including transport, food, guide, and admission fees for 350B ($14) per person. Contact your hotel or an agency for bookings.

Many people who come to Nong Khai contemplate a visit to **Laos.** It is tantalizingly close, but you'll have to plan in advance or have a lot of time and money to get there. The procedures are expected to change (they seem to change constantly), but as of 1994 the following guidelines were in effect: A visa, costing approximately 2,500B ($100), is required; this entitles you to a 15-day visit. If you arrange your visa in Nong Khai it will take about one week to get a copy of your passport and four passport photos. If you are able to apply at the Laotian embassy in Bangkok, the charge is 300B ($12), but it's generally approved only if you book a tour, have a sponsor in Loas, or intend to conduct business. Once you've arranged for a visa, you are only allowed to travel to Vientiane; once there, you may apply for permission to travel around the country; however, when we investigated this we were told that they had stopped issuing internal travel permits. In other words, many people spend both time and money to discover that they could only go as far as the capital. For those who need to leave Thailand in order to renew their Thai visa, this isn't such a terrible deal, but we hope that travel eases again (it used to be much easier to visit other parts of Laos), making a real tour of Laos a possibility. An alternative to this is to book a packaged tour with companies in Bangkok or the United States, such as Adventures in Paradise in New York City.

Even if you don't go to Laos, avail yourself of the opportunity to read the greetings that await travelers from Laos upon their entry into Thailand. In the interests of history, we shall record a few morsels of the published regulations entitled "Definition of Alien with Hippy Characteristics: A person who is dressed in an impolite and dirty looking manner; a person who wears a singlet or waistcoat without underwear; a person who wears any type of slippers or wooden sandals except when they are a part of a national costume; an alien with such characteristics will be prohibited from entering the Kingdom." Waistcoat owners beware!

7. NAKHON PHANOM

740km (459 miles) NE of Bangkok; 252km (156 miles) E of Udon Thani;
481km (298 miles) NE of Khorat; 271km (168 miles) N of Ubon Ratchathani;
303km (188 miles) E of Nong Khai; 93km (58 miles) E of Sakon Nakhon

GETTING THERE By Plane One flight daily leaves from Bangkok to Sakon Nakhon (flying time: 65 minutes; 1,750B [$70] on Thai Airways).

By Bus Four air-conditioned buses a day leave from Bangkok (trip time: 13 hours; 350B [$14]). Three buses leave daily from Udon Thani (trip time: 5 hours; 100B [$4]). Many buses travel to Ubon Ratchathani daily (trip time: 4½ hours; 90B [$3.60]).

By Car The most direct route from either Bangkok or Khorat is on Route 2 (Friendship Highway) either north to Udon Thani and east on Route 22 or east on Route 24, north on Route 219 to Buriram, northeast on Route 213, and east on Route 22. The former includes a visit to Phimai and Ban Chiang, while the latter passes through Prasat Hin Phanom Rung and the less explored central Isan region.

ESSENTIALS The **area code** is 042. There is a small **TAT** information office at City Hall (tel. 513490; fax 513492). The closest **Thai Airways** office (tel. 712259) is located in Sakon Nakhon at 1446/73 Yuvapatana Rd. The **Nakhon Phanom Provincial Hospital** (tel. 511422) is on Sumthon Wichit Road; the emergency number for the **police,** on Sumthon Wichit Road, is 511266.

SPECIAL EVENTS Nakhon Phanom hosts two river spectacles to celebrate the end of the Rains Retreat. The first is the renowned **Mae Khong longboat race,** while the second is an illuminated **boat procession** that is agumented by cultural programs, Buddhist rituals, and a craft and food fair. Both celebrations normally take place in October, specifically on the 13th day of the waxing moon during the

11th lunar month. The **Phra That Phanom Festival** takes place in February (see "Easy Excursions," below).

"N akhon" translates to religious, and it's this spiritual connectin that attracts many travelers to Nakhon Phanom: They come to visit Phra That Phanom, the Northeast's most sacred Buddhist site, located about 76km (47 miles) south of the town on Route 212. The town is set along the Mae Khong, bordering Laos; across the way is the smaller Loatian town of Ta Kaek. Although there's a fair amount of traffic between the two towns, Nakhon Phanom is not an official cross-over point for foreign tourists—you'll have to travel northwest to Nong Khai or south, down to the outskirts of Ubon, in order to officially enter Laos.

You can, however, take an excursion on the river; boats leave from the pier more or less hourly (20B [80¢]). Nakhon Phanom is a good place to buy silver—in several shops near the pier—some of it fashioned by the skillful local craftsmen, some by Laotians in nearby refugee settlements, even some machine-made in Bangkok (though it's considerably cheaper here). It's pleasant enough, though few people speak English. If you're traveling south to Ubon you might consider staying at the Phra That Phanom site, where there are some rudimentary accommodations, and continuing your journey after a morning visit.

WHERE TO STAY

There are several adequate hotels, including the River Inn, with rates from about 100B to 400B ($4 to $16). The attractive new Mae Khong Grandview Hotel on the river just south of town wasn't open during our last visit, but if you're going to stay more than a night you'll probably want to check it out.

NAKHON PHANOM HOTEL, 403 Aphiban-Bancha Rd., Nakhon Phanom 48000. Tel. 042/511074. Fax (66)042/511074. 58 rms. A/C TEL **Directions:** South center of town, near bus stations.
$ Rates: 300B ($12) single with A/C; 350B ($14) double with A/C. MC, V.
The NKP is centrally located, clean, comfortable enough, air-conditioned, and the friendly manager speaks English. There's a good restaurant, pool, and snooker parlor. Insist on a rear-facing room, as the plaza out front is a popular late-night gathering place for local young people.

OUT OF TOWN

There are three guest houses located near the site of Phra That Phanom that, while being merely functional, may be just the thing for those who're heading south to Ubon. Although none are very clean, travel maven Marvin Rosen wrote us to suggest the **Saeng Thong** (no phone) at 34 Mu 1, Phanom-Phanarak Road where fan-cooled doubles run 140B ($5.60); singles cost 85B ($3.40). Another, possibly cleaner alternative, is the **Lim Charoen** (tel. 042/541019) at 167/67 Mu 13, Chayangkun Road; fan-cooled rooms range from 110B to 175B ($4.40 to $7) for singles and doubles, respectively.

EASY EXCURSIONS
PHRA THAT PHANOM

The origins of this most sacred shrine are somewhat undetermined, though archeologists have concluded that the first building was put up about 1,500 years ago (the spire is said to date from the 9th century). The legend associated with the temple is that the monk Maha Kasapa brought a breastbone of the Buddha to this location, whereupon five local princes built a stupa to house the relic. After that, successive rulers built smaller shrines, and most importantly, rebuilt the original structure; it's been restored seven times. The most recent restoration took place in 1977 after the tower had collapsed in 1975.

The shrine is venerated throughout the year by both Thai and Laotian people; however, for seven days beginning on the full moon during the third lunar month, Phra That Phanom hosts a fair for worshipers. The fair, in honor of the Buddhist Rains Retreat, features food-and-craft stalls and a variety of cultural programs.

On the way to the shrine, at **Renu Phanom**, is a crafts center where locals produce a wide range of embroidered material. There is also a diminutive version of the shrine with the appropriate name, Phra That Renu Nakhon.

Public buses travel between Nakom Phanom and the site for 20B (80¢).

8. UBON RATCHATHANI

629km (390 miles) NE of Bangkok; 271km (168 miles) S of Nakhon Phanom; 370km (229 miles) E of Khorat; 227km (141 miles) E of Surin

GETTING THERE By Plane   One flight a day leaves from Bangkok (flying time: 65 minutes nonstop, 2 hours via Khorat; 1,600B [$64] on Thai Airways).

By Train   Ubon is connected by rail to Bangkok via the Khorat, Buriram, Surin line. One express (10 hours), three rapid (12 hours), and three ordinary (14 hours) trains a day leave from Bangkok (second-class ordinary 300B [$12], express 340B [$13.60]). Seven trains daily leave from Khorat, with stops in Si Saket, Surin, and Buriram (trip time: 6 hours; 70B [$2.80]).

By Bus   There are seven air-conditioned and VIP buses departing daily from the Northern Bus Terminal (tel. 02/271-0101 or 279-4484) in Bangkok on Paholythin Road (trip time: 9½ hours; 325B [$13] and 500B [$20]). Seven buses daily leave from Khorat (trip time: 5 hours; 150B [$6]). Many buses travel daily to Nakhon Phanom (trip time: 4½ hours; 80B [$3.20]).

By Car   The most direct road from Bangkok is along Route 1 to Saraburi, turning east on Route 2 into Khorat (trip time: 4 hours); travel south on Route 304 and continue east on Route 24 (taking side trips to Buriram, Surin, and Si Saket); proceed north on Route 212 into Ubon (trip time: 5 hours).

ESSENTIALS   The **area code** is 045. The **Thai Airways office** (tel. 254431) is located at 364 Chayanggoon Rd.; they operate a shuttle to and from the airport that departs 2 hours prior to departures for 60B ($2.40). The **Rom Gao Hospital** (tel. 254053) is on Auparat Road, on the south side of town; the emergency number for the **police** is 191 or 254216. Most national **banks** have branch offices in Ubon, with the largest concentration on Prommaraj Road, a block south of the TAT office; hours are Monday to Friday 8:30am to 3:30pm. The airport has a **currency exchange** bureau open every day; hours are determined by Thai Airways flights. Ch. Watana (tel. 242202) operates a **car-rental** agency; expect to pay about 1,200B ($48) a day without gas.

SPECIAL EVENTS   Normally beginning in July (the full moon during the eighth lunar month), Ubon hosts its **Candle Festival** to honor the start of the 3-month-long Buddhist Rains Retreat. The highlight of this period is the Candle Parade in which giant decorated beeswax cast figures and floats are trekked through the town. During this celebration there are also bazaars, a beauty parade, Buddhist rituals and merit making, and dance performances.

A visit to Ubon Ratchathani is most compelling for its proximity to the prehistoric cave paintings at Pha Taem, located north of the confluence of the Mae Khong and Moon rivers. The city, one of Isan's most developed, is being positioned as Thialand's international gateway to nearby Laos (it's near one of two official cross-over points for foreigners), Cambodia, and beyond, to Vietnam. The proximity of these politically turbulent countries to Ubon Province accounts for the overwhelming military presence of the Thai army; wherever you wander from the town you're likely to encounter a well-established base.

Although there is little to see and do within Ubon, it's a fine place to start or end a tour of the region's southern cities, as it is connected by plane to Bangkok and close to Si Saket. Lastly, if you can manage to visit during the Candle Festival (usually in late July) you'll be rewarded with a genuine Thai spectacle.

ORIENTATION

Information   The TAT (tel. 243770; fax 243771) operates a branch office in Ubon that is very helpful in providing information about the city and its environs. They publish a good map of the town and will, if requested, arrange a car and driver for those who wish to tour the area; expect to pay approximately 1,200B ($48) without gasoline. The office is located at 264/1 Kaenthani Rd.; hours are daily 8:30am to 4:30pm.

City Layout   The town is built along the banks of the Moon River. The most important area for travelers is within a four-square-block area proceeding north from the river. Running parallel to the river are Prommathep Road, followed by Prommaraj (with many banks), Kaenthani Road (where you'll find the TAT) and Srinarong Road, with the General Post Office (open Monday to Friday 8:30am to 4:30pm; Saturday 8:30am to noon, closed Sunday; telephone office open daily 24 hours) and, three blocks west, the National Museum. The main north-south intersecting artery is Auparat Road, which is an extension of the bridge that spans the Moon River (the lesser suburb of Warinchamrab is located on the other side of the Moon). As Auparat extends northward, it becomes Chayangkul Road where the public bus terminal and Thai Airways office are located. The air-conditioned bus terminal is located on Phalorangrit Road, 1½ blocks north of the TAT office. The international airport is located on Ubon's outskirts; plan on taking a tuk-tuk or taxi to reach the center of town.

WHAT TO SEE & DO

The National Museum provides a good overview of the historical development of lower Isan. It's particularly interesting for its diverse collection of Indian, Khmer, and Thai art and objects that demonstrate interaction of these competing cultures. There is also an ethnographic section that highlights Thai and Laotian costumes and customs.

The structure that houses the collection was built in the mid-19th century and served as the provincial governor's office.

Admission is 25B ($1). It's open Wednesday to Saturday 8:30am to 4:30pm (the museum is often closed during lunch).

The **Wat Supatanaram Warawihan** complex demonstrates how Ubon is a significant crossroad in Southeast Asia. Originally built in 1853 by Vietnamese craftspeople in a Vietnamese/European style, it was financed by the Thai king Rama IV to house 7th-century Khmer lintels, an ancient figure of the Indian Hindu deity Ganesha, Dvaravati stone boundary markers—all placed in front of the viharn as memorials—and a Buddha of Chinese influence, Pra Sapphayu Chao. This aesthetically eclectic shrine is revered by both Thai and Laotian people, adding to the cultural mélange of historic and regional modes. Within the complex is a sonorous wooden bell that is reputed to be the largest of its kind in Thailand. The wat is located along the Moon River, a good place to take in the sunset.

Wat Tung Sri Muang, a temple complex situated smack in the center of town and around the corner from one of our favorite Ubon restaurants, is worth a visit. Okay, we admit that the erotic paintings did catch our eye, but what the heck, we'd been on the road for a long time. Actually this wat is renowned for its mural paintings as well as the gracefully designed compound, including a pond and an all-teak library with a collection of antique books.

The best single place to buy silk, *khit* patterned cloth, ready-made garments, silver, and other local wares is **Phanchat Esan Folk Arts and Handicrafts,** 158/1-2 Ratchabut Rd. (between TAT and the Ratchathani Hotel), tel. 243433. It's open 9am to 8pm daily except Wednesday; Mastercard and VISA are accepted. The friendly English-speaking owner is knowledgeable and informative.

Watanasilp, 104 Ratchabut Rd., tel. 255661, has a large selection of silver, ranging from cultural handicrafts to sophisticated machine-made items from Bangkok (less expensive here than in the capital), as well as exquisite pieces in gold and hematite.

WHERE TO STAY

PATHUMRAT HOTEL, 337 Chayangkul Rd., Ubon Ratchathani. Tel. 045/241501. 138 rms. A/C MINIBAR TV TEL **Directions:** To the northwest of the river.
$ Rates: 800B ($32) single with A/C; 1,500B ($60) double with A/C; family room 2,000B ($80); extra bed 300B ($12). AE, DC, MC, V.

This modern seven-story high rise offers rather plain but comfortable furnishings both in its guest quarters as well as public spaces. The lobby is often crowded with Thai tourists who congregate in the coffee-shop area around the large television or who're reading the newspaper while waiting for their tour bus. There is a swimming pool just off of the lobby. The management is a bit friendlier than in most Isan accommodations and the level of service is adequate.

RATCHATHANI HOTEL, Kaenthani Rd., Ubon Ratchathani 34000. Tel. 045/244838. Fax 045/243561. 100 rms. A/C TV TEL **Directions:** Across from TAT.
$ Rates: 275B ($11) single with fan; 420B ($16.80) single with A/C; 350B ($14) double with fan; 600B ($24) double with A/C. MC, V.

This is an aging hotel that, after a recent renovation, offers very good value for money. Some rooms have air-conditioning and the restaurant is okay. We like its central location, two blocks from the Mun River, and its proximity to the in-town sites and services, but don't expect much help from the staff.

WHERE TO DINE

BONGKOT RESTAURANT, 10/24 Nakhon Ban Rd. Tel. 241443.
Cuisine: THAI/CONTINENTAL/AMERICAN. **Directions:** West of Wat Tung Sri Muang.
$ Prices: Appetizers 40B–60B ($1.50–$2.40); main courses 50B–120B ($2–$4.80). No credit cards.
Open: Daily 11am–midnight.

We stumbled upon this charming new little place during our last trip. Wood walls and ceilings, pastel tablecloths, and families enjoying an intimate meal by candlelight while a pretty, well-dressed woman sang Thai ballads at a piano, put us in mind of a quiet bistro in Provence. The menu is large and various, including American sandwiches.

KHUN DEI RESTAURANT, 10/18 Nakhon Ban Rd. Tel. 242278.
Cuisine: THAI. **Directions:** Around the corner from Wat Tung Sri Muang.
$ Prices: Main courses 10B–50B ($40¢–$2). No credit cards.
Open: Daily (except Sunday) 10am–10pm.

There won't be a word of English spoken here and the menu won't help either, but we found the food at the Khun Dei to be about the best we sampled in Ubon. The specialties are Isan-style Thai food, which basically means hotter than hot. The *som tam* (papaya salad with a cornucopia of accompanying ingredients) was incendiary but utterly fresh and delicious. Similarly tasty but considerably toned down was a plate of chicken *larb*. Our *gai yang* (fried chicken) was crisp and inexpensive. Speaking of price, a complete meal for two should run no more than about 150B ($6).

EASY EXCURSIONS

PHA TAEM CLIFF PAINTINGS & SAO CHALIANG   Well-preserved cliff paintings, dating from 4,000 to 2,000 years ago, are the principle attraction of Pha Taem, located 95km (59 miles) northeast of Ubon. The site is located along the base of sandstone cliffs that overlook the broad Mae Khong basin; we like this particular stop as much for its panorama as for the paintings. After arriving at the site, you'll have to walk down, a shade less than a mile, to the cliffs.

The prehistoric abstracted forms are thought to have been painted by a migrating tribe that had a developed agricultural society. Figures of humans, domestic animals, and fish seem to connect with similar images found at such neolithic sites as Ban Chiang. There are two basic stretches of cliff paintings which are thought to be the longest in Southeast Asia. For the best view, we suggest climbing up the low observation towers. For the more intrepid hiker, you can either continue along the trail or scramble down to the village below. In any case, be sure to wear a hat and good shoes and plan on buying a bottle of water (there are stalls up top, adjacent to the parking lot) to take with you.

Along the road to Pha Taem is a wonderful rock formation, **Sao Chaliang,** that is especially popular with kids who enjoy climbing. Although it's small, it might remind them of a real-life Bedrock—minus the Flintstones. We like this diversion for picture taking and, if you plan ahead, it'd be a fun place for a picnic.

The best way to get to Pha Taem is by hired car (contact the TAT for car and driver), especially as there is no direct public transportation to Pha Taem. It is possible to take a bus to Wat Phokhaokaew (every hour from Ubon); switch to the Khong Chiam–bound bus (14km [9 miles] from Pha Taem), and try to hire a tuk-tuk to the site; however, you should contact the TAT for the current bus schedule to ensure that this is still a viable option.

The site is open dawn to dusk. Admission is free.

KAENG TANA NATIONAL PARK   There are several scenic overlooks and parks along the Mae Khong and its confluence with the Mae Moon. The Kaeng Tana National Park includes both the confluence as well as inland, forested areas that have hiking trails, bungalows, and rock formations similar to Sao Chaliang's. During low water, roughly February through May, there are islets to explore, while waterfalls are best seen during and after the rains, from June through November. There is a short ferry that traverses the Moon River from Khong Chiam (50B [$2] per vehicle). In the town of Khong Chiam, there are a few restaurants, a market, and an emerging cluster of primitively equipped guest houses; we suggest a stay here for those who're really trying to escape the tourist hordes.

Traveling west, back toward Ubon, is the well-developed overlook at Sapue Rapids. Here you'll find a wide stretch of water with fisherpeople casting nets into the rushing water. There are food-and-drink stalls immediately adjacent, so it's possible to join the many Thai families picnicking on the rocks while taking in the lovely river scenery.

Just a few kilometers west is the newly built, ceramic tile covered temple at Wat Phokhaokaew. It's gaudy, but if you're in the neighborhood it might be worth a stop.

CHONGMEK   For those who have arranged their Laotian visa in advance (at the Bangkok embassy), Chomgmek is an official crossing point. We went to this border settlement because we were told that they had an ethnically interesting market. Instead, we found a dreary fenced-in hamlet that a few lucky Laotians are permitted to visit in order to buy Thai and foreign goods. Other than that, there is no compelling reason to visit.

EN ROUTE TO SURIN

We discovered that there are two wats—**Wat Pa Pong** and **Wat Pa Nanachat**—located midway between Ubon and Si Saket that are home to forest-dwelling

Buddhist monks, many of whom hail from the United States, Canada, and Europe. The spiritual leader at Wat Pa Pong, 12km (7 miles) from Warinchamrab (south of the Ubon–Si Saket Highway), is Acharn Cha, who leads a contingent of devoted acolytes in the study of Vipassana (insight oriented) meditation. Visitors are welcome at Wat Pa Pong, but they are requested to arrive in the morning, as the afternoon is devoted to silent meditation. The related complex, Wat Pa Nanchat (temple of the International Forest), is located north of the main highway and is home exclusively to farang monks; visitors are similarly welcomed and advised.

The best way to get there, other than by private car, is to take a bus to Warinchamrab and hire a tuk-tuk or take a song tao.

SI SAKET

Pronounced "SEE-Sket," this province is among the most ancient in Isan and, correspondingly, has several excellent Khmer sites worth visiting.

PRASAT HIN WAT KAMPHAENG NOI Located about 8km (5 miles) off Route 226 on the road to Surin, this Khmer sanctuary is thought to have served as a so-called healing house. Intact are the foundation and central prang, but the structure of the site can be imagined based on the crumbling laterite remains and the familiar style developed during the 13th-centruy reign of King Jayavarman VII. Among th highlights of this ruin are the decorative lintels that depict Hindu scenes, such as Baruna carried by three swans. It's open daily 8:30am to 4:30pm. Admission is 25B ($1).

PRASAT HIN WAT KAMPHAENG YAI The largest of the Khmer sanctuaries in this part of Isan, Kamphaeng Yai is though to have been finished in 1042 and was dedicated to the Hindu deity Shiva. Although the Angkor architectural design is evident, there is a strong direct Indian influence throughout, particularly on the northern (vishnu in slumber) and southern (Shiva with Uma riding on Nandi the bull) lintels adorning the central prang. Like Phimai, the temple was converted from a Brahmanic Khmer–based shrine into a Mahayana Thai–Buddhist complex after the 13th century.

Much of the Prasat has been reconstructed using modern bricks, but the governmental Fine Arts Department has made an attempt to integrate as many of the decorated columns and lintels as possible. Kamphaeng Yai is located on Route 2080, about 15 minutes farther west from Kamphaeng Noi. It's open daily 8:30am to 4:30pm. Admission is 25B ($1).

PRASAT PHRA WIHARN For the truly dauntless traveler there is a visit to Khao Phra Wiharn, which is actually in Cambodia. Hm, Cambodia, you say? The Thai government has negotiated a special right for foreign visitors who wish to visit this impressive Khmer temple set in the hills overlooking that war-weary country. Like the vista at Phanom Rung, the view from Khao Phra Wiharn is remarkable and, in its day (in the 12th century), it was on par with Phimai and Phanom Rung as one of the major Khmer satellite stops from Angkor Wat. (During our last visit in late 1993, the border was closed due to renewed Khmer Rouge activitiy in the area, but we remain hopeful.) It's a big-time site and it takes a major effort to get there.

You must apply for permission by writing to: Kong Kamlang Surnari, Suan Yaek, Kong Thap Phak Thi 2, Amphoe Muang, Jangwat Surin 32000. You'll be asked to present your authorized pass at the military checkpoint (don't even think about trying to get by these guys). To get there, take a bus (trip time: 1½ hours; 25B [$1]) or song tao from Si Saket, 64km (40 miles) south to Kantharalak. From there, either take a motorcycle tuk-tuk or, if you're lucky, a timely song tao (which the TAT informed us may not take you into Camobdia, even if you have permission). Prior to heading to the site, you'll have to check in with the army barracks at Ban Nam Yen. We repeat: This is only to be done by the authorized and the brave.

9. SURIN

457km (283 miles) NE of Bangkok; 227km (141 miles) W of Ubon
Ratchathani; 111km (69 miles) E of Buriram; 198km (123 miles) E of Khorat

GETTING THERE By Plane   Currently there is no regularly scheduled air service to Surin, but Bangkok Airways has had daily flights there in the past and may again in the future.

By Train   Surin is connected by rail to Bangkok via the Khorat, Buriram, Ubon line. Two trains a day leave from Bangkok (trip time: 10 hours on ordinary train, 8-½ hours by express train; second-class ordinary 260B [$10.40], express 300B [$12]). Several trains daily leave from Khorat, with a stop in Buriram (trip time: 3 hours; 60B [$2.40]).

By Bus   There are four air-conditioned buses departing daily from the Northern Bus Terminal (tel. 02/271-0101 or 279-4484) in Bangkok on Paholyothin Road (trip time: 6 hours; 220B [$8.80]). Seven buses depart daily from Khorat (trip time: 3 hours; 60B [$2.40]). Many buses depart daily to Ubon (trip time: 3½ hours; 70B [$2.80]).

By Car   The most direct road from Bangkok is along Route 1 to Saraburi, turning east on Route 2 into Khorat (trip time: 4 hours); travel south on Route 304 and continue east on Route 24.

ESSENTIALS   The **area code** is 044. The **Bangkok Airways office** (tel. 511274) is located in the Petchkasem Hotel at 104 Chitbumrung Rd. The **Provincial Hospital** (tel. 511006) is on Tambon Nai Muang Road; the emergency number for the **police** is 191 or 511007; the border police number is 511386. Most national **banks** have branch offices in Surin, with the largest concentration on Thanasarn Road; hours are Monday to Friday 8:30am to 3:30pm. Mengthai Hongyen (tel. 511715) and Gopchai (tel. 511775) both **rent cars** and are located on Tesabarn III and Tesabarn I, respectively; expect to pay 1,200B ($48) a day without gas.

SPECIAL EVENTS   Many people associate Surin solely with its famed **Elephant Roundup,** and though we think there are other compelling reasons to come here, this event is certainly a regional highlight. Each year, on the third Saturday and Sunday in November, the main events of the roundup take place in the town stadium. Accompanying the roundup is a week-long **Elephant Fair,** a greatly expanded version of a typical Thai market, with food-and-crafts stalls, performances (including Surin folktales), a rocket show, and rides; the fair begins about a week in advance of the roundup.

There are some pretty great elephant activities that take place during the festival, all of which should prove utterly cool for kids. Aside from the actual roundup, there are elephant tugs-of-war, an elephant talent contest, elephant soccer games, an elephant procession over their trainers (!), and a re-creation of a war formation involving elephants and soldiers.

Since Surin is jammed with tourists from around the world during this event, you are well advised to make hotel and travel reservations as soon as possible. If you find that it's impossible, consider staying in a nearby town or, if you can only travel in January, try the Chaiyaphum Roundup.

Surin is elephant country. Its festivals, excursions, and identity are intricately tied to ethnic Suay history and one of the great legends in Thai history. It seems that a tribal people, who were of either Laotian or Thai ancestry, migrated from the Mae Khong valley into what was later to become Ayutthaya-ruled Thailand. The villages that became Surin weren't under the direct rule of the kingdom, caught between Thai and Cambodian factions, yet when a royal white elephant escaped from

Ayutthaya, the Suay were brought in to capture King Suriyamarin's prized pachyderm. As a reward, the king conferred the honorific "Luang" on six men, one of whom was Luang Surintarapakdee Srinarongchangwang. He later moved his village to the site of present day Surin, which officially become a Thai-ruled city under the Chakri dynasty in 1756. By the way, Kyle believes that since everyone wanted a white elephant, the Thai deities decided to protect them by camouflaging them in a dull, unattractively colored exterior, which is why all elephants are gray! Okay, have you got a better story?

Victoria Westhead, or designated shopper, informs us that Surin is home to some of the best silver working in Thailand. We have seen finely made silver bracelets, baubles, and beads that are from Surin in high-end Bangkok shops (such as Gifted Hands) and would suggest that would-be buyers attend Surin's markets to sample the locally made wares.

ORIENTATION

Information There is no official information office in Surin; however, we found the people at the Pirom Guest House (tel. 44/515140) at 242 Krungsrinai Rd. to be friendly and helpful; they also ran daily excursions in and around Surin. For transport information, contact the three private bus companies: Theparat Tours (tel. 512081), S. K. Sethee Tour (tel. 511496), and Kajakarn Rajasrima (tel. 512161).

City Layout Surin is a compact—though growing—city with a central market and a main street, Thanasarn Road. Behind Thanasarn is the train station (on the northern end of Surin), and along it are nearly all of the foreign exchange banks. Near Thanasarn are Tesabarn I, II, and III roads, where you'll find a large number of tourist services and establishments such as rental-car agencies, department stores, and restaurants. The two most central landmarks in town are the market and the post office, just about in the exact center of Surin. In the same central area is Chitbumrung Road, the location of the Petchkasem Hotel, which hosts the Bangkok Airways office. The bus station is located in the northeast quadrant of town, a very short tuk-tuk or samlor ride to most hotels.

WHAT TO SEE & DO

We wondered where the elephants who participate in the annual roundup live during the rest of the year and learned that many of them reside in **Tha Klang Elephant Village** in the village of Tha Klang, located 58km (37 miles) north of Surin. The villagers are reputed to be descendants of the Suay who have long worked as elephant capturers and trainers, largely in and around the Cambodian border area. Today they train elephants for labor as well as to perform in the region's two roundups, in Surin during November and Chaiyaphum in January. Visitors are welcome in the village; however, few elephants are in Tha Klang during the day. They only return in the evening hours after putting in their work near the river. Some tours, such as that organized by Mr. Pirom (see "Where to Stay," below, for details), include an overnight in Tha Klang—in fairly primitive accommodations—to best see the elephants in their domestic setting with their handlers. A typical tour departs in the afternoon and returns to Surin on the following day; expect to pay about 700B ($28) per person including meals, accommodations, transport, and guide.

Once again the govermental Fine Arts Department is restoring and reconstructing a Khmer temple, and as with most in this part of Thailand, it was built during the 11th century in Angkor style. Like many of its kind, **Prasat Sikhoraphum (Prasat Ban Ra-ngaeng)** was converted during the 17th century from a Hindu to a Buddhist shrine. Of particular note are the carvings, excellent examples of Khmer limestone work, adorning the doorway columns as well as the Shiva carved lintel above the main doorway of the central prang. It's open daily 8:30am to 4:30pm. Admission is 25B ($1).

Located about 30km (19 miles) north of Surin, the recently restored **Prasat Ban Phuluang** is admired as much for its surroundings as for its elegantly carved sandstone and laterite Khmer architecture. As with most Khmer sites in Isan, Phuluang is thought to have been built in the 11th or 12th century during the reign of King Suriyaworamun I. The highlight here is the east-facing lintel above the main entrance with a delightful scene of Indra riding an elephant. We visited Phuluang at sunset and were knocked out by the soft light and the well-landscaped setting.

In the modern village of Ban Pluang, there are opportunities to watch and pur-chase silk weaving. It's open daily 8:30am to 5:30pm. Admission is 25B ($1).

Located 12km (7 miles) east of Surin, off Route 226, is **Butom**, a rural **basket-weaving village.** If you wander into the village you're bound to see a group of women weaving sturdy and attractive baskets under their stilt houses, usually accom-panied by a Thai soap opera on a generator-run television. It's a pretty weird sight but the work is great; people come from Bangkok to make their purchases. We bought several baskets and paid no more than about $5 for the most intricately wo-ven design. There are several roadside stands that sell baskets, but you can also buy directly from the craftspeople.

Two **silk-weaving villages,** both within about 20km (13 miles) of Surin, are open to visitors who wish to see demonstrations of traditional methods of manufac-turing silk. Khawao Sinrin and Chanrom (the former on Route 214 north of Surin, the latter on Route 2077 to the east of town) are centers of handmade silk prod-ucts, from thread to finished lengths of material, which are sold locally and in shops in Surin.

WHERE TO STAY

Some hotels will add a surcharge during the Elephant Roundup, so if you plan on visiting during the festival expect to pay as much as a 50% premium. The prices quoted are the normal prices.

PETCHKASEM HOTEL, 104 Chitbumrung Rd., Surin 32000. Tel. 044/ 511274. Fax 044/514041. 162 rms. A/C TV TEL **Directions:** In the center.

$ Rates: 425B ($17) single; 725B ($29) double; family room 1,450B ($58). Extra bed 300B ($12). MC, V.

Until recently, this six-story high rise offered the best that Surin had to offer (it's since been surpassed by the Tharin), but don't expect much in the way of luxury or service: It's rather Spartanly furnished, poorly maintained, and a tad worn. Neverthe-less, the Petchkasem has a restaurant, coffee shop, disco, pool, and other services that make it a center, not only for its guests, but for residents as well.

THARIN HOTEL, Sirirat Rd., Surin 32000. Tel. 044/514281. 240 rms. A/C TV TEL **Directions:** In the center.

$ Rates: 700B ($28) single; 1,250B ($50) double; suite from 2,000B ($80). Extra bed 300B ($12). MC, V.

Since the tourist explosion hit Thailand, there have been few hotels built in Surin; however, the town finally has a good standard in the Tharin Hotel, which has a good restaurant, a nightclub, and a very nice pool. All rooms are equipped in a clean and modern fashion, and when we were there, we felt the service and mainte-nance to be a notch better than in other Isan hotels. If you plan on visiting during the roundup try to reserve a room as early as possible.

MEMORIAL HOTEL, 186 Lak Muang Rd., Surin 32000. Tel. 044/511288. 56 rms. A/C TEL **Directions:** In the center.

$ Rates: 200B ($8) single with fan; 325B ($13) single with A/C; 275B ($11) double with fan; 400B ($16) double with A/C. No credit cards.

This is a small hotel, that, nevertheless, offers decent value for money, especially for the fan-cooled rooms; some rooms have air-conditioning. We like its central location, clean rooms, and proximity to restaurants and services.

PIROM GUEST HOUSE, 242 Krungsrinai Rd., Surin. Tel. 044/515140. 6 rms and dormitory. **Directions:** West of the center, 2 blocks west of the market.

$ Rates: 70B ($2.80) single with fan; 120B ($4.80) double with fan; 60B ($2.40) dor-mitory room. No credit cards.

The Pirom is a small guest house with style and personal attention. Located in a dark-wood, older Thai house, it avoids the banality of the modern-style hotels so ubiquitous in Isan. There are no amenities to speak of (bathing facilities are outside the rooms), and the rooms themselves are very basic and small, but Mr. Pirom (who speaks excellent English) and his wife, Aree, are lovely hosts and both are extremely well informed about the area. Pirom leads daily excursions (see "What to See & Do," above) to the more remote destinations around Surin, especially to Tha Klang elephant village. He also guides cultural tours through Isan.

WHERE TO DINE

There are several attractive new restaurants on the small street between the bus station and the Tharin Hotel. Among the other Thai eateries in Surin, we suggest **Sai Yen** on Chitbumrung Road (the same road as the Petchkasem Hotel), **Pae Tee** on Tesabarn I, and **Somboonpochana** near the Bor Kor Sot bus station; all serve a combination of Isan and Thai specialties at low to moderate prices.

LOW JAR, 5-7-9 Tesabarn II Rd. Tel. 512354.
  Cuisine: THAI. **Directions:** In the center.
$ Prices: Main courses 15B–85B (60¢–$3.40). MC, V.
  Open: Daily 8am–8pm.
This is our favorite restaurant in Surin and, a bonus to those looking for the local and exotic, it features Isan specialties along with a full complement of Thai dishes.

EASY EXCURSIONS

BURIRAM

Buriram, about halfway between Surin and Khorat (and easily reached by either bus, train, or car), is the capital of the province of the same name. The main reason for a stop there would be a visit to **Phanom Rung,** one of the best Khmer ruins in the world—but as facilities for foreign tourists have not developed as anticipated, we currently recommend you visit the site from Khorat or Surin.

If you have the time, there are a number of interesting lesser sites in the province, and the TAT in Khorat publishes a good guide pamphlet. For additional information write the **Nang Rong Tourism Promotion Club,** 8/1 Soi Srikoon, Amphoe Nang Rong, Buriram 31110, or contact Mr. Phanna at the Nang Rong School (tel. 631383) or Mr. Phaisan at the Prakhonchai Phittayakhom School (tel. 671131). **Phanom Rung Tours** (formed by two assistant professors at Buriram Teachers College), 131 Buriram-Prakhnochai Rd., Buriram (tel. 044/612046; fax 612691), can arrange tours, accommodations, and meals, with packages starting at about 1,500B ($60).

Should you wish to overnight in Buriram, we recommend the **Thep Nakron Hotel,** 139 Isan Rd., tel. 044/613400, on the main highway, where air-conditioned singles go for about 600B ($24) and doubles for 800B ($32). VISA and MasterCard are accepted. An acceptable downtown alternative is the **Thai Hotel,** 38/1 Romburi Rd., tel. 044/611112, with rooms ranging from 300B ($12) for a single with fan to 500B ($20) for an air-conditioned double. VISA and MasterCard are accepted. There's an inexpensive Chinese restaurant adjacent to it and an unnamed shop about 100 yards south that sells groceries and baked goods.

In the first week of November the annual **Longboat Races** are held at Amphoe Satuk; an elephant procession and elephant swimming contest are part of the festivities. **Songkran** (full moon of the fifth lunar month) is celebrated by a special pilgrimage to Phanom Rung. Early December brings a colorful **Kite Festival.** Contact the TAT in Khorat for more information.

Phanom Rung

Perhaps due to its isolated hilltop location, **Prasat Hin Phanom Rung** (Great Mountain), one of the major stops on the road to Angkor Wat, was deserted from its fall in the late 13th century until its "rediscovery" in 1935. Full-scale restoration began in 1972, and in early 1988, it opened to the public, instantly becoming one of the region's most popular Khmer sites. The shrine was the subject of an international dispute when one of its exceptionally well-carved sandstone lintels, depicting a reclining Vishnu, showed up in the Art Institute of Chicago. It was returned to Thailand and reinstalled just after the site's opening.

The temple, built on the summit of an inactive volcano, sits majestically above the wide plains, facing southeast toward Angkor in Cambodia. The approach is via a stairway, interrupted by pavilionlike bridges, lined on both sides with a multiheaded cobra or *naga* (mythical serpent) in Angkor style. The base of the central structure was built in the 10th century and almost certainly housed Shiva imagery, such as a phallic lingam (the pipe that allowed water to cascade over the lingam is still in place) in a small temple enclosure; this building was expanded by the 12th century and is the main prang of the site. Above the finely carved Lopburi-period doors are lintels, each portraying an important Hindu character or incident, the most famous of which is that of the reclining Vishnu. Look carefully at the columns and supporting stones on the central buildings, as many are festooned with ornately carved Shivas, galloping elephants, and shapely Khmer dancers. At the periphery of the central buildings are several 13th-century structures which are thought to have functioned as libraries.

If you visit on your own, we suggest buying a copy of Dr. Sorajet Woragamvijya's English-language guide to the site, *The Sanctuary Phanomrung* (Lower Northeast Study Association, Buriram); it is both authoritative and concise.

To reach Phanom Rung by public transport from Khorat, take a Surin-bound bus to Ban Tak (trip time: 2 hours; 50B [$2]) and take a tuk-tuk or song tao to the site. It's open daily 8am to 5pm. Admission is 25B ($1).

Down the hill and about 8km (5 miles) from Phanom Rung in Ban Chorake (Village of Crocodiles) is **Prasat Muang Tam,** a largely unreconstructed Khmer site that features a series of ponds framed by nagas (similar to the stairway at Phanom Rung) surrounding a gallery of prangs or stupas. Again, lintel carvings indicate a Brahmanic tradition, with the most significant frieze illustrating Shiva riding on the back of Nandi the Bull. We like this site as a companion to its neighbor not only because of its great carving, but also because it highlights the difference between a "found" site and one that has been reconstructed.

There is no public transportation to Muang Tam; however, taxis or tuk-tuks will take you there from Ban Tako (and sometimes from Phanom Rung). The site is open daily 7:30am to 6pm. Admission is 25B ($1).

Prasat Ta Muen Toj and **Ta Muen Tom,** two halts on the Angkor road, are part of a larger cluster of Khmer buildings, constructed in the 11th century, that are located exactly on the current Thai-Cambodian border. At Muen Toj, the main stupa is, like Ban Pluang, of square design. Muen Tom is a larger complex which incorporates a remarkable sandstone wall and base with a triple stupa on the central porch.

When we arrived, soldiers came out of their tents, armed with automatic weapons, and carefully guided us through the sites, aware that mines have not been completely cleared in the adjoining area. The buildings, which may have had religious or possibly healing functions attached to them, are a jumble of sandstone and laterite bricks and columns. Thick trunk banyans have grown up in the midst of this cacophony of stones; brush fires, lit by the armed soldiers to keep the jungle from overwhelming the site, complete the scene. It's no wonder that we felt a strong kinship with Indiana Jones at the Muen Toj and Tom.

You'll likely be the only ones at this particular stop, so we suggest making the most of it. This is the kind of place where, once you overcome the feeling that a band of Khmer Rouge soldiers might open fire at any moment, you'll relax and attend to the sounds, sites, and smells of a little-visited, wild location.

You'll have to hire a car in order to visit. Plan on being stopped by no less than six military checkpoints. At each stop we felt organized society recede (just like in *Apocalypse Now*), so by the final checkpoint we knew that we were on the cusp of civilization. Not for the faint of heart.

CHAPTER 11

EXPLORING NORTHERN THAILAND

Exotic Northern Thailand is home to the majority of Thailand's half-million plus tribal peoples, many of whom emigrated from Laos and southwestern China. Because of the ethnic, cultural, and language ties to these neighbors, the hill tribes have retained their traditional costumes, religion, art, and way of life. These distinctive ethnic cultures continue to make the rural north one of the country's most popular tourist destinations.

Most of the hill tribes have traditionally subsisted on shifting agriculture: burning forests to clear land, planting poppies as a food and cash crop, then setting up new bamboo and thatch villages whenever their farmlands became depleted. This nomadic existence has meant that travelers interested in hill-tribe culture have had to go out and look for it. Contact with the pure cultural traditions and simple rural life of these hospitable peoples is only one of the attractions of trekking, a popular way to explore this region.

Other parts of the north are affiliated with the historic Lan Na Kingdom. Thailand's second city after Bangkok, Chiang Mai was the Lanna Thai capital from the 13th to 18th centuries, when it was a powerful ally of the central Sukhothai Kingdom. Using this exciting city as a base for travel by bus, car, or motorcycle, you can visit the ruins of fortifications, see ornately decorated wats, and tour fine museums preserving the Lanna culture.

1. GEOGRAPHY, HISTORY & PEOPLE

GEOGRAPHY

Northern Thailand is comprised of 15 provinces, many of them sharing borders and peoples with Myanmar to the north and west and Laos to the northeast (Thailand's eastern areas bordering Laos and Cambodia are covered in Chapter 10, "Exploring the Northeast: Thailand's Frontier"). This verdant, mountainous terrain (including Thailand's largest mountain, Doi Inthanon, at 2,563m [8,408 ft.]) supports nomadic farming and teak logging at high altitudes and systematic agriculture in the valleys. The hill tribes' traditional poppy crops have largely been replaced with rice, tobacco, soybeans, corn, and sugarcane.

Due north and east of Chiang Mai, lowland farmers also cultivate seasonal fruits such as strawberries, longan, mandarin oranges, mango, and melon; the lush, tended fields and winding rivers make sightseeing, particularly in the spring, a visual treat.

In addition to agriculture, lumber (especially teak), textiles, some mining, and handicrafts and tourism-related cottage industries contribute to making Northern Thailand one of the country's fastest growing economies.

HISTORY

In the late 13th century, King Mengrai united several Tai or Thai tribes that had migrated from southern China and built the first capital of the Lan Na Kingdom in Chiang Rai. Mengrai, whose brilliant rule was aided by useful alliances, saw a threat in the Mongol emperor Kublai Khan's incursions into Myanmar and quickly forged ties with the powerful Kingdom of Sukhothai in the south. The Lanna Thai king moved quickly to consolidate his position when he vanquished the vestiges of the Mon Empire in Nakorn Hariphunchai (Lamphun) and in 1296 moved his new capital south to what is now Chiang Mai. There is a monument to King Mengrai, across from Chiang Mai's Wat Phan Tao, where he was supposedly struck by lightning and killed in 1317.

For the next century, Chiang Mai prospered and the Lan Na Kingdom grew, absorbing most of the present-day northern provinces. Allied with Sukhothai, they were able to repulse any significant attacks from Khmer and Mon neighbors. With the rise of the Siam Kingdom at Ayutthaya came the eventual destruction of the Sukhothai Empire, long the Lanna Thai's guarantor of power. Ayutthaya forces repeatedly tried to take Chiang Mai, but the kingdom did not yield. Instead, Chiang Mai strengthened itself, and from the late 14th century until the eventual fall to the Burmese in 1556, it enjoyed tremendous affluence and influence.

After 200 years of relentless warfare with the Burmese, the Lan Na Kingdom was destined for ruin. Most northern provinces were already allied with Bangkok's Kingdom of Siam. After Siam's King Taksin recaptured Chiang Mai from the Burmese army in 1775, the city was so weakened that Taksin moved its surviving citizens to nearby Lampang. For two decades Chiang Mai was literally a ghost town, bringing an end to the Lan Na Kingdom's supremacy in the north. The city continued to decline in power and was formally incorporated into the modern Thai nation in 1938.

PEOPLE

It is the ethnic hill-tribe peoples of the north that make this area a unique destination for visitors to Thailand. Most tribes migrated from China or Tibet to Myanmar, Laos, and Vietnam and ultimately settled in Thailand's northern provinces such as Chiang Rai, Chiang Mai, Mae Hong Son, Phayao, and Nan. The six main tribes are the Karen, Akha (also known as the Kaw), Lahu (Mussur), Lisu (Lisaw), Hmong (Meo), and Mien (Yao), each with subgroups that are linked by historical lineage, language, costume, social organization, and religion.

Hill tribes are divided into two linguistic categories, the Sino-Tibetan and Austro-Asiatic, though only descendants of the Mon-Khmer speak a dialect of the latter category. In addition, tribes are divided geographically into lowland or valley dwellers who grow cyclical crops, such as rice or corn, and high-altitude dwellers who grow opium poppies. The so-called indigenous tribes, who have occupied the same areas for hundreds of years, are those that tend to inhabit the lower valleys in organized villages of split-log huts. The nomadic groups generally live above 1,000m (3,250 feet) in easy-to-assemble bamboo and thatch housing, ready to resettle when nearby fields grow less fertile or when political strife overspills the Myanmar and Laos borders.

Many of the highland minorities (especially the Akha) have experienced problems with opium addiction. It begins when the larger villages host a local trader, usually of Chinese or Thai extraction, who funnels the poppies into the lucrative Golden Triangle opium pipeline. The Thai government has tried, through education and financial incentives, to wean the hill tribes away from cultivating opium poppies, both for health reasons as well as international pressure to stem the heroin trade.

Nearly all tribal villages have a headman who performs most of the political and social functions, including welcoming guests. The nomadic, high-altitude villages are led by village elders or a shaman who consults spirits. If there is a change in condition—agriculturally, from disease or death, or as a result of security (there are bandits in the area)—the whole village may disband and move to a more advantageous location. Villages also break up over internal disputes, leading the inhabitants to wander in families and take up residence in a new region. Most often the social unit is characterized as the extended family; this is especially true among the Hmong (Meo) and Mien (Yao), who practice polygamy.

Highland minorities believe in spirits, and it is the role of the shaman, or head religious figure, to read into every situation the workings of the spiritual pantheon. Most villages practice rites that are meant to appease the spirits, with the shaman or headman chosen to determine the problem, prescribe the solution, and perform the ritual. Remarkably enough, neither the shamans nor headmen are considered to be of higher stature than the other villagers. They merely render a service and are on equal footing with all other inhabitants. If a shaman or headman becomes too grandiose in his political aspirations, the villagers will often decide collectively to disband.

Karen The 265,000 Karen are the largest tribal group in Thailand, accounting for more than half of all tribal people in the country. In nearby Myanmar it's estimated that there are over four million people of Karenic descent (and of Buddhist belief), many of whom have settled along the Thai-Burmese border. For several years, the Burmese government has battled Karen rebels seeking an autonomous homeland. In Thailand, the Karen are geographically dispersed, living as far north as Chiang Rai and as far south as Kanchanaburi. Among the Karen are several subgroups: the Sgaw (White Karen), the Pwo (also White Karen), Kayah (Red Karen), Pa O (Black Karen), and the Padung (the Long Necks, who elongate their necks with brass bands). The Sgaw and Pwo represent 95% of Karen tribespeople, with the other three groups living in remote areas of Mae Hong Son Province.

The Karen have lived in Thailand since the 18th century, though they date their culture back to the 8th century B.C. Based on language and mythology, scholars place the Karen's geographic origin west of Tibet. Today the Karen engage in swidden agriculture, an excellent form of land rotation that is being threatened by overpopulation. The crops themselves are watched over by a ritual landlord who makes sacrifices to the spirits. The most commonly mentioned spirit to placate is the so-called Crop Grandmother who sits perched on the stumps of felled trees. The major deity is the lord of land and water, and it is to him that most sacrifices are made. Karen tribes mostly occupy lower-lying areas and are not significant growers of opium poppies, but they are well-known as weavers of cotton.

The Karen are among the most assimilated among the hill tribes of Thailand, making it difficult to identify them by any outward appearance; however, the most traditional tribespeople wear silver armbands and don a beaded sash and headband, and the single women wear all white.

Hmong (Meo) The Hmong are a nomadic tribe scattered throughout Southeast Asia and China. About 65,000 Hmong live in Thailand, with the greatest number residing in Chiang Mai, Chiang Rai, Nan Phetchabun, and Phrae provinces; there are approximately four million Hmong living in China. Within Thailand are several subgroups: the Hmong Daew (White Hmong) and the Hmong Njua (Blue Hmong) are the main divisions; the Hmong Gua Mba (Armband Hmong) is a subdivision of the Hmong Daew. Until last year, a substantial Hmong Daew population from Laos was concentrated in refugee camps near the border. Those immigrants have been absorbed into other Hmong communities, gone back to Laos, and 4,000 are currently squatting in the famous drug addiction treatment center and temple in Soraburi, in central Thailand.

The Hmong speak a Sino-Tibetan dialect that uses many words from Chinese. As with other ethnic minorities (especially the Mien, with whom the Hmong have a deep affinity), the Chinese government attempted to restrict the freedom of the fiercely independent Hmong to speak their own language and pursue their Non-Han Chinese social customs.

In Thailand, the Hmong generally dwell in the highlands, where they cultivate opium poppies at a greater rate than any other tribal group; corn, rice, and soybeans are also grown as subsistence crops. The Hmong are also excellent animal breeders; their ponies are especially prized.

As with other nomadic tribes, the Hmong maintain much of their wealth in silver jewelry. Neck rings are given to Hmong babies as a sign of their acceptance into the material world. During the December New Year festival, families wear their silver jewelry and ornaments in a fabulous display of craftsmanship. The women are particularly distinctive with knotted, long dark hair woven with horse- or human-hair switches to create an enormous bun on the top of their heads. Though most men take one wife, it is a sign of wealth to take two.

Also like most of the other tribes, the Hmong are pantheistic and rely on shamans to perform spiritual rites, though their elite is staunchly Catholic. The shamans practice animal sacrifice and perform many rituals in the event of a spiritual emergency. They contact the spirit world in a trancelike state. They place particular emphasis on the spirit of doors: doors for entering and exiting the human world, doors to houses, doors to let in good fortune and to block bad spirits, and doors to the afterlife. The Hmong also are ancestor worshipers, again an echo from their Chinese past.

Like the Chinese, with whom they resided for so many centuries, Hmong are an entrepreneurial lot, and they are beginning to move down from the hills to pursue a less rigorous and more profitable life in other occupations. But as long as the lucrative opium trade continues, the Hmong will remain in the highlands, cultivating poppies.

Lahu (Mussur) The Lahu people, of which 40,000 abide in Thailand, are a fractured group with a great many subdivisions. The differences can even be seen from their clothing. The two main bands are the Lahu Na (Black Lahu) and the Lahu Shi (Yellow Lahu), with the Lahu Hpu (White Lahu), La Ba, and Abele comprising a minuscule number. Most Lahu villages are situated above 1,000m (3,250 feet) in the mountains around Chiang Mai, Chiang Rai, Mae Hong Son, Tak, and Kamphaeng Phet, where poppies, dry rice, corn, and other cash crops are grown.

The Lahu first arrived during the late 19th century, having migrated from southwestern China into Myanmar, then later into Thailand. Their language, Lahu Na, similar to Tibetan, is so well accepted that other tribal people and Yunnanese Chinese have adopted it as their common tongue. The Lahu are skilled musicians, and their bamboo and gourd flutes are the most common instrument (we bought such a flute in the Night Market in Chiang Mai; it makes a lovely sound and is easy to play). These flutes are often used by young men to woo the woman of their choice.

If any tribe reflects the difficulties of maintaining a singular cultural identity in the tumult of migration, it's the Lahu. Consider Lahu religion: Originally animist, they adopted the worship of a deity called G'ui sha (possibly Tibetan in origin), borrowed the practice of merit making from Buddhism (Indian or Chinese), and ultimately incorporated Christian (British/Burmese) theology into their belief system. G'ui sha is the supreme being who created the universe and rules over all spirits. Spirits inhabit animate and inanimate objects, making them capable of benevolence or evil, with the soul functioning as the spiritual force within people. In addition, they practice a kind of Lahu voodoo as well as following a messianic tradition. They welcome strangers more than any other tribe in Thailand.

Mien (Yao) There are now estimated to be 33,000 Mien living in Thailand, concentrated in Chiang Rai, Phayao, Lampang, and Nan provinces. The Mien are still numerous in China as well as in Vietnam, Myanmar, and Laos. Like the Hmong, tens of thousands of Mien fled to northern Thailand from Vietnam and Laos after the end of the Vietnam War.

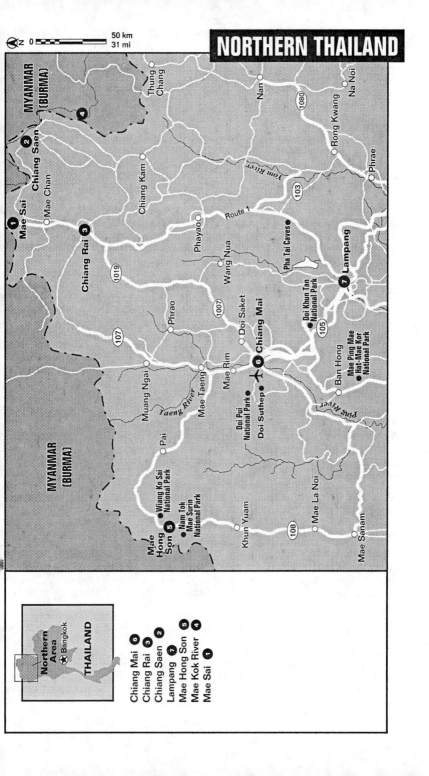

NORTHERN THAILAND

0 | 50 km
0 | 31 mi

MYANMAR (BURMA)

Thung Chang

Nan

1080

Na Noi

Rong Kwang

Chiang Saen

Mae Sai

Mae Chan

Chiang Kam

Yom River

103

Phrae

Chiang Rai

Route 1

Phayao

Pha Tai Caves

Lampang

1019

Wang Nua

Doi Khun Tan National Park

Phrao

1007

Doi Saket

105

107

Chiang Mai

Mae Ping Mae Kat-Mae Kor National Park

Muang Ngai

Mae Taeng

Mae Rim

Ban Hong

Taeng River

Doi Pui National Park

Doi Suthep

Ping River

Pai

Wiang Ko Sai National Park

Nam Tok Mae Surin National Park

Mae Hong Son

Khun Yuam

Mae La Noi

Mae Sanam

108

MYANMAR (BURMA)

Chiang Mai ⑥
Chiang Rai ③
Chiang Saen ②
Lampang ⑦
Mae Hong Son ⑤
Mae Kok River ④
Mae Sai ①

THAILAND

Northern Area

★ Bangkok

Even more than the Hmong, the Mien (the name is thought to be from the Chinese word for "barbarian") are closely connected to their origins in southern China. They incorporated the Han spoken and written language into their own, and many Mien legends, history books, and religious tracts are recorded in Chinese. The Mien people also assimilated ancestor worship and a form of Taoism into their theology, in addition to celebrating their New Year on the same date (relying on the same calendar system) as the Chinese.

Mien farmers practice shifting agriculture but do not rely on opium poppies; instead they cultivate dry rice and corn. The women produce rather intricate and elegant embroidery, which often adorns their clothing. Their silver work is intricate and highly prized even by other tribes, particularly the Hmong. Much of Mien religious art appears strongly influenced by Chinese design, particularly Taoist motifs, clearly distinguishing it from other tribes' work.

Courting rituals appear absolutely libertine in comparison with Western traditions. Young men and women are free to have premarital sexual relations; as long as an agreeable price can be found for the bride, nearly anything goes. Adoption of other Mien children or children from other suitable tribes is a common practice.

Lisu (Lisaw) The Lisu are one of the smaller ethnic minorities in northern Thailand, representing less than 5% of all hill-tribe people. They arrived in Chiang Rai Province in the 1920s, migrating from nearby Myanmar. The Lisu occupy high ground, which allows them to grow poppies for the opium harvest as well as other subsistence crops. Lisu people, like their Chinese cousins (many have intermarried) are reputed to be extremely competitive and hardworking. They also frequently intermarry with the Lahu. Even their clothing is brash, incorporating a multitude of brightly colored tunics, embellished with hundreds of silver beads and trinkets. All of which is to say that the Lisu are achievers.

The Lisu also live well-structured lives. Their rituals rely on complicated procedures which demand much from the participants. Everything from birth to courtship to marriage to death is ruled by an orthodox tradition, liberally borrowed from Chinese ideas. Perhaps because of their structured, achievement-oriented society, the Lisu have the highest suicide rate among Thailand's tribal people.

Akha (Kaw) Perhaps of all the tradition-bound tribes, the Akha, accounting for only 3% of all minorities living in Thailand, have maintained the most profound connection with their past. At great events in one's life, the full name (often more than 50 generations of titles) of an Akha is proclaimed, with each name symbolic of a lineage dating back over a thousand years. All aspects of life are governed by the Akha Way, an all-encompassing system of myth, ritual, plant cultivation, courtship and marriage, birth, death, dress, and healing.

It may be that the strength of the Akha Way is the key to maintaining the identity of such a nomadic people, for the Akha are widely spread throughout southern China, Laos, Vietnam, and Myanmar. The first Akha migrated from Myanmar to Thailand in the beginning of the 20th century, originally settling in the highlands above the Mae Kok River in Chiang Rai Province. Now they are moving down to lower heights in search of more arable land. They are the so-called shifting cultivators, depending on subsistence crops, planted in rotation, and raising domestic animals for their livelihood.

We found the clothing of the Akha among most attractive of all the hill tribes. Skillful embroidery on simple black jackets is the everyday attire for both men and women. The Akha shoulder bags are adorned with silver coins, baubles, and found beads and are woven with exceptional skill.

The Akha are ancestor worshipers, but they also attach great importance to separating the human world from the spirit world. Each year, in front of every village, large open gates are built and consecrated to symbolize the segregation of these two worlds, in effect trying to create harmony through isolation.

2. WHEN TO GO

Northern Thailand has three distinct seasons. The hot season (March to May) is dry with temperatures up to 86°F (30°C), the rainy season (June to October) is cooler, with the heaviest daily rainfall in September, and the cool season (November to February) is brisk, with daytime temperatures as low as 59°F (21°C) in Chiang Mai town, and 41°F (5°C) in the hills. November to May is the best time for trekking, with February, March, and April (when southern Thailand gets extremely hot) usually being the least crowded months.

Northern Thailand celebrates many unique festivals, as well as many nationwide festivals in an unusual way. Check the calendar below so that you can plan your trip to coincide with one of them. Many Thais also travel to participate in these festivals (particularly the Winter Fair, Flower Festival, Songkran, and Loi Krathong) and advance hotel reservations are a must.

CALENDAR OF EVENTS

Many of these annual events are based on the lunar calendar. Contact the TAT in Bangkok for the exact dates.

JANUARY

□ **Winter Fair,** Chiang Mai. Special theatrical events, a Beauty Queen pageant, and art exhibits are held at the Municipal Stadium (December 30–January 8).
□ **Umbrella Festival,** Bo Sang. Held in a village of umbrella craftspeople and painters about 15km (9 miles) east of Chiang Mai, there are handicraft competitions, an elephant show, and a local parade.

FEBRUARY

□ **Flower Festival,** Chiang Mai. Celebrates the city's undisputed position as the "Flower of the North" with concerts, flower displays and competitions, a food fair, and a beauty contest. The space of the mammoth parade—the focal point of the festival—is decidedly Asian, and not nearly as rushed as something like Macy's Thanksgiving Day Parade, but the streets are just as jammed (first weekend).

The Buak Hat park is the location for most of Chiang Mai's other events, including an exquisite orchid competition/display, flower-arranging demonstrations, and a pageant to elect a Miss Chiang Mai Flower Festival.
□ **King Mengrai Festival,** Chiang Rai. Known for its special hill-tribe cultural displays and a fine handicrafts market (early February).
□ **Sakura Blooms Flower Fair,** Doi Mae Salong. Celebrates the sakura of Japanese cherry tress, imported to this northwestern hill village by former members of China's nationalist Kuomintang party (early February).

MARCH

□ **Poy Sang Long.** A traditional Shan ceremony honoring Buddhist novices, widely celebrated in the northwestern village of Mae Hong Son (late March or early April).

APRIL

☐ **Songkran (Water) Festival.** Celebrated over the Lanna Thai New Year, most of the ceremonies take place at the wats. Presents and merit-making acts are offered, and water is sprinkled over Buddhas, monks, elders, and tourists, to celebrate the beginning of the harvest and to ensure good fortune. The festival is celebrated in all northern provinces, and throughout the country (mid-April).

MAY

☐ **Visakha Bucha.** Honors the birth, enlightenment, and death of the Lord Buddha on the full moon, this month. Celebrated nationwide, it's a particularly dramatic event in Chiang Mai, when residents walk up Doi Suthep in homage.

☐ **Harvest Festival,** Kho Loi Park. In the north and in Chiang Rai, this festival honors the harvest of litchis. There is a parade, litchi competition and display, a beauty contest to find Miss Chiang Rai Litchi Nut, and lots of food (mid May).

☐ **Mango Fair,** Chiang Mai. A fair honoring mangoes, the local's favorite crop (second weekend).

AUGUST

☐ **Lamyai or Longan Fair,** Lamphun. Celebrates the town's favorite fruit and one of Thailand's largest foreign-exchange earners. Yes, there is a Miss Longan competition, too (first or second weekend).

OCTOBER

☐ **Nan Province** sponsors two days of boat racing, with wildly decorated, long, low-slung craft zipping down the Nan River. The Lanna Boat Races are run seven days after the Rains' Retreat, marking the beginning of the dry season.

NOVEMBER

☐ **Loi Krathong.** Occurs around the country over two nights of the full moon in the 12th lunar month. Crowds float small banana-leaf boats bearing candles, incense, a flower, and a coin as an offering to wash away the previous year's sins. Since this festival dates from the Sukhothai era, in Chiang Mai brightly colored lanterns are strung everywhere, enormous, flaming hot-air balloons are released in the night sky and there is a parade of women in traditional costumes, as well as a Miss Noppamas Beauty Pageant. The offering boats or krathongs are floated on the Ping River. In Sukhothai there is a spectacular sound and light show.

DECEMBER

☐ **Day of Roses,** Chiang Mai. Held in Buak Hat Park, there are exhibitions and cultural performances (first weekend).

3. GETTING THERE & GETTING AROUND

GETTING THERE

Before the 1920s, when the railway's Northern Line to Chiang Mai was completed, one traveled either by longboat or elephant; the trip took over two weeks and was considered fairly arduous. Today, commerce and tourism together have generated several transportation operations. See Chapter 12, "Chiang Mai," and Chapter 13 "Touring The Northern Hills," for more specific schedule and price information.

BY PLANE Thai Airways (tel. 02/280-0070 or 280-0080 in Bangkok) flies from Bangkok to Chiang Mai, Lampang, Chiang Rai, Mae Hong Son, Nan, and Phrae. There are also flights between many of these destinations and between them and Phitsanulok in central Thailand.

BY TRAIN Express and rapid trains leave Bangkok for Chiang Mai several times a day. Sleeper cars are available on certain trains, and should be reserved as early as possible.

BY BUS There are dozens of daily and nightly private, air-conditioned buses to Chiang Mai and other northern cities, as well as cheaper, less comfortable, public buses from Bangkok's Northern Bus Terminal.

GETTING AROUND

BY BUS There is frequent, inexpensive, and slow bus service between Chiang Mai and other northern cities. You'll also find *song tao*, pickup trucks fitted with long bench seats (also known locally as *seelor* or four wheels), that ply all the major roads throughout the north, with no fixed schedule or stopping points.

BY CAR Hertz and Avis rent cars with or without driver; both have offices at many of the north's larger hotels, and reservations can also be made in Bangkok. Don't forget the Thais use the British left-hand drive system. Self-drive rental rates for cars and Jeeps range from 1,200B ($48) to 4,000B ($160) a day or 7,200B ($288) a week for unlimited kilometers. Expect to pay from 300B to 400B ($12 to $16) an hour for a car and driver, with a 3-hour minimum.

Local rental-car companies rent sedans for 850B to 1,200B ($34 to $48) per day, and can arrange a car and driver for about 1,440B ($57.60) per day, depending on your destination. Make certain that you inspect the vehicle before paying or you may be stuck with the oldest one on the lot.

BY MOTORCYCLE Seven- to ten-day circuits of northern Thailand are becoming popular, particularly with European travelers, but are only recommended to very experienced riders. Most riders rent motorcycles in Chiang Mai, and average 100km to 150 km (62 to 93 miles) a day. Cheaper motorcycles give you the same flexibility as a car; off-road dirt bikes provide access to remote hill-tribe villages.

Plan your itinerary carefully. *Pocket Guide for Motorcycle Touring in Northern Thailand* or *The Mae Hong Son Loop* are popular, locally published guides for sale in Chiang Mai, but even the best Thai maps are never up-to-date on road conditions or on which dirt paths link small villages. Serendipity is almost assured, and there are many primitive guest houses and small noodle shops along the roads.

Friends from Munich gave us the low-down on equipment: 250cc Honda off-road bikes are commonly available and good because of their added power and large fuel tanks. In the winter of 1993 they rented for 450B ($18) per day or 350B ($14) per day on a weekly basis. Small 150cc motorbikes are sometimes the only thing available in the smaller villages outside of Chiang Mai. Small fuel tanks make them impractical for longer trips, and they usually aren't sturdy enough for off-road adventure, but they have enough power for most day trips. In 1993, these motorbikes rented for 150B ($6) a day or 130B ($5.20) a day on a weekly basis.

Karl and Ilse also had some warnings: Most rental motorcycles are very old and patched together from several different models. Before you make a deal with a rental shop, read the contract. Make sure it includes insurance (only liability coverage for the other party is sold, not for damage to your bike), and make sure that if the motorcycle breaks down due to wear, it is the rental company's responsibility to transport it back home.

Other tips: Once you've located the perfect bike and bargained for it, test it on the local streets before departing on a long journey. Always wear a helmet and drive slowly and cautiously. Be on the defensive with Thai drivers; they use the British left-hand drive system and often just drive down the middle of uncrowded roads. Watch out for stray dogs, chickens, and water buffalo, who never behave as you would expect. Always move to the shoulder of the road if a bus tries to overtake you. Be extra careful on the narrow, steeply winding roads in the west near the Burmese border. Avoid driving at night. Be as cautious as you would be in a heavily trafficked urban area in the West and you'll have a safe journey.

SUGGESTED ITINERARIES

IF YOU HAVE 3 DAYS

Day 1: Visit the wats in the Old City, then have a traditional northern Thai massage at Rinkaew Complex and try a khan toke dinner/cultural show.

Day 2: Visit Doi Suthep and Wat Mahatat, and in the afternoon visit the National Museum or shop along Sankamphaeng Road or the Nantawan Arcade. If you didn't shop in the afternoon, explore the Night Market in the evening.

Day 3: Visit the Elephant Training Camp in Lampang, see the historic wats in Lampang and Lamphun, and explore the Night Market if you haven't already.

IF YOU HAVE 5 DAYS

Days 1–2: Fly to Chiang Mai and follow the suggested itinerary above.

Days 3–5: Join a 2-night/3-day trek from Chiang Mai to nearby hill-tribe villages, in the vicinity of Chiang Rai. If you hate the idea of walking, use Days 3–5 for an air or land excursion to Mae Hong Son. In Mae Hong Son, take a longboat ride to the Padung village or an elephant ride into the jungle.

IF YOU HAVE 7 DAYS

Days 1–2: Fly to Chiang Mai and follow the suggested itinerary above.

Days 3–6: Join a 3-night/4-day trek to a more remote area, perhaps around Mae Salong or Mae Hong Son.

Day 7: Enjoy civilization in Chiang Mai, shop, sightsee, or visit the Elephant Training Camp in Lampang. If trekking doesn't interest you spend Days 1–2 as above.

Day 3: Drive to Chiang Rai, visit PDA Hill Tribe museum, take a longboat ride on the Mae Kok River.

Day 4: Drive to Chiang Saen, visit National Museum and historical sites, continue on to Golden Triangle, overnight.

Day 5: Drive to Mae Sai to see border, then continue onto Mae Salong, overnight.

Day 6: Drive to Mae Hong Son, overnight, or drive to Chiang Khong and shop for weaving and silver and visit Tai Lue or Hmong shops in town.

Day 7: Drive the southern route back to Chiang Mai.

IF YOU HAVE 10–14 DAYS

Days 1–4: Explore Chiang Mai as suggested above, but more fully.

Days 5–7: Join a 3-night/4-day trek in the region east of Chiang Rai.

Days 8–10: Drive to the Golden Triangle and use it as a base to explore Chiang Rai, Chiang Saen, and Mae Sai.

Days 11–14: Use this time to explore the northwest by driving, or by trekking, using Mae Hong Son as a base. (If you find a trek going to Mae Salong or Mae Hong Son from Chiang Mai, use Days 8–10 to see whatever your trek didn't cover, then use Days 11–14 to explore the Golden Triangle, Chiang Rai, Chiang Saen, and Mae Sai.)

4. TREKKING THROUGH THE NORTHERN HILLS

Trekking in northern Thailand is a relatively new phenomenon. Until the mid-1970s few people took to the trails, preferring the dramatic peaks and striking foliage of Nepal, Pakistan, and India to the low hills and semitropical terrain. Those few who did headed for the Golden Triangle, at the borders of Thailand, Myanmar, and Laos, attracted by the concentration of indigenous and nomadic hill tribes, their traditional culture, and their infamous, illicit opium fields.

Today hundreds of people head to the trails, with organized tours along well-beaten paths to Akha, Karen, Lahu, Lisu, Hmong, and Mien villages, most often within a 2-to-3-day Jeep ride and walk from Chiang Mai. Nearly all tours from this city now combine treks with river rafting and elephant walks, adding a kind of visceral thrill to the often easygoing hikes.

Trekking has become well organized. The flow of trekkers on well-trafficked trails is restricted; prices are fixed. In Chiang Mai, only certified guides who have a basic knowledge of several hill-tribe languages and who have posted a 10,000B bond with TAT are permitted to operate. After suffering through a season in which bandits attacked foreign trekkers, the Tourist Police in Chiang Mai, Mae Hong Son, and Chiang Rai now insist that all routes and trekking participants be registered before departure.

If this sounds like trekking has lost some of its pioneer spirit, it has and it hasn't. It is true that many of the villages (particularly near the paved roads) and their tribal residents now depend on revenue generated by treks and, accordingly, don traditional costumes, perform music and dancing and other ceremonies, produce crafts, and offer the obligatory opium pipe to well-paying Western guests. And it is true that most treks visit the same places, increasing the likelihood of running into other groups. But if you are willing to walk a little farther, or to start your journey from smaller, northern villages, you can still explore territories little known to any but the most knowledgeable adventurer.

TREKKING COMPANIES

The TAT publishes a list of trekking companies that operate out of Chiang Mai, but elsewhere, you're on your own. However, the problem isn't finding a trek (there are several leaving every day from Chiang Mai, and a surprising number from Chiang Rai, Mae Hong Son, and Pai), it's finding one that combines experienced and knowledgeable guides, an intelligent itinerary, a compatible group, appropriate timing, all at an acceptable price. Let's examine what you should look for in a trek.

The Guide If there is one single element of a trek that will make or break the experience, it is the guide. Although most claim to speak a number of hill-tribe languages, it's impossible to be fluent in so many different dialects with no written alphabet; besides, their command of English is the most important thing. Hill-tribe guides usually know key phrases in other tongues, know the best trails, are well informed about the area and people, and are usually pretty interesting characters themselves. Try to meet your prospective guide and ask lots of questions.

The Itinerary Several well-known Chiang Mai agencies offer prepackaged routes that leave on a regularly scheduled basis. If you intend to climb to more remote spots, you might either have to arrange a custom tour (more expensive) or call around to see if anyone happens to offer such a trip.

If you intend to visit the Golden Triangle or Mae Salong or Pai in the northwest, most trekking companies offer a 2- or 3-day trek. Those who want to travel east to Phayao or Nan will have to dig a little to find an appropriate outfit. If you can't stand the idea of trekking (though most consist of easy days of three to six hours of gentle walking), but want to visit some of the hill-tribe villages, inquire about Jeep trips. Nearly all trekking itineraries list the various hill-tribe villages visited; try to read as much as you can and decide for yourself which you'd most like to see.

Most treks start with a Jeep or minibus drive, or a raft or boat trip, to the head of the trail—such trips can take a full day. Plan on spending two or three days for a nearby trek and between five days and two weeks to reach the more remote spots.

The Group   Trips are often transformed into wonderful experiences or disasters by the composition of the group. If you're planning a long, arduous trip, try to meet your fellow travelers before committing; you might find that they aren't up to the rigors of the adventure or, conversely, you may not meet their expectation. Also, look for an agency that limits the number of people to about 10 per trek. We think at least four in the group minimizes personality clashes and adds conviviality.

The Season   Seasonality plays some part in trekking; see "When to Go," above, for more information.

What to Bring   Most trekkers come to Thailand on holiday, totally unprepared for a serious trek. That's fine, because most treks are on well-traveled paths, up and down rolling, cultivated hillsides, and require no special equipment. Good sneakers or walking shoes are usually adequate, though rainy season trekkers will probably prefer waterproof, nonskid hiking boots. A wool sweater for evenings and some outerwear to sleep in (many trekking companies only provide blankets) will come in handy. We prefer wearing long pants to shorts because of the sometimes dense underbrush and the nightly mosquito raids. A flashlight, supply of tissues or toilet paper, mosquito repellent, and a basic first-aid kit with blister remedies is also recommended.

Price   The last criterion is price, though you shouldn't get too stingy here because even the most expensive treks cost less than one night at a hotel and three restaurant meals. As with everything in Thailand, some negotiating is in order. In Chiang Mai or any of the smaller trekking cities, determine the current price for the region you're interested in, find the type of trek you might want to join, and offer about 30% less than the average asking price. On our 1993 visit, treks ranged from about 300B ($12) to 500B ($20) per person per night, with prices changing inversely with the number of participants and length of a longer trek. In Chiang Rai, which attracts well-heeled European tourists, the treks were often cushier and prices steeper, going up to $100 for two people per day.

Typically, trekkers' fees will pay for food; some budget operators charge separately for transportation to and from the trail head. Some companies provide sleeping bags, backpacks, and water bottles free of charge, while others rent them. Any optional activities: the opium cocktail hour with the village headman; an elephant walk; and river rafting all cost more.

CHIANG MAI

Founded in 1296 by King Mengrai, Chiang Mai ("new city") was the capital of the first independent Tai state, Lan Na Thao (Kingdom of One Million Rice Fields). It became the cultural and religious center of the Tai, and remained so throughout the turbulent period of recurring Burmese occupation (1558–1774), absorbing its occupier's influence on religion, architecture, language, cuisine, and culture. After years of decreasing power, Chao Intanon (1871–97) was appointed to Chiang Mai's throne. Fearful of continuous encroachment by the British (who had teak-logging interests as occupiers of Myanmar), King Chulalongkorn of Bangkok forced the Lan Na Kingdom to give up much of its autonomy. Like the surrounding mountainous regions long inhabited by hill-tribe peoples, Lan Na became a northern province under the rule of Bangkok's Siamese Kings.

In the last 40 years, the population has grown fivefold to about 160,000, making this once-sleepy hill station Thailand's second city after Bangkok. Significant recent changes include air pollution, rush-hour traffic, water shortages, and the displacement of tribal people in the nearby hills and valleys to make way for the development of retirement- and vacation-home communities.

Local civic groups such as the conservation group *For Chiang Mai* are becoming politically active. Cofounder Sirichai Narumit-Rekagarn told the *Nation* (November 29, 1990), "I have seen the results of unplanned development . . . Although about 40 high-rise condos have either already been built or are in the process of construction, it is still better to do something about it now than never." Plans are underway to preserve the Old City by shifting new construction to the village of Sankamphaeng, creating yet another chiang mai ("new city") as a role model for the country's future.

It would be difficult to find a city that reflects more of the country's diverse cultural heritage and modern aspirations than Chiang Mai. Tour buses crowd Burmese-style wats ablaze with the color of saffron and abuzz with the chanting of monks. Traditional open-air markets sell handicrafts, produce, and motorcycle parts. Narrow streets lined with ornately carved teak houses lie in the shadow of contemporary skyscrapers. Chiang Mai's heart is its Old City, an area surrounded by vestiges of walls and moats originally constructed for defense. Yet Chiang Mai as a whole is a modern city, with the usual advantages and disadvantages. No visitor to Thailand should miss it.

Because of its temperate climate (similar to the hill stations in nearby Myanmar) and central location, Chiang Mai is an excellent base for exploring the north of Thailand.

WHAT'S SPECIAL ABOUT CHIANG MAI

Events/Festivals

- The Chiang Mai Flower Festival, replete with floats, traditional and modern music, and masses of orchids, jasmine, and roses (February).
- The Thai New Year (Songkran), celebrated with lively processions and religious ceremonies (April).

Religious Shrines

- Numerous wats of historical and architectural significance, dating from the 13th to 19th centuries.
- Wat Phra That Doi Suthep, one of the country's holiest sites set on a hill overlooking the scenic Ping River valley.

Shopping

- The Night Market, a huge indoor and outdoor bazaar offering a wide range of new and old clothing, souvenirs, artworks, and tribal handicrafts.
- Sankamphaeng Road, a 15km (9 mile) stretch of factories and showrooms with the country's largest variety of handicrafts.

TV & Film Locations

- *Rambo III* was filmed in Chiang Mai Province.
- *Air America* was shot in the forests south of Chiang Mai.

1. ORIENTATION

ARRIVING

BY PLANE The Chiang Mai International Airport (tel. 270222) houses several banks open daily from 8am to 8pm, a post and overseas call office which is open daily from 8:30am to 8pm, and a TAT booth (tel. 270222, ext. 2122) open daily 8 to 10am, 12 to 2pm, and 5 to 8:30pm. There is a luggage storage office ($1 per bag per day) near the Security Booth, open daily to meet flights.

Thai Airways (240 Propokklao Rd., tel. 210042) flies from Bangkok to Chiang Mai 10 times daily. The cost is 1,650B ($66) per person one-way. Flights connect Chiang Mai with Phitsanulok three times daily, and the cost is 650B ($26) per person one-way.

There are four flights daily between Chiang Mai and Mae Hong Son, each 345B ($13.80) per person one-way; and twice daily from Chiang Mai to Chiang Rai, costing 420B ($16.80) per person.

BY TRAIN **Express** trains leave Bangkok for Chiang Mai at 6pm and 7:40pm daily taking 13½ hours; **Rapid** trains leave three times daily taking 14 hours. For a round-trip, second-class air-conditioned sleeper (express only), the cost is 1,010B ($40.40); round-trip, third-class (rapid) tickets cost 300B ($12). Sleeper cars, available on certain express and rapid trains should be reserved as early as possible. Purchase tickets at Bangkok's Hua Lampong Railway Station (tel. 02/223-7020) up to 90 days in advance. For local train information in Chiang Mai call 247462, for reservations call 242094.

BY BUS Approximately 10 different private companies offer frequent, air-conditioned service to Chiang Mai from Bangkok. Public buses run eight times daily. The public bus cost for the 10-hour trip is approximately 470B ($18.80). Buses depart Bangkok's Northern Bus Terminal. There is also frequent service between Chiang Mai and Mae Hong Son, Phitsanulok, and Chiang Rai. For schedules in Chiang

Mai, check with the TAT, a travel agent, or call the Arcade Bus Station by the Superhighway at tel. 242664 or the Chang Puak Station at tel. 211586.

BY TAXI Taxis are not efficient in Chiang Mai's twisting streets (and there aren't many around), but a cab from the airport is a good idea. Ask first at the Taxi Counter; expect to pay 100B ($4) to your hotel. The Thai Airways limo service costs 30B ($1.20) for the hotel-drop minibus or 100B ($4) for a private car.

TOURIST INFORMATION

The **TAT** office is at 105/1 Chiang Mai–Lamphun Rd., 400 meters south of the Nawarat Bridge on the east side of the Ping River (tel. 053/248604; fax 248605). The office is open daily from 8:30am to 4:30pm. You can call the airport TAT branch (tel. 270222, ext. 2122) for information until 8:30pm.

CITY LAYOUT

A triumvirate of 13th-century kings, representing the Lanna Thai, Phayao, and the powerful Sukhothai kingdoms, chose the site of medieval Chiang Mai. Always keen to spot metaphysical spirits and signs, the royals selected an area that was inhabited by a triumvirate of forces symbolized by two white barking deer, two white sambar deer, and a family of white mice. The land was a fertile plain, bordered by the Mae Nam Ping (Ping River) to the east and the verdant, cool Doi Suthep (Suthep Mountain) on the west, and was to be called Nopphaburi Si Nakhonphing Chiang Mai (the formal title of the new city).

The Old City was completely surrounded by a massive wall and a moat. Only the moat (it was rebuilt in the 19th century) and restored gates remain as reminders of the original wall. Within the Old City are three of the area's more important wats, **Wat Chedi Luang, Wat Phra Singh,** and **Wat Chiang Man.**

Most of the major streets radiate from the Old City (passing through a series of gates) and fan out in all directions. The main business and shopping area is the half-mile stretch between the six gates on the east side (along Moon Muang Road) of the Old City and east to the Ping River. Here you will find the Night Market, many shops, better hotels, guest houses and restaurants, a slew of trekking companies (especially along Tha Pae Road), and some of the most picturesque back streets in the area. The main post office and train station are farther east, across the Ping River over the Nawarat Bridge (follow Charoen Muang, the continuation of Tha Pae Road).

As you exit the Old City on the west side from the Suan Dok Gate, Suthep Road leads out to Wat Suan Dok, with its justly famous traditional massage center. The road leading out from the northwest corner of the Old City is Huai Kaeo, with a strip of modern hotels, the zoo, university, and ultimately Doi Suthep mountain. Atop the latter is the most regal of all Chiang Mai Buddhist compounds.

2. GETTING AROUND

In 1882 traveler Carl Bock wrote in *Temples and Elephants* about Chiang Mai's transport system: "I doubt . . . when novelty of [carriages] died away, the people would care to adopt this mode of locomotion in preference to elephant-riding . . . Even then, roads would have to be constructed for this purpose and the Laosian is not yet educated up to that high pitch of civilization." Things have changed. Not only are there bicycle-drawn carriages, but there are taxis, tuk-tuks, rental cars, buses, minibuses, motorcycles, and best of all, cheap truck taxis.

BY BUS Local minibuses cost 8B to 35B (32¢ to $1.40) for edge-of-town destinations. The minibus to Wat Pra That on Doi Suthep mountain costs 35B ($1.40); 25B ($1) return.

There is frequent, inexpensive (8B to 22B or 32¢ to 88¢) bus service to the nearby villages of Sankamphaeng, Lamphun, Bo Sang, and Hang Dong. Contact TAT for a printed schedule or check your hotel for the nearest minibus station.

BY TRUCK TAXI (SONG TAO) Red pickup trucks fitted with long bench seats are known locally as *song tao* or *seelor* (four wheels). They ply all the major roads throughout the city, day and night, with no fixed stopping points. Hail one going in your general direction and tell the driver your destination (it helps to have it written out in Thai). If it fits in with those of other passengers, you'll get a ride to your door for only 5B to 15B (20¢ to 60¢). It's our favorite transport: They're cheap, fast, and the drivers are honest.

BY TUK-TUK The ubiquitous tuk-tuk is the next best option. The fare within Chiang Mai is always negotiable, but expect to pay about 30B to 100B ($1.20 to $4) for an in-town ride. These motorized three-wheel vehicles are the same as those in Bangkok but are never called *samlor* (three wheels). In Chiang Mai, samlor is reserved for the old bicycle trishaws which frequent a very limited part of the city near the markets and the Ping River.

Warning: Many tuk-tuk drivers will hustle you with a 3-hour 30B ($1.20) shopping tour of their "favorite" shops and factories, then pocket hefty commissions on your purchases. However, many drivers have emigrated from Bangkok, speak good English, and are fun to ride with. Just make sure you go where *you* want to go: a favorite ploy is pretending they have never heard of your choice.

BY TAXI There are always private taxis (car services) stationed at the large hotels. At some, the concierge desk will give you the rates. At others, you'll have to negotiate with the driver. Plan on paying 60B to 120B ($2.40 to $4.80) for destinations within the city.

BY CAR **Hertz**, at 90 Sri Donchai (tel. 279474, fax 270184), rents cars, with or without driver, by the day or week. **Avis** has an office at 14/14 Huai Kaeo Rd. (tel/ fax 221316) opposite the Chiang Mai Orchid Hotel, with similar services. Self-drive rental rates for cars and Jeeps start at 1,200B ($48) a day or 7,500B ($300) a week for unlimited kilometers. Expect to pay from 250B ($10) an hour for a car and driver, with a 2-hour minimum and 20 free kilometers.

Local rental-car companies (there are dozens) rent self-drive sedans for 850B to 1,200B ($34 to $48) per day, but they are not insured. Most travel agents will arrange a car and driver for about 1,300B ($52) per day. We loved our driver, Mr. Song Muang, from the Inthanon Tours office (tel. 212373), and also had luck with World Travel Service (tel. 210030).

BY BICYCLE OR MOTORCYCLE We saw a few brave souls pedaling away on bikes in the traffic and air pollution, but we don't recommend it. Some of the budget guest houses do rent bikes for about 25B ($1) per day if you're determined to do it.

Many guest houses along the Ping River and shops around Chaiyapoom Road (north of Tha Pae Road in the Old City) rent 100cc motorcycles for about 175B ($7) per day. Make sure you have the necessary insurance, try to rent a helmet, and expect to leave your passport or credit card as security. Traffic congestion makes driving within the city very dangerous, but many Europeans enjoy renting larger, off-road motorcycles on a weekly basis for touring the northern areas, especially hilly or mountainous areas where biking is arduous.

FAST FACTS   *CHIANG MAI*

American Express Sea Tours Co. Ltd., 2/3 Prachasampan Road, off Chang Klan Road (tel. 271401), is the American Express representative.

Area Code The area code is 053 for the Chiang Mai region.

Babysitters Most of the hotels will provide babysitters if given a few hours' notice.

Bookstores Suriwong Book Centre, 54/1-5 Sri Dornchai (tel. 281052), is open daily 8am to 7:30pm, Sunday till 12:30pm. D. K. Book House, 234 Tha Pae Road (tel. 251555), is open daily 8:30am to 8:30pm. Both stores sell English language books, Nancy Chandler's wonderful, colorful *Map of Chiang Mai* (70B or $2.80), and the excellent P+P Chiang Mai Bus Map (50B or $2). DC, MC, and V accepted.

Business Hours See Chapter 2.

Car Rentals See "Getting Around" in this chapter.

Climate See "When to Go" in Chapter 2.

Currency See "Information, Entry Requirements & Money" in Chapter 2.

Currency Exchange There are dozens of conveniently located bank exchanges open daily 8am to 8pm. Around the Night Market, most of the bank exchanges are open 7am to 10pm. You can always exchange currency at your hotel.

Dentist/Doctor The American Consulate (see below) will supply you with a list of English speaking dentists and doctors. There are also several medical clinics; check with your hotel about the best and nearest facility.

Drugstores There are dozens of pharmacies throughout the city; most open daily 7am to 12am.

Embassies/Consulates The American Consulate is located at 387 Wichayanon Rd., near the Ping River and adjacent to the Chiang Mai Municipality Building (tel. 252665 or 252644). Open Monday to Friday 7:30am to 4:30pm. There are no consulates or embassies for Britain, Canada, New Zealand, or Australia.

Emergencies Dial 191 in case of emergency.

Eyeglasses Charoensilp Optic Co. Ltd., 101-5 Tha Pae Road (tel. 274499) or at the Gad Saun Kaew Shopping Center (tel. 22444, ext. 12018), can repair or replace your eyeglasses. Open daily 8am to 6:30pm; MasterCard, Visa accepted.

Hairdressers/Barbers Several expensive hotels have in-house salons. The Ann Beauty Salon on Loi Droa Road next to the Novotel Suriwongse Hotel is recommended for women. We had good luck at Two Plus One, in the Old City on Moon Muang, a few blocks east of Tha Pae Gate.

Holidays See "When to Go" in Chapter 2 and the "Calendar of Events" in Chapter 11, "Exploring Northern Thailand."

Hospitals Lanna Hospital on the superhighway north of the Old City (tel. 211037) and McCormick Hospital on Kaew Nawarat Road northeast of the Nawarat Bridge (tel. 241311) are private, recommended hospitals.

Information Call the TAT (tel. 248604 or 248607). Also see "Information, Entry Requirements & Money" in Chapter 2.

Language Study You can study the Thai Language at the AUA Language Center, 24 Rajdamnern Rd. (tel. 211377, fax 211377). Director Stephen Thibeault says you can learn some Thai in as little as one month! Contact the school for more information.

Laundry/Dry Cleaning Every hotel and guest house offers 1-day service at reasonable prices.

Luggage Storage/Lockers There are storage facilities at the railroad station, open daily 5am to 8:30pm (25¢ per bag/day) and at the airport, open daily to meet flights ($1 per bag/day).

Lost Property Contact the Tourist Police (see below).

Newspapers/Magazines English language local and imported newspapers, as well as international magazines, are widely available.

Photographic Needs Broadway Photo, 251-3 Tha Pae Rd. (tel. 275578), will repair cameras. Open daily 7am to 9pm.

Police Dial 221444 in emergencies. The Tourist Police (tel. 248974 or 248130) are at 105/1 Chiang Mai–Lamphun Rd. on the east side of the Ping River, on the ground floor of the TAT building.

Post Office General Post Office is on Charoen Muang, near the train station (tel. 241070). Open Monday to Friday 8:30am to 4:30pm; Saturday 8:30am to noon, Sunday and holidays closed. There are several others scattered around the city.

The Overseas Call Office, open 24 hours, is upstairs from the GPO and offers phone, fax, and telex services. There are also international direct daily booths at the airport, TAT, Thai Airways, the Chiang Inn by the Night Market, and just outside Tha Pae Gate. The city is dotted with private fax and overseas call offices. Expect to pay 60B ($2.40) for a 3-minute call to the United States and 170B ($6.80) for one fax sheet.

Religious Services   English-language Catholic services are held at the Assembly of God at 87/14 Huai Kaeo Rd. and at the Seven Fountains Catholic Chapel at 92 Huai Kaeo Rd.

Restrooms   Large hotels and most restaurants have public restrooms. Outside the city, small restaurants may charge 2B (8¢) for the use of an Asian toilet. Bring your own toilet paper.

Safety   In general, the city is quite safe and not yet infested with pickpockets and petty thieves. However, always lock your valuables up at hotels and guest houses. Trekkers' safety is monitored by the Tourist Police, who require every guide to register the particulars of his clients and their route before departing the city.

Shoe Repairs   There are several small shops near the Warorot Market, or around the Night Market off Chang Klan Rd.

Taxes   As in Bangkok, there is an 8% tax on hotel rooms and an 8.25% tax on restaurant bills.

Taxis   See "Getting Around" in this chapter.

Telegrams/Telex   See "Post Office," above.

Television   See "Fast Facts: Bangkok" in Chapter 3.

Transit Info   Chiang Mai International Airport (tel. 270222 or 270234); Thai Airways (tel. 211044); railroad reservations (tel. 244795 or 242094) and information (tel. 247462 or 245363); Arcade Bus Station (tel. 242664).

3. ACCOMMODATIONS

The quality of Chiang Mai's hotels has not yet caught up with its recent surge in popularity, though a recent building boom has yielded a few deluxe hotels. However, there are several newly constructed, first-class hotels. Family-run guest houses provide the best value in town.

We've divided our choices into three geographic areas: near the Ping River, around the Old City, and the Westside/Huai Kaeo Road. Most of the higher-priced hotels and some excellent guest houses are concentrated near the Ping River, an area closest to the bustling heart of the city and the Night Market. This is the best neighborhood for walking, but it's noisier than the westside.

The strip of high-rise hotels on Huai Kaeo Road extends west from the Old City. The new city's congestion has pushed recent developments out along this verdant road, almost up Doi Suthep mountain. The Holiday Inn Green Hills Chiang on the westside near Chiang Mai University is the city's first deluxe hotel. Although this strip is undistinguished, and dining options are limited, this is where some of the nicest shops are located and it's only a brief tuk-tuk ride to the Old City and a 15- to 20-minute ride to the Night Market.

Inexpensive hotels and guest houses have sprung up around the Old City, particularly inside the eastern wall and moat, and outside of it, near Tha Pae Road. This brusque and noisy thoroughfare extends 1km (⁶/₁₀ mile) east to the Ping River, fortunately most of these tiny hotels are tucked into narrow, picturesque sois, and are fairly quiet. They offer very good value, plus plenty of shopping, dining, and nightlife within walking distance.

Note: You must add an 8% tax and a 10% service charge to all rates below, unless otherwise noted.

NEAR THE PING RIVER

VERY EXPENSIVE

CHIANG INN HOTEL, 100 Chang Klan Rd., Chiang Mai 50000. Tel. 053/ 270070. Fax 053/27499. Telex TH 43503. 170 rms. A/C MINIBAR TV TEL

$ Rates (including breakfast): 2,100B–2,400B ($84–$96) single; 2,400B–2,700B ($96–$108) double. AE, DC, MC, V.

The recently renovated Chiang Inn is south of Tha Pae Road, near the Night Market, but it's set back from the lively street and is quieter at night than you'd expect. Unfortunately it's right across the street from the Chiang Inn Plaza, an arcade of flashy Western chain eateries like Burger King and Dunkin Donuts. The compact, teak-paneled lobby has a homey yet elegant feel and is always crowded with Europeans. Spacious, recently renovated, rooms are decorated with local homespun textiles and are clean.

The Chiang Inn has also recently opened an attractive Spanish-style "lodge" in the area across the Narawat Bridge, past the railroad station. It's surprisingly tranquil though some traffic noise is still audible. The Spanish theme is well carried out in black ironwork details, glazed tile floors, and woven bedspreads. The manicured golf course–like grounds include a good-sized freeform pool with a planted island, two tennis courts, and a watchtower with a view of Chiang Mai. Rates are the same as in the Night Market facility.

Dining/Entertainment: There is a popular coffee shop, a French restaurant (see "Dining," below), a lobby cocktail bar, and the city's favorite disco, the Wall.

Services: Room service, concierge, laundry service, complimentary airport transfer.

Facilities: Large pool with sun deck, tennis, business center, shopping arcade.

CHIANG MAI PLAZA HOTEL, 92 Sri Dornchai Rd., Chiang Mai 50000. Tel. 053/270040. Fax 053/272230. Telex PLAZAHO TH 49329. 444 rms, 87 suites. A/C MINIBAR TV TEL

$ Rates: 2,000B–2,400B ($80–$96) single; 2,200B–2,600B ($88–$104) double; from 9,000B ($360) suite. AE, DC, MC, V.

These two 12-story towers, completed in 1986, form a typically bland, modern Western hotel, but guest rooms are large, plush, and offer city and mountain views. The lobby is so enormous that the helpful staff and decorative furniture are almost lost in acres of brilliantly polished granite. However, the fine service, large swimming pool, good restaurant, shopping arcade, and a huge suite were enough to lure Elizabeth Taylor here on a 1989 visit to Thailand. The Plaza is also well located: in town, but just far enough away, toward the Ping River, to be out of the congestion. It's between Chang Klan and Charoen Prathet roads.

Dining/Entertainment: The huge Phai Khum restaurant serves Thai and continental cuisine. We like the lobby bar, where a classical Thai quartet performs traditional music nightly. For more action, try the Twinkle Lounge hostess club or the popular Plaza Disco.

Services: 24-hour room service, concierge, limousine service, babysitting (with notice), laundry service.

Facilities: Large swimming pool, fitness center, pool hall, shopping arcade.

ROYAL PRINCESS, 112 Chang Klan Rd., Chiang Mai 50000. Tel. 053/ 281033. Fax 053/281044. Telex 49325 TH. 190 rms, 8 suites. A/C MINIBAR TV TEL

$ Rates: 2,650B–2,875B ($106–$115) single; $3,125B–3,350B ($125–$134) double; 9,600B ($384) suite. Extra bed 720B ($28.80). AE, DC, MC, V.

The northern cousin of Bangkok's deluxe Dusit Thani is a first-rate city hotel less than 200 yards from Chiang Mai's Night Market on the corner of Loi Kroa Road. Furnishings are tasteful, with elements of Thai art and discreet luxury. During our stay over the New Year, the extremely busy staff was always helpful and courteous. Our quiet room overlooked the glittering lights of the city and was a good size, clean, and—though not new—impressively well maintained. We found the cotton bathrobes and slippers welcome after a day of sightseeing; they, as well as a hairdryer and personal safe, are standard amenities.

Dining/Entertainment: The sometimes frenetic lobby has a comfortable bar. The pleasant coffee shop serves an elaborate breakfast buffet with delicious pastries (300B or $12 per person), and the Jasmine restaurant (see "Dining," below) serves excellent dim sum at lunch. For get-away-from-it-all entertainment, check out the live bands in the Music Room.

Services: 24-hour room service, concierge, limousine service, babysitting (with notice), laundry service.

Facilities: Small swimming pool.

THE EMPRESS HOTEL, 199 Chang Klan Rd., Chiang Mai 50000. Tel. 053/270240 or 272977. Fax 053/272467. Telex 43516 EMPETEL TH. 375 rms. A/ C MINIBAR TV TEL

$ Rates: 1,600B–2,600B ($64–$104) single; 1,900B–2,900B ($76–$116) double; suites from 7,000B ($280). Extra bed 400B ($16). AE, DC, MC, V.

This 17-story tower, opened in 1990, is a bit out of town (2km [1.2 miles] south of the Night Market) but in a quiet spot. The impressive public spaces are filled with glass, granite, and chrome and well-integrated touches of Thai style. Large rooms with picture windows are a tasteful, modern interpretation of Oriental decor, using primarily rose-and-peach tones. Bathrooms are small but include many toiletries. In time, we think this place may rival the more seasoned Chiang Mai Plaza.

Dining/Entertainment: Pranda Palace, a Peking-style Chinese restaurant, is located on the mezzanine level. La Brasserie is a formal continental grill with an attached wine cellar. There's a coffee shop, an Asian cocktail lounge with live entertainment, and several bars and lounges, plus the very popular Crystal Cave Disco.

Services: 24-hour room service, concierge, limousine service, babysitting (with notice), laundry service.

Facilities: Swimming pool.

NOVOTEL SURIWONGSE, 110 Chang Klan Rd., Chiang Mai 50000. Tel. 053/270051. Fax 053/270063. Telex 49311 NVTS TH. 168 rms. A/C MINIBAR TV TEL

$ Rates: 1,900B ($76) single; 2,100B–2,500B ($84–$100) double; from 4,500B ($180) suite. Extra bed 400B ($16). AE, DC, MC, V.

The French-managed hotel on the corner of Loi Kroa Road has a hardwood-paneled lobby giving it a richness that belies its moderate price. The spacious, teak-trimmed twin bedrooms are among Chiang Mai's better values. Higher-priced rooms offer a balcony and better view, yet all are equipped with first-class amenities. Unlike the woody decorative scheme downstairs, the colors in the upstairs guest areas are cheerier off white and pastel.

Dining/Entertainment: The northern-style Thai restaurant, Fueng Fah, is well regarded and very popular. The newly installed Bistro and its sidewalk café serve very pricey French fare but are crowded at teatime, when real shoppers stoke up for a Night Market assault.

Services: Room service, concierge, laundry service, fitness center, small arcade.

EXPENSIVE

MAE PING HOTEL, 153 Sri Dornchai Rd., Chiang Mai 50000. Tel. 053/ 270160. Fax 053/270181. Telex 49343 MAETEL TH. 350 rms, 24 suites. A/C MINIBAR TV TEL

$ Rates: 1,600B ($64) single; 1,800B ($72) double; from 3,000B ($120) suite. Extra bed 300B ($12). AE, DC, MC, V.

This newly built tower hotel is one of the city's best values because of its attractive style and terrific location. It's two blocks from the Night Market, on soi parallel to Chang Klan Road, between Loi Kroa and Sri Dornchai roads, so you can get a good night's sleep without springing for the 14th and 15th floor Executive Club rooms. The unusual double height lobby interprets Thai architectural elements in bold white-and-gold decor, with shops, a tour desk, and other services discreetly included. Large, bright guest rooms have contemporary blond teak furnishings upholstered in peach, jade, or blue, modern conveniences, and mountain views. Sculpted lamp bases and reproductions of temple murals add a classic touch.

Dining/Entertainment: There is a coffee shop with a bounteous international lunch buffet (140B or $5.60), the elegant Venezia Ristorante, and a cocktail terrace. The popular, landscaped Larn Mae Ping Beer Garden serves beer and snacks from Thai pushcarts.

Services: Room service, concierge, limousine service, babysitting (with notice), laundry service.

Facilities: Small swimming pool, shopping arcade.

PORNPING TOWER, 46-48 Charoen Prathet Rd., Chiang Mai 50000. Tel. 053/270099. Fax 053/270119. Telex 43557 PPHOTEL TH. 325 rms. A/C MINIBAR TV TEL

$ Rates: 1,800B ($72) single; 2,200B ($88) double. Extra bed 350B ($14). AE, DC, MC, V.

This 20-story hotel, the tallest in the city, bustles with evening activity at the Bubble Discotheque, the lower-level cocktail lounge, the lobby bar, and even in the coffee shop. The Hong Kong–style public spaces are of polished marble, glass, and mirrors. Hallways are burnished a cinnabar red. Rooms are elegantly furnished in cool colors and contemporary styles. The Pornping has a great pool with an inviting sun deck, a friendly staff, a popular Chinese restaurant, a rooftop international grill room, and other services which make it one of the best buys in the city. It's located south of Tha Pae Road.

DUANGTAWAN HOTEL, 132 Loi Kroa, Chiang Mai 5000. Tel. 053/270384 or 02/55525 in Bangkok. Fax 053/275304 or 02/2555529 in Bangkok. Telex 49352 DTWHTL. 554 rms. A/C MINIBAR TV TEL

$ Rates: 1,900B–2,100B ($76–$84) single; 2,100B–2,300B ($84–$92) double; 6,000B ($240) and up, suite. Extra bed 400B ($16). AE, DC, MC, V.

This recently completed 25-floor white tower stands out from the others near the Night Market because of its subdued elegance. No unnecessary details here, though marble floors and gold accents lend luxury to public areas, which are furnished Western-style in green and burnt orange. The large rooms are simply and tastefully furnished in white and green with dark-wood accents. Bathrooms are huge and come with separate shower-rooms.

Dining/Entertainment: A well-regarded dining room serves good Chinese and Thai fare, also some Western food, with local songbirds at night.

Services: Room service, concierge, laundry service, fitness center, swimming pool, sauna.

RIVER VIEW LODGE, 25 Charoen Prathet Rd., Soi 2, Chiang Mai 50000. Tel. 053/271109. Fax 053/279019. 36 rms. A/C TEL

$ Rates (including breakfast): 1,200B–1,450B ($48–$58) single/double; 1,800B ($72) triple. MC, V.

Where does veteran shopper and mapmaker Nancy Chandler stay when in Chiang Mai? The River View Lodge, run by a delightful couple, tucked away on Ping River, south of Tha Pae Road, and just a 5-minute walk from the Night Market. You, too, can breakfast informally on the deck and look out over lawns that stretch down to the river. Aesthetically pleasing details abound. The main white-stucco building has a row of dormers, each gable decorated with local carvings. Teak furniture is locally crafted; the lamp bases are modeled after local Buddha figures. Large, impeccable rooms have terra-cotta tile floors and contain a table, chairs, dresser, and bathroom with shower. (Our favorite room is the small one with its own garden terrace, but many have balconies.) The open-sided restaurant serves traditionally prepared Thai cooking as well as European food, and there's even a swimming pool. Rates depend on view and are higher than those at most guest houses, but this place is a delight.

STAR INN, 36 Soi 4, Loi Kroa Rd., Chiang Mai 50000. Tel. 053/270360. Fax 053/273082. 82 rms. A/C TV TEL
$ Rates: 1,200B ($48) single; 1,400B ($56) double; 2,000B ($80) suite. Extra bed 300B ($1.20). AE, MC, V.

This small, comfortable white stucco hotel offers good value for its location, tucked away behind the Duangtawan and right by the Night Market. Many of its visitors are from other parts of Asia, but the staff seemed at home in English. The lobby is dominated by a patterned granite floor and massive, carved dark-wood furniture. Though the rooms and bathrooms are smaller than many in this price category, they're handsomely furnished in grays and greens with local homespun covers and are well maintained.

Dining/Entertainment: Star caters to its Asian guests with a karaoke bar and a popular Korean restaurant that's arranged in traditional booths of low tables and pillow seats.

MODERATE

BAAN KAEW GUESTHOUSE, 142 Charoen Prathet Rd., Chiang Mai 50000. Tel. 053/271606. 20 rms. TEL
$ Rates (including tax and services): 350B ($14) single/double with fan; 450B ($18) single/double with A/C. No credit cards.

This motel-style guest house, south of Sri Dornchai Road opposite Wat Chaimongkol, forms an L-shaped courtyard enclosing a manicured lawn and well-attended garden. Rooms are simple, spotless, fan-cooled, and have screened windows overlooking the grounds. Tiled bathrooms have hot-water showers. Breakfast is served in a shaded pavilion and snacks can be had all day at picnic tables on the lawn. Baan Kaew is in a refreshingly peaceful neighborhood with a large enough lawn for kids to play.

GALARE GUEST HOUSE, 7 Charoen Prathet Rd., Soi 2, Chiang Mai 50000. Tel. 053/273885. 35 rms. MINIBAR TEL
$ Rates (including tax and service): 725B ($29) single/double. DC, MC, V.

If the River View Lodge is booked or you want to save the baht, try the smaller Galare, almost next door. It's a modern, Thai-style, three-story, brick and wood motel on the Ping River, south of Tha Pae Road. Broad covered verandas, glistening with polished teak and rattan furniture, overlook a pleasant garden and courtyard. Rooms are small but have screened windows and fans. They are comfortable and tastefully furnished. The cheap, no frills snack bar serves breakfast and beverages on a covered deck overlooking the river. Sam's Trekking, based at the Galare, organizes treks to hill-tribe villages as well as local tours of Chiang Mai.

ONCE UPON A TIME, 385/2 Charoen Prathet Rd., Chiang Mai 50000. Tel. 053/274932. Fax 053/273675. 11 rms. A/C MINIBAR
$ Rates (including tax and service): 600B–1,800B ($24–$72) single/double; 2,525B ($101) triple. AE, MC, V.

⭐ Many of you who toured the Vimanmek Palace in Bangkok probably imagined life in a traditional Rattanakosin mansion. Here in Chiang Mai, Pierre Delalande and his partner have opened a guest house with a restaurant and 11 delightful guest rooms in the Lanna Thai style. The elegantly restored compound of teak pavilions clusters around a landscaped garden. Ducks and birds (you can actually hear their song!) populate the grounds. Mr. Pierre has taken great care: The plethora of beaded curtains, pink lace, and gingerbread wood trimming lends a very homey, slightly overdone, "Victorian Thai Gay" aesthetic that is totally pleasing. Unique guest quarters, tended by 24-hour butler service, range in price according to size (most are around 950B [$38] or 1,450B [$58]). All are teak, with tables

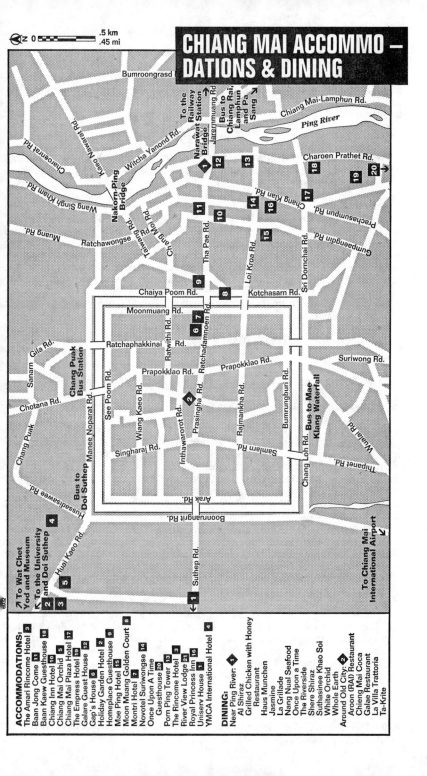

CHIANG MAI ACCOMMO – DATIONS & DINING

0 .5 km
.45 mi

Bumroongrasd

Ping River

Chiang Mai-Lamphun Rd.

Charoen Prathet Rd.

To the Railway Station

Bus to Chiang Rai, Lamphun and Pa Sang

Jatermmuang Rd.

Narawat Bridge

Nakorn Ping Bridge

Witcha Yanond Rd.

Keo Nawarat Rd.

Charoenrat Rd.

Wang Singh Kham Rd.

Tawarat Rd.

Chang Moi Rd.

Chang Klan Rd.

Prachasumpon Rd.

Gumpaengdin Rd.

Sri Dornchai Rd.

Muang Rd.

Ratchawongse

Tha Pae Rd.

Loi Kroa Rd.

Chaiya Poom Rd.

Kotchasarn Rd.

Moonmuang Rd.

Ratchadamnoen Rd.

Ratwithi Rd.

Ratchaphakkinai Rd.

Prapokklao Rd.

Prapokklao Rd.

Prapokklao Rd.

Rajmankha Rd.

Suriwong Rd.

Sanarn

Gila Rd.

See Poom Rd.

Chang Puak Bus Station

Wiang Kaeo Rd.

Prasingha Rd.

Intthawarorot Rd.

Bumrungburi Rd.

Bus to Mae Klang Waterfall

Chang Loh Rd.

Chotana Rd.

Chang Puak

Manee Noparat Rd.

Singharaj Rd.

Samlan Rd.

Wualai Rd.

Thipanet Rd.

Bus to Doi Suthep

Hussadisawee Rd.

Huai Kaeo Rd.

To Wat Chet Yod and Museum

To the University and Doi Suthep

Arak Rd.

Boonruangrit Rd.

Suthep Rd.

To Chiang Mai International Airport

ACCOMMODATIONS:
The Amari Rincome Hotel **3**
Baan Jong Come **11**
Baan Kaew Guesthouse **18**
Chiang Inn Hotel **10**
Chiang Mai Orchid **5**
Chiang Mai Plaza Hotel **17**
The Empress Hotel **19**
Galare Guest House **12**
Gap's House **6**
Holiday Garden Hotel **2**
Homeplace Guesthouse **9**
Mae Ping Hotel **15**
Moon Muang Golden Court **8**
Montri Hotel **7**
Novotel Suriwongse **14**
Once Upon A Time Guesthouse **20**
Porn Ping Tower **13**
The Rincome Hotel **3**
River View Lodge **21**
Royal Princess Inn **16**
Uniserv House **1**
YMCA International Hotel **4**

DINING:
Near Ping River: ◆
Al Shiraz
Grilled Chicken with Honey
Restaurant
Haus Munchen
Jasmine
La Grillade
Nang Nual Seafood
Once Upon a Time
The Riverside
Shere Shiraz
Suthasinee Khao Soi
White Orchid
Whole Earth
Around Old City: 2
Aroon (RAI) Restaurant
Chieng Mai Coca
Galae Restaurant
La Villa Trattoria
Ta-Krite

of complimentary, long-ago toiletries (like ginger soap and eau de cologne), Victorian brass wall sconces, and rattan armchairs. Framed historical photos and unique accessories add enormous style; it's historically playful and utterly au courant. Located a 20-minute walk south of the Night Market, on the Ping River between the Monfort College and Mengrai bridge, this is a special place to sample traditional Thai hospitality.

INEXPENSIVE

CHIANG MAI YOUTH (CYH2) HOSTEL, 21/8 Chang Klan Rd., Mooban Oon-Ruen, Chiang Mai 50000. Tel. 053/236735. 16 rms with bath, dormitory with shared bath.
$ Rates (including tax and service): 125B ($5) dorm bed; 145B ($5.80) single/double. MC, V.

Don't confuse the Chang Klan hostel with Youth's Hostel at 4 Rajchaphakinai Road near the Chiang Mai Gate in the Old City. Youth's is actually the city's original IYH affiliate, but by comparison, it's worn and faded. The newer Chang Klan City Hostel (or CYH2 as it's known) is less convenient but almost luxurious. Spotless, twin-bedded rooms have private hot-water showers, fan or air-conditioning; bunks in the spick-and-span dorm are fan-cooled; there's laundry service and a highly recommended trekking company. Breakfast is served in a proper dining room! CYH2 runs a free nightly shuttle to the Night Market (about 4km [2½ miles] north of CYH2), and the good spirit we've come to expect at IYH affiliates prevails.

AROUND THE OLD CITY

MODERATE

BAAN JONG COME, 47 Soi 4, Tha Pae Rd., Chiang Mai 50000. Tel. 053/274823. 28 rms.
$ Rates (including tax and service): 300B–450B ($12–$18) single/double; 600B ($24) triple. No credit cards.

We thought this attractive, three-story lodge was one of the best guest houses in this part of town. It's conveniently located, three blocks east of Tha Pae Gate, yet fairly quiet. Bright, airy rooms, as well as bathrooms with shower, are fully tiled and very clean. All have a comfortable seating area, screened windows, and fans; higher-priced rooms also have air-conditioning, though we never needed it in Chiang Mai's pleasant climate. The open-sided ground floor has a TV lounge, a good, inexpensive restaurant (try their kuai tiao rice noodles), and a reputable trekking office. Mr. Oud and his friendly staff run the place like an efficient hotel.

GAP'S HOUSE, 3 Soi 4, Ratchadamnoen Rd., Chiang Mai 50000. Tel. 053/213140. 18 rms.
$ Rates (including tax and service): 175B ($7) single; 200B ($8) double; 350B ($14) suite. Rates include American breakfast. MC, V.

This place is a rare find—centrally located yet quiet, comfortable yet traditional, newly built yet with plenty of Lanna Thai style. Superb values, but book ahead for the less expensive rooms. Most of the rooms are tucked into free-standing teak houses, with polished floors and walls, woven rattan beds, kitschy upholstered chairs, and clean, tiled bathrooms. There's a block of four attached rooms which are smaller and usually rented to singles, as well as a double suite with a TV and minibar (often booked by U.S. government workers). This is, at last, a place with the homey advantages and charm of a guest house plus the comforts of a hotel. Bargain rates include breakfast, served in the teak dining pavilion in the middle of their flower-filled garden. The manager, Mr. Preecha, is friendly and informative; he and his staff are one of Gap's greatest assets. The guest house is one block west of Tha Pae Gate, down the soi opposite USIS.

MONTRI HOTEL, 2-6 Ratchadamnoen Rd., Chiang Mai 50000. Tel. 053/211069. Fax 053/217416. 80 rms. TEL

$ Rates (including tax and service): 450B ($18) single/double with fan; 535B ($21) single/double with A/C. MC, V.

If you like the group dynamics of a big hotel, this is a good, inexpensive choice located on the west side of Tha Pae Gate. Older guest rooms are fan cooled and worn but clean. Newly renovated rooms have air-conditioning and more attention to decor, at the higher rate. They're brighter and much better value, especially the quieter, high-floor ones. The Montri also boasts JJ's Coffeeshop and Bakery, the most popular watering hole in Chiang Mai. Most of the hundreds of travelers who pass this busy corner every hour manage to stop in for coffee, cake, a sandwich, or a burger (open daily 6:30am to 10:30pm). It's also just a couple of blocks north of Chiang Mai's modest go-go girl district.

INEXPENSIVE

HOMEPLACE GUESTHOUSE, 9 Soi 6, Tha Pae Rd., Chiang Mai 50000. Tel. 053/273439. Fax 053/273494. 16 rms. A/C TEL

$ Rates (including tax and service): 300B ($12) single/double with fan; 500B ($20) single/double with A/C. MC, V.

A gregarious family (that speaks little English) manages this newly built walk-up that resembles a small apartment house. Sky-blue walls and tiled floors enhance the bright, cheery ambience. The third floor has a simple roof deck with concrete tables and stools—perfect for eating breakfast with a view or getting some sun. Bargain-rate, compact, tidy rooms have private hot-water showers, a small seating area, ceiling fan, and air-conditioning. They are cleaned thoroughly every day too.

MOON MUANG GOLDEN COURT, 95/1 Moon Muang Rd., Chiang Mai 50000. Tel. 053/212779. 20 rms.

$ Rates (including tax and service): 130B–150B ($5.20–$6) single/double with fan; 280B ($11.20) single/double with A/C; hot showers 15B (60¢) extra. No credit cards.

An Irish couple Kyle met really liked this drab, three-story inn one block west of Tha Pae Gate because of its cleanliness and low price. The simplest rooms with twin beds, fan, and screened windows share access to cold-water showers and toilets. Even though the hotel is at the foot of a long driveway, off the busy road, request a back-facing room.

WESTSIDE/HUAI KAEO ROAD

VERY EXPENSIVE

CHIANG MAI ORCHID, 100-102 Huai Kaeo Rd., Chiang Mai 50000. Tel. 053/222099. Fax 053/221625. Telex 49337 CHIOR TH. 262 rms. A/C MINIBAR TV TEL

$ Rates: 2,875B–3,700B ($115–$148) single; 3,350B–4,200B ($134–$168) double; suite from 10,800B ($432). Extra bed 550B ($22). AE, DC, MC, V.

The Chiang Mai Orchid, just west of the Old City, and right next door to the enormous Western-style Gad San Kaew/Central Shopping Complex, has a fine reputation for sophisticated facilities and friendly service. It deserves it. The lobby and other public spaces are festooned with flowers and decorated with clusters of chic, low-slung rattan couches and chairs. Spacious, quiet rooms are pleasantly furnished with local wood carvings. The Orchid also has a childrens' play center and a knowledgeable tour desk.

Dining/Entertainment: There's an excellent continental restaurant, Le Pavillon; an open-air Thai restaurant/coffee shop for northern specialities; a new Chinese restaurant; and a poolside snack bar. The lobby's coffee bar serves European pastries, tea, and 11 brewed coffees, from 2 to 9pm.

Services: 24-hour room service, concierge, limousine service, babysitting (with notice), laundry service.

Facilities: Large swimming pool, health club with aerobics classes, traditional Thai massage parlor, shopping arcade.

THE AMARI RINCOME HOTEL, 301 Huai Kaeo Rd., at Nimanhemin Rd., Chiang Mai 50000. Tel. 053/221130. Fax 053/221915. Telex TH 49313. 158 rms. A/C MINIBAR TV TEL

$ **Rates:** 2,300B ($92) single; 2,500B ($100) double; 8,400B ($336) suite. Extra bed 500B ($20). AE, DC, MC, V.

This tranquil hotel complex is one of our favorites because of its elegant, yet traditional, Thai atmosphere. Public spaces are decorated with local handicrafts. The professional staff wears intricately embroidered costumes. Large, balconied guest rooms are elaborately adorned with Burmese tapestries and carved wood accents. Pretty, plush bathrooms have been totally redone. The Amari's grounds are expansive; across the street is the posh Nantawan Arcade, a minimall with some of the city's best shops.

Dining/Entertainment: The Thong Kwow is a handsome teak restaurant serving a hearty lunch buffet and international cuisine by candlelight. The moderately priced coffee shop has a ceiling covered with painted umbrellas from nearby Bo Sang.

Services: 24-hour room service, concierge, limousine service, babysitting (with notice), laundry service.

Facilities: Two swimming pools (one Olympic-size and open to the public for 75B or $3), tennis courts, jogging track, shopping arcade.

HOLIDAY INN GREEN HILLS, 24 Chiang Mai–Lamphang Super Highway, Chiang Mai 50000. Tel. 053/220100 or 2482263 in Bangkok. Fax 053/221612 or 2482264 in Bangkok. Telex 49353 HICM TH. 200 rms. A/C MINIBAR TV TEL

$ **Rates:** 2,600B–2,800B ($104–$112) single/double; suites from 6,300B ($252). AE, DC, MC, V.

This recently completed deluxe facility offers the bland Western comfort and gloss characteristic of the chain. It's 6km (about 3½ miles) north of the airport, and right around the corner from the Nimhaeminda Arcade which houses some of Chiang Mai's nicest stores. At our last visit, surrounding buildings were in the last stages of construction; when they are completed (probably in 1995), the Holiday Inn will really start to fill up. In the meantime it's even attracted members of the Thai royal family—the elder sister of the king paid a visit here in 1993.

The lobby has a striking peaked orange ceiling with dark green inset circles and some surprising touches of Thai style in carved furniture and wall hangings, but the large rooms are strictly Western, with flowered spreads, blond wood, and plush armchairs around small tables. The staff is warm, efficient, and speaks especially good English.

Dining/Entertainment: There's a wealth of options here: The ornate Cherry Blossoms restaurant specializes in Chinese banquets with exotic dishes like shark-fin soup, and the Salathong Thai restaurant serves up traditional local dishes. For a lower-key, lower-priced Italian meal, try Pinocchio's, which has a more-than-life-sized statue of the wooden doll on the door that's especially inviting to children. There's also the Mariko Karaoke bar and a poolside café for lighter fare.

Services: Room service, concierge, laundry service, free shuttle to Night Market.

Facilities: Swimming pool, sauna, fitness center, free access to golf-and-squash facilities, small arcade, business center, parking.

EXPENSIVE

HOLIDAY GARDEN HOTEL, 16/16 Huai Kaeo Rd., Chiang Mai 50000. Tel. 053/210901-4. Fax 053/210905. Telex 49320 HOLIDAY TH. 200 rms. A/C MINIBAR TV TEL

$ **Rates:** 1,400B–1,700B ($56–$68) single; 1,600B–1,900B ($64–$76) double in tower; 800B ($32) single, 900B ($36) double garden wing. AE, DC, MC, V.

Most of the hotel, opened in 1987, is in well-kept buildings set in a U-shape around a small pool and garden. In 1990, a sparkling 12-story tower was built, adding an ultramodern glass-walled elevator, a large, gray granite lobby, a pool-view coffee shop, and more than 100 compact, well-designed, tasteful guest rooms. Rates vary according to location and view. The older, high-ceilinged garden wing rooms seem more colonial by comparision and are more worn. Yet, they're very comfortable and excellent value. The hotel retains its Thai homeyness and the management is very friendly. Besides the coffee shop, there is a casual Thai restaurant and outdoor bar by the pool. The hotel is 4km (2.4 miles) west of the Old City.

INEXPENSIVE

UNISERVE HOUSE, Chiang Mai University, Huai Kaeo Rd., Chiang Mai 50002. Tel. 053/221699, ext. 3601.
$ Rates (including tax and service): 475B ($19) single; 600B ($24) double. No credit cards.

Some of you might enjoy being tenants in dorms used for the training of professional hospitality managers. You can sleep late, have a private air-conditioned room and toilet, yet feel like a student again for very little money. Little English is spoken (although languages are part of the curriculum) and it may be difficult to arrange a room, but the TAT can assist you. The extensive grounds of Chiang Mai University offer a pleasant respite from the busy city, and easy access to the zoo. It's an inconvient location, about 6km (3.6 miles) west of the Old City, but a unique glance at Thai life. Chiang Mai Teachers College (tel. 053/214138) also rents dorm space to visitors at its main building.

YMCA INTERNATIONAL HOTEL, 11 Sermsuk Rd., Mengrairasmi, Chiang Mai 50000. Tel. 053/221819. Fax 053/215523. Telex 49341 YMCACMT TH. 31 rms. TEL
$ Rates (including tax and service): 85B ($3.30) dormitory; 145B ($5.80) single, 220B ($8.80) double with shared bath; 220B ($8.80) single, 290B ($11.60) double with fan; 300B–600B ($12–$24) single, 350B–725B ($14–$29) double with A/C. Extra bed 170B ($6.80). AE, MC, V.

The YMCA is convenient, but tough to find. It's off Hatsadhisawee Road, north of the Thai Public Library on Huai Kaeo Road, and just a few blocks walk northeast of the Chiang Mai Orchid Hotel. The hotel has a studious, clean-cut aura and the modern, carpeted rooms are clean, quiet, and cheap. There are many choices, ranging from a suite with minibar and TV, to private rooms with fans, air-conditioning, and private shower, to dorm-style with common bath. Access to the YMCA's good cafeteria, tour desk, crafts shop, laundry, recreation and business center facilities is included in the price.

4. DINING

Northern-style or Lanna Thai cooking is influenced by the ethnic minorities (including the Burmese) who live in the area. Even the Chinese food is different, influenced by the Muslims who've migrated south from Yunnan Province (there are many restaurateurs from Kunming). Among the most distinctive northern Thai dishes are *khao miao,* glutinous or sticky rice (often served in a knotted banana leaf); *sai-ua,* Chiang Mai sausage; *khao soi* (a spicy, curried broth with vegetables and glass noodles), and many other, slightly sweet, meat and fish curries. You may be relieved to know that chili peppers are used less than in pure Thai cuisine.

The formal northern meal is call *khan toke,* referring to the custom of sharing a variety of main courses (eaten with hands) with guests seated around *khan toke* (low, lacquered teak tables). Most of the restaurants that serve in the khan-toke style combine a dance performance with the meal, making it a full evening's entertainment (see "Evening Entertainment," below, for details).

Chiang Mai is also blessed with wonderful street food and food markets. The best food markets for tasting local favorites are the Anusarn Market, on the corner of Sri Dornchai and Chang Klan roads near the Night Market, and Somphet Market, on the northwest interior perimeter road in the Old City. You can also try the food stalls on

Moon Muang Road at the southwest corner of the Old City or the outdoor restaurants and stalls on the east side of the Old City at the gate near Loi Kroa Road.

Prices range from the expensive European restaurants in the best hotels (up to $70 for two with wine) to food stalls where you can treat yourself and a friend for $5. Some restaurants include the 8.25% tax and standard 10% service charge in their rates, others don't. Most restaurants do not require reservations. If they do, it will be noted.

NEAR THE PING RIVER

EXPENSIVE

If the west side of town is more convenient, the fine continental restaurant at the Chiang Mai Orchid Hotel, Le Pavillon (tel. 22209), also comes highly recommended by local expatriates.

LA GRILLADE, in the Chiang Inn Hotel, 100 Chang Klan Rd. Tel. 270070.
   Cuisine: FRENCH. **Reservations:** Recommended at dinner.
$ **Prices:** Appetizers 50B–275B ($2–$11); main courses 240B–500B ($9.60–$20). AE, MC, V.
   Open: Lunch daily 11:30am–2pm, dinner daily 6:30pm–10pm.
The hotel's formal Thai-style dining room serves some of the best continental fare in the city, with a strong leaning toward French cuisine. Comfortable armchairs, crisp linens, gleaming crystal, and attentive service distinguish this from your average casual Thai dining experience. For starters, enjoy fresh asparagus with hollandaise, vegetable salads, and several potages. The red snapper, panfried with capers, is flown in daily from the south and imported Australian tenderloin is marinated in red wine and cooked with artichoke hearts; both are excellent. Luckily for the pocketbook, French wines are served by the bottle or glass.

JASMINE, in the Royal Princess, 112 Chang Klan Rd. (south of Loi Kroa Rd.). Tel. 281033.
   Cuisine: CHINESE. **Reservations:** Recommended at dinner.
$ **Prices:** Appetizers 150B–425B ($6–$17); main courses 225B–1,200B ($9–$48). AE, DC, MC, V.
   Open: Lunch daily 11am–1pm, dinner daily 6–10pm.
Jasmine is an intimate, quiet, tastefully decorated and expensive Cantonese restaurant that specializes in dim sum (about 60B [$2.40] for each three- to five-piece serving) at lunch. The variety changes often, but there are normally 12 different mildly spiced, freshly steamed treats from which to choose. Dinner and lunch main courses are deliciously prepared by a Chinese chef, who came from the Bangkok Dusit Thani's gourmet Mayflower Restaurant to supervise this establishment. Specialities include bird's-nest soup, barbecued pig, crystal prawns, minced squab with lettuce, and shark's fin (sometimes available in their set-price lunch [475B or $19] or dinner [1,500B or $60] menus).

WHITE ORCHID, in the Hotel Diamond, 33/10 Charoen Prathet Rd. (south of Tha Pae Rd.). Tel. 270080.
   Cuisine: CHINESE. **Reservations:** Recommended at dinner.
$ **Prices:** Appetizers 70B–300B ($2.80–$12); main courses 70B–500B ($2.80–$20). MC, V.
   Open: Lunch daily 11am–2pm, dinner daily 5–10:30pm.
Go past the tolerable coffee shop and teak Lanna khan-toke house to find this riverside restaurant at the back of the courtyard. Diners are served around tables large enough for 10 (the restaurant can also accommodate couples or small groups). You can either sit under the covered pavilion or outside in the garden café overlooking the river. We enjoyed a sensational meal including Peking duck, roast duck, sliced noodles with shrimp, chicken with cashews, and stir-fried mixed vegetables.

PICCOLA ROMA, 3/2-3 Charoen Prathet Rd. Tel. 271256.
   Cuisine: ITALIAN. **Reservations:** Recommended at dinner.

$ Prices: Appetizers 70B–220B ($2.80–$8.80); main dishes 140B–340B ($5.60–$13.60). AE.
Open: Lunch daily 11am–2pm, dinner daily 4pm–11pm.

Locals praise this *taverna* just north of the Pornping Tower and the Diamond Riverside as the best of the city's many new Italian restaurants, and we thought it would be perfect for a romantic candlelight dinner. The setting is elegant, with dark paneled wood walls and crisp white tablecloths, and the menu as genuinely northern Italian as the management. One Canadian couple we met raved about their meal of focaccia, carpaccio, fettucine with pesto, and thick, creamy homemade ice cream.

LE COQ D'OR, 68/1 Tanon Koh Klano Hoi. Tel. 282024.
Cuisine: FRENCH. **Reservations:** Recommended.
$ Prices: Appetizers 95B–360B ($3.80–$14.40); main dishes 260B–680B ($10.40–$27.20). AE.
Open: Lunch daily noon–2pm, dinner daily 6–10pm.

Coq d'Or, long purveyors of the best French food in the Old City, have relocated to the area east of the Ping River, not far from the Mengrai Bridge, on the old Chiang Mai–Lamphun Road on the lush, tranquil grounds of the Wood Estate (once the home of WAR Wood, the former British consul of Chiang Mai, whose hilarious memoirs are available all over Chiang Mai). The setting is a beautiful 50-year-old villa, with parrots in cages outside that shriek "Sawadi krup." Inside, the food is classic French, from goose pâté, to escargots in butter and herbs, to consommé with sherry to the crêpe Suzette. The main courses run the gamut from filet of sole with lemon and capers or whole red snapper, to duck à l'orange and rack of lamb.

MODERATE

NANG NUAL SEAFOOD RESTAURANT, 27/2 Koa Klang Rd., Nong Hoi. Tel. 281974. Fax 281972.
Cuisine: THAI/CHINESE/WESTERN. **Directions:** 7km (4.2 miles) south of town on the Lamphun Highway.
$ Prices: Appetizers 30B–145B ($1.40–$5.80); main courses 50B–180B ($2–$7.20). AE, MC, V.
Open: Daily 10am–11pm.

Geared to tour groups and large parties, this place is south of town on the Lamphun Highway. You enter a garden with pet birds, monkeys, and a waterfall; huge dining areas include an air-conditioned interior or outdoor patio overlooking a lagoon with a small playground. There are 63 (Kyle counted!) full meals cast in colored plastic, displayed in the entrance foyer, each numbered for easy ordering. Edible Thai desserts and fruit are displayed on a traditional teak bed. The food's not bad—good shrimp cocktail and barbecued spareribs, a decent steak with a real baked potato, OK Chinese fare, and toned-down Thai standards—it's just a little too wild for us. Might be fun for kids.

ONCE UPON A TIME, 385/2 Charoen Prathet Rd. Tel. 274932.
Cuisine: THAI. **Reservations:** Recommended.
$ Prices: Main courses 70B–170B ($2.80–$6.80). AE, MC, V.
Open: Daily 4:30pm–midnight. Lunch is served during festivals or by request.

If you want the best Thai food, in the most beautiful compound of restored teak houses, there's no better choice. The same restaurateurs who created Bangkok's fondly-remembered Once Upon A Time have brought their many talents north. The two-story teak dining pavilion (other houses in the garden have been turned into charming Lanna Thai guest rooms) is on the tranquil banks of the Mae Ping; south of the Night Market.

Downstairs, specialties such as *hohmok*, an array of seafood soufflés made with prawn, mussels, or fish and coconut milk; mildly spiced grilled duck in a coconut-milk curry, and other delicacies (*pla chon*—fresh river fish served with dipping sauces—is a favorite) illustrated in the hand-drawn menu are served. Upstairs, under the peaked roof, diners can sit on cushions in the khan-toke style and sample the same specials or an array of northern Thai dishes, including pork curry and piquant chili pastes.

WHOLE EARTH RESTAURANT, 88 Sri Dornchai Rd. off Chang Klan Rd. Tel. 282463.
Cuisine: VEGETARIAN/ASIAN. **Reservations:** Recommended.
$ **Prices:** Appetizers 40B–80B ($1.60–$3.20); main courses 50B–180B ($2–$7.20). No credit cards.
Open: Daily 11am–10pm.

If you're looking for Asian food in the typically California/health food/Western vein, head for this New Age Thai pavilion. The food is prepared by a gifted Pakistani chef and is part vegetarian, Thai, Chinese, and Indian. There is often an acoustic guitarist (and a long wait for tables on the balcony or overlooking a garden) in the evenings. This is also Chiang Mai's center for transcendental meditation.

INEXPENSIVE

SHEVE SHIRAZ, 23-35 Charoen Prathet, Soi 6. Tel. 276132.
Cuisine: INDIAN.
$ **Prices:** Appetizers 12B–90B (48¢–$3.60); main courses 50B–110B ($2–$4.40). No credit cards.
Open: Daily 9:30am–11pm.

A terrific Indian/Pakistani/Arabic restaurant near the Night Market. One step in the door, and the scent of coriander, cardamom, and anise will convince you the tastes are going to be authentic. It's also especially good for vegetarians—the *aloo paratha* (potato-stuffed bread) and the *bindi* masala (okra in tomato) melt in your mouth.

HAUS MÜNCHEN, 115/3 Loi Kroa Rd. at the corner of Chang Klan Rd. Tel. 274027.
Cuisine: GERMAN/CONTINENTAL.
$ **Prices:** Appetizers 25B–50B ($1–$2); main courses 80B–115B ($3.20–$4.50). No credit cards.
Open: Daily 9am–11pm.

The popular Haus München is around the corner from the Night Market, so it fills up with shoppers each evening. You can eat wurst, delicious Kasseler (smoked pork), fish-and-chips, spaghetti, or many other German favorites (including homemade brown bread). You can also drink draft Amarit beer (45B or $1.80 per stein) and check in with the international expatriate community.

BUDGET

GRILLED CHICKEN WITH HONEY RESTAURANT, 40-42 Charoen Prathet Rd., next to Pornping Hotel. Tel. 271488.
Cuisine: THAI.
$ **Prices:** Main courses 18B–120B (75¢–$4.80). MC, V.
Open: Daily 9:30am–11pm.

Chicken gai yang is a northern Thai specialty (one we New Yorkers call "chickens die young"),—a honey-grilled fowl that puts Colonel Sanders to shame. This place serves Chiang Mai's best (55B [$2.20] for a chicken large enough for two). The sauce is the key: a sweet and slightly hot condiment that should be used liberally. Continuing on the chicken theme, try the spicy chicken soup, with plump and abundant mushrooms. The atmosphere at this open-air restaurant is totally casual, with local Thai families and few foreigners, all eating with their fingers.

SUTHASINEE KHAO SOI, 134/10 Chang Klan Rd. No phone.
Cuisine: THAI.
$ **Prices:** Main courses 18B–35B (75¢–$1.40). No credit cards.
Open: Daily 9am–8:30pm.

This small, Formica and fluorescent shop house, just south of Dusit Inn Hotel, isn't easy to find, but it's a sure bet for purely local, authentic *khao soi*. This aromatic

FROMMER'S COOL FOR KIDS:
DINING

Chiangmai Coca *(see p. 331)* The huge dining areas, the minislides out front, and the cook-it-yourself sukiyaki draw lots of Thai families.

Grilled Chicken with Honey Restaurant *(see p. 328)* Kids love the yummy barbecued chicken and eating with their hands.

concoction (18B or 75¢) is a large bowl of coconut curry soup with noodles, *gai* (chicken), or *moo* (pork), including greens and seasonable vegetables such as tangy green eggplant. It's a big-time, unusual taste sensation. The restaurant's not touristy; if you can't find it, a resident should be able to point you in the right direction.

WANGKUN-RENA RESTAURANT, 149/53 Chang Klan Rd. Tel. 274588.
 Cuisine: THAI.
$ Prices: Appetizers 30B–45B ($1.20–$1.80); main courses 70B–150B ($2.80–$6). No credit cards.

If you like shrimp, you'll love this clean open-air restaurant in the middle of the Anusarn Night Market with its big white-tiled tanks of giant prawns. They also serve all kinds of fish, but we loved the shrimp sautéed with tiny whole cloves of garlic; the grilled shrimp was also good, delectably smoky and subtle. This place is always jammed with Thai families and European visitors; it's a great place to take a break from a hard night of bargaining in the Night Market.

AROUND THE OLD CITY

MODERATE

LA VILLA PIZZERIA, Pensione La Villa, 145 Ratchadamnoen Rd., west of Prapokkiao Rd. Tel. 277403.
 Cuisine: ITALIAN.
$ Prices: Appetizers 45B–175B ($1.80–$7); main courses 50B–150B ($2–$6). MC, V.
 Open: Daily 11am–10pm.

You can sit under a thatch canopy and watch flames leaping in the brick pizza oven, or sit upstairs at a picnic table, away from the whir of the cappuccino machine. La Villa is part of a friendly, Italian-run guest house, where an occasional "Ciao, bambina!" is heard. Main courses include fegato alla veneziana (beef liver fried with onions and butter) and several pastas, including our favorite, Tarantina, tossed with imported olive oil, chili, and local mussels. Various vegetable-and-meat combo pizzas start at 70B ($2.80) for the small (two person) size. The crust is thinner than Kyle prefers, but the authentic mozzarella, oregano, and tomato topping is delicious.

INEXPENSIVE

TANEM, Chaiya Poom. No phone.
 Cuisine: NORTHERN THAI.
$ Prices: Appetizers 12B–40B (48¢–$1.60); main dishes 20B–75B (80¢–$3). No credit cards.
 Open: Lunch daily noon–2pm, dinner daily 6pm–8pm.

It's easy to walk by the gates of this drab open-air restaurant outside the Old City, just north of Tha Pae Gate, and thereby miss an outstanding northern Thai meal. In addition to the usual tourists, you'll see plenty of Thai couples drawn by the excellent *khao soi* (spicy curried noodles with crispy noodles on top) and *khanom jin nam giaw* (chicken with curried noodles, Chinese style). But be warned: no alcohol, no sleeveless shirts, and the kitchen closes by 8pm.

AMERICA, 402/1-2 Tha Pae Rd. Tel. 232017.

Cuisine: MEXICAN/ITALIAN/THAI.

$ Prices: Appetizers 20B–45B (80¢–$1.80); main dishes 30B–180B ($1.20–$7.20). No credit cards.

Open: Daily 11am–10pm.

Tony Moon, a warm, relaxed restaurateur from Salt Lake City, recently took over this smallish restaurant on Tha Pae Road, and it's been the hangout of the most interesting expatriate crowd in Chiang Mai ever since. The place is by no means fancy, but Tony is sure to come by your table to see that the service and food are to your liking, and it's easy to fall into conversation with fellow travelers or Western residents if you so desire. Or you can just watch the world go by Tha Pae through the big plate-glass windows. The food is also worth the trip: the Mexican tacos and fresh salads here are authentic and tasty, and the ice cream is good, particularly the chocolate chip.

THE CRUSTY LOAF BAKERY 24-24/1 Ratwitti Rd. Tel. 214554.

Cuisine: WESTERN.

$ Prices: Appetizers 15B–40B (60¢–$1.60); main dishes, 25B–30B ($1–$1.20). No credit cards.

Open: Daily, 8am to 9pm.

Even if you don't notice the handsome display of different breads in the front windows, the smell of fresh-baked loaves will draw you into this cheerful, unpretentious little joint in the Old City, a few blocks northwest of Tha Pae Gate. It's run by a nice Irish-Thai couple, and the long tables covered with green-checked oilcloth, wooden benches, clutter of plants, and lighthearted Irish pictures on the wall make this a very pleasant place to start a day of exploring wats in the Old City. A substantial American breakfast with good coffee costs 50B ($2), and they even have Irish soda bread!

AROON [RAI] RESTAURANT, 45 Kachasarn Rd. Tel. 276947.

Cuisine: NORTHERN THAI.

$ Prices: Appetizers 12B–35B (50¢–$1.40); main courses 18B–50B (75¢–$2). No credit cards.

Open: Daily lunch 11:30am–2:30pm, dinner 5:30–10pm.

For authentic northern food, adventurous eaters should stroll into this nondescript garden restaurant two blocks south of the Tha Pae Gate. Their *khao soi*, filled with egg noodles and crisp-fried chicken bits and sprinkled with dried, fried noodles, is spicey and coconut-sweet at the same time. Chiang Mai sausages are served sliced over steamed rice; puffed-up fried pork rinds are the traditional (if not cholesterol-free) accompaniment. Dishes are all made to order in an open kitchen, so you can point to things that interest you, including the myriad fried insects, beetles, and frogs for which this place is famous.

TA-KRITE, 17-19 Samlarn Rd., Soi 1. Tel. 216333.

Cuisine: THAI/CHINESE.

$ Prices: Appetizers 30B–45B ($1.20–$1.80); main courses 30B–60B ($1.20–$2.40). MC, V.

Open: Daily 10am–midnight.

⭐ This maze of small Lanna Thai houses offers the city's best "pure Thai" food (no northern influence). Potted ferns, bougainvillea, impatiens, and poinsettias screen diners, who are tucked in alcoves, verandas, and myriad dining spaces from one another, creating a surprisingly romantic atmosphere. The food is superb! We devoured their *mee krob*, sweetly crisp, noodles flavored with dried shrimp and bean curd; the *yam mah krua*, cold grilled eggplant spiced with onions and minced fish; a tangy *gaeng phet*, tender duck curry; plus standard Chinese fare like sweet-and-sour spareribs, all served on locally made blue-and-white ceramic. If you enjoyed Bangkok's Lemon Grass, try this. It's located just west of Samlarn Road, one block south of Wat Phra Singh.

BUDGET

AUM VEGETARIAN RESTAURANT, 65 Moon Muang Rd., opposite Tha Pae Gate. No phone.
Cuisine: VEGETARIAN.
$ Prices: Appetizers 12B–25B (50¢–$1); main courses 18B–45B (75¢–$1.80). No credit cards.
Open: Daily 9am–2pm, dinner 5–9pm.

This recently refurbished hole-in-the-wall restaurant seems to receive divine inspiration for its vegetarian cuisine. Cheap, simple noodle and rice dishes, excellent tofu served in several ways, and fresh vegetables with exotic seasoning comprise the small menu. There's a spacious upstairs dining room which is usually quieter than the Spartan seating on the busy, commercial avenue.

WESTSIDE/HUAI KAEO ROAD

CHIANGMAI COCA, 9912 Huai Kaeo Rd. Tel. 220569.
Cuisine: THAI.
$ Prices: Main courses 25B–70B ($1–$2.80). No credit cards.
Open: Daily 10am–10:30pm.

The 10m-tall (30 feet) illuminated logo is unmistakable if you've been in Thailand more than 24 hours, but this time it's a Coke sign with a steaming sukiyaki cooker above it. This lively restaurant has seating outdoors in a huge gravel lot or under a huge, fan-cooled hangar. It's a good thing, too, because it's always packed with Thai families enjoying the cook-it-yourself, inexpensive fare. The roast duck is tender, and served with a bittersweet plum sauce. Delicious "fresh" spring rolls are steamed with rice-flour wrappers filled with mushrooms, bean curd, fish, and chopped vegetables. There's a choice of 29 items you can boil in the sukiyaki cooker, but we stuck with shrimp dumplings, meatballs, sliced chicken, and cabbage—all fresh and wonderfully spiced by our tray of condiments. The waitresses are young and energetic, even helping kids get on and off the slides out front. Chiangmai Coca is across the street and one block east of Chiang Mai Orchid Hotel.

GALAE RESTAURANT, 65 Suthep Rd. Tel. 222235.
Cuisine: THAI.
$ Prices: Appetizers 30B–60B ($1.20–$2.40); main courses 60B–120B ($2.40–$4.80). V.
Open: Mon–Fri 9am–9pm, Sat–Sun 9am–10pm.

Galae is 5km (3 miles) west of the Old City in a wooded compound up the hill toward Doi Suthep. Dining is casual, with tables on several grass plateaus under cool shade trees, overlooking a lake. The place serves typical Thai rice and noodle dishes, including Chiang Mai sausage, but it's famous for beef that's cooked on a spit nearby. The fragrance of roasting chili, lemon juice, and garlic used as seasoning is very tempting. Their pomelo and fried catfish salad is a deliciously pungent, unusual combination of flavors.

SANKAMPHAENG ROAD/SHOPPING DISTRICT

BAAN SUAN RESTAURANT, 51/3 Sankamphaeng Rd., Moo 1. Tel. 242116.
Cuisine: THAI.
$ Prices: Appetizers 50B–110B ($2–$4.40); main courses 60B–200B ($2.40–$8). AE, DC, MC, V.
Open: Daily noon–10pm.

Baan Suan is an ideal spot for those scouring this busy road for exotic shopping bargains. It's located 7km (4.2 miles) east of the Nawarat Bridge. The restaurant is quite large, with both outdoor garden tables and indoor seating (air-conditioned) in a traditional teak house. The menu is varied with typical northern Thai dishes and other regional main dishes. We particularly liked their Burmese pork curry, spicy Chiang Mai sausage salad, and fiery morning glories northern style. Dishes are moderately priced and well prepared, but the service can be very slow and aggravating if a tour bus has arrived.

5. ATTRACTIONS

Chiang Mai offers superb sightseeing, shopping, trekking, elephant riding, and rafting all within a compact geographical area. No matter what you choose, be sure to explore the city: Stroll along the Ping River and into the Old City, visit the food-and-flower markets, search for elegant teak homes, and stop along the way to sample some of the world's best street food.

SUGGESTED ITINERARIES

IF YOU HAVE 1 DAY

Visit the wats in the Old City, shop on Tha Pae Road or the Nantawan Arcade, experience a khan toke dinner/cultural show, and stroll through the Night Market on your way home.

IF YOU HAVE 2 DAYS

Day 1: Visit the wats in the Old City, get a northern-style traditional massage at Rinkaew Porech, and try a khan toke dinner/cultural show.
Day 2: Visit Wat Mahatat and Doi Suthep and in the afternoon visit the National Museum or shop along Sankamphaeng Road or the Nantawan Arcade. Explore the Night Market in the evening.

IF YOU HAVE 3 DAYS

Day 1: Visit the wats in the Old City and try a khan toke dinner/cultural show.
Day 2: Visit Doi Suthep and Wat Mahatat and in the afternoon visit the National Museum or shop along Sankamphaeng Road or the Nantawan Arcade. If you didn't shop this afternoon, explore the Night Market in the evening.
Day 3: Visit the Elephant Training Camp in Lamphang, see the historic wats in Lamphang and Lamphun, and explore the Night Market if you haven't already.

IF YOU HAVE 5 DAYS OR MORE

See "Suggested Itineraries" in Chapter 11, "Exploring Northern Thailand."

THE TOP ATTRACTIONS

Except for Bangkok, Chiang Mai, with more than 700, has the greatest concentration of exquisitely crafted wats in the country. If you start in the early morning you can see all of the principal sights in one day, particularly if you travel by tuk-tuk. This tour is by no means exhaustive; there are hundreds of wats, shrines, and other sites of interest, but these few highlights are a "must" for anyone interested in Buddhist culture.

WAT CHEDI LUANG, Prapokklao Rd. south of Ratchadamnoen Rd.

Because it's near the Tha Pae Gate, most visitors begin their sightseeing at Wat Chedi Luang, where there are two wats of interest. This complex, which briefly housed the Emerald Buddha now at Bangkok's Wat Phra Kaeo, dates from 1411 when the original chedi was built by King Saen Muang Ma. The already-massive edifice was expanded to 280 feet in height in the mid-1400s, only to be ruined by a severe earthquake in 1545, just 11 years before Chiang Mai fell to the Burmese (it was never rebuilt). A Buddha still graces its exterior; it's not unusual to spot a saffron-robed monk bowing to it as he circles the chedi.

The remarkable *nagas* guarding the stairway entrance to the typical northern viharn are exceptionally ornate and ferocious. Next to the tall gum tree on the left as you enter the compound is the shrine honoring Sao Inthakhin, also referred to as the city's pillar. It is believed that the upkeep of this wat is directly related to the well-being of Chiang Mai. During festivals, young girls often sell small sparrows trapped in rattan cages for 20B (80¢). The Buddhist custom known as making merit is fulfilled by setting them free, bringing good fortune to the liberator.

The other wat on the grounds is the **Wat Phan Tao**, with its wooden viharn and bot, reclining Buddha, and fine carving on the eaves and door. After leaving the temple, walk around to the monks' quarters on the side, taking in the traditional, teak northern architecture and delightful landscaping.

Admission: 10B (40¢) suggested contribution.

Open: Daily 6am–5pm.

WAT PHRA SINGH, Samlarn Rd. and Ratchadamnoen Rd.

This compound was built during the zenith of Chiang Mai's hegemony over the north; consequently it became one of the more venerated shrines in the city. Today it's still the site of many important religious ceremonies, particularly during the Songkran Festival. More than 700 monks study here, and we found them to be especially friendly and curious.

King Phayu, of Mengrai lineage, built the chedi in 1345, principally to house the cremated remains of King Kamfu, his father. As you enter the grounds, head to the right toward the 14th-century library. Notice the graceful carving and the characteristic roof line with four separate elevations. The sculptural *devata* (Buddhist spirits) figures, in both dancing and meditative poses, are thought to have been made during King Muang Kaeo's reign in the early 16th century. They decorate a stone base designed to keep the fragile *sa* (mulberry bark) manuscripts elevated from flooding and vermin.

On the other side of the temple complex is the 200-year-old Lai Kham ("Gilded Hall") viharn, housing the venerated image of the Phra Singh or Sighing Buddha, brought to the site by King Muang Ma in 1400. Tragically, in 1922, the original Buddha's head was stolen; the reproduction in its place doesn't diminish the homage paid to this figure during Songkran. Inside are frescoes illustrating the stories of Sang Thong (the Golden Prince of the Conchshell) and Suwannahong. These images convey a great deal about the religious, civil, and military life of 19th-century Chiang Mai during King Mahotraprathet's reign.

Admission: 10B (40¢) suggested contribution.

Open: Daily 6am–5pm.

WAT SUAN DOK, Suthep Rd.

We like this complex less for its architecture (the buildings, though monumental, are undistinguished) than for its contemplative spirit and pleasant surroundings.

The temple was built amid the pleasure gardens of the 14th-century Lanna Thai monarch, King Ku Na. Unlike most of Chiang Mai's other wats (more tourist sights, working temples, and schools), Wat Suan Dok houses quite a few monks who seem to have completely isolated themselves from the frenzy of the outside world.

Among the main attractions in the complex are the bot, with a very impressive Chiang Saen Buddha (one of the largest bronzes in the north) dating from 1504 and some garish murals; the chedi, built to hold the miraculous relics of the Buddha prophesied by Sumana Thera (the same monk who inspired Wat Phra That on Doi Suthep); and a royal cemetery with some splendid shrines. Traditional Thai herbal massage (like that at Wat Po in Bangkok) is offered on the grounds of the wat. To reach Wat Suan Dok, take the Suan Dok Gate one mile west of the Old City.

Admission: 10B (40¢) suggested contribution.

Open: Daily 6am–5pm.

WAT CHET YOT, superhighway near the Chiang Mai National Museum.

Wat Chet Yot (also called Wat Maha Photharam) is one of the central city's most elegant sites. The chedi was built during the reign of King Tilokkarat in the late 15th century (his remains are in one of the smaller chedis), and in 1477 the World Sangkayana convened here to revise the doctrines of the Buddha.

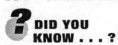

DID YOU KNOW . . . ?

- The provincial seal of Chiang Mai, depicting the auspicious white elephant given by a local ruler to King Rama II, was the inspiration for the flag of the Kingdom of Siam—a white elephant on a red ground.
- Doi Inthanon, at 2,565m (8,336 feet), is the highest mountain in Thailand and one of the southernmost foothills of the Himalayas.

The unusual design of the main rectangular chedi with seven peaks was copied from the Maha Bodhi Temple in Bodh Gaya, India, where the Buddha first achieved enlightenment. The temple also has architectural elements of Burmese, Chinese Yuan, and Ming influence. However, the extraordinary proportions, the angelic, levitating devata figures carved into the base of the chedi, and the juxtaposition of the other buildings make Wat Chet Yot (Seven Spires) a masterpiece.

The Lanna-style Buddha hidden in the center was sculpted in the mid-15th century; a door inside the niche containing the Buddha leads to the roof on which rests the Phra Kaen Chan (Sandalwood Buddha). There is a nice vista from up top (only men are allowed to ascend the stairs). The wat is located north of the intersection of Nimanhemin and Huai Kaeo roads. It is on your left, about a half mile up the superhighway.

Admission: 10B (40¢) suggested contribution.
Open: Daily 6am–5pm.

WAT CHIANG MAN, Wiang Kaeo and Ratchaphakkinai Rds.

This wat, in the Old City near the Chang Puak Gate, thought to be Chiang Mai's oldest, was built during the 14th century and was the home of King Mengrai. Like many of the wats in Chiang Mai, this complex reflects many architectural styles. Some of the structures are pure Lanna, some are influenced by Ceylonese (Sri Lanka) designs: Notice the typical row of elephant supports. Wat Chiang Man is most famous for its two Buddhas: Phra Sritang Khamani (a miniature crystal image also known as the White Emerald Buddha) and the marble Phra Sri-la Buddha. Unfortunately, the viharn that safeguards these religious sculptures is almost always closed.

Admission: 10B (40¢) suggested contribution.
Open: Daily 6am–5pm.

CHIANG MAI NATIONAL MUSEUM, superhighway. Tel. 221308.

Just north of the seven-spired Wat Chet Yot is the modern complex housing the province's fine collection of Lanna Thai art. Woodwork, stonework, and the many religious images garnered from local wats are well labeled. They help to chronicle the distinct achievements of the Lan Na Kingdom from the 14th to 18th centuries, and reveal how Burmese religious art grew more influential over the years of occupation. (Note the weapons on display that were used to combat the Burmese.) After you've aborbed this museum, try to visit the university's Tribal Research Institute. Knowledge of both cultures will serve you well while touring the north.

Admission: 10B (40¢)
Open: Wed–Sun 9am–noon and 1–4pm. **Closed:** Holidays.

MORE ATTRACTIONS

TRIBAL RESEARCH INSTITUTE, Chiang Mai University. Tel. 221332.

If you plan to go trekking or have an interest in the hill-tribe people, visit this facility. The institute conducts research, publishes excellent books and brochures, coordinates trekking groups, and runs a small, informative museum devoted to the ethnographic legacy of the northern tribal groups. Don't miss the informative library next door. It's 4km (2.4 miles) west of the Old City, off Huai Kaeo Road.

Admission: Free.
Open: Mon–Fri 8:30am–noon and 1–4:30pm.

THAI COOKING CLASS, Home of Somphon and Elizabeth Nabnian, 101/2 Moon Muang Rd. Tel. 490456.

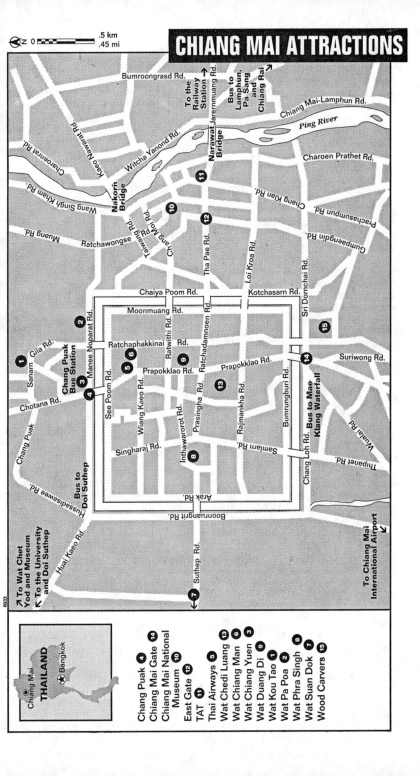

CHIANG MAI ATTRACTIONS

.5 km
0
.45 mi

Bumroongrasd Rd.

To the Railway Station

Bus to Lamphun, Pa Sang, and Chiang Rai

Chiang Mai-Lamphun Rd.

Ping River

Charoen Prathet Rd.

Witcha Yanond Rd.

Kaeo Nawarat Rd.

Charoenrat Rd.

Narawat Jarernmuang Rd.
Bridge

Nakorn Bridge

Wang Singh Kham Rd.

Muang Rd.

Ratchawongse

Tawee Rd.

Chang Moi Rd.

Ratchaphakkinai

Moonmuang Rd.

Chaiya Poom Rd.

Kotchasarn Rd.

Ratwithi Rd.

Ratchadamnoen Rd.

Prapokklao Rd.

Chang Klan Rd.

Prachasumpan Rd.

Gumpaengdin Rd.

Tha Pae Rd.

Loi Kroa Rd.

Sri Dornchai Rd.

Suriwong Rd.

11
10
12
2
1
6
5
3
4
9
13
8
15
14
7

Sanarn Gila Rd.

Chang Puak Bus Station

Manee Noparat Rd.

See Poom Rd.

Wiang Kaeo Rd.

Singharaj Rd.

Inthawaroot Rd.

Prasingha Rd.

Rajmankha Rd.

Samlarn Rd.

Arak Rd.

Boonruangrit Rd.

Suthep Rd.

Chotana Rd.

Chang Puak

Hussadisawee Rd.

Bus to Doi Suthep

Huai Kaeo Rd.

To Wat Chet Yod and Museum
To the University and Doi Suthep

Chiang Loh Rd.
Bus to Mae Klang Waterfall

Bumrungburi Rd.

Wualai Rd.

Thipanet Rd.

To Chiang Mai International Airport

THAILAND

Chiang Mai

Bangkok

Chang Puak **4**
Chiang Mai Gate **14**
Chiang Mai National Museum **10**
East Gate **12**
TAT **11**
Thai Airways **5**
Wat Chedi Luang **13**
Wat Chiang Man **6**
Wat Chiang Yuen **3**
Wat Duang Di **9**
Wat Kou Tao **1**
Wat Pa Poa **2**
Wat Phra Singh **8**
Wat Suan Dok **7**
Wood Carvers **15**

Some travelers think the fiery, savory cuisine is the best thing about Thailand. If you want to learn more about it, try these 1- or 2-day courses with an experienced Thai chef who also speaks excellent English. In each 6-hour session, he demonstrates the preparation of six different simple Thai dishes which the students get to copy—and eat! These include such favorites as *tom yam gam* (hot-and-sour prawn soup), *pad thai*, and spicy glass noodle salad. Seasonal fruit tastings and copies of recipes are also included, as is a list of alternatives for hard-to-find Thai ingredients in different countries. Classes cost 500B ($20) per day including transportation and ingredients and are held from 10am to 3pm daily. There are only 3 to 10 students in each class, so call a day ahead for reservations.

THAI TRADITIONAL MASSAGE

RINKAEW POVECH COMPLEX, 183/4 Wualai Rd. Tel. 274565.
The gentle but penetrating Thai massage, thought to have developed as a healing tool over 2,000 years ago, is widely practiced at wats throughout Thailand. Many urban hotels now offer traditional massage (as opposed to physical or sexual massage), but nowhere is it as widely promoted as in Chiang Mai. Here, a huge complex, with several nonprivate rooms containing two to eight beds, sends its minivan around to collect clients (10B or 40¢ one-way). On arrival, you purchase a ticket and are guided to a room to don loose-fitting rayon slacks and top. Uniformed masseuses appear and set to work, starting with the feet and rubbing their magic throughout the body. A "tourist pleaser" massage lasts one hour, but the traditional Thai method takes two to two and a half hours. There are also Finnish, Western, and Thai herbal saunas. Your daytime massage can be combined with a visit to the Lanna Folk Museum, and your nighttime one with a khan-toke dinner, both at the Old Chiang Mai Cultural Center.

This complex is south of the Old City, opposite the Old Chiang Mai Cultural Center. The Petngarm Hat Wait Massage Center in the Diamond Hotel on Charoen Prathet is also recommended (tel. 270080).
Admission: 225B ($9) per hour.
Open: Daily 8am–8pm.

COOL FOR KIDS

Half a mile west of the Tribal Research Center on Huai Kaeo Road is Thailand's largest zoo—Chiang Mai Zoo. Though hardly the most impressive, it's fun and of some interest to older children. There is also a children's playground and parklike arboretum with many well-labeled trees and plants (open daily 8:30am to 4:30pm). This hilly and cool setting is perfect for a picnic before the 1.2km (less than a mile) switchback road to Doi Suthep. Admission is 10B (40¢). It's open daily 8am to 5pm.

6. SPORTS & RECREATION

SPECTATOR SPORTS

HORSE RACING In Chiang Mai there is horse racing throughout the year, usually every Saturday and Sunday from noon to 4pm. The race track is near the Lanna Golf Course on Chotana Road, north of the city on Route 107, on the Mae Rim road. Check with the TAT for the latest schedule.

THAI BOXING It isn't for everyone, but it's more of an authentic Thai experience than almost anything else. The ring is rope and canvas. The promoter chants the boxers' names and hawks at potential spectators over blaring loudspeakers. As fight time approaches, the crowd swarms in. Serious fans hover over tables where the fighters are oiled, massaged, taped, and counseled, hoping for an edge on the unofficial betting line. Betting begins just before a bout opens and continues through the fight, with bets shifting so many times it's a wonder anyone can keep track. The stakes range from about 2,000B ($80) to 20,000B ($800), depending on boxers' ranking.

The fights usually begin around 9pm and last into the early morning. The first are between flyweights—kids really, who look about 12 to 14 years old. Heavyweight fights start later. Unlike Western-style boxing, the long, lean fighters are more flexible and likely to win. One aficionado told us to look for the slimmest hips and best developed calves.

Each bout lasts three rounds, the last the most feverish. As one match ends, the next begins; spectators move in and out with food and drinks, making the whole scene feel like a Thai country fair. There are few if any farangs at such events.

Check with the TAT for the latest schedule (they were Saturday and Sunday at 8pm at our visit). Fights are held at the **Boxing Stadium** on Kongsai Road. Ringside seats are 130B to 250B ($5.20 to $10); standing room is around 45B ($1.75).

RECREATION

GOLF   The best public golf course is the 18-hole Lanna Golf Course, 4km (2.4 miles) north of the Old City, on Route 107. It's open daily 6am to 7pm; clubs are available for rent (tel. 221911).

Another popular club, Inthanon Resort, is south of the city at Nong Rong, Pasang, in the Lamphun district (about a half-hour drive). Call for more information (tel. 235886).

SWIMMING   There is an Olympic-size swimming pool open to the public at the Amari Rincome Hotel, Huai Kaeo Road, west of the Old City. Admission is 75B ($3). Call for more information (tel. 221044).

TENNIS   The Anantasiri Tennis Courts, opposite the Chiang Mai National Museum on the superhighway north of the Old City, are open to the public. Call for admission fees and hours (tel. 222210).

7. SAVVY SHOPPING

Chiang Mai, indisputably the country's center for handicrafts, is a shopper's paradise. In less than a decade, the famous Night Market has blossomed from an evening street fair where hill-tribe people displayed their wares on the ground to a huge indoor Night Bazaar mall and several blocks of late-night stalls and shops. Along with the number of merchants, the quantity and quality of merchandise have mushroomed. Compared with tackling Bangkok's horrific traffic and pollution to shop, Chiang Mai's centralized district and easily accessible showrooms are much more pleasant and easier to peruse.

THE SHOPPING SCENE   Prices of contemporary clothing and accessories are still cheap by our standards, styles are up-to-the-minute, and workmanship is getting better and better. The opposite is true when it comes to certain hill-tribe handicrafts, but there are now dozens of "antique" stores offering fabulous used traditional textiles and jewelry. New Thai arts and souvenirs are widely available; the time and skill that goes into their handcrafting make them delightful, inexpensive purchases.

Tragically, the British conservation group, Care for the Wild, recently uncovered a huge trade in elephant-hide products, particularly in Night Market stalls. They estimate 50 Asian elephants (an endangered species) are being killed each week by Burmese Karen tribesmen, who are using the illegal export to fund rebel activities. We urge you not to buy elephant-skin products (importation is illegal in many countries anyway), and to report these vendors to the Tourist Police.

🅕 FROMMER'S SMART TRAVELER: SHOPPING

1. If you're only interested in one shop, call ahead to inquire if they'll pick you up, as many places provide free transportation.
2. Pay with cash or traveler's checks if possible. Credit card purchases (particularly American Express) are often marked up 3% to 5%.
3. Shopping is easiest in your own vehicle. Be prepared to battle with your taxi or tuk-tuk driver about which shops you're willing to see. They all get a 10% to 30% commission from most shops, but obviously have their favorites, and can be very tough about steering you this way. Be persistent—or hail another car.
4. Hand carry your purchases. Shipping is surprisingly expensive, by sea or air mail, and some items will be subject to import duties (check with your consulate to determine current Customs regulations). We found one highly recommended shipper: World Express (tel. 272383). Call daily between 8am and 6pm to arrange for merchandise to be picked up from your hotel. In 1994, shipping rates to the U.S. East Coast were 4,500B ($180) per 10kg (minimum) by air, 6,500B ($260) per cubic meter (minimum) by sea, including packing, Customs forms, and delivery to the airport/port nearest to the destination.
5. Except in the most modern shops, bargaining is the rule. Shop around and compare prices; decide what you want to pay and, in most cases, subtract a substantial percentage for your opening bid. There is no rule. Sometimes prices are hiked 200%, while at other times prices are listed at close to the eventual sales price.
6. If you're traveling throughout northern Thailand, you'll see lots of hill-trade handicrafts. Prices are about the same, and most of the best merchandise goes straight to Chiang Mai, but if it's a unique item that speaks to you, don't wait—buy it.

Daytime shopping is scattered throughout the Old City and along Tha Pae Road. A new upscale shopping complex, known locally as the **Nantawan Arcade,** is on Nimanhemin Road off Haui Kaeo Road, directly across from the Amari Rincome Hotel (see below for specific recommendation). Most shops here are open daily 9:30am to 6:30pm. At night, everyone flocks to the Night Market (see "Markets" later in this section) on Chang Klan Road, open daily 6 to 11pm. Be sure to visit the Anusarn Market, just southwest of the Novotel, for extra cheap prices, less crowded aisles, and a generally less touristy experience. But remember, it closes at 10pm, one hour before the rest of the Night Market. For contemporary crafts, teak furniture, traditional umbrellas, and an embarrassment of riches, spend a day on Sankamphaeng Road (see "Sankamphaeng Road" later in this section). It's a 15km (9-mile) highway of factories and showrooms that will be less overwhelming if you've visited the in-town shops first. Most places will ship your merchandise; they're open daily 8:30am to 5:30pm.

SHOPPING A TO Z

ANTIQUES

DUANGJITT HOUSE, 95/10 Nimanhemin Rd. Tel. 215167.
Part of the Nanatawan Arcade, this three-story, contemporary teak house is the elegant gallery of Duangjitt Thaveesri, a distinguished woman who has spent her life collecting Thai and tribal clothing and Southeast Asian handwoven materials. Her

small shop holds a stunning display of antique textiles, Cambodian and Thai "mutmee" silk ikat (sarong lengths start at 3,500B [$140]), paintings, and silver jewelry. Mrs. Duangjitt numbers Princess Diana and Elizabeth Taylor among her many collectors. The house feels like a private museum, with her or her daughter, Ms. Chitlada, as your learned guides. Interested collectors are sometimes invited to the Thaveesri home to view even more valuable artworks and paintings, but must visit the shop first to discuss such a visit.

MANEESINN ANTIQUES, 289 Tha Pae Rd. Tel. 276586.

Look here for traditional Thai, Chinese, and Burmese antiques. We were especially impressed with their exquisite lacquerware and baskets. The shop is small but has a good selection of decorative furniture (old lacquer khan toke tables cost 16,000B [$400]), wood carvings, and sculpture. There are many carrying baskets of finely woven vine, used by elegant Burmese ladies of another era, from 6,000B ($240).

CERAMICS

Thai ceramics—often imitating traditional celadon shapes from Sukhothai and Si Satchanalai—are also prized purchases. Having been burned with a phony "antique" purchase, we really enjoyed seeing how these new antiquities are created by hand.

MENGRAI KILNS, 31/1 Ratuthit Rd. Tel. 241802.

This high-quality collection is located on the east side of the Ping River near the Chiang Mai Gymkhana Club. Mengrai produces beautiful, handcrafted celadon and stoneware, with a large variety of traditional patterns and shapes based on Chinese and Thai classics. Prices are certainly more reasonable than what's sold as "antique" in most shops. There is a new branch at 79/2 Araks Rd., Soi Samlarm 6 (tel. 272063).

THAI CELADON KILNS, 62 Chotana Rd., Hwy. 107. Tel. 213541.

If you avoid the noon to 1pm lunch break, you can watch the many steps of celadon making. Craftspeople, all trained at this kiln, work in open wood sheds to prepare the clay, shape it on a potter's wheel (or mold pieces that cannot be hand-sculpted), incise it with traditional patterns, and leave it to dry. Within a few days, preliminary firing prepares the clay for the lustrous greenish glaze that marks it as celadon. Cups, serving dishes, even decorative furnishings are sold, in celadon as well as patterned or colored glazes.

HILL-TRIBE CRAFTS & CLOTHING

Because of its proximity to Thailand's northern borders at the Golden Triangle, the bustling commercial hub of Chiang Mai is the major center for tribal crafts. Goods from Myanmar (often smuggled), Laos, northern Thailand, and even Cambodia find their way here, mostly via Chinese traders.

Older objects and used textiles are real treasures. The dyes are natural, there is more attention to traditional designs, and workmanship tends to be much better. Scarcity of the older items has driven prices way up over the past few years. We liked the shops listed below for their quality, but the variety of goods is astonishing and many shops carry similar things. Don't forget the Night Market; it's also a huge source of cheap, newly made hill-tribe goods.

ANONGPORN, 208-10 Tha Pae Rd. Tel. 236654 or 252654. Fax 252899.

This is one of the best shops for older hill-tribe crafts, particularly for textiles—though the wares are a little dusty. Their selection seems almost endless: intricately embroidered Hmong collars, colorful Akha jackets, baskets, and bags, Mien coats; a small selection of silver jewelry, including belts, bracelets, necklaces, and silver beads. The quality of their old and new goods seems to be higher than what sells in the typical market stalls, yet prices are comparable. Used appliqué and embroidered jackets sell for 800B to 2,250B ($32 to $90).

CHATRAPORN THAI SILK, 194 Tha Pae Rd. Tel. 234691.
This large shop has a particularly good collection of locally made cotton and silk garments (most incorporating panels of hill-tribe embroidery or appliqué work), plus old hill-tribe clothing and jewelry and newly woven bags and pouches. Several items are sized and fit better than the huge, one-size tops and slacks sold elsewhere. Cool, cotton dresses adorned with hill-tribe textile bodices cost 600B to 800B ($24 to $32). Newly made evening jackets of mutmee, Thai silk ikat, start at 1,200 ($48).

HILLTRIBE PRODUCTS FOUNDATION, 21/17 Suthep Rd. Tel. 277743.
This large shop near Wat Suan Dok is under the patronage of His Majesty the King, and was established to sell Akha, Karen, Yao, Hmong, Lisu, and Lahu crafts to provide an alternative income to poppy cultivation. Profits are used to fund handicraft training and the Border Patrol Police, who monitor the region's opium trade. There's a broad selection of silver jewelry (sold by weight at 20B [80¢] per gram), traditional costumes, bags, stylish mutmee jackets, finished pillow covers (from 100B to 250B [$4 to $10]), and many gift items, all reasonably priced and sold for a good cause.
There's a second branch at 100/61-62 Huai Kaeo Rd., opposite the entrance to Chiang Mai University (tel. 212978).

THE LOOM, 27 Rajmanka Rd. Tel. 278892.
This small wooden house, located a few blocks east of Wat Chedi Luang in the Old City, showcases a superb collection of antique and new textiles from Thailand, Laos, Cambodia, China, and Burma at affordable prices. We snapped up long contemporary silk-ikat scarves from Thailand's Northeast for 200B ($8) each, and gorgeous, colorful old silk sarongs from Cambodia and Laos for 300B to 400B ($12–$16) apiece. You will never see anything this nice in the Night Market, but look around first for a rough idea of prices and be sure to bargain.

STUDIO NAENNA, 188 Soi 9, Nimhaeminda Rd. Tel. 226041.
Patricia Cheesman Naenna, the internationally known textile expert and author of books on Thai textiles, makes long, blousy jackets of originally designed silk ikat (priced for export at 3,300B [$132] each). They're gorgeous and extremely wearable, as are her dresses, fitted skirts, range of pants styles for women, and muted silk-ikat shirts for men, which are all made in her own workshops. She also keeps a library of traditional silk-ikat patterns available in the large widths convenient to Western tailoring at 900B ($36) per meter. Handsome leather-trimmed silk-ikat attaché cases go for 460B ($18.40) and scarves start at 500B ($20). Everything here is exquisitely chosen, a welcome respite from weeding through the good and bad at the Night Market, and the atmosphere of the place (one block south of the Nantawan Arcade and parallel to Huai Kaeo Road) is wonderfully serene. One of our favorites. The store is open daily from 8:30am to 5pm. Major credit cards are accepted.

YMCA INTERNATIONAL HOTEL Y SHOP, 11 Sermsuk Rd. Tel. 221819.
Another shop whose earnings are returned to the community through rural development programs, handicraft training, and marketing and export assistance. The Y Shop displays a small but varied selection of goods produced by villagers they work with. From the contemporary ceramics, we liked the small blue-and-white elephant pitchers, a great present at only 100B ($4). Brightly painted paper umbrellas, bamboo baskets, jewelry and handbags, cosmetic pouches, travel kits, etc., of hill-tribe textiles start at 100B ($4).

BRONZE & SILVER

Chiang Mai's metalsmiths still produce the superb utilitarian and decorative work they've made for centuries. Besides jewelry, many studios produce flatware, everyday table settings, and formal repoussé silver tea sets, often elaborately decorated. The longtime silver shopping area has been **Wua Lai Road** (Route 108), about two miles south of the Chiang Mai Gate, on the south side of the Old City, where you can hear silversmiths' hammers ringing all day long. Bronze and silver shops are now opening on Sankamphaeng Road as well.

CHIANG MAI SILVERWARE, 62/10-11 Sankamphaeng Rd. Tel. 246037.
The classic Patanaanunwong Company has a factory where you can watch silversmiths hammer and polish their work (most of it serving pieces and utilitarian items). The majority of goods are ornate and expensive—although tiny herb pots cost as little as 175B ($7). A single demitasse spoon costs around 475B ($19), and picture frames run as high as 6,200B ($248).

SIAM SILVERWARE, 5 Wua Lai Rd., Soi 3. Tel. 279013.
This is one of the oldest and largest dealers. There's a large selection of new tableware and serving pieces (some in beautiful, traditional Thai designs) and a few decorative objects, plus a variety of well-priced jewelry. Prices are based on weight and workmanship.

SIPSONG PANNA, 95/19 Nimanhemin Rd. Tel. 216096.
The finest collection of hill-tribe silverware and folk jewelry can be found at this small, crowded Nantawan Arcade shop. The handiwork of Tai, Burmese, Chinese, and Laotian artisans is a browser's delight. There are dozens of old, hand-beaten serving bowls, jars, and other useful objects, as well as intricately fashioned ornaments, beads, pipes, and accessories. Shop around before you come here, so you have a sense of local prices for newly made goods, then bargain.

THAI SHOP, 106 Moo 6, Sankamphaeng Rd. Tel. 242366.
In the back, you can watch the manufacture of bronzeware. You must be careful about quality when purchasing it: Some vendors don't use enough nickel (so the bronze tarnishes easily), or use too much, leaving little bronze patina. Thai Shop's formula is 3% nickel, 79% copper, and 18% tin, for a positively handsome, gleaming product. A 12-person, 144-piece service costs about $200. The shop also sells lacquer ware, some of which is hand painted. and some coated with an eggshell application. The creation of strong, durable lacquer ware is very time intensive; each of typically 19 coats must dry before the next one is applied, and the whole process can take many months, even for small pieces.

JEWELRY

The distinctive jewelry sold in Chiang Mai is made by the northern hill tribes. These hand-sewn, exotic, ethnic ornaments are often unique, expensive older pieces (see "Bronze & Silver" for other shops). Orchid jewelry, those odd but lovely earrings, brooches, and pendants made by lacquering live orchids and mounting them in gold, is sold throughout the country. However, the greatest variety and best prices are here because most is manufactured in the north.

NEW ORCHID JADE FACTORY, 7/7 Doi Suthep, at the base of Wat Phra That. Tel. 248413.
One of many shops with a wide variety of lacquered orchid jewelry. Kyle's favorite are the petal earrings which come in the most vivid, unreal (though natural) colors. They're featherweight, perfect in this hot climate, and cost about 250B ($10) a pair.

There's also beautiful jade jewelry and carved standing pieces, exported to Gumps in San Francisco, among others. Although the Chinese and traditional Thais prefer green jade, the superior Burmese jade or jadeite (as opposed to nephrite, Chinese jade) comes in shades of gold, white, red, or lilac. A well-cut pendant costs anywhere from $145 for an unusual blue jade to $295 and up. Rubies, sapphires, and semiprecious stones are sold here, and at their other branch at 109 Airport Rd. (tel. 277774).

P. N. PRECIOUS STONES, 95/4-7 Nimanhemin Rd. Tel. 222396. Fax 216800.
The only precious gems dealer whom our sources would recommend without hesitation. P. N. is known for the quality of stones, workmanship of the settings, and reasonable prices. They have an especially good collection of Burmese rubies. If you're only making one jewelry purchase, shop around in Bangkok, where you'll have much greater variety and the bargaining power that comes from several nearby competitors.

MARKETS

In a shopper's paradise, some consider the Night Market (also called the Night Bazaar) the city's premier attraction. There are several daytime food (see "Dining" earlier in this chapter) and dry goods markets as well.

THE NIGHT MARKET, Chang Klan Rd. between Tha Pae and Loi Kroa Rds.

The actual Night Bazaar is a modern, antiseptic, three-story building, but the indoor and outdoor market extends south to Sri Dornchai Road and far beyond. Many shops and stalls remain open throughout the day and evening, especially along Chang Klan Road. The Anusarn section and the Night Market closes at 10pm, so if you want a chance to browse through some of the best deals, come early.

The stalls have grandiose names, like Harrods (with the familiar logo), and most carry Bangkok-produced counterfeits of international name-brand clothing, watches, and luggage. A skillfully reproduced Lacoste shirt will cost about 120B ($4.80)—the little alligator logo alone is 25B ($1). There are hundreds of pirated audio tapes and videocassettes as well, though if the U.S. Government succeeds in enforcing international copyright laws, this patent piracy may dwindle. Until then, it's all here.

Inside the Night Bazaar building itself (a currency-exchange booth guards the entrance) are primarily modern, mass-manufactured goods, with an occasional stand selling wonderful tribal chotchkas. The range is from pretty good, low-cost Thai fashions to typical schlock souvenirs. The top floor has booths selling locally produced handicrafts, some "antiques," and some decorative arts.

If you have any complaints that you wish to register with the authorities regarding "unsportsmanlike conduct," visit the Tourist Police booth, on the sidewalk at the foot of the stairs leading to the bazaar.

Open: Daily 6–11pm.

WAROWOT MARKET, Changmoi and Wichayanon Rds.

This central indoor market is the city's largest. Produce, colorful fruits, spices, and food products jam the ground floor. On the second floor, things are calmer, with dozens of vendors selling cheap cotton sportswear, Thai-made shoes, and some hill-tribe handicrafts and garmets. It's the Thai way to shop, fun and inexpensive.

Open: Daily 7am–4pm.

SANKAMPHAENG ROAD

Dedicated shoppers will have to devote at least half a day to shopping along the Chiang Mai–Sankamphaeng Road (Route 1006). It runs due east out of Chiang Mai, and after several kilometers becomes lined with shops, showrooms, and factories extending another 9km (5.4 miles). For quick reference, the following shops, some of which we've reviewed elsewhere, are in order of proximity to Chiang Mai: **Chiang Mai Tusnaporn** (Woodwork & Furniture); **Chiang Mai Silverware** (Bronze & Silver); **Thai Shop** (Bronze & Silver); **Lanna Lacquerware** (Thai Arts & Crafts); **Borisoothi Art Gallery** (Antiques); **Shinawatra** (Silk); **Chiang Mai Sudaluk** (Woodwork & Furniture); **Bo Sang Umbrella Center** (Thai Arts & Crafts); **Baan Celadon** (Ceramics).

SILK

SHINAWATRA THAI SILK, 145/1-2 Sankamphaeng Rd. Tel. 338053.

This is an outlet of the high quality Bangkok chain, rivaled only by Jim Thompson's in Bangkok. Shinawatra sells handwoven and hand-painted silk and cotton by the meter, a wide range of men's and women's conservative silk fashions, cushions, drapery, ties, and dozens of silk accessories; it also does custom tailoring. A man's aloha shirt in brightly patterned silk costs 1,250 ($50). One square meter (1.2 square yard) of two-ply silk is 525B ($21); upholstery-grade silk 650B ($26). A second shop is across from the Chiang Mai Orchid Hotel at 18 Huai Kaeo Rd. (tel. 221076).

Sankamphaeng is a tiny village known for fine cotton and silk. As with the umbrella village of Bo Sang (see "Thai Arts & Crafts," below), there are several workshops where you can observe the weaving process and buy locally made fabric. Many local women told us that they buy much of their silk for dressmaking here.

THAI ARTS & CRAFTS

BAN PHOR LIANG MEUN'S TERRA COTTA ARTS, 36 Prapakklao Rd. Tel. 278187.

This unusual store sells terra-cotta reproductions of Khmer, Indian, Burmese, Chinese, and Thai statuary of all sizes, from all periods, which are displayed in a handsome old teak house and garden just inside the Chiang Mai Gate. The work is highly detailed and the choices appealing. We particularly admired a pair of large, snarling *nagas* (the snake deities often found flanking temple doors) for 1,500B ($60) apiece, and the wide variety of Buddhas which range in price from 5,000B to 50,000B ($200 to $2,000). Owner Maliwan Maivun guarantees all their shipping and swears that her goods travel well.

BO SANG UMBRELLA MAKING CENTER, 111/2 Bo Sang–Sankamphaeng Rd. Tel. 338324.

The hamlet of Bo Sang (also known as the Umbrella Village) is a craft center where you can watch women make paper and bamboo umbrella frames, then hand-paint them with traditional Thai scenes or floral patterns. This shop/factory is typical of many, and will duplicate your design if you bring them a rough sketch.

GONG DEE LTD., 301/11 Soi 2, Nimanhemin Rd. No phone.

This elegant shop opposite the Nantawan Arcade displays the contemporary wood sculpture and painting of artist Vichit Chaiwong. Mr. Vichit, a trained painter from Sankamphaeng, has recently turned to carving rounded bowls, art sculpture, cups, decorative items, and even furniture from mango wood, then inlaying decorative hand-tooled pieces of nickel. The contrast between the polished golden wood and rough-hammered metal is startling, interesting, and unusual. Small cigarette boxes (some painted) start at 200B ($8); items range up to several hundred dollars for furniture and paintings.

JOHN GALLERY, 330 Tha Pae Rd. Tel. 232245.

We couldn't resist the hand-painted T-shirts created by this local artist. He's got a great eye for universal symbols and a penchant for oft-quoted rock lyrics, but his designs are imaginative and skillful and his interpretations of 20th-century abstract and cubist masterpieces are wonderful. Short- and long-sleeved, washable cotton T-shirts cost 200B to 425B ($8 to $17).

MICHI GALLERY, 3rd floor, Duangjitt House, 95/10 Nimanhemin Rd. Tel. 217767.

On the top floor of this Nantawan Arcade gallery devoted to dazzling textiles and ornate antique jewelry is a small shop dedicated to the craft of papermaking. Artisan Chitlada Thaveesri designs, and has manufactured locally, different grades of *sa* paper (mulberry bark), traditionally made to copy Buddhist scriptures. The cottonlike, off-white paper is sold in large sheets, bound into diaries and sketch pads (250B or $10) with dried vines and silk cords, cut into foldout books for calligraphy, and made into stationery or gift cards (from 60B or $2.40). Covers are often dyed or stamped or have rice kernels or wild flowers embedded in them. It's an impressive collection, with many reasonably priced (great gift ideas!) items.

NANDAKWANG, 95/1-2 Nimanhemin Rd. Tel. 222261.

This branch of the popular Bangkok store sells first-rate goods of homespun Thai cotton and is a real treat for anyone interested in weaving. We found a lot of household items too pastel and decorative, but there's a huge selection of table linens (napkins start at only 18B or 75¢), and some conservatively styled, nubby cotton womens' clothing (wraparound skirts start at 1,000B ($40). Their factory can be visited. It's in Lamphun at 330 Pasang Rd. (tel. 521001).

WOODWORK & FURNITURE

CHIANG MAI SUDALUCK CO., 99/9 Ban Nong Khong, Sankamphaeng Rd. Tel. 338006.

One of the biggest furniture factories, this is located at the turnoff for the Bo Sang umbrella village. There's a huge selection of teak furniture, reproductions of seated, standing, reclining, gilded and plain wood Buddhas, and a good collection of ornate, traditionally carved spirit houses (small ones start at $120).

CHIANG MAI TUSNAPORN, 123 Moo 3, Sankamphaeng Rd. Tel. 241188.

Tusnaporn is one of the first teak factory/showrooms along the Sankamphaeng shopping strip. You can watch craftspeople fashioning the most intricate carving with simple hand chisels. Popular purchases include cocktail cabinets and elephants (sized from toys to tables). John went straight for the heavy teak coffee tables (masterfully carved with scenes from the *Ramakien*), which cost about $1,300 including packing and shipping.

8. EVENING ENTERTAINMENT

There are two activities that interest most visitors to Chiang Mai: shopping and participating in a traditional khan-toke dinner. For festivals (see "Calendar of Events" in Chapter 2) and special events, check with the TAT, pick up a free copy of the biweekly Chiang Mai Newsletter, the monthly *Welcome to Chiang Mai and Chiang Rai* magazine, or TAT's excellent free booklet, *Trip Info*, published monthly.

THE PERFORMING ARTS

Every night of the year, from 7:30 or 8pm to about 10pm, there's a free performance at the Night Market. The large, open plaza just south of the Night Bazaar building seems empty and too civic-minded during the day, but after sundown it comes to life. A thatch-roof stage set, decorated with traditional water-filled candi and scoopers to sate thirsty passersby, is the scene for a classical Thai orchestra. After they play their gong, bell, and xylophone-like instruments for a while, a trio of classical dancers in vivid silk costumes and extravagant jewelry appears. Each show varies, but there is often folk dancing by hill-tribe performers or a folk-music performance after the classic numbers. Some evenings, a local rock band plays after the culture hounds are satisfied. The casual ambience seems to attract children, and even rabid shoppers stop browsing to watch!

The other way to enjoy a cultural show is with a traditional Lanna Thai meal—khan-toke dinners make the exotic northern Thai food, the oddly discordant and intriguing music, and the slow, deliberate dancing palatable to everyone. *Note:* Many local travel agents sell one of these evening programs at a 10% to 20% discount including transportation, because they purchase seats in bulk.

LANNA KHAN TOKE, 33/10 Charoen Prathet Rd. Tel. 270080.

This is a popular dining room open nightly from 7 to 10pm where guests can sample the food and dance of northern culture. It's in a Victorian-style building dating from the 1880s, hidden between the modern Diamond Hotel and the Ping River. Guests remove their shoes and sit on pillows at reserved, low tables. The menu is fixed and filling: sticky rice, *cap moo* (fried pork skins), *kang kai* (a meat-and-vegetable curry), stir-fried chicken, *larb* (minced beef with chili peppers), and *namprik ong* (a spicy pork-and-vegetable dish). Thai classical musicians and dancers perform while you dine. After dinner, everyone adjourns to the lower-floor amphitheater for a program of traditional northern hill-tribe dances. Reserve in advance.

Prices: Dinner and show 250B($10).

OLD CHIANG MAI CULTURAL CENTER, 185/3 Wua Lai Rd. Tel. 275097.
The Cultural Center is an interesting complex about 15 minutes south of town. There are hill-tribe craftmaking displays, shops, and a Lanna Folk Museum (open Friday to Wednesday 10am to 4pm). The menu and performance are similar to the more commercial fare at Lanna Khan Toke, but the venue is not as traditional. Instead, after a six-course meal (Muslim or vegetarian food can be requested in advance) where the hardworking staff offers continuous refills, guests can walk through the grounds and see examples of traditional hill-tribe housing. Hill-tribe vendors in costume sell their wares until everyone is seated at the nearby amphitheater. The emcee reiterates that performers are "genuine and are not city people dressed up as hill-tribe people." Their shy, awkward, dispirited rendition of simple folk dances convinced us this was true. Nonetheless, it's a worthwhile evening.
Nearby is the Rinkaew Povech herbal massage center (see "Attractions" earlier in this chapter)—just the thing before a khan-toke meal and dance performance. Call ahead for reservations and they will pick you up at your hotel; a return bus is provided free.
Prices: Dinner and show 220B ($8.80).

THE CLUB & MUSIC SCENE

NIGHTCLUBS

BLUE MOON, 5/4 Moon Muang Rd. off Soi 2. Tel. 214040.
This popular nightclub has live singers, usually performing current Latin music and ballroom dance tunes. There's dancing, plus traditional massage, steam baths, and physical massage available upstairs at the J. R. II Massage Parlor. Mixed drinks start at 135B ($5.40) and bottled whisky is very expensive. Female dance partners are available at 120B ($4.80) per hour.
Admission: Two-drink minimum for men; 120B ($4.80) for women.

RINKAEW NIGHTCLUB AND LOUNGE, 183/4 Wualai Rd. Tel. 274565.
Rinkaew is another popular, large nightclub. Here you can dance, drink, watch a Thai floor show, and even get a traditional massage at their massage parlor next door. The intimate lounge stays open after the nightclub closes. Mixed drinks start at 150B ($6); bottled whisky is very expensive. Female dance partners are available at 100B ($4) per hour.
Admission: Two-drink minimum for men; 100B ($4) for women.

DISCOTHEQUES

BUBBLES DISCO, in the Pornping Hotel, 46-48 Charoen Prathet Rd. Tel. 270100.
Bubbles has a live band. It's nothing great, but if you want to dance, and don't mind the predominantly teenage crowd, it's fun.
Admission: 100B ($4), includes one drink.

CRYSTAL CAVE, in the Empress Hotel, 199 Chang Klan Rd. Tel. 27049.
The newest and currently most popular disco in town. It attracts a foreign crowd slightly younger than the one at the Wall, so the scene is more energetic.
Admission: 90B ($3.60), includes one drink.

THE WALL, in the Chiang Inn Hotel, 100 Chang Klan Rd. Tel. 270070.
It attracts an older crowd that goes for the selection of latest European and U.S. disco and pop hits.
Admission: 100B ($4), includes one drink.

THE BAR SCENE

Most of Chiang Mai's bars (and many restaurants) offer musical entertainment. None charge an admission fee but some have a one-drink minimum; mixed drinks cost 80B to 200B ($3.20 to $8) and a small Singha or Kloster beer will range from

45B to 70B ($1.80 to $2.80). If bars sounds too tame, you can check out the local nightclubs, go-go clubs, or massage parlors. Before going in, make sure you understand all the charges: They can mount up faster than you realize.

Our favorite area in Chiang Mai by night is on the east banks of the Ping River, overlooking the city. It's particularly nice during the festival of Loy Krathong, when thousands of banana-leaf boats with candles and flowers are launched on the river and fireworks go off overhead. On other nights the setting is lovely and tranquil, with night breezes and the lights of the Night Market in the distance. There are three great outdoor places in a row off Charoen Raj Road, just across from the Chinda Hospital, that serve good food and drinks at modest prices. They start to rock at about 8pm and keep going till about 1am.

If you're looking for a lively, young crowd, make the scene at the **Riverside Pub & Restaurant** (9/11 Charoen Raj Rd., tel. 243239), which has been around the longest. Mixed sets of C&W and R&B start at 10pm; though locals call the selections predictable, we thought the music was fine. **The Brasserie** (37 Charoen Raj Rd., tel. 241665) is notable for its lead guitarist, Tak (late of the Riverside). Many Chiang Mai residents make sure to hit the Brasserie every weekend night at 11pm to catch his searing solos; call on weeknights to make sure he'll be there. The **Gallery** (25-29 Charoen Raj Rd., tel. 248601), which doesn't have music, is the most sophisticated of the lot. It's housed in a 100-year-old teak villa, with an airy, whitewashed front gallery that showcases a choice selection of pottery, hill-tribe textiles, and contemporary Thai paintings (which start at 5,000B or $200). Locals praise specialties like the minced chicken wrapped around sugarcane, and sautéed asparagus with prawns.

On the other side of the river, there's **Ban Kao Restaurant,** Anusarn Market, Charoen Prathet Road (tel. 275623). Ban Kao (literally "old village") is a compound of teak houses in a peaceful garden just one block east of the Night Market. It attracts an older crowd. There's an intimate ground-floor bar and several dining levels; after 7pm the music ranges from classical piano to Thai pop, but it's always soft enough so you can talk. On our visit, we were so famished from shopping that we noshed at several food stalls on the way here and only sampled their yummy appetizers (dried beef, pork on egg-dipped toast, fried cashews, shrimp rolls, and prawn fritters).

GAY BARS

THE COFFEE BOY, 248 Tunghotel Rd. Tel. 244458.
Classical music serenades visitors to this classical teak house near the Chiang Mai Arcade bus station. Popular with young Thais and their friends; so much so, that they've added a cottage compound. Cabaret show Friday and Saturday nights after 11pm.

SIAMESE CAT COCKTAIL LOUNGE, 19/39 Singharaj Rd. No phone.
One of the oldest and most popular clubs, this bar is located near the Chiang Mai Arcade bus station. There is a male cabaret show on weekends after 11pm and a Katoey (drag) show nightly at 7pm and 8:30pm.

MORE ENTERTAINMENT
MOVIES

At most cinemas there are four daily shows starting at noon. They usually consist of commercials followed by Thai, Chinese, or junky American action pictures, almost always dubbed into the Thai language. However, many theaters have an English-language viewing room where a translated sound track is broadcast. One of the largest movie theaters is at the corner of Sri Dornchai and Chang Klan roads. Admission is 25B to 40B ($1 to $1.60); it's cheaper farther from the screen. Another movie theater is at Gad Suan Kaew Shopping Complex, near the Chiang Mai Orchid (tel. 252303).

Cinephiles might want to contact the **Alliance Française,** 138 Charoen Prathet Rd. (tel. 275277). They show French classics and some new releases a few nights per week; admission is 25B ($1).

PHYSICAL MASSAGE PARLORS

The Chiang Mai sex scene is tame in comparison to Bangkok, but there were several go-go clubs clustering around Moonmuang Road in the Old City on our last visit. They provide plenty of opportunities for companionship. Several centers offer traditional herbal massage for men and women until 8 or 10pm (see "Attractions,"above).

Chiang Mai Turkish Bath and Massage, 88/1 Viang Ping Trade Center on Chang Klan Road (tel. 274459), is one of the classiest places for physical massage, etc. Activities start at 600B ($24) per hour.

Sayuri, Soi 2, Bumrung Rat Road (tel. 242361), has 100 staff masseuses. Body and hand massage cost 800B ($32) and 500B ($20) an hour respectively.

9. EASY EXCURSIONS FROM CHIANG MAI

If you have time for only one day trip, we recommend taking a minibus up to Wat Phra That and touring Suthep Mountain. If you have more time, you might want to journey to Lamphun or to an elephant training camp in Lampang.

The jewel of Chiang Mai, **Wat Phra That,** can be caught glistening in the sun on the slopes of Doi Suthep mountain. One of four royal wats in the north, at 1,000m (3,250 feet) it occupies an extraordinary site with a cool refreshing climate, expansive views over the city, the mountain's idyllic forests, waterfalls, and flowers.

Wat Phra That was built to house a relic of the Buddha that was prophesied and found by Sumana Thera in the 14th century. During the installation of the relic in Wat Suan Dok (in the Old City), Sumana Thera discovered that the holy object had split in two, with one part equaling the original size. A decision was made, in order to honor the miracle, to build another wat to house the "new" relic. King Ku Na placed the relic on a howdah of a sacred white elephant and let him wander freely through the hills. After several false starts, the prophetic pachyderm blew his horn three times, made three counterclockwise circles, and knelt down. A site had been found atop Doi Suthep.

The original chedi was built to a height of 26½ feet. Subsequent kings contributed to it, first by doubling the size, then by adding layers of gold and other ornamentation to the exterior. The gilded-copper decorative umbrellas around the central chedi, and the murals showing scenes from the Buddha's life, are delightful.

Other structures were raised to bring greater honor to the Buddha and various patrons. The most remarkable is the naga staircase, added in 1557, a steep 290 steps leading up to the wat. The nagas (with their incredibly long scaly bodies) deserve careful examination as they comprise one of the most dramatic approaches to a temple in all of Thailand (try to ignore the many shops selling trinkets at the base). The road winding up the mountain (to shorten the 5-hour climb) was finished in 1935 by Kruba Srivichai (a Lanna Thai monk) and thousands of volunteers after only 175 days of excavation and grading.

Within the temple grounds the sanctity of the pilgrimage becomes more apparent. Anyone with exposed legs is offered a sarong at the entrance. Most Thai visitors come to make an offering—usually flowers, candles, incense, and small squares of gold leaf that are applied to one's favored Buddha or to the exterior of a chedi—and to be blessed. Believers kneel down and touch their foreheads to the ground in worship, then often shake prayer sticks to learn their fortune. It's not unusual to see a Westerner take part in these public ceremonies.

It's worthwhile coming in the early morning or evening to avoid the crowds. The suggested contribution is 10B (40¢).

Wat Phra That is open daily from 7am to 5pm. To get there, take the minibus from Chang Puak (White Elephant) Gate on the north side of the Old City. The fare is 35B ($1.50) going up and 25B ($1) for the descent (the ride is cool, so bring a sweater). The bus stops at the base of the naga staircase. If you'd rather not climb the 290 steps (a great part of the experience), there's a motorized gondola to the top for 5B (20¢).

If you're lucky (we never are), you can enter the grounds of the **Phuping Palace, Doi Bua Ha,** the summer residence of Thailand's royal family. The palace, built in 1962, is 4km (2½ miles) beyond Doi Suthep, and is reputed to have fabulous gardens. All we can say is that if members of the royal family are in residence admission is verboten; often, several weeks prior to or following a royal visit, it's also closed. Check with a local tuk-tuk driver.

Admission is free. The grounds are open from Friday to Sunday from 8:30am to 4:30pm. For transportation there, the Doi Suthep minibus continues to the Phuping Palace from Wat Phra That (see above). It's located 22km (14 miles) west of the Old City off Route 1004, on Doi Bua Ha.

LAMPHUN

The oldest existing city in Thailand, just 26km (16 miles) south of Chiang Mai, was founded in A.D. 663 by the Mon Queen Chammadevi as the capital of Nakorn Hariphunchai. Throughout its long history, the Hariphunchai Kingdom was fought over, often conquered, yet remained one of the powers of the north until King Mengrai established his capital in neighboring Chiang Mai.

In the 13th century, the overload of the city, Ai Fa, built a canal linking Lamphun's Kuang River with the Mae Nam Ping to forge a link with the growing Lan Na Kingdom. After taking complete control over the city he treasonably delivered it to a rival king, Muang Rai, marking the advent of Lamphun's decline.

The most direct way to get there is by car, taking the old highway Route 106S south to town. The Superhighway no. 11 runs parallel and east of it, but you'll miss the tall yang or rubber trees, which shade the old highway until Sarapi, and the bushy yellow-flowered *khilik* (cassia) trees. Buses to Lamphun and Pasang leave from the Chang Puak Gate or the east side of the Nawarat Bridge in Chiang Mai; the 45-minute ride costs 10B (48¢).

WHAT TO SEE & DO

Attractions here (aside from the legendary beauty of the local women) are the historical wats, including some excellent Dvaravati-style chedis, a fine museum, and the unique and tasty fruit called longan. On the second weekend in August, Lamphun goes wild with its Longan Festival, celebrating with a parade of floats decorated only in longans, a fruit exhibition, market, and a beauty contest to select that year's Miss Longan. The ubiquitous trees can be spotted by their narrow, crooked trunks and large, droopy oval leaves. Lamphun and Pasang (to the south) are also popular with shoppers for excellent cotton and silk weaving.

The highlight of Lamphun is **Wat Phra That Hariphunchai,** one of the most striking temples in all of Thailand. (Wat Phra Ihat Doi Suthep was modeled after the 15th-century Sri Lankan restoration done here.) The central chedi, in Chiang Saen style, is more than 150 feet high and dates from the 9th century, when it was built over a royal structure. The nine-tiered umbrella at the top is 6,498.75 grams of gold (it's also said that a hair of the Buddha is inside); The chedi's exterior is faced with bronze. Also of interest in the temple complex are an immense bronze gong (reputedly the largest in the world), several viharns (rebuilt in the 19th and 20th centuries) containing Buddha images (in legend, he visited a hill about 16km [10 miles] from the town where he left his footprints; the site is marked by Wat Phra Bat Tak Pha). During the full-moon day in May, There is a ritual bathing for the Phra That.

The new **Hariphunchai National Museum,** Amphur Muang (tel. 511186), houses a wonderful collection of Dvaravati- and Lanna-style votive and architectural objects. It's just across the street from Wat Phra That Hariphunchai's back entrance, and worth a visit to see the many bronze and stucco religious works removed from the wat for display. We really liked the canopied, baroquely ornate howdah belonging to Lamphun's last king, on the lower level. Admission is 10B (40¢). It's open Wednesday to Sunday 9am to noon and 1 to 4pm.

Wat Chammadevi (Wat Kukut) is a large complex located less than 1km (⁶/₁₀ mile) northwest of the city center. The highlights here are the late Dvaravati-style chedis, Suwan Chang Kot and Ratana, built in the 8th and 10th centuries respectively, and modeled on those at Bodha Gaya in India. The central one is remarkable for the 60 standing Buddhas that adorn its four corners. The wat itself was built by Khmer artisans for King Mahantayot around A.D. 755. The relics of his mother, Queen Chammadevi, are housed inside, but the gold-covered pagoda was stolen, earning this site its nickname Kukut (topless).

McKean Rehabilitation Institute

If you are driving to Lamphun, and have an interest in medicine, you might want to take a detour off Route 1008, to the McKean Rehabilitation Institute. This is a fascinating leprosy clinic and park dating from the beginning of this century. It's set on an island that can be driven around in a few minutes. There are free tours conducted Monday to Friday from 8am to noon.

A Nearby Village

Continue south on Route 106 another 8km (5 miles) to **Pasang.** Like Lamphun, this village's market is noted for its fine weaving, particularly of cotton thread. Small workshops and stands that sell locally woven textiles are open for inspection.

LAMPANG

The sprawling town (originally called Khelang Nakhon) is romanticized in older publications for its exclusive reliance on the horse and carriage for transportation, a throwback to the 19th-century European legacy. There's still little traffic, but it's only darting tuk-tuks and noisy motorcycles; the modern town offers little in the way of enchantment.

However, Lampang is graced with some of the finest Burmese temples in Thailand and supports the nearby, celebrated Young Elephant Training Camp. Because of the regions fine kaolin, there are dozens of ceramics factories producing the new and "antique" pottery sold in Chiang Mai. For a lunch break or an overnight sojourn, the Tipchang Lampang Hotel, 54/22 Tarkraonoi Rd. (tel. 054/226501; fax 225362; telex 42503 TIPCH TH), is the most comfortable in town, with large, air-conditioned rooms from 420B to 590B ($16.80 to $23.60) for two. For more information, contact the **Lampang District Tourist Center,** Chatichai Road near the central clock tower (tel. 226810). It's open daily from 8:30am to noon and 1 to 4:30pm.

The most direct way to reach Lampang is by car, taking the old highway Route 106 south to Lamphun, then superhighway no. 11 southeast for another 64km (40 miles). Buses to Lampang leave from the eastern terminal, just over the Nawarat Bridge on Charoen Rat Road or the bus arcade. The 2¹/₂-hour trip costs 29B ($1.15).

WHAT TO SEE & DO

The following wats are most easily seen by car or taxi.

WAT PHRA KAEO DON TAO, Tambon Wiang Nua; 12km (6.2 miles) southwest of the town center.
This highly revered 18th-century Burmese temple is known for housing the Emerald Buddha, now in Bangkok's Wat Phra Kaeo, for 32 years. Legend has it that one

day the prince of Chiang Mai decided to move the Emerald Buddha (found in Chiang Rai in 1436) from its home to Chiang Mai. His attendants traveled the great distance to Chiang Rai with a royal elephant to transport the sacred icon, then found that it refused to go to Chiang Mai with its burden. This wat was built where the elephant came to rest in Lampang. There is an impressive carved wooden chapel and Buddha, and a 162-foot-high pagoda housing a strand of the Buddha's hair. Poke around in the small Laan Thai Museum to the left of the entrance, it contains some fine woodwork and old *phra viharns* (spirit houses).

WAT PHRA THAT LAMPANG LUANG, Tambon Lampang Luang, Ko Kha; 18km (11 miles) south of the center of town.

This impressive complex is considered one of the finest examples of northern Thai architecture. If you mount the main steps toward the older temples, you'll see a site map, a distinguished viharn (inspired by Wat Phra That Haripunchai in Lamphun), and behind it to the west, a chedi with a fine seated Buddha. Go back to the parking area and cross through the lawn filled with contemporary, painted-plaster Chinese gods. Past the old, old Bodhi tree whose stems are supported by dozens of bamboo poles and ribbons, you'll see signs for the Emerald Buddha House. The small Phra Kaeo Don Tao image wears a gold necklace and stands on a gold base; it's locked behind two separate sets of gates and is very difficult to see.

YOUNG ELEPHANT TRAINING CENTER, Lampang-Ngao Hwy., 54km (33 miles) east of Lampang.

This center is run by the Veterinary Section of the Northern Lumber Production Division of the Forest Industry Organization, and is unlike the other elephant camps which are set up for tourists. The 3- to 5-year-old elephants train at this facility to harvest hardwoods, specifically teak, in the government-controlled forests. There are about 100 elephants at any one time at the center, all supervised by a veterinary staff and *mahouts* (handlers and trainers). Among the tasks that the elephants learn are bathing (the Huai Mae La provides enough water for frolicking), pushing logs with both trunk and tusks, log hauling and walking in procession, piling logs, and crouching down to allow mahouts to mount and dismount, as well as learning their various commands. Elephants train throughout the year, except the hot season (March to May).

Admission: 50B ($2) suggested contribution to mahouts.

Open: Daily demonstrations 9–11am; closed holidays. (Check with the TAT office in Chiang Mai before going to confirm the elephants are in training.)

DOI INTHANON NATIONAL PARK

Thailand's tallest mountain—2,563m (8,408 feet)—is Doi Inthanon. It crowns a 360-square-mile national park filled with impressive waterfalls and wild orchids, all only 47km (29 miles) south of Chiang Mai.

Doi Inthanon Road climbs 48km (30 miles) to the summit of the mountain. Along the way is 100-foot-high Mae Klang Falls (a popular picnic spot with food stands) and nearby Pakan Na Falls (less crowded, because it requires a bit of climbing along a path to reach). The main road continues to the top, where there is a fine view and two more falls, Wachirathan and Siriphum, both suitable for exploration.

Camping is allowed in the park, but you must check with the TAT or the national park office to obtain permits, schedule information, and regulations. The area is a popular day-trip destination for residents of Chiang Mai. If you travel by private car, you can take an 8-mile side trip to Lamphun on Route 1015.

Admission: 10B (40¢).

Open: Sunrise–Sunset. **Transportation/Directions:** Take a blue bus to Chom Thong from the Chiang Mai Gate (1 hour ride costs 15B [60¢]). Day trips organized by local tour companies cost 1,000B ($40), including lunch. By car, take Route 108 south through San Pa Tong; continue south following signs to the national park.

MAE SA VALLEY

This lovely area, more developed than south toward Doi Inthanon National Park, is about 20km (12 miles) northwest of Chiang Mai. A rash of condo construction and the sprouting of roadside billboards all indicate the Mae Sa Valley is being developed as a rural tourist resort, but it still has an unhurried feel. Current attractions include an elephant show (including rides), a cascade, and a nature park, as well as orchid nurseries. Most of these attractions are packaged by local tour operators as a half-day trip costing 450B ($18).

CHIANG DAO

This town and its environs offer several small resort hotels and a few fun **activities,** but if you don't have a car, the easiest way to sightsee is by joining a day trip organized by local tour operators (800B or $32 per person)

YOUNG ELEPHANTS TRAINING CAMP, Chiang Dao.
Our favorite destination is the second best, and fairly authentic, elephant training camp after that in Lampang. The adventure begins as you cross a rope bridge and walk through a forest to the camp. After the elephants bathe in the river (showering themselves and their mahouts) they demonstrate log hauling and log rolling. Read the pamphlet that's available—elephant lore (an elephant sleeps four hours a day) is fascinating.
After the show, you can climb into a howdah and take a safari across the Ping River and through the forest to a Lisu village. It's a 2½ hour trip and costs 275B ($11) per person. Brief elephant rides on the grounds are only 15B (60¢).
Admission: 60B ($2.40) adults, 25B ($1) children.
Open: Daily shows 9am, 10am. **Transportation/Directions:** Take the bus from Chiang Puak Gate; the 1½ -hour ride costs 25B ($1). By car, take Route 107 north; it's 56km (35 miles) from Chiang Mai.

CHIANG DAO CAVE, (Wat Tham Chiang Dao).
Lest you think we've forgotten about all matters historical, think again, because Chiang Dao has one of Greater Chiang Mai's more fascinating sites. The road from town leads through a wonderful stretch of hardwood forests and open land, finally ending at a delightful parking lot (you'll understand when you arrive) below the opening of the cave. Local guides with lanterns will escort you to see a series of Buddhist statues (including a 13-foot-long reclining one); the row of five seated Buddhas in the first cavern is particularly impressive. The cave (a spelunker's delight) extends well into the mountain, but is forbidden to all but the brave and experienced.
Admission: 10B (40¢).
Open: Daily 8:30am–4:30pm. **Directions:** Take Route 107 north; it's 72km (45 miles) north of Chiang Mai or 16km (10 miles) north of the Young Elephants Training Camp.

10. TREKKING FROM CHIANG MAI

Trekking from Chiang Mai has been a tourist activity only since the mid-1970s, but it's become so popular that dozens of agencies sell 2-night/3-day expeditions led by "fluent, multilingual tribal leaders." Even the unfit, the elderly, or the disabled who might never have contemplated a traditional trek including daily 15km (9-mile) hikes and sleeping on the floor of tribal chief's huts, can now enjoy day treks of rafting, riding on elephant back, or driving by Jeep to see the northern hill tribes.
Because of their popularity and easy access, most trekking routes within a close range of Chiang Mai return to the same tribal villages, which then grow to depend on trek revenue. Accordingly, villagers don traditional costumes, perform music, dance, produce crafts, and offer the obligatory opium pipe to well-paying Western

guests. But if you are willing to pay more, and walk a little farther over more rigorous trails to the unusual places, you can still explore territory little known to any farang.

Everyone always enjoys and learns something from their chosen trek; the key to making it an unforgettable experience is the research you put into studying the hill tribes, questioning the trek operators, and interviewing the leader and participants. See Chapter 11, "Exploring Northern Thailand," for more information about choosing the right trek. Below are some recommended firms offering treks from Chiang Mai.

Trekking Companies The TAT publishes a list of companies that operate out of Chiang Mai. Companies go into and out of business regularly and favorite guides move to new agencies, so it takes some effort to find a trek that suits your needs. Most companies are concentrated along Tha Pae and Moon Muang roads near the Old City. It's best to allow a day just for research, but if you're pressed for time, contact the TAT and explain your specific needs to them. They often know the schedules and rates of the larger trekking outfits and can make suggestions.

Several friends have had good experiences with Pinan Tours, 235 Tha Pae Rd. (tel. 053/276081; fax 053/217416), considered one of the best in the business. Other locally recommended companies are Sam's Trekking Service, c/o Galare Guesthouse, 7 Charoen Prathet Rd. (tel. 053/273885; fax 053/279088); Singha Travel, 277 Tha Pae Rd. (tel. 053/282579; fax 053/279260); Summit Tour and Trekking, 30 Tha Pae Rd. (tel. 053/233351; fax 053/270119); Youth's Tour, c/o IYH Chiang Mai Youth Hostel, 31 Prapokklao Rd. (tel. 053/212863); and Eagle House Trekking, 16-18 Chang Moi Rd. (tel. 235387).

The Itinerary Several well-known agencies offer prepackaged routes that leave on regular schedules. For the better-traveled trails, you'll have no problem finding a company; if you intend to climb to more remote spots, you might have to call around to see if anyone offers such a trip or arrange a custom tour (more expensive).

The standard beginner's trek is usually two nights, three days, with about three hours of non-strenuous walking each day. Most companies offer this trek north to the Golden Triangle or southwest near Mae Sariang and Hong Son. Those who want to go north to Mae Salong or east to Phayao or Nan or northwest to Pai and the Myanmar border will have to dig a little to find an appropriate outfit. The more serendipitous can review Chapter 13 "Touring the Northern Hills," and arrange a trek once they've arrived at one of these more remote starting points.

Price Some negotiating is in order. Visit a few of the Tha Pae Road or Moon Muang Road agencies, determine the price ranges of the trip you want to join, and offer about 30% less. Many trekking companies arrange custom trips, even on short notice, with a corresponding increase in price. (Singha Travel charges 1,200B to 6,000B [$48 to $240] for one to eight days.)

On our visit in 1994, Pinan Tours had a 3-day trek to the area around Mae Sariang for 1,600B ($64) per person; a more remote 4-day trek to see the primitive Mbabri tribes in the Ngao area southeast of Chiang Mai (near Nan) was 3,000B ($120). Prices are based on four people in a group; they rise if the number of people declines. Sam's Trekking had a 4-day trek to Pai and Mae Hong Son (including one night in a hotel) for 4,000B ($160). Summit Tours 6-day trek to Mae Hong Son (including rafting and an elephant ride) cost 3,000B ($120).

Jeep treks can be arranged by several of these agencies. Consult with them about your itinerary (often determined by road conditions); the cost averaged about 750B ($30) per day for a Jeep holding a driver, guide, and two or three passengers, plus 300B ($12) per person for supplies, expenses, etc.

CHAPTER 13

TOURING THE NORTHERN HILLS

1. CHIANG RAI
• WHAT'S SPECIAL
  ABOUT THE NORTH
2. CHIANG SAEN & THE
  GOLDEN TRIANGLE
3. MAE HONG SON
4. PAI
5. NAN

Once you leave the bustle of urban Chiang Mai and its satellite cities, you begin to discover the heart of the north. The area's mountainous terrain, its proximity to the Myanmar and Laos borders, and the diverse ethnic hill tribes that have colored its history and culture are what distinguish northern Thailand from the rest of the country.

There are dense jungles and teak forests logged by elephants. The Mae Khong River flows downstream from the Golden Triangle, the heroin-producing region straddling Myanmar and Laos. And, of most interest to the traveler, this is the area where nomadic, self-reliant hill tribes have been left alone to lead traditional lives.

Treks, by foot, Jeep, elephant back, or boat, through the forested hill-tribe homelands, either north from Chiang Mai to Chiang Rai, north from Chiang Rai to the Myanmar/Laos/Thai border at the Golden Triangle, or northwest around Pai and Mae Hong Son, are a popular means to explore this region and get to know its unique peoples.

1. CHIANG RAI

780km (485 miles) NE of Bangkok; 180km (112 miles) NE of Chiang Mai

GETTING THERE By Plane Four flights a day leave from Bangkok (flying time: 85 minutes; 1,885B [$74]); two flights a day leave from Chiang Mai (flying time: 40 minutes; 420B [$16.80]).

By Bus Five air-conditioned buses leave daily from Bangkok (trip time: 12 hours; 283B [$11.60]); 17 buses leave daily from Chiang Mai (trip time: 3 ½ hours; 79B [$3.15]).

By Car The fast, not particularly scenic, route from Bangkok is Highway 1 North, direct to Chiang Rai. A slow, scenic approach on blacktop mountain roads is Route 107 north from Chiang Mai to Fang, then Route 109 east to Highway 1.

By Boat One long-tail boat taxi daily plies the Mae Kok River between the village of Thaton and Chiang Rai (trip time: 4 to 6 hours; 170B [$6.80] per person). Five buses daily leave Chiang Mai to catch the Thaton boat taxi (trip time: 3 ½ hours; 50B [$2]).

Chiang Rai is Thailand's northernmost province; the mighty Mae Khong River (known to most readers as the Mekong of Vietnam fame) shares borders with Laos to the east and Myanmar to the west. The scenic Mae Kok, which supports many hill-tribe villages along its banks, flows right through the provincial capital Amphur Muang, or Chiang Rai.

WHAT'S SPECIAL ABOUT THE NORTH

Events/Festivals
☐ Nan's colorful Boat Races pit multicolored, twin-prow longboats against one another to honor the Buddhist Lent (October to November).

Museums
☐ Chiang Saen's National Museum with excellent Buddhist sculpture and folk arts.
☐ Nan National Museum's particularly fine ethnographic displays.

People
☐ The Karen, Hmong, Mien, Akha, Lisu, Lahu, and Tai Lue are the fascinating tribal groups.

Religious Shrines
☐ Chiang Saen's Wat Pa Sak, built in 1295, still towers over its namesake grove of 1,000 teak trees.

Trekking
☐ Chiang Rai's variety of itineraries: from minivan trips to long-tail boat cruises to rugged jungle hikes.
☐ Mae Hong Son's more rigorous, hill-hiking treks to see the Padung women.
☐ Pai's low budget, student-oriented adventure treks to the newest, least-explored areas.

King Mengrai put Chiang Rai on the map in A.D. 1262. Born to the ruler of Chiang Saen's Yonok Kingdom and the princess of Yunnan's Chiang Hung Kingdom, the ambitious Mengrai attacked his neighbors to the north and east as soon as he ascended to the Yonok throne. To consolidate his conquests into the Lan Na Kingdom, he established a new capital at the central city of Chiang Rai. With greater success in his imperial campaign, including the annexation of the Lamphun-based Nakorn Haripunchai Kingdom, he relocated the capital farther south to Chiang Mai. After 30 years as the center of attention, Chiang Rai's position faded until it suffered under the hands of Burmese occupiers. In 1786 it became part of the Siam Kingdom and in 1910 was proclaimed an official province of Thailand by King Rama VI.

This small city, set in a fertile valley with a cool, refreshing climate, (Chiang Rai is 1,885 feet above sea-level), has achieved new prominence with European group tourists disappointed in urban Chiang Mai. Its tree-lined riverbank, small Night Market, and easy-to-get-around layout lures travelers weary of traffic congestion and pollution. Although Chiang Rai has some decent hotels, good restaurants, and a convenient location to recommend it, we suggest that anyone seeking a really rural alternative to bustling Chiang Rai consider spending a few nights in Chiang Saen, the Golden Triangle, or Mae Hong Son.

ORIENTATION

ARRIVING The new Chiang Rai International Airport is about 10km (6.2 miles) north of town. There's a bank exchange open daily 9am to 5pm and a gift shop. Taxis hover outside expectantly: 1994 rates were 50B ($2) to town; 200B ($8) to Mae Chan; or 400B ($16) to Chiang Saen.

INFORMATION The TAT is located right next to the Tourist Police at 445 Singhakai Rd. in the Mai Kok Villa Hostel; both are very helpful (tel. 711786). The monthly *Welcome to Chiang Mai and Chiang Rai* and the monthly *Chiang Rai Discovery* are distributed free by most hotels.

CITY LAYOUT   Chiang Rai is a small city, with most services grouped around the main north-south street, Paholyothin. There are three noteworthy landmarks: the small Clock Tower in the city's center, one block west of Paholyothin; the statue of King Mengrai (the city's founder) at the northeast corner of the city, on the super-highway to Mae Chan; and the Mae Kok River at the north edge of town. Singhakai Road is the northernmost, riverside road. The bus station is off Paholyothin at Prasopsuk Road, across from the Wiang Inn Hotel. The Night Market is on Paholyothin Road between Prasopsuk and the other Paholyothin Road (a confusing offshoot of the main street).

GETTING AROUND

BY TRISHAW OR TUK-TUK   You'll probably find walking the best method of transport. However, there are bicycle trishaws parked outside the Night Market and on the banks of the Mae Kok River, which charge 10B to 20B (40¢ to 80¢) for in-town trips. During the day there are tuk-tuks; they charge 35B to 75B ($1.40 to $3) for in-town trips.

BY BUS   Frequent local buses are the easiest and cheapest way to get to nearby cities. All leave from the bus station (tel. 711369).

BY MOTORCYCLE   A lot of travelers like to rent motorcycles; read our words of caution in Chapter 11, "Exploring Northern Thailand." Two local companies are recommended: Soon Motorcycle, 197/2 Trirath Rd. (tel. 714068) and Lek House, 95 Thanalai Rd. (tel. 713337). Daily rates run about 460B ($18.40) for a 250cc motor-cycle, 150B ($6) for a 100cc moped, and 10B (40¢) for a helmet.

BY CAR   Avis (tel. 715777) has a branch at the Dusit Island Resort where self-drive vehicles cost from 1,200B ($48) for a Jeep to 1,500B ($60) for a sedan, and cars with driver cost 2,700B ($108) per day, including insurance and 200km (120 miles) free. At **P. D. Tour & Car Rental Services** a Jeep goes for 800B ($32) per day and a sedan for 1,000B ($40), not including gas.

FAST FACTS: CHIANG RAI

Area Code   It's 053.
Climate   This river valley and its surrounding areas have a general climate similar to that of all northern Thailand, but the rainy season lasts longer here, usu-ally April to July.
Currency Exchange   Several bank exchanges on Paholyothin are open daily 8:30am to 10pm.
Hospitals   The new Sriburin Hospital (tel. 717499) is south of town near Little Duck hotel complex on the superhighway.
Police   The Provincial Police is at Rattanakhet Road (tel. 711444). Call 191 in case of emergency.
Post Office   The post office is two blocks north of the Clock Tower on Uttarakit Road. Open Monday to Friday 8:30am to 4:30pm.
Telephone/Telex/Fax   The Overseas Call Office is right behind Wat Phra Kaeo on Ngum Muang Road. Open daily 7am to 11pm.
Transit Info   The Thai Airways office is at 870 Paholyothin Rd. near the Wiang Inn Hotel (tel. 711179). Open daily 8am to 5pm.

WHAT TO SEE & DO

In town, there are three historic wats and a small folk museum worth visiting. In the vicinity of Chiang Rai, you can visit hill-tribe villages, tour historic Chiang Saen or visit the scenic Golden Triangle (see below), take a long-tail boat ride on the Mae Kok River, shop at the Mae Sai border, or explore the cool hillsides of Doi Mae Salong.

EXPLORING CHIANG RAI'S WATS

Wat Phra Kaeo is the best known of the northern wats, because it once housed the Emerald Buddha now at Bangkok's royal Wat Phra Kaeo. Near its Lanna-style chapel is the chedi, which (according to legend) was struck by lightning in 1436 to reveal a plaster-covered Buddha image. Only later, when the plaster shell was damaged, did the monks discover the solid green jasper Buddha. The wat compound is at the northwest side of town off Singhakai Road.

Wat Phra Singh is two blocks east on Singhakai Road. Although it's been heavily restored, the wat is thought to date from the 15th century. Inside is a replica of the Phra Singh Buddha, a highly revered Theravada Buddhist image whose original was removed to Chiang Mai's Wat Phra Singh. The recently rebuilt, Burmese-style Wat Doi Tung sits atop a hill above the northwest side of town (it's up a steep staircase off Kaisornrasit Road) and offers scenic views of the Mae Kok valley. It's said that King Mengrai himself chose the site for his new Lan Na capital from this very hill.

The Population and Community Development Association, PDA, 620/25 Thanalai Rd. (tel. 713410), is a nongovernmental organization responsible for some of the most effective tribal development projects in the region. Through their family planning, waterworks, and agricultural projects, they have gotten to know their clients well. As part of their educational program, the top floor of the PDA offices has been turned into a small, but very interesting, ethnography museum—the Hill Tribe Education Center and Museum. With the help of international volunteers, a fascinating 20-minute slide show has been created to help visitors understand the different cultures of the nine major hill tribes. Its informative narration and the museum's well-labeled displays will teach you more, in less than an hour, than a day trip through the countryside. Children will enjoy touching many of the objects, making the tools work, and peeking into the model houses. There is a handicraft/clothing shop in front of the office where high-quality items for sale fund the PDA's work, and a new restaurant (see "Dining," below). Admission is a suggested contribution of 25B ($1) or 50B ($2) for the slide show. It's open daily from 8:30am to 5pm and is located off Wiset Wiang Road in the center of town.

TOURING THE HILL-TRIBE VILLAGES

Most of the hill-tribe villages within close range of Chiang Rai have become somewhat assimilated by the routine visits of group tours. Nonetheless, if your time is too limited to consider a trek, several in-town travel agencies offer day trips to the countryside. Prices are based on a two-person minimum and decline as more people sign up; rates include transportation and a guide.

Sea Tours Ltd. at the Dusit Island Resort combines a visit to Mien and Akha villages with a drive to the border at Mae Sai, through the Golden Triangle and up to Doi Mae Salong to a KMT (Kuomintang) settlement. The 8-hour trip costs 1,340B ($53.60) per person (tel. 715346). Far-East North Tours at 873/8 Paholyothin Rd. (tel. 713625) has a half-day trip by long-tail boat to a Karen village, then a short elephant ride, and a short walk to a Lahu village. It costs 950B ($38) per person. The Chiang Mai Travel Center, 893 Paholyothin Rd. (tel. 714799), has a more exotic day drive east along the Mae Khong to Chiang Khong, to visit Kamu, Hmong, and Mien villages, stopping on the return in Chiang Saen. It costs 1,500B ($60) per person.

CHIANG SAEN & THE GOLDEN TRIANGLE

The ancient village of Chiang Saen and the geographic curiosity of the Golden Triangle are usually seen as day trips from Chiang Rai. All of the tour operators above offer guided tours; both destinations can also be easily visited by public bus. We've included them in a separate section of this chapter because we think both are

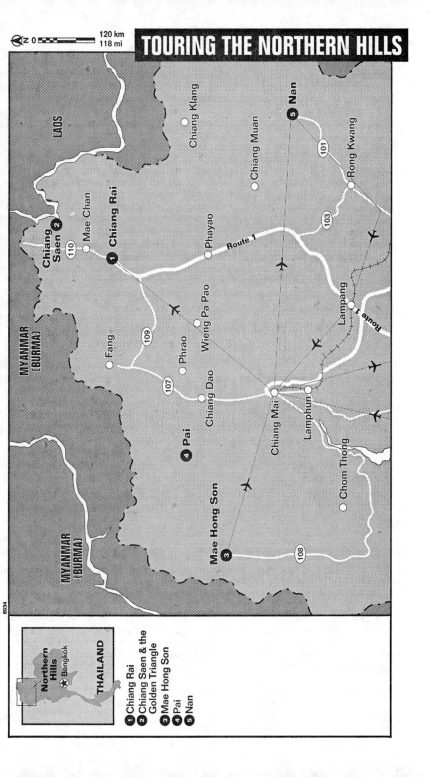

TOURING THE NORTHERN HILLS

0 120 km
   118 mi

LAOS

MYANMAR
(BURMA)

MYANMAR
(BURMA)

THAILAND

Northern
Hills
★ Bangkok

1 Chiang Rai
2 Chiang Saen & the
  Golden Triangle
3 Mae Hong Son
4 Pai
5 Nan

Chiang Saen 2
Mae Chan
110
1 Chiang Rai

Chiang Klang

Chiang Muan

5 Nan
101
Rong Kwang

Phayao

Route 1

103

109
Fang
Wieng Pa Pao
Phrao
107
Chiang Dao

Lampang

Route 1

4 Pai

Chiang Mai
Lamphun

Chom Thong

Mae Hong Son
3
108

6934

deserving of an overnight stay. Chiang Saen's small, Spartan accommodations make it a natural base for budget tourists, while the Golden Triangle's two rural resorts make it a better sightseeing base for those with the resources for a private car.

LONG-TAIL BOAT TRIPS ON THE KOK RIVER

The Mae Kok is one of Chiang Rai's best assets. Though shallow and silted much of the year, it's still the most picturesque avenue for sightseeing in the region. Budget tourists may enjoy hopping on the Thaton long-tail boat taxi service that leaves the Chiang Rai pier each morning at 10am. Although it stops at a Karen tribal village en route, you'll only stay at each stop for a moment—the fun is in the ride itself.

For about 300B ($12) per hour, you'll be able to charter your own noisy long-tail boat (from the pier off the river road opposite the Dusit Island Resort) to sightsee in the area. Most local travel agents do this, chartering boats to the Karen village, continuing to the elephant parking lot where these delightful creatures await their charges, then returning to Chiang Rai by minivan.

EASY EXCURSIONS FROM CHIANG RAI

MAE SAI & THE MYANMAR BORDER

Mae Sai, 60km (36 miles) due north of Chiang Mai, is Thailand's northern border with Myanmar. A short concrete bridge leading to Tha Khi Lek spans the narrow stream separating the two countries. It's crossed daily by hundreds of Thai and Burmese nationals, their arms laden with goods to trade or sell. Citizens of other countries are not permitted to cross the border, and there's little to see.

Some people hate the crass commercialism of this ugly, newly built town. Dozens of girls bedecked in hill-tribe festival costumes and lipstick offer to pose for photographers (10B [40¢] per child or 20B [80¢] for four children, per snapshot). More than a hundred cotton and thatch-shaded shops and stalls sell everything from hill-tribe clothing, Burmese-made acessories and wood carvings, ruby and jade jewelry, and *kalaga* (the lovely sequined Burmese tapestries) to sandalwood and herbal products bought by the Thais. Border shops are usually open daily 8am to 6pm. Bargain hard!

If you need to spend the night, the 32-room Top North Hotel at 305 Paholyothin Rd. is about 110 yards from the border post (tel. 053/731955). Acceptable rooms with air-conditioning cost 500B ($20) single or double; simpler, fancooled rooms with cold-water showers cost 350B ($14) single or double. VISA is accepted. There are several small restaurants nearby.

Public buses leave every 15 minutes from Chiang Rai; the 1½ hour trip costs 18B (75¢). Private cars can take the superhighway Route 110 north direct to Mae Sai or combine this with a side trip to Chiang Saen.

DOI MAE SALONG & DOI TUNG

Doi Mae Salong and Doi Tung are neighboring mountains whose forested slopes are inhabited by hill-tribe peoples. Both make scenic, interesting day trips, though Doi Mae Salong's good accommodations are popular with those seeking peace and quiet.

Phra That Doi Tung, at 2,000m (6,500 feet) above sea level, is a 10th-century monastery considered one of Chiang Rai's most venerated shrines. Locals believe that the wat's twin chedis contain relics of the Buddha's collarbone, making them also a site of pilgrimage for residents of Myanmar's Shan state and Laos's Luang Prabang and Vientiane provinces. You'll notice better paved roads and cleaner, more modern settlements than at Mae Salong, thanks to the presence of Her Majesty the Queen Mother, who occupies a palace on Doi Tung's western slopes.

Doi Mae Salong is a more rugged mountain, best known for its 5,000 sakura, or Japanese cherry trees, which cover the hillsides in a profusion of pink. The trees, imported by the region's immigrants from as far away as China and Myanmar, are celebrated each January with a Sakura Festival.

The hilltop site of **Ban Santikhiri Jienho,** the "KMT village," was settled in 1960 by General Tuan sae Tuan, former chief of staff of China's 93rd Division. He led 2,000 soldiers, their families, and elders (mixed Kuomintang allies or peoples of Chinese Haw descent) who emigrated from China through Myanmar (then Burma) into Thailand, some settling and others continuing their exodus to Taiwan. Tea cultivation is the village's primary source of income, and many Chinese act as merchants for the hillside's original Akha, Lahu, Shan, and Yao inhabitants, now rice and maize farmers.

Development has come quickly; newly paved roads extend from Santikhiri to far-off hill-tribe villages, and adverse effects are slowly being recognized. Says Mr. Prayong Norlamyai of the Hill Area Development Foundation, "If the hill tribes are not well prepared for the change, their societies will collapse. Because the influence of the tourism boom is very strong, their traditions and culture will become no more than game show presentations for the tourists . . . . Even the Chinese in Mae Salong can't adjust themselves. Only big shops can grow while many small shops just can't survive . . ." The HADF and governmental groups are working on ways to help Doi Mae Salong's mixed residents face change, including establishing locally managed "cultural guest houses," which would serve as arts-and-crafts repositories for each village and provide profitable lodging for tourists.

At our visit, the hilltop **Maesalong Resort,** Chiang Rai–Maechan Road, Amphur Maechan, 57110 Chiang Rai (tel. 053/714047; fax 053/714047), was the best choice. A triple-arched pagoda gate leads to a complex of comfortable bungalows and rooms with mountainview balconies. Rattan furnishings, simple decor, fans, and hot showers make them as luxurious as any around. Rates are 600B to 2,400B ($24 to $96), including tax and services, for a single or double room, with spacious suites at the highest rate (American Express, MasterCard, and VISA accepted). There's a souvenir shop and the Sakura Restaurant, which specializes in south Chinese or Yunnanese cuisine and also serves Thai and continental dishes. The tiny **Shin Sane** (no phone) in the heart of the village was highly recommended by a Peace Corps friend, who paid the friendly Chinese hosts 60B ($2.40) for a private room and hot shower.

Within the village, there are several small noodle shops, northern Thai restaurants featuring the spicy *khao soi* soup, and, of course, pretty good Yunnanese Chinese restaurants. Imported Chinese beer, Chinese-brand cigarettes, toiletries, food products, and locally grown Chinese tea are sold in this Thai settlement.

Doi Tung can be reached by superhighway Route 110 south from Mae Sai (18km or 11 miles) or north from Chiang Rai (45km or 28 miles), then Route 1149 west, uphill through the verdant, refreshing countryside. To Doi Mae Salong, take superhighway Route 110 north from Chiang Rai (33km or 20½ miles), then Route 1130 west through the countryside. There are several smaller, jeepable roads (also accessible to off-road motorcycles) from Mae Chan or Mae Sai; check with a local on current road conditions before attempting them.

There is no practical public transportation for anyone attempting a day trip. However, Sea Tours Ltd. and other Chiang Rai agencies offer a drive up Doi Mae Salong to see a Kuomintang settlement, which costs about 1,200B ($48) per person.

WHERE TO STAY

To say that Chiang Rai has undergone a recent tourism boom is an understatement; at last count this city of 37,000 had more than 2,000 hotel rooms! Hotels are all within walking distance of the sights and shopping, with the exception of our two very expensive choices, which are within a 15-minute walk of the town center. You must add 7% government tax and 10% service charge to the rates quoted below unless otherwise noted.

VERY EXPENSIVE

DUSIT ISLAND RESORT HOTEL, 1129 Kraisorasit Rd., Amphur Muang 57000, Chiang Rai. Tel. 053/715777. Fax 053/715801. Telex TH 41322 IRH. 226 rms, 45 suites. A/C MINIBAR TV TEL **Directions:** Over bridge at northwest corner of town.

$ Rates: 2,875B–3,250B ($115–$130) single; 3,150B–3,500B ($126–$140) double; suite from 6,000B ($240). Extra bed 700B ($28). AE, DC, MC, V.

This is the newest and certainly the splashiest addition to Chiang Rai's expanding tourist scene. Occupying a large delta island in the Mae Kok River, the Dusit Island continues the respected tradition set by the Dusit Thani Hotels. In a town known only for small guest houses and local hotels, it's sure to please those looking for international luxury and resort comforts, though at the expense of local flavor and homeyness.

The dramatic lobby is a soaring space of teak, marble, and glass, as grand as any in Thailand, with panoramic views of the Mae Kok. Rooms are luxuriously appointed in cotton pastels and teak trim; higher priced ones offer more amenities than the standard bathrobe, hair dryer, and magazines. However at our visit, we found the connecting rooms very noisy, with our neighbor's normal conversation entirely audible. The Dusit Island's manicured grounds, pool, and other facilities create a resort ambience that shouldn't dissuade you from exploring the town.

Dining/Entertainment: The hotel's most formal dining room is the semicircular peak on the 10th floor, with sweeping views and a grand terrace overlooking the Mae Kok. The fine continental fare will run $25 to $45 per person. Chinatown is a more casual Cantonese restaurant, with a large, tasty dim sum offering at lunch and excellent Chinese fare at dinner. The sunny coffee shop extends into an outdoor poolside terrace and makes for scenic dining. In the evening, there's the cozy Music Room bar and a new nightclub.

Services: 24-hour room service, concierge, limousine service, babysitting (with notice), laundry service.

Facilities: Swimming pool, tennis courts, health club, billiards, kiddie pool and playground, tour desk.

RIMKOK RESORT, 6 Moo 4, Tathorn Rd., Amphur Muang, 57000 Chiang Rai. Tel. 053/716445. Fax 053/715859. 200 rms, 30 suites. A/C MINIBAR TV TEL **Directions:** On north shore of Kok River, about 6km (3.7 miles) north of town center.

$ Rates: 1,500B ($60) single; 1,700B ($68) double; suite from 4,000B ($160). Extra bed 300B ($12). AE, DC, MC, V.

Though inconvenient, this riverside resort offers fine views from not-too-expensive rooms. Well decorated and plush with first class amenities, they offer comforts rarely found in this town. The public spaces are also quite grand—thoroughly done over in Thai decor and arts and crafts—and lushly planted lawns open off large verandas. The Rimkok Resort is actually only a 15-minute walk from town via a pedestrian bridge; free regular shuttle service is offered to those who prefer the quick drive.

Dining/Entertainment: For evening meals, there is the attractive Sipsong Panna Thai restaurant, as well as the pleasant, moderately priced coffee shop.

Services: 24-hour room service, concierge, limousine service, babysitting (with notice), laundry service.

Facilities: Swimming pool.

EXPENSIVE

WANGCOME HOTEL, 896/90 Penawibhata Rd., Chiang Rai Trade Center, Amphur Muang 57000, Chiang Rai. Tel. 053/711800. Fax 053/712973. Telex WANGCOME TH 41307. 221 rms. A/C MINIBAR TV TEL **Directions:** Off Paholyothin.

$ **Rates:** 1,200B ($48) single; 1,400B ($56) double; suite from 1,600B ($64). Extra person 300B ($12). AE, DC, MC, V.

While not our favorite choice, the Wangcome provides an adequate alternative to the better-value Wiang Inn across the street. Rooms are small but comfortable, detailed with Lanna Thai style (such as carved teakwook trim on headboards). The lobby is centered, very dramatically, on a mounted pair of ivory tusks, a sad but interesting trophy of the old Lanna culture.

Dining/Entertainment: There's a lively coffee shop and a moody cocktail lounge, a popular rendezvous spot after the Night Market (across the street) closes.

Services: Limousine service, laundry, beauty parlor.

WIANG INN, 893 Paholyothin Rd., Amphur Muang 57000, Chiang Rai. Tel. 053/711533. Telex 41308 WIANG IN TH. 256 rms. A/C MINIBAR TV TEL

Directions: Center of town, off Prasopsuk Road.

$ **Rates:** 1,200B ($48) single; 1,450 ($58) double; suite from 6,000B ($240). Extra person 250B ($10). AE, DC, MC, V.

This place has lots going for it: full amenities, helpful staff, several dining venues, a large pool, a reputable tour desk, and a convenient location, around the corner from the bus station and opposite the Night Market. Large rooms are trimmed in dark teak, with pale teak furniture and Thai artwork. Murals of long-ago Lan Na hang over the beds and ceramic vases support table lamps. There's been a recent renovation and it's extremely well maintained, despite the steady stream of group tours. It's popular, so book early.

Dining/Entertainment: The Golden Teak, overlooking the pool and garden, serves a varied international menu. There's a casual Thai restaurant and a dimly lit bar off the lobby that's a popular gathering spot. There's also an infrequently used disco.

Services: Limousine service, laundry service.

Facilities: Swimming pool, the Hill Massage Parlor has traditional Thai massage for 300B ($12) per hour; open 4pm to midnight.

MODERATE

THE GOLDEN TRIANGLE INN, 590 Paholyothin Rd., Amphur Muang 57000, Chiang Rai. Tel. 053/711339. Fax 053/713963. Telex 41311 TRIANGL TH. 39 rms. AC **Directions:** East of town center.

$ **Rates** (including tax, service, and breakfast): 600B ($24) single; 650B ($26) double. MC, V.

Now and again, you find those special little hotels whose charm and character set them apart from all others. The Golden Triangle is a small hotel and, while neither luxurious nor fancy, offers a lot of comfort in a style that's traditionally Thai. Rooms are paved in pastel tiles; thatched walls are dotted with Thai paintings and wood carvings; fabrics and furniture are quietly tasteful and thoroughly native. The owners Junlaphan Sithiwong and his American wife, Rebecca, lend a homey air to the place and also run a very good restaurant and a trekking agency which is well respected, if high priced. Behind the Golden Triangle building, Rebecca has started a gift shop with a choice selection of the nicest goods available in the North (ranging from silver and textiles to ceramics and inlaid antique furniture), and a gallery with six exhibits a year. During our visit, the gallery was showing the work of artists from Chiang Rai, including Tawan Dutchanee, one of Thailand's best-known artists.

BUDGET

BOONBUNDAN GUESTHOUSE, 1005/13 Jedyod Rd., Chiang Rai. Tel. 053/727040. 53 rms.

$ **Rates:** 350B ($14) single or double with A/C; 120B ($4.80) single or double with fan. Extra bed 100B ($4). No credit cards.

This popular budget choice behind Wat Jedyod offers huge rooms with air-conditioning, private cold shower and toilet, and a garden view at low prices; it also has smaller fan-cooled rooms with shared hot shower at rock bottom prices. They have an open pavilion restaurant crowded with budget travelers, a safe for valuables, and an inexpensive in-house trekking service.

MON RONG COME, 339 Soi Homnuan, Paholyothin Rd. Tel. 053/712821.
18 rms. **Directions:** On banks of Mae Kok River, north of King Mengrai Monument off superhighway.
$ Rates: 200B–300B ($8–$12) bungalows with fan; 550B–650B ($22–$32) single or double with A/C. Extra bed 100B ($4). No credit cards.

This is a good compromise between rustic serenity and near-town convenience, highly recommended by the local TAT. The modern one-story attached villas have private hot showers and toilet, TV, and telephones; the more worn wooden bungalows are fan-cooled, with individual cold showers and toilet. Neither is exactly plush, but they're clean and have lovely views of the landscaped grounds and the Mae Kok River flowing by. The Thai family who runs this place is gentle and helpful.

WHITE HOUSE GUESTHOUSE, 789 Paholyothin Rd., Amphur Muang 57000, Chiang Rai. Tel. 053/713427. 15 rms. **Directions:** Northeast edge of town, about 450 yards north of King Mengrai Statue.
$ Rates (including tax and service): 110B ($4.40) single; 145B ($5.80) double. AE.

This is a popular inn despite its location on the superhighway to Mae Sai (not as noisy as it sounds). The place is pleasant and well run by an English-speaking staff. Simple, clean rooms are fan-cooled, with private hot showers and toilet. The White House also has a small restaurant, rents vehicles, and runs treks at very reasonable prices.

WHERE TO DINE

There are several good restaurants in the heart of town, many of which serve northern Thai cuisine. Don't forget to try some of the pork and curry dishes and some local specialties: the huge *ching kong* catfish caught in April–May, litchis which ripen in June to July, and the sweetest-ever nanglai pineapple and pineapple wine, sold December to January.

THE NIGHT MARKET/FOOD STALLS, Trairat and Tanarai Rds.
Every night after 7pm, the cavernous, tin-roofed lot south of the Rama Hotel comes alive with dozens of chrome-plated food stalls, where purveyors of many steamed, grilled, and fried Thai treats feed passersby. This is a fun sight (about a 10-minute walk from the souvenir Night Market), but not so hygienically pure as we would like. The hungry might prefer Hawanariga, around the corner at 402/1-2 Banphaprakan Rd. instead.

BIERSTUBE, 897/6 Paholyothin Rd. Tel. 714195.
Cuisine: GERMAN/THAI. **Directions:** 1 block south of Wiang Inn.
$ Prices: Main courses 35B–120B ($1.40–$4.80). No credit cards.
Open: Daily 9am–midnight.

Karl Heinz Krost from Mainz runs a friendly German beer hall that serves what expatriates claim is the town's best continental fare. In the shade of rattan blinds and thatch fringe, regulars dine on imported cheeses and locally made wursts, layered together on real German bread. Come early for the hearty onion-and-potato *Bauernfrühstück* (Kyle's favorite omelet). Standards such as Weisswurst, served with mashed potatoes and sauerkraut, taste like the genuine thing. The only Thai spices that creep into the menu are in the Bangkok-style (lighter than the northern foods) Thai dishes prepared by Karl's wife. No German beer is served but there is beer on tap, and the bar's a comfortable place to hang out.

T. HUT, Paholyothin Rd. Tel. 712162.
   Cuisine: THAI. **Directions:** 300m (330 yards) south of Satharn Payabarn Road, near gas station.
   $ Prices: Appetizers 35B–50B ($1.40–$2); main courses 45B–55B ($1.80–$2).
   Open: Daily 5pm–midnight. MC, V.
This contemporary Thai house has peaked roofs, stucco walls, and a large garden surrounding a spirit house. Inside, rattan tables and chairs are so comfortable that it feels like you're eating in a Thai friend's living room. The gentle staff speak little English but understand *mai pet* (not spicy). T. Hut has delicious, northern cuisine, all authentically spiced and potent. *Yam moo yaw* is a favorite Chiang Rai ham that's especially good combined with their salad *kai*, a green mango and chicken vinaigrette cold salad. John liked the *Nua Yan T. Hut*, their special, very spicy grilled beef. Their deep fried taro crab and beef *penang* were also memorable.

CABBAGES & CONDOMS, 620/25 Thanalai Thanon. Tel. 713410.
   Cuisine: THAI. **Directions:** Downstairs from the PDA hill tribe museum. AE, MC, V.
   Open: Daily 10am–10pm.
In 1994, the Population & Community Development Association (PDA) is slated to open a Chiang Rai branch of its popular Bangkok restaurant. Good Thai food at reasonable prices, and all profits go to fund the PDA's excellent projects, which range from AIDS education to getting plumbing and electricity for local hill-tribe villages.

SHOPPING

The recent influx of tourists has made Chiang Rai a magnet for hill-tribe clothing and handicrafts products. You'll find many boutiques in the Night Market (see "Evening Entertainment," below), as well as some fine shops scattered around the city. Most are open daily from 8:30am to 10pm and accept credit cards. There's much less available than in Chiang Mai, but prices are reasonable.

LITTLE GOLDEN TRIANGLE, superhighway opposite the Little Duck Hotel. Tel. 715005.
   A large shop in a new minimall about 4km (2.4 miles) south of town, Little Golden Triangle has more pretension than most of the hill-tribe shops, but carries good quality old and new homespun, embroidered fabrics, "ancient" beads, and pretty silver jewelry.

CHIANG RAI HANDICRAFTS CENTER, 273 Moo 5, Paholyothin Rd. Tel. 713355.
   This is the largest of the hill-tribe shops, with a huge selection of well-finished merchandise, an adjoining factory, a good reputation for air-mail shipping, and a helpful sales staff that passes out hot tea to wilting shoppers. Aisle after aisle of newly made celadon and ceramics, textiles, pillow covers and table linens, carved woodwork, jewelry, and Thai handicrafts from other regions are sold at reasonable prices. The center is 4km (2.4 miles) north of town on the superhighway; call ahead for a free pickup. Open daily 8am to 6pm.

EGO, 869/81 Pemawiphat Rd. Tel. 712090.
   The dark-wood interior and subtle lighting of this shop (soon to move to the river area) make it feel like a hill-tribe house. Dozens of jackets, shirts, skirts, jewelry, and handicrafts are sold. Owner Wicha Promyong has a great eye for ethnic fashions and accessories that will wear well outside of Thailand.

THE SILVER BIRCH, 891 Paholyothin Rd. Tel. 414844.
   This popular new shop near the Wiang Inn sells lovely old and new silver hill-tribe jewelry in addition to a wide variety of carved, unpainted wooden objects. They run the gamut from tasteful flowers and bird mobiles to sculptures in more dubious taste, like giant hands with male organs instead of fingers. There's a little table outside where drinks are served, and you can sit and watch the world go by on Paholyothin after making your purchases. Open from 10am to 10pm. No credit cards are accepted.

EVENING ENTERTAINMENT

There is little to do in Chiang Rai at night; most visitors stroll through the Night Market and souvenir shop. It's really a miniversion of the more famous conterpart in Chiang Mai. Shops clustered along Paholyothin Road near the Wiang Inn, and around the two lanes leading off it to the Wangcome Hotel, stay open till 10pm to sell kitschy souvenirs, embroidered hill-tribe fabrics and simple clothes made from them, some silver jewelry, lots of T-shirts, postcards, and some Thai woodwork found in other cities. Concentrate on the mirror-and-sequin *kalagas* (Burmese embroideries) and on the black-and-navy cotton embroidered with geometric motifs. At certain times of year, a deep gold beverage (locally brewed pineapple wine) is also sold. Lantna Plaza and Chiang Rai Plaza are two minimalls with postcards and cheap, print Thai cotton sportswear, both on Paholyothin. Bakery snacks and soda are widely available.

You can also hit the disco or karaoke bar at the **Inn Come,** across from Little Duck on the superhighway (admission is 90B or $3.60 including one drink), or have a beer for 40B ($1.60) at the congenial **Panama Jack's,** a little wooden bar-restaurant on Jedyod Road, a couple of blocks north of Wat Jedyod. There's always someone in there talking to the cheerful Scottish owner. Finally, there's also a small red-light district behind the Wang Come, which is, shall we say, no great shakes: a few deserted go-go bars and some massage parlors nearby.

EASY EXCURSIONS

TREKKING FROM CHIANG RAI

Most of the trekking and tour operators in Chiang Rai specialize in day trips, repeatedly taking groups to the same nearby villages. Longer treks usually begin with a minivan or long-tail boat ride away from the city, so that hikers can explore less-touristed areas when they walk. The hilly, scenic region bordering the Mae Khong River around Chiang Khong (137km [85 miles] northeast of Chiang Rai) is one of the newest, therefore less developed, areas of exploration. Other travelers prefer to head southeast to the forested Phayao, or south to Nan, to look for the newly discovered, primitive Mbabri nomads or the Tai Lue tribes.

If you're pressed for time, call or write to one of the recommended trek operators for information about scheduled trips or custom itineraries that can be put together quickly. Remember the rainy season extends from April to July here, so check on the weather patterns if you're booking far ahead. Large parties can command their own schedule and get a better price than small groups; single travelers may have to wait a few days after arrival before finding other like-minded trekkers. The prices quoted below are based on a two-person minimum and include transportation, guide, food, and lodging.

Golden Triangle Tours, c/o Golden Triangle Inn, 590 Paholyothin Rd. (tel. 711339, fax 053/713963), has an excellent reputation for leading environmentally sensitive and ethnographically interesting treks. They recommend a 4-day trip to see Hmong, Mien, and Tai Lue villages in the Chiang Khong region: with three days of four to six hours hiking per day, and one day by boat. The 1993 cost was 3,000B ($120) per person not including accommodations. You can also contact **Adventures in Paradise Tours** in Bangkok for more information (tel. 02/279-2153 or 271-2818).

Mr. Kems of the **White House Guesthouse,** 789 Paholyothin Rd. (tel. 713427), also runs treks enjoyed by many guests. He runs a regular 3-day trek which includes daily hiking, an hour's long-tail boat ride, and a 2-hour elephant ride to explore some Akha, Yao, Lahu, Lisu, Karen, Hmong, or Shan villages north and east of the city. The 1993 cost was 1,800B ($72) per person.

Far East Tours, c/o Wang Come (tel. 713615) is another recommended outfit; the average cost of a 3-day package is 1,500 ($60) per person. See Chapter 11, "Exploring Northern Thailand," for more information about setting up a trek.

2. CHIANG SAEN & THE GOLDEN TRIANGLE

935km (581 miles) NE of Bangkok; 239km (148 miles) NE of Chiang Mai

GETTING THERE **By Bus** Twelve buses a day from Chiang Mai via Chiang Rai (trip time: 5 hours; 160B ($6.40). Forty buses a day from Chiang Rai (trip time: 1½ hours; 15B [60¢]).

By Car Take the superhighway Route 110 north from Chiang Rai to Mae Chan, then route 1016 Northeast to Chiang Saen.

ESSENTIALS **Orientation** Route 1016 is the village's main street, which intersects after 500m (550 yards) with the Mae Khong River. Along the river road are a few guest houses to the west, and an active produce, souvenir, and clothing market to the east.

Information There is no TAT, but the staff at the few guest houses speak some English and try to be helpful.

Fast Facts The **area code** is 053. Siam Commercial Bank (open Monday to Friday 8:30am to 3:30pm and Saturday from 8:30am to 12 noon), the **bus stop**, **post** and **telegram office** (no overseas service and few local telephones), **police station**, and the Chiang Saen National Museum are all on main street. There is a **currency exchange** booth (open daily 8:30am to 5:30pm) at the Golden Triangle.

The small village of Chiang Saen has the sleepy, rural charm of Myanmar's ancient capital of Pagan. The single lane road from Chiang Rai (59 km [37 miles]) follows the small Mae Nam Chan River past coconut groves and rice paddies guarded by lingering water buffalo. Thatched Lanan Thai houses with gladiola and poinsettia bushes out front have peaked rooflines that extend into Xs like buffalo horns. Deep irrigation ditches paralleling the road are busy with women swinging fishing nets or sorting their catch in baskets balanced on inner tubes. Whole families in brightly patterend *lungi* (Burmese-style sarong) carefully tend fields of tobacco, strawberries, and pineapple.

Fortunately for the birthplace of expansionary King Mengrai, little Chiang Saen was abandoned for the new Lanna Thai capitals of Chiang Rai, then Chiang Mai, in the 13th century. With the Mae Khong River and the Laos border hemming in its growth, modern developers went elsewhere. Today, the slow rural pace, decaying regal wats, crumbling fort walls, and overgrown moat contribute greatly to its appeal. After visiting the excellent museum and local sites, most travelers head west along the Mae Khong to the Golden Triangle, the north's prime attraction.

GETTING AROUND

BY FOOT There's so little traffic it's a pleasure to walk; all of the in-town sights are within 15 minutes' walk of each other.

BY BICYCLE OR MOTORCYCLE It's a great bike ride (45 minutes) from Chiang Saen to the prime nearby attraction, the Golden Triangle. The roads are well paved and pretty flat. **Chiang Saen House Rent Motor,** on the river road just 10m (33 feet) east of the main street intersection, has good one-speed bicycles for 25B ($1) per day and 100cc motorcyles (no insurance, no helmets) for 150B ($6) per day.

BY MOTORIZED PEDICAB The vultures hovering by the bus stop in town are pedicab drivers who will take you to the Golden Triangle for 50B ($2) one-way. Round-trip fares with waiting time are negotiable to about 200B ($8) for about two hours.

BY SONG TAO   On the main street across form the market, you will find **Song Tao** (truck taxis) offering rides for only 10B (40¢) each way. Between 8am and 10am or 2pm and 3pm are good times to try.

BY LONG-TAIL BOAT   Long-tail boat captains offer Golden Triangle tours for 375B ($15) per boat (seating eight) one-way. Many people enjoy the half-hour cruise, take a walk around the village of Sob Ruak after they've seen the Golden Triangle, and then continue on by bus.

WHAT TO SEE & DO

Allow at least half a day to see all of Chiang Saen's historical sights, before exploring the Golden Triangle. To help with orientation, make the museum your first stop.

The **Chiang Saen National Museum** houses a small but very fine collection of this region's historic and ethnographic products. The ground floor's main room has a collection of large bronze and stone Buddhas dating from the 15th to 17th century Lan Na Kingdom. Pottery from Sukhothai-era kiln sites is displayed downstairs and on the balcony.

The handicrafts and cultural items of local hill tribes are fascinating. We particularly like the display of Nam Bat, an ingenious fishing tool. One long-tail boat could take out a few fishermen and 20 *nam bat* (gourds hung with strings and small hooks), which were floated simultaneously to catch quite a haul, especially between May and June when the Mae Kok's freshwater fish are at their plumpest. Burmese-style lacquer ware, Buddhas, and wood carvings scattered through the museum reinforce the similarities seen between Chiang Saen and its spiritual counterpart, Pagan. Allow an hour to go through the museum carefully. Admission is 10B (40¢). It's open Wednesday to Sunday from 9am to 4pm; closed holidays.

EXPLORING CHIANG SAEN'S WATS

Wat Pa Sak, the best preserved, is the focus of a landscaped historical park that contains a large, central, square-based stupa and six smaller chedis and temples. The park preserves what is left of the compound's 1,000 teak trees ("Pa Sak"). It was constructed in 1295 by King Saen Phu to house relics of the Buddha, though historians believe its ornate combination of Sukhothai and Pagan styles dates it later. The historical park is about 220 yards west of the Chiang Saen Gate (at the entrance to the village) and is open daily from 8am to 5pm. Admission is 25B ($1).

The area's oldest wat is still an active Buddhist monastery. Rising from a cluster of wooden dorms, **Wat Phra Chedi Luang** (or Jadeeloung) has a huge brick chedi which dominates the main street. The wat complex was established in 1331 under the reign of King Saen Phu and was rebuilt in 1515 by King Muang Kaeo. The old brick foundations, now supporting a very large, plaster seated Buddha flanked by smaller ones, are all that remain. Small bronze and stucco Buddhas excavated from the site are now in the museum. It's open daily from 8am to 5pm. Admission is free.

There are several other wats of note in and around the town. **Wat Mung Muang** is the 15th-century square-based stupa seen next to the post office. Above the bell-shaped chedi are four small stupas. Across the street, you can see the bell-shaped chedi from **Wat Phra Bouj.** It's rumored to have been built by the prince of Chiang Saen in 1346, though historians believe it's of the same period as Mung Muang. As you leave Chiang Saen on the river road, going northwest to the Golden Triangle, you'll pass **Wat Pha Kao Pan,** with some sculpted Buddha images tucked in niches and on its stupa, then the unrestored vihara mound of **Wat Sangakaeo Don Tan.** Both are thought to date from the 16th century. (The museum has a good map about local historical sites on its second floor.)

THE GOLDEN TRIANGLE

The infamous Golden Triangle (12km [7.5 miles] northwest of Chiang Saen) is a delta-shaped sandbar formed by the confluence of the broad, slow, and silted Mae

Khong and Mae Ruak rivers. They create Thailand's north border, separating it from overgrown jungle patches of Myanmar to the east and forested, hilly Laos to the west. The area's appeal as a vantage point over forbidden territories is quickly diminishing. Even as we go to press, the Burmese are constructing a deluxe hotel for foreigners on their side of the triangle, and the Laotians are eagerly greeting tourists at their new land border at Nong Khai, almost 800km (500 miles) southeast.

Nonetheless, a "look" at the home of ethnic hill tribes and their legendary opium trade is still fascinating. Each Feburary, after the dry-season harvest, mule caravans transport poppy crops from the mountains to heroin factories in the Golden Triangle; the annual yield of 4,000 tons represents 50% of the heroin sold in the United States. Despite years of DEA-financed campaigns, the crops continue to emanate from this area due to the Myanmar's notorious drug lord, Khun Sa, and his Muang Tai Army.

The appeal of this geopolitical phenomenon has created an entire village—Sob Ruak—of thatch souvenir stalls, cheap river-view soda and noodle shops, and very primitive guest houses (see "Where to Stay and Dine," below, for two fine hotels). The Opium House Museum and the Marijuana Pipe Shop are typical of what's available on the commercial strip, almost a quarter-mile long. Need we say more?

WHERE TO STAY & DINE

There are a few tiny guest houses in Chiang Saen, and two fine resort hotels in the Golden Triangle area. We recommend the former to budget tourists who don't mind Spartan conditions, and the resorts to anyone who can afford them. It's a very scenic, relaxing place from which to explore all of the north.

The best restaurant ambience in tiny Chiang Saen is at the interesection of main street and the river road, with a large veranda overlooking the river. This is Salathai, known for its moderate prices and fine, simple Thai and Chinese fare geared to foreigners.

LE MERIDIEN BAAN BORAN HOTEL, Golden Triangle, Chiang Saen 57150, Chiang Rai. Tel. 053/716678. Fax 053/716702. Telex 086/49131 BBHOTEL TH. 106 rms, 4 suites. A/C MINIBAR TV TEL **Directions:** Above river, 12km (7.5 miles) northwest of Chiang Saen.

$ Rates: 2,400B ($96) single or double; suite from 7,200 ($288). Extra bed 350B ($14). AE, DC, MC, V.

In stunning contrast to most new hotels, this one is a triumph of ethnic design. You'll never question whether you're in the scenic hill-tribe region because the Le Meridien Baan Boran's elegance and style depend on locally produced geometric and figurative weavings, carved teak panels, and pervasive views of the juncture of the Ruak and Mae Khong rivers. On a hilltop just 2km (1.2 miles) west of the infamous Golden Triangle, balconied rooms have splendid views. This oasis of comfort has attached rooms that are so spacious and private you'll feel like you're in your own bungalow or the home of a fabulously wealthy tribal chief. Tile foyers lead to large bathrooms with bathrobes and hairdryers, then to a bedroom furnished in teak and traditionally patterned fabrics. Deep navy and burgundy accents set off the bronze figurines framed in glass lamp bases at every bedside.

Giant gilded columns support the Chiang Rai–style peaked lobby roof, where impressive wood carvings and prayer umbrellas decorate the cocktail lounge. The staff is excellent and friendly. Several Jeep tours and sightseeing options are carefully planned, making this an option for long-staying guests.

Dining/Entertainment: The Yuan Lue Lau is the lovely, riverview casual dining pavilion. Thai and continental set menus or main courses, snacks, and breakfast are served. Frequent barbecues and buffets are done on a lower, riverview terrace.

Services: Concierge, car rental, babysitting (with notice), laundry service, tour desk.

Facilities: Swimming pool, Jacuzzi.

DELTA GOLDEN TRIANGLE RESORT, 222 Golden Triangle, Chiang Saen, 57150 Chiang Rai. Tel. 053/777031. Fax 053/777005. Telex 41306 GOLDEN

TH. 71 rms, 2 suites. A/C MINIBAR TV TEL **Directions:** In Sob Ruak, 11km (7 miles) northwest of Chiang Saen.

$ Rates: 2,000B–2,700B ($80–$108) single; 2,400B–2,700B ($96–$108) double; suite from 5,400B ($216). Extra bed 500B ($20). AE, DC, V.

This five-story hotel block looms over the west corner of tiny, souvenir-soaked Ban Sob Ruak. Modern, spacious guest rooms with pastel and rattan decor have large balconies overlooking the Golden Triangle. It's a fine, totally comfortable choice if you're passing through, but not nearly the tribal experience that the Le Meridien Baan Boran provides.

Dining/Entertainment: There's a three-story, Lanna Thai–style restaurant with multipeaked roofs which serves northern Thai specialties and some continental cuisine and has an evening cocktail lounge.

Services: Concierge, car rental, laundry service.

Facilities: Small outdoor pool.

GIN'S GUEST HOUSE, Chiang Saen. No Phone. 16 rms, 1 bungalow. **Directions:** 1½ km from the bus station, on the road to the Golden Triangle.

$ Rates 100B–120B ($4–$4.80) single; 120B–160B ($4.80–$6.40) double. No credit cards.

This big, old two-story teak affair, with wide-plank floors and beautiful carved balconies and doors, is the most luxurious of the budget choices in Chiang Saen. The higher rates are for rooms with private hot bath and toilet. There's a porch that makes the most of the Mekong River view as well as a pleasant garden. Gin's lends bicycles at no charge for an hour; 15B (60¢) per half day.

J.S. GUESTHOUSE, Chiang Saen. Tel. 053/777060. Fax 053/771313. **Directions:** About 100 meters west of the post office.

$ Rates 50B–100B ($2–$4) single; 75B–200B ($3-$8) double; 300B ($12) triple. No credit cards.

J.S. is spankingly bright and fresh, with white tiled floors in the public areas and a little outdoor garden overlooking a wide, rural road. The more expensive rooms come with private toilet and cold showers, and there's a communal hot shower available, all exceptionally clean and well tended. Though it's not close to the Mekong, which is one of the town's greatest assets, this is a pretty convenient location: across the street is an inexpensive laundry place, and you're not far from the post office, the bus station, the national museum, and the archeological site of Wat Pa Sak.

3. MAE HONG SON

924km (574 miles) NW of Bangkok; 355km (220 miles) NW of Chiang Mai via Pai; 274km (170 miles) NW of Chiang Mai via Mae Sariang

GETTING THERE **By Plane** One Thai Airways flight a day leaves from Bangkok (flying time: 80 minutes); four flights a day leave from Chiang Mai (flying time: 45 minutes). Reserve as early as possible—these flights are booked weeks ahead in the busy season.

By Bus Five buses a day leave from Chiang Mai via Mae Sariang (trip time: 6 hours; 175B [$7]); five buses a day from Chiang Mai via Pai (trip time: 9 hours; 155B [$6.20]).

By Car The worthwhile scenic route is longer, with steep, winding roads and occasional stretches of unpaved laterite: Take Route 107 north from Chiang Mai to Route 1095 northwest through Pai. The faster route is paved and broader: Take Route 108 southwest from Chiang Mai to Mae Sariang, then continue north on Route 108.

Mae Hong Son is a province bordering Myanmar where visitors can discover large areas of scenic woodlands, waterways, and hill-tribe villages little affected by change. The verdant hills, mist-shrouded year-round, burst into color each October and November when *tung buatong* (wild sunflowers) come into bloom. The province's crisp air and cool climate guarantee a refreshing, relaxing sojourn.

This forested, mountainous region was little known until recently. Mountains scarred by slash-and-burn agriculture and logged teak forests indicated hill-tribe habitation, but the lack of infrastructure kept Mae Hong Son from public view. Change came in the mid-1980s, when Thailand's rapid industrialization began to incorporate hill-tribe peoples into the modern economy. Roads, airfields, and public works projects opened up the scenic province to all. Poppy fields gave way to terraced rice paddies and garlic crops. Simultaneously, the surge in tourism brought foriegners trekking into villages where automobiles were still unknown.

The completion of two large hotels in the early 1990s augured even greater change for the rapidly expanding provincial capital. Although Mae Hong Son will continue to be the focus of major development for several years, we think its picturesque valley setting and lovely Burmese-style wats are worthy of a visit.

By the way, readers intrigued by the American CIA's private airline and its role in the Vietnam War, will be pleased to learn the feature film *Air America* was shot at the tiny Mae Hong Son Airport (5km [3 miles] east of town). Shell casings and combat sheds used as set dressing are still in place, and residents will long marvel at the 6-week occupation of their town by 400 filmmakers in 1990. Wouldn't you like to know where Mel Gibson and Robert Downey, Jr. slept?

ORIENTATION

INFORMATION There is no TAT, but the **Tourist Police** at 12 Khunlumprapas by the market are very helpful (tel. 611259).

CITY LAYOUT Amphur Muang (literally "capital city") or Mae Hong Son is quite small, but contains three noteworthy landmarks: Wat Phra That Doi Kung Mu, on a hill at the west side of town; the statue of King Singhanat Rajah (the city's founder) on a small green at the town's center; and Nong Chongkam Lake on the east. Khunlumprapas, part of the Pai-Mae Sariang "highway" linking other provincial centers, is the town's main street and home to several travel agents, small hotels, and restaurants. Singhanat Bamrung Road, at the only traffic light, is the largest east-west street. The Night Market and Tourist Police are just south of this intersection, the bus station is just north of it. Walking is the best method of transport, but there are a few tuk-tuks parked outside the market for longer trips. A number of restaurants and guest houses rent 100cc motorbikes for day trips. Prices quoted ranged from 150B to 450B ($6 to $18) so be sure to shop around.

FAST FACTS: MAE HONG SON

Area Code It's 053.

Climate The mountains create more extreme weather here. The hot season (March to April) has temperatures as high as 40°C (104°F); and the rainy season is longer (May to October), with several brief showers daily.

Currency Exchange The Bangkok Bank exchange on Khunlumprapas is open Monday to Friday 8:30am to 5pm. Krung Thai Bank on Singhanat Road is open seven days 8:30am to 5pm. In addition, several banks open for each flight arrival at the airport.

Hospitals The Sri Sangawan Hospital is east of town on Singhanat Bamrung Road (tel. 611378).

Post Office The post office is opposite the King Singhanat Rajah statue. Open Monday to Friday 8:30am to 4:30pm.

Telephone/Telex/Fax The Overseas Call Office is upstairs from the post office. Open daily 7am to 10pm.

Transit Info The Thai Airways office is a 10-minute walk east on Singhanat Bamrung Road (tel. 211044).

WHAT TO SEE & DO

In town, there are many beautiful wats worth visiting. In the vicinity of Mae Hong Son, you can visit a village of long-necked Padung women, take a long-tail boat ride on the Pai River, or try an elephant ride in the nearby jungle.

In 1993, one of my favorite hotels, the Mae Hong Son Resort, offered a 2-night/3-day tour package from Chiang Mai that included tours to most of the sights mentioned below, round-trip airfare, room, board, and airport transfers for the great price of 3,700B ($148) per person (tel. 053/611406 in Mae Hong Son or 053/251217 in Chiang Mai).

EXPLORING MAE HONG SON'S WATS

Wat Chongklan and **Wat Chongkham** are reflected in the serene waters of Nong Chongkam Lake, in the heart of town. Their striking white chedis and dark teak vihara are the most telling elements of Burmese influence. Wat Chongklan was constructed from 1867–71 as an offering to Burmese monks who made the long journey here to the funeral of Wat Chongkham's abbot. Inside are a series of folk-style glass paintings depicting the Buddha's life and a small collection of dusty Burmese wood carvings. The older Wat Chongkham (ca. 1827) was built by King Singhanat Rajah and his queen and is distinguished by gold-leaf columns supporting its vihara.

Wat Phra That Doi Kung Mu (also known as Wat Plai Doi) dominates the western hillside above the town, particularly at night, when the strings of lights rimming its two Mon pagodas are silhouetted against the dark forest. The oldest part (ca. 1860) of this compound was constructed by King Singhanat Rajah, and the 15-minute climb up its new naga staircase is rewarded by grand views of the mist-shrouded valley, blooming pink cassia trees, and Nong Chongkam Lake below. Each April, the national **Poy Sang Long Festival** honoring Prince Siddhartha's decision to become a monk is celebrated here by a parade of novices. Below Wat Phra That, there's a 40-foot-long reclining Buddha in Wat Phra Non.

THE PADUNG: VILLAGE OF LONG-NECKED WOMEN

Postcards, T-shirts, and dish towels emblazoned with the head of a young woman wearing a tall gold collar advertise one of Mae Hong Son's most intriguing attractions. She is from the Padung tribe, with a heart-shaped face framed by short black bangs that's different from that of most Thai tribal peoples.

The Padung, originally from Myanmar, are thought to be an aristocratic subgroup of the Karen tribe. Legend has it that many generations ago, when their kingdom was threatened by attacking Burmese troops, the Padung princess uprooted a solid gold tree that grew near the border of their territory and tied it around her neck for safekeeping. As victory approached, the ruthless Burmese chopped off the princess's head in order to capture the tree. Thus, Padung women came to wear *moodee* or golden collars (now made of shiny brass) in her honor.

At the age of nine, Padung girls get their first half-inch-wide collar; they add one per year until they get married. A foot-long neck is highly prized; you'll see women with brass bands around their forearms and shins as well. The rings are mysteriously added by a local witch doctor; these women become so accustomed to them that by the time they are adults, the Padung can no longer hold up their heads without the rings' support. The practice is dying out, but young women have been sighted wearing their first rings in other areas.

Unfortunately, seeing the Padung has become a political decision in our complicated world. It's estimated that fewer than 50 currently live in Thailand, mostly in Karen villages, on provincial land donated by the Thai government to Karen rebel groups expelled by Myanman's military dictatorship. Because the Karen charge each visitor a 250B ($10) fee to see and photograph them (no video cameras are allowed), it's widely assumed that the Padung are kept at these villages to help fund rebel activities. We were told that the women are obligated to weave and sell small items in order to pay for room and board. While many tourists are turned off by the zoolike atmosphere, we found it an honor to be able to meet and support these unique, regal people.

If you decide to go, there are two villages that can be visited in day trips from Mae Hong Son. The first (with six Padung women in residence) is on the Pai River, about 20 minutes by long-tail boat from town. Several in-town travel agents and the riverside **Maehongson Resort** (tel. 611406) offer this excursion for about 400B ($16) for the 2-hour boat rental, plus 250B ($10) per person "viewing" fee. The **Single Travel office,** in town on Khunlumprapas, has a full-day Jeep excursion (five hours' drive each way) to a jungle village with 15 Padung women in residence. They sell this as a more "authentic" tour, for 1,000B ($40) for the Jeep, plus 250B ($10) per person viewing fee (tel. 612388).

RAFTING ON THE PAI RIVER

The Pai River originates in northern Myanmar and runs 180km (112 miles) downstream through Pai and Mae Hong Son until it meets the Salween River in Burmese territory. During October and November, when the water is at its highest (30m wide by 7m deep [99 by 23 feet deep]), easygoing raft trips are a popular way to see the countryside. **Sam Mok Tours** (tel. 611439) and **Tomas Tours** (tel. 611313) can organize 6-hour trips near the village of Pai.

Several in-town travel agents and the riverside **Hong Son Resort** (tel. 611406) offer 2- to 3-hour long-tail boat cruises to the police check post at Ban Nam Phiang Din (there's a small wat to see there) and then downstream to the Burmese border. You can study the teak and redwood stands along the riverbank and watch waist-deep fishermen trying to catch baklin and catfish in the fast-flowing water.

ELEPHANT RIDES

The region's mahouts keep their elephants primarily to help with teak harvesting on the steep hillsides. However several work with in-town travel agents and the Hong Son Resort (tel. 611406) to offer 2-hour "jungle safaris" on elephant-back. We were alternately delighted and numbed by the repetitive, rolling pitch of our cushioned howdah, yet think it's worth a try. The ride costs 500B ($20) for two hours, 750B ($30) for four hours.

WHERE TO STAY

Just a few years ago, the first two grand hotels were built in Mae Hong Son to meet the influx of upscale tourists, overshadowing the pleasant but more modest accommodations that were available. The combination of luxury and landscape at the Holiday Inn or Tara Imperial is a great experience if you can afford it, but the best value is found in the budget family-style guest houses clustering around Jong Kahm Lake, the base of Doi Kung Moo, or out of town.

EXPENSIVE

HOLIDAY INN, 114/5-7 Khunlumprapas Rd., Mae Hong Son 58000. Tel. 053/611390, 612108, or 612212. Fax 053/611524. Telex 41204 HOLIDAY TH (in Bangkok 02/276-1233). 114 rooms. A/C MINIBAR TV TEL
$ Rates: 2,000B ($80) single; 2,200B ($88) double; 3,500B ($140) suite. Extra bed 400B ($16). AE, DC, MC, V.

This recently completed four-story deluxe facility gleams with sophistication on the outskirts of sleepy little Mae Hong Son. The handsome marble lobby has some touches of Thai style in the carved wooden paneling and reception desk, but it's furnished with British colonial wicker furniture and the rooms are strictly Western, with twin beds of blond wood and quilted floral bedcovers. Exceptional here are the balcony views of mountains towering above the beautifully landscaped grounds and two free-form swimming pools—they're especially ravishing in the morning, before the famous Mae Hong Son mists have blown away.

The guests we saw were a suprisingly mixed crew, from a rollicking group of backpackers on a splurge to honeymooners and old Continental couples, all made equally welcome. The staff is friendly and helpful, though not as fluent in English as we expect from this chain.

Dining/Entertainment: Prominent locals flock to the handsome, tile-floored dining room with more mountain views, which serves good Thai, Chinese, and Western fare at prices quite a bit higher than others in town. There's also a snooker club and a nightclub downstairs with local singers.

Services: Room service, concierge, laundry service, free airport transfer, in-house trekking services.

Facilities: Swimming pool, tennis court, pharmacy, gift shop.

TARA MAE HONG SON, 149 Moo 8, Tampon Pang Moo, Mae Hong Son, 58000. Tel. 053/611473, 622373, or 611483. Fax 053/611252. Telex 41202 TARA HGN (in Bangkok: tel. 02/261-9000; fax 02/225-2680). 114 rooms. A/C MINIBAR TV TEL

$ Rates 1,872B ($75) single; 2,223B ($89) double; 3,500B ($140) suite. Extra bed 400B ($16). AE, DC, MC, V.

Another recently completed deluxe hotel competing for the upscale traveler in Mae Hong Son. Although this place is about two kilometers (a little over a mile) out of town and deliberately rustic in style, the good taste, services, and upkeep mark it as one of Bangkok's Imperial chain of hotels. It's set in the edge of teak woods and overlooks a lush garden with a stream running through it. The rooms are furnished in blond wood and wicker, with big wooden balconies, and the suites are positively enormous. There's a small fitness center, a medium-sized free-form pool set into a wooden deck, and an open-air lobby restaurant with big round tables and a fine view. This place draws more Americans than other upscale resorts in the area—good or bad depending on your point of view.

Services: Room service, concierge, laundry service, free airport transfer, in-house guide services.

Facilities: Swimming pool, tennis courts, pharmacy, gift shop.

MODERATE/INEXPENSIVE

BAI YOKE CHALET, 90 Khunlumprapas, Amphur Muang 58000, Mae Hong Son. Tel. 053/611466. Fax 053/611533. 40 rms. AC TEL

$ Rates (including tax and service): 850B–1,500B ($34–$60) single, double, triple. MC, V.

This hotel offers decent, midsize rooms; though simple, they have some Thai style. Lower-priced rooms are good value but plain; for 1,300 ($52) you get the same hardwood floors and hot, private showers, plus a little more decor. The top-priced ones have a minibar also. There's a pleasant second-floor terrace; rooms overlooking the back share access and are quieter.

PIYA COMPLEX, 1/1 Khunlumprapas, Soi 3, Mae Hong Son 58000. Tel. 053/611260 or 612307. Fax 053/612308. 8 rms. **Directions:** On the east side of Jong Kham Lake.

$ Rates (including tax and service): 250B ($10) single or double with fan; 350B ($14) single or double with A/C. No credit cards.

This is the best budget choice on beautiful Jong Kham Lake (easily the nicest part of town), and it's wise to book ahead because it usually has a waiting list. Piya's is a one-story wooden house with a garden courtyard; the airy rooms come with their own hot showers and toilets. The restaurant/bar has shaded tables outside with a scenic view of the lake and a rustic, wood-paneled interior where you'll often find travelers gathered around the pool table. Piya Grongpherpoon the well-organized Thai owner, also runs a trekking service and rents out bikes and motorbikes at reasonable prices.

PENPORN GUESTHOUSE, 6/1 Phadung Moi Tan, Amphur Muang 58000, Mae Hong Son. Tel. 053/611577. 10 rms.

$ Rates (including tax and service): 200B ($8) single/double. No credit cards.

This in-town lodge is more than a typical guest house; it is similar to a Spartan motel. Basic, bright rooms in an L-shaped wing surround a manicured lawn with potted flowers at the base of Doi Kung Moo Hill, off Khunlumprapas. Each is fan cooled and includes a private hot water bathroom with shower. There is a simple rooftop breakast terrace offering continental breakfast for 20B (80¢), plus open views of the mist-shrouded mountains.

Nearby Places to Stay

Some of our favorite establishments are about 6km (3.6 miles) south of town, inconvenient, but ideal for bookworms.

MAE HONG SON RESORT, 24 Ban Huaidea, Amphur Muang 58000, Mae Hong Son. Tel. 01/611406 or 053/251217 in Chiang Mai. Fax 053/251121 or 053/251135 in Chiang Mai. 42 rms. A/C
$ Rates (including tax and service): 775B ($31) single/double; suite from 3,600B ($144). Extra bed 200B ($8). MC, V.
Though not a luxurious resort, this collection of bungalows on the banks of the Pai River provides a convenient base for exploring the area (their minivan shuttles into town for 200B [$8] round-trip). Rooms are comfortable, though minimal in style; most are gracefully and privately placed around the grounds. Only three suites with big verandas actually front the river; if you can't afford one, reserve a midpriced room, as some of the cheapest bungalows face the driveway. Advanced reservations are a must. The open-air restaurant offers a fine view of the morning elephant baths across the river. The level of service is fairly sophisticated, and manager Mr. Charlie Chunahacha gives all guests a personal attention that distinguishes this from its neighbors.

RIM NAM KLANG DOI RESORT, 108 Ban Huey Daer, Amphur Muang 58000, Mae Hong Son. Tel. 053/612142. Fax 053/612086. 39 rms.
$ Rates (including tax and service): 500B–750B ($20–$30) single/double. Extra bed 100B ($7). MC, V.
With the longest name of any hotel we saw in Thailand, the Riverside Among the Hills Resort is a good-value, rural venue. (Their minivan shuttles into town for 100B [$4] round-trip.) Many rooms have good river views; they're simpler than at the neighboring Mae Hong Son Resort, and the small staff's English is lacking, but the resort grounds are lushly planted and attentively groomed. We preferred the 500B ($24) river-view, fan-cooled rooms with private hot showers from the myriad choices. However, campers get the best deal, because they can pitch their own tents or the resort's on the banks of the Pai for only 140B ($5.60) and have access to a toilet and cold shower.

WHERE TO DINE

The local Night Market on Khunlumprapas is the busiest venue for budget travelers. Tiny tables are crowded with people sampling noodle soups, crisp-fried beef, dried squid, roast sausage, fish balls, and other snacks sold by various vendors. Prices run 8B to 30B (35¢ to $1.20). Early risers (5:30 to 7am) will find it crowded with local merchants and vendors at breakfast.

KAI-MOOK, 23 Udom Chaonited Rd., Tel. 612092.
   Cuisine: THAI. **Directions:** East of main street.
$ Prices: Main courses 25B-110B ($1-$4.40) MC, V.
   Open: Lunch daily 11am–2pm, dinner daily 5pm–3am.
Kai-mook is a tin-roofed pavilion with more style than most: Overhead lights are shaded by straw farmer's hats, and Formica tables are interspersed between bamboo columns. The southern Thai menu includes Kai-mook salad, a tasty blend of crispy fried squid, cashews, sausage, and onions. There are several soup dishes, including the popular chicken with coconut milk and galenga, fluffy-light spring rolls, superspicy pork sausage, and deep-fried pashon fish—all pretty good.

EVENING ENTERTAINMENT

For such a small town, Mae Hong Son offers a surprising number of nighttime diversions. The favorite student and hip farang hangout is the **Fern Bar,** on Khunlumprapas opposite the Police Booth. It's a good place for beer (30B or $1.20) and some music; it stays open till midnight. Another popular rock and country-and-western (occasionally) bar is **Blue Jean,** (tel. 611350) at 4 Khunlumprapas, Soi 3, on the south side of Nong Chongkam Lake. You can catch a Thai songbird with some nifty synthesizer accompaniment nightly at the **Maehongson Mountain Inn.** It's loud, but frothy fresh fruit drinks cost only 35B ($1.40).

Strollers can take in some hill-tribe handicraft shopping on Khunlumprapas until about 11pm or inspect the dozens of large stuffed animals sold by vendors near the bus station.

EASY EXCURSIONS

TREKKING FROM MAE HONG SON

There are more trekking and tour operators on the main street than hotels and restaurants combined. Unfortunately, the region's increased popularity means that trekkers have to go farther away (usually 4- to 5-day treks) to see villages unspoilt by tourist visits. Ironically, several day treks by Jeep or minivan have been created for visitors with little time, little inclination to walk, and more money.

Travelers interested in a rigorous trek to little seen hill-tribe villages will probably want to head northwest, to the area around Pai and the Burmese border. The following guides and companies were recommended to us: Johnnie, the Karen proprietor of Johnnie House, a guest house on Jong Kham Lake; Chumlong Orchai, the co-owner of Jong Kham Guesthouse, who is Suan; Mr. Ayme at Mae Hong Son Tours Ltd., 25 Khunlumprapas (tel. 612414), and the two guides of Burmese origin leading treks from the Mae Hong Son Guesthouse (tel. 612510), a very Spartan establishment a 15-minute walk west of Khunlumprapas.

Rates vary according to size of group and destination, usually about 300B to 450B ($12 to $18) per day, per person, including guide, meals, and village lodging. See Chapter 11, "Exploring Northern Thailand," for more information about setting up a trek.

Of the many day treks, most combine a morning in-town temple visit with a Karen and Hmong village if you're headed south, or with a Lisu, Black Lahu, Hmong, "KMT" Chinese refugee, or Shan village to the north. Depending on the season, the Pha Sua Waterfall, the Fish Cave, or a sunflower viewing might be added attractions. These day treks cost about 500B to 800B ($20 to $32) per person, depending on the number of people going and the vehicle required.

EN ROUTE TO PAI

The **Tham Pla Park** is 17km (10.5 miles) north of Mae Hong Son on Route 1095, the winding mountain road to Pai. This small landscaped park has been created around the Tham Pla or fish cave. It's actually a grotto crowded with carp (legend says there are 10,000 of them) who mysteriously prefer it to the clear, flowing streams all around. There's a parking lot filled with young boys selling fish pellets (2B [8¢] per packet, but whoa!! The carp wouldn't eat them!), a fancy visitors center (long closed), a Non-Formal Education Center with a Ping-Pong table, and a pretty promenade through the woods to the grotto.

There, under the watchful eyes of a religious shrine, are young girls selling papaya (6B [25¢] per packet) and hard-boiled eggs (12B [50¢] per packet)—both much preferred by the swollen carp—and candles and incense offerings for the shrine. The grotto, once unsuccessfully explored by Thai Navy divers, is said to be several meters deep and to extend for miles.

Ten kilometers (6 miles) away in the park is the huge **Pha Sua Waterfall,** which tumbles over limestone cliffs in seven cataracts. The water is at its most powerful after the rainy season, in August and September. The Meo hill-tribe village of Mae Sou Yaa is beyond the park on a jeepable road, just a few kilometers from the Myanmar border.

The **Lod or Spirit Cave** is off Route 1095 (40km [24 miles] northwest of Pai), about 8km (5 miles) north of the "highway" on a laterite road. This large, striking cave is filled with colorful stalagmites and stalactites, but more importantly, was discovered in the 1960s to be filled with antique pottery dating from the Ban Chiang culture.

4. PAI

831km (516 miles) NW of Bangkok; 135km (84 miles) NW of Chiang Mai

GETTING THERE   By Bus   Five buses a day leave from Chiang Mai (trip time 4 hours; 100B [$4]). Four buses daily from Mae Hong Son (trip time: 4 hours; 30B [$1.20]).

By Car   The scenic route is long, with steep, winding roads and occasional stretches of unpaved laterite: Take Route 107 north from Chiang Mai, then Route 1095 northwest to Pai.

ESSENTIALS   Orientation   Tiny Pai consists of four streets; Route 1095 or the Pai–Mae Hong Son Highway is the main one. The bus station is at the northeast end of town. You can walk the town in five minutes. Some travelers like to rent a bicycle or motorcycle for day trips (Northern Green Pai rents bikes for 40B [$1.60] a day, 100cc motorcycles for 175B [$7] a day, with helmet).

Information   There is no TAT, but guest house and restaurant staff speak good English and are very helpful.

Fast Facts   Area code is 053. The **Krung Thai Bank** is the only one, open Monday to Friday 8:30am to 3:30pm. The **Pai Hospital** (a tiny clinic) is one block west of the bus station. The **Town Police** is ½km (³/₁₀ mile) north of the intersection with Route 1095, on the road parallel to it. The **post office**, where overseas calls can also be made, is about 1km (.62 mile) south of the police station. There are very few phones in town. A private **telephone** office is about 10 yards north of the police station; open Monday to Friday 8am to 3pm.

Pai is a small village in the crook of the narrow, meandering Pai River, located about a third of the way between Chiang Mai and Mae Hong Son. The twisting, hilly road from Chiang Mai leads through small groves of litchi, longan, and banana trees, plummets into valleys filled with mist, then rises again past fields where summer rice crops give way to garlic in the fall, then to soybeans over the cold winter. Though not particularly picturesque or ethnically interesting itself, Pai's fortuitous location and lack of urban bustle have made it the new mecca for young, low-budget tourists. Several even begged us not to praise Pai too highly! We enjoyed the easy, Bohemian appeal of the place. With two restaurants that bake their own whole wheat bread, two outstanding traditional massage places, outfits like Peace Trekking, and signs everywhere urging us to "Save the Burmese forests," Pai bears a definite resemblance to northern California.

The parade of buildings—concrete with tin roofs, woven rattan shaded by thatch, and split logs covered by teak-leaf shingles—demonstrates the town's recent haphazard growth. Pai's four commercial streets are lined with small guest houses and advertising. There's an amazing array of shoes, sandals, and boots on sale here (for obvious reasons) and also a few stores selling handicrafts.

Large oak-tag billboards in front of little thatch trekking offices show dotted lines connecting Pai with Karen, Lisu, Lahu, Shan, and KMT (Kuomintang) tribal villages.

These offices are usually a one-man band: The guy who plans your itinerary will probably carry your pack and guide you around. Most visitors make their trek choice within 24 hours of arrival and take off, eventually to return for a day or so of relaxation here before taking the next day's long-distance bus.

WHAT TO SEE & DO

No one comes to Pai because there's a lot to do. In the midst of relaxing, you can stroll around to the four small in-town wats. The principal one is **Wat Klang** next to the bus station, with several small pagodas surrounding a large one topped by a mondop. **Wat Hodana** and **Wat Nam Hu** are west of Route 1095; Nam Hu is known for its Chiang Saen–era Buddha, whose hollow head is filled with holy water. There's a waterfall about 7km (4.2 miles) west of town past the two wats, and a hot spring about 7km (4.2 miles) to the east, past the Pai High School.

Our favorite shopping experience was buying handicrafts from the young Lisu women in bright traditional garb who wander past the cafés in town with their wares. The goods are beautiful, you're buying directly from the hill people, and at the end of the transaction the vendor will often thank you on behalf of herself and her village—an altogether unique and satisfying encounter.

Tiny Pai boasts two terrific traditional massage places. Mr. Jan's Herbal Sauna and Massage, which is Burmese style and done through a cloth, soothing for those who find Thai style too rigorous. Sessions start at 80B ($3.20); with herbal sauna 150B ($6). There's also Mr. Charlie's Herbal Sauna & Massage, with two graduates from Chiang Mai's famous Old Medicine Hospital program. We had one of the best traditional massages ever here, for 120B ($4.80) per hour. Contact Thai Yai or Charlie's House for more information.

WHERE TO STAY

There are half a dozen guest houses in and around Pai, and many more are sure to be built by the time you visit.

CHARLIE'S HOUSE, 9 Rungsiyanon Rd., Pai 58130, Mae Hong Son. Tel. 053/699039. 16 dorm rms, 3 bungalows.

$ Rates (including tax and service): 40B ($1.60) single; 80B ($3.20) double; 140B ($5.60) single/double bungalow. No credit cards.

This small guest house is set in a nicely planted garden just off the main street, next to the Krung Thai Bank. Three fancy wooden bungalows with the luxury of bedside lamps and hot-water showers dominate the tranquil setting, but most rooms are very simple twin-bedded affairs in a block next to the clean communal toilets and showers. All rooms have fans and screened widows and are well maintained. His place is very good value, with a new restaurant, a safe for valuables, and a more clean-cut crowd than most.

NUNYA'S, Rungsiyanon Rd. Tel. 053/699051.

$ Rates (including tax and service): 80B–120B ($3.20–$4.80) single or double. No credit cards.

If Charlie's is full, you can try Nunya's just up the street. This new little wooden house is set in a garden of bright flowers with tables and benches. The fan-cooled rooms are scrupulously clean, and the more expensive ones come with their own hot-water showers and toilets.

RIM PAI COTTAGES, Pai 58130, Mae Hong Son. No phone. 16 rms. **Directions:** Northeast side of town, 85m (94 yards) east of bus station.

$ Rates (including breakfast, tax, and service): 400B–600B ($16–$24) single/double. No credit cards.

These attractive Swiss chalet–style A-frames on the bank of the lazy Pai River are almost luxurious compared to everything else around. Ten log cottages and six attached rooms have verandas for river watching, simple twin-bed interiors, hot-water showers, private toilets, fans, and screened windows. It's a very peaceful setting, far from the nearest paved road, with an elevated breakfast pavilion for truly scenic dining.

WHERE TO DINE

OWN HOME VEGETARIAN RESTAURANT, 6/9 Rungsiyanon Rd. Tel. 699125.
   Cuisine: VEGETARIAN. **Directions:** On cross street near the Pai High School.
$ Prices: Main courses 18B–60B (75¢–$2.40). No credit cards.
   Open: Daily 6pm–10pm.
At this open-air, thatch dining area around the corner from the long-distance telephone office, you'll find an international clientele eating hummus, felafel, eggplant-and-cheese moussaka, adequate pizza, veggie variations on pad thai noodles, and an amazingly diverse international collection of vegetarian dishes. The proprietors are very helpful and warm.

THAI YAI, Pai. Tel. 699093.
   Cuisine: WESTERN/THAI. **Directions:** On main street, just south of Ratchamrong Road.
$ Prices: Appetizers 18B–35B (72¢–$1.40); main dishes 25B–40B ($1–$1.60). No credit cards.
   Open: Daily 7:30am–10:30pm.
Thai Yai serves breakfast, lunch, and dinner, and there's always someone hanging out here, probably because Andrea and Tao, the Scottish-Thai owners, serve up such terrific food and atmosphere at low prices. It's a clean, peaceful wooden room filled with picnic tables and plants, and there's a chessboard, music, and Andrea's small but excellent library to browse. On the walls you'll find information about projects that benefit the local hill-tribe people, including the ones that produce the raw materials for Thai Yai's excellent fresh-brewed coffee and whole wheat bread.

   The Thai food here is fine, but baked potatoes, garlic bread, homemade soups, and salads are what draw the homesick here—only the whole-wheat pizza was a little too heavy and doughy for our taste. The desserts are truly outstanding: we devoured the moist, chewy carrot-and-ginger cake and banana-and-coconut cake with some of the best homemade ice cream we've had anywhere.

EASY EXCURSIONS

TREKKING FROM PAI

There are at least a dozen trekking and tour operators on the two main streets, most affiliated with the guest houses and restaurants. Since the office manager and trek leader are usually one and the same person, take the time to visit several of these shops and meet your guide before you settle on a trip. If you're not in Pai during the busy winter season (December to February) it may take a few days to gather other clients for your intended trek. While you're waiting, you can enjoy several day treks in the vicinity of Pai, where you can visit nearby hill-tribe villages.

   At our visit, trekkers looking for unexplored villages were heading north of Pai to Karen and Lisu villages near the Pai River. (The area south from Pai to Mae Hong Son, though rich with hill-tribe villages, was becoming crowded with trekking parties originating in Mae Hong Son.) Travelers looking for a rigorous trek will find it in this hilly, forested region. One operator's sign read, "No Mercy, no elephants, no fanfare."

   The following companies were recommended to us: Seela, a local Karen guide, at Karen Trekking (ask for directions at Thai Yai), and Happy at P. S. Riverside Guesthouse, and Mr. Nann, c/o Charlie's House, 9 Rungsiyanon Road. Walking treks from the Pai area cost 1,000B to 1,300B ($40 to $52) per person for a 4-day trek.

5. NAN

668km (415 miles) NE of Bangkok; 318km (198 miles) SE of Chiang Mai

GETTING THERE   By Plane   Three flights a week leave from Chiang Mai (flying time: 50 minutes; 510B [$20.40]); three flights a week leave from Phitsanulok via Phrae (flying time: 95 minutes; 57B [$2.30]).

By Bus   Eight buses a day leave from Bangkok (trip time: 12 hours; 300B [$12]); one bus a day leaves from Chiang Rai (trip time: 6 hours; 70B [$2.80]).

By Car   Take superhighway Route 110 South through Phayao to Rong Kwang, then Route 101 Northeast to Nan. Take Route 11 southeast from Chiang Mai to Den Chai, then Route 101 northeast through Phrae to Pai.

ESSENTIALS   Area code is 054. There is no TAT office. The town's few **hotels** are within a block of the Night Market, near the bus station. **Pedicabs** (bicycle trishaws) are available for local sightseeing and charge about 50B ($2) per half hour.

Because of its awkward location, you're unlikely to go through Nan in your travels around Thailand. Some tour operators do package it (along with the highway stops Phayao and Phrae) on a North Thailand itinerary—Nan's heavily wooded villages provide "jungle" elephant trips, and its historical wats are of some interest. We say if time is limited, pass it by, unless you're here in late October or early November and can attend the annual Lanna Boat Races.

Nan was of more interest during the era of Sukhothai's supremacy, when the first settlers arrived. Chao Khun Fong of the Phuka dynasty decided in 1358 to move his capital south from Pua to the east bank of the Nan River. Within a decade, the city had run out of potable water and was relocated to Ban Huay Kai, on the west bank of the river, the site of today's Nan. (The celebrated Wat Phra That Chae Haeng dates from this time.) From 1560 to 1785, the Nan and the Lan Na kingdoms succumbed to Burmese rule. After years of fighting, the capital was abandoned, resettled at various times, abandoned again, and finally rebuilt at its present site.

EN ROUTE FROM CHIANG RAI: NAN

The superhighway south of Chiang Rai is well paved but busy; as you approach **Phayao** (92km or 57 miles), the landscape becomes more rural. Phayao is a large town built on the shores of scenic Kwan Pha Yao, a freshwater lagoon which supports over 5,000 acres of fish breeding. On its east bank is **Wat Si Khom Kham,** a recently built wat housing a 55-foot-tall seated Buddha whose play area most intrigued us. As if in a Brueghel fantasyland, larger-than-life plaster figures of dinosaurs, snakes, Buddhas, and monks fill the courtyard. In a playground setting, several groups of emboweled and wounded (Dante inspired?) mortals, including a giant E.T., struggle to overcome their fate. You really need a break after this experience; luckily there are many food stalls and soda shops around the nearby lagoon.

Turning toward Nan, you'll pass dozens of roadside stands selling mandarins and tamarind pods. These small, sweet, gold oranges, Nan's favorite product, were bred by a local educator from a Yunnan breed and have become a profitable industry. The tamarind is used for sweetening spicy Thai sauces or in desserts.

WHAT TO SEE & DO

Once you're here, spend half a day seeing some historic wats (open daily 8am to 5:30pm; admission free) and the fine museum.

The 600-year-old **Wat Phra That Chae Haeng** (Doi Bhubhiang Chae Haeng, Nan) sits atop Mount Bhubhiang, about a 5-minute drive east of town on the Mae

Charim Road, on the site of Chao Khun Fong's original city. The glistening copper-covered base and gilded copper chedi are said to house relics of the Buddha. The multitiered rooftops of the more recent temples are typical of the Tai Lue architectural style. The wat is celebrated annually on the full moon of the first lunar month.

Local chronicles note the construction of the unusual compound of **Wat Bhumin** (Baan Bhumin), just a short walk from Nan's Night Market, in 1603. Unlike most wats, the main place of worship was the vihara, and it's a very beautiful frescoed building worthy of close inspection. Ignore the current restoration work and peek inside. Wall murals depict the daily life of this agrarian society, while the coffered ceiling is adorned with rich gilt, red, and black patterns. Lanna Thai artisans were imported to complete the main four carved teak doors.

Nearby in the heart of town is **Wat Chang Kham Wora Vihara,** a monastery built for royalty in 1547, and still actively used to train novices. In a style typical of Sri Lanka, the main stupa has six elephant sculptures striding forth from each face, as if in search of freedom. Note the striking bell tower at the rear of the compound, and the old teak vihara with its painted, carved pediment and doors.

Each Songkran the people of Nan come to **Wat Suan Tan** (Nai Wiang) to venerate the large bronze Chao Thong Thit Buddha installed in the main pagoda. The ornately carved roof, with its restored, charming mural of devotees listening to the Buddha's teachings, caps a base punctuated by niches representing the four cardinal points. This wat is two blocks north of the Night Market.

The excellent **Nan National Museum,** Pa Gong Road, Amphur Muang, Nan (tel. 710561), is known to locals as Ho Kham, the title it had when it served as residence for Nan's ruling family. To Thais, the museum is best known for the Black Elephant Tusk, a well-guarded relic on the second floor. This darkened ivory tusk was brought from Chiang Tung by an early ruler and displayed in the palace until the death of the last king.

The museum is terrific on many other counts. There are informative ethnographic displays, particularly the reconstructed kitchen and bedroom on the main floor. The history of Thai art, with explanations and examples of varying styles, is a small but fascinating exhibit. Upstairs, there is a collection of locally carved wood Buddhas that are lovely and very unusual. Try to allow at least one hour to see the collection in depth. The museum is open Wednesday to Sunday frm 9am to noon and 1 to 4pm; closed holidays; admission is 10B (40¢). It's located right in the heart of town.

NAN PROVINCIAL BOAT RACES

Races between longboats manned by teams of oarsmen began in the late 19th century in celebration of Songkran. These popular competitions were then held as part of monastic fairs, but eventually became the main event after the Buddhist Lent (late October to early November). In Nan, the Lent is also celebrated by the giving of an elephant tusk and robe to Wat Chang Kahm Wora Vihara, but the races have become a regional event drawing Thais and tourists from around the country.

Now Save Money on All Your Travels by Joining
FROMMER'S ™ TRAVEL BOOK CLUB
The World's Best Travel Guides at Membership Prices

FROMMER'S TRAVEL BOOK CLUB is your ticket to successful travel! Open up a world of travel information and simplify your travel planning when you join ranks with thousands of value-conscious travelers who are members of the FROMMER'S TRAVEL BOOK CLUB. Join today and you'll be entitled to all the privileges that come from belonging to the club that offers you travel guides for less to more than 100 destinations worldwide. Annual membership is only $25 (U.S.) or $35 (Canada and foreign).

The Advantages of Membership

1. Your choice of *three* free FROMMER'S TRAVEL GUIDES (any *two* FROM-MER'S COMPREHENSIVE GUIDES, FROMMER'S $-A-DAY GUIDES, FROMMER'S WALKING TOURS *or* FROMMER'S FAMILY GUIDES—plus *one* FROMMER'S CITY GUIDE, FROMMER'S CITY $-A-DAY GUIDE *or* FROMMER'S TOURING GUIDE).
2. Your own subscription to **TRIPS AND TRAVEL** quarterly newsletter.
3. You're entitled to a **30% discount** on your order of any additional books offered by FROMMER'S TRAVEL BOOK CLUB.
4. You're offered (at a small additional fee) our **Domestic Trip-Routing Kits.**

Our quarterly newsletter **TRIPS AND TRAVEL** offers practical information on the best buys in travel, the "hottest" vacation spots, the latest travel trends, world-class events and much, much more.

Our **Domestic Trip-Routing Kits** are available for any North American destination. We'll send you a detailed map highlighting the best route to take to your destination—you can request direct or scenic routes.

Here's all you have to do to join:

Send in your membership fee of $25 ($35 Canada and foreign) with your name and address on the form below along with your selections as part of your membership package to **FROMMER'S TRAVEL BOOK CLUB, P.O. Box 473, Mt. Morris, IL 61054-0473.** Remember to check off your *three* free books.

If you would like to order additional books, please select the books you would like and send a check for the total amount (please add sales tax in the states noted below), plus $2 per book for shipping and handling ($3 per book for foreign orders) to:

> **FROMMER'S TRAVEL BOOK CLUB**
> P.O. Box 473
> Mt. Morris, IL 61054-0473
> (815) 734-1104

[ ] **YES.** I want to take advantage of this opportunity to join FROMMER'S TRAVEL BOOK CLUB.
[ ] **My check is enclosed.** Dollar amount enclosed_____*
        (all payments in U.S. funds only)

Name_____
Address_____
City_____ State_____ Zip_____
        All orders must be prepaid.

To ensure that all orders are processed efficiently, please apply sales tax in the following areas: CA, CT, FL, IL, NJ, NY, TN, WA and CANADA.

*With membership, shipping and handling will be paid by FROMMER'S TRAVEL BOOK CLUB for the three free books you select as part of your membership. Please add $2 per book for shipping and handling for any additional books purchased ($3 per book for foreign orders).

Allow 4–6 weeks for delivery. Prices of books, membership fee, and publication dates are subject to change without notice. Prices are subject to acceptance and availability.

Please Send Me the Books Checked Below:

FROMMER'S COMPREHENSIVE GUIDES
(Guides listing facilities from budget to deluxe,
with emphasis on the medium-priced)

	Retail Price	Code		Retail Price	Code
☐ Acapulco/Ixtapa/Taxco 1993–94	$15.00	C120	☐ Japan 1994–95 (Avail. 3/94)	$19.00	C144
☐ Alaska 1994–95	$17.00	C131	☐ Morocco 1992–93	$18.00	C021
☐ Arizona 1993–94	$18.00	C101	☐ Nepal 1994–95	$18.00	C126
☐ Australia 1992–93	$18.00	C002	☐ New England 1994 (Avail. 1/94)	$16.00	C137
☐ Austria 1993–94	$19.00	C119	☐ New Mexico 1993–94	$15.00	C117
☐ Bahamas 1994–95	$17.00	C121	☐ New York State 1994–95	$19.00	C133
☐ Belgium/Holland/ Luxembourg 1993–94	$18.00	C106	☐ Northwest 1994–95 (Avail. 2/94)	$17.00	C140
☐ Bermuda 1994–95	$15.00	C122	☐ Portugal 1994–95 (Avail. 2/94)	$17.00	C141
☐ Brazil 1993–94	$20.00	C111	☐ Puerto Rico 1993–94	$15.00	C103
☐ California 1994	$15.00	C134	☐ Puerto Vallarta/Manzanillo/ Guadalajara 1994–95 (Avail. 1/94)	$14.00	C028
☐ Canada 1994–95 (Avail. 4/94)	$19.00	C145	☐ Scandinavia 1993–94	$19.00	C135
☐ Caribbean 1994	$18.00	C123	☐ Scotland 1994–95 (Avail. 4/94)	$17.00	C146
☐ Carolinas/Georgia 1994–95	$17.00	C128	☐ South Pacific 1994–95 (Avail. 1/94)	$20.00	C138
☐ Colorado 1994–95 (Avail. 3/94)	$16.00	C143	☐ Spain 1993–94	$19.00	C115
☐ Cruises 1993–94	$19.00	C107	☐ Switzerland/Liechtenstein 1994–95 (Avail. 1/94)	$19.00	C139
☐ Delaware/Maryland 1994–95 (Avail. 1/94)	$15.00	C136	☐ Thailand 1992–93	$20.00	C033
☐ England 1994	$18.00	C129	☐ U.S.A. 1993–94	$19.00	C116
☐ Florida 1994	$18.00	C124	☐ Virgin Islands 1994–95	$13.00	C127
☐ France 1994–95	$20.00	C132	☐ Virginia 1994–95 (Avail. 2/94)	$14.00	C142
☐ Germany 1994	$19.00	C125	☐ Yucatán 1993–94	$18.00	C110
☐ Italy 1994	$19.00	C130			
☐ Jamaica/Barbados 1993–94	$15.00	C105			

FROMMER'S $-A-DAY GUIDES
(Guides to low-cost tourist accommodations and facilities)

	Retail Price	Code		Retail Price	Code
☐ Australia on $45 1993–94	$18.00	D102	☐ Israel on $45 1993–94	$18.00	D101
☐ Costa Rica/Guatemala/ Belize on $35 1993–94	$17.00	D108	☐ Mexico on $45 1994	$19.00	D116
☐ Eastern Europe on $30 1993–94	$18.00	D110	☐ New York on $70 1994–95 (Avail. 4/94)	$16.00	D120
☐ England on $60 1994	$18.00	D112	☐ New Zealand on $45 1993–94	$18.00	D103
☐ Europe on $50 1994	$19.00	D115	☐ Scotland/Wales on $50 1992–93	$18.00	D019
☐ Greece on $45 1993–94	$19.00	D100	☐ South America on $40 1993–94	$19.00	D109
☐ Hawaii on $75 1994	$19.00	D113	☐ Turkey on $40 1992–93	$22.00	D023
☐ India on $40 1992–93	$20.00	D010	☐ Washington, D.C. on $40 1994–95 (Avail. 2/94)	$17.00	D119
☐ Ireland on $45 1994–95 (Avail. 1/94)	$17.00	D117			

FROMMER'S CITY $-A-DAY GUIDES
(Pocket-size guides to low-cost tourist accommodations
and facilities)

	Retail Price	Code		Retail Price	Code
☐ Berlin on $40 1994–95	$12.00	D111	☐ Madrid on $50 1994–95 (Avail. 1/94)	$13.00	D118
☐ Copenhagen on $50 1992–93	$12.00	D003	☐ Paris on $50 1994–95	$12.00	D117
☐ London on $45 1994–95	$12.00	D114	☐ Stockholm on $50 1992–93	$13.00	D022

FROMMER'S WALKING TOURS

(With routes and detailed maps, these companion guides point out
the places and pleasures that make a city unique)

	Retail Price	Code		Retail Price	Code
☐ Berlin	$12.00	W100	☐ Paris	$12.00	W103
☐ London	$12.00	W101	☐ San Francisco	$12.00	W104
☐ New York	$12.00	W102	☐ Washington, D.C.	$12.00	W105

FROMMER'S TOURING GUIDES

(Color-illustrated guides that include walking tours, cultural and historic
sights, and practical information)

	Retail Price	Code		Retail Price	Code
☐ Amsterdam	$11.00	T001	☐ New York	$11.00	T008
☐ Barcelona	$14.00	T015	☐ Rome	$11.00	T010
☐ Brazil	$11.00	T003	☐ Scotland	$10.00	T011
☐ Florence	$ 9.00	T005	☐ Sicily	$15.00	T017
☐ Hong Kong/Singapore/			☐ Tokyo	$15.00	T016
Macau	$11.00	T006	☐ Turkey	$11.00	T013
☐ Kenya	$14.00	T018	☐ Venice	$ 9.00	T014
☐ London	$13.00	T007			

FROMMER'S FAMILY GUIDES

	Retail Price	Code		Retail Price	Code
☐ California with Kids	$18.00	F100	☐ San Francisco with Kids		
☐ Los Angeles with Kids			(Avail. 4/94)	$17.00	F104
(Avail. 4/94)	$17.00	F103	☐ Washington, D.C. with Kids		
☐ New York City with Kids			(Avail. 2/94)	$17.00	F102
(Avail. 2/94)	$18.00	F101			

FROMMER'S CITY GUIDES

(Pocket-size guides to sightseeing and tourist accommodations and
facilities in all price ranges)

	Retail Price	Code		Retail Price	Code
☐ Amsterdam 1993–94	$13.00	S110	☐ Montréal/Québec		
☐ Athens 1993–94	$13.00	S114	City 1993–94	$13.00	S125
☐ Atlanta 1993–94	$13.00	S112	☐ Nashville/Memphis		
☐ Atlantic City/Cape			1994–95 (Avail. 4/94)	$13.00	S141
May 1993–94	$13.00	S130	☐ New Orleans 1993–94	$13.00	S103
☐ Bangkok 1992–93	$13.00	S005	☐ New York 1994 (Avail.		
☐ Barcelona/Majorca/Minorca/			1/94)	$13.00	S138
Ibiza 1993–94	$13.00	S115	☐ Orlando 1994	$13.00	S135
☐ Berlin 1993–94	$13.00	S116	☐ Paris 1993–94	$13.00	S109
☐ Boston 1993–94	$13.00	S117	☐ Philadelphia 1993–94	$13.00	S113
☐ Budapest 1994–95 (Avail.			☐ San Diego 1993–94	$13.00	S107
2/94)	$13.00	S139	☐ San Francisco 1994	$13.00	S133
☐ Chicago 1993–94	$13.00	S122	☐ Santa Fe/Taos/		
☐ Denver/Boulder/Colorado			Albuquerque 1993–94	$13.00	S108
Springs 1993–94	$13.00	S131	☐ Seattle/Portland 1994–95	$13.00	S137
☐ Dublin 1993–94	$13.00	S128	☐ St. Louis/Kansas		
☐ Hong Kong 1994–95			City 1993–94	$13.00	S127
(Avail. 4/94)	$13.00	S140	☐ Sydney 1993–94	$13.00	S129
☐ Honolulu/Oahu 1994	$13.00	S134	☐ Tampa/St.		
☐ Las Vegas 1993–94	$13.00	S121	Petersburg 1993–94	$13.00	S105
☐ London 1994	$13.00	S132	☐ Tokyo 1992–93	$13.00	S039
☐ Los Angeles 1993–94	$13.00	S123	☐ Toronto 1993–94	$13.00	S126
☐ Madrid/Costa del			☐ Vancouver/Victoria 1994–		
Sol 1993–94	$13.00	S124	95 (Avail. 1/94)	$13.00	S142
☐ Miami 1993–94	$13.00	S118	☐ Washington, D.C. 1994		
☐ Minneapolis/St.			(Avail. 1/94)	$13.00	S136
Paul 1993–94	$13.00	S119			

SPECIAL EDITIONS

	Retail Price	Code		Retail Price	Code
☐ Bed & Breakfast Southwest	$16.00	P100	☐ Caribbean Hideaways	$16.00	P103
☐ Bed & Breakfast Great American Cities (Avail. 1/94)	$16.00	P104	☐ National Park Guide 1994 (avail. 3/94)	$16.00	P105
			☐ Where to Stay U.S.A.	$15.00	P102

Please note: if the availability of a book is several months away, we may have back issues of guides to that particular destination. Call customer service at (815) 734-1104.